Prepare with The Power of Classroom Practice

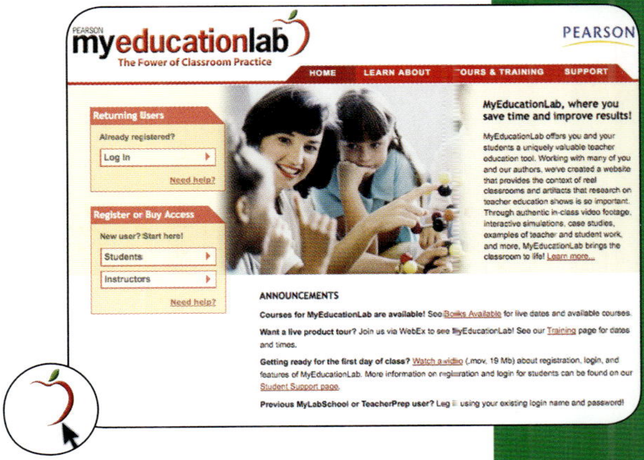

Register for **MyEducationLab** today at www.myeducationlab.com

What is MyEducationLab?

MyEducationLab is easy to use and integrate into this book.
Wherever you see the MyEducationLab logo in the margins or elsewhere in the text, follow the simple instructions to access the videos, strategies, cases, and artifacts associated with these assignments, activities, and learning units on MyEducationLab. MyEducationLab is organized topically to enhance the coverage of the core concepts discussed in the chapters of your book. For each topic on the course you will find most or all of the following resources:

Students:

- Take **Practice Tests** for each chapter of your text.
  - Completion of each practice test generates a **study plan** that is unique to you.
  - The study plan links to text excerpts, activities with feedback, and videos and other media that can help you master concepts covered in your text.
- Complete **Assignments and Activities** to apply text content to real classroom situations.
- Explore the **Building Teaching Skills and Dispositions** exercises to practice and strengthen the skills that are essential to teaching.

MyEducationLab offers:

- Authentic **classroom video** shows real teachers and students interacting, and helps prepare you for the classroom.
- **Case studies** offer real-life perspectives on common issues and challenges faced in the classroom.
- Authentic student and teacher **classroom artifacts** provide you with the actual types of materials encountered every day by teachers.

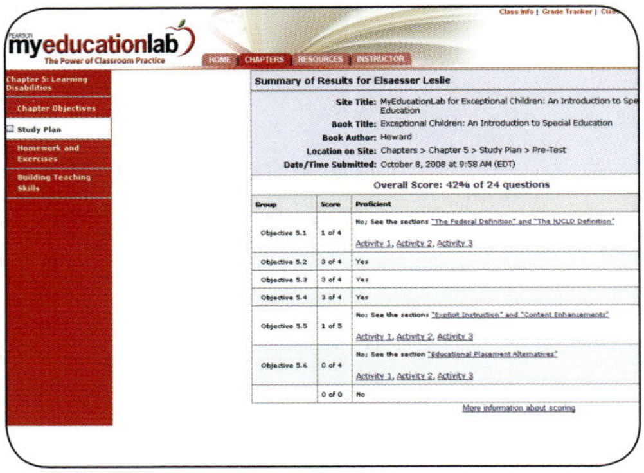

CONNECTION TO NATIONAL STANDARDS: Now it is easier than ever to see how coursework is connected to national standards. Each topic on MyEducationLab lists intended learning outcomes connected to the appropriate national standards. And all of the Assignments and Activities and all of the Building Teaching Skills and Dispositions in MyEducationLab are mapped to the appropriate national standards and learning outcomes.

ASSIGNMENTS AND ACTIVITIES: Designed to save instructors preparation time and enhance student understanding, these assignable exercises show concepts in action (through video, cases, and/or student and teacher artifacts). They help students synthesize and apply concepts and strategies they read about in the book.

BUILDING TEACHING SKILLS AND DISPOSITIONS

These learning units help students practice and strengthen skills that are essential to quality teaching. Students are presented with the core skill or concept and then given an opportunity to practice their understanding of this concept multiple times by watching video footage (or interacting with other media) and then critically analyzing the strategy or skill presented.

STUDY PLAN

A MyEducationLab Study Plan is a multiple choice assessment tied to chapter objectives and supported by study material. A well-designed Study Plan offers multiple opportunities to fully master required course content as identified by the objectives in each chapter:

- **Chapter Objectives** identify the learning outcomes for the chapter and give students targets to shoot for as they read and study.
- **Multiple Choice Assessments** assess mastery of the content. These assessments are mapped to chapter objectives, and students can take the multiple choice quiz as many times as they want. Not only do these quizzes provide overall scores for each objective, but they also explain why responses to particular items are correct or incorrect.
- **Study Material: Review, Practice and Enrichment** give students a deeper understanding of what they do and do not know related to chapter content. This material includes text excerpts, activities that include hints and feedback, and interactive multi-media exercises built around videos, simulations, cases, or classroom artifacts.
- **Flashcards** help students study the definitions of the key terms within each chapter.

GENERAL RESOURCES ON YOUR MYEDUCATIONLAB COURSE

The Resources section on MyEducationLab is designed to help students pass their licensure exams, put together effective portfolios and lesson plans, prepare for and navigate the first year of their teaching careers, and understand key educational standards, policies, and laws. This section includes:

- **Licensure Exams:** Contains guidelines for passing the Praxis exam. **The Practice Test Exam** includes practice multiple-choice questions, case study questions, and video case studies with sample questions.
- **Lesson Plan Builder:** Helps students create and share lesson plans.
- **Licensure and Standards:** Provides links to state licensure standards and national standards.
- **Beginning Your Career:** Educate Offers tips, advice, and valuable information on:
  - o Resume Writing and Interviewing: Expert advice on how to write impressive resumes and prepare for job interviews.
  - o Your First Year of Teaching: Practical tips on setting up a classroom, managing student behavior, and planning for instruction and assessment.
  - o Law and Public Policies: Includes specific directives and requirements educators need to understand under the No Child Left Behind Act and the Individuals with Disabilities Education Improvement Act of 2004.

What if I need help?

We've got you covered 24/7.
There is a wealth of helpful information on the site, under "Tours and Training "and" Support."
Technical support is available 24 hours a day, seven days a week, at http://247pearsoned.custhelp.com.

Content Area Reading

TENTH EDITION

Content Area Reading

Literacy and Learning Across the Curriculum

Richard T. Vacca
Emeritus, Kent State University

Jo Anne L. Vacca
Emerita, Kent State University

Maryann Mraz
University of North Carolina at Charlotte

PEARSON

Boston ■ Columbus ■ Indianapolis ■ New York ■ San Francisco ■ Upper Saddle River
Amsterdam ■ Cape Town ■ Dubai ■ London ■ Madrid ■ Milan ■ Munich ■ Paris ■ Montreal ■ Toronto
Delhi ■ Mexico City ■ Sao Paulo ■ Sydney ■ Hong Kong ■ Seoul ■ Singapore ■ Taipei ■ Tokyo

Editor-in-Chief: Aurora Martínez Ramos
Senior Development Editor: Mary Kriener
Series Editorial Assistant: Meagan French
Director of Marketing: Quinn Perkson
Executive Marketing Manager: Krista Clark
Marketing Assistant: Kate Monea
Editorial Production Service: Omegatype Typography, Inc.
Manufacturing Buyer: Megan Cochran
Electronic Composition: Omegatype Typography, Inc.
Interior Design: Omegatype Typography, Inc.
Photo Researcher: Annie Pickert
Cover Administrator: Linda Knowles

Credits and acknowledgments borrowed from other sources and reproduced, with permission, in this textbook appear on appropriate page within text.

Photo Credits: Bob Daemmrich/The Image Works, pp. xiv, xv, 166, 168, 194, 196; Bob Daemmrich Photography, pp. ix, x, xii, xiii, xvi, xix, xxxiv, 2, 50, 52, 84, 86, 124, 126, 234, 236, 354, 356; Robin Nelson/PhotoEdit, pp. x, 28, 30; Michael Newman/PhotoEdit, pp. xxi, 398, 400; Frank Siteman, pp. xvii, xviii, 278, 280, 316, 318.

Library of Congress Cataloging-in-Publication Data

Vacca, Richard T.
Content area reading : literacy and learning across the curriculum / Richard T. Vacca, Jo Anne L. Vacca, Maryann Mraz.—10th ed.
p. cm.
Includes bibliographical references and index.
ISBN-13: 978-0-13-703511-3 (hardcover)
ISBN-10: 0-13-703511-X (hardcover)
1. Content area reading. I. Vacca, Jo Anne L. II. Mraz, Maryann E. III. Title.
LB1050.455.V33 2011
428.4'3—dc22 2009032672

10 9 8 7 6 5 4 3 2 1 EDW 14 13 12 11 10

PEARSON

www.pearsonhighered.com

ISBN-10: 0-13-703511-X
ISBN-13: 978-0-13-703511-3

To Karen Brothers and Clis Stauffer,
longtime colleagues who taught us by example:
"Let us be who we are and let us be it well."

—Rich and Jo Anne Vacca

To my wonderful parents, Marilyn and Steve,
for teaching me from childhood forward that pursuing
knowledge is always worth the effort, and for enthusiastically
supporting my educational adventures to this day.
And to Jo Anne and Rich Vacca for being inspiring
mentors and extraordinary friends.

—Maryann Mraz

About the Authors

‹ **Richard and Jo Anne Vacca** are professors emeriti in the School of Teaching, Learning and Curriculum Studies in the College of Education, Health and Human Services at Kent State University. They met as undergraduate English majors at SUNY Albany and have been partners ever since. Jo Anne taught language arts in middle schools in New York and Illinois, and received her doctorate from Boston University. Rich taught high school English, and earned his doctorate at Syracuse University. He is a past president of the International Reading Association.

The Vaccas live in Vero Beach, Florida, where they golf, volunteer, and walk their toy poodles, Tiger Lily and Gigi Marie. They especially enjoy visiting and traveling with their daughter, Courtney; son-in-law, Gary; and grandsons, Simon, Max, and Joe.

‹ **Maryann Mraz** is an associate professor in the Reading and Elementary Education Department at the University of North Carolina at Charlotte (UNCC). She earned her Ph.D. from Kent State University under the guidance of Jo Anne and Rich Vacca. Maryann is a board member of the Association of Literacy Educators and Researchers (ALER) and the author of numerous articles, chapters, and instructional materials on literacy education, including the co-authored books *The Literacy Coach's Companion* and *Independent Reading*. She teaches graduate courses in literacy education and provides professional development workshops to teachers and literacy coaches.

Brief Contents

Contents

CHAPTER 4

CHAPTER 5
Planning Instruction for Content Literacy 124

PART TWO / Instructional Practices and Strategies

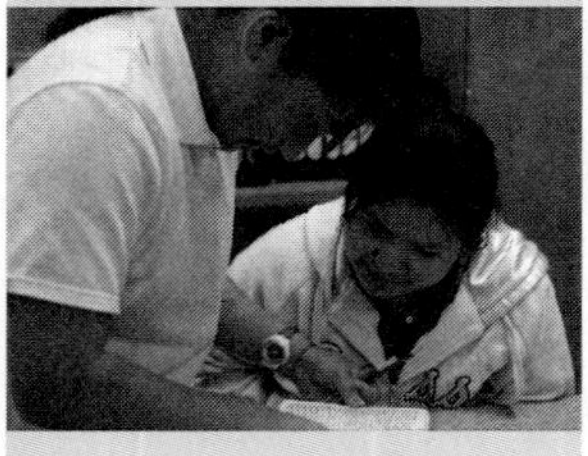

CHAPTER 8

Developing Vocabulary and Concepts 234

CHAPTER 10

Studying Text 316

CHAPTER 11

Learning with Trade Books

CHAPTER 12

Preface

This edition represents a personal milestone for us as we celebrate the thirtieth anniversary of *Content Area Reading: Literacy and Learning Across the Curriculum*. The first edition was drafted on dozens of legal-size writing pads, revised by hand, and then transcribed on a mechanical typewriter, a concept foreign to many of today's adolescent learners. Some of you may be wondering—with good reason—why revise the same book ten times? Have content literacy practices changed enough in three decades to warrant ten editions of the same book? While we have remained true to the original intent of the book, our answer to these questions is an enthusiastic "Yes!" During the past thirty years, we have witnessed dramatic changes in the way we think about literacy, what it means to be literate, and the ways we use literacy to learn and socially network with others. When we compare earlier editions to the present one, we are both delighted and surprised by how much the book has changed while maintaining its core beliefs and assumptions. There is much in this edition that is new and revitalized.

New to This Edition

First published in 1981, this book has undergone multiple revisions over the years to reflect an ever-expanding knowledge base grounded in research and practice in the areas of literacy, cognition and learning, educational policy, technology, and student diversity. Moreover, we have learned from teachers how they have gone about putting into practice the ideas and instructional strategies contained in this and previous editions. Numerous teachers have shared what features of the book they like, what has worked for them, and what might need changing. As a result, the revised content in this edition underscores ways of thinking about literacy and learning that are grounded in the current knowledge base as well as in the professional insights of teachers.

Chapter content has been rigorously updated to reflect current theory, research, and practice related to literacy and learning across the curriculum. Expanded emphasis has been given throughout many of the chapters on what it means to be literate in the twenty-first century, including a detailed analysis of the instructional concept of *disciplinary literacy* and how it is similar to and different from *adolescent literacy* and *content literacy.* How content area teachers plan and adapt literacy and learning to meet the needs of struggling adolescent readers and writers is a predominant theme that runs throughout the book. New features of this text include the following:

- **Complete reorganization** of the text into two main parts: Part One, Learners, Literacies, and Texts; and Part Two, Instructional Practices and Strategies.
- A new **Chapter 2, Learning with New Literacies,** replaces a now outdated discussion on electronic texts from previous editions. This chapter was developed by William Kist, Kent State University, one of the leading scholars in the area of socially networked classrooms and new literacies.

- A new **Chapter 7, Guiding Reading Comprehension,** underscores the importance of comprehension strategies that guide reader–text interactions and consolidates instructional strategies from several chapters of the previous edition.
- A new **Chapter 12, Literacy Coaching,** expands on the discussion of the literacy coach, who has become an indispensable ally to content area teachers and specialists in middle and high schools. This chapter addresses the roles and expectations associated with literacy coaching, giving particular attention to collaboration, professional development, and explicit literacy instruction for struggling adolescent learners.
- **Voices from the Classroom** features include interviews with content area teachers related to instructional practices. In these interviews, teachers reflect on particular challenges that they have encountered in their classroom relative to the chapter topic. They then describe how they applied and adapted the strategies and/or concepts presented in the chapter to address that challenge.
- **RTI for Struggling Adolescent Learners** features take a relatively new approach to instructional intervention, Response to Intervention (RTI), and show how it may be adapted to various aspects of content literacy instruction.
- **New instructional examples** throughout many of the chapters replace examples that have been in previous editions.
- **Updates of new research** and ways of thinking about literacy, learning, and instructional practice appear throughout the chapters.

Organization of This Edition

Weaving literacy practices into the fabric of content area instruction requires teachers to rethink business as usual, just as we have found ourselves rethinking, rewriting, and fine-tuning a vision of literacy and learning across the curriculum. More often than not, there is a disconnect between students and disciplinary tasks that require reading to learn. Academic texts, whether printed in typesetter's ink or viewed electronically on a computer screen, are pivotal tools in the development of strategic, independent learners. Yet students are often disengaged from the process of learning with texts in their classrooms. We believe that teachers are in a strategic position to make a difference in the way their students approach literacy and learning in their classrooms.

As part of the revision process, therefore, we decided to simplify the structure of this edition by organizing chapters into two main parts. Part One, Learners, Literacies, and Texts, places the focus on the cultural, linguistic, and academic diversity of today's learners; their personal and academic literacies; and the kinds of texts that are integral to their lives in and out of school. Part Two, Instructional Practices and Strategies, contains a multitude of evidence-based instructional strategies waiting to be adapted to meet the conceptual demands inherent in disciplinary learning.

Within this simplified organizational structure of the text, chapter changes include the following:

- **CHAPTER 1** incorporates an increased emphasis on the changing nature of literacy in the twenty-first century with particular attention on contemporary definitions of literacy; the importance of *new literacies* and *adolescent literacy* in today's schools; the meaning of *disciplinary literacy,* and ways in which disciplinary literacy is similar to and different from *content literacy.*
- **CHAPTER 2** is new to this edition and addresses the following questions: What are new literacies? What is different about learning with new literacies? What is the same? Why is learning with new literacies essential for students? What are some strategies that can be used to help students learn using new literacies? How do the roles of teachers change when they make new literacies an integral part of subject matter learning?
- **CHAPTER 3** provides an expanded discussion and new information and research about culturally responsive instruction and the use of multicultural texts, including books for English learners.
- **CHAPTER 4** brings an up-to-date discussion and new research to topics such as high-stakes testing, legislation, standards, and accountability. In addition, it provides new information and examples related to behavior frequency observations, rubrics for self-evaluation, and informal assessment tools such as the writing conference log and learning participation inventory. The section on readability has been expanded to include a discussion of *lexile levels.*
- **CHAPTER 5** provides a detailed description of an explicit strategy model useful for planning instruction for struggling readers.
- **CHAPTER 6** includes updated and expanded sections on self-efficacy and motivation, the IEPC strategy, and the ReQuest strategy. New instructional examples are interspersed with previous ones throughout the chapter.
- **CHAPTER 7** synthesizes comprehension strategies from various chapters of the previous edition and provides updated research and new examples of strategy use for guiding reading comprehension.
- **CHAPTER 8** updates research and supplies new information on tiered levels of vocabulary learning and the use of graphic organizers.
- **CHAPTER 9** now features recent information on the effects of text messaging on students' writing and includes new examples, activities, and strategies for writing to learn.
- **CHAPTER 10** provides a comprehensive treatment of the use of study strategies in core content areas with new examples and illustrations.

- **CHAPTER 11** includes updated information and research on the use of books—other than textbooks—for disciplinary-related learning. New titles and an updated list of trade books are provided for instructional purposes.

- **CHAPTER 12** is new to this edition and explores the roles and expectations associated with literacy coaching, placing particular emphasis on building learning communities within schools, supporting professional development, and providing instructional support for struggling readers.

Features in the Tenth Edition

The tenth edition of *Content Area Reading* retains many of the features of the previous edition while improving its overall coverage of content literacy topics. It continues to emphasize a contemporary, functional approach to content literacy instruction. In a functional approach, content area teachers learn how to integrate literacy-related strategies into instructional routines without sacrificing the teaching of content. Our intent is not to morph a content teacher into a reading specialist or writing instructor. Rather, our goal has always been, and shall continue to be, to improve the overall coverage of instructional strategies and practices that remain at the heart of this book. In every chapter, special pedagogical features are provided to aid in this effort.

Features at the beginning of each chapter include the following:

- **Chapter opening quotes** help readers reflect on the underlying theme of the chapter.

- **An organizing principle** provides readers with a "heads-up" by introducing the rationale for the chapter and highlighting its underlying theme.

- **A graphic organizer** depicts the relationships among ideas presented in the chapter.

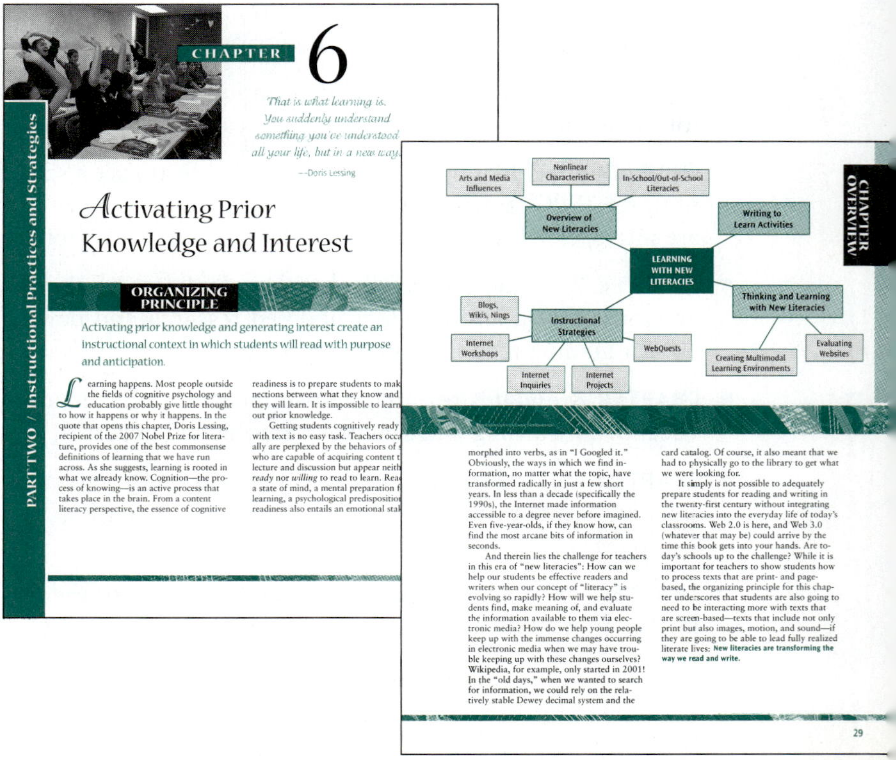

- **Frame of Mind** questions help readers approach the text in a critical frame of mind as they analyze and interpret information presented.

In-text features include the following:

- **Voices from the Classroom** include interviews with content area teachers related to instructional practices.

- **RTI for Struggling Adolescent Learners** occur in many of the chapters and show how Response to Intervention (RTI) may be adapted to various aspects of content literacy instruction.

- **Evidence-Based Best Practices** highlight the steps and procedures involved in using high-visibility strategies that are supported by theoretically sound rationales and/or evidence-based, scientific research.

Special marginal notations and callouts provide opportunities to enhance the basic instruction within the chapters:

- **Response Journal** marginal icons signal readers to use a "response journal" while reading to make personal and professional connections as they react to ideas presented in each chapter.

- **MyEducationLab** assignments in the margin correlate chapter content with special online activities designed to help readers develop instructional skills and knowledge. (See the following MyEducationLab discussion.)

- **Classroom Artifact** figures throughout the book illustrate instructional procedures and materials developed by teachers for authentic teaching situations.

Chapters conclude with additional features that help readers review and practice the concepts introduced in the chapter:

- **Looking Back, Looking Forward** sections at the end of each chapter offer a summative review of the concepts introduced and a perspective on where the discussion will lead to next.
- **Minds On** activities engage students in thinking more deeply about some of the important ideas that they have studied.
- **Hands On** activities engage students in applying some of the important ideas that they have studied.
- **eResources** signal readers to investigate online resources to enrich and extend the topics presented.

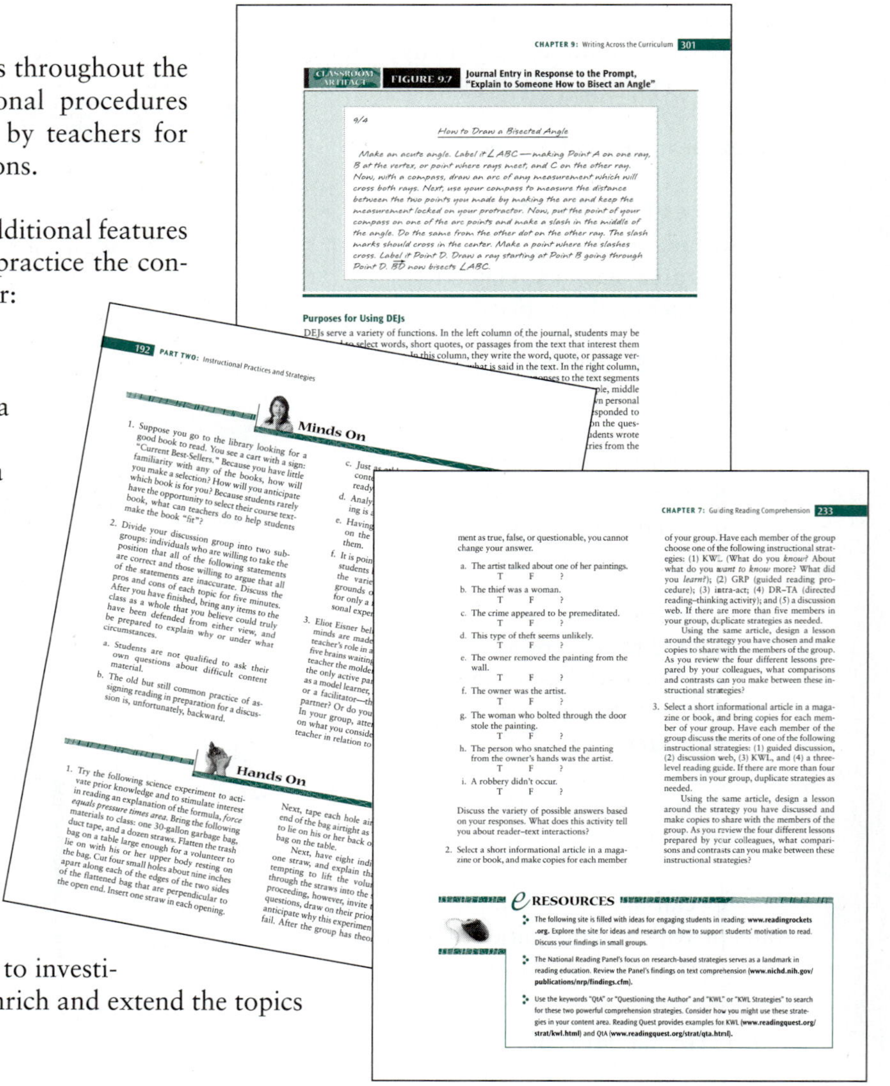

CHAPTER 9: Writing Across the Curriculum 301

CLASSROOM ARTIFACT FIGURE 9.7 Journal Entry in Response to the Prompt, "Explain to Someone How to Bisect an Angle"

9/4

How to Draw a Bisected Angle

Make an acute angle. Label it ∠ABC—making Point A on one ray, B at the vertex, or point where rays meet, and C on the other ray. Now, with a compass, draw an arc of any measurement which will cross both rays. Next, use your compass to measure the distance between the two points you made by making the arc and keep the measurement locked on your protractor. Now, put the point of your compass on one of the arc points and make a slash in the middle of the angle. Do the same from the other dot on the other ray. The slash marks should cross in the center. Make a point where the slashes cross. Label it Point D. Draw a ray starting at Point B going through Point D. BD now bisects ∠ABC.

Purposes for Using DEJs

DEJs serve a variety of functions. In the left column of the journal, students may be ...

192 PART TWO: Instructional Practices and Strategies

Minds On

1. Suppose you go to the library looking for a good book to read. You see a cart with a sign: "Current Best-Sellers." Because you have little familiarity with any of the books, how will you make a selection? How will you anticipate which book is for you? Because students rarely have the opportunity to select their course textbook, what can teachers do to help students make the book "fit"?
2. Divide your discussion group into two subgroups: individuals who are willing to take the position that all of the following statements are correct and those willing to argue that all of the statements are inaccurate. Discuss the pros and cons of each topic for five minutes. After you have finished, bring any items to the class as a whole that you believe could truly have been defended from either view, and be prepared to explain why or under what circumstances.
   a. Students are not qualified to ask their own questions about difficult content material.
   b. The old but still common practice of assigning reading in preparation for a discussion is, unfortunately, backward.

Hands On

1. Try the following science experiment to activate prior knowledge and to stimulate interest in reading an explanation of the formula, *force equals pressure times area.* Bring the following materials to class: one 30-gallon garbage bag, duct tape, and a dozen straws. Flatten the trash bag on a table large enough for a volunteer to lie on with his or her upper body resting on the bag. Cut four small holes about nine inches apart along each of the edges of the two sides of the flattened bag that are perpendicular to the open end. Insert one straw in each opening.

CHAPTER 7: Guiding Reading Comprehension 233

ment as true, false, or questionable, you cannot change your answer.

a. The artist talked about one of her paintings. T F ?
b. The thief was a woman. T F ?
c. The crime appeared to be premeditated. T F ?
d. This type of theft seems unlikely. T F ?
e. The owner removed the painting from the wall. T F ?
f. The owner was the artist. T F ?
g. The woman who bolted through the door stole the painting. T F ?
h. The person who snatched the painting from the owner's hands was the artist. T F ?
i. A robbery didn't occur. T F ?

Discuss the variety of possible answers based on your responses. What does this activity tell you about reader–text interactions?

2. Select a short informational article in a magazine or book, and make copies for each member of your group. Have each member of the group choose one of the following instructional strategies: (1) KWL (What do you *know*? About what do you *want to know* more? What did you *learn*?); (2) GRP (guided reading procedure); (3) intra-act; (4) DR–TA (directed reading–thinking activity); and (5) a discussion web. If there are more than five members in your group, duplicate strategies as needed.

Using the same article, design a lesson around the strategy you have chosen and make copies to share with the members of the group. As you review the four different lessons prepared by your colleagues, what comparisons and contrasts can you make between these instructional strategies?

3. Select a short informational article in a magazine or book, and bring copies for each member of your group. Have each member of the group discuss the merits of one of the following instructional strategies: (1) guided discussion, (2) discussion web, (3) KWL, and (4) a three-level reading guide. If there are more than four members in your group, duplicate strategies as needed.

Using the same article, design a lesson around the strategy you have discussed and make copies to share with the members of the group. As you review the four different lessons prepared by your colleagues, what comparisons and contrasts can you make between these instructional strategies?

eRESOURCES

- The following site is filled with ideas for engaging students in reading: www.readingrockets.org. Explore the site for ideas and research on how to support students' motivation to read. Discuss your findings in small groups.
- The National Reading Panel's focus on research-based strategies serves as a landmark in reading education. Review the Panel's findings on text comprehension (www.nichd.nih.gov/publications/nrp/findings.cfm).
- Use the keywords "QtA" or "Questioning the Author" and "KWL" or "KWL Strategies" to search for these two powerful comprehension strategies. Consider how you might use these strategies in your content area. Reading Quest provides examples for KWL (www.readingquest.org/strat/kwl.html) and QtA (www.readingquest.org/strat/qta.html).

MyEducationLab

Teacher educators who are developing pedagogies for the analysis of teaching and learning contend that analyzing teaching artifacts has three advantages: it enables new teachers time for reflection while still using the real materials of practice; it provides new teachers with experience thinking about and approaching the complexity of the classroom; and in some cases, it can help new teachers and teacher educators develop a shared understanding and common language about teaching.*

*Darling-Hammond, L., & Bransford, J. (Eds.). (2005). *Preparing teachers for a changing world.* San Francisco: John Wiley & Sons.

As Linda Darling-Hammond and her colleagues point out, grounding teacher education in real classrooms—among real teachers and students and among actual examples of students' and teachers' work—is an important, and perhaps even an essential, part of training teachers for the complexities of teaching in today's classrooms. For this reason, we have created a valuable time-saving website—MyEducationLab—that provides you with the important context of real classrooms and artifacts. The authentic in-class video footage, interactive exercises, and other resources available on MyEducationLab offer you a uniquely valuable teacher education tool.

MyEducationLab is easy to use and integrate into both your assignments and your courses. Wherever you see the MyEducationLab logo in the margins or elsewhere in the text, follow the simple instructions to access the videos, strategies, cases, and artifacts associated with these assignments, activities, and learning units on MyEducationLab. For each chapter in this book you will find most or all of the following resources:

- **Connection to National Standards.** Now it is easier than ever to see how your coursework is connected to national standards. In each chapter of MyEducationLab you will find intended learning outcomes connected to the appropriate national standards for your course. All of the activities in MyEducationLab are mapped to the appropriate national standards and learning outcomes as well.
- **Assignments and Activities.** Designed to save instructors preparation time, these assignable exercises show concepts in action (through videos, cases, or student and teacher artifacts) and then offer thought-provoking questions that probe your understanding of theses concepts or strategies. (Feedback for these assignments is available to the instructor.)
- **Building Teaching Skills and Dispositions.** Designed to help the reader develop a core teaching skill or build a core teaching disposition, these assignable exercises scaffold development built around various media assets (video, artifact, case, etc.).
- **IRIS Center Resources.** The IRIS Center at Vanderbilt University (http://iris.peabody.vanderbilt.edu), funded by the U.S. Department of Education's Office of Special Education Programs (OSEP), develops training enhancement materials for preservice and in-service teachers. The Center works with experts from across the country to create challenge-based interactive modules, case study units, and podcasts that provide research-validated information about working with students in inclusive settings. On your MyEducationLab course we have integrated this content where appropriate to enhance the content coverage in your book.
- **General Resources on Your MyEducationLab Course.** The Resources section of your MyEducationLab course is designed to help you pass your licensure exam, put together an effective portfolio and lesson plan, prepare for and navigate the

first year of your teaching career, and understand key educational standards, policies, and laws. This section includes the following:

— *Licensure Exams.* Access guidelines for passing the Praxis exam. The Practice Test Exam includes practice questions, Case Histories, and Video Case Studies.

— *Portfolio Builder and Lesson Plan Builder.* Create, update, and share portfolios and lesson plans.

— *Preparing a Portfolio.* Access guidelines for creating a high-quality teaching portfolio that will allow you to practice effective lesson planning.

— *Licensure and Standards.* Link to state licensure standards and national standards.

— *Beginning Your Career.* Educate yourself—access tips, advice, and valuable information, including:

Expert advice on how to write impressive resumes and prepare yourself for job interviews.

Practical tips to set up your classroom, manage student behavior, and learn to more easily organize for instruction and assessment.

Specific directives and requirements you need to understand under the No Child Left Behind Act and the Individuals with Disabilities Education Improvement Act of 2004.

— *Special Education Interactive Time Line.* Build your own detailed time lines based on different facets of the history and evolution of special education.

Supplements for Instructors and Students for the Tenth Edition

Pearson Education is committed to preparing the best quality supplements for its textbooks, and the supplements for the tenth edition of *Content Area Reading* reflect this commitment. For more information about the instructor and student supplements that accompany and support the text, ask your Pearson Publisher's Representative.

- **Instructor's Resource Manual and Test Bank.** The Instructor's Resource Manual and Test Bank includes a wealth of interesting ideas and activities designed to help instructors teach the course. Each chapter includes a chapter-at-a-glance grid, the chapter purpose, underlying concepts, student objectives, vocabulary and key terms, activities and discussion questions, MyEducationLab extension activities, plus test questions for each chapter.

- **Computerized Test Bank.** The printed Test Bank is also available electronically through the Pearson Education computerized testing system. **Pearson MyTest** is a powerful assessment generation program that helps instructors easily create and print quizzes and exams. Questions and tests are authored online, allowing ultimate flexibility and the ability to efficiently create and print assessments anytime, anywhere! Instructors can access Pearson MyTest and their test bank files by going to **www.pearsonmytest.com** to log in, register, or request access. Features of Pearson MyTest include the following:

  — **Premium Assessment Content**

  Draw from a rich library of assessments that complement your Pearson textbook and your course's learning objectives.

  Edit questions or tests to fit your specific teaching needs.

  — **Instructor-Friendly Resources**

  Easily create and store your own questions, including images, diagrams, and charts using simple drag-and-drop and Wordlike controls.

  Use additional information provided by Pearson, such as the question's difficulty level or learning objective, to help you quickly build your test.

  — **Time-Saving Enhancements**

  Add headers or footers and easily scramble questions and answer choices—all from one simple toolbar.

  Quickly create multiple versions of your test or answer key, and when ready, simply save to MS Word or PDF format and print.

  Export your exams for import to Blackboard 6.0, CE (WebCT), or Vista (WebCT).

- **PowerPoint Presentation.** Ideal for lecture presentations or student handouts, the PowerPoint presentation provides dozens of ready-to-use graphic and text images.

- **Study Guide for Students.** A Study Guide provides opportunities for student practice and support for student understanding for each chapter.

Acknowledgments

Many people deserve our thanks and merit recognition for demonstrating the care that reveals a true professional. New to this book is a third co-author, Maryann Mraz, from the University of North Carolina at Charlotte (UNCC). Maryann brought a renewed sense of enthusiasm to the revision process, inspiring us to think harder and write better. Thank you to Dr. Jean Vintinner at University of North Carolina at Charlotte (UNCC) for sharing her experiences, strategies, and insights. We also wish to thank William Chamberlain, Tim Fitzpatrick, Jennifer Boysko, Wendy Maldonado, Lynne Newton, Sarah VanWyhe, Aaron Cooper, and Tracy Willey for their contributions to the Voices from the Classroom segments in this edition.

Applause to our contributing authors for making our job easier: William Kist, Kent State University, for Chapter 2, Learning with New Literacies; Patricia Ruggiano Schmidt and Wen Ma, Le Moyne College; for their revision of Chapter 3, Culturally Responsive Teaching in Diverse Classrooms; and Barbara Moss and Virginia Loh, San Diego State University, for their revision of Chapter 11, Learning with Trade Books.

We would be remiss if we failed to acknowledge the thoughtful and thought-provoking suggestions of our colleagues who responded to questionnaires and reviewed the text for this edition: Sharon E. Andrews, Augustana College; Lee A. Dubert, Boise State University; Stephenie Hewett, The Citadel; Deborah Jinkins, Tarleton State University; Ann K. Petersen, Buena Vista University; and Anita F. Thompson, Chapman University College.

We also would like to recognize the outstanding work of Mary Kriener, our senior developmental editor, for her excellent insights, questions, and suggestions for improving the manuscript for this edition. And, finally, a special thanks to Aurora Martínez Ramos, vice president and editor-in-chief for Literacy and ELL, who has been a model for us in the art and skill of juggling many balls at once!

Content Area Reading

CHAPTER 1

I always wondered why somebody didn't do that. Then I realized I was somebody.

—Lily Tomlin, actress and comedienne

Literacy Matters

ORGANIZING PRINCIPLE

All content area teachers play a critical role in helping students to think, learn, and communicate with texts.

Lily Tomlin's observation does more than put a smile on our faces. It reminds us that when it comes to learning across the curriculum, literacy matters. All teachers have a role to play in making a difference in the literate lives of their students. In this chapter, we explore what that role is for the content area teacher, and in the process of doing so, we clarify several core concepts related to literacy and learning: *content literacy, disciplinary literacy, adolescent literacy, new literacies,* and *reading to learn.*

If you're a content area teacher, or studying to be one, you may be wondering why you're even taking a course that has the terms *reading* and/or *literacy* in its title. No doubt you view your primary role as teaching the important ideas and concepts of your discipline. Yet, as a content area teacher, you also have an important role to play in showing students how to use literacy-related strategies in your discipline. Literacy is an evolving concept that changes with society over time. Perhaps it's best to think of literacy in terms of the *multiple literacies* that we use to make and communicate meaning. In this book, we explore how to support students' literacies by helping them make and communicate meaning with the various kinds of texts—both print and nonprint—they use in content areas.

Our primary emphasis throughout this book is on reading and writing to learn

CHAPTER OVERVIEW

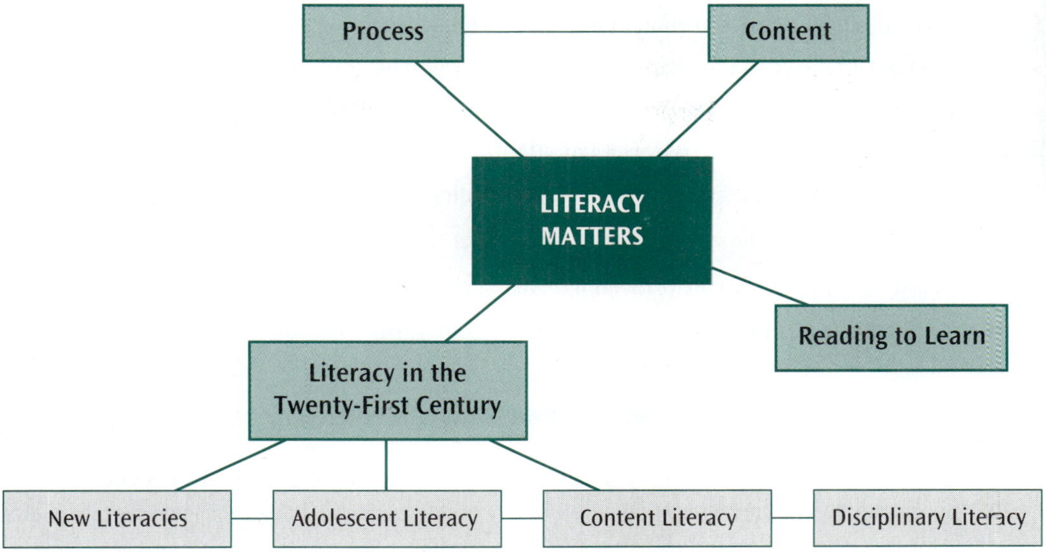

in middle and high school. Unfortunately, many adolescent learners struggle with academic texts. One of the realities facing teachers across all content areas is that many students make little use of reading as a tool for thinking and learning. They either read on a superficial level or find ways to circumvent content literacy tasks altogether. All too often, adolescent learners give up on reading with the expectation that teachers will impart information through lecture and class discussion. When students become too dependent on teachers as their primary source of information, they are rarely in a position to engage actively in reading to think and learn.

This need not be the case. As the organizing principle of this chapter underscores: **All content area teachers play a critical role in helping students to think, learn, and communicate with texts.**

Study the Chapter Overview. It's your map to the major ideas that you will encounter in the chapter. The graphic display shows the relationships that exist among the concepts you will study. Use it as an organizer. What is the chapter about? What do you know already about the content to be presented in the chapter? What do you need to learn more about?

RESPONSE JOURNAL

Write a "five-minute essay" in your response journal on your initial reaction to the organizing principle.

In conjunction with the Chapter Overview, take a moment or two to study the Frame of Mind questions. This feature uses key questions to help you think about the ideas that you will read about. When you finish reading, you should be able to respond fully to the Frame of Mind questions.

FRAME OF MIND

1. Explain the difference between content and process knowledge.
2. What are new literacies and how are they changing the way we think about learning and literacy in the twenty-first century?
3. What is adolescent literacy and why is it important to twenty-first-century society?
4. Why do many adolescents have difficulty comprehending academic texts?
5. How are content literacy and disciplinary literacy alike? How are they different?
6. Why is reading to learn a strategic, meaning-making process?
7. What comprehension strategies are critical to reading to learn? What role does prior knowledge play in comprehension?

There are no pat formulas for teachers who want students to develop core concepts and good habits of thinking within a discipline. Nor are there magic potions in the form of instructional strategies that will make a difference with all students, all the time. Teaching is a problem-solving activity: There's just you, the academic texts and instructional strategies that you use, and the students whose lives you touch in the relatively brief time that they are under your wing. Teaching is a daunting but immensely rewarding enterprise for those who are up to the challenge.

Highly effective content area teachers plan lessons that are engaging. These teachers recognize that "engaging the disengaged" is not an easy task. Yet they continually strive to make learning intellectually challenging for the students they are teaching. A top instructional priority, therefore, is to involve students actively in learning the important ideas and concepts of the *content* they are studying. But the effective teacher also knows that an intellectually challenging instructional environment engages students not only in the acquisition of content but also in the *thinking processes* by which they learn that content.

No wonder the classroom is like a crucible, a place where the special mix of teacher, student, and text come together to create wonderfully complex human interactions that stir the minds of learners. Some days, of course, are better than others. The things that you thought about doing and the classroom surprises that you didn't expect fall into place. A creative energy imbues teaching and learning.

Sometimes, however, lessons limp along. Others simply bomb—so you cut them short. The four or so remaining minutes before the bell rings are a kind of self-inflicted wound. Nothing is more unnerving than waiting for the bell to ring when students don't have anything meaningful to do.

Consider a high school science teacher's reflection on the way things went in one of her chemistry classes. "Something was missing," she explains. "The students aren't usually as quiet and passive as they were today. Excuse the pun, but the chemistry wasn't there. Maybe the text assignment was too hard. Maybe I could have done something differently. Any suggestions?"

This teacher's spirit of inquiry is admirable. She wants to know how to improve her teaching—how to engage students in learning the important concepts of her chemistry course and how to involve them in thinking like scientists. ■

Content and Process: Two Sides of the Same Coin

Like all good teachers, the chemistry teacher in the preceding example cares about *what* she does and *how* she does it. *Content* and *process*, after all, are two sides of the same instructional coin. She knows a lot about the what of instruction—the content of chemistry—and how to teach that content in ways that develop important ideas and concepts in an intellectually challenging instructional environment. A strong attraction to academic content is one of the reasons teachers are wedded to a particular discipline. Yet it is often much more difficult to teach something than to know that something: "The teacher of the American Revolution has to know both a great deal about the American Revolution and a variety of ways of communicating the essence of the American Revolution to a wide variety of students, in a pedagogically interesting way" (Shulman 1987, p. 5).

What to teach (content) and how to teach it (process) represent nagging problems for today's teachers. On one hand, researchers have shown that subject matter mastery is essential for effective teaching (Allen 2003; Sanders 2004; Walsh & Snyder 2004). Indeed, a strong connection exists between teachers' content knowledge preparation and higher student achievement.

The Educational Testing Service (ETS) study *How Teaching Matters* (Wenglinski 2000) concluded, not surprisingly, that teachers' content knowledge is an important factor in student achievement. Student achievement, for example, increases by 40 percent of a grade level in both mathematics and science when teachers have a major or minor in the subject. However, the study also concluded that content knowledge alone is not the only factor necessary to help increase student achievement. Indeed, the classroom instructional practices and strategies of teachers significantly influence student achievement. The study found that students who engage in active, hands-on learning activities and respond to higher-order thinking questions outperform their peers by more than 70 percent of a grade level in mathematics and 40 percent in science. In addition, the study showed that students whose teachers have received professional development training in working with special populations outperform their peers by more than a full grade level. The findings of the ETS study indicate that greater attention, not less, needs to be paid to improving the pedagogical knowledge of teachers and the classroom aspects of teacher quality.

myeducationlab

To enhance your understanding of connecting with standards, go to the IRIS Center Resource section of Topic 10: "Planning for Instruction" in the MyEducationLab for your course and complete the module entitled "Content Standards: Connecting Standards-Based Curriculum to Instructional Planning."

Balancing Content and Process in Content Area Classrooms

In their book *A Good Teacher in Every Classroom,* Linda Darling-Hammond and Joan Baratz-Snowden (2005) argue that the conventional view of teaching is simplistic in that teaching is viewed as proceeding through a set curriculum in a manner that *transmits* information from teacher to student. Moreover, they contend that there is much more to teaching than knowing the subject matter that students should learn. Among the many classroom practices characteristic of effective teachers, they "carefully organize activities, materials, and instruction based on students' prior knowledge . . . and engage students in active learning" (pp. 2–3).

Many of the literacy practices and strategies that you will learn about in this book will help you organize instruction around students' prior knowledge and their active engagement in text-related activities. As a result, students will be in a better position to understand the structure of your discipline and the important ideas and concepts underlying the subject matter that you teach. Balancing content and pedagogical knowledge in a standards-based curriculum means at the very least

- Knowing the standards for your content area and grade level;
- Making instructional decisions based on authentic assessments throughout the school year about students' abilities to use reading and writing to learn; and
- Integrating content literacy practices and strategies into instructional plans and units of study.

Standards, in a nutshell, are expected academic consequences defining what students should learn at designated grade levels and in content areas. Since the mid-1990s, a proliferation of national, state, and local standards have provided a road map to what students *should know* and *be able to do* at each grade level and for each content area.

The underlying rationale for the creation of standards is that high learning expectations—clearly stated and specific in nature—will lead to dramatic increases in student achievement. With high learning expectations comes an accountability system based on "high-stakes" assessment to determine how well students meet the standards formulated in each content area. Some states tie high-stakes assessment to the threat of grade-level retention for students who perform below predetermined levels of proficiency in critical areas such as reading. We explore in more detail the nature of high-stakes assessment in Chapter 4.

Pressure on Teachers

In a high-stakes educational environment, standards are bound to increase the pressure on teachers as well as students. In order for standards-based instruction to be effective in improving student performance, it needs to be aligned with the curriculum. As a result, numerous states have developed content standards, and school districts have subsequently redesigned their curricula to ensure consistency with the content area and grade-level standards outlined by the state.

The pressure to teach content standards well is omnipresent for many teachers. Yet teaching content well means helping students discover and understand the structure of a discipline (Bruner 1961). The student who discovers and understands a discipline's structure will be able to contend with its many detailed aspects. From an instructional perspective, teachers must help students see the "big picture" and develop the important concepts and powerful ideas that are part of each subject. Teachers who are wedded to a discipline walk a tightrope between content and process. It is certainly a balancing act every time the attempt is made to influence what is learned and how it should be learned.

To become literate in a content area, students must understand how to use reading, writing, talking, and viewing to learn. Integrating these thinking/learning processes helps students to better understand what they are reading about, writing about, talking about in classroom discussion, or viewing on a computer screen or video monitor. Using literacy-based learning strategies doesn't require specialized training on the part of content area teachers. And the pursuit of literacy does not diminish the teacher's role as a subject matter specialist. To help students become literate in a discipline does not mean to teach them *how* to read or write or talk as might be the case in a reading or English classroom. Instead, reading, writing, talking, and viewing are tools that students use to learn with texts in content areas. Who's in a better, more strategic position to show students how to learn with texts in a particular content area and grade level than the teacher who guides *what* students are expected to learn and *how* they are to learn it?

Teaching and Learning with Texts

Teaching and learning with texts are challenges in today's classrooms, where the demands inherent in the teaching of content standards can easily lead to "covering" information without much attention given to *how* students acquire core concepts.

Why does literacy matter? Discipline-literate students know how to think and learn with texts. Texts, whether in print or nonprint form, are indispensable sources of information, meaning-making, and knowledge construction. Learning how to teach with texts contributes significantly to the way you think about teaching, learning, and curriculum. Throughout this book, we invite you to examine content area literacy practices, and the assumptions underlying those practices, in the light of promising strategies for text learning and active student engagement.

Although texts come with the territory, using them to help students acquire content doesn't work well for many teachers. Teaching with texts is more complex than it appears on the surface. Whether you're a novice or a veteran teacher, using texts effectively requires a willingness to explore instructional strategies and to move beyond *assigning* and *telling*.

RESPONSE JOURNAL

What do you do as a reader to make meaning and construct knowledge as you interact with a text?

What are assigning and telling? Think back to when you were in school. You probably had a teacher or two who used an instructional strategy for teaching with text that included the following: *Assign* a text to read (usually with questions to be answered for homework); then in subsequent lessons *tell* students what the material they read was about, explaining and elaborating on the ideas and information in the text through lecture and question-and-answer routines. The interaction between teacher and students no doubt involved calling on a student to answer a question, listening to the student's

Calvin and Hobbes **by Bill Watterson**

Source: "Calvin and Hobbes," copyright © 1992 Bill Watterson. Reprinted with permission of Universal Press Syndicate. All rights reserved.

response, and then evaluating or modifying the student's response. Such is the ebb and flow of assign-and-tell instructional routines.

There is more to teaching with texts than assigning and telling. Assigning and telling are common but uninspired teaching practices that bog students down in the mire of passive learning. Assign-and-tell, more often than not, dampens active involvement in learning and denies students ownership of and responsibility for the acquisition of content. Teachers place themselves, either by design or by circumstance, in the unenviable position of being the most active participants during classroom interactions with students.

When teachers impart knowledge with little attention to how learners acquire that knowledge, students soon become nonparticipants in the academic life of the classroom. Assign-and-tell practices not only result in passive reading but also influence the way students view themselves in relation to texts. The accompanying *Calvin and Hobbes* cartoon has Calvin thinking of himself as "informationally impaired."

RESPONSE JOURNAL

When you were in middle or high school, did you know students who were "informationally impaired"? Why do you think some students give up on reading and doing homework assignments?

Teaching with texts requires its fair share of strategy. But it involves more than assigning pages to be read, lecturing, or using questions to check whether students have read the assigned material. To use texts strategically, you must first be aware of the powerful bonds that link literacy and learning in a discipline. Let's begin by taking a closer look at some of the meanings attached to the term *literacy*.

Literacy in the Twenty-First Century

To better understand what it means to be literate in a discipline or content area, we need to first examine some of the ways the term *literacy* has been used in our twenty-first-century, techno-savvy, media-driven society. Literacy is a dynamic concept that is continually evolving. In the United States and other technologically advanced countries, becoming literate carries with it strong cultural expectations. Society places a premium on literate behavior and demands that its citizens acquire literacy for personal, social, academic, and economic success. But what does it actually mean to be literate in the twenty-first century?

The meaning of *literacy* often fluctuates from one social context to another and from one group to another. For example, the term *computer literacy* has been used in recent times to describe the level of expertise and familiarity someone has with computers and computer applications. *Digital literacy* is often defined as the ability to use digital technology, communication tools, or networks to locate, evaluate, use, and create information. In today's multimedia world, *information literacy* denotes the ability to identify, locate, and access appropriate sources of information to meet one's needs. The broad definition of *media literacy* is even more encompassing in that it refers to someone's ability to access, analyze, evaluate, and produce communication and information in a variety of media modes, genres, and forms. And in the health and wellness field, *health literacy* is a more specific type of information-based competence denoting someone's ability to obtain, process, and understand the basic health information and services needed to make appropriate health decisions.

The above examples are but a few ways the term *literacy* has morphed to characterize someone's level of knowledge or competence in a particular area or subject in a multimodal society. For centuries the most common use of the term *literacy* had been to denote one's ability to read and write a language with competence. Today, however, the dynamic nature of literacy is such that it encompasses more than the ability to read and write black marks on a printed page. Literacy has come to represent a synthesis of language, thinking, and contextual practices through which people make and communicate meaning. Yet the more society evolves, the more complex and multidimensional the concept of literacy becomes:

> Today information about the world around us comes to us not only by words on a piece of paper but more and more through the powerful images and sounds of our multi-media culture. Although mediated messages appear to be self-evident, in truth, they use a complex audio/visual "language" which has its own rules (grammar) and which can be used to express many-layered concepts and ideas about the world. Not everything may be obvious at first; and images go by so fast! If our children are to be able to navigate their lives through this multi-media culture, they need to be fluent in "reading" and "writing" the language of images and sounds just as we have always taught them to "read" and "write" the language of printed communications. Furthermore, they need the skills to interact, to share their ideas and to collaborate constructively, making it possible to participate in today's media-driven culture. (Thoman and Jolls 2008, p. 8)

As notions of literacy expand with the times, so does the concept of *text*. Literate activity is no longer limited by conventional notions of text (Neilsen 2006). Texts include not only print forms of communication but also nonprint forms that are digital, aural, or visual in nature. Texts in content area classrooms represent sets of potential meanings and signifying practices, whether the text is a novel in an English class, the instructional conversation that takes place about the novel, or the made-for-television movie based on the novel. Helping students to *think* and *learn* with all kinds of text is an important responsibility of the content area teacher. Johannes Gutenberg's invention of movable type in the fifteenth century resulted in a revolution of ideas. Printed texts in the hands of the masses changed the face of literacy and learning in much the same way that multimodal information and communication technologies (ICT) are creating new literacies and new ways of learning.

myeducationlab

Go to the Building Teaching Skills and Dispositions section of Topic 9: "Integrating Technology" in the MyEducationLab for your course. As you complete the activity, consider how electronic texts can help students learn essential concepts across the curriculum.

New Literacies, New Ways of Learning

The potential for media and technology to make a difference in students' literacy development and learning was evident in the early 1980s, when computers began to play an increasingly important role in classrooms. However, the digital technologies available two decades ago were primitive compared to today's powerful technologies. Today's adolescents represent the first generation of youth who have grown up since the emergence of digital technologies, video games, cell phones, instant messaging, and the World Wide Web. Because they are the first generation to be immersed in ICT for their entire lives, they have at their fingertips more information than any generation in history (Considine, Horton, & Moorman 2009).

With continuously emerging ICT a reality in the twenty-first century, new literacies are necessary to use ICT effectively and to fully exploit their potential for learning (Kist 2005; Leu 2000). The new literacies are grounded in students' abilities to use reading and writing to learn but require new strategic knowledge, skills, and insights to meet the conceptual and technological demands inherent in complexly networked environments. To be sure, the Internet is one of the most powerful ICT extant, and it depends on literacy.

Nevertheless, there are real differences between reading printed texts and reading texts in a digital medium. As Kist (2005) explains, printed texts such as books are written for the reader to proceed from the front of the book to the back of the book, reading from left to right, "and most readers of a book will read the text with the order of the words coming in the same order for him or her as for every other reader of that book" (p. 5). However, one reader on the Internet might click on a hyperlink that another online reader would not. As a result, the first online reader would then process the text in a completely different sequence from that of the second reader.

Reading texts in a digital environment is not a linear activity. New literacies, therefore, are crucial in the search for content area information on the Internet and other ICT. As Leu, Leu, and Coiro (2006) point out, new literacies allow readers "to *identify* important questions, *navigate* complex information networks to locate important information, *critically evaluate* that information, *synthesize* it to address those questions, and then *communicate* the answers to others. These five functions help to define the new literacies that your students need to be successful with the Internet and other information and communication technologies (ICT)" (p. 1).

What, then, are some of the classroom implications for the development of new literacies? First and foremost, teachers need to help students "learn how to learn" new technologies. From a new literacies perspective, knowing how to learn continuously changing technologies is more critical than learning any particular ICT. Moreover, teachers need to provide instructional support in the development and use of strategies that, among other things, help students critically read and evaluate information. According to Leu (2002), learners will need to know how to put into play

> new forms of strategic knowledge necessary to locate, evaluate, and effectively use the extensive resources available within complexly networked ICT such as the Internet. The extent and complexity of this information is staggering. . . . How do we best search for information in these complex worlds? How do we design a Web page to be useful to people who are likely to visit? How do we communicate effectively with videoconference technologies? Strategic knowledge is central to the new literacies. (p. 314)

RESPONSE JOURNAL

How proficient are you with the use of new literacies associated with ICT? Are you proficient enough to help students "learn how to learn" ICT such as the Internet? Elaborate.

A teacher should not automatically assume that today's adolescents already are strategic in their use of ICT for academic purposes. The extensive use of ICT by adolescents in social and personal contexts often creates a false sense of competence in an academic context. As Considine, Horton, and Moorman (2009) put it, "hands-on is not the same as heads-on" when it comes to making assumptions about how effectively adolescents use ICT to learn (p. 472).

Print resources, such as textbooks and trade books, in combination with digital texts, sound, and images create powerful learning environments in an academic discipline. Learning with new literacies, which we will explore in Chapter 2, involves many of the same thinking processes that print forms of text involve. However, teachers who work with adolescent learners in middle and high school may find that some, if not many, of their students struggle with assignments that require thinking and learning with academic text in print or nonprint forms. No wonder *adolescent literacy* is a hot topic in education today (Cassidy & Cassidy 2009). Let's take a closer look at the concept of adolescent literacy and its implications for thinking and learning with texts.

Adolescent Literacy

According to Bob Wise (2009), president of the Alliance for Excellent Education and a former governor of West Virginia, adolescent literacy is the cornerstone of students' academic success. The literacy learning that takes place in adolescents is of critical importance in preparing them for life in and out of school. The Commission on Adolescent Literacy of the International Reading Association (IRA) asserts that

> adolescents entering the adult world in the 21st century will read and write more than at any other time in human history. They will need advanced levels of literacy to perform

> their jobs, run their households, act as citizens, and conduct their personal lives. They will need literacy to cope with the flood of information they will find everywhere they turn. They will need literacy to feed their imaginations so they can create the world of the future. In a complex and sometimes even dangerous world, their ability to read will be crucial. Continual instruction beyond the early grades is needed. (Moore, Bean, Birdyshaw, & Rycik 1999, p. 3)

In the early grades of elementary school, many students learn basic skills related to reading and writing; however, by fourth grade and on, they need to continue to develop skill and sophistication in the use of literacy strategies and practices specific to different disciplines, texts, and situations. As the emphasis on disciplinary learning increases in middle and high schools, adolescents must develop both confidence in themselves and the thinking processes necessary for academic success in various content areas. Ironically, adolescents often experience difficulty with disciplinary literacy and learning, even though they may regularly use literacies for social purposes outside of school in ethnic, online, and popular culture communities (Moje 2007).

Since 1992, when periodic National Assessment of Education Progress (NAEP) surveys in reading began for students in grades 4, 8, and 12, it has become evident that there is an adolescent literacy crisis in the United States (Alliance for Excellent Education 2006; Kamil 2003; Vacca 1998; Vacca & Alvermann 1998). Few would argue with the importance of early reading development. Yet the emphasis on learning to read in the primary grades in the United States has served to magnify the lack of attention and commitment given to adolescent learners and their literacy needs.

From a historical perspective, the literacy needs of middle and high school students have received marginal attention by policy makers and curriculum planners. In the latter half of the twentieth century, students who struggled with reading often were identified as "remedial readers" and were assigned to "reading labs" or "remedial reading" classes, where they typically received piecemeal instruction apart from the content areas. As Vacca and Alvermann (1998) indicated, there has been an apparent lack of a national policy and schoolwide commitment for the ongoing literacy development of learners beyond the primary grades. Recently, however, there have been positive initiatives taking place focusing on the literacy needs of adolescents.

In a landmark report entitled *Reading Next,* Biancarosa and Snow (2004) address the current state of adolescent literacy and identify fifteen critical elements of effective adolescent literacy programs. These elements are highlighted in Box 1.1. In addition, a 2005 federal initiative, the Striving Readers program, provides competitive, discretionary grants to school districts to raise the reading achievement levels of middle and high school–aged students in Title I–eligible schools with significant numbers of students reading below grade level. One of the goals of the Striving Readers program is to enhance reading achievement in middle and high schools through improvements to the quality of literacy instruction across the curriculum.

Evidence-Based Best Practices

BOX 1.1

Fifteen Elements of Effective Adolescent Literacy Programs

Reading Next, a report to Carnegie Corporation of New York, provides a "vision for action and research" in the development of adolescent literacy programs. The report delineates fifteen elements for improving middle and high school literacy achievement.

1. *Direct, explicit comprehension instruction,* which is instruction in the strategies and processes that proficient readers use to understand what they read, including summarizing, keeping track of one's own understanding, and a host of other practices
2. *Effective instructional principles embedded in content,* including language arts teachers using content-area texts and content-area teachers providing instruction and practice in reading and writing skills specific to their subject area
3. *Motivation and self-directed learning,* which includes building motivation to read and learn and providing students with the instruction and supports needed for independent learning tasks they will face after graduation
4. *Text-based collaborative learning,* which involves students interacting with one another around a variety of texts
5. *Strategic tutoring,* which provides students with intense individualized reading, writing, and content instruction as needed
6. *Diverse texts,* which are texts at a variety of difficulty levels and on a variety of topics
7. *Intensive writing,* including instruction connected to the kinds of writing tasks students will have to perform well in high school and beyond
8. *A technology component,* which includes technology as a tool for and a topic of literacy instruction
9. *Ongoing formative assessment of students,* which is informal, often daily assessment of how students are progressing under current instructional practices
10. *Extended time for literacy,* which includes approximately two to four hours of literacy instruction and practice that takes place in language arts and content-area classes
11. *Professional development* that is both long term and ongoing
12. *Ongoing summative assessment of students and programs,* which is more formal and provides data that are reported for accountability and research purposes
13. *Teacher teams,* which are interdisciplinary teams that meet regularly to discuss students and align instruction
14. *Leadership,* which can come from principals and teachers who have a solid understanding of how to teach reading and writing to the full array of students present in schools
15. *A comprehensive and coordinated literacy program,* which is interdisciplinary and interdepartmental and may even coordinate with out-of-school organizations and the local community

Source: Reading Next: A Vision for Action and Research in Middle and High School Literacy (2004). www.all4ed.org/files/ReadingNext.pdf, pp. 12–13.

Teaching adolescents is no easy task. Their lives are complex. Not only are they undergoing great physical changes, but they also are faced with ongoing cognitive, emotional, and social challenges. Adolescents who struggle with literacy in academic disciplines often go through the motions of reading without engaging in the process.

Even skilled adolescent readers will struggle with reading sometimes, in some places, with some texts. Some students may lack the prior knowledge needed to connect to important ideas in the text. Others may get lost in the author's line of reasoning, become confused by the way the text is organized, or run into unknown words that are difficult to pronounce, let alone define. Often comprehension problems are only temporary. However, the difference between proficient adolescent readers and those who struggle all the time is this: When proficient readers struggle with text, they know what to do to get out of trouble. They have confidence in themselves as readers and learners. When a text becomes confusing or doesn't make sense, good readers recognize that they have an array of skills and strategies that they can use to work themselves out of difficulty.

Average and above-average adolescent learners, who are usually on track to go to college, might also struggle with reading without their teachers being cognizant of it. Often these students feel helpless about their ability to engage in academic literacy tasks, but go through the motions of "doing" school. Since 1992 periodic national assessments of reading conducted by the National Center for Education Statistics (NCES) show that the majority of U.S. students in grades 4, 8, and 12 have obtained, at best, only "basic" levels of literacy. These NAEP surveys for reading (NAEP 2007) reveal that the vast majority of adolescent learners in grades 4 and 8 have difficulty with complex literacy tasks. For example, they may be able to read with some degree of fluency and accuracy but might not know what to do with text beyond saying the words and comprehending at what is essentially a literal level of performance. In the classroom, these students may appear *skillful* in the mechanics of reading but aren't *strategic* enough in their abilities to handle reading tasks that require interpretation and critical thinking. Throughout this book we explore the role of motivation in the academic lives of adolescents who struggle with school-based literacy even though they are likely to use new literacies *outside* of school for personal and social purposes (Lenters 2006; Moje 2007; Moje, Overby, Tysvaer, & Morris 2008).

The terms *content literacy* and *disciplinary literacy* are frequently used to describe a discipline-centered instructional approach to literacy and learning in content area classrooms. From our perspective, content literacy and disciplinary literacy reflect many of the same instructional attributes, although critics of content literacy pedagogy claim some real differences between the two approaches to literacy and learning (Draper 2008; Moje 2007, 2008). In the next section, we explore the common ground between content literacy and disciplinary literacy and discuss how the two concepts may differ in terms of teaching practices.

Disciplinary Literacy in Perspective

For many years the term *content area reading* was associated with helping students better understand what they read across the curriculum. However, the concept of content area reading was broadened in the 1990s to reflect reading as well as other language processes. Hence, the relatively new construct of *content literacy* refers to the ability to use reading, writing, talking, listening, and viewing to learn subject matter in a given discipline (Vacca 2002a). Content literacy involves the use of research-based cognitive learning strategies designed to support reading, writing, thinking, and learning with text. Most recently, the concept of *disciplinary literacy* is having an impact on the way researchers and educators think about literacy and learning in content areas (Buehl & Moore 2009; Lee 2004; Moje 2007, 2008; Shanahan & Shanahan 2008).

William S. Gray, one of the early titans in the field of reading, articulated the relationship between reading and learning that remains today the underlying rationale for reading in content areas. Not only did he forge the beginnings of content area reading, but he is also credited with what has become an often used, and often confused, mantra in education, "Every teacher is a teacher of reading." More than seventy-five years ago, Gray (1925) published one of the first descriptive studies to identify reading and study skills by content area. He determined that each content area requires different sets of skills for effective reading and study of text material. These different skill sets are related to one's purpose for reading and the conceptual demands of the text.

Many other researchers in the 1940s, 1950s, and 1960s designed "content-centered" studies to investigate the effectiveness of guiding students' reading within the context of disciplinary instruction. Harold Herber (1964), for example, developed "guide materials" to assist high school physics students in the development of core concepts in their textbook. He found that the students who used "study guides" to read physics text significantly outperformed those students who did not use guides to read the content under study. Herber (1970) later wrote the first comprehensive textbook, *Teaching Reading in Content Areas,* exclusively devoted to content area reading instruction. The guiding principle underlying Herber's book is as powerful today as it was nearly forty years ago: *Content determines process*. Even though the majority of students learn how to read in elementary school with some degree of proficiency, they must learn how to adapt reading and thinking strategies to meet the peculiarities and conceptual demands of each discipline they study. The shift from skills to learning strategies was first felt in the 1970s and 1980s when numerous research studies were conducted to better understand the role of thinking and learning processes in reading and to validate learning strategies grounded in cognitive principles (Conley 2008).

Content literacy and disciplinary literacy are extensions of the concept of content area reading, where "content determines process" in a given discipline. The underlying goal of a discipline-specific approach to literacy is to show students how to think and learn with text as they develop a deep understanding of concepts and ideas encountered in texts. Each discipline poses its own challenges in terms of purposes for reading, vocabulary, concepts, texts, themes, and topics. How students read, think, and learn with text more than likely varies from content area to content area: "Even casual observation shows that students who struggle with reading a physics text may be excellent readers of poetry; the student who has difficulty with word problems in math may be very comfortable with historical narratives" (National Council of Teachers of English 2008).

The big idea behind disciplinary literacy is that literacy development in a discipline is inextricably related to content knowledge and thinking. Doug Buehl (2009), a longtime advocate of adolescent literacy and a former social studies teacher and literacy coach in Madison, Wisconsin, argues that middle and high school curricula must focus not only on what students should know and be able to do, but also on how "experts within a discipline read, write, and think" (p. 535). He contends that content area teachers are sometimes frustrated by "generic literacy practices" encountered in professional development workshops that are not relevant to reading and learning in their disciplines.

Buehl (2009) advocates for continued research on discipline-specific literacy practices, which seem "to be an especially fertile ground for determining how to mentor students to read, write, and think through the lens of a mathematician, biologist, musician, historian, artist, novelist, and so forth" (p. 537). He cites a statewide project in Wisconsin called Thinking Like a Historian in which history teachers are encouraged to engage in questioning routines around five core themes crucial to thinking and learning with historical text:

1. Cause and effect: "What happened and why?"
2. Change and continuity: "What changed and what remained the same?"
3. Turning points: "How did events of the past affect the future?"
4. Through their eyes: "How did people in the past view their lives and world?"
5. Using the past: "How does studying the past help us understand our lives and world?" (Wisconsin Historical Society 2009)

In a similar vein, Lee (2004) describes disciplinary literacy as "the ability to understand, critique, and use knowledge from texts in content areas" (p. 14). She links disciplinary literacy directly to the needs of culturally diverse adolescent readers who struggle with academic texts and suggests that an important dimension of a discipline-specific approach to literacy is to draw on adolescent learners' "cultural funds of knowledge"—that is, the kinds of knowledge that culturally diverse students bring to learning situations. As we explain in Chapter 3, how teachers adjust instruction to the sociocultural strengths of students in diverse classrooms is an important aspect of literacy and learning in a discipline.

Moje (2007) provides a complex view of disciplinary literacy as she discusses some of the theory, research, and pedagogical practices supporting instructional approaches to disciplinary literacy. She describes one such approach found on the website of the Institute for Learning at the University of Pittsburgh (www.instituteforlearning.org/dl.html):

> This approach to teaching and learning integrates academically rigorous content with discipline-appropriate habits of thinking. The driving idea is that knowledge and thinking

must go hand in hand. To develop deep conceptual knowledge in a discipline, one needs to use the habits of thinking that are valued and used by that discipline. . . . The ultimate goal of Disciplinary Literacy is that all students will develop deep content knowledge and literate habits of thinking in the context of academically rigorous learning in individual disciplines. (Quoted in Moje 2007, p. 10)

Others have called for a rethinking of the way literacy is embedded within various disciplinary-specific learning situations. For example, Shanahan and Shanahan (2008) conducted a descriptive research project in which they studied how disciplinary experts (university professors and classroom teachers) from mathematics, history, and chemistry engaged in reading to learn. In the first year of the project, the researchers adapted a pedagogical practice called "think-alouds" to identify the "specialized reading skills" used by the experts to comprehend texts in their respective disciplines. During the think-aloud sessions, the researchers discovered that "[e]ach of the disciplinary experts emphasized a different array of reading processes, suggesting the focused and highly specialized nature of literacy at these levels" (Shanahan & Shanahan 2008, p. 49).

In the second year of the project, the teams of disciplinary experts studied the viability of generic literacy strategies and explored ways to develop instructional strategies that were discipline-specific. These strategies are similar in intent to the kinds of cognitive-based strategies found in this and other books dealing with literacy and learning across the curriculum. However, the teams of discipline-specific experts modified and adapted generic literacy strategies to meet the textual and conceptual demands inherent in their specific disciplines.

Whether you call it *content area reading, content literacy,* or *disciplinary literacy,* the guiding principle behind each instructional approach remains as powerful today as it has for nearly a century. *Content determines process.* The conceptual demands and structure of a discipline-specific text determines how a reader will interact with that text, make sense of it, and learn from it. As Kamil (2003) concluded, teaching literacy strategies has value for all teachers. However, a disciplinary literacy perspective reminds us that teachers, as subject matter specialists, must also have a solid understanding of the reading, writing, and thinking processes necessary to adapt and modify literacy strategies, tailoring them to meet the conceptual and textual demands of the content under study.

As recent National Assessments of Educational Progress (NAEP) show, far too many adolescents struggle with academic reading tasks (Lee, Grigg, & Donahue 2007; Perie, Grigg, & Donahue 2005). Many school districts have begun to use a *tiered* approach to intervention for students who significantly struggle with reading and learning. This approach, known as *Response to Intervention* (RTI), holds much promise for improving literacy and learning across the curriculum. RTI underscores the importance of responsive teaching, assessment, and differentiated instruction in the academic lives of adolescents who struggle with reading. Throughout various chapters of this book, we will highlight RTI and the role it might play in helping students, especially adolescent learners, who struggle with text.

RTI for Struggling Adolescent Learners

BOX 1.2

Implications for Content Literacy

What is Response to Intervention (RTI) and how does it affect the work of content area teachers? RTI is a relatively new, promising approach to providing the most appropriate instruction, service, and research-based strategy interventions to significantly struggling learners. In response to the growing number of students recommended for special education programs, a new version of the Individuals with Disabilities Education Act was passed in 2004. This act redefines the way students with learning disabilities are identified. Because previous protocols for special education referrals did not require students to have interventions within general education classrooms, it was often difficult to determine whether literacy-related learning problems were due to a student's cognitive disabilities or to a lack of exposure to effective literacy instruction (Johnson, Mellard, Fuchs, & McKnight 2006).

The goal of RTI, therefore, is to use schoolwide assessments to identify at-risk learners and to provide various levels of strategy interventions before students fall behind their peers. According to the National Research Center on Learning Disabilities (NRCLD), RTI is "an assessment and intervention process for systematically monitoring student progress and making decisions about the need for instructional modifications or increasingly intensified services using progress monitoring data" (Johnson, Mellard, Fuchs, & McKnight 2006, p. 2). The International Reading Association (2008) describes RTI as a multi-tiered process that provides services and interventions to struggling learners at increasing levels of intensity. In the RTI instructional framework, all stakeholders are expected to work collaboratively to make instructional decisions. Teachers, parents, literacy coaches, special education teachers, and additional staff members work together to determine the needs of each student and to plan and deliver appropriate instruction.

RTI is much more prevalent at the elementary school level than at middle and secondary levels. However, many middle and high schools have begun to implement RTI in their school districts. Although there are several RTI models to follow, a three-tier approach to strategy intervention is used in many school districts.

TIER 1

All students in Tier 1 receive high-quality, research-based instruction differentiated to meet their needs, and are screened periodically to identify struggling learners who need additional support. Content area teachers have an important role to play at this level of intervention. Throughout this book, we describe many potentially useful assessment procedures and literacy strategies grounded in cognitive theory and research that support and monitor students' ability to learn with text.

TIER 2

Tier 2 provides targeted intervention for students who have not been successful in classroom learning situations and have not made adequate progress in core curriculum studies. Their progress is monitored frequently to determine whether strategy interventions have been successful. Content area teachers typically receive support, as needed, from literacy coaches and specialists to ensure that students "on the edge" are making adequate progress at their grade level. For example, in some RTI models, students who are at risk of failure are assigned to tutoring centers within a school for more intensive instruction and support. Moreover, handheld electronic devices, which provide more intensive instructional programs for the 10 to 15 percent of students who are at Tier 2, are also being used within content area classrooms to prevent struggling adolescent learners from falling behind their peers.

TIER 3

At this level, students receive individualized, intensive interventions that target the students' skill deficits for the remediation of existing problems and the prevention of more severe problems. Literacy specialists and special education personnel are responsible for providing Tier 3 interventions and work closely with classroom teachers.

Reading to Learn

A variety of classroom-related factors influence reading to learn in a given discipline, including

- The learner's prior knowledge of, attitude toward, and interest in the subject;
- The learner's purpose for engaging in reading, writing, and discussion;
- The vocabulary and conceptual difficulty of the text material;
- The assumptions that the text writers make about their audience of readers;
- The text structures that writers use to organize ideas and information; and
- The teacher's beliefs about and attitude toward the use of texts in learning situations.

Writers of texts communicate with readers in the same way that speakers use language to communicate with listeners, or filmmakers use sound and moving images to tell a story or communicate meaning to viewers. Teaching with textbooks or other types of written text involves more than assigning pages to be read, lecturing, or using questions to check whether students have read the material the night before. To use written texts strategically and effectively, you must first be aware of the powerful bonds between reading and knowledge construction. With this in mind, consider how reading to learn relates to meaning-making and text comprehension.

Reading as a Meaning-Making Process

Language helps a learner to make sense of the world, to understand and to be understood. As a result, language and meaning cannot be severed from one another. Language isn't language unless meaning-making is involved. Oral language without meaning is mere prattle—a string of senseless, meaningless speech sounds. Written language without meaning is a cipher of mysterious markings on paper.

To be literate in content area classrooms, students must learn how to use reading to construct knowledge in the company of authors, other learners, and teachers. Using reading in the classroom to help students to learn doesn't require specialized training on the part of content teachers, although many of today's middle and high schools employ *literacy coaches* (a topic discussed in Chapter 12) to develop, support, and extend content area teachers' use of literacy strategies. Content literacy practices do not diminish the teacher's role as a subject matter specialist. Instead, reading is a tool students use to construct, clarify, and extend meaning in a given discipline.

Why are you able to read a text such as Lewis Carroll's "Jabberwocky" with little trouble, even though Carroll invents words such as *chortled* and *toves* throughout the poem? Try reading "Jabberwocky" aloud:

JABBERWOCKY

'Twas brillig, and the slithy toves
Did gyre and gimble in the wabe;
All mimsy were the borogoves,
And the mome raths outgrabe.

"Beware the Jabberwock, my son!
The jaws that bite, the claws that catch!
Beware the Jubjub bird and shun
The frumious Bandersnatch!"

He took his vorpal sword in hand:
Long time the manxome foe he sought—
So rested he by the Tumtum tree,
And stood awhile in thought.

And, as in uffish thought he stood,
The Jabberwock, with eyes of flame,
Came whiffling through the tulgey wood,
And burbled as it came!

One, two! One, two! And through and through
The vorpal blade went snicker-snack!
He left it dead, and with its head
He went galumphing back.

"And hast thou slain the Jabberwock?
Come to my arms, my beamish boy!
O frabjous day! Callooh! Callay!"
He chortled in his joy.

'Twas brillig, and the slithy toves
Did gyre and gimble in the wabe;
All mimsy were the borogoves,
And the mome raths outgrabe.

What is quickly apparent from your reading of the poem is that going from print to speech is a hollow act unless meaning-making is involved in the transaction.

Try rewriting the poem using your own words. If you and a colleague or two were to compare your rewrites, you undoubtedly would find similarities in meaning, but also important differences. These differences undoubtedly reflect the knowledge of the world that you as a reader bring to the text as well as the *strategies* you used to make meaning.

Reading as a Strategic Process

Throughout this book, we argue that the real value of reading lies in its uses. Whether we use reading to enter into the imaginative world of fiction; learn with academic texts; meet workplace demands; acquire insight and knowledge about people, places, and things; or understand a graphic on an Internet website, readers, to be successful, must use strategies to meet the demands of the task at hand.

For example, a skilled reader will approach the following passage as a challenge and use a repertoire of reading strategies to construct meaning.

A PLAN FOR THE IMPROVEMENT OF ENGLISH SPELLING*

For example, in Year 1 that useless letter "c" would be dropped to be replased either by "k" or "s," and likewise "x" would no longer be part of the alphabet. The only kase in which "c" would be retained would be the "ch" formation, which will be dealt with later. Year 2 might reform "w" spelling, so that "which" and "one" would take the same konsonant, wile Year 3 might well abolish "y" replasing it with "i" and Iear 4 might fiks the "g/j" anomali wonse and for all.

Jenerally, then, the improvement would kontinue iear bai iear with Iear 5 doing awai with useless double konsonants, and Iears 6–12 or so modifaiing vowlz and the rimeining voist and unvoist konsonants. Bai Iear 15 or sou, it wud fainali bi posibl tu meik ius ov thi ridandant letez "c," "y" and "x"—bai now jast a memori in the maindz ov ould doderez—tu riplais "ch," "sh," and "th" rispektivli.

Fainali, xen, aafte sam 20 iers ov orxogrefkl riform, wi wud hev a lojikl, kohirnt speling in ius xrewawt xe Ingliy-spiking werld.

In order to comprehend text successfully, skilled readers must be able to *decode* or pronounce words quickly and accurately, read with *fluency,* activate *vocabulary knowledge* in relation to the language of the text, and put into play *text comprehension* strategies to understand what they are reading. As Figure 1.1 suggests, decoding, reading fluency, vocabulary, and comprehension are interrelated processes. If readers have trouble decoding words quickly and accurately (e.g., analyzing and recognizing sound–letter relationships), it will slow down their ability to read fluently in a smooth, conversational manner. Moreover, if they struggle to decode words accurately, various reading errors (e.g., mispronunciations, word omissions, and substitutions), if significant, will cause cognitive confusion and limit readers' abilities to bring meaning and conceptual understanding to the words in the text.

When students lack decoding and fluency skills, the act of reading no longer becomes automatic. As you read "A Plan for the Improvement of English Spelling," did the letter substitutions cause you to struggle as a reader? Perhaps. The progressive substitution of letters undoubtedly slowed down your ability to read in a smooth, conversational manner and may even have affected your accuracy in recognizing some words. Just think about some of the students in classrooms today who lack the ability to decode words accurately and read fluently. They may

RESPONSE JOURNAL

Describe some of the reading strategies you use to successfully complete an academic reading assignment. What are some of the strategies you use for writing essays or papers that will be graded or shared with others?

*Although on the Internet this passage is widely attributed to Mark Twain, there is uncertainty as to its actual author.

FIGURE 1.1 Reading Involves the Use of Decoding, Fluency, Vocabulary, and Comprehension Strategies

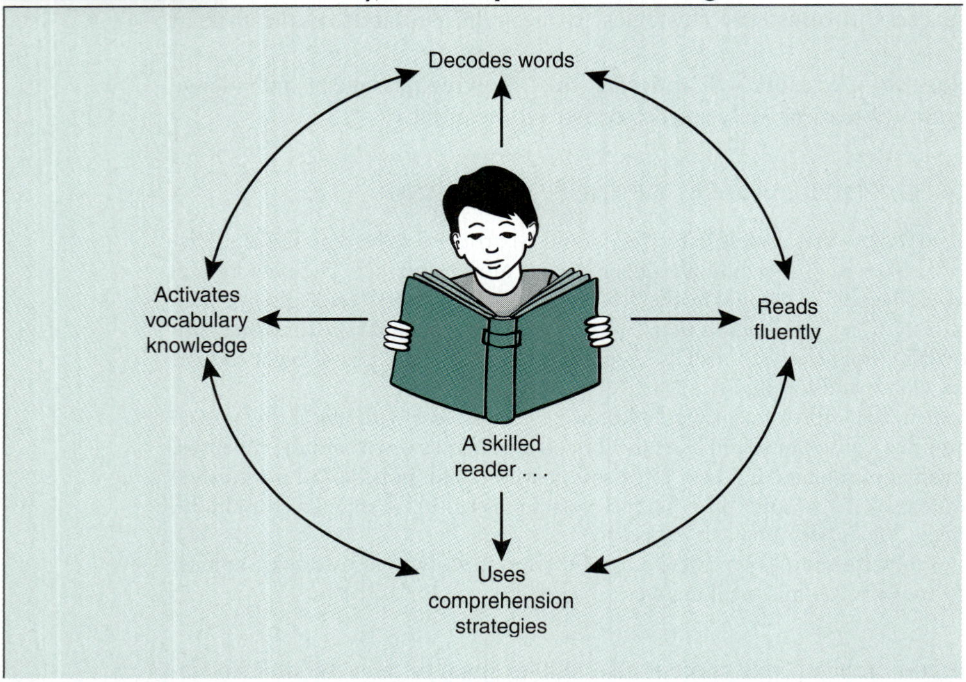

experience difficulty because they read in a slow and halting manner, word-by-word, and have trouble pronouncing words quickly and accurately. They spend so much time and attention on trying to "say the words" that comprehension suffers and, as a result, the reading process breaks down for them. Such students will benefit from *direct, explicit* instruction in decoding and fluency strategies from trained literacy specialists.

Our guess is that the reading process did not break down for you as you read the passage. Even though the substitution of letters slowed down your reading, chances are you were still able to comprehend the passage and construct meaning from it. This is because skilled readers do not use a single strategy to comprehend text. They know how to "think with print" as they search for and construct meaning from text. Skilled readers have at their command *multiple strategies* for comprehending text.

Reading as a Comprehension Process

When skilled readers have difficulty comprehending what they are reading, they often become *strategic* in the way they approach challenging and difficult text. That is to say, good readers have developed *strategies* that they use to understand what they are reading. As Duke and Pearson (2002) explain, we know a great deal about what good

TABLE 1.1

What Do Good Readers Do When They Comprehend Text?

Characteristics of Good Readers	Strategies of Good Readers
Good readers are ■ Active ■ Purposeful ■ Evaluative ■ Thoughtful ■ Strategic ■ Persistent ■ Productive	Good readers ■ Have clear *goals* in mind for their reading and evaluate whether the text, and their reading of it, is meeting their goals. ■ *Look over* the text before they read, noting such things as the *structure* of the text and text sections that might be most relevant to their reading goals. ■ *Make predictions* about what is to come. ■ Read *selectively,* continually making decisions about their reading—what to read carefully, what to read quickly, what not to read, what to reread, and so on. ■ *Construct, revise,* and *question* the meanings they make as they read. ■ Try to determine the meanings of *unfamiliar words and concepts* in the text. ■ Draw from, compare, and *integrate their prior knowledge* with material in the text. ■ Think about the *authors* of the text, their styles, beliefs, intentions, historical milieu, and so on. ■ *Monitor their understanding* of the text, making adjustments in their reading as necessary. ■ *Evaluate the text's quality and value,* and react to the text in a range of ways, both intellectually and emotionally. ■ *Read different kinds of text differently.* ■ *Attend closely* to the setting and characters when reading narrative. ■ Frequently *construct* and *revise summaries* of what they have read when reading expository text. ■ Think about text before, during, and after reading.

Source: Adapted from "Effective Practices for Developing Reading Comprehension" by N. K. Duke and P. D. Pearson, in *What Research Has to Say about Reading Instruction* (pp. 205–242), A. E. Farstrup & S. J. Samuels (eds.). Copyright © 2002 by the International Reading Association. Reproduced with permission of International Reading Association via Copyright Clearance Center.

readers do when they read: "Reading comprehension research has a long and rich history . . . much work on the process of reading comprehension has been grounded in studies of good readers" (p. 205). Table 1.1 delineates what good readers do when they engage in the process of comprehending text.

The research-based findings of two influential reports, *The Report of the National Reading Panel* (National Reading Panel 2000) and the *RAND Report on Reading Comprehension* (RAND Reading Study Group 2002), indicate that much is known about comprehension instruction. These reports, for example, draw several conclusions about effective comprehension instruction, including the following:

RESPONSE JOURNAL

Describe the relationships among *reader*, *text*, and *activity* in the reading comprehension model described in Chapter 2 of the RAND report.

- Instruction can be effective in helping students develop a repertoire of strategies that promotes and fosters comprehension.
- Strategy instruction, when integrated into subject matter learning, improves students' comprehension of text.
- Struggling readers benefit from *explicit instruction* in the use of strategies.
- Vocabulary knowledge is strongly related to text comprehension and is especially important in teaching English learners.
- Effective comprehension strategies include *question generation, question answering routines, comprehension monitoring, cooperative learning, summarizing,* visual displays known as *graphic organizers,* and knowledge of different *text structures.*
- Students benefit from exposure to different types or *genres* of texts (e.g., informational and narrative texts).
- Teachers who provide choices, challenging tasks, and collaborative learning experiences increase students' motivation to read and comprehend texts.

Learners position themselves to comprehend texts whenever they use *prior knowledge* to construct meaning for new material that they are studying. Prior knowledge reflects the experiences, conceptual understandings, attitudes, values, skills, and strategies a student brings to a text learning situation. Let's take a closer look at the role prior knowledge plays in comprehending and learning with text.

Prior Knowledge and Comprehension: A Closer Look

In workshops for content teachers, we occasionally read the short story "Ordeal by Cheque" by Wuther Crue (first published in *Vanity Fair* magazine in 1932). The story is extraordinary in that it is told entirely through the bank checks of the Exeter family over a twenty-eight-year span. The workshop participants interact in small groups, and each group is assigned the task of constructing the meaning of the story. At first glance, the groups don't know what to make of their task. "You must be kidding!" is a typical response. At this point, we engage the groups in a *prereading activity* to activate prior knowledge, declare the purposes for reading, and arouse interest in the story. We assign them the activity in Table 1.2, which depicts in chart form the essential bits of information contained on the first nine checks of the story. Group members collaborate as they respond to the task of answering the three questions that accompany the chart: What is the story about? How would you describe the main

TABLE 1.2

Prereading Activity for "Ordeal by Cheque"

Here are the essential bits of information contained in the first few checks of the story:

Entry Date:	Paid To:	Amount:	Signed By:
8/30/03	A baby shop	$ 148.50	Lawrence Exeter
9/2/03	A hospital	100.00	Lawrence Exeter
10/3/03	A physician	475.00	Lawrence Exeter Sr.
12/19/03	A toy company	83.20	Lawrence Exeter Sr.
10/6/09	A private school for boys	1,250.00	Lawrence Exeter Sr.
4/18/10	A bicycle shop	52.50	Lawrence Exeter Sr.
8/26/15	A military academy	2,150.00	Lawrence Exeter Sr.
9/3/21	A Cadillac dealer	3,885.00	Lawrence Exeter Sr.
9/7/21	An auto repair shop	288.76	Lawrence Exeter Sr.

What is the story about? How would you describe the main characters? What do you think will happen in the remainder of the story?

characters? What do you think will happen in the remainder of the story? We invite you to analyze the information in the chart. Are you able to construct what has taken place so far in the story? What inferences did you make about the characters?

Your predictions and inferences are probably rooted in your "knowledge of the world" as well as your knowledge of how stories work. Some of you, for example, may have used your knowledge of *story structure* to infer a setting for "Ordeal by Cheque" and identify a problem around which the remainder of the story will unfold. Based on the information in Table 1.2, what appears to be the problem of the story? The fifteen or so minutes that it takes to complete the prereading activity is time well spent. Not only have you developed a general sense of what the story is about but also your curiosity and interest may have been aroused about the content of the remaining checks in the story.

Not only do readers activate prior knowledge *before* reading but they also use prior knowledge *during* and *after* reading to infer meaning and elaborate on the text content. You will find this to be the case as you read "Ordeal by Cheque" in its entirety (see Appendix A on pages 418–421). As you read, you will undoubtedly find yourself using your knowledge of the world as well as what you know (or think you know) about the characters, the historical era in which the story is set, and the plot to make inferences, to evaluate, and to elaborate on the story content. Why is this the case?

Cognitive scientists use the technical term *schema* to describe how people use world or prior knowledge to organize and store information in their heads. Furthermore, *schema activation* is the mechanism by which people access what they know and match it to the information in a text. In doing so, they build on the meaning they already bring to a learning situation. Indeed, schemata (the plural of schema) have been called "the building blocks of cognition" (Rumelhart 1982) because they represent elaborate networks of information that people use to make sense of new stimuli, events, and situations. When a match occurs between students' prior knowledge and text material, a schema functions in at least three ways.

First, a schema provides a framework for learning that allows readers to *seek and select* information that is relevant to their purposes for reading. In the process of searching and selecting, readers are more likely to *make inferences* about the text. You make inferences when you *anticipate* content and *make predictions* about upcoming material, or you *fill in gaps* in the material during reading.

Second, a schema helps readers *organize* text information. The process by which you organize and integrate new information into old facilitates the ability to *retain and remember* what you read. A poorly organized text is difficult for readers to comprehend. We illustrate this point in more detail when we discuss the influences of text structure on comprehension and retention in later chapters.

Third, a schema helps readers *elaborate* information. When you elaborate what you have read, you engage in a cognitive process that involves deeper levels of insight, judgment, and evaluation. You are inclined to ask, "So what?" as you engage in conversation with an author.

LOOKING BACK LOOKING FORWARD

In this chapter, we invited you to begin an examination of content literacy practices and the assumptions underlying those practices. Teachers play a critical role in helping students use literacy strategies to think and learn with text. Learning with all kinds of text, whether in print or nonprint forms, is an active process. In today's standards-based educational environment, the pressure to teach content standards well can easily lead to content-only instruction with little attention paid to how students acquire information and develop concepts. Yet teachers must balance content (what they teach) and process (how they teach) as they engage students in thinking and learning with text.

To this end, we explored the role that literacy plays in the acquisition of content knowledge. The concept of literacy must be viewed from a twenty-first-century perspective. In an era of digital media, many of today's adolescents have developed "new literacies" that they use for personal and social purposes. New literacies are having a major influence on learning in academic contexts. To shift the burden of learning from teacher to student requires an understanding of the relationships among literacies, texts, and learning across the curriculum. As a result, we attempted to put content literacy and disciplinary literacy practices into perspective, contending that the two approaches to instruction share much common ground. Our emphasis throughout this book is on reading and writing to learn. Learning how to comprehend text across disciplines is what content area reading is all about.

The next chapter puts the spotlight on new literacies in the adolescent lives of twenty-first-century learners. Digital texts are highly engaging and interactive. New literacies make it possible to interact with text in ways not imaginable even a short while ago. Literacy-related learning opportunities in multimodal environments are interactive, enhance communication, engage students in multimedia, create opportunities for inquiry, and support socially mediated learning. Whether students are navigating the Internet or interacting with popular media such as video games, an array of learning experiences await them.

Minds On

1. During a job interview, the principal of a middle school asks if you are "highly qualified" for the position. How would you respond?

2. Imagine that during lunch, several teaching colleagues comment that because many students in their courses "can't read," these teachers rarely use books. They argue that students learn content just as well through audiovisual aids and discussions.

   Divide a small group of six class members into two smaller groups of three: one representing the teachers who believe books are unnecessary and one representing those who believe books are essential. For ten minutes, role-play a lunchtime debate on the pros and cons of using reading in content areas. After the time has elapsed, discuss the arguments used by the role players. Which did you find valid, and with which did you disagree?

3. Your supervisor observes a lesson in which you use a large block of time for students to read. Afterward, the supervisor says that you should assign reading as homework, rather than "wasting" valuable class time. She adds that if you continue with lessons like this, your students will be lucky to finish one or two books over the entire year. Consequently, you request a meeting with the supervisor. What arguments might you bring to this meeting to help convince her of the validity of your approach?

4. Picture a science class of twenty-five students from very diverse backgrounds—different social classes, different ethnicities, and varying achievement levels. Many of the students struggle with text materials. Describe some classroom strategies you might use to respond to struggling readers while maintaining high standards of content learning.

5. Your group should divide into two teams, one pro and one con. Review each of the following statements, and discuss from your assigned view the pros and cons of each issue.

   a. We read to discover meaning (to understand), as much as we talk to communicate meaning to others (to be understood).

   b. Students need to know the purpose for a text assignment if they are going to read effectively.

   c. Reading strategies are so interrelated that a knowledge of them is of little practical value for students.

Hands On

1. With a small group, examine the following well-known passage and attempt to supply the missing words. Note that all missing words, regardless of length, are indicated by blanks in the passage.

   Besides, Sir, we shall not fight our battles alone. There is a just God, who presides over the destinies of nations, who will raise up friends to fight our _______ for us. The battle, Sir, is not to the strong alone: it is to the vigilant, the active, the _______. Besides, Sir, we have no election. If we were base enough to desire it, it is now too late to retire from the contest.

   There is no _______, but in submission or slavery. Our chains are forged. Their _______ may be heard on the plains of Boston! The war is inevitable—and let it come—I repeat, Sir, let it come! It is in vain, Sir, to extenuate the matter. Gentlemen may cry, "Peace! Peace!" But there is no peace. The war has actually begun!

   The next gale that sweeps from the North will bring to our ears the clash of resounding _______! Our brethren are already in the field! Why stand we here idle? What is it that the Gentlemen wish? What would they have? Is life so _______, or peace too _______, as to be purchased at the price of chains and _______? Forbid it, Almighty God! I know not what _______ others may take, but as for me, give me _______ or give me death!

   After you have filled in the blanks, discuss the processes by which decisions on possible responses were made and any problems encountered. How did prior knowledge of the passage's topic assist your reading process? (After you have completed this experiment, review Patrick Henry's speech at the end of the "Hands On" section in Chapter 5.)

   In what ways was your experience similar to that of a student who attempts to decipher a content passage but who has little background knowledge of its content?

2. Bring the following materials to class: a large paper bag, five paper plates, four buttons, three cardboard tubes, scraps of material, six pipe cleaners, three sheets of construction paper, scissors, tape, and a stapler. Your instructor will silently give each group a written directive to create a replica of a living creature (cat, dog, rhinoceros, aardvark, etc.) with no verbal communication permitted.

   After your group has constructed its creature, list the communication difficulties, and discuss how each was overcome. Finally, have a spokesperson from each group share these difficulties with the rest of the class.

3. As suggested in the chapter, rewrite Lewis Carroll's poem "Jabberwocky" on page 18 using "real" words.

   Compare your efforts with those of other members of your small group, and discuss the following questions:

   - Why are there differences in the translations?
   - Does your translation change the intended meaning of the poem?
   - Do the differences affect your enjoyment of the poem?
   - What personal experiences and prior knowledge that you brought to your reading of the poem may have influenced your translation?

*e*RESOURCES

- Think about a highly abstract concept, such as *dream* (**www.dreamtree.com**) or universe (**www.handsonuniverse.org**), and go to the websites devoted to the topics. Bring a physical object to class that represents the concept. Verbally report your criteria for choosing the object to your class.
- Explore the website **www.literacymatter.org/lessons/contentoverview.htm.** Select a lesson plan sample that is appropriate for the content area and grade level you plan to teach. Discuss how you could adapt this lesson for use in your classroom.
- Find out how national and state content standards in your content area are similar or different. Go to *Education World* online **(www.education-world.com/standards/state/toc/index.shtml)** to explore National Standards and State Standards.

CHAPTER 2

We can't e-mail her and there's little prospect of the Queen blogging, conducting a webchat or indeed twittering.

—Peter Hunt, BBC News, on the launch of Queen Elizabeth's website

Learning with New Literacies

ORGANIZING PRINCIPLE

New literacies are transforming the way we read and write.

In the fifty-seventh year of her reign, Queen Elizabeth II officially entered the era of "new literacies" with the unveiling of her redesigned, state-of-the-art website. The queen even has her own channel on YouTube! Nevertheless, many in the British press are somewhat skeptical of how far the queen will go in cyberspace. Will she e-mail? Blog? Tweet? Webchat? All speculation (and humor) aside, the launching of the queen's website marks not only a historic occasion in Great Britain but also a symbolic one: It signifies in a very public way that we live in a new media age, where technological advances brought on by the digital forces of the computer are transforming the way we communicate, collect information, make meaning, and construct knowledge.

Walk into any middle or high school classroom today and you may very well hear the following snippets of instructional conversations between students:

Jon: Where did you find out that list of Revolutionary War battles?

Brittany: I looked it up on Wikipedia.

Danielle: Where did you find out who played Ophelia in that movie?

Nate: I found it on the Internet Movie Database.

Andy: How did you find out the title of that poem?

Heather: I Googled the first line of the poem.

These exchanges reflect the types of information gathering students typically engage in as they interact with digital texts in and out of today's content area classrooms. As you can see, even the way we and our students use language is changing! In today's new media age, the names of some search engines have

Written in collaboration with William Kist, Kent State University.

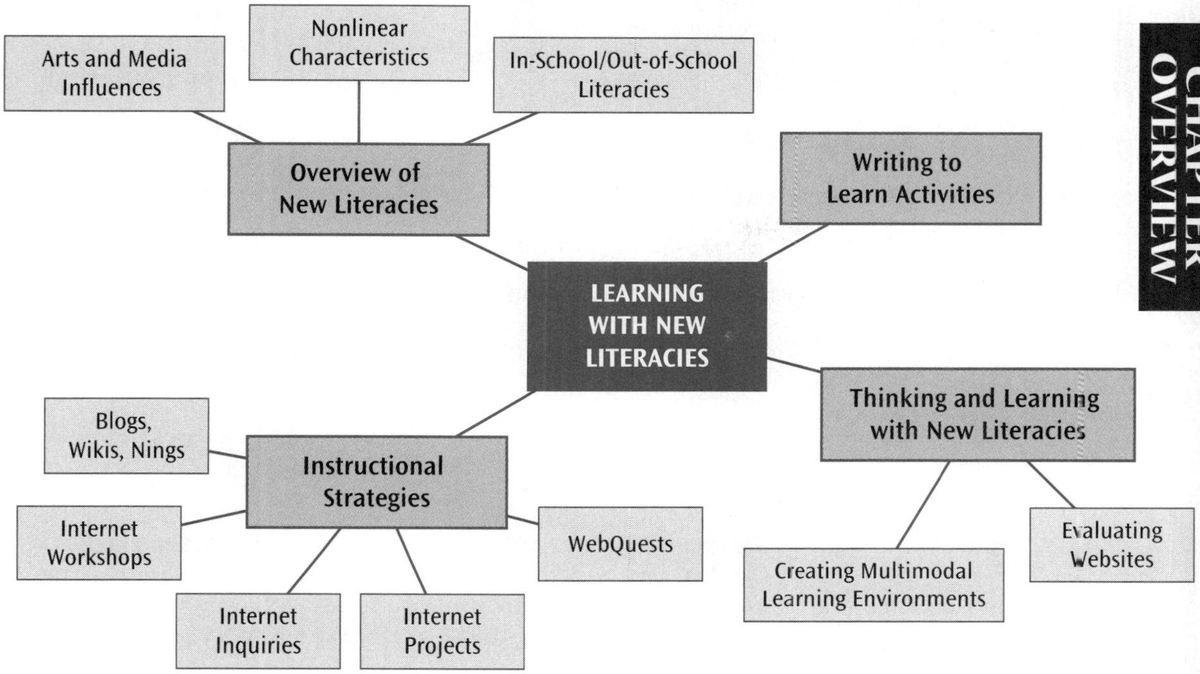

morphed into verbs, as in "I Googled it." Obviously, the ways in which we find information, no matter what the topic, have transformed radically in just a few short years. In less than a decade (specifically the 1990s), the Internet made information accessible to a degree never before imagined. Even five-year-olds, if they know how, can find the most arcane bits of information in seconds.

And therein lies the challenge for teachers in this era of "new literacies": How can we help our students be effective readers and writers when our concept of "literacy" is evolving so rapidly? How will we help students find, make meaning of, and evaluate the information available to them via electronic media? How do we help young people keep up with the immense changes occurring in electronic media when we may have trouble keeping up with these changes ourselves? Wikipedia, for example, only started in 2001! In the "old days," when we wanted to search for information, we could rely on the relatively stable Dewey decimal system and the card catalog. Of course, it also meant that we had to physically go to the library to get what we were looking for.

It simply is not possible to adequately prepare students for reading and writing in the twenty-first century without integrating new literacies into the everyday life of today's classrooms. Web 2.0 is here, and Web 3.0 (whatever that may be) could arrive by the time this book gets into your hands. Are today's schools up to the challenge? While it is important for teachers to show students how to process texts that are print- and page-based, the organizing principle for this chapter underscores that students are also going to need to be interacting more with texts that are screen-based—texts that include not only print but also images, motion, and sound—if they are going to be able to lead fully realized literate lives: **New literacies are transforming the way we read and write.**

FRAME OF MIND

1. What are new literacies?
2. What is different about learning with new literacies? What is the same?
3. Why is learning with new literacies essential for students?
4. What are some strategies that can be used to help students learn using new literacies?
5. How do roles of teachers change when they make new literacies an integral part of subject matter learning?

Jeremy Duncan, the main character of the popular *Zits* cartoon strip, is a fifteen-year-old aspiring rock musician whose life is a mix of teenage angst and perpetual boredom. Making music turns him on, but everything else, especially academic-related tasks like reading and writing, represents a slow death. One of the few joys in Jeremy's perfectly miserable life, besides music, is his computer. Jeremy is convinced his parents don't understand anything, especially the world of teenagers, cyberspace, and computers. In the cartoon reproduced here, Jeremy is dutifully explaining something or other to his father, Walt, about using a computer. He might as well be talking to his perplexed dad in a foreign language. When it's Walt's turn on the computer . . . well, a picture's worth a thousand words!

Jeremy is a digital native. He and his adolescent counterparts are the first generation of youth to have grown up with digital technologies. Consequently, as the cartoon illustrates, Jeremy has developed skills and "new literacies" Walt Duncan can only dream of mastering in his lifetime. ■

Source: Zits © Zits Partnership, King Features Syndicate.

An Overview of New Literacies

Ironically, the first person to use the term *new literacy,* John Willinsky, coined the phrase before the advent of many of the new media that have driven the "new literacies" revolution. Willinsky's idea of a "new" literacy revolved more around a different mind-set for approaching reading and writing in the classroom than around technological advances. In his 1990 book, Willinsky describes classrooms that are driven not by textbooks and teacher talk, but instead by inquiry and student choice—a "new" literacy that wasn't dependent on students regurgitating "right" answers. Of course, the roots of a student-centered concept of curriculum, literacy, and learning can be traced back to the groundbreaking work of John Dewey (1899/1980) and many other educational pioneers and literacy researchers who followed in his footsteps.

A recent line of research—the New Literacy Studies—underscores the importance of "a specific sociocultural approach to understanding and researching literacy" (Lankshear & Knobel 2003, p. 16). A sociocultural approach views literacy as social practice. That is to say, New Literacy Studies examine literacy as completely situated in all of the many "discourses" (i.e., uses of language) in people's lives—as they act at work, at school, within the family, and in any social situation (Barton & Hamilton 1998; Street 1995; Gee 1996).

As the new media became more and more a part of our lives, teachers learned how to surf the Internet and bookmark; in today's classrooms, they're learning how to blog and build a wiki. Being a literate person in today's society involves more than being able to construct meaning from a printed text. A literate person needs to be able to "read" and "write" and learn with texts that have multimodal elements such as print, graphic design, audio, video, and nonstop interaction. In a twenty-first-century, media-driven society, a teacher needs to have at least a basic mastery of reading and writing using modes of communication that were previously left to the art, music, theater, and film teachers. Reading and writing aren't just about print anymore, as we move from a page-dominated literacy to a screen-dominated literacy (Kress 2003).

From the Arts to Media: Expanding Definitions of Literacy

Over the past few decades, in a not unrelated development, many educators have advocated for more inclusion of the arts in classrooms. Arts integration advocates such as Eisner (1997) and Greene (1997) have urged teachers to bring into every classroom multiple forms of representation such as painting, music, and theater. Leland and Harste (1994) discuss "ways of knowing" that need to be honored in our classrooms regardless of whether the Internet has brought these arts elements into the everyday lives of readers and writers. Those who have described what arts-integrated classrooms can look like have given us a glimpse into what all classrooms may need to look like when all reading and writing is done in a multimodal environment.

In fact, it is art educator Eliot Eisner who provides us with a particularly useful overarching definition of literacy:

> In order to be read, a poem, an equation, a painting, a dance, a novel, or a contract each requires a distinctive form of literacy, when literacy means, as I intend it to mean, a way of conveying meaning through and recovering meaning from the form of representation in which it appears. (Eisner 1997, p. 353)

At the same time that some educators were urging arts integration, television had already been an impetus to the development of another key strand of the new literacies movement. Many educators, particularly from the United Kingdom and Australia, called for young people to be educated about the ways of television and all media (Buckingham 1993), arguing that all students should be exposed to at least the basics of media education, including elements of consumerism as well as production (Buckingham 2003; Hobbs & Frost 2003).

Paralleling the work of media educators are the critical literacy theorists who have urged educators to help students explore and examine the power dynamics in the discourses that surround us (Freire 1970/2000; McLaren 1989). Essentially, students need to learn how to be consumers of both "fiction" and "nonfiction" media, and to be able to recognize when they're being manipulated, as when, for example, they see their favorite television character drinking Dr Pepper. Students are now exposed to advertising even when doing simple research for a school project, and are at risk of being "branded" by corporations even when attempting to perform literacy tasks that used to be free of any kind of advertising (Klein 2000).

Nonlinear Characteristics of New Literacies

Along with the multimodal aspects of the new literacies, there are additional characteristics of reading on the screen that differentiate new literacies from print-based literacy. For example, new media are usually read in a nonlinear fashion. That is to say, the reader may jump from element to element within a digital text in a completely random way. Traditional printed texts such as books are written for readers to proceed from front to back, reading from left to right. However, readers of electronic texts have the option of clicking on any one of a number of hyperlinks that can take them on a path that digresses completely from the path other readers might take. Linear reading, of course, still occurs. Though many adolescents have probably read the latest *Harry Potter* or *Twilight* book, and perhaps even last night's assignments in their textbooks, much of their personal reading now is done with digital texts. As a result, reading is individualized and proceeds in nonlinear fashion, based on the immediate interests and characteristics of the reader (Reinking, 1997).

In addition, a reader can now interact with other readers and even the author of the text being read. A reader no longer has to wait for an author to respond to a letter or to conduct research at the library about a question that comes up. In many cases, a reader can e-mail the author to answer a question (if the author keeps up with e-mail!). Or, if the author is not available, with several keystrokes, the reader is able to find a community of readers via a bookselling site with whom to engage in some social networking revolving around the text. If there were ever a doubt that reading is a socially constructed activity, these characteristics of new media completely negate the stereotype of the lonely reader being "shushed" by the librarian. Though individualized, reading is becoming a truly social and interactive experience.

Linking In-School with Out-of-School Literacies

The literacies that students have access to outside of school are much different than they were even a decade ago. As adolescent learners develop their use of new literacies for personal and social purposes, there seems to be more of a gap between students' in-school literacies and their out-of-school literacies. For example, while students say that they always intend to read books on paper (Scholastic 2008), there is a general tapering off of print-based reading frequency among adolescents, with an even larger decline in reading among boys, who report they read much less frequently as teenagers than they did as eight-year-olds (Scholastic 2006). Historically, reading researchers have concentrated more attention on the cognitive side than the affective, motivational side of reading (Guthrie & Wigfield 1997). This is why it is more critical than ever to continue to make curricular content more relevant, especially in the modes in which content is presented.

There is also an economic argument for using new literacies in the classroom: Helping students to learn with new literacies is part of making sure that they are prepared for life in the twenty-first century. The Pew Internet project recently reported that 73 percent of respondents (representing 147 million adults) are Internet users, and 55 percent of Americans have broadband access at home as of 2008 (Pew Internet and American Life Study 2006, 2008). Moreover, the emphasis on new literacies does not necessarily have a negative impact on students' print literacy. Some studies have shown a link between using activities that involve nonprint-dominated materials and an increase in print literacy.

Voices from the Classroom

BOX 2.1

William
Fifth-Grade Teacher

CHALLENGE

I was always interested in computer use. Ten years ago my school district bought teacher desktops for us to use. I loved having the resource in the classroom, but never could figure out a way to use it effectively with the students. One day I was getting a desk out of storage when I found a bunch of old Apple IIs and some software. It wasn't long before I had set them up in my classroom for my students to use.

Unfortunately, I had trouble with using the old computers because I didn't have a printer. I could have my students use them to do drill and skill and play some of the great old education games such as "The Oregon Trail." After the year was over, I put the old Apples back into storage.

Five years ago, my school received a grant for setting up three classrooms through the eMINTS program (www.emints.org). I spent two years receiving extensive training through the program. The grant paid for the training and setup of three classrooms with twelve student desktops, a SMART board with projector, a teacher desktop, and a teacher laptop. We learned how to use the technology to do project-based, small-group learning. The idea was to transform our teaching. We learned about creating websites and using online sites. This was still in the Web 1.0 days.

After several years of using the new tools I had, I read a book called *The World Is Flat* by Thomas Friedman. Reading it made me realize how important learning how to use technology was for my students. I immediately began to explore what more it could do for us.

I was really unhappy about the static web pages I was creating in Dreamweaver. I couldn't change the pages easily, and I couldn't figure out how to do the dynamic content I saw on other people's sites. I started looking at blogs and decided that I needed to set up my own blog. I thought it would be a great way to share with the community what we were doing. I set up a Gaggle blog, but I wasn't really happy with it. Then I found out that Blogger had comment moderation and in December of 2006 I set up my blog.

STRATEGY

At first I used the blog to communicate with my students. I would ask questions and get some responses. Sometimes I just used it for fun stuff. My students told me that they couldn't tell what I wanted them to actually post on "for real" so I created another blog just for fun things.

By the end of the spring semester in 2007, I decided I wanted my students to be able to write on their own blogs. I thought that they would enjoy creating on "their space" and that others would be able to comment on their posts. This would encourage them to do a good job. I finally figured out how I wanted to make the blogs work at the end of the fall of 2007. In the spring semester of 2008 my homeroom finally got to work on their own blogs.

After the school year was over, I realized that my students spent a lot of time posting to their blogs, but they didn't spend much time commenting on others. I decided that with my next class I would give them more time to comment.

I really wanted all my students to be able to create posts and get comments instead of just my homeroom. I also decided that creating over sixty blogs for them to work on was way too much work. So now I am busy setting them up as coauthors on a blog so that they all will publish on one blog. This will save me tons of setup and monitoring time. It will also help me minimize the amount of time my students are changing their themes or adding widgets to their blogs.

This summer I attended NECC in San Antonio and was amazed by the number of people there, but I wasn't surprised by what they were using. I discovered the Classroom 2.0 Ning, and started using Twitter. Both of these sites really helped me find new and innovative tools to use. I have experimented with many different tools to see what can be useful to me and to my class. I also use an RSS feed through Bloglines to keep track of the posts of my favorite education bloggers.

One example of a great tool I found from another online educator was Voicethread. Voicethread allows narration of pictures or video with the addition that other people can also comment on the Voicethread. I incorporated it into a science assignment at the end of last year.

REFLECTION

The most positive changes I have seen through the journey have been my own. The students have very little understanding of the power of the tools we use; they think they are cool and they like having people from other countries comment on their work. That does encourage them. The biggest positive change has been with my excitement over using the new tools and the experiences I am sharing with my students. I love finding tools that they can use that are different from my personal experience. I love sharing with other educators what my class is doing. I have more enthusiasm for teaching and for learning.

Using activities that involve visual art—another form of text in the classroom—such as the well known "sketch-to-stretch" activity has been shown to further students' comprehension of print and learning in general (Bustle 2004; Hibbing & Rankin-Erickson 2003; Short, Harste, & Burke 1996; Whitin 2002). The sketch-to-stretch activity involves asking students to take a break from reading by stretching and then sketch what is being visualized while reading, thus linking print literacy with visual literacy. There have also been studies that have compared and contrasted reading and writing strategies when reading and writing traditional print text with reading and writing hypertext (Coiro 2003; Dreher 2000; Patterson 2000; Schmar-Dobler 2003).

Many teachers are embracing new literacies, in combination with printed texts, as motivational tools in their classrooms; new literacies, in essence, become "the spoonful of sugar to help the print go down" (Kist 2005). Read about William Chamberlain's gradual journey into new literacies in Voices from the Classroom (see Box 2.1).

New Literacies and Content Standards

Knowing how to use new literacies is integral to the strategic knowledge and skills that every student in all content areas will need to develop to be discipline-literate in the twenty-first century. Practically all of the national education associations in the various academic disciplines have developed content standards or statements of principle that implicitly or explicity acknowledge the proficient use of technologies for information and communication. The International Reading Association and the National Council of Teachers of English are explicit in their standard for using new literacies:

> Students use a variety of technological and information resources (e.g., libraries, databases, computer networks, video) to gather and synthesize information and to create and communicate knowledge. (IRA 1996, p. 3)

Actually, new literacies are embedded in more state and national standards than many people assume. Though the term *new literacies* is absent from most state standards within the United States, *media* and *media literacy* are more than likely mentioned.

Frank Baker has studied state teaching standards since 1999 and has found many elements of media literacy throughout standards documents in all subject areas:

> Though only a few states actually use the phrase "media literacy," you can find plenty of references to advertising, bias, critical viewing, informational texts, the language of film, mass media, propaganda, techniques of persuasion and more. . . . Although the teaching of media literacy concepts is not happening in most US schools, there is increased interest in education because of the new literacies and 21st century literacy skills movements. Both movements include strong recommendations for critical thinking—and to me, media literacy is all about applying critical thinking to media messages, and giving students opportunities not only to analyze media messages, but create and produce them as well. (Baker 2009)

Study the content standards and state proficiency assessments in your content area. To what extent do these assessments, where they exist, reflect the literacies that students need to communicate effectively as well as search for and interpret information on the Internet?

Thinking and Learning with New Literacies

The Internet is quickly changing the way we think, inquire, read, and write. This revolutionary way of communicating includes elements of print, visual art, sound, motion pictures, and advertising. Based on a review of new literacies research and a long-term study of classrooms that are embracing new literacies, Kist (2005, 2007a) has proposed some characteristics of new literacies classrooms:

- New literacies classrooms feature daily work in multiple forms of representation.
- In new literacies classrooms, there are explicit discussions of the merits of using certain symbol systems in certain situations with much choice.
- In new literacies classrooms, there are meta-dialogues, such as think-alouds, by teachers who model working through problems using certain symbol systems.
- In new literacies classrooms, students take part in a mix of individual and collaborative activities.
- New literacies classrooms are places of student engagement in which students report achieving a "flow" state.

There are numerous instructional strategies for using new literacies in content area classrooms that can be grouped into at least two overarching categories: (1) helping students to think and learn in a multimodal environment, and (2) using new literacies to help students learn content.

Thinking and Learning in Multimodal Environments

Most students probably are well aware of the basic conventions of the Web such as the idea of clicking on a link and going to another website. However, one of the most helpful discussions to have with students is to simply have them discuss the differences in thinking and learning about a multimodal text versus reading to learn in a print-based environment. A good way to get the discussion going is to model a typical (that is to say, nonlinear) reading progression on the Internet.

myeducationlab

Go to the Assignments and Activities section of Topic 9: "Integrating Technology" in the MyEducationLab for your course. Complete the activity "Using Technology to Enhance Instruction" and consider the preparation students need in order to use technology effectively.

If a person wants to find out about space exploration, for example, he or she can access NASA's website on the Internet. Within that site, one might click on "Space Shuttle" for a definition and a computer-generated model of the shuttle, click on the highlighted "History" link for a brief overview and history of the space program, digress to an audio recording and videoclip of Neil Armstrong as he set foot on the moon, or engage in a live interview with a NASA scientist or astrononaut. Later in the "e-document," the reader might click on the "Projects" link to find out about many of the online projects that NASA offers to students. Following this sequence of reading experiences, the teacher could demonstrate a completely different line of reading, both stemming from the same first Internet text.

The concepts of *hypertext* and *hypermedia* are crucial to understanding the interactions between reader and text in a multimodal environment. Hypertext differs from printed text in that its structure is much less linear. The hypertext format offers a "web" of text that allows the reader to link to other related documents and resources on demand. When sound, graphics, photographs, video, and other nonprint media are incorporated into the hypertext format, the electronic environment is called "hypermedia."

From an instructional perspective, the branching options offered in hypertext and hypermedia serve two important functions: to scaffold students' learning experiences and to enhance and extend thinking. For readers who may struggle with text or with difficult concepts, the resources available on demand in a hypertext environment include pronunciations, definitions, and explanations of keywords and terms, audio versions of the text, video recordings, video files, photographs, graphics, interactive exercises, and student-centered projects.

One of the most profound ways of getting students to fully realize the interactivity of the Web is to give them practice in writing this way, by insisting that they embed hyperlinks in their writing. To get started, students can look at examples of famous texts embedded with hyperlinks, such as the Magna Carta or the Declaration of Independence found at the site called "From Revolution to

RTI for Struggling Adolescent Learners BOX 2.2

Strategy Intervention and New Literacies

RTI strategy interventions in Tier 1 and Tier 2 should capitalize on students' use of new literacies. Offering struggling adolescent readers an opportunity to interact with electronic text may lead to greater motivation and engagement in literacy activities. The novelty and variety of using multiple media in the classroom may attract students to reading who had long ago given up the pursuit. Technology, as we'll learn about in this chapter, has created a wealth of new opportunities for learning and has influenced how content area teachers implement instruction. Yet teachers must go beyond incorporating technology into lessons. Adolescent learners facing academic challenges must be taught how to navigate their own learning and think critically while interacting with these resources.

Computers and other electronic devices are both a "facilitator of knowledge and medium for literacy" (Biancarosa & Snow 2004). Technology allows teachers to plan higher levels of differentiation and to meet the academic needs of a greater number of students during instruction. Electronic databases, such as EBSCO, provide middle and high school students a wealth of information at various degrees of reading difficulty, allowing teachers to find multiple texts related to course content.

For example, EBSCO has created The Student Research Center, a search interface designed specifically for middle and high school students. The Student Research Center provides adolescent learners with appropriate research tools for easily obtaining the information that they seek from EBSCO databases, including electronic magazines, newspapers, biographies, film, and video. Students can also search databases by topic and limit their searches according to appropriate *lexile reading levels* (see Chapter 4 for a discussion of lexile reading levels and other tools for determining the readability or difficulty level of texts).

Through the use of electronic texts, content area teachers can create flexible groups within their classes that allow all students access to text appropriate to their needs and relevant to course objectives. In addition, interactive computer programs, such as PLATO and Academy of Reading, adapt to a student's reading performance by providing text passages that are written at a level consistent with the student's needs. Doing so increases the comprehensibility of the text for the student. Additionally, such programs provide students with immediate feedback on assignments and allow teachers to track student progress towards goals outlined in intervention plans. Some programs that include voice recognition software allow students to record themselves while reading so that miscues can be tracked and appropriate feedback provided. These resources can be useful for providing students with multiple interactions with texts and for offering independent practice (Biancarosa & Snow 2004).

Reconstruction" (http://odur.let.rug.nl/~usa). Students can then take any text—an excerpt from a textbook or a novel—and type the excerpt into a word processing document, embedding the text with a certain number of hyperlinks. If, for instance, the text mentions Yosemite National Park, students could be shown how to turn the words "Yosemite National Park" into a hyperlink taking them to the official Yosemite site (www.nps.gov/yose). Once students have practice embedding their own writing with hyperlinks, a logical follow-up is a discussion prompted by such questions as: How is reading hypertext different from reading text in a book? How is writing with embedded hyperlinks different from writing with pencil and paper?

What are some things that a writer can do when writing in a hypertext environment that can't be done when writing in a paper-based environment? What are the advantages and disadvantages of communicating in each environment?

Learning How to Evaluate Websites

Along with the benefits of interactive web texts come the risks of quality control. Because a hyperlink can take the reader to potentially untested sites, students need to be taught from an early age how to evaluate the links they come across and how to use them wisely. There are many models for helping students to search effectively online. Don Leu and his New Literacies Research Team at the University of Connecticut (www.newliteracies.uconn.edu) have come up with a framework for student practice that uses four different lenses when evaluating online resources: (1) examining what bias the site may contain; (2) determining how reliable the site is; (3) determining the accuracy of information on the site; and (4) synthesizing the information presented on the site in a meaningful way (see Figure 2.1).

An entertaining and instructive way to help students see how easily readers of the Internet can be misled is to show them some of the well-known hoax sites, such as the MalePregnancy site that purports to follow a man through the first recorded male pregnancy. Students can list and discuss design elements of the hoax sites that make them seem as if they are presenting legitimate information. The following hoax sites can be used to teach students the principle that not all sites that appear to be valid are in fact valid:

- Male Pregnancy: www.malepregnancy.com
- Dihydrogen Monoxide: www.dhmo.org
- McWhortle Enterprises, Inc.: www.mcwhortle.com
- Northwest Tree Octopus: http://zapatopi.net/treeoctopus

Blogs, Wikis, and Nings

Readers frequently access information from "homemade" collaborative texts found online in the form of *blogs, wikis,* and *Nings.*

Blogs

Blogs, short for *weblogs,* are essentially online journals or diaries that are often personal accounts of life experiences. In many instances, blog readers rely on these stream-of-consciousness accounts for serious information, whether in regard to political races, social issues, or even weather conditions. Teachers are now assigning students to read preselected blogs related to class projects, make comments on the blogs, and then report back to the class, perhaps in the form of their own student blogs. A class can set up its own blog with space available for each student to have personal *blogspace.* Commonly used sites to host blogs are www.blogger.com and www.typepad.com.

FIGURE 2.1 A Framework for Critically Evaluating Websites

Bias and Stance

- Identify, evaluate, and recognize that all websites have an agenda, perspective, or bias.
- Identify and evaluate bias, given a website with a clear bias.
- Identify and evaluate the author of a website whenever visiting an important new site.
- Use information about the author of a site to evaluate how information will be biased at that site.

Reliability

- Investigate multiple sources to compare and contrast the reliability of information. Identify several markers that may affect reliability such as:

  Is this a commercial site?
  Is the author an authoritative source (e.g., professor, scientist, librarian, etc.)?
  Does the website have links that are broken?
  Does the information make sense?
  Does the author include links to other reliable websites?
  Does the website contain numerous typos?
  Does the URL provide any clues to reliability?
  Do the images or videos appear to be altered?
- Understand that Wikipedia is a reasonable, but imperfect, portal of information.
- Identify the general purpose of a website (entertainment, educational, commercial, persuasive, exchange of information, social, etc.).
- Identify the form of a website (e.g., blog, forum, advertisement, informational website, commercial website, government website, etc.) and use this information when considering reliability.

Accuracy

- Evaluate information based on the degree to which it is likely to be accurate by verifying and consulting alternative and/or especially reliable sources.

Synthesize Information

- Understand both the specific information related to the task as well as the broader context within which that information is located.
- Synthesize information from multiple media sources including written prose, audio, visual, video, and/or tables and graphs.
- Separate relevant information from irrelevant information.
- Organize information effectively.
- Manage multiple sources both on- and offline, including:

  Choose tools to meet the needs of managing information, including file folders, electronic file folders, notebooks, e-mail, and so on.
  Cite sources.
  Take notes with paper and pencil, when appropriate.
  Take notes with a word processor, when appropriate.
  Type notes using shortcut strokes such as highlight/cut/copy/paste.

Source: Leu, D. J., Coiro, J., Castek, J., Hartman, D. K., Henry, L. A., & Reinking, D. (2008). Research on instruction and assessment in the new literacies of online reading comprehension. In C. C. Block, S. Parris, & P. Afflerbach (Eds.), *Comprehension instruction: Research-based best practices.* New York: Guilford Press. Reprinted by permission of Guilford Press.

Study how Heidi Whitus, an English teacher from Communication Arts High School, begins the year with a class activity that asks students to perform certain tasks related to media study and respond in the form of a blog (see Figure 2.2).

Blogs can be set up so that only members of the class can access them and only the blog owner can post entries. The teacher can be notified via e-mail each time an entry is posted or comment made so that appropriateness of content can be monitored. Teachers are using blogs for such functions as classroom management, learning logs and online notebooks, class discussions, and, of course, personal expression (Echlin

FIGURE 2.2 **Heidi Whitus's Blog Assignment**

Please do at least one of the following before December 4 and report on it in your blog:

	Advanced	Proficient	Partially Proficient	Not Proficient
Activity 1 Listen to the podcast of "On the Media" at least twice during the semester. You can subscribe to it from iTunes or go to www.onthemedia.org. Summarize the stories you heard on your blog. Be sure to make a note of the dates of the podcasts you listened to.	■ More than two shows listened to ■ Detailed summaries and reflections of both stories ■ Dates included	■ Two or more shows listened to ■ Summaries of both stories ■ Dates included	■ Two or more shows listened to ■ Insufficient summaries of stories ■ Dates not included	■ Two or more shows listened to ■ No summaries of stories ■ Dates not included
Activity 2 Read the San Antonio *Express-News* **and** a newspaper from another city on at least three different days. Compare the types of stories covered, the amount of advertising, and the kinds of feature stories ("soft" news) in the two papers.	■ Read papers on more than three days ■ Detailed comparison and reflections of both papers	■ Read papers on three days ■ Comparison of both papers	■ Read papers on fewer than three days ■ Slight comparison of both papers	■ Read papers on fewer than two days ■ No comparison of papers
Activity 3 Watch television news from at least three different channels (WOAI, KENS-5, KSAT, PBS, KABB are the local stations, and if you have cable you should also include CNN, FOX News and/or MSNBC); **compare** their approach to broadcast journalism by choosing a specific story and describing the differences in how the different channels cover the story.	■ Watched more than three channels ■ Detailed comparison and reflections of all stories	■ Watched three channels ■ Comparison of all stories	■ Watched fewer than three channels ■ Slight comparison of stories	■ Watched fewer than two channels ■ No comparison of stories
Activity 4 Watch at least two of the following movies about mass media outside of class, and summarize the films and your reflections of them in your blog: ■ *All the President's Men* ■ *Broadcast News* ■ *The China Syndrome* ■ *Shattered Glass* ■ *Network* ■ *Good Night and Good Luck* ■ *His Girl Friday* ■ *Citizen Kane*	■ Watched more than two films ■ Detailed summaries of all films	■ Watched two films ■ Summaries of both films	■ Watched two films ■ Slight summaries of film	■ Watched fewer than two films ■ No summaries of films

Source: Adapted from Kist, W. (2010). *The socially networked classroom: Teaching in the new media age.* Thousand Oaks, CA: Corwin Press.

FIGURE 2.3 Blogging Guidelines

1. Students working online are expected to treat all of these spaces as classroom spaces. Writing, photos, or videos that are inappropriate for the classroom are not appropriate for these places either. While I encourage you to talk and connect with others, I also expect that you will conduct yourself in ways that would be acceptable inside the classroom.
2. Never give out personal information over the Internet. Sites that we use such as Flickr, Youtube, Ning, and all of your blogs are all open to the public. Don't share anything that you don't want the world to know. For your own safety, be careful what you say. Don't give out your phone number, home address, email address, or MSN name. Be especially careful of any videos or photos of yourself that you post online. This is also important to remember if you have a personal blog, Youtube channel, or Facebook account.
3. If you put it on the Internet, the odds are very good that it will stay on the Internet. Always. That means ten years from now when you are looking for a job, it will be possible for an employer to discover immature things that you said or posted when you were younger. Be sure that anything you post you are proud of. They can come back to haunt you if you don't.
4. Working online, you have the chance to connect with people from around the world. You must remember to be respectful of the people and beliefs from all cultures, nations, and religions. This means working to understand how and why people around the world are both similar and different. It is important to remember that differences do exist but that much can be learned by working to understand these things.

Source: From Clarence Fisher, Joseph H. Kerr School, Snow Lake, Manitoba. Retrieved February 22, 2009, from www.evenfromhere.org/?p=1061

2007). When introducing blogs, it's important to establish guidelines for blogging such as those suggested in Figure 2.3.

Wikis and Nings

Wikis and Nings are more collaborative in nature, as readers seek to build knowledge on a specific topic and upload the text to a common environment. *Wiki* is a Hawaiian word meaning "fast" and has come to signify a collaboratively built text in which volunteers contribute facts and help to edit and shape the presentation of the information. Many teachers are using sites such as www.pbwiki.com or www.wikispaces.com to host wikis that they build with their students. Such wiki building can also serve to facilitate a discussion about the pitfalls (and advantages) of using wikis for information: When anyone and everyone can contribute information to a wiki, readers need to make sure the information being read is accurate.

Nings have come on strong since the startup of www.Ning.com in 2004. At this site, readers can join discussions on a growing number of topics and start a social network of their own focusing on a common topic of interest. Nings are rapidly becoming sources of information for people interested in delving deeply into a topic. Nings and wikis can be set up to engage students with many different topics.

Social studies teacher Tom Daccord set up a wiki combined with a Ning to help students research the presidential race of 2008 as part of the Great Debate Wiki/

Ning Project (www.greatdebate2008.wikispaces.com). This project was a collaboration of approximately ten schools across the United States. Students who never met each other face-to-face had the opportunity to collaboratively build a knowledge base about the presidential race and also to make persuasive arguments about their positions. They were assigned to research and collect information on topics related to the candidates' positions and then post them on the wiki. They began the project by exploring several presidential positions assigned by their teachers, but were also encouraged to inquire into other issues related to the candidates' positions. One group of students chose to research the issue of the death penalty, even though this was not a major issue in the presidential campaign. This topic, for whatever reason, generated much research and then much passionate debate, once students moved to the second part of the project. After the positions were thoroughly researched, students went to the Ning and participated and debated in the various forums according to the topics they had researched. The Ning was password-protected, so that only members of the classes involved could make comments.

Another interesting blogging project called YouthVoices (http://youthvoices.net) attempts to bring together schools from around the world as students write blog entries and collaborate on various writing activities. Students are also allowed and encouraged to create their own groups about topics as diverse as rap music and world peace. As they communicate with each other online about their various topics of inquiry, students are expected to adhere to some simple but direct rules of conduct:

- Speak directly to the student or teacher whose post you are responding to;
- Quote from the post or describe specific details (of an image or video);
- Relate the work to your own experiences or to another text, image, video, or audio that this one reminds you of; and
- Be encouraging and generous with your remarks. End on a positive note.

Following these guidelines leads to a greater citizenship potential for students, as they will increasingly have to collaborate and interact with people online over the course of their lives.

The advantage of having students document their process via a blog, wiki, and/or Ning is that teachers and students have a running record of the journey taken. Moreover, a teacher has the ability to guide and redirect student thinking, if necessary, via a well-placed blog comment or comment in a Ning forum. The fact that the teacher's comment appears alongside the students' gives a clear visual representation that the teacher and students are colearners.

Showing students how to use strategies to think and learn in multimodal environments and participate in blogs, wikis, and Nings is often initiated within the context of demonstration lessons known as Internet workshops. The Internet workshop allows teachers to model and demonstrate skills and strategies related to new literacies.

Internet Workshops

An Internet workshop is characterized by its flexibility. In some respects, it is similar in purpose to a writing workshop or a reading workshop in an English/language arts classroom (Atwell 1998). In writing and reading workshops, teachers who use a workshop model in their classrooms set aside regularly scheduled time for students to engage in reading and writing activities. In the process of doing so, students share their reading and writing with others in the class, typically in small-group book discussions or writing response groups. During workshop time, teachers often conduct "minilessons" to respond to content- and process-related issues and problems students are having during reading or writing sessions. Minilessons may also be designed for strategy instruction. In these explicit instructional situations, a teacher may take several minutes or more of workshop time to show students how to use a set of procedures that will help them become more skillful as readers and writers.

Like reading and writing workshops, an Internet workshop provides an instructional framework for students allowing for regularly scheduled time to engage in activity on the Internet. The activity may range from specific electronic text assignments to individual or group research to collaborative projects on the Internet. For example, a teacher might assign a website or several websites for students to visit. With younger learners, the website(s) are bookmarked in advance by the teacher so that the class has easy access to them. Students are directed to the website(s) to engage in a content literacy activity in much the same way as they would in a textbook or other print resources. Many of the content literacy activities in this book can be adapted for this purpose.

On other workshop occasions, students may work individually or in collaboration with one another on WebQuests, Internet inquiries, or Internet projects. These instructional strategies are much more extensive than specific assignments on the Internet and may take one to several weeks to accomplish. Regardless of the type of instructional focus, teachers should bring students together intermittently during workshops to share their work or to build strategic knowledge and skills related to the effective use of the Internet as a tool for learning. In these situations, workshop time is devoted to problems students are having searching for information or communicating with others. Internet workshops can also be designed around explicit strategy instruction. For example, a workshop might revolve around using search engines effectively, thinking critically about information, or designing a web page.

Internet Inquiries

The Internet inquiry engages students in research using information sources on the Internet. Inquiries can be conducted individually or collaboratively and often take one or more weeks to complete. Internet inquiries are typically part of larger thematic units and are used in conjunction with Internet workshops. The Internet inquiry broadly follows the tenets of a discovery model for investigating hypotheses or questions. Students are invited to (1) generate questions about a topic or theme under discussion in class, (2) search for information on the Internet to answer the questions, (3) analyze the information, (4) compose a report or some other form of dissemination related to findings, and (5) share findings with the whole class.

Question generation is one of the keys to conducting a successful Internet inquiry. Many teachers use the KWL strategy (see Chapter 7) to help students raise questions. Others use brainstorming techniques to generate a list of questions. Whatever strategy is used for generating questions, the questions should come from the students rather than the teacher whenever possible. An Internet workshop minilesson might focus on asking good questions to guide the information search. A teacher may also use workshop time to scaffold instruction on how to use search engines effectively or how to record and analyze information through the use of "inquiry charts" (I-charts) and other tools for recording and analyzing findings (Hoffman 1992; Randall 1996). In Chapter 5, we provide steps to guide the various phases of any type of inquiry or research investigation.

An Internet Inquiry in Elementary Science

Students in a third-grade elementary classroom have been engaged in a thematic unit related to the study of monarch butterflies. As part of the unit, the class developed a plan for raising monarch butterflies and visited several websites on the Internet related to specific workshop activities that the teacher had planned. The students also read trade books such as *Discovering Butterflies* by Douglas Florian, *Monarch Butterfly* by Gail Gibbons, and *Animal World: Butterflies* by Donna Bailey. As a result of these classroom learning experiences, the class embarked on an Internet inquiry designed around the students' "personal questions" regarding monarch butterflies. The class first brainstormed a list of questions that the teacher recorded on chart paper. Some of the questions included: Do monarch butterflies eat anything besides milkweed? Are monarch butterflies found all over the world? How long do monarch butterflies live? and How many eggs can one monarch butterfly lay? Using the list of questions on chart paper as a guide, each student selected three questions to research. The questions did not have to come from the brainstormed list but could be generated by students as they engaged in their information search on the Internet and from trade books that were available in the classroom.

The teacher conducted an Internet workshop on how to use the search engine Ask.com (www.ask.com). She also explained to students how to use I-charts to record information they found on individual websites or in trade books related to each of their questions. Across the top of the I-chart, each student recorded his or her name and a personal question about monarch butterflies. The remainder of the I-chart was divided into two columns. The left column provided space for a student to record the name of the website or trade book that was used to gather information. The right column was used to record information that students found to answer their questions. Across the bottom of the I-chart was space for students to record "new questions" based on their research.

When students completed their information searches, they collected their I-charts and began analyzing the information to answer their questions. The teacher facilitated the analysis by walking around the room helping individuals as needs arose. Students used the analysis to create a poster portraying the answers to their questions. The inquiry culminated with a "poster session" in which students shared the information related to their questions.

Internet Projects

An Internet project involves collaborative approaches to learning on the Internet. Often students engage in project learning with other students who may be from different schools in different parts of the country or the world. Other types of projects may involve collaborative interactions between students and experts from various fields. For example, Internet projects are regularly posted on websites such as NASA Quest, where students have the opportunity to discuss space science and many other topics with one another and with NASA personnel.

Many Internet projects are designed by teachers as part of units of study. Advanced planning is essential for teacher-designed projects. Generally the following steps need to be considered:

- *Plan a project for an upcoming unit and write a project description.*
- *Post the project description and time line several months in advance* seeking classroom partnerships with other teachers.
- *Post the project at a location on the Internet where teachers advertise their projects,* such as Global SchoolNet's Internet Project Registry (www.gsn.org/pr/index.cfm).
- *Arrange collaboration details* with teachers in other classrooms who agree to participate.
- *Complete the project using Internet workshop sessions* for project-related activities and e-mail information exchanges with students and teachers in other classrooms involved in the project.

Leu, Leu, and Coiro (2006) provide numerous examples at different grade levels of Internet projects for various content areas that are posted on websites or have been designed by teachers.

WebQuests

WebQuests have become a popular instructional model for engaging learners on the Internet. A WebQuest is a teacher-designed web page that packages various learning tasks and activities for students to complete using Internet resources. WebQuests are typically organized around several components: introduction, task, process, resources, learning advice, and conclusion.

> **myeducationlab**
>
> Go to the Assignments and Activities section of Topic 9: "Integrating Technology" in the MyEducationLab for your course and complete the activity "Wireless WebQuests." Notice the steps one teacher takes to plan and implement WebQuests in a high school classroom.

The introduction to a WebQuest provides an overview of the learning opportunity available to the students. Often the introduction places the learner(s) in a hypothetical situation somewhat similar to RAFT writing activities (see Chapter 9). As a result, students are assigned a role and a purpose for engaging in the learning activity. The task component of the WebQuest describes the task(s) students will complete and lists the questions that guide the information search.

The process component outlines the steps and procedures students will follow to complete the learning task. The resources component of a WebQuest provides links to information resources on the Internet that students will need to access to complete the learning task. The "learning advice" component provides directions to students on how to organize information, whether in outlines, time lines, graphic organizers (see Chapter 10), notebook entries such as the double-entry journal format (see Chapter 5), or I-charts. And finally, the conclusion to the WebQuest brings closure to the activity and summarizes what students should have learned from participation in the WebQuest.

Writing to Learn in a New Literacies Paradigm

Essentially, many of these Internet inquiry, project, and WebQuest strategies incorporate "writing to learn" activities. As we explain in Chapter 9, writing to learn is an essential component of literacy and learning across all disciplines because students are often expected to represent their knowledge through writing. What makes the new literacies applications different is that the concept of "writing" has expanded to include nonprint representations of knowledge, and the texts themselves may be shaped collaboratively, over time and distance.

There are many new literacies applications for writing to learn. Allowing students to represent the content in a PowerPoint presentation is one type of writing to learn activity that allows them to think about core ideas and concepts. However, with new literacies, students have at their command the ability to think and learn with content not only using print but also graphics, sound, and even video. For example, a common project in social studies classrooms is to have students do research on local histories, videotaping local participants in historical events, and then uploading their memories to a website devoted to this project. If students are not able to collect their own primary source documents, they can go online to such sites as the Library of Congress's American Memory Project (http://memory.loc.gov/ammem/amhome.html).

Two examples of local history projects can be found at the following websites:

Mound Builder Indians
Charles Russell Elementary, Ashland, Kentucky
http://library.thinkquest.org/CR0212160

Social History of Beverly Public Schools
Beverly High School, Beverly, Massachusetts
www.primaryresearch.org/PRTHB/schoolhistory/about.php

For additional ideas and lessons on incorporating writing to learn activities into a new literacies paradigm, explore the websites in Figure 2.4.

It is obvious by now that we are truly living in a new media age. Many educators are concerned about this and are worried that we will lose "book knowledge" as a society, that people will be so tuned into their iPods and laptops, they won't know

FIGURE 2.4 **Related Read/Write/Think Lesson Plans**

These lesson plans elaborate on ideas suggested in this chapter. Read/Write/Think is a joint project of the International Reading Association and the National Council of Teachers of English. See www.readwritethink.org/index.asp for more ideas.

Annotating Poems with Hyperlinks
www.readwritethink.org/lessons/lesson_view.asp?id=36

Blogging About Utopian Societies
www.readwritethink.org/lessons/lesson_view.asp?id=942

Critical Media Literacy: Commercial Advertising
www.readwritethink.org/lessons/lesson_view.asp?id=97

Conducting Collaborative Internet Research: Harlem Renaissance
www.readwritethink.org/lessons/lesson_view.asp?id=252

Examining the Content of Internet Sites
www.readwritethink.org/lessons/lesson_view.asp?id=29

Using Wikis to Catalog Protest Songs
www.readwritethink.org/lessons/lesson_view.asp?id=979

how to speak and write and read anymore. It's clear, however, that what many people are doing on their iPods and Blackberries and laptops is a form of reading and writing and that these new literacies are shaping our communication in ways we never could have envisioned just twenty years ago. It seems that many educators around the world are indeed realizing the potentials (and dangers) of these new reading and writing forms. Whether or not we embrace these new forms, the screen-based society to which Kress (2003) referred is now upon us, and our students will need to have practice in navigating the rich sources of communication that are now available in greater abundance and in more alternative forms than ever before.

LOOKING BACK LOOKING FORWARD

Digital texts and media are highly engaging and interactive. Hypertext and hypermedia make it possible to interact with text in ways not imaginable even a short while ago. Text learning opportunities in multimodal environments are interactive, enhance communication, engage students in multimedia, create opportunities for inquiry through information searches and retrieval, and support socially mediated learning. Reading and writing with computers has changed the way we think about literacy and learning. Whether students are navigating the Internet or interacting with others through blogs and Nings, an array of electronic text learning experiences await them. Various instructional strategies, including Internet workshops, Internet inquiries, Internet projects, and WebQuests are approaches to online learning in various content areas.

In the next chapter, we take a closer look at one type of student who often struggles with content literacy tasks—the English learner. With every passing year, the United States becomes more linguistically and culturally diverse. English learners struggle with academic language and are often tracked in lower ability classes than language majority students. The dropout rate among English learners is alarmingly high. How can content area teachers plan instruction to account for cultural and linguistic differences in their classrooms? Let's read to find out.

Minds On

1. To what extent do you believe students should participate in the selection of documents from websites for use in a content course? Would you answer this question differently for students of various ages?
2. How often have you used electronic texts as part of subject matter learning? In your estimation, did the teacher use an electronic text assignment to its full potential? If not, in what additional ways might the electronic text resource have been explored?
3. Why do many students seem to dislike doing research in a library but are enthusiastic about surfing the Net for information resources?
4. What are the similarities between learning with new literacies and traditional print texts? What are the differences?
5. What are the barriers facing teachers who want to assign more projects involving new literacies? What are ways to overcome those barriers? Are the benefits worth the effort?
6. What are the challenges of assessing new literacy projects?

Hands On

1. Assign students to write an essay with embedded links. Look at some examples of hypertext such as any Wikipedia article or online text. Discuss with students what is different about writing in a hypertext environment versus a traditional pencil-and-paper environment.
2. Instead of a paper-and-pencil anticipation guide, set up an electronic version, in which students e-mail you whether they disagree or agree with statements you have worded that preview a text they will be reading. (See Chapter 6 for more details.)
3. Select a recent news event and conduct a search for information resources on the Web. Select several resources and compare them for treatment, reliability, and accuracy. What does it mean to develop a healthy skepticism when interacting with texts on the Web?
4. Using the keywords "Examples of WebQuests," conduct a search on the Internet for teacher-designed WebQuests in the content area of your choice. Evaluate three or four of the WebQuest websites. Based on your search, what are some of the strengths of a WebQuest instructional model? What are some of the weaknesses? Discuss the strengths and weaknesses of these WebQuests in a small group.
5. Search the Global SchoolNet's Internet Projects Registry or other locations similar to it for Internet project descriptions in your content area. Use these project descriptions to guide the development of a project description that you have in mind at a grade level of your choice. Share your project descriptions with others in your group.

eRESOURCES

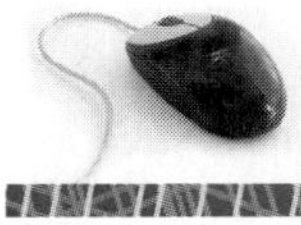

- Conduct an Internet inquiry of your own by going to Reading Online (**www.readingonline.org**) and Global SchoolNet's Internet Project Registry (**www.gsn.org/GSH/pr/index.cfm**). Study several reports and Internet projects in your content area.
- Find out more about the WebQuest strategy by going to **http://webquest.org/index.php**. Explore existing WebQuests and consider how you could create a WebQuest for your content area.

CHAPTER 3

We may have all come on different ships, but we're in the same boat now.

—Martin Luther King, Jr.

Culturally Responsive Teaching in Diverse Classrooms

ORGANIZING PRINCIPLE

Teachers respond to linguistic and cultural differences by scaffolding instruction in culturally responsive classrooms.

The Civil Rights Movement of the 1960s and, in more recent years, the political, social, and economic upheavals around the world have brought diverse groups of people to our schools. The Martin Luther King quote that opens this chapter is particularly relevant in today's classrooms. When it comes to teaching and learning with texts in diverse classrooms, we're all in the same boat, and the ship's captain—the teacher—is responsible for the welfare of everyone on board.

Different languages and cultures are gifts in our classrooms; they bring us fresh perspectives and vibrant new ideas that have the potential to animate classroom interactions. Yet teaching with texts is more challenging in today's classroom, where cultural and linguistic diversity has been increasing steadily since the 1960s. More often than not, students from different backgrounds struggle with literacy and learning in academic contexts. As a result, the strengths that they bring to instructional situations usually go untapped. Lee Gunderson, a well-known literacy educator, believes we need to make connections between the content that we teach and students' cultures and languages. This notion is often defined as *culturally responsive teaching* or *culturally relevant pedagogy.*

Written in collaboration with Patricia Ruggiano Schmidt and Wen Ma, Le Moyne College.

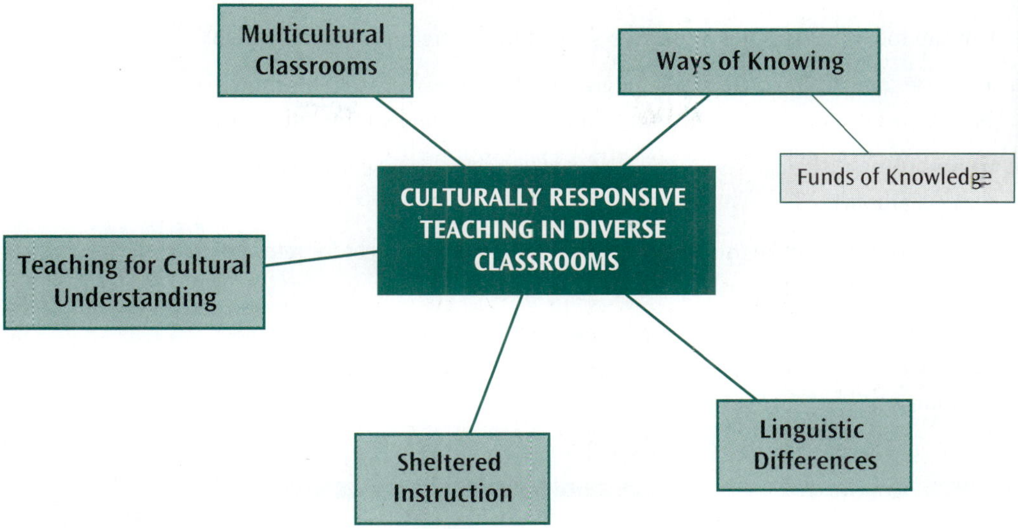

Culturally and linguistically diverse learners often are caught in a cycle of school failure that contributes to marginal achievement and high dropout rates. Typically, they are placed in low-ability groups where instruction is based on a limited, watered-down version of the curriculum. As a result, the strengths that diverse learners bring to instructional situations usually go untapped. Nowhere is the reality of a marginal school experience more pronounced than in the academic lives of English learners. Their school experience is often characterized by failure, disconnection, and resistance to reading and writing in academic contexts. The increasing number of learners whose first language is one other than English demands literacy-related instruction that is strategic and culturally responsive, with high learning expectations for all students.

How can teachers be responsive to linguistic and cultural diversity in their classrooms while maintaining high standards for content literacy and learning? Understanding the cultural and linguistic differences between mainstream and nonmainstream learners is an important first step, as the organizing principle of this chapter suggests: **Teachers respond to linguistic and cultural differences by scaffolding instruction in culturally responsive classrooms.**

FRAME OF MIND

1. Why are today's classrooms more diverse than they were several decades ago?
2. What are some of the cultural and linguistic differences that students from various racial and ethnic backgrounds bring to classroom learning situations?
3. What is culturally responsive instruction and what does it look like in content area classrooms?
4. How can teachers make use of community and family resources for relevant instruction?
5. Why do English learners struggle with content literacy tasks, and how does sheltered instruction make content more accessible to them while providing additional language support?

RESPONSE JOURNAL

If you currently are teaching, how would you describe the cultural and linguistic differences of your students? If you are studying to be a teacher, describe the cultural and linguistic differences that existed in your school experiences.

The purpose of this chapter is straightforward enough: to help teachers successfully respond to linguistic and cultural differences in their classrooms and to promote academic achievement for all learners. In culturally responsive classrooms, teachers draw on students' backgrounds, languages, and experiences to make connections with the discipline-specific content under study. In doing so, students find that academic experiences are more meaningful in their lives, and therefore, they become more interested and focused on content area learning. This is not a simple process but one that occurs in small increments as teachers and students experience positive results.

Tim Fitzpatrick, a science teacher in an urban high school, captures the essence of culturally responsive instruction by "keeping it real" in his science classes. His voice is featured in Box 3.1. As diverse learners become more engaged, they are motivated to focus on topics, complete assignments, and contribute to the classroom community with thoughtful questions and appropriate comments (Izzo & Schmidt 2006; Schmidt & Finkbeiner 2006). ■

Voices from the Classroom

BOX 3.1

Tim

High School Science Teacher

Tim Fitzpatrick has been teaching for twelve years in one of the most impoverished urban high schools in his state. More than 95 percent of the students receive free or reduced lunches and 50 percent are labeled as special education or English language learner (ELL). Students in Tim's school identify their cultural backgrounds as European American (10%), African American (25%), Latino (25%), Native American (5%), and racially mixed (10%). In addition, about 25 percent of the students claim China, Vietnam, Bangladesh, Nigeria, Thailand, Ghana, Sudan, Egypt, Kenya, or Zaire as their countries of origin.

Tim teaches several science courses, including a ninth-grade Survey of Sciences course, Biology, and Environmental Science. English learners are exclusively enrolled in the freshman survey course that includes introductions to chemistry, physics, biology, and earth science. Environmental Science is an elective for all seniors and deals with ecology, weather, and human effects on the natural world. Biology requires a state standardized test at the end of the school year. From Tim's perspective, "Science is a subject that may be easier to teach to ELL students than other content area courses. The sciences have their own languages, new to all of the students. We're also able to use many visuals and hands-on activities."

KEEPING IT REAL

Tim's approach to instruction is culturally responsive: "I keep it real. I use a lot of common sense and dialogue with my students both in and out of the classroom. My student–teacher relationships are a number one priority. I respect my students and constantly ask them to explain to each other and to me. They'll learn more when they are comfortable and know that I care." Tim also communicates regularly with the English as second language (ESL) teacher, since many of his students have had little, if any, formal schooling in their countries of origin and have trouble reading or writing in their home languages. Early in the school year, he makes it a point to label all tools and equipment in the science lab in both English and the students' home languages so they can begin to identify them. Because he sees culture and language as inextricably intertwined, Tim has discovered that recognizing the students' home languages and writing them next to English words is an essential element in his class.

Moreover, Tim attempts to connect culture to content whenever it makes sense to do so:

> Biology is great for drawing upon my students' cultures because of genetics, and the study of plant and animal life in their countries of origin. Studying world scientific problems in terms of cultural understandings, such as energy, immunities, birth control, uses and abuses of automobiles are all topics for great discussion and practice communicating. I took my classes to see the Ernie Davis movie *The Express* in the fall, and they were blown away by the racism. It made for great discussions in all of my science classes.

At the beginning of the school year, Tim's classes go through a modified version of the ABCs of Cultural Understanding and Communication in which students develop autobiographic sketches and share aspects of their life stories with one another (see Box 3.2 on page 57). According to Tim, the exercise is well worth the time:

> It takes one class period and students get the message that I welcome dialogue. Students are also encouraged to sit near a different person daily, so they can learn and develop as a learning community. I want them to express their informed opinions . . . not regurgitate facts.

As part of his instructional routines, Tim begins classes with a question for journal writing. For example, he reads a short passage regarding a man being attacked by a mountain lion, explains the meaning of predator and prey, and then asks the students to write about another example, possibly from their own experiences. They then share responses with one another. He also uses PowerPoint presentations for lectures, designs word walls with technical vocabulary related to the content under study, and uses graphic organizers such as concept maps (see Chapter 8 for further explanations). In addition, Tim is selective about assigning text material to read. He only selects paragraph sections that are most important in text chapters and, if the text is too difficult, he will even rewrite material that is crucial for understanding core concepts.

So now we know what Tim means when he says, "I keep it real."

Most people, other than those who study culture, probably don't think much about what it means to be immersed in a culture, just as fish probably don't think much about what it means to be immersed in water. The term *culture* represents a complex and multidimensional concept at best. Culture has been defined by Peregoy and Boyle (2008) as the shared beliefs, values, and rule-governed patterns of behavior that define a group and are required for group membership. On one level are the surface features of a culture—its foods, dress, holidays, and celebrations. On another level are deeper elements, which include not only values and belief systems but also "family structures and child-rearing practices, language and non-verbal communication, expectations, gender roles, biases—all the fundamentals of life that affect learning" (Díaz-Rico & Weed 2002, p. 197).

Language and culture are inextricably connected. Native speakers learn language in social settings, and in the process, they also learn their culture's norms for using language. As you might expect, different cultures have different rules that are always culturally defined and culturally specific. When a student's norms differ from the teacher's expectations, communication is often hindered. Because language use is culturally specific, it is easy for teachers not to recognize that language rules are indeed in effect for speakers of other dialects or speakers with different cultural norms for communicating.

RESPONSE JOURNAL

Brainstorm a list of words and idiomatic expressions that are specific to a cultural group with whom you identify. Why would someone outside of your cultural group have difficulty understanding these words and expressions?

Teaching and Learning in Multicultural Classrooms

The rapidly changing demography of the United States and its schools is transforming the country into a society that is increasingly *multicultural*. Guofang Li (2009), for example, explored the extent to which cultural and linguistic diversity prevails in today's classrooms as well as the conflicts and struggles of diverse learners trying to make sense of a curriculum dominated by mainstream European American cultures. Li's book *Multicultural Families, Home Literacies and Mainstream Schooling* provides a powerful lens for better understanding the lives and home practices of underrepresented students and their families.

Sturtevant (1992) studied content literacy practices in a multicultural context in a northern Virginia high school. An American history teacher in her study began the school year with twenty-nine students, but by May, the size of the class had dwindled to eighteen. Most of the Hispanic students in this class had moved from the school district, many returning to their home countries. Of the remaining students, there were five African Americans, two whites, three Asians (a Chinese, a Korean, and a Cambodian), two Africans (one from Ethiopia and the other from Zambia), one European (from Germany), and five Latin Americans (four from El Salvador and one from Peru). All of the immigrant students spoke English with limited proficiency but well enough to be mainstreamed into the regular classroom.

The American history teacher, born in a small, all-white Ohio town, drew on his own experiences in the Peace Corps to build positive social relationships in the classroom. While in the Peace Corps, he had learned what it meant to be a member of a minority cultural group on a small Caribbean island of almost entirely black inhabitants. In class, he was sensitive to cultural and language differences, and his willingness to understand these differences enabled him to teach more effectively. For example, he recognized that "kids become distrustful" if the teacher views their culture as inferior or their language as deficient. In class discussions, he avoided correcting students' English, believing that it was more important for them to explore ideas openly and critically without fear of humiliation than to speak "correct" English. His sensitivity to cultural and dialect differences allowed his students to interact with one another and with him in the way they spoke to peers and adults in their home or community. The teacher's response to student diversity in his classroom made a difference in the academic lives of his students. In diverse classrooms, cultural and linguistic sensitivity is a crucial first step in working with students to achieve academic standards. Teaching for cultural understanding will also make a difference in the way diverse learners respond to instruction.

myeducationlab

To hear an expert discuss cultural considerations in the classroom, go to the IRIS Center Resource section of Topic 1: "Diversity, Culture, and Literacy" in the MyEducationLab for your course and listen to the podcast entitled "Episode 2: Diane Torres-Velasquez on Diverse Learners."

Teaching for Cultural Understanding

Various instructional perspectives reflect different belief systems related to the teaching of multicultural concepts in today's classrooms. Diaz (2001) describes these perspectives within the context of four distinct instructional approaches. In the *contributions approach,* teachers typically emphasize culturally specific celebrations and holidays within the curriculum, such as Martin Luther King Day. The contributions approach reflects the surface level of a culture but does not make provisions for in-depth study of its deeper elements.

Somewhat related to the contributions approach is an instructional perspective that is additive in nature. The *additive approach* underscores the teaching of various themes related to multicultural concepts and issues. These concepts and issues are integrated into the curriculum through the development of a thematic unit of study, but on the whole the curriculum remains relatively the same throughout the year.

When teachers attempt to help students understand diverse ethnic and cultural perspectives by providing them with ongoing opportunities to read about concepts and events, make judgments about them, think critically, and generate their own conclusions and opinions, they are using a *transformative approach*. This approach, combined with the next one, lends itself well to content literacy strategies that emphasize critical analysis and interpretation. According to Diaz (2001), an extension of the transformative approach involves project learning. The *decision-making/social action approach* provides learners with

myeducationlab

To enhance your understanding of cultural influences, go to the IRIS Center Resource section of Topic 1: "Diversity, Culture, and Literacy" in the MyEducationLab for your course and complete the module entitled "Cultural and Linguistic Differences: What Teachers Should Know."

opportunities to engage in activities and projects related to cultural concepts and issues, particularly those issues and problems dealing with social action.

Teachers need to go beyond limiting the content of instructional lessons to celebrations or one-time-only thematic units related to multicultural concepts. Today's teachers need to provide students with literacy and learning experiences that will provide them with the cross-cultural knowledge and skills they will need as future adults in a nation that has become increasingly diverse. Multicultural literature helps students develop cross-cultural knowledge and skills.

One model used to help teachers become more culturally aware and sensitive to those from diverse backgrounds and experiences is the ABCs of Cultural Understanding and Communication (Schmidt 1998, 1999b, 2000, 2001, 2003, 2005a,b). Teachers who participate in this process have also adapted the model for their own classrooms. Their students learn to appreciate the differences around them and classrooms become learning communities, a reality often difficult to create in secondary classrooms. Box 3.2 briefly explains the model.

After completing the ABCs model's first four steps, teachers design lesson plans for connecting home, school, and community for children's reading, writing, listening, speaking, and viewing based on numerous modifications of the model. They see ways to develop collaborative relationships with families in an atmosphere of mutual respect, so that students gain the most from their education.

The ideas depicted in Box 3.2 may be adapted in any content area and are usually implemented at the beginning of a course of study or the school year. Students create lifeline stories depicting key events; interview each other; compare and contrast life stories of famous mathematicians, scientists, and politicians; and use the Internet to explore the reasons for cultural differences related to geography and architecture.

The ABCs of Cultural Understanding and Communication helps teachers learn about family and community values and shows them how to value communities and families.

Integrating Multicultural Literature Across the Curriculum

When teachers use multicultural literature in the classroom, they provide students with texts that not only are engaging but also recognize the unique contributions of each culture and the similarities of the human experience across cultures. At the same time, they help nonmainstream cultures appreciate and value their heritage and give all students the benefits of understanding ways of knowing about the world that are different from their own. Choosing multicultural texts to integrate into the curriculum is no easy task. Asking several questions can help you select those books that will be most useful to students in your classroom (Yokota 1993):

- Is this book good literature? Is the plot strong? Is characterization true to experience?
- Are setting, theme, and style well developed?

Evidence-Based Best Practices BOX 3.2

ABCs of Cultural Understanding and Communication

1. Students write their autobiographies, starting with their earliest memories of family traditions, religion, education, victories, defeats, and so forth. The life stories are shared only with the instructor, so personal information may be confidentially included.
2. Teachers interview parents or family members of students who are culturally different from themselves. This occurs on neutral ground, usually not at school. They interview at a local coffee shop, park, or community center. A student's home is also acceptable if the teacher is willing to visit. The teacher begins by asking the family member what he or she would like to see happen in school for the student. The teacher attempts to discover student interests and routines outside of school. The teacher also shares his or her own life experiences at appropriate times during the interview.
3. The teacher then creates a chart comparing and contrasting the life of the family member and the life of himself or herself (the teacher).
4. Next, the teacher analyzes the differences. He or she writes why certain differences are admired and why certain differences make one feel uncomfortable. The purpose of this exercise is to examine one's own culture in relation to the culture of the person interviewed. This helps develop an awareness of ethnocentricity, the idea that your own culture guides your existence.
5. Finally, the teacher begins to make connections by studying the curriculum and exploring ways to make studies meaningful to specific students and their families and communities. Inviting a mother and her new baby into the classroom to discuss human development may be one way to bring relevance to learning. Inviting a new arrival from Puerto Rico to teach a song or dance to the class and discuss the island's geography is another way to include differences. Inviting a carpenter to discuss house framing when students study trigonometry connects school and community in positive, memorable ways.

- Is this book culturally accurate? Will it help readers gain a true sense of the culture?
- Is the book rich in cultural details? Do details that give readers insight into the nuances of daily life enhance the story? Or is the culture overgeneralized?
- Are cultural issues presented comprehensively? Do they have enough depth and realism for readers to get a true sense of how culture affects the lives of people?
- Are minorities relevant? Are members of a minority group present for a reason, or could the story be told as easily about any cultural group? Token involvement of minority characters gives little sense of their unique, culturally rooted experience.
- Are dialogue and relationships culturally authentic?

Multicultural Books: A Closer Look

Multicultural books encompass every genre, including picture books, poetry, fiction, and nonfiction. A defining characteristic of multicultural books is their focus on people of color. These books provide diverse students with rich opportunities not only to see themselves reflected in the books they read but also to appreciate and celebrate the experiences of people of color from the past. As such, multicultural books also provide mainstream students with opportunities to learn about other cultures and peoples. For example, Suzanne Fisher Staples's (1991) *Shabanu: Daughter of the Wind* draws readers into the life of a girl growing up among camel-trading nomads in modern Pakistan.

Such books can help students understand cultural norms related to family, morality, sex roles, dress, and values of other cultures. Most importantly, however, multicultural literature brings the people of a particular group into focus and can help students realize that in spite of our differences all people share many common emotions, dreams, and hopes for the future. Through interactions with characters representing a variety of cultures, young people begin to view members of parallel cultures as individuals who are unique, and yet have universal feelings and experiences. Pam Muñoz Ryan's (2000) *Esperanza Rising* is a wonderful coming-of-age novel focused on a "riches to rags" story of a wealthy young Mexican girl and her mother who end up becoming migrant workers in the fields of California. The book is based on the real-life experiences of the author's grandmother. Teenagers can relate to it because it tells a story of identity and family, common themes in all of our lives.

Multicultural books portray members of a wide variety of cultures including African and African American, Asian and Asian American, Native American, Latino, and so on. It is important to note that there is a difference between being Mexican and being Mexican American. When selecting multicultural books for the classroom, teachers must differentiate between these groups. For example, a Mexican person living in Mexico has remarkably different experiences from a Mexican American person living in the United States. Teachers cannot assume, for example, that a modern Mexican American child will be able to relate to a book about Mexico.

Studying the folklore of diverse cultures is a common practice in schools, especially in the lower grades; however, the protagonists of many folktales are adolescents who have much to say to today's young adults. The human dimension of slavery is powerfully told, for example, in Virginia Hamilton's *The People Could Fly* (1985); true multicultural understanding is also enhanced by her compilation of creation myths entitled *In the Beginning* (1988). A host of folktale collections from around the world can add insight to the study of history, social studies, and geography. Folk literature is the "cement" or "mirror" of society (Sutherland & Arbuthnot 1986, p. 163), and thus gives readers an insider's view of a culture's beliefs and attitudes that is not typically found in textbooks. That said, scholars of multicultural literature such as Cai (1994) caution against using folktales exclusively, a practice that can perpetuate perceptions of exoticism and otherness. Ideally, folktales are typically studied in conjunction with contemporary, realistic depictions of the cultures in question. For example, it would be ideal to pair a substantial library of Chinese folktales about Mulan with more contemporary stories about Chinese American females such as Grace Lin's (2007) *The Year of the Dog* and/or Joyce Lee Wong's (2007) *Seeing Emily.*

Many students in today's ethnically diverse urban classrooms prefer books about young people living in challenging circumstances that may parallel their own experiences. These titles describe teens' personal struggles with drugs, gangs, abuse, and similar issues. Many urban students feel a strong connection with characters in these books, for whom daily survival in today's world is often a challenge. Short story anthologies like *Big City Cool: Short Stories About Urban Youth* (Weiss & Weiss 2002), contain selections by Walter Dean Myers, Amy Tan, and other authors familiar with what it means to grow up in urban America.

The memoir *Always Running: La Vida Loca: Gang Days in L.A.* (Rodriguez 1993) is what high school teacher Carol Jago calls a "disappearing book"—a book that mysteriously leaves the shelves of her classroom library and seldom returns, which is a clear indicator of its popularity. *Always Running* is the controversial memoir of Luis Rodriguez's life in a gang, which was written in an effort to get his son to leave gang life and create a different future for himself. Other factual books of interest to urban students include Loung Ung's (2000) *First They Killed My Father: A Daughter of Cambodia Remembers,* which graphically portrays one family's struggle to survive the horrors of the Khmer Rouge in Cambodia. In *Voices from the Fields: Children of Migrant Farm Workers Tell Their Stories* (Atkin 1993), ten Mexican American children of migrant farmworkers describe their lives in their own words. One of the young people featured is a gang member, one an unmarried teenage mother, and one is making plans to attend college and become a physician. The author portrays the uncertainty of their lives, at the same time recognizing the strong bonds that bind these young people to their families.

Research suggests that despite the availability of high-quality and interesting multicultural books, many teachers are not using these books to full advantage. Teachers often cite lack of time and knowledge about these books as reasons for limiting their use (Loh 2006). Because of the canon or other required readings dictated by the school district, teachers sometimes report that they do not have time or opportunity to expose their students to multicultural books that fall outside of the prescribed curricula.

According to Wills and Mehan (1996), however, diverse experiences need to be viewed as part of the American narrative, not as a separate entity. For example, when teaching a unit on World War II, teachers should also include texts about the Japanese internment such as *Looking Like the Enemy: My Story of Imprisonment in Japanese American Internment Camps* (Gruenewald 2005) and texts about African American women during this time such as *Bitter Fruit: African American Women in World War II* (Honey 1999). Considering and studying multiple perspectives about any given topic and/or unit only enhances and deepens the content and cultural knowledge; in this way the lives of our students are further enriched.

To learn more about the many resources for identifying multicultural books for students, teachers can refer to lists and guides developed by the Cooperative Children's Book Center, the North Central Regional Education Laboratory, the

American Library Association, and so on. Other sources include magazines such as *BookList, School Library Journal, Kirkus Review,* and the *Horn Book Magazine.* Lastly, teachers can consider books that have won awards such as the Asian/Pacific American Award for Literature, the International Board on Books for Young People (IBBY) Honour List, the Pura Belpre Award, and the Coretta Scott King Award, among others.

Teachers report that they often fear offending other cultures by choosing the "wrong" book. For this reason, some teachers opt out of using multicultural books altogether (Loh 2006; Bishop 2003). The resources mentioned above can help teachers select appropriate multicultural books with confidence and avoid the temptation to ignore diversity in our classroom libraries and in our curricula and instruction.

Ways of Knowing in a Culturally Responsive Classroom

It is crucially important to be aware that students from diverse cultural backgrounds bring different ways of knowing, different styles of questioning, and different patterns of interaction to school. For example, different cultures may have different attitudes, expectations, and assumptions about the value of reading and writing and what it means to be a reader and writer. Alicia, a Latina student, didn't want to be a "schoolgirl." To be a schoolgirl meant always having her head in a book, always doing homework. However, Alicia had little trouble getting involved in school activities that revolved around meaningful, collaborative literacy activities, such as tutoring younger students and writing social studies texts for them (Heath & Mangiola 1989).

Different cultures may place a different emphasis and value on various cognitive activities and styles of questioning. Some societies, for example, emphasize memorization and analytical thinking over the ability to experiment or to make predictions (Fillmore 1981). The cognitive styles of culturally diverse students may differ. Heath (1983) discovered that African American students experienced academic difficulty in their classrooms partly because of their lack of familiarity with the kinds of questions they were expected to answer in school. For example, based on family interaction patterns in the African American community that she studied, Heath found that students were not familiar with school questions asking them to describe or identify the attributes of objects or concepts. The students were much more familiar with analogy-type questions comparing one object or concept with another. When teachers became aware of the differences between the kinds of questions they asked and the kinds of questions familiar to the students, they were able to make adjustments in their questioning style. As a result, the teachers noticed a marked contrast in their students' participation and interest in lessons.

myeducationlab

Go to the Building Teaching Skills and Dispositions section of Topic 1: "Diversity, Culture, and Literacy" in the MyEducationLab for your course. As you complete the activity, consider how a teacher can meet the needs of all students.

Ways of knowing are intertwined with ways of interacting and learning. Rather than emphasize individual competition, some cultural groups prize group interaction, helping one another, and collaborative activity. Reyes and Molner (1991), for example, suggest that cooperative learning is more "culturally congruent" with students from Mexican American backgrounds. The research support for cooperative classroom strategies, especially in diverse learning situations, is impressive (Little Soldier 1989; Slavin 1987).

Many students from diverse linguistic and cultural backgrounds are discriminated against not only because of race and language but also because of their struggles to exist in high-poverty areas. The daily struggles to survive in poverty also yield funds of knowledge that are often overlooked in schools. It is each teacher's responsibility to develop relationships that nourish trust. By seriously drawing on students' interests and popular culture, teachers can make connections that demonstrate a respect for students' lives (Payne 2003; Schmidt 2005a).

When teaching for linguistic and cultural diversity, motivational activities are based on the same principles as those learned for any successful teaching and learning situation. Teachers must draw on student prior knowledge and interests. Therefore, family and community cultures and languages, popular culture, and individual student interests are all necessary considerations when motivating students for learning. Teachers differentiate instruction and plan for the inclusion of relevant information in their content areas. Ideas interspersed throughout this book will demonstrate and expound on these motivational principles for engaging diverse groups of students in content area classrooms.

Funds of Knowledge

The powerful role that culture plays in shaping students' behaviors and their knowledge of the world often goes unnoticed in classrooms. Understanding the sociocultural dynamics of home and community gives us a broader perspective on the worldviews students bring to school. Culturally and linguistically diverse students typically come from working-class families where their individual lives are inseparable from the social dynamics of the household and community in which they live. A teacher who makes a point of understanding the home culture, ethnic background, and community of students is in a better position (1) to understand the kinds of knowledge that culturally diverse students bring to learning situations and (2) to adjust the curriculum to their sociocultural strengths.

Luis Moll (1994) contends that much is to be gained from understanding the "social networks" of the households in a cultural group. These networks are crucial to families, who often engage in exchanging "funds of knowledge." These funds of knowledge may represent occupationally related skills and information that families share with one another as a means of economic survival. Moll argues that the social and cultural resources that students bring to school—their funds of knowledge—are rarely tapped in classroom learning contexts. Using

RESPONSE JOURNAL

Think about the funds of knowledge that you possess based on your cultural background and heritage. Describe how you make use (or will make use) of such knowledge in your teaching.

the community's rich resources and funds of knowledge builds on one of students' greatest assets: the social networks established within a cultural group. One such resource is its people. Moll (1994) puts it this way: "One has to believe that there are diverse types of people that can be helpful in the classroom even though they do not have professional credentials. Wisdom and imagination are distributed in the same way among professional and nonprofessional groups" (p. 194).

In a middle-level classroom, Mexican American students in Tucson, Arizona, engage in a study of construction which includes inquiry into the history of dwellings and different ways of building structures. The students have access to a wide array of reading materials from the library to focus their investigation: trade books, magazines, newspapers, and reference resources, to name a few. The teacher builds on students' reading by inviting parents and community members to speak to them about their jobs in the construction industry. For example, a father visits the class to describe his work as a mason.

Showing interest in students' home cultures and ethnic backgrounds builds trust in the classroom. Jackson (1994) believes that building trust with students of diverse backgrounds is a culturally responsive strategy that is often overlooked. One way to create trust may be as simple as learning students' names and pronouncing them correctly, and perhaps having them share the unique meanings and special significance of their first names. Teachers may also invite them to research and share information about their family's ethnic background, using questions suggested by Cover (1989): What generation in the United States do you represent? Are you and your siblings the first of your family to be born in this country? Were you foreign born? From where did you or your ancestors migrate? What made them wish to come here? Does your immediate or extended family practice ethnic or cultural customs which you or they value or with which you or they identify? Do you or your relatives speak your ethnic group's language? What occupations are represented in your family background?

The instructional strategies in Boxes 3.3 and 3.4 show how teachers may draw on students' funds of knowledge in science, mathematics, and the arts.

Characteristics of Culturally Responsive Instruction

Culturally responsive instruction, as you can see, is related to students' ways of knowing, motivation for learning, and their funds of knowledge. In other words, instruction that is responsive to cultural differences in the classroom makes connections with students' backgrounds, origins, and interests to teach the required standards associated with a curriculum. Learning becomes more relevant as teachers draw on students' prior knowledge and experiences. So how can teachers tell that culturally responsive instruction is happening in classrooms?

Research on culturally responsive instruction has discovered seven key characteristics (Au 1993; Boykin 1978, 1984; Ladson-Billings 1994, 1995; Moll 1992; Osborne 1996; Reyhner & Garcia 1989; Schmidt 2003, 2005a,b; Tatum 2005). When lessons in secondary mathematics, social studies, science, language, and English content areas incorporate the seven characteristics, students stay more focused, become invested

Evidence-Based Best Practices **BOX 3.3**

Drawing on Students' Funds of Knowledge in Science and Mathematics

Science and mathematics are all around us. To help students understand how meaningful these content areas are, it is important to help them see the relevancy in their own lives as well as the community's life. Teachers may invite community or family members to various content area classes to discuss occupations related to particular content areas. As a result, students might consider future occupations more seriously when they hear from community or family members (Schmidt & Ma 2006).

1. Read through student registration cards to determine what kinds of work family members do. Mechanics and repair people know about simple machines. Nurses' aides and doctors know about the human body systems. Carpenters and architects understand many principles of trigonometry related to framing and designing homes. Cooks and pharmacists know a lot about chemical change. Electricians and engineers have knowledge about what powers our world. Companies will often allow workers to go to a school as part of their public relations programs.
2. At the beginning of a unit of study, ask students who they know in these occupations. In class, list the people and discuss the occupations. Encourage students to invite family members to discuss their work. If this doesn't work, make phone calls and send letters to invite family and community members to class.
3. At the end of a unit of study, discuss other occupations that might relate to the content of mathematics and science.

The following are specific examples of people who may visit the class. Of course, there are many more.

Invite a family member or members who have stopped smoking to discuss the respiratory system in biology class.

1. Persons talk about the stopping process.
2. Students interview them about their feelings physically and emotionally.
3. After the visitors leave, students may discuss the interviews in relation to respiratory functions.

Invite a professional cook to chemistry class.

1. The cook discusses the various ingredients used in cooking such as baking soda, sugar, vinegar, yeast, salt, and more. The cook explains the functions of these chemicals.
2. Students record information, write formulas, and discuss and demonstrate chemical reactions in food preparation (e.g., carbon, sodium chloride, acetic acid, and sodium hydroxide). Discuss chemical formulas.

Invite a carpenter to mathematics class.

1. Students study plans for a home in relation to trigonometry.
2. Students prepare questions to be given to the carpenter to discuss with the class.
3. The carpenter explains tools used to build homes and constructs a small frame in the classroom from 2" × 4" wood.
4. Students study more complex house plans and what is necessary to pursue carpentry.

Reading, writing, listening, speaking, and viewing are all part of culturally responsive teaching and learning. Students will link their community to the units of study and see the relevance of the lessons to their own lives. They will meet people from differing backgrounds and experiences who make significant contributions to the community.

Source: Adapted from *50 Literacy Strategies for Culturally Responsive Teaching, K–8* (Paper) by P. R. Schmidt and W. Ma. Copyright 2006 by Sage Publications, Inc., Books. Reprinted by permission of Sage Publications, Inc., via Copyright Clearance Center.

Evidence-Based Best Practices

BOX 3.4

Drawing on Students' Funds of Knowledge in the Arts

An understanding and appreciation of cultures is often taught through the arts. Working with the school's art, music, and drama teachers may help enrich this strategy. Also local musicians and artists can be additional resources. Seeing and listening to artistic endeavors may inspire the students to think about their own talents (Schmidt & Ma 2006).

1. Picture books are a means of introducing students to various art media. Encourage the students to choose what they like and try to make it in their own way. For example, I like that tree in the picture. I am going to make one that is sort of like that tree. I like the colors in that picture. I am going to use those colors in my picture. I like that statue of a dolphin. I am going to make a little one with this clay.
2. Musicians or older students may visit the class to talk about various musical instruments and play short pieces of music from different cultures—steel drums, sitar, maracas, or flute. Students may want to touch and play these instruments.
3. Local theater groups may be invited to perform and actually teach students about mime and other forms of acting.
4. A costume corner or center may be a place where the actors decide what is authentic for a particular theater or dance production.
5. Local dancers from Latino, Arabic, African, or Asian cultures may perform in classrooms and teach the students dance steps using music from the cultures.
6. Students may present a performance entitled Appreciating the Arts Around the World for the local community.
7. After reading *Honoring Our Ancestors: Stories and Pictures by Fourteen Artists* (Rohmer 1999) and *Just Like Me: Stories and Self-Portraits by Fourteen Artists* (Rohmer 1997), students may select an artist to study and should be ready to tell the life story. Also, try to recreate a sample of their work.

Source: Adapted from *50 Literacy Strategies for Culturally Responsive Teaching, K–8* (Paper) by P. R. Schmidt and W. Ma.

in what is happening, and actually step onto the road of academic success and social achievement (Tatum 2000). Additionally, literacy development is promoted, because reading, writing, listening, speaking, and viewing provide the foundation for the seven characteristics of culturally responsive teaching (Schmidt 2005a,b). These characteristics, with brief definitions, follow (Schmidt 2003):

1. *High expectations.* Supporting students as they develop the literacy appropriate to their ages and abilities;
2. *Positive relationships with families and community.* Demonstrating clear connections with student families and communities in terms of curriculum content and relationships;
3. *Cultural sensitivity.* Reshaped curriculum mediated for culturally valued knowledge, connecting with the standards-based curriculum as well as individual students' cultural backgrounds;

4. *Active teaching methods.* Involving students in a variety of reading, writing, listening, speaking, and viewing behaviors throughout the lesson plan;
5. *Teacher as facilitator.* Presenting information, giving directions, summarizing responses, and working with small groups, pairs, and individuals;
6. *Student control of portions of the lesson ("healthy hum").* Talking at conversation levels around the topic studied while completing assignments in small groups and pairs; and
7. *Instruction around groups and pairs to create low anxiety.* Completing assignments individually, but usually in small groups or pairs with time to share ideas and think critically about the work.

Culturally responsive instruction helps to create classroom learning environments that celebrate languages and cultures (Cazden 2001; Cummins 1986; Igoa 1995; Schmidt 1998). Literacy coaches support content area teachers in the development of classroom learning environments by providing training around the following ideas and others found in this chapter:

- Label objects in the classroom in two or three languages, such as desk, chair, book, teacher, students, and so on. Have the student or a family member assist the teacher if necessary. Labeling is common in primary classrooms. It works great in secondary classrooms too. A daily practice pronouncing the vocabulary highlights other cultures and languages. The small amount of time necessary to implement this idea not only recognizes linguistic differences but also teaches and brings an awareness to second language learning.
- Invite students or family members to present information or artifacts from their country of origin. Many students have jewelry and art objects they can share. Storytelling in some cultures is a powerful record of history.
- Use paired learning.
- Give opportunities for students to speak, read, or write in their home language each day in school.
- Include visuals wherever and whenever possible, such as videos, overhead transparencies, disposable cameras, and posters when teaching.
- Present opportunities for hands-on classroom experiences and field trips.
- Put up the daily class schedule and provide a predictable environment for learning.
- Have a map of the world or globe for students to view.
- Use choral reading for students with limited English fluency.
- Have bilingual dictionaries available.
- Use nonfiction picture books to teach key concepts in content areas.

- Include different cultures in curriculum topics (e.g., famous Latino chemists, famous Chinese artists).
- Encourage drawing and writing.
- Keep a personal journal.
- Help students keep an assignment pad.

Linguistic Differences in Today's Schools

Linguistic differences among today's student population are strikingly evident in many school districts throughout the United States. From the East Coast to the West Coast, and from the Gulf to the Northern Great Lakes, the increasingly large number of immigrants from non-European nations is influencing how content area teachers approach instruction. It is no exaggeration to suggest that in some urban school districts more than fifty languages are spoken (Banks 2001).

When immigrant students maintain a strong identification with their culture and native language, they are more likely to succeed academically, and they have more positive self-concepts about their ability to learn (Banks 2001; Diaz 2001; Garcia 2002). Schools, however, tend to view linguistically diverse students whose first language is one other than English from a deficit model, not a difference model. For these English learners, instructional practices currently are compensatory in nature: "That is, they are premised on the assumption that language diversity is an illness that needs to be cured" (Diaz 2001, p. 159).

In addition, regional variations in language usage, commonly known as dialects, are a complicated issue for teachers. In truth, all English language users speak a dialect of English, which is rooted in such factors as age, gender, socioeconomic status, and the region of the country where one was born and grew up. Even presidents of the United States speak dialects! The difficulty with dialect differences in the classroom is the *value* assigned to dialects—the perceived goodness or badness of one particular language variation over another. Roberts (1985), however, suggests that language variations are neither good nor bad, and that such judgments are often about the people who make them rather than about clarity or precision. Delpit (1988) argues quite convincingly that teachers need to respect and recognize the strengths of diverse learners who use dialects in the classroom.

Dialect Use in the Classroom

Cultural variation in the use of language has a strong influence on literacy learning. Even though students whose first language is not English do not have full control of English grammatical structures, pronunciation, and vocabulary, they can engage in reading and writing activities (Goodman & Goodman 1978). When students use their own culturally acceptable conversational style to talk and write about ideas they read in texts, they are likely to become more content literate and to improve their literacy skills. Au and Mason (1981), for example, describe how minority Hawaiian learners improved their reading abilities when they were allowed to use their home language to talk about texts.

Language *differences* should not be mistaken for language *deficits* among culturally diverse students. Many of the low-achieving high school students in the rural Georgia classroom that Dillon (1989) studied were African Americans who spoke a dialect commonly referred to as black English vernacular. Black dialect is acquired through family interactions and participation in the culture of the community. The teacher in Dillon's study had much success in leading text-related discussions because of his sensitivity to his students' dialect as a tool for communication in the class. As Dillon put it, the teacher "allowed students to use dialect in his classroom because they were more comfortable with it and more effective communicators" (p. 245).

Shouldn't students from minority backgrounds learn to use standard American English? The question is a rhetorical one. As teachers, our stance toward the use of standard American English is critical. Standard American English, often thought of as the "news broadcast–type" English used in the conduct of business, is the language of the dominant mainstream culture in U.S. society—the "culture of power," according to Delpit (1988). Delpit explains that the rules and codes of the culture of power, including the rules and codes for language use, are acquired by students from mainstream backgrounds through interaction with their families. Minority students, however, whose families are outside the mainstream culture, do not acquire the same rules and codes. If students are going to have access to opportunities in mainstream society, schools must acquaint students from minority backgrounds with the rules and codes of the culture of power. Not making standard American English accessible to students from minority backgrounds puts them at a disadvantage in competing with their mainstream counterparts.

Although it is important for culturally diverse learners to receive explicit instruction in the use of standard American English, *when* and *under what circumstances* become critical instructional issues. All students should understand how cultural contexts influence what they read, write, hear, say, and view. Language arts classes are probably the appropriate place to provide explicit instruction in the functional use and conventions of standard American English. Although becoming proficient in standard American English may be an important school goal for all students, it should not be viewed as a prerequisite for literate classroom behavior (Au 1993). When it is viewed as a prerequisite, teachers deny students the opportunity to use their own language as a tool for learning. Increasing their command of standard American English, in and of itself, will not improve students' abilities to think critically, "since students' own languages can serve just as well for verbal expression and reasoning" (p. 130).

English Language Learning

English learners (ELs) are those students who speak English as a nonnative language. Because their home language is that of a minority group—for example, Spanish,

Navajo, or Vietnamese—they are considered to be *language minority* students. English learners are, for the most part, the children of immigrants who left their homelands for one reason or another. Some English learners, however, are born in the United States. As Peregoy and Boyle (2001) explain:

> Many recent immigrants have left countries brutally torn by war or political strife in regions such as Southeast Asia, Central America, and Eastern Europe; others have immigrated for economic reasons. Still others come to be reunited with families who are already here or because of the educational opportunities they may find in the United States. Finally, many English language learners were born in the United States and some of them, such as Native Americans of numerous tribal heritages, have roots in American soil that go back for countless generations. (p. 3)

Immigration patterns have changed dramatically in the past one hundred years. At the onset of the twentieth century, the vast majority of immigrants (87 percent) were from Europe. At the beginning of the twenty-first century, however, the majority of immigrants have come from Latin America (57 percent). Based on data from the U.S. Census Bureau (2000), as displayed in Table 3.1, there were nearly 25,800,000 foreign-born individuals living in the United States at the onset of the twenty-first century.

TABLE 3.1

Number and Percentage of U.S. Foreign Born and Country of Origin

Country of Origin	Foreign Born March 1997 Number (percentage)
All Countries	25,779,000 (100.0%)
Mexico	7,017,000 (27.2%)
Philippines	1,132,000 (4.4%)
China and Hong Kong	1,107,000 (4.3%)
Cuba	913,000 (3.5%)
Vietnam	770,000 (3.0%)
India	748,000 (2.9%)
Dominican Republic	632,000 (2.5%)
El Salvador	607,000 (2.4%)
Great Britain	606,000 (2.4%)
Korea	591,000 (2.3%)

Source: Table from Lucy Tse. (2001). *"Why Don't They Learn to Speak English?" Separating Fact from Fallacy in the U.S. Language Debate.* New York: Teachers College Press, p. 11.

Bilingual and ESL Programs

English learners vary in their use of English. Some may have little or no proficiency in the use of English. Others may have limited English skills; still others may use English proficiently and are mainstreamed into the regular curriculum. What is language proficiency? It has been defined as "the ability to use a language effectively and appropriately throughout the range of social, personal, school, and work situations required for daily living in a given society" (Peregoy & Boyle 2001, p. 29). Language proficiency, therefore, encompasses both oral and written language processes, including speaking, listening, reading, and writing.

In the United States, there is an array of instructional programs for English learners. Programs vary greatly, depending on the number of ELs enrolled in a school district. Many with limited English proficiency are placed in bilingual and English as a second language (ESL) programs. Bilingual and ESL programs are designed specifically to meet the academic, cultural, and linguistic needs of English learners until they are proficient enough in English to be mainstreamed into the regular curriculum.

Bilingual programs are designed to teach English and to provide instruction in the core curriculum using the home language of the English learner. Bilingual programs reach only a small percentage of students, despite a growing body of research that suggests that immigrant students who maintain a strong identification with their culture and native language are more likely to succeed academically and have more positive self-concepts about their abilities to learn (Banks 2001; Diaz 2001; Garcia 2002). ESL programs differ from bilingual programs in that they are taught entirely in English in schools where there are many language minority groups represented, making it difficult to implement bilingual instruction.

Bilingual and ESL teachers provide invaluable compensatory services for language minority students with limited English proficiency. When these students are mainstreamed into the regular curriculum, however, they often struggle with content literacy tasks. Let's take a closer look at some of the reasons diverse learners struggle with reading and writing in content area classrooms.

What Makes Content Literacy Difficult for English Learners?

Once they are mainstreamed into the regular curriculum, English learners often struggle with content area texts. In schools where tracking is used as an organizational tool, a disproportionate number of English learners have been placed in lower-track classrooms, even though the notion that students learn best with others of similar achievement levels has not been supported by research (Allington 2001; Oakes 1985). In mainstream classes, reading textbooks is one of the most cognitively demanding, context-reduced tasks that minority language students will encounter (Cummins 1994). Some students may become frustrated by texts because of issues related to background knowledge. According to Kang (1994):

> **myeducationlab**
>
> Go to the Assignments and Activities section of Topic 1: "Diversity, Culture, and Literacy" in the MyEducationLab for your course. Complete the activity "Cultural and Language Experiences" and hear educators discuss the needs of students who are English learners.

> Some information or concepts in textbooks may presuppose certain background knowledge that native speakers may take for granted but that may

> be different or lacking in some ESL students. Culture-specific background knowledge developed in students' native country, community, or home may affect their comprehension, interpretation, and development of social, cultural, historical, and even scientific concepts. Even if students possess the background knowledge presumed for a particular text, they may not be able to activate it to relate and organize new information. (p. 649)

The vocabulary load of content area textbooks is also a problem for some ESL learners. The academic language of texts is not the language of conversational speech. If students have limited literacy skills in their own native language, they will obviously experience a great deal of frustration and failure with English texts. Moreover, if students are good readers in their native language but have minimal proficiency in English, the language barrier may inhibit them from making effective use of their literacy skills.

Other researchers, however, have discovered that students learning English as a second language are more capable of comprehending subject area content than previously thought, especially in activity-based classes such as science. They may not be able to easily express ideas orally in English, but when given opportunities to write and answer written questions, they demonstrate clear understandings (Bernhardt 1998; Bernhardt & Kamil 1998). Similarly, Ma (2004), in his case study of college-level Korean international students, discovered that they preferred listening activities rather than discussion activities in class. They explained that listening to others in small groups was helpful in hearing multiple perspectives and interpretations necessary for understanding the culture and language of the United States. Additionally, these students relate to a Confucian learning culture (Watkins & Biggs 1996) that emphasizes deep reflective listening. Unfortunately, they may be placed at a disadvantage in classrooms in the United States, where those who are talkative in discussion groups are privileged (Li 2005; Pang & Cheng 1998).

Books for English Learners

English learners have become a recognizable force in today's classrooms. ELs face a triple challenge compared to mainstream students: They need to learn academic content, develop nativelike English proficiency, and achieve comfort with American culture. It is important to note that ELs have language, not cognitive, obstacles.

One way to address these challenges is to have ELs interact with authentic trade books. In doing so, teachers can increase students' content and vocabulary knowledge, offer more practice with authentic language, and provide scenarios that describe the life of American teenagers, which will expose ELs to a variety of cultural behaviors and ways of thinking. Books, TV shows, and movies can be excellent venues for ELs to learn about real-life experiences. For example, Jeff Kinney's *Diary of a Wimpy Kid* (Kinney 2007) can introduce ELs to the dynamics of junior high school hierarchies. The book's humor, simple vocabulary, and graphics will engage ELs, which increases their motivation to read.

Knowing that English learners need additional support with language learning, teachers may find *graphic novels* to be a perfect alternative for these students. Graphic

RTI for Struggling Adolescent Learners BOX 3.5

Responding to the Language Needs of English Learners

In recent years, there has been a surge in the percentage of English learners. This population of students is often disproportionately represented in special education programs—not as a result of cognitive disabilities, but rather because of their struggle with using the English language. The overrepresentation of English language learners in special education programs spotlights the need for appropriate materials for assessing and supporting non–English-speaking students (James 2004). By following RTI guidelines, remediation sensitive to the needs of English language learners should be provided within the classroom to lessen the amount of inappropriate special education referrals.

In an era of high-stakes assessments, it is important that appropriate RTI-related assessment measures be used to evaluate the progress and achievement of students with limited English proficiency. While some states provide standardized assessments in alternate languages, most prominently Spanish, others rely on test modifications or accommodations, such as extended time and alternative placement for testing, the use of a language translation dictionary, or additional support from the test administrator to simplify, reiterate, or read aloud test items. In some cases, students who face language challenges are exempt from testing altogether based on the length of time they have been exposed to English education.

In an effort to uphold the ideals of RTI, assessments should be provided in a language and format familiar to each English learner so that the results represent the student's abilities rather than language difficulties (James 2004). For example, classroom teachers can provide texts and trade books in students' native languages; students can be permitted to give their initial response to a reading in their primary language and then translate their work. This allows English learners to fully process reactions to text before attempting to translate their thoughts. When more formal methods of assessment are required, educators can locate resources that will meet the needs of culturally diverse classrooms.

Some examples of assessments provided in alternative languages include the following:

- *The Woodcock-Muñoz Achievement Battery–Revised.* This assessment by Riverside Publishing is parallel to the English language version and measures cognitive abilities and academic achievement.
- *The Native Language Literacy Screening Device.* This assessment created by the New York State Department of Education is available in 26 languages and measures students' literacy levels in their native languages.
- *Spanish Reading Inventory.* This reading inventory written by Jerry L. Johns and published by Kendall Hunt allows teachers to conduct running records with passages in Spanish to determine students' reading levels and plan appropriate instruction.

novels, already popular with adolescents for independent reading, combine words with pictures that can support the learning of students for whom English poses particular difficulties. Using graphic novels in the classroom is an increasingly popular way to scaffold ELs' understanding of content. Illustrations in graphic novels provide valuable context clues about the meaning of the written content and offer particular support for students who lack the ability to visualize as they read. Graphic novels are available in a variety of genres, including biographies, fiction, nonfiction, and fantasy. These texts have particular appeal for reluctant readers and can be used to teach a variety of literacy skills including dialogue, inferencing, story elements, literary terms like *writing, satire, irony,* and *parody,* and much more.

Using Will Eisner's (2000) *New York: The Big City,* Kelly Faust developed a lesson for her urban English learners, many of whom had been in this country for only one year. The purpose of the lesson was to further student understanding of story elements and encourage writing. She began the lesson by showing the students six frames of a wordless story from the book on the overhead projector. She then used the think-aloud strategy to point out the events of the story and the ways in which the visual techniques of the illustrator supported it. She reviewed the basic elements of a story with her students, and asked students whether the frames represented a story. Students pointed out that these frames contained characters, setting, and a simple plot. Students then discussed the story with a partner, creating their own version of the events portrayed in the frames. At this point, one team of students dictated their story to the group. Kelly recorded this story on chart paper, so that other students could see the concepts recorded. She modeled for the students how to use quotation marks to designate the exact words of a speaker. At strategic points, Kelly involved specific students in recording the text on paper. Next, Kelly directed the students to identify the characters, the setting, and the events of the plot in the recorded story.

Following this, Kelly presented students with a new series of wordless frames from the Eisner book. She reviewed the think-aloud strategy and students took turns thinking aloud with a partner about the text. Students then worked in teams to draft their own stories on notebook paper. At this point, Kelly conducted minilessons reviewing areas of need reflected in the student drafts. After revising, the students transferred their stories to chart paper and shared them with the class, pointing out the elements of story as reflected in their own writing. For more information on using comics and graphic novels in the classroom, see Chapter 12 and also check out the Graphic Classroom website at http://graphicclassroom.blogspot.com.

Vocabulary in areas such as mathematics, social studies and science can be overwhelming, causing content to be inaccessible for many English Learners. More vocabulary is introduced in social studies and science textbooks than in textbooks used to teach students a foreign language. Using picture books with ELs is a good practice because pictures can aid comprehension (see Box 3.6). Also, the vocabulary and language patterns of picture books are simple, which also aids comprehension. But one concern about picture books is that adolescents want to read stories about other adolescents. Chapter book series such as Mary Pope Osborne's *Magic Tree House* and Jon Scieszka's *Time Warp Trio* bring various science and social studies concepts to life in an easy-to-read but content-rich manner.

English learners need to learn to navigate nonnarrative texts because much of secondary schooling is based on the ability to read this text type. For social studies topics, check out books by Russell Freedman. Freedman includes a lot of primary and secondary sources and illustrations in his works. Furthermore, his books are rich in content but more concise and interesting than textbooks. *Immigrant Kids* (Freedman 1995), for example, is ideally suited for ELs as are other books about teens who share their struggles. Shaun Tan's wordless graphic novel *The Arrival* (2007) depicts the journey of an immigrant who grapples with loneliness and the strangeness of learning a new language and culture. There are also several anthologies that address this topic,

BOX 3.6

Picture Books in Mathematics

A variety of picture books may be used not only to help young adolescent English learners develop mathematical concepts but also to draw on their prior knowledge and experience (Schmidt & Ma 2006). Here are several suggestions for using math picture books in middle grade classrooms:

1. To spark interest and develop an understanding of mathematical concepts, have English learners read stories about famous mathematicians and cultures that have been mathematically oriented. The Internet provides wonderful leads on famous mathematicians from different cultures.
2. Have English learners read math-oriented picture books to younger siblings. Picture books explain in ways that help students understand mathematical concepts. In addition, students may create and design their own math books to be shared in other classrooms and with younger audiences.
3. Use math picture books as a strategy for motivating interest in mathematics and providing a greater depth of understanding of mathematical concepts.

Create an area in the classroom to display picture books such as the following:

Burns, M.	*The Greedy Triangle*
Heller, R.	*More Geometrics*
Wisniewski, D.	*Rain Player*
Tang, G.	*Math for All Seasons*
Tang, G.	*Math-terpieces*
Tang, G.	*The Grapes of Math*
Scieszka, J.	*Math Curse*
Schwartz, D.	*How Much Is a Million*
Neuschwander, C.	*Sir Cumference and the First Round Table*
Seife, C.	*Zero: Biography of a Dangerous Idea*
McKellar, D.	*Kiss My Math: Showing Pre-Algebra Who's Boss*

These books enhance the study of mathematics with humor and delightful stories and illustrations, bringing added joy to the study of math while encouraging related reading, writing, listening, speaking, and viewing activities.

such as *First Crossing: Stories About Teen Immigrants* (Gallo 2007) and *Kids Like Me: Voices of the Immigrant Experience* (Blohm & Lapinsky 2006). Series such as Ellen Levin's *If You . . .* (e.g., *If Your Name Was Changed at Ellis Island* [1996] and *If You Traveled West in a Covered Wagon* [1992]) and David Adler's picture book biographies are also welcome additions to content area learning for ELs.

Teaching for cultural understanding and using multicultural literature create a community of learners within the four walls of the classroom. Within such learning communities, it is important for teachers to understand the ways in which diverse learners "come to know" and to tap into students' "funds of knowledge."

Sheltered Instruction for English Learners

Sheltered instruction does not focus specifically on second language development issues. Instead, teachers often use a variety of instructional aids to let students who have limited skills in reading, writing, listening, and speaking "see" challenging, and often abstract, content visually. This may be done by contextualizing the learning tasks through hands-on cooperative activities, pictures, relevant media, artistic representations of meaning, and reading-to-learn strategies modeled for the students (Campano 2007; Haynes 2007). As a result, sheltered instruction often provides opportunities for nonnative students to learn discipline-specific content while improving their English language skills (Díaz-Rico 2008; Faltis & Coulter 2008).

RESPONSE JOURNAL

What does the term *sheltered* suggest to you? Why do you think it is used to describe an instructional approach for English learners?

When English learners struggle with content literacy tasks, instruction should be specially designed to meet their academic and linguistic needs, which often include (1) learning grade-appropriate and academically demanding content; (2) learning the language of academic English as reflected in content subjects, texts, and classroom discourse; (3) engaging in appropriate classroom behavior and understanding participation rules and expectations in small groups and whole-class instructional routines; and (4) mastering English vocabulary and grammar (Echevarria, Vogt, & Short 2008). Sheltered instruction, also known as SDAIE (specially designed academic instruction in English), is an approach to content area learning and language development that provides the instructional support needed to make grade-level content more accessible for ELs while promoting English development (Echevarria & Graves 2003).

Although the concept of "sheltering" English learners is similar to the concept of scaffolding instruction for all learners who need instructional support to be successful with content literacy tasks, it has been adapted for use in two types of instructional contexts: (1) in mainstreamed, core curriculum classrooms made up of native speakers and nonnative speakers who are at an *intermediate* level of language proficiency and (2) in ESL classrooms made up of nonnative speakers who are at similar levels of language proficiency.

The SIOP Model

One model for sheltered instruction, SIOP (sheltered instruction observation protocol), provides a comprehensive instructional framework that can be used in several ways to shelter instruction for English learners. First, the SIOP model serves as a blueprint for designing lessons that integrate content learning with additional language support for English learners. Second, the SIOP model enhances instructional delivery by making teachers aware of highly effective practices and behaviors that will make a difference in the academic and language development of students. And third, the SIOP model provides an observational framework for rating teachers in sheltered classrooms. Figure 3.1 depicts the major components within the SIOP model: lesson preparation, instruction, strategies, interaction, practice/application, lesson delivery, and assessment (Echevarria, Vogt, & Short 2008).

Sheltered instruction is a powerful approach to content area learning and language development. The literacy strategies described throughout this book may be

FIGURE 3.1 The Sheltered Instruction Observation Protocol (SIOP)

Observer: ______________________ Teacher: ______________________

Date: ______________________ School: ______________________

Grade: ______________________ ESL level: ______________________

Class: ______________________ Lesson: Multi-day Single-day

I. Preparation

1. Clearly defined *content objectives* for students
2. Clearly defined *language objectives* for students
3. *Content concepts* appropriate for age and educational background level of students
4. *Supplementary materials* used to a high degree, making the lesson clear and meaningful (graphs, models, visuals)
5. *Adaptation of content* (e.g., text, assignment) to all levels of student proficiency
6. *Meaningful activities* that integrate lesson concepts (e.g., surveys, letter writing, simulations, constructing models) with language practice opportunities for reading, writing, listening, and/or speaking

II. Instruction

(1) Building Background

7. *Concepts explicitly linked* to students' background experiences
8. *Links explicitly made* between past learning and new concepts
9. *Key vocabulary emphasized* (e.g., introduced, written, repeated, and highlighted for students to see)

(2) Comprehensible

10. *Speech* appropriate for students' proficiency level (e.g., slower rate, enunciation, and simple sentence structure for beginners)
11. *Explanation* of academic tasks clear
12. Uses a variety of *techniques* to make content concepts clear (e.g., modeling, visuals, hands-on activities, demonstrations, gestures, body language)

(3) Strategies

13. Provides ample opportunities for student to use *strategies*
14. Consistent use of *scaffolding* techniques throughout lesson, assisting and supporting student understanding
15. Teacher uses a variety of *question types throughout the lesson including those that promote higher-order thinking skills* throughout the lesson (e.g., literal, analytical, and interpretive questions)

(4) Interaction

16. Frequent opportunities for *interactions* and discussion between teacher/student and among students, which encourage elaborated responses about lesson concepts
17. *Grouping configurations* support language and content objectives of the lesson
18. Consistently provides sufficient *wait time for student response*
19. Ample opportunities for students to *clarify key concepts in L1*

(5) Practice/Application

20. Provides *hands-on* materials and/or manipulatives for students to practice using new content knowledge
21. Provides activities for students to *apply content and language knowledge* in the classroom
22. Uses activities that integrate all *language skills* (i.e., reading, writing, listening, and speaking)

(6) Lesson Delivery

23. *Content objectives* clearly supported by lesson delivery
24. *Language objectives* clearly supported by lesson delivery
25. *Students engaged* approximately 90–100% of the period
26. *Pacing* of the lesson appropriate to the students' ability level

III. Review/Assessment

27. Comprehensive *review* of key vocabulary
28. Comprehensive *review* of key content concepts
29. Regularly provides *feedback* to students on their output (e.g., language, content, work)
30. Conducts *assessment* of student comprehension and learning of all lesson objectives (e.g., spot checking, group response) throughout the lesson

Source: Echevarria, J., Vogt, M., & Short, D. (2008). *Making content comprehensible for English language learners: The SIOP model*, 3rd ed. Published by Allyn & Bacon, Boston, MA.

incorporated into instructional routines for students in sheltered or nonsheltered classrooms. Many of these strategies have been recommended by English language educators for use with language minority students (Díaz-Rico & Weed 2002; Echevarria & Graves 2003; Echevarria, Vogt, & Short 2008; Peregoy & Boyle 2001). In the next section, we highlight several strategies and suggest ways to adapt instruction for diverse learners.

Adapting Instruction in Content Classrooms

Content area teachers are in a strategic position to make adaptations in the way they design and deliver instruction in classrooms with native and nonnative speakers. These adaptations in instructional design and delivery lead to additional language support for English learners, as well as increased learning opportunities in the core curriculum.

Provide Comprehensible Input

Support nonnative speakers in your classroom by showing sensitivity to their language needs. An important component of sheltered instruction is to provide *comprehensible input* for English learners (Echevarria & Graves 2003). Make content learning comprehensible by simplifying your language when giving directions, leading whole-class discussions, or facilitating small-group interactions. When talking to a class that includes ELs, especially students at a beginning or intermediate level of language proficiency, it may be necessary to speak clearly and speak at a slightly slower rate than you normally would if you had only native speakers in your classroom. During discussions, it may also be necessary to repeat yourself, define new words in a meaningful context, or paraphrase when you use more sophisticated language than ELs can understand. Providing comprehensible input also means being aware of your use of idiomatic expressions and limiting them when students find idiomatic expressions difficult to understand. Moreover, keep in mind that gestures and facial expressions help to dramatize what you are saying during discussion. Barton (1995) reminds teachers not only to simplify and clarify the language they use but also to check for understanding frequently throughout classroom conversations. As we explained earlier in the chapter, scaffold instruction during discussion by supporting students in their use of home languages and their own culturally acceptable conversational styles.

Use Strategies for Vocabulary Development

Linguistically diverse learners, whether they are good or poor readers, will encounter unfamiliar content area vocabulary during reading that may pose comprehension problems for them. In a study of bilingual readers, researchers discovered that good readers focused on increasing vocabulary (Jimenez, Garcia, & Pearson 1995, 1996). In addition, English learners who struggle as readers benefited from vocabulary strategy instruction (Jimenez & Gamez 1996). Vocabulary strategy instruction is effective when a teacher helps ELs to develop a few key terms in depth rather than attempting to have them learn many words superficially (Gersten & Jimenez 1994). Such instruction should take into account strategies and procedures that will help students build meaning for important concept terms.

For example, whenever the opportunity presents itself, it's important to help students recognize and use the relationship between cognates and the context in which they are used. *Cognates* are words that are culturally and linguistically related in both the nonnative speaker's language and in English. As part of cognitive strategy instruction for struggling readers, Latina/o students in a middle school special education classroom were shown how to approximate word meaning through the cognate relationships they encountered in the texts that they were reading. The researchers used a think-aloud strategy, as discussed in the previous chapter, to scaffold instruction (Jimenez & Gamez 1996, p. 88):

> ***Researcher:*** You know the word in Spanish, so we can use a Spanish clue to help us figure out what it means. Victor, what does *espectacular* mean?
>
> ***Victor:*** That it's useful?
>
> ***Researcher:*** It's something very . . .
>
> ***Sara:*** Special?
>
> ***Researcher:*** Special, you got it! I like this. So (for) something very special, you can say wonderful, *maravilloso*. The Spanish clue helped us with *spectacular* because that is exactly the same in English and Spanish. Have you guys heard that word on the radio, *spectacular?* [The researcher writes this on the chalkboard.] That's English, and here's Spanish *espectacular.* The only difference between English and Spanish is that we put an *e* in the front in Spanish. That's exactly the same word. It almost sounds exactly the same, only a little bit different. But when you guys can do this you're taking advantage of your bilingualism and you're using what you already know to help you understand. OK? I think it's really cool when Latino kids do that. That makes a lot of sense to me.

In addition to emphasizing cognate-related vocabulary building, showing linguistically diverse learners how to approximate word meaning through *word structure* and context is another important aspect of vocabulary building. In Chapter 8, we will examine in more detail how to use context and word structure in content classrooms.

Chapter 8 also explores a variety of strategies for vocabulary and concept development, including the use of *graphic organizers.* A variety of organizers may be employed to help English learners see how the new concepts they are learning are related to other concepts they already know. The *plus* (+) strategy developed by Wen Ma, for example, involves students making connections with a parallel concept, a bigger concept, and a smaller concept in a given content area. Jeff Cretchen uses this strategy with native and nonnative learners while teaching the concept of electromagnetic energy in his twelfth-grade physics class.

CLASSROOM ARTIFACT **FIGURE 3.2** **Graphic Organizer for Electromagnetic Energy**

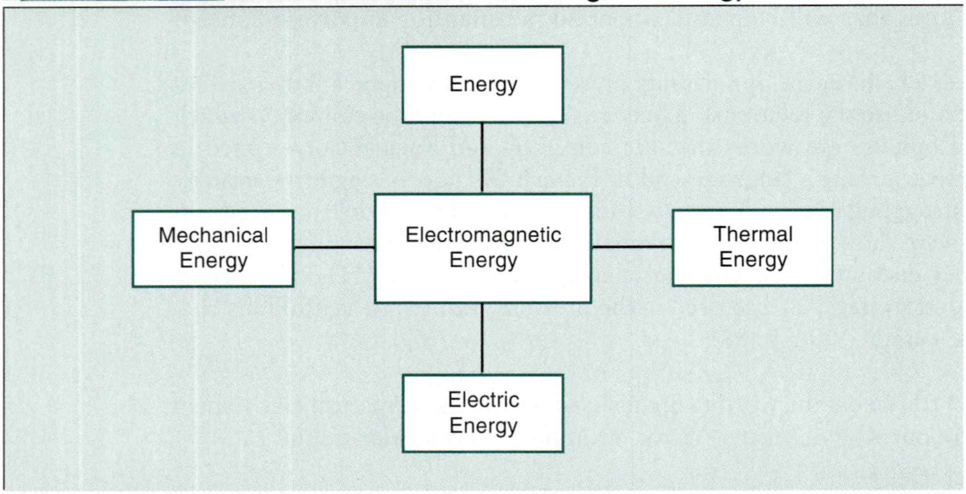

1. Jeff asked his students to draw five boxes on a page, with one box in the middle and the other four each to its left, right, top, and bottom, as shown in Figure 3.2.
2. The new concept *electromagnetic energy* that they were working on was written inside the middle box.
3. Jeff's students brainstormed to discover the overarching concept *energy,* which was put inside the top box.
4. Students continued to brainstorm. Two parallel concepts, *mechanical energy* and *thermal energy,* emerged. Each term was entered in the left and right boxes, which represented concepts parallel to the concept *electromagnetic energy.*
5. The bottom box is for a specific example, specific attribute, or defining characteristic of electromagnetic energy. *Electric energy* is one type of electromagnetic energy and is written in the bottom box. These boxes, as shown in Figure 3.2, help students view the term *electromagnetic energy* in relation to other related concepts.
6. As English learners acquire more knowledge about various kinds of electrical appliances, they may continue to elaborate on relationships among concepts. They may note that electric energy may be converted to light, sound, kinetic, or thermal energy in the household. This strategy may be easily adapted for studying different groups of concepts in different content areas. No matter what group of concepts students study, each time they develop links with a new concept.

Differentiate Between Intensive and Extensive Reading

English learners need to be taught that not all texts need to be read and understood at the same level of detail, and that they may employ different strategies for different reading tasks. Kristin Berry, a tenth-grade global studies teacher, introduced *intensive reading* and *extensive reading* strategies to her interdisciplinary English/global studies class while working on a unit of study about World War II. She followed these four steps to help English learners and native language speakers recognize when to use intensive reading and extensive reading strategies:

1. Kristin required her students to engage in an intensive reading of the core textbook to understand the big picture. They read about Germany's aggression in Europe, Japan's aggression in Asia, diplomacy and the Allied forces, major events and figures, and the fall of Germany and Japan, as well as the relationships among the social, political, military, and economic factors.

2. To help her students comprehend the chapters, Kristin not only worked with them on important vocabulary but also clarified the meaning of difficult sentences through rereading, paraphrasing, summarizing, group discussion, and written response. Through reading intensively, Kristin helped her students develop a solid understanding of the textbook.

3. In collaboration with her language arts colleague, Kristin incorporated a variety of learning activities and assignments into her lessons. She required students to read extensively some of the books that addressed various aspects of the war, such as *The Diary of Anne Frank: Play and Related Readings* (Goodrich & Hackett 2000), *Night* (Wiesel 2006), *Rumors of Peace* (Leffland 1979), and *Summer of My German Soldier* (Greene 1999). Then Kristin asked her students to select one novel to read for a general understanding. They were to connect what they read with what they had learned from reading the textbook.

4. To help students cope with the large volume of reading, Kristin also gave explicit instruction in the use of two study strategies that we elaborate on in Chapter 10: *skimming* (i.e., reading quickly to grasp the main ideas of a text) and *scanning* (i.e., reading quickly to locate specific detail). These varied reading experiences extended, diversified, and brought life to the textbook. As a result of Kristin's sheltered approach to instruction, intensive reading and extensive reading helped both English learners and mainstream students learn during the unit of study.

Use the Repeated Reading Strategy

For English learners who are still in the process of developing reading fluency, the *repeated reading strategy* may be a useful intensive reading approach to fully comprehend a content area text across varied grade levels. A three-step reading process may help students better understand a text through the use of repeated readings of text material:

1. The first reading focuses on breaking down the linguistic barriers for the English learners. To begin, each student is required to skim a given text and mark any language

item not understood. Before explaining the terms in class, the teacher encourages responses from other students. This is useful in developing students' ability to guess the meaning of a word from its context. The teacher may call students' attention to some "key points." The teacher also helps ELs differentiate between *denotation* (the literal meaning a word has) and *connotation* (the implied or suggested meaning of a word in context). Thus the students will not do a rigid word-for-word interpretation of every sentence in English. It is worth mentioning that because of the linguistic subtleties and intricacies of English figurative expressions, special consideration should be given to the unique difficulty of learning "language forms."

2. The next reading centers on the ideas expressed in the text. Clearly, the students should be allowed more time for this second reading so that they may chew over the main ideas and important details in the text for in-depth comprehension. As the language form is but a vehicle for carrying meaning, the students should be encouraged to learn how the main ideas, viewpoints, and so on are presented; how the ideas flow from beginning to end; and how all the separate sentences and paragraphs are tightly knitted semantically. In other words, now the central task is to understand the ideas that are presented and the way they are connected in the text.

3. The third stage primarily aims to help students size up how the material is organized in order to have an overview of the text. The organizational pattern; the effect of the style, tone, and attitude achieved; and the basic writing techniques (such as diction and rhetoric) can all be dealt with in this final reading.

After the three readings, students would better know the language forms involved in the text and the ideas these forms express. As a result, students' knowledge of the text is likely to be more comprehensive because of the text-centered method employed throughout the reading process. It is important to remember that the three steps are interchangeable. When used in combination with other group discussion and/or writing activities, the repeated reading strategy would be even more effective.

Use Learning Strategies for Active Engagement

Throughout the remainder of this book, we will be focusing on learning strategies that will engage students in comprehending texts. These strategies can be as simple and straightforward as creating posters for a chapter. This strategy allows teachers to use a variety of group and collaborative activities in different content areas. Betty Vrooman, for example, uses posters with the English learners in her middle school social studies class. She followed these three steps:

1. After her students read a particular chapter, Betty asked them to create a poster to visually represent the main ideas expressed by this chapter. Based on the length and complexity of the chapter, she varied the requirement for the total number of key concepts to be included in a poster, from five to twelve. Her students used illustrations, color, lettering, and so on to present the chapter's information in an inviting and creative manner.

2. Betty's students shared their posters in a small group consisting of three to five students (including both English learners and mainstream learners). All members took turns sharing their posters with each other. While sharing, they were encouraged to use the ideas from the poster as "talking points." Betty asked the other students to point out at least one thing that they particularly liked in the poster and to offer one suggestion about how to better interpret the chapter's content as well.

3. After the group sharing, Betty invited all students to share in a whole-class session, and each individual student could share some of the highlights from his or her own reading, writing, or group sharing. Meanwhile, she provided further explanation about the main ideas, concepts, or additional background information related to the chapter under study. When needed, she also gave feedback to clarify any unclear points or misunderstandings as reflected from the students' posters or presentations.

In summary, Betty feels that asking her students to create posters for a text they read helps deepen their engagement with the text. The sharing provides further opportunities for both the English learners and mainstream students to exchange ideas about what they thought and understood. This strategy may be easily adjusted for use in other content areas. In each case, the poster helps to support English learners' critical engagement with a text in a socially supported context. Chapter 5 provides a more extended discussion of collaborative learning strategies.

Use Writing Strategies

English learners sometimes get stuck while engaging in specific writing activities. By involving them in a variety of writing strategies, as emphasized in Chapter 9, students will come to view writing as a tool to understand as well as to be understood. One such strategy, "mental composition," is particularly useful in composing an essay or reflecting on a learning task. The strategy helps students, especially ELs, think about what they are going to write without having to worry about "getting it down on paper." In her seventh-grade language arts class, Stephanie Kent introduces the strategy by thinking aloud with students and modeling the process. For example, after the class reads the young adult novel *Walk Two Moons* (Creech 1996), she uses her response to the novel to model the steps for mental composition.

> **myeducationlab**
> Go to the Assignments and Activities section of Topic 1: "Diversity, Culture, and Literacy" in the MyEducationLab for your course and complete the activity "Common Cultural Goals." Consider how one student's writing transcends cultural borders.

This is how Stephanie shares her mental composition with her students:

> In my paper, I want to have an introduction, the body, and some kind of ending. So first I want to introduce the title and the author of the book to the readers of my paper. I may begin with *Walk Two Moons* by Sharon Creech. This is the story of a young girl named Salmanca (Sal) Tree Hiddle.
>
> To lead to the main discussion of the story or the body of my response, I think I want to continue by discussing how the novel follows a story structure; that is, there is a story within a story. One story is about Sal's trip with her grandparents to visit her mother's

> burial place, and the other focused on her best friend Phoebe Winterbottom, whose mother also left her. Then I want to mention Sal's memories of her mom, the story of Phoebe's mom, and how the two stories intertwine. I also want to mention how Sal's journey ends.
>
> Then I want to mention some of the important issues related to the novel, such as coping with death in the family by young adolescents. Anyway, this is how I may write my paper. What do you think?

Stephanie models the procedures for mental composition, or in her words, "seeing a paper unfolding in one's head." She realizes the importance of engaging English learners in actual writing as well. Therefore, in addition to mental composition, she selects some topics to involve her students in practicing brainstorming, planning, drafting, revising, and completing the writing. At the same time, she provides some concrete suggestions to help them generate ideas: journal entries, informal nongraded writing, one-page think pieces, in-class free writing, microtheme paragraphs, practice exam questions/topics, small-group discussions, rewrites, and so on. In other words, mental composition and regular writing become supplementary and complementary.

Mental composition may be adapted for helping students notice varied learning tasks. For example, students may use it to recall what was learned at various stages of reading a novel or text and review what was taught after a particular class. When used in combination with other writing practices, such mental composing promotes active intellectual participation through writing, reading, speaking, and listening across content areas.

LOOKING BACK LOOKING FORWARD

Changes in the racial and ethnic composition of our student population have been dramatic. Today's classrooms are more linguistically and culturally diverse than they were in the 1960s. The linguistic, cultural, and achievement differences of students contribute to the complexities of classroom diversity. Students of diverse backgrounds (who may be distinguished by their ethnicity, social class, language, or achievement level) often struggle in classrooms. English language learners especially challenge teachers to look for and experiment with instructional strategies that will actively involve them in the life of the classroom. Sheltered instruction makes a difference in the academic and language development of English learners.

Teachers reach diverse learners by scaffolding instruction in ways that support content literacy and learning. Throughout this book, we explore scaffolded instruction designed to help all students learn with texts.

In the next chapter, we explore another dimension of standards-based curriculum as we shift our attention to different forms of assessment in the content area classroom. Concern about assessment is one of the major issues in education in the United States today. What role do standardized "high-stakes" assessments play in the lives of classroom teachers? How do authentic forms of assessment inform instructional decisions? How can teachers use portfolios and make decisions about the texts they use? The key to assessment in content areas, as we contend in the next chapter, is to make it as useful as possible. Let's find out how and why this is the case.

Minds On

1. Picture a content area class of twenty-five students from very diverse backgrounds—different native languages, different ethnicities, and varying achievement levels. Describe some classroom strategies you might use to respond to individual differences while maintaining high standards of content literacy and learning.

2. According to the latest census projections, by the year 2020 half of all public school students will be from minority backgrounds. How do you believe this change will influence learning strategies in the classroom?

3. In some classes, teachers do most of the talking, and students recite one- or two-word answers. What learning strategies are denied to students in this type of classroom design? How can teachers share their knowledge with students and still avoid overlecturing?

4. Create a culturally responsive lesson for your content area using the seven characteristics of culturally responsive teaching and learning listed on pages 64 and 65.

5. Write your life story from earliest memories to the present. Reflect on your life and your students' lives as you write your autobiography.

Hands On

1. For fifteen minutes in a four-member small group, discuss the topic "how technology might transform popular sports by the year 2121." After the discussion, reflect on how the unique background of each member of the group contributed to the views expressed. Did any of the following factors influence individual participation: background knowledge of sports or technology, past experience playing sports, individual understanding of sports language or technological applications, or personal definitions of "popular" sports? What parallels might you draw with classroom lessons in which students bring cultural and linguistic differences to the learning activities?

2. Come to class prepared to share a piece of your personal "fund of knowledge"—knowledge and information that your family has passed on—with your small group. For example, you might share a passed-on craft, a skill, a family hobby, or a recipe. How did this sharing "connect" you to the group and the group to your culture?

3. Teach a culturally responsive content area lesson and reflect on it in writing. Report your process of designing and implementing the lesson in class.

4. Interview one of your students' parents in a neutral location. (Meet him or her for coffee at a local spot.) Find out what you can do to make learning more interesting or meaningful for your student.

eRESOURCES

- The following sites are filled with ideas for engaging English learners of all levels: **http://literacy connections.com/SecondLanguage.php** and **www.literacynet.org/esl.** Browse these sites for engaging activities and suggestions for working effectively with ELs. Adapt those activities and suggestions to content area lessons.

- Visit the Multicultural Education Internet Resource Guide (**http://jan.ucc.nau.edu/~jar/Multi.html**) and a special project of *The Internet TESL Journal* (**http://a4esl.org**). Explore the various activities available to assist English-learning students.

- Go to SIOP Central (**www.cal.org/siop**) to study lesson plans based on the SIOP model.

CHAPTER 4

Don't tell us the only way to teach a child is to prepare him to fill in bubbles on a standardized test.

—Barack Obama, forty-fourth president of the United States

Assessing Students and Texts

ORGANIZING PRINCIPLE

Instructional assessment is a process of gathering and using multiple sources of relevant information about students for instructional purposes.

How effectively are students learning to use reading, writing, talking, and viewing as tools to comprehend and respond to material in content areas? Assessing students and texts to provide this kind of information means that there is a direct connection between teaching and learning, between instruction and the improvement of practice. Assessment in content area classrooms means that students and teachers are actively engaged in a process of evaluation and self-evaluation. Instead of measuring learning exclusively by a score on a standardized test or proficiency exam, the learning process includes assessment of authentic tasks.

Teachers and students want useful assessment; that is, they want to make sense of how and what is taught and learned at any given time. Teachers want to make instructional decisions based on their students' content literacy skills, concepts, and performance. They must also deal with the very real pressure of state and federal mandates for standards-based curriculum and testing. Yet, as President Barack Obama suggests, testing alone won't yield improvements in student learning.

To understand assessment, you need to differentiate between two major contrasting approaches: a formal, high-stakes approach

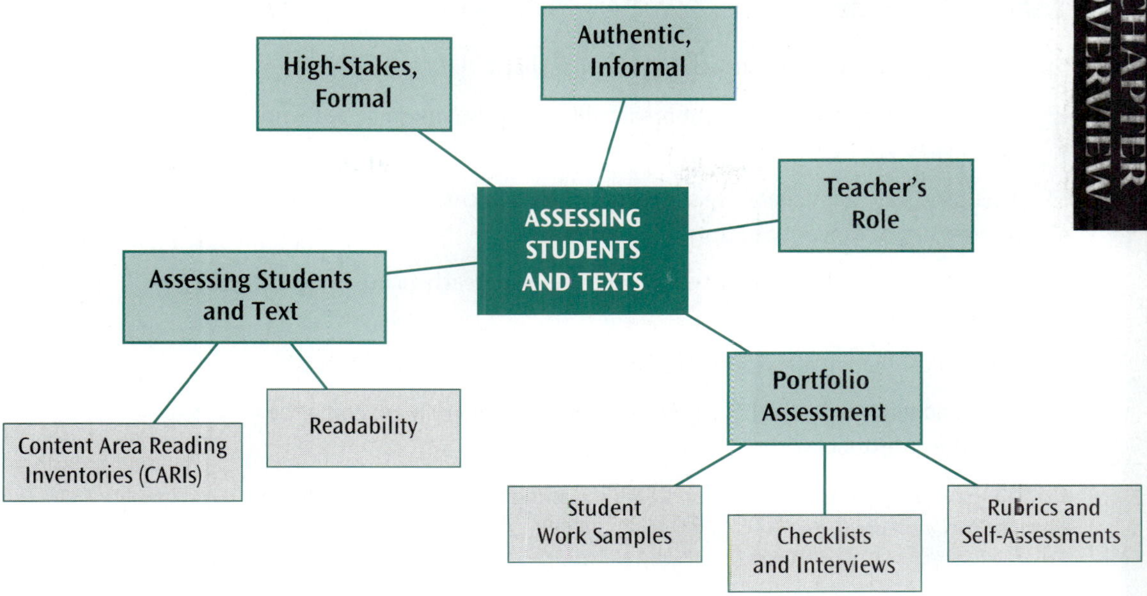

and an informal, authentic approach. When standards were initially developed by professional organizations and state governments, testing was thought to be necessary to ensure that schools would meet high standards of achievement. Soon, students' performances on state-mandated tests became the focus of debate among educators, policy makers, and constituency groups. The public's attention today is often on this formal, high-stakes approach to assessment. Many teachers have become adept at alternative, authentic assessment practices to help them make decisions about instruction appropriate for each student. As depicted in the graphic organizer, portfolios, observations, anecdotal records, checklists, interviews, inventories, and conferences with students are some of the methods and techniques that make authentic assessment possible.

Assessing for instruction should, first and foremost, provide the opportunity to gather and interpret useful information about students as they learn, including their prior knowledge; their attitudes toward reading, writing, and subject matter; and their ability to use content literacy to learn with texts. Through the portfolio assessment process—collecting authentic evidence of student work over time—teachers and students gather useful information about an individual's comprehension and response to content area material. The organizing principle of this chapter maintains that assessment should be useful, authentic, and responsive to teacher decision making: **Instructional assessment is a process of gathering and using multiple sources of relevant information about students for instructional purposes.**

FRAME OF MIND

1. How does assessment help us set instructional goals?
2. How does a formal, high-stakes approach differ from an informal, authentic approach?
3. What have state and federal legislators done to try to ensure students' success on high-stakes standardized tests?
4. What are some of the informal assessment strategies teachers use in the context of their classrooms?
5. How can content area teachers involve students in the portfolio process?
6. When and how might teachers use professional judgment in analyzing the difficulty of textbooks?
7. What are predictive measures of readability, and how do they differ from performance measures?

Teachers sometimes know intuitively that what they do in class is working. More often, however, information for making decisions is best obtained through careful observation of students. Their strengths and weaknesses as they interact with one another and with texts can be assessed as they participate in small groups, contribute to class discussions, respond to questions, and complete written assignments. This approach to assessment is *informal* and *authentic;* it is student centered and classroom based. This approach, however, isn't the only one operating in schools today. If teachers are in a school district guided by standards-based curricula, they need to understand the differences between *high-stakes* and *authentic* approaches to assessment. ■

RESPONSE JOURNAL

Write about a time when a teacher had an intuition about you as a student. Was it on target? Off target?

High-Stakes Testing and Authentic Approaches to Assessment

The two major views of assessment, high-stakes and authentic, are like different sides of the same coin. They represent the almost opposite perspectives of policy makers on one side and teachers on the other. Policy makers are responding to the public demand for assurances that students will leave school well prepared to enter either the workforce or college. Teachers and other educators are calling for better, more authentic assessment practices that will improve instruction and result in learning. As Tierney (1998) put it, one focuses on "something you *do to* students," and the other focuses on "something you *do with* them or help them *do for themselves*" (p. 378).

Authentic methods often include some combination of observations, interviews, anecdotal records, and student-selected performances and products. The information gained from an authentic assessment can be organized into a rich description or portrait of your content area classroom or into student *portfolios*. Concerns that emerge, whether about individual students or about the delivery of instructional strategies, are likely to make sense because they come directly from the classroom context and often result from teacher–student or student–student interaction.

Consider how an authentic approach differs from a more formal, high-stakes one. In Table 4.1, the two approaches are compared in several categories. Certainly, there are many gray areas in assessment, where the formal and informal overlap. In this table, however, differences between the two approaches are emphasized. Traditional, formal assessments are product oriented. They are more tangible and can be obtained at predetermined points in time. Authentic assessments are informal and process oriented. The process is ongoing, providing as much information about the student as learner as about the product. Together, they permit a more balanced approach through a combination of traditional, formal and authentic, informal practices. The end result is an understanding of *why* particular results are obtained in formal assessment, which informs the *how* of the teacher decision-making process.

High-Stakes Testing: Issues and Concerns

Never have the stakes been higher. With virtually every state adopting content standards in multiple content areas, such as English, mathematics, social studies, and science, standardized testing systems have been mandated, developed, and put in place throughout the United States. And under No Child Left Behind, states are required to use standardized tests results to determine whether schools are achieving adequate yearly progress (AYP).

RESPONSE JOURNAL

When did you take your first "big" test in school? What kind of an experience was it?

Thus, although standardized testing has been used to evaluate student achievement since Thorndike developed the first standardized tests in the early part of the twentieth century, the amount of

TABLE 4.1

Comparisons of Two Approaches to Assessment

	High-Stakes, Formal	Authentic, Informal
Orientation	Formal; developed by expert committees and test publishers	Informal; developed by teachers and students
Administration	Testing one time performance; paper-and-pencil, multiple-choice; given to groups at one seating	Continuously evolving and intermittent throughout an instructional unit; small group, one on one
Methods	Objective; standardized reading achievement tests designed to measure levels of current attainment; state proficiency testing of content knowledge	Classroom tests, checklists, observations, interviews, and so on, designed to evaluate understanding of course content; real-life reading and writing tasks
Uses	Compare performance of one group with students in other schools or classrooms; determine funding, support for districts and schools; estimate range of reading ability in a class; select appropriate materials for reading; identify students who need further diagnosis; align curriculum; allocate classroom time	Make qualitative judgments about students' strengths and instructional needs in reading and learning content subjects; select appropriate materials; adjust instruction when necessary; self-assess strengths and weaknesses
Feedback format	Reports, printouts of subtest scores; summaries of high and low areas of performance; percentiles, norms, stanines	Notes, profiles, portfolios, discussions, recommendations that evolve throughout instructional units; expansive (relate to interests, strategies, purpose for learning and reading)

mandatory testing has increased. And the stakes—significant rewards and penalties—have risen. Furthermore, in recent years, mandatory tests have been administered to younger and younger students and with greater frequency than ever before (Hoffman et al. 1999).

Several issues and concerns about the role of high-stakes testing are being discussed widely. Proponents of high-stakes testing contend that such testing is a sound strategy to use to ensure that standards are met and students are achieving at an appropriate level of proficiency. They seek to effectively end the practice of social promotion, that is, promoting students from one grade level to the next regardless of whether the students have demonstrated on tests the potential to work successfully at the next grade level. Proponents of high-stakes tests assert that test results can help schools to identify areas of weakness and to allocate resources where they are most needed in order to improve their programs and the performance of individual students (ECS 2008). Some proponents also point to generally positive popular attitudes about the fairness and utility of standardized testing. For example, despite claims to the contrary, many people believe that standardized tests are inherently fair and scientific (Afflerbach 2004).

Though use of mandated, high-stakes testing has spread, questions abound about the implications of such tests. One concern centers on the narrowing of the school curriculum as a result of the heavy emphasis placed on test preparation (Nichols & Berliner 2007). As Guilfoyle (2006) explains, "In this culture of 'What gets measured gets done,' the question that begs to be asked [is], 'What happens to what *doesn't* get measured?'" (p. 9). What doesn't get tested can include subjects such as social studies, visual arts, music, and physical education as well as school-sponsored extracurricular activities. In one California school, for example, funding was dropped for music, art, Spanish, and industrial design classes and students were required to take two periods of core subjects for which high-stakes tests were administered (Zastrow & Janc 2006).

What about the validity of certain assessment tools? Some studies have raised questions about the reasons behind student gains on state-mandated assessment, suggesting that the scores produced may be substantially higher than the students' understanding of the subject area material (Koretz 2008). Research has not shown a link between increased standardized testing and increased reading achievement (Afflerbach 2004). Some researchers suggest that students' improved performances on standardized tests can be attributed not only to achievement but also to factors such as the increased class time spent on test preparation, students' growing familiarity with test questions and procedures, and a large proportion of low-scoring students being exempted from taking tests in order to avoid the sanctions connected with low test scores (Klein, Hamilton, McCaffrey, & Stecher 2000; Nichols & Berliner 2007). Additionally, some are concerned that students referred to as "bubble kids"—those who are close to attaining a passing score—receive targeted instruction in order to raise their scores to the required marks, but students whose scores are not close to passing don't receive the instruction they need to progress.

Additional concerns about high-stakes testing include the contention that high-stakes tests require a significant amount of time and resources that could be directed more effectively toward other ways of increasing reading achievement. In addition, although high-stakes tests paint an incomplete picture of students' reading capabilities, students are being labeled at earlier ages based on the result of these test scores (Afflerbach 2004). High-stakes testing encourages educators to view students as test score "increasers" or test score "suppressors" (Nichols & Berliner 2008). For students who struggle academically, high-stakes testing can diminish both their self-efficacy for learning and their motivation to attempt academic pursuits. For students who are academically capable, an academic routine centered on achieving a mandated test score often fails to focus on their potential as learners. Nichols and Berliner (2008) point out that research has yet to examine the impact of high-stakes testing on students' attitudes and dispositions toward learning. Other critics claim that, far from being fair, high-stakes testing has led to a disproportionate number of minority and low-income students being retained or dropping out of school (Darling-Hammond 2003).

School leaders face the challenge of blending student needs with needed scores and have expressed additional concerns about mandated high-stakes tests. Some assert that the tests are not grounded in child development theory, pointing out that students of the same chronological age should not be expected to be at the same point in terms of cognitive development and academic achievement. Others express concern that the high-stakes nature of the tests results in classroom instruction that focuses more on the drilling of skills and less on the application of knowledge (Mraz 2000).

Some professional organizations, such as the International Reading Association, advise against attaching rewards and penalties to single test scores and encourage the use of multiple measures, which honor the complexity of reading, to inform important decisions (Ransom et al. 1999). The National Reading Conference (NRC) recommends that assessment be aligned with classroom curricula and instruction, provide clear suggestions for improved instruction to meet learner needs, and be consistently reviewed and revised by stakeholders, including school boards, teachers, and parents (Afflerbach 2004).

No single test can meet the needs of all groups who require information about school and student performance. Different constituencies need different types of information, presented in different forms, and made available at different times. Policy makers and the general public may benefit from information provided by norm-referenced tests that are administered on an annual basis. Parents, teachers, and students need information specific to individual students on a more consistent basis. Observations, portfolios, samples of student work over time, and conferences about student progress are more effective than standardized tests in providing that type of information. The purpose of the assessment selected, and the goals for its use, should be carefully considered so that the assessment tool selected will ultimately serve to provide information that can be used to improve learning opportunities for all students (Farr 1992).

RESPONSE JOURNAL

Do you feel competent in making assessment part of teaching? What do you think is the best preparation you could receive?

Legislation, Standards, and Accountability

Traditionally, the role of the federal government in educational policy was to provide funding to individual states. Authority over curriculum and assessment was delegated by state policy makers to local school districts. Districts, in turn, relied on teachers and building administrators to make instructional decisions with little guidance or interference from legislative authorities (Massell, Kirst, & Hoppe 1997). In the past decade, however, the federal government has played an increasingly more prominent role in educational policy making.

In 2002, the No Child Left Behind Act (NCLB), a reauthorization of the original Elementary and Secondary Education Act (ESEA) of 1964, instituted new accountability requirements that marked an unprecedented level of federal involvement in K–12 schools. In order for schools to receive federal funding for education, NCLB requires states to develop and implement a standardized accountability program that shows whether their public schools have achieved adequate yearly progress (AYP). AYP has been described as "an all or nothing" model (NCDPI 2008), and the

RTI for Struggling Adolescent Learners

BOX 4.1

Identifying Students at Risk for Failure

Because assessment is one of the cornerstones of RTI, teachers need resources that will help them to identify which students are at risk for failure, pinpoint specific areas of strength and weakness, and offer insight into the effectiveness of instructional strategies (Berman & Biancarosa 2005). RTI is a process by which students are screened to determine their present level of performance and then intermittently assessed thereafter to determine their progress and reaction to instruction. Furthermore, curriculum-based measurements are used to assess students' progress toward course goals and objectives (Stecker, Fuchs, & Fuchs 2008). In this chapter, we suggest a variety of assessment tools that will help content area teachers document students' progress and plan appropriate instruction over the course of the school year. Most RTI models, especially at the elementary level, recommend weekly assessments for students identified as struggling readers and monthly assessments for all students to determine whether instruction is effective (National School Boards Association 2006; NCTE 2006; Torgesen, Houston, Rissman, Decker, Roberts, et al. 2007; Stecker, Fuchs, & Fuchs 2008). The data created by these assessments should drive instructional decision making.

Results of such measures allow teachers to accurately gauge the reading levels of students and determine particular strengths and weaknesses. With this information, teachers are in a strategic position to select materials for whole-class or individualized instruction that align with the needs of the students. Often, trade books and anthologies provided by publishers provide direction on how to match resources to students' abilities through leveling systems such as Lexile scores or grade equivalencies, which analyze difficulty by considering characteristics such as sentence and word length or complexity of vocabulary and syntax. Several informational databases also include the reading levels of texts and articles relevant to subject area topics. This allows content area teachers access to texts of varying levels of difficulty in order to differentiate instruction for their students.

consequences of not achieving AYP are serious. Schools that do not make AYP for two or more consecutive years face sanctions under the federal law. Those sanctions include losing federal funding, being restaffed, or being closed altogether (Guilfoyle 2006; Toppo 2001).

Critics of the legislation contend that, although high standards of educational achievement are desirable, NCLB unfairly penalizes schools and actually lowers standards as states adjust their proficiency requirements downward to preserve federal funding, thus giving an illusion of progress when test scores increase (Koretz 2008). Additional concerns have been raised about the disproportionate number of mandates in relation to the actual funding offered to schools to fulfill those mandates (Maguire 2001). Some have even challenged the constitutionality of NCLB, questioning whether the federal government is infringing on states' rights, coercing rather than inducing states to meet requirements in order to receive federal funding (McColl 2005). In 2007–2008, more schools across the nation failed to meet test score targets than in any previous year. Some attribute this change to the fact that minimal gains in improvement were required in the early years of the legislation, while rapid gains in improvement are currently required (Dillon 2008). Unfortunately, Congress made no concerted attempt to revise the NCLB law during its 2007 reauthorization (Dillon 2008).

As of 2008, NCLB requires states to administer standardized assessments in reading, mathematics, and science to students in grades 3 through 8 and in high school. The results of those standardized tests determine whether schools are making adequate yearly progress. To meet NCLB requirements, the Education Commission of the States (ECS) reports that state policy makers have actively engaged in assessing student performance and imposing consequences for schools that do not meet required standards. Monetary incentives are often granted by states to schools and teachers who attain high or expected standards of growth.

In response, some states, such as North Carolina, have revised their comprehensive plans to link standards with mandated assessments. North Carolina's ABC Accountability Model was originally organized around the goals of ensuring strong accountability, emphasizing high educational standards, and providing schools and districts with some degree of local control. Students who do not meet required standards are given opportunities for retesting as well as interventions, such as instructional opportunities, personalized education plans, and increased monitoring and evaluations. In 2006, revisions to the ABC program included the implementation of new growth formulas and, at the high school level, assessment of student performance on ten mandated end-of-course tests in algebra I, algebra II, biology, English, geometry, U.S. history, civics and economics, chemistry, physical science, and physics. Additional revisions to the state's accountability system are expected to be announced (North Carolina Department of Public Instruction 2008). Clearly, the implications of high-stakes testing reach into the content area classroom.

Standardized Testing: What Teachers Need to Know

Standardized reading tests are formal, usually machine-scorable instruments in which scores for the tested group are compared with standards established by an original normative population. The purpose of a standardized reading test is to show where students rank in relation to other students based on a single performance.

To make sense of test information and to determine how relevant or useful it may be, you need to be thoroughly familiar with the language, purposes, and legitimate uses of standardized tests. For example, as a test user, it is your responsibility to know about the norming and standardization of the reading test used by your school district. Consult a test manual for an explanation of what the test is about, the rationale behind its development, and a clear description of what the test purports to measure. Not only should test instructions for administering and scoring be clearly spelled out but also information related to norms, reliability, and validity should be easily defined and made available.

Norms represent average scores of a sampling of students selected for testing according to factors such as age, sex, race, grade, or socioeconomic status. Once a test maker determines norm scores, those scores become the basis for comparing the test performance of individuals or groups to the performance of those who were included in the norming sample. *Representativeness*, therefore, is a key concept in understanding student scores. It's crucial to make sure that the norming sample used in devising the reading test resembles the characteristics of the students you teach.

Norms are extrapolated from raw scores. A *raw score* is the number of items a student answers correctly on a test. Raw scores are converted to other kinds of scores so that comparisons can be made among individuals or groups of students. Three such conversions—percentile scores, stanine scores, and grade-equivalent scores—are often represented by test makers as they report scores.

Percentile scores describe the relative standing of a student at a particular grade level. For example, the percentile score of 85 of a student in the fifth grade means that his or her score is equal to or higher than the scores of 85 percent of comparable fifth graders.

Stanine scores are raw scores that have been transformed to a common standard to permit comparison. In this respect, stanines represent one of several types of standard scores. Because standard scores have the same mean and standard deviation, they permit the direct comparison of student performance across tests and subtests. The term *stanine* refers to a *sta*ndard *nine*-point scale, in which the distribution of scores on a test is divided into nine parts. Each stanine indicates a single digit ranging from 1 to 9 in numerical value. Thus a stanine of 5 is at the midpoint of the scale and represents average performance. Stanines 6, 7, 8, and 9 indicate increasingly better performance; stanines 4, 3, 2, and 1 represent decreasing performance. As teachers, we can use stanines effectively to view a student's approximate place above or below the average in the norming group.

Grade-equivalent scores provide information about reading-test performance as it relates to students at various grade levels. A grade-equivalent score is a questionable abstraction. It suggests that growth in reading progresses throughout a school year at a constant rate; for example, a student with a grade-equivalent score of 7.4 is supposedly performing at a level that is average for students who have completed four months of the seventh grade. At best, this is a silly and spurious interpretation: "Based on what is known about human development generally and language growth specifically, such an assumption [underlying grade-equivalent scores] makes little sense when applied to a human process as complex as learning to read" (Vacca, Vacca, Gove, et al. 2002).

Reliability refers to the consistency or stability of a student's test scores. A teacher must raise the question, "Can similar test results be achieved under different conditions?" Suppose your students were to take a reading test on Monday, their first day back from vacation, and then take an equivalent form of the same test on Thursday. Would their scores be about the same? If so, the test may indeed be reliable.

Validity, by contrast, tells the teacher whether the test is measuring what it purports to measure. Validity, without question, is one of the most important characteristics of a test. If the test purports to measure reading comprehension, what is the test maker's concept of reading comprehension? Answers to this question provide insight into the *construct validity* of a test. Other aspects of validity include *content validity* (Does the test reflect the domain or content area being examined?) and *predictive validity* (Does the test predict future performance?).

In general, information from standardized tests may help screen for students who have major difficulties in reading, compare general reading-achievement levels or different classes or grades of students, assess group reading achievement, and assess the reading growth of groups of students (Allington & Strange 1980). However, teachers also need useful information about students' text-related behavior and background knowledge. You would be guilty of misusing standardized test results if you were to extrapolate about a student's background knowledge or ability to comprehend course materials on the basis of standardized reading-test performance. Alternatives to high-stakes, formal assessments are found in an informal, authentic approach to assessment. One of the most useful tools for inquiry into the classroom is observation.

Authentic Assessment: The Teacher's Role

In a high-stakes approach to assessment, the *test* is the major tool; in an authentic approach, the *teacher* is the major tool. Who is better equipped to observe students, to provide feedback, and to serve as a key informant about the meaning of classroom events? You epitomize the process of assessing students in an ongoing, natural way because you are in a position to observe and collect information continuously (Valencia 1990). Consequently, you become an observer of the relevant interactive and independent behavior of students as they learn in the content area classroom.

myeducationlab

Go to the Building Teaching Skills and Dispositions section of Topic 2: "Assessment" in the MyEducationLab for your course. As you complete the activity, consider how ongoing assessment can inform instruction.

Observation is one unobtrusive measure that ranges from the occasional noticing of unusual student behavior to frequent anecdotal jottings to regular and detailed written field notes. Besides the obvious opportunity to observe students' oral and silent reading, there are other advantages to observation. Observing students' appearance, posture, mannerisms, enthusiasm, or apathy may reveal information about self-image. However, unless you make a systematic effort to tune in to student performance, you may lose valuable insights. You have to be a good listener to and watcher of students. Observation should be a natural outgrowth of teaching; it increases teaching efficiency and effectiveness. Instructional decisions based on accurate observations help you zero in on what and how to teach in relation to communication tasks.

Today's teachers are expected to meet the special needs of all students. Consequently, the challenges of teaching diverse learners in the classroom may cause nonspecialist teachers to feel frustrated and unprepared. Understanding and accepting differences in students can, however, lead to effective instructional adaptations. Lynne, a middle school literacy coach, explains how she has used observational assessment to help address the needs of students with behavioral issues that affect their learning:

> I am often asked by teachers for advice on how to address behavioral concerns that they have about particular students. I begin by recommending that they use a Behavior Frequency Observation Checklist as a diagnostic-prescriptive measure to record the instances of inappropriate or inattentive behaviors they observe. I've used the checklist with

individual teachers, and also with teachers across subject areas to document student behaviors observed in different content area classes. For example, I've given teachers across content areas the same frequency observation form to document the existence of the targeted behaviors of a particular student or a group of students. This orderly observation and documentation allowed the teachers to determine if the same behaviors occurred across content area classes, or if the behaviors were isolated to a specific class. Based on this documentation, appropriate intervention strategies could be developed and implemented. After an agreed-upon period of time, the frequency checklist can be repeated to determine to what extent intervention strategies were effective.

There are several advantages to using a frequency observation form: The observer can identify specific target behaviors or academic skills; when completed, the form provides objective data about targeted behaviors that can be used when communicating concerns to parents or to school support personnel; data collected can be used to develop intervention strategies to enhance the learning environment for the student; and the form can serve as both a preassessment tool to establish a baseline for future intervention and as a postassessment tool to judge the impact of an intervention. In addition to the basic format for behavior frequency data, Lynne included two other sections: *other pertinent information,* where she noted the reason for the observation as well as any support the student might be receiving in or out of school, and *tentative conclusions,* where she made comments about what she just observed and what to focus on in the next observation. Figure 4.1 illustrates Lynne's observation of Thomas.

CLASSROOM ARTIFACT **FIGURE 4.1** **Behavior Frequency Observation**

Student Name: *Thomas* Date: *October 12, 2008*

Start time: *10:00 a.m.* Stop time: *10:30 a.m.*

School: *Edison Middle School* Grade: *6*

Subject: *Mathematics*

Other pertinent information: *Thomas is being observed to determine if a referral for possible ADHD evaluation is appropriate.*

Target Behavior	**Frequency of Occurrence**	**Total**
Calls out of turn	| | | | | | | | | | | | |	13
Moves out of seat	| | | | | |	6
Distracts others (e.g., drops things, moves the desk, touches others)	| | | | | | | | | |	10
Makes unnecessary noises (e.g., taps desk, hums)	| | | | | | |	7
Off task (e.g., not working; does not start assignment)	| | | | | | | | | | | | | | |	15

Tentative Conclusion: *Additional observations across content area classes are recommended.*

To record systematic observations, to note significant teaching–learning events, or simply to make note of classroom happenings, you need to keep a notebook on hand or online. Information collected purposefully aids in classifying information, inferring patterns of behavior, and making predictions about the effectiveness of innovative instructional procedures. As they accumulate, these "field notes" provide documentary evidence of students' interactions over periods of time.

Teachers and others who use informal, authentic tools to collect information almost always use more than one means of collecting data, a practice known as *triangulation*. This helps ensure that the information is valid and that what is learned from one source is corroborated by what is learned from another source. A fifth-grade science teacher recounted how he combined the taking of field notes with active listening and discussion to assess his students' current achievement and future needs in the subject:

> I briefly document on individual cards how students behave during experiments conducted individually, within a group, during reading assignments, during phases of a project, and during formal assessments. Knowing which students or what size group tends to enhance or distract a student's ability to stay on task helps me organize a more effective instructional environment. When students meet to discuss their projects and the steps they followed, I listen carefully for strategies they used or neglected. I sometimes get insights into what a particular student offered this group; I get ideas for topics for future science lessons and projects or mini-lessons on time management, breaking up a topic into "chunks," and so on.

In Box 4.2 Cindy, a high school social studies teacher, shares her experience using frequency observation with class discussion.

Informal assessment strategies are useful to teachers during parent–teacher conferences for discussing a student's strengths and weaknesses. They also help build an ongoing record of progress that may be motivating for students to reflect on and useful for their other teachers in planning lessons in different subjects. And finally, the assessments themselves may provide meaningful portfolio entries from both a teacher's and a student's perspective, serving "as the essential link among curriculum, teaching, and learning" (Wilcox 1997, p. 223).

RESPONSE JOURNAL

How can parent–teacher conferences make a difference in students' academic performance? What can a teacher do to enhance the effectiveness of these conferences?

Many students want to establish a personal rapport with their teachers. They may talk of myriad subjects, seemingly unrelated to the unit. It is often during this informal chatter, however, that you find out about the students' backgrounds, problems, and interests. This type of conversation, in which you assume the role of active listener, can provide suggestions about topics for future lessons and materials and help the student's voice emerge.

Discussion, both casual and directed, is also an integral part of assessment. You need to make yourself available, both before and after class, for discussions about general topics, lessons, and assignments. For an assessment of reading comprehension, nothing replaces one-on-one discussion of the material, whether before, during, or after the actual reading. Finally, encourage students to verbalize their positive and

Voices from the Classroom

BOX 4.2

Cindy

Tenth-Grade Social Studies Teacher

CHALLENGE

When preparing my lessons for our reading of *The Kite Runner* with my social studies honor students, I was concerned that many of the complexities presented in that story would be lost on the students if they didn't have a basic understanding of Afghanistan. I decided that I needed to get a sense of what the students already knew, or what they thought they knew, about Afghanistan before we opened the book. Understanding these topics might help them to better comprehend the book we were about to read together.

STRATEGY

I had, on occasion, used a Frequency Observation Form to record data on students' behavior, but I had not yet adapted it for observations of students' academic skills. I decided to try. I began by listing topics that would be addressed through their reading of the book such as details about Afghan history and culture. Then we engaged in a prereading discussion about these topics. Through their responses during this discussion, which included asking students for a show of hands to indicate how many of them agreed or disagreed with statements about Afghanistan, I was able to gauge the extent to which my students' knowledge and assumptions about Afghanistan were accurate.

REFLECTION

My Frequency Observation Chart indicated that, prior to reading the book, only four out of twenty students had prior knowledge of Afghanistan that was detailed and accurate. This meant that I had had some work to do to help build their background knowledge before I assigned them chapters of the book to read on their own! Knowing that they lacked relevant information on the book's key focus helped me to select strategies and questioning techniques throughout our reading to enhance their knowledge of the topic and to check for comprehension as they read. When we had finished reading and discussing *The Kite Runner,* I revisited the Frequency Observation Chart again to see if my students' understanding of Afghan culture and history had improved. This time, I found that seventeen of the twenty students had acquired knowledge needed to understand the many nuances in the story. Also, I noticed that students' responses during our class discussions were often more insightful than I had expected, and almost all of the students participated in those discussions. Had I simply plunged into reading this book without ascertaining what they already knew or didn't know, I'm not sure that would have happened.

negative feelings about the class itself as well as about topics, readings, and content area activities.

A note of caution: It's important to realize that "no matter how careful we are, we will be biased in many of our judgments" (MacGinitie 1993, p. 559). Yet teachers who observe with any sort of regularity soon discover that they are able to acquire enough information to process "in a meaningful and useful manner" (Fetterman 1989, p. 88). They can then make reliable decisions about instruction with observation and other techniques in portfolio assessment.

Portfolio Assessment

One of the most exciting and energizing developments in assessment continues to be portfolios. As a global, alternative, balanced practice in gathering information about students, *portfolio assessment* is a powerful concept that has immediate appeal and potential for accomplishing the following purposes:

- Providing and organizing information about the nature of students' work and achievements
- Involving students themselves in reflecting on their capabilities and making decisions about their work
- Using the holistic nature of instruction as a base from which to consider attitudes, strategies, and responses
- Assisting in the planning of appropriate instruction to follow
- Showcasing work mutually selected by students and teacher
- Revealing diverse and special needs of students as well as talents
- Displaying multiple student-produced artifacts collected over time
- Integrating assessment into the daily instruction as a natural, vital part of teaching and learning
- Expanding both the quantity and the quality of evidence by means of a variety of indicators

Portfolios are vehicles for ongoing assessment. They are composed of purposeful collections that examine achievement, effort, improvement, and, most important, processes (selecting, comparing, sharing, self-evaluation, and goal setting) according to Tierney, Carter, and Desai (1991). As such, they lend themselves beautifully to instruction in content areas ranging from math and science to English, history, and health education.

Significant pieces that go into student portfolios are *collaboratively* chosen by teachers and students. Selections represent processes and activities more than products. A distinct value underlying the use of portfolios is a commitment to students' evaluation of their own understanding and personal development.

Contrasting portfolios with traditional assessment procedures, Walker (1991) submits that instead of a contrived task representing knowledge of a subject, portfolios are an "authentic" assessment that measures the process of the construction

TABLE 4.2

Portfolios Versus Testing: Different Processes and Outcomes

Portfolio	Testing
Represents the range of learning activities in which students are engaged	Assesses students across a limited range of assignments that may not match what students do
Engages students in assessing their progress or accomplishments and establishing ongoing learning goals	Mechanically scored or scored by teachers who have little input
Measures each student's achievement while allowing for individual differences between students	Assesses all students on the same dimensions
Represents a collaborative approach to assessment	Assessment process is not collaborative
Has a goal of student self-assessment	Student self-assessment is not a goal
Addresses improvement, effort, and achievement	Addresses achievement only
Links assessment and teaching to learning	Separates learning, testing, and teaching

Source: Tierney, R. J., Carter, M. A., & Desai, L. E. (1991). *Portfolio Assessment in the Reading–Writing Classroom.* Copyright © 1991 Christopher Gordon Publishers, Inc. Reprinted by permission of Christopher Gordon Publishers, Inc.

of meaning. The *students* make choices about what to include; these choices in turn encourage self-reflection on their own development, their own evaluation of their learning, and personal goal setting. Advantages of portfolios are more easily visualized when compared with traditional assessment practices as displayed in Table 4.2, adapted from Tierney, Carter, and Desai (1991, p. 44).

Adapting Portfolios to Content Area Classes

You can, by making some individual adjustments, adapt portfolios to meet your needs. Techniques such as interviewing, observing, and using checklists and inventories provide good sources of information about students in the classroom. The use of portfolios is in many ways a more practical method of organizing this type of information. Linek (1991) suggests that many kinds of data be collected for a thorough documentation of attitudes, behaviors, achievements, improvement, thinking, and reflective self-evaluation. For example, students may begin a math course with poor attitudes and may constantly challenge the validity of the content by saying things such as, "What are we learning this for anyway? It's got nothing to do with me and my life." If you provide opportunities for functional application in realistic situations, comments may change over time to "Boy, I never realized how important this was going to be for getting a job in real life!"

Much more than a folder for housing daily work, a record file, or a grab bag, a portfolio is a comprehensive profile of each student's progress and growth. Most professional associations have endorsed the use of portfolios. For example, if you are preparing to teach a math class, whether it's arithmetic, algebra, or trigonometry, consult the National Council for Teachers of Mathematics (NCTM)

Evidence-Based Best Practices **BOX 4.3**

Steps in the Implementation of Portfolios

To get started implementing the portfolio assessment process, certain logical steps must be taken and certain decisions need to be made:

1. *Discuss with your students the notion of portfolios as an interactive vehicle for assessment.* Explain the concept and show some examples of items that might be considered good candidates for the portfolio. Provide some examples from other fields, such as art and business, where portfolios have historically recorded performance and provided updates.
2. *Specify your assessment model.* What is the purpose of the portfolio? Who is the audience for the portfolio? How much will students be involved? Purposes, for example, may be to showcase students' best work, to document or describe an aspect of their work over time (to show growth), to evaluate by making judgments by using either certain standards agreed on in advance or the relative growth and development of each individual, or to document the process that goes into the development of a single product, such as a unit of work on the Vietnam era or the Middle East or nutrition.
3. *Decide what types of requirements will be used, approximately how many items, and what format will be appropriate for the portfolio.* Furthermore, will students be designing their own portfolios? Will they include videos or computer disks? Or will they have a uniform look? Plan an explanation of portfolios for your colleagues and the principal; also decide on the date when this process will begin.
4. *Consider which contributions are appropriate for your content area.* The main techniques for assessing students' behavior, background knowledge, attitudes, interests, and perceptions are writing samples, video records, conference notes, tests and quizzes, standardized tests, pupil performance objectives, self-evaluations, peer evaluations, daily work samples, and collections of written work (such as vocabulary activities, graphic organizers, concept maps, inquiry/research projects, and reports).

assessment guidelines. Then, decide with students what types of samples of student-produced work should be included. Box 4.3 outlines a procedure for implementing portfolios.

Cherrie Jackman, a fifth-grade teacher, wanted to experiment with portfolios as an assessment tool for writing and science. Here's how she described the process of implementation that she followed:

> To begin implementing portfolios in my class, I followed certain steps:
>
> - First, I explained the concept of portfolios and discussed why they are important. We thought of how local businesses use portfolios, and how certain types of professions (architecture, art, journalism) depend on them.
> - Next, I explained the purposes of our portfolio: to describe a portion of students' work over the quarter, showing how it has improved; to reflect on and evaluate their own work in writing and science; and to compile a body of work that can travel with them from year to year.

- Then we discussed the requirements for our portfolio: to select one or two pieces of work from science and writing that each student feels is representative of the best that he or she has done for the quarter; to add one piece for each subject area each quarter; and at the end of the school year, to evaluate students' overall progress.
- I gave examples of the kinds of contributions that would be appropriate: writing samples, self-evaluations (reflections) on a particular project, semantic maps, group projects, peer evaluations—all are acceptable pieces of work to place into the portfolio.
- Finally, we discussed the ongoing process of conferencing that will occur in our classroom. I will meet with students on an individual basis to discuss work in progress and assist in deciding which pieces might be placed in the portfolio. Time in class will be scheduled during the week for students to write reflections, ask for peer evaluations, or hold discussions with teachers about the portfolios. Although the actual work may be done at another time (writing, science), the assessment of the work could be done during this regularly scheduled time.

Portfolios are a process! I really want students to understand that their portfolios are a work in progress. I want them to feel comfortable selecting a piece, critiquing others' work, and asking questions. I want them to feel ownership for their own work!

An example of a portfolio contribution made by one of Cherrie's students is a personal reflection on an experiment done in science (see Figure 4.2).

FIGURE 4.2 A Personal Reflection for Science

Experiment:

They're All Wet—Determine what effect soaking seeds has on the time it takes them to sprout. In a group of four, develop an experiment using the scientific procedure. Evaluate your group from a scientific and cooperative point of view.

Reflection:

I selected the experiment "They're All Wet" as my best work in science for a number of reasons.

(1) My group worked very well together. Everyone was assigned a job (reader, recorder, speaker, organizer), and everyone got to talk.

(2) We wrote a sound hypothesis and design for our experiment because we took our time and we thought about the process.

(3) We kept very good records of our observations, and then everyone participated in telling about them.

(4) Even though our experiment did not prove our hypothesis, I learned many things from this experiment (see above).

Next time maybe my results will support my hypothesis, but I did learn the proper way to conduct an experiment.

As Scott's math teacher discovered, an array of assessment possibilities, including writing conference logs and learning participation inventories, are useful in high school. Figure 4.3 depicts the writing conference log for Scott developed during a geometry unit on quadrilaterals. First, students were asked to take double-entry journal notes that connected the information they read in their geometry textbook to information presented during class discussions. Next, the students worked together in small groups to create a *semantic feature analysis* (see Chapter 10) that compared and contrasted the characteristics of different types of quadrilaterals. After completing the semantic feature analysis, students were asked to write a paragraph that summarized their findings. Finally, in preparation for a mandatory standardized test, students completed a series of word problems that required them to apply their knowledge of quadrilaterals. They were asked to show their computations and to write a summary explaining how they solved each word problem. In addition to the writing conference log, Scott's teacher also used the learning participation survey, shown in Figure 4.4 (p. 104), to assess Scott's participation throughout the quadrilaterals unit.

myeducationlab

Go to the Assignments and Activities section of Topic 2: "Assessment" in the MyEducationLab for your course and complete the activity "Problem-Based Assessment." Consider how observation helps the teacher learn more about the students' strengths and needs.

Checklists and Interviews

Informal assessment techniques, such as checklists, interviews, and content area reading inventories (discussed later in this chapter), are different from natural, open-ended observation. They often consist of categories or questions that have already been determined; they impose an a priori classification scheme on the observation process. A checklist is designed to reveal categories of information the teacher has preselected. When constructing a checklist, you should know beforehand which reading and study tasks or attitudes you plan to observe. Individual items on the checklist then serve to guide your observations selectively.

The selectivity that a checklist offers is both its strength and its weakness as an observational tool. Checklists are obviously efficient because they guide your observations and allow you to zero in on certain kinds of behavior. But a checklist can also restrict observation by limiting the breadth of information recorded, excluding potentially valuable raw data. Figure 4.5 (p. 105) presents sample checklist items that may be adapted to specific instructional objectives in various content areas.

In addition to checklists, observations, logs, and inventories, interviews should be considered part of the portfolio assessment repertoire. There are several advantages of using interviews, "be they *formal,* with a preplanned set of questions, or *informal,* such as a conversation about a book" (Valencia, McGinley, & Pearson 1990, p. 14). First, students and teachers interact in collaborative settings. Second, an open-ended question format is conducive to the sharing of students' own views. Third, it reveals to what extent students are in touch with their internal disposition toward reading subject matter material.

In general, there are three *types of interviews:* structured and semistructured, informal, and retrospective. As described by Fetterman (1989, pp. 48–50), these types blend and overlap in actual practice.

FIGURE 4.3 **Writing Conference Log**

Name: *Scott*

Date: *1-22-09*

Title: *Double-entry journal for class notes on quadrilaterals*

Focus of conference: *Self-checking knowledge*

Genre: *Nonfiction*

Progress Observations

Strengths:

- *Scott was able to note the main characteristics of each type of quadrangle.*
- *He consistently spelled most terms correctly, and knew how to find the spelling of unfamiliar terms.*
- *Scott makes connections between new and prior learning.*

Areas to work on:

- *Scott needs more practice organizing information.*
- *Needs to improve his use of punctuation when writing sentences*

Date: *1-15-09*

Title: *Comparing the structures of quadrilaterals (Semantic feature analysis and summary paragraph)*

Focus of conference: *Compare/Contrast*

Genre: *Nonfiction*

Progress Observations

Strengths:

- *Is able to identify the types of quadrilaterals (Square, rectangle, rhombus, trapezoid, parallelogram) and compare attributes*
- *Correctly uses the semantic features analysis to compare and contrast*
- *Uses evidence to support his claims about the characteristics of each quadrilateral*

Areas to work on:

- *Work on use of grammar and punctuation when writing summary paragraph*

Date: *1-27-09*

Title: *Answering word problems completely and correctly*

Focus of conference: *Practicing for standardized assessments*

Genre: *Nonfiction*

Progress Observations

Strengths:

- *Good application of knowledge of quadrilaterals*
- *Mastery of basic math problem solving*

Areas to work on:

- *Elaborate explanation of work in completing word problems*
- *Consider a problem from multiple perspectives to determine the best answer*
- *Use complete sentences and proper punctuation in formal written responses*

FIGURE 4.4 **Learning Participation Inventory**

Name: Scott

Observations for work completed January '09	Often	Occasionally	Seldom
1. Shows enthusiasm for learning Scott always begins work promptly and remains engaged throughout the lesson; makes appropriate connections to previously learned concepts.	★		
2. Raises questions Scott asks questions of both the teacher and of his classmates but his questions do not usually make use of higher-order thinking skills.		★	
3. Listens attentively during discussions Scott often listens during small-group discussions but tunes out during whole-class instruction.		★	
4. Shares ideas Shares his ideas in small-group settings, but seldom participates during whole-class discussions.			★
5. Responds thoughtfully to the ideas of others Scott usually considers the perspectives of other students.	★		
6. Participates in projects enthusiastically Scott understands how class concepts link together and works hard to make connections between assignments and course goals.	★		

Observations:
While Scott seems hesitant to share ideas in whole-group settings, once he understands the material and how concepts fit together, he works diligently with classmates in small-group settings to complete assignments.

1. *Formally structured and semistructured.* Verbal approximations of a questionnaire; allow for comparison of responses put in the context of common group characteristics; useful in securing baseline data about students' background experiences.

2. *Informal.* More like conversations; useful in discovering what students think and how one student's perceptions compare with another's; help identify shared values; useful in establishing and maintaining a healthy rapport.

FIGURE 4.5 Sample Checklist Items for Observing Reading and Study Behavior

Reading and Study Behavior	Fred	Pat	Frank	JoAnne	Jerry	Courtney	Mike	Mary
Comprehension								
1. Follows the author's message	A	B	B	A	D	C	F	C
2. Evaluates the relevancy of facts								
3. Questions the accuracy of statements								
4. Critical of an author's bias								
5. Comprehends what the author means								
6. Follows text organization								
7. Can solve problems through reading								
8. Develops purposes for reading								
9. Makes predictions and takes risks								
10. Applies information to come up with new ideas								
Vocabulary								
1. Has a good grasp of technical terms in the subject under study								
2. Works out the meaning of an unknown word through context or structural analysis								
3. Knows how to use a dictionary effectively								
4. Sees relationships among key terms								
5. Becomes interested in the derivation of technical terms								
Study Habits								
1. Concentrates while reading								
2. Understands better by reading orally than silently								
3. Has a well-defined purpose in mind when studying								
4. Knows how to take notes during lecture and discussion								
5. Can organize material through outlining								
6. Skims to find the answer to a specific question								
7. Reads everything slowly and carefully								
8. Makes use of book parts								
9. Understands charts, maps, tables in the text								
10. Summarizes information								

Grading Key: A = always (excellent)
B = usually (good)
C = sometimes (average)
D = seldom (poor)
F = never (unacceptable)

3. *Retrospective.* Can be structured, semistructured, or informal; used to reconstruct the past, asking students to recall personal historical information; may highlight their values and reveal information about their worldviews.

One technique developed to interview students about the comprehension process is the Reading Comprehension Interview (RCI) (Wixson, Boskey, Yochum, & Alvermann 1984). Designed for grades 3 through 8, it takes about thirty minutes per student to administer in its entirety. The RCI explores students' perceptions of (1) the purpose of reading in different instructional contexts and content areas, (2) reading task requirements, and (3) strategies the student uses in different contexts.

The RCI's main uses are to help identify patterns of responses (in the whole group and individuals) that then serve as guides to instruction and to analyzing an individual's flexibility in different reading activities.

Several questions on the RCI are particularly appropriate for content area reading. Although the RCI was developed for grades 3 through 8, high school teachers can make good diagnostic use of some of the questions.

Rather than interviewing each student individually, we suggest the following adaptation: Have each student keep a learning log. In these logs, students write to themselves about what they are learning. For example, they can choose to focus on problems they are having with a particular reading assignment or activity. A variation on this general purpose would be to ask students to respond to some of the more pertinent questions on the RCI—perhaps one or two at any one time over several weeks.

In relation to a particular content area textbook, examine the kinds of questions students can write about from the RCI:*

1. What is the most important reason for reading this kind of material? Why does your teacher want you to read this book?
2. Who's the best reader you know in (*content area*)? What does he/she do that makes him/her such a good reader?
3. How good are *you* at reading this kind of material? How do you know?
4. What do you have to do to get a good grade in (*content area*) in your class?
5. If the teacher told you to remember the information in this story/chapter, what would be the best way to do this? Have you ever tried (*name a strategy, e.g., outlining*)?
6. If your teacher told you to find the answers to the questions in this book, what would be the best way to do this? Why? Have you ever tried (*name a strategy, e.g., previewing*)?
7. What is the hardest part about answering questions like the ones in this book? Does that make you do anything differently?

Having students respond to these questions in writing does not deny the importance of interviewing individuals. However, it does save an enormous amount of time while providing a teacher with a record of students' perceptions of important reading tasks related to comprehension.

*From "An Interview for Assessing Students' Perceptions of Classroom Reading Tasks" by K. Wixson, A. Boskey, M. Yochum, and D. Alvermann, *The Reading Teacher*, January 1984.

Rubrics and Self-Assessments

Students need to play a role in the assessment of their own literacy products and processes. Teachers who want to help students get more involved in assessment invite them to participate in setting goals and to share how they think and feel. What are the students' perceptions of their achievements? McCullen (1998) described how she begins this process with middle grade students:

> I usually start by envisioning the possible outcomes of each assignment. Then the students and I develop a standard of excellence for each facet of the process and convert the outcomes into a rubric. Thus, before the students begin their research, they know the goals of the assignment and the scope of the evaluation. (p. 7)

myeducationlab
Go to the Assignments and Activities section of Topic 2: "Assessment" in the MyEducationLab for your course and complete the activity "Using Rubrics to Clarify Expectations" to see how one teacher prepares her students to use a rubric to assess presentations.

Rubrics are categories that range from very simple and direct to comprehensive. Rubrics provide students with detailed, consistent guidelines about the expectations for their papers or projects. Some are designed to help individual students self-assess; often they are designed to be used by small groups or by an individual student and teacher. In Figure 4.6, a basic rubric, sometimes referred to as a *holistic rubric,* serves the dual purpose of involving each student in evaluating the group's work on an inquiry project involving the Internet and in self-evaluating. This type of scoring rubric provides a list of criteria that correspond to a particular grade or point total.

FIGURE 4.6 **Rubric for Self-Evaluation**

Sixth-Grade Inquiry Project

Name: ______________________

Directions: Evaluate your performance in each of the following categories. Feel free to make comments about areas of this project in which you believe you were successful and areas in which you thought you could improve.

Content	Points Possible	Points Earned	Comments
Selection of topic and identification of subtopics	5		
Planning and organization of project	10		
Annotated bibliography of print resources: thoroughness and focus (minimum 4)	20		
Annotated bibliography of Web resources: thoroughness and focus (minimum 4)	20		
Effective use of time in the computer lab	5		
Presentation of findings to classmates	15		

More detailed types of rubrics include *analytic rubrics* and *weighted trait rubrics*. Analytic rubrics break down the total score for an assignment into separate traits on which the assignment will be evaluated. Weighted trait rubrics, although similar to analytic rubrics, assign higher values to some traits than to others. The weighted trait rubric, shown in Figure 4.7, was developed in a seventh-grade life science class by the teacher and her students for a unit on exploring the five senses. The teacher gave the students copies of the rubric in advance so they could monitor themselves. Using a scale of 0 to 3, students were graded individually and as part of a group by their teacher and by themselves. Note that 70 percent of the total grade was based on their individual scores, whereas 30 percent was based on the group score. A rubric such as this can be time consuming to develop. Rubrics containing less detail and those developed in partnership with students may take less time to construct. They surely help involve students in monitoring their own learning in an authentic, meaningful way that takes the guesswork out of assessment.

Assessing Text Difficulty

Evaluating texts and assessing students' interactions with texts are crucial tasks for content area teachers and students—and they call for sound judgment and decision making. One of the best reasons we know for making decisions about the quality of texts is that the assessment process puts you and students in touch with their textbooks. To judge well, you must approach text assessment in much the same manner as you make decisions about other aspects of content area instruction. Any assessment suffers to the extent that it relies on a single source of or perspective on information rather than on multiple sources or perspectives. Therefore, it makes sense to consider evidence in the student's portfolio along with several other perspectives.

One source of information to consider is publisher-provided descriptions of the design, format, and organizational structure of the textbook along with grade-level readability designations. Another information source is your acquired knowledge of and interactions with the students in the class. A third is your own sense of what makes the textbook a useful tool. A fourth source is student perspective, so that instructional decisions are not made from an isolated teacher's perception of the students' perspectives. To complement professional judgment, several measures can provide you with useful information: Lexile levels, readability formulas, the Fry graph, the cloze procedure, readability checklists, and a content area framework for student analysis of reading assignments. The first order of business, then, if content area reading strategies are to involve students in taking control of their own learning, is to find out how students are interacting with the text.

Content Area Reading Inventories

Teacher-made tests provide another important indicator of how students interact with text materials in content areas. A teacher-made *content area reading inventory*

FIGURE 4.7 **Detailed Rubric for an Inquiry Project on the Five Senses**

	Group Evaluation	Individual Evaluation
3	■ Worked well together every day ■ Thoroughly completed the lab activity ■ Developed a well-organized, very neatly presented handout that combined all group members' work, including at least one visual aid ■ Worked independently on most days	■ Used at least four sources, including one website and one traditional source; correctly listed the sources ■ Thoroughly answered the assigned question ■ Came up with and answered thoroughly two related questions ■ Participated in an experiment and engaged in a thoughtful reflection around that experiment ■ Cooperated with and helped group members every day
2	■ Worked well together most days ■ Completed the lab activity with some effort ■ Developed a well-organized, fairly neatly presented handout that combined all group members' work; may or may not have included a visual aid ■ Worked independently on some days	■ Used at least three sources, including one website and one traditional source; listed the sources ■ Thoroughly answered the assigned question ■ Came up with and tried to answer two related questions ■ Participated in an experiment and engaged in a thoughtful reflection around that experiment ■ Cooperated with and helped group members most days
1	■ May or may not have worked well together ■ Completed the lab activity ■ Developed a handout that combined all group members' work; did not include a visual aid ■ Did not work independently	■ Used at least two sources; listed the sources ■ Answered the assigned question ■ Came up with and tried to answer one related question ■ Participated in an experiment and engaged in a reflection around that experiment ■ Cooperated with and helped group members some days
0	■ Did not work well together ■ Did not complete the lab activity ■ Did not develop a handout that combined all group members' work ■ Did not work independently	■ Used fewer than two sources ■ Did not answer the assigned question ■ Did not come up with any related questions ■ May have participated in an experiment but did not reflect on that experiment ■ May or may not have cooperated

Grading Scale

- 70% of your grade is based on your individual score
- 30% of your grade is based on the group score

Final Score	Letter Grade
2.5–3.0	A
2.0–2.4	B
1.4–1.9	C
0.6–1.3	D
Below 0.6	F

(CARI) is an alternative to the standardized reading test. The CARI is informal. As opposed to the standard of success on a norm-referenced test, which is a comparison of the performance of the tested group with that of the original normative population, success on the CARI test is measured by performance on the task itself. The CARI measures performance on reading materials actually used in a course. The results of the CARI can give a teacher some good insights into *how* students read course material.

Administering a CARI involves several general steps. First, explain to your students the purpose of the test. Mention that it will be used for evaluation only, to help you plan instruction, and that grades will not be assigned. Second, briefly introduce the selected portion of the text to be read and give students an idea direction to guide silent reading. Third, if you want to find out how the class uses the textbook, consider an open-book evaluation, but if you want to determine students' abilities to retain information, have them answer test questions without referring to the selection. Finally, discuss the results of the evaluation individually in conferences or collectively with the entire class.

A CARI can be administered piecemeal over several class sessions so that large chunks of instructional time will not be sacrificed. The bane of many content area instructors is spending an inordinate amount of time away from actual teaching.

A CARI elicits the information you need to adjust instruction and meet student needs. It should focus on students' abilities to comprehend text and to read at appropriate rates of comprehension. Some authorities suggest that teachers also evaluate additional competency areas, such as study skills—skimming, scanning, outlining, taking notes, and so forth. We believe, however, that the best use of reading inventories in content areas is on a much smaller scale. A CARI should seek information related to basic reading tasks. For this reason, we recommend that outlining, note taking, and other useful study techniques be assessed through observation and analysis of student work samples.

Levels of Comprehension

Teachers estimate their students' abilities to comprehend text material at different levels of comprehension by using inventories similar to the one shown in Figure 4.8 for American history. The teacher wanted to assess how students responded at literal (getting the facts), inferential (making some interpretations), and applied (going beyond the material) levels of comprehension. At this time you can also determine a measure of reading rate in relation to comprehension.

You can construct a comprehension inventory using these steps:

1. *Select an appropriate reading selection from the second fifty pages of the book.* The selection need not include the entire unit or story but should be complete within itself in overall content. In most cases, two or three pages will provide a sufficient sample.
2. *Count the total number of words in the excerpt.*

FIGURE 4.8 **Sample Comprehension Inventory in American History**

General directions: Read pages 595–600 in your textbook. Then look up at the board and note the time it took you to complete the selection. Record this time in the space provided on the response sheet. Close your book and answer the first question. You may then open your textbook to answer the remaining questions.

STUDENT RESPONSE FORM

Reading time: _____________ min. _____________ sec.

I. *Directions:* Close your book and answer the following question: In your own words, what was this section about? Use as much space as you need on the back of this page to complete your answer.

II. *Directions:* Open your book and answer the following questions.

1. To prevent the closing of banks throughout the country, President Roosevelt declared a national "bank holiday."

   a. True b. False

2. The purpose of the Social Security Act was to abolish federal unemployment payments.

   a. True b. False

3. The National Recovery Administration employed men between the ages of 18 and 25 to build bridges, dig reservoirs, and develop parks.

   a. True b. False

4. President Roosevelt established the Federal Deposit Insurance Corporation to insure savings accounts against bank failures.

   a. True b. False

III. *Directions:* Answers to these questions are not directly stated by the author. You must "read between the lines" to answer them.

1. Give an example of how FDR's first 100 days provided relief, reform, and recovery for the nation.

   ____

2. How is the Tennessee Valley Authority an example of President Roosevelt's attempt to help the poorest segment of American society?

   ____

3. How did the purpose of the Civil Works Administration differ from the purpose of the Federal Emergency Relief Act?

   ____

IV. *Directions:* Answers to these questions are not directly stated by the author. You must "read beyond the lines" to answer them.

1. If FDR had not promoted his New Deal program through his fireside chats, do you think it would have been successful? Why or why not?

   ____

2. Why did FDR's critics fear the New Deal? Do you think their concerns were justified? Why or why not?

   ____

3. Which New Deal program would you call the most important? Why?

   ____

3. *Read the excerpt and formulate ten to twelve comprehension questions.* The first part of the test should ask an open-ended question such as, "What was the passage about?" Then develop three or more questions at each level of comprehension.

4. *Prepare a student response sheet.*

5. *Answer the questions.* Include specific page references for discussion purposes after the testing is completed.

While students read the material and take the test, the teacher observes, noting work habits and student behavior, especially of students who appear frustrated by the test. The American history teacher whose inventory is illustrated in Figure 4.8 allowed students to check their own work as the class discussed each question. Other teachers prefer to evaluate individual students' responses to questions first and then to discuss them with students either individually or during the next class session.

Rates of Comprehension

To get an estimate of students' rates of comprehension, follow these steps:

1. *Have students note the time it takes to read the selection.* This can be accomplished efficiently by recording the time in five-second intervals by using a "stopwatch" that is drawn on the board.

2. *As students complete the reading, they look up at the board to check the stopwatch.* The number within the circle represents the minutes that have elapsed. The numbers along the perimeter of the circle represent the number of seconds.

3. *Later, students or the teacher can figure out the students' rates of reading in words per minute.* For example:

   Words in selection: 1,500

   Reading time: 4 minutes 30 seconds

   Convert seconds to a decimal fraction. Then divide time into words.

   $$\frac{1{,}500}{4.5} = 333 \text{ words per minute}$$

4. *Determine the percentage of correct or reasonable answers on the comprehension test.* Always evaluate and discuss students' rates of reading in terms of their comprehension performance.

In summary, information you glean from a CARI will help you organize specific lessons and activities. You can decide on the background preparation needed, the length of reading assignments, and the reading activities when you apply your best judgment to the information you have learned from the assessment.

Readability

There are many readability formulas that classroom teachers can use to estimate textbook difficulty. Most popular formulas today are quick and easy to calculate. They typically involve a measure of sentence length and word difficulty to determine a grade-level score for text materials. This score supposedly indicates the reading achievement level that students need to comprehend the material. Because of their ease, readability formulas are used to make judgments about materials. These judgments are global and are not intended to be precise indicators of text difficulty.

A readability formula can best be described as a "rubber ruler" because the scores that it yields are estimates of text difficulty, not absolute levels. These estimates are often determined along a single dimension of an author's writing style: sentence complexity (as measured by length) and vocabulary difficulty (also measured by length). These two variables are used to predict text difficulty. But even though they have been shown to be persistent correlates of readability, they only indirectly assess sentence complexity and vocabulary difficulty. Are long sentences always more difficult to comprehend than short ones? Are long words necessarily harder to understand than short ones? When a readability formula is used to rewrite materials by breaking long sentences into short ones, the inferential burden of the reader actually increases (Pearson 1974–1975).

Keep in mind that readability measures don't account for the experience and knowledge that readers bring to content material. They are not designed to tap the variables present in readers. Our purpose, interest, motivation, and emotional state as well as the environment that we're in during reading contribute to our ability to comprehend text.

Lexile Levels

In recent years, the Lexile framework has become a commonly used measure of text difficulty. Many publishers have defined Lexile measures for the books they produce; newspapers and magazine articles, available through commonly used periodic databases, frequently include Lexile measures. The Lexile framework for reading consists of two measures: The Lexile reader measure represents a student's reading ability on the Lexile scale, and the Lexile text measure represents a text's difficulty on the Lexile scale. Lexile text measures are based on two components: semantic difficulty (word frequency) and syntactic complexity (sentence length). A Lexile text measure is determined by dividing a text into 125-word segments. Each segment is compared to a Lexile database. The words in each sentence of the segment are counted. Calculations, based on a psychometric model, are computed in order to determine the Lexile measure for the text.

Lexile measures are intended to assist teachers in selecting reading materials that are at an appropriate level of difficulty for their students. Typically, if a Lexile reader measure is below a Lexile text measure, a student's comprehension of that text is likely to decrease. Lexile measures are written as a number followed by the letter *L*. The Lexile scale ranges from below 200L for beginning reader texts to above 1700L for advanced texts. While Lexile measures are not intended to be prescriptive for specific grade levels, guidelines for text measure and reader measure ranges at various grade levels are:

GRADE	READER MEASURES	TEXT MEASURES
5	565L to 910L	750L to 950L
6	665L to 1000L	850L to 1050L
7	735L to 1065L	950L to 1075L
8	805L to 1100L	1000L to 1100L
9	855L to 1165L	1050L to 1150L
10	905L to 1195L	1100L to 1200L
11 and 12	940L to 1210L	1100L to 1300L

It is important to remember that a Lexile measure is not intended to reflect the quality or content of any printed text, nor can a Lexile measure take into account the background knowledge that students bring to a text. A Lexile measure can, however, help teachers to consider how content area reading materials correspond to students' reading levels so that a compatible match between the two can be made.

The Fry Graph

The readability graph developed by Edward Fry (1977) is a quick and simple readability formula. The graph was designed to identify the grade-level score for materials from grade 1 through college. Two variables are used to predict the difficulty of the reading material: sentence length and word length. Sentence length is determined by the total number of sentences in a sample passage. Word length is determined by the total number of syllables in the passage. Fry recommended that three 100-word samples from the reading be used to calculate readability. The grade-level scores for each of the passages can then be averaged to determine overall readability. According to Fry, the readability graph predicts the difficulty of the material within one grade level. See Figure 4.9 for the graph and expanded directions for the Fry formula.

Cloze Procedure

The cloze procedure does not use a formula to estimate the difficulty of reading material. Originated by Wilson Taylor in 1953, a cloze test determines how well students can read a particular text or reading selection as a result of their interaction with the material. Simply defined, then, the *cloze procedure* is a method by which you systematically delete words from a text passage and then evaluate students' abilities to accurately supply the words that were deleted. An encounter with a cloze passage should reveal the interplay between the prior knowledge that students bring to the reading task and their language competence. Knowing the extent of this interplay will be helpful in selecting materials and planning instructional procedures. Figure 4.10 (p. 116) presents part of a cloze test passage developed for an art history class. Here is how to construct, administer, score, and interpret a cloze test.

FIGURE 4.9 **Fry Readability Graph**

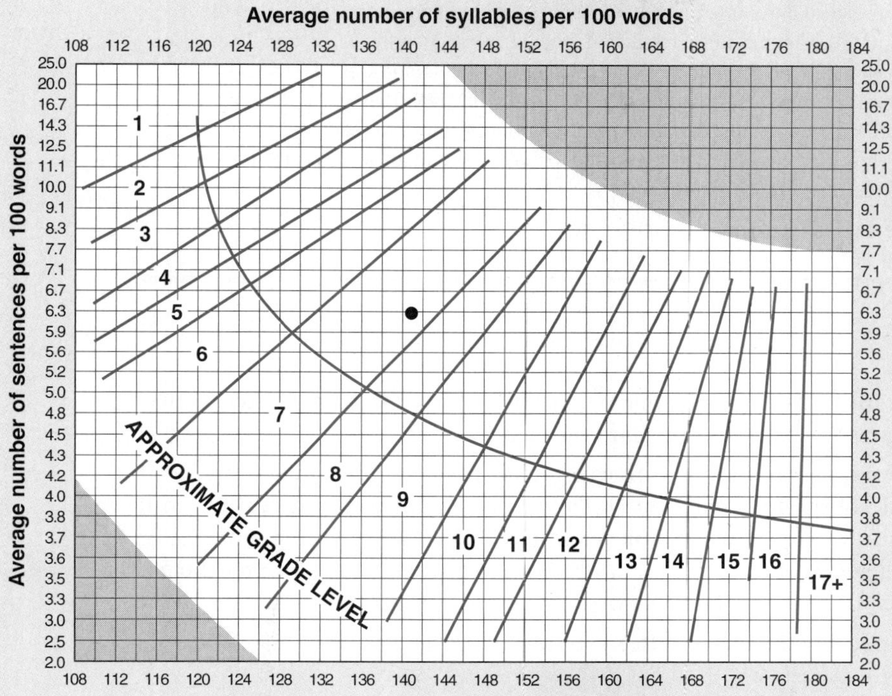

EXPANDED DIRECTIONS FOR WORKING READABILITY GRAPH

1. Randomly select three (3) sample passages and count out exactly 100 words each, beginning with the beginning of a sentence. Do count proper nouns, initializations, and numerals.
2. Count the number of sentences in the 100 words, estimating length of the fraction of the last sentence to the nearest one-tenth.
3. Count the total number of syllables in the 100-word passage. If you don't have a hand counter available, an easy way is simply to put a mark above every syllable over one in each word; then, when you get to the end of the passage, count the number of marks and add 100. Small calculators can also be used as counters by pushing numeral 1, then pushing the + sign for each word or syllable.
4. Enter graph with *average* sentence length and *average* number of syllables; plot dot where the two lines intersect. Area where dot is plotted will give you the approximate grade level.
5. If a great deal of variability is found in syllable count or sentence count, putting more samples into the average is desirable.
6. A word is defined as a group of symbols with a space on either side; thus *1945* is one word.
7. A syllable is defined as a phonetic syllable. Generally, there are as many syllables as vowel sounds. For example, *stopped* is one syllable and *wanted* is two syllables. When counting syllables for numerals and initializations, count one syllable for each symbol. For example, *1945* is four syllables.

Source: Edward Fry, *Elementary Reading Instruction*. Copyright © 1977 by McGraw-Hill Companies. Reprinted by permission.

FIGURE 4.10 **Sample Portion of a Cloze Test**

If the symbol of Rome is the Colosseum, then Paris's symbol is without doubt the Eiffel Tower. Both are monuments unique (1) planning and construction; both (2) admiration by their extraordinary (3) and bear witness (4) man's inborn will to (5) something capable of demonstrating (6) measure of his genius. (7) tower was erected on (8) occasion of the World's (9) in 1889. These were the (10) of the Industrial Revolution, (11) progress and of scientific (12). The attempt was made (13) adapt every art to (14) new direction which life (15) taken and to make (16) human activity correspond to (17) new sensibility created by (18) changing times.

Answers to the cloze test sample may be found on page 122.

1. *Construction*
   a. Select a reading passage of approximately 275 words from material that students have not yet read but that you plan to assign.
   b. Leave the first sentence intact. Starting with the second sentence, select at random one of the first five words. Delete every fifth word thereafter, until you have a total of fifty words for deletion. Retain the remaining sentence of the last deleted word. Type one more sentence intact. For children below grade 4, deletion of every tenth word is often more appropriate.
   c. Leave an underlined blank of fifteen spaces for each deleted word as you type the passage.
2. *Administration*
   a. Inform students that they are not to use their textbooks or to work together in completing the cloze passage.
   b. Explain the task that students are to perform. Show how the cloze procedure works by providing several examples on the board.
   c. Allow students the time they need to complete the cloze passage.
3. *Scoring*
   a. Count as correct every *exact* word students apply. *Do not* count synonyms even though they may appear to be satisfactory. Counting synonyms will not change the scores appreciably, but it will cause unnecessary hassles and haggling with students. Accepting synonyms also affects the reliability of the performance criteria, because they were established on exact word replacements.
   b. Multiply the total number of exact word replacements by two to determine the student's cloze percentage score.
   c. Record the cloze scores on a sheet of paper for each class. For each class, you now have one to three instructional groups that can form the basis for differentiated assignments (see Figure 4.11).

FIGURE 4.11 **Headings for a Cloze Performance Chart**

Subject ______________________________

Period ______________________________

Teacher ______________________________

Below 40 percent	Between 40 and 60 percent	Above 60 percent

4. *Interpretation*
   a. A score of 60 percent or higher indicates that the passage can be read competently by students. They may be able to read the material on their own without guidance.
   b. A score of 40 to 60 percent indicates that the passage can be read with some competency by students. The material will challenge students if they are given some form of reading guidance.
   c. A score below 40 percent indicates that the passage will probably be too difficult for students. They will need either a great deal of reading guidance to benefit from the material or more suitable material.

RESPONSE JOURNAL

How did you do on the sample cloze passage? Do you think it is a useful assessment tool?

The cloze procedure is an alternative to a readability formula because it gives an indication of how students will actually perform with course materials. Unfortunately, the nature of the test itself will probably be foreign to students. They will be staring at a sea of blank spaces in running text, and having to provide words may seem a formidable task. Don't expect a valid score the first time you administer the test. It's important to discuss the purpose of the cloze test and to give students ample practice with and exposure to it.

Readability Checklist

Despite the many factors to be considered in text evaluation, *teachers ultimately want texts that students will understand, be able to use, and want to use*. To help guide your assessment and keep it manageable, a checklist that focuses on *understandability, usability,* and *interestability* is useful. One such checklist is shown in Figure 4.12; it is an adaptation of the Irwin and Davis (1980) Readability Checklist.

The domain of *understandability* provides information about how likely a given group of students is to comprehend the text adequately. It helps the teacher assess relationships between the students' own schemata and conceptual knowledge and

FIGURE 4.12 General Textbook Readability Checklist

In the blank before each item, indicate ✓ for "yes," + for "to some extent," or x for "no" or "does not apply."

Understandability

_______ 1. Are the assumptions about students' vocabulary knowledge appropriate?

_______ 2. Are the assumptions about students' prior knowledge of this content area appropriate?

_______ 3. Are the assumptions about students' general experiential background appropriate?

_______ 4. Does the teacher's manual provide the teacher with ways to develop and review the students' conceptual and experiential background?

_______ 5. Are new concepts explicitly linked to the students' prior knowledge or to their experiential background?

_______ 6. Does the text introduce abstract concepts by accompanying them with many concrete examples?

_______ 7. Does the text introduce new concepts one at a time, with a sufficient number of examples for each one?

_______ 8. Are definitions understandable and at a lower level of abstraction than the concept being defined?

_______ 9. Does the text avoid irrelevant details?

_______ 10. Does the text explicitly state important complex relationships (e.g., causality and conditionality) rather than always expecting the reader to infer them from the context?

_______ 11. Does the teacher's manual provide lists of accessible resources containing alternative readings for very poor or very advanced readers?

_______ 12. Is the readability level appropriate (according to a readability formula)?

Usability

External Organizational Aids

_______ 1. Does the table of contents provide a clear overview of the contents of the textbook?

_______ 2. Do the chapter headings clearly define the content of the chapter?

_______ 3. Do the chapter subheadings clearly break out the important concepts in the chapter?

_______ 4. Do the topic headings provide assistance in breaking the chapter into relevant parts?

_______ 5. Does the glossary contain all the technical terms in the textbook?

_______ 6. Are the graphs and charts clear and supportive of the textual material?

_______ 7. Are the illustrations well done and appropriate to the level of the students?

_______ 8. Is the print size of the text appropriate to the level of student readers?

_______ 9. Are the lines of text an appropriate length for the level of the students who will use the textbook?

_______ 10. Is a teacher's manual available and adequate for guidance to the teachers?

_______ 11. Are the important terms in italic or boldface type for easy identification by readers?

_______ 12. Are the end-of-chapter questions on literal, interpretive, and applied levels of comprehension?

FIGURE 4.12 **General Textbook Readability Checklist *(continued)***

Internal Organizational Aids

_________ 1. Are the concepts spaced appropriately throughout the text, rather than being too many in too short a space or too few words?

_________ 2. Is an adequate context provided to allow students to determine the meanings of technical terms?

_________ 3. Are the sentence lengths appropriate to the level of students who will be using the text?

_________ 4. Is the author's style (word length, sentence length, sentence complexity, paragraph length, number of examples) appropriate to the level of students who will be using the text?

_________ 5. Does the author use a predominant structure or pattern of organization (compare–contrast, cause–effect, time order, problem–solution) within the writing to assist students in interpreting the text?

Interestability

_________ 1. Does the teacher's manual provide introductory activities that will capture students' interests?

_________ 2. Are the chapter titles and subheadings concrete, meaningful, or interesting?

_________ 3. Is the writing style of the text appealing to the students?

_________ 4. Are the activities motivating? Will they make the student want to pursue the topic further?

_________ 5. Does the book clearly show how what is being learned might be used by the learner in the future?

_________ 6. Are the cover, format, print size, and pictures appealing to the students?

_________ 7. Does the text provide positive and motivating models for both sexes as well as for a variety of racial, ethnic, and socioeconomic groups?

_________ 8. Does the text help students generate interest as they relate experiences and develop visual and sensory images?

Summary Rating

Circle one choice for each item.

The text rates highest in understandability / usability / interest.

The text rates lowest in understandability / usability / interest.

My teaching can best supplement understandability / usability / interest.

I would still need assistance with understandability / usability / interest.

Statement of Strengths:

Statement of Weaknesses:

Source: Adapted from "Assessing Readability: The Checklist Approach" by Judith Irwin and Carol Davis, *Journal of Reading, 24*(2), 124–130.

the text information. When teachers judge textbooks for possible difficulties, it is imperative to decide whether the author has considered the knowledge students bring to the text. The match between what the reader knows and the text will have a strong influence on the understandability of the material.

Armbruster and Anderson (1981) indicate that one way to judge the author's assumptions about students' background knowledge and experiences is to decide if enough relevant ideas are presented in a text to satisfy the author's purpose. Often, authors use headings to suggest their purposes for text passages. Convert the headings to questions. If the passage content answers the questions, the authors have achieved their purposes and the passage is *considerate*. If an author hasn't provided enough information to make a passage meaningful, the passage is *inconsiderate*.

The second major domain is *usability.* Is the text coherent, unified, and structured enough to be usable? Divided into two subsections on the Readability Checklist, this section provides information about the presentation and organization of content. It will help the teacher assess factors contributing to the day-to-day use of the text in teaching and the students' use in learning. These items help pinpoint for a teacher exactly what needs supplementing or what may take additional preparation time or class time.

The third domain, *interestability,* is intended to ascertain whether features of the text will appeal to a given group of students. Illustrations and photos may have instant appeal; students can relate to drawings and photographs depicting persons similar to themselves. The more relevant the textbook, the more interesting it may be to students.

Experiment with the Readability Checklist by trying it out on a textbook in your content area. Once you've completed the checklist, sum up your ratings at the end. Does the text rate high in understandability, usability, or interestability? Is a low rating in an area you can supplement well through your instruction, or is it in an area in which you could use more help? Also, summarize the strengths and weaknesses of the textbook. If you noted two areas in which you'd still need assistance, this text is unlikely to meet your needs. Finally, decide how you can take advantage of the textbook's strengths and compensate for its weaknesses.

LOOKING BACK LOOKING FORWARD

Assessing students and texts is a process of gathering and using multiple sources of relevant information for instructional purposes. Two major approaches to assessment prevail in education today: a formal, high-stakes one and an informal, authentic one. Pressure from policy makers and other constituencies has resulted in the adoption of curriculum standards specifying goals and objectives in subject areas and grade levels in most states. Hence, student performance on state-mandated tests must also be considered by teachers who need to make instructional decisions based on their students' content literacy skills, concepts, and performance.

An informal, authentic approach is often more practical in collecting and organizing the many kinds of information that can inform decisions, including (1) students' prior knowledge in relation to instructional units and text assignments, (2) students' knowledge and use of reading and other communication strategies to learn from texts, and (3) assessment of materials. The use of portfolios and careful observation and documentation of students' strengths and weaknesses as they interact with one another and with content-specific material sheds light on the *why* as well as the *what* in teaching and learning.

In this chapter, the key terms, major purposes, and legitimate uses of standardized tests were presented. Contrasts were drawn between portfolios and testing. As teachers engage learners in a process of portfolio assessment, they make adaptations appropriate for their subject matter and consider issues that have been raised about using portfolios. Suggestions for assessing students' background knowledge included interviews, pretesting, and instructionally based strategies. Interpreting interviews, surveys, scales, and observations, and developing rubrics, logs, and inventories help both teachers and students assess performance, behavior, and perspectives. For insights into how students interact with text material and a measure of performance on the reading materials used in a course, teacher-made content area reading inventories were suggested.

Assessing the difficulty of text material requires both professional judgment and quantitative analysis. Text assessment considers various factors within the reader and the text, the exercise of professional judgment being as useful as calculating a readability formula. Teachers, therefore, must be concerned about the quality of the content, format, organization, and appeal of the material. We supplied several procedures for assessing text difficulty: Lexile levels, readability formulas, the cloze procedure, and readability checklists.

How do teachers incorporate instructional practices and strategies into lessons *before, during,* and *after* assigning texts to read? In the next chapter, we explore the design of content literacy lessons and units of study. These lessons and units bring students and texts together in content learning situations.

Minds On

1. You are planning for the new school year in a district whose scores on the statewide proficiency tests have not shown much improvement. As long as you don't stray from the district's curriculum standards, you may use any assessment strategies to meet the needs, abilities, and interests of your students. Outline your plan for instructional assessment.

2. For keeping records, most portfolios of student work include a cover page, one that reflects the teacher's philosophy of assessment. With a group of classmates, select a content area and design a cover page that reflects your vision of authentic assessment.

3. Imagine that you are a new teacher reviewing the required text you will be using in the fall. Initially, you find the book fascinating, and you are certain it will excite many of your students. Yet after analyzing the work, you discover that its readability appears to be above the reading level of most of your students. How might you use this text effectively?

4. Readability formulas are predictive measures. How do predictive measures differ from performance measures in helping you determine how difficult reading materials will be for your students?

Hands On

1. In groups of three, turn to the "Legislation, Standards, and Accountability" section of this chapter. How has your state (or region or province) taken action to put standards for curriculum content in place? Describe any recent revisions in process or testing procedures or personnel that may affect your local school district. Rewards? Consequences?

2. Develop an observation checklist for the assessment of reading and study behavior in your content area. Compare your checklist with those developed by others in the class for similar content areas. What conclusions might you draw?

3. Each member of your group should locate one sample of text material on the same topic from these sources: an elementary content area text, a secondary content area text, a newspaper, and a popular magazine. Determine the readability of a sample passage from each by using two different readability formulas. Compare your findings by using two additional readability formulas. What conclusions can you draw from the comparison?

4. Two members of your group of four are designated as observers. The other members should collaboratively attempt to solve the following mathematics problem:

   Calculate the surface area of a cylinder that is 12 inches long and 5 inches in diameter.

   Note any observations that you believe might be useful in assessing the group's performance. What types of useful information do observations like these provide?

ANSWERS TO FIGURE 4.10

1. in	5. build	9. Fair	13. to	17. the
2. stir	6. the	10. years	14. every	18. rapidly
3. dimensions	7. The	11. of	15. had	
4. to	8. the	12. conquests	16. every	

eRESOURCES

- Go to the website for the International Reading Association (**www.reading.org**), select "About IRA," and open the IRA Position Statements (**www.reading.org/General/AboutIRA/PositionStatements.aspx**). Examine IRA's position statement on the rights of students. Read and discuss the ten principles listed and how each relates to authentic assessment.

- Go to the website **www.carnegie.org/literacy/national.html.** There you will find information about NAEP scores and state resources. Discuss these scores and resources in the context of other types of assessments used or required in your school.

- Read the full text of the IRA's position on high-stakes testing (**www.reading.org/downloads/positions/ps1035_high_stakes.pdf**).

CHAPTER 5

Plans are nothing; planning is everything.

—Dwight D. Eisenhower

Planning Instruction for Content Literacy

ORGANIZING PRINCIPLE

Instructional planning brings students and texts together in ways that support content literacy and learning.

Planning is essential, whether fighting a war, leading a country, running a business, or teaching a class of middle or high school learners. When Dwight Eisenhower was asked what the key to victory was during the Normandy invasion of World War II, he minimized the product of planning—the battle plan—with the now famous quote that opens the chapter. It was the strategic planning that went into the lead-up to the invasion—the process of thinking through the actions needed for victory—that made the difference between success and failure. It was the thinking through of objectives, activities, unintended consequences, and strategic alternatives in case something went wrong that were of primary concern to Eisenhower and his military commanders.

Likewise, the key to content literacy and learning is the forethought that goes into planning *instructional frameworks* that support thinking and learning with text. Engaged learning is the result, quite often, of well-planned lessons and units of study. Someone

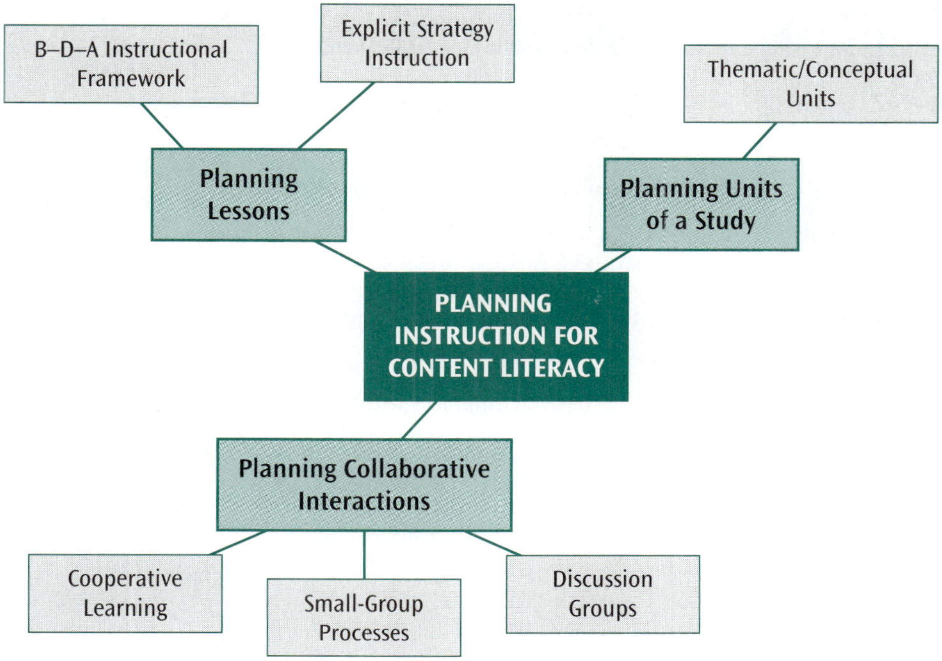

CHAPTER OVERVIEW

in the world of business once said that 90 percent of your results come from activities that consume 10 percent of your time. When this saying is applied to an instructional context, the time teachers take to plan engaged learning environments is time well spent. Planning appropriate frameworks for instruction includes the thinking through of text-centered lessons and units of study revolving around what students need to learn, strategies and activities that will facilitate learning, and texts that serve as vehicles for learning. The organizing principle of this chapter underscores the planning of active text learning environments in content area classrooms: **Instructional planning brings students and texts together in ways that support content literacy and learning.**

FRAME OF MIND

1. How can content area teachers plan and design instruction so that students will actively engage in literacy-related activities?
2. What planning components are involved in explicit strategy instruction?
3. What is involved in designing a text lesson based on a B–D–A instructional framework?
4. How does designing a unit of study help teachers plan a variety of instructional activities that connect literacy and learning?
5. How do teachers create an inquiry/research emphasis within units of study?
6. How can teachers incorporate collaborative/cooperative learning activities within lessons and units of study?
7. How are guided discussions different from reflective discussions?

Content literacy has the potential to play an important role in the academic lives of children and adolescents. In order to plan instruction effectively, a teacher needs to be aware of the *explicit* and *functional* dimensions of content literacy. The explicit aspects of content literacy emphasize direct instruction in the development of skills and strategies that enable students to comprehend what they are reading. Instruction is explicit in the sense that teachers overtly engage in the teaching of procedures to develop students' understanding and use of strategies. In a schoolwide curriculum, the primary responsibility for explicit strategy instruction often falls on the shoulders of reading/language arts teachers and literacy specialists. And this is as it should be. Yet classroom teachers also have a responsibility to show students how to learn with discipline-specific texts, especially those students who struggle with literacy tasks in an academic context.

As crucial as explicit strategy instruction may be to students' literacy development, another equally important dimension of content literacy is the functional nature of strategy use in content areas. Functional instruction emphasizes the application of strategies needed to learn from a variety of print and nonprint sources of information. When the functional aspects of content literacy are operating in the classroom, the teacher is able to integrate literacy and learning in seamless fashion. To the casual observer in a content area classroom, the functional use of strategies would be difficult to categorize as a "strategy lesson." What the observer might conclude, however, is that the teacher used a variety of instructional activities and strategies that actively engage students in learning the content under study. ■

Explicit Strategy Instruction

When texts serve as tools for learning in content area classrooms, teachers have a significant role to play. That role can be thought of as "instructional scaffolding." Content-literate students know how to learn with texts independently. Yet many students have trouble handling the conceptual demands inherent in text material when left to their own devices to learn. A gap often exists between the ideas and relationships they are studying and their prior knowledge, interests, attitudes, cultural background, language proficiency, or reading ability. Instructional scaffolding allows teachers to support students' efforts to make sense of texts while showing them how to use strategies that will, over time, lead to independent learning.

Used in construction, scaffolds serve as supports, lifting up workers so that they can achieve something that otherwise would not have been possible. In teaching and learning contexts, scaffolding means helping learners to do what they cannot do at first. Instructional scaffolds support text learners by helping them achieve literacy tasks that would otherwise have been out of reach. Instructional scaffolding provides the necessary support that students need as they attempt new tasks; at the same time, teachers model or lead the students through effective strategies for completing these tasks. Providing "necessary support" often means understanding the diversity that exists among the students in your class, planning active learning environments, and supporting students' efforts to learn with texts. All learners will benefit from explicit, scaffolded instruction in the use of literacy strategies.

Strategy instruction helps students who struggle with text become aware of, use, and develop control over learning strategies (Brown & Palincsar 1984). Explicit teaching provides an alternative to "blind" instruction. In blind instructional situations, students are taught what to do, but this is where instruction usually ends. Although directed to make use of a set of procedures that will improve reading and studying, students seldom grasp the rationale or payoff underlying a particular strategy. As a result, they attempt to use the strategy with little basis for evaluating its success or monitoring its effectiveness. Explicit instruction, however, attempts not only to show students *what* to do but also *why, how,* and *when.* Pearson (1982) concludes that such instruction helps "students develop independent strategies for coping with the kinds of comprehension problems they are asked to solve in their lives in schools" (p. 22).

As Figure 5.1 shows, explicit strategy instruction has several components: *awareness and explanation, modeling and demonstration, guided practice,* and *application.* By way of analogy, teaching students to be strategic readers provides experiences similar to those needed by athletes who are in training. To perform well with texts, students must understand the rules, work on technique, and practice. A coach (the teacher) is needed to provide feedback, guide, inspire, and share the knowledge and experiences that she or he possesses in the same way literacy coaches support teachers.

FIGURE 5.1 **Instructional Model for Explicit Strategy Instruction**

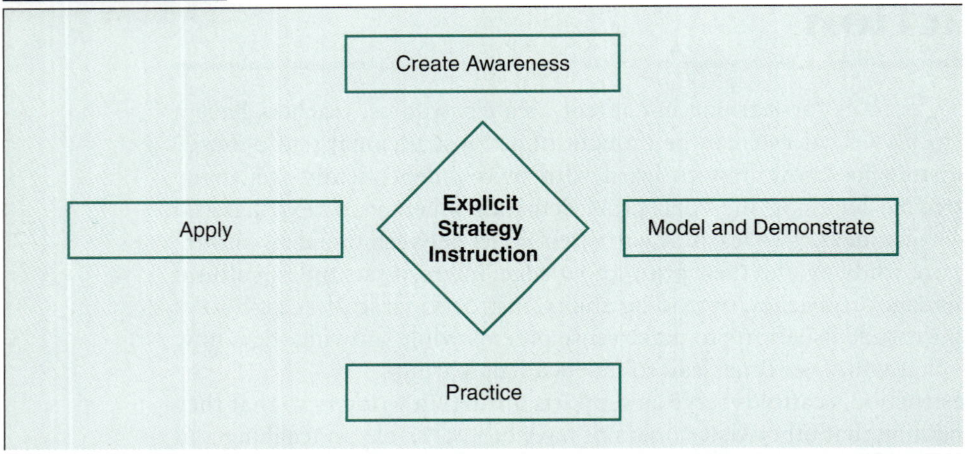

Strategy Awareness and Explanation

To begin the awareness and explanation stage of explicit strategy instruction, first conduct an informal assessment of students' ability to use a particular literacy strategy. Students should think of the assessment as a "tryout" rather than as some kind of test of their ability to use the strategy. Assessment gives the teacher an opportunity to determine the degree of knowledge that students have about a strategy under discussion. Moreover, it yields insight into how well the students use a strategy to handle a reading task. For these reasons, assessing the use of a strategy should occur in as natural a context as possible. Assessment can usually be accomplished within a single class period if these steps are followed:

1. *Assign students a text passage of approximately 500 to 1,500 words.* The selection should take most students ten to fifteen minutes to read.

2. *Direct students to use a particular strategy.* For example, suppose the strategy involves writing a summary of a text selection. Simply ask students to do the things they normally do when they read a passage and then write a summary of it. Allow adequate time to complete the task.

3. *Observe the use of the strategy.* Note what students do. Do they underline or mark important ideas as they read? Do they appear to skim the material first to get a general idea of what to expect? What do they do when they begin actually constructing the summary?

4. *Ask students to respond to respond in writing to several key questions about the use of the strategy.* For example: What did you do to summarize the passage? What did you do to find the main ideas? Did you find summarizing easy or difficult? Why?

During the awareness step, a give-and-take of ideas takes place between teacher and students. As a result, students should recognize the rationale and process behind the use of the strategy. It is important to first discuss the assessment. Teachers should use their observations and students' reflective responses to the questions for this purpose. Continue the strategy discussion with the following activities:

- Lead a discussion of why the strategy is useful. What is the payoff for students? How does it improve learning?
- Engage in a discussion that explains the rules, guidelines, or procedures for being successful with the strategy.
- Have students experience using the strategy. They can practice the rules or procedures on a short text selection.

Awareness and explanation provide students with a clear picture of the learning strategy. The *why* and *how* are solidly introduced, and the road has been paved for more intensive modeling and demonstration of the strategy.

Strategy Demonstration and Modeling

Once the *why* and a beginning sense of the *how* are established, the students should receive careful follow-up in the use of the strategy. Follow-up sessions are characterized by demonstration through teacher modeling, explanations, practice, reinforcement of the rules or procedures, and more practice. The students progress from easy to harder practice situations and from shorter to longer text selections. The following activities are recommended:

- *Use a chart, PowerPoint presentation, or overhead transparency to review the steps students should follow.*
- *Demonstrate the strategy.* Walk students through the steps. Provide explanations. Raise questions about the procedures.
- *As part of a demonstration, initiate a think-aloud procedure to model how to use the strategy.* By thinking aloud, the teacher shares with the students the thinking processes he or she uses in applying the strategy. Thinking aloud is often accomplished by reading a passage out loud and stopping at key points in the text to ask questions or provide prompts. The questions and prompts mirror the critical thinking required to apply the strategy. Once students are familiar with the think-aloud procedure, encourage them to demonstrate and use it during practice sessions. In Chapter 7, we explain in more detail the role that think-alouds play in modeling strategies.

Guided Practice

Use trial runs with short selections from the textbook. Debrief the students with questions after each trial run: Did they follow the steps? How successful were they?

What caused them difficulty? Have them make learning-log entries. Often, a short quiz following a trial run shows students how much they learned and remembered as a result of using the study strategy.

The practice sessions are designed to provide experience with the strategy. Students should reach a point where they have internalized the steps and feel in control of the strategy.

Strategy Application

The preceding components of strategy instruction should provide enough practice for students to know *why*, *how*, and *when* to use the study strategies that have been targeted by the teacher for emphasis. Once students have made generalizations about strategy use, regular class assignments should encourage its application. Rather than assign for homework a text selection accompanied by questions to be answered, frame the assignment so that students will have to apply the strategies they are learning.

Planning Lessons

A lesson usually revolves around all of the students in a class reading the same text. Text-centered lessons provide a blueprint for action. Planning in advance of actual practice is simply good common sense. Planning is essential because learners respond well to structure. When reading text, learners need to sense where they are going and how they will get there. Lessons should be general enough to include all students and flexible enough to allow the teacher to react intuitively and spontaneously when a particular plan is put in actual practice. In other words, lessons shouldn't restrict decisions about the instruction that is in progress; instead, they should encourage flexibility and change.

Lesson Plan Formats

Lesson plan formats vary from school district to school district. However, a comprehensive lesson plan undoubtedly will be aligned with standards (sometimes referred to as *benchmarks* in some local and state curricular guides) within a particular content area at a particular grade level. Moreover, a comprehensive lesson plan will not only address the standards in a discipline but also will include instructional goals or objectives, essential questions, assessment, instructional strategies and activities, instructional materials and resources, and technology. What questions do teachers need to consider when planning lessons?

- *Standards (benchmarks).* What local, state, or national standards will be addressed?
- *Instructional goals.* What will students need to know and be able to do? What knowledge, attitudes, skills, and strategies will students gain from participation in the lesson?

- *Essential questions.* What "big" questions will generate discussion about the topic under study? What questions will be asked to help students focus on important aspects of the topic?
- *Instructional strategies and activities.* What instructional practices, strategies, and activities will be used in the lesson? How will the learning environment support collaborative interactions among students and active engagement in the topic?
- *Instructional materials and resources.* What textbook assignments, trade books, newspaper and magazine articles, reference materials, electronic texts, and so on will students need to engage in learning?
- *New literacies.* How will the use of new literacies support student learning? How will technology and media extend and enhance the lesson?
- *Assessment.* What assessment tools will be needed to evaluate student learning? Will students engage in self-assessment?

Figure 5.2 (pp. 132–134) shows how Judith Roman, an American history teacher, developed a five-day lesson plan designed to help students engage in a cooperative learning strategy called *jigsaw learning,* which we discuss in detail later in this chapter. The "jigsaw puzzle" lesson helped students evaluate the roles of various U.S. presidents who dealt with the issue of Vietnam.

Throughout Part I of this book we have discussed various instructional practices, strategies, and activities to engage students in reading content area text materials. These content literacy practices and strategies fit nicely within the Strategy Awareness and Explanation section of the lesson plan format we just described. Teachers can plan lessons in what we call a B–D–A instructional framework.

B–D–A Instructional Framework

What a teacher does *before reading, during reading,* and *after reading* (B–D–A) is crucial to active and purposeful reading. The B–D–A instructional framework can help teachers incorporate instruction strategies and activities into lessons involving content literacy and learning. A lesson doesn't necessarily take place in a single class session; several class meetings may be needed to achieve the objectives of the lesson. Nor do all the components of a B–D–A lesson necessarily receive the same emphasis in any given reading assignment; the difficulty of the material, students' familiarity with the topic, and your judgment all play a part when you decide on the sequence of activities you will organize. What the structure of a B–D–A instructional framework tells you is that readers need varying degrees of guidance. As we show throughout this book, there are before-reading, during-reading, and after-reading activities that support students' efforts to construct meaning. The components of a B–D–A instructional framework can be examined in Figure 5.3 (p. 135).

> **myeducationlab**
>
> Go to the Building Teaching Skills and Dispositions section of Topic 7: "Planning for Instruction" in the MyEducationLab for your course. As you complete the activity, consider how your instructional choices can affect student thinking and interest.

FIGURE 5.2 Lesson Plan for Vietnam and the Presidential Jigsaw

Goal/Objective

Identifying the key decision makers and the decisions they made about U.S. involvement in the Vietnam War.

Essential Questions

Who were the presidents who involved the United States in Vietnam and where did that involvement lead? What was the specific role of each president?

Standards

This lesson could be used while studying twentieth-century American history.

Correlation with Ohio Academic Content Standards: K–12 Social Studies

- *History.* Students use materials drawn from the diversity of human experience to analyze and interpret significant events, patterns, and themes in the history of Ohio, the United States, and the world.
- *Government.* Students use knowledge of the purposes, structures, and processes of political systems at the local, state, national, and international levels to understand that people create systems of government as structures of power and authority to provide order, maintain stability, and promote the general welfare.

Correlation with National Standards

- *Social studies.* U.S. history, grades 5–12

Correlation with Information Power Standards

- *Standard 1.* The student who is information literate accesses information efficiently and effectively.
- *Standard 7.* The student who contributes positively to the learning community and to society is information literate and recognizes the importance of information to a democratic society.

Timeframe

This lesson will take five class days with some additional time being spent out of class either at home or in the media center.

End Product

Each team of students will construct a five-piece jigsaw puzzle using either poster board, wood, Styrofoam, or any other type of material. Each piece of the puzzle will represent a president and his part in the Vietnam legacy using pictures, graphs, and keywords. Students will also

- Analyze data;
- Draw conclusions from a variety of sources;
- Understand the complexities of the Vietnam War and its legacy for America;
- Work collaboratively; and
- Present the work to their class.

Activities

Students will work in groups of five either in the classroom with their teacher or in the media center with the librarian, depending on their needs.

Day 1

With teacher, revisit the powers of the office of the president and the Congress with relation to the War Powers Act. Discuss the position of commander in chief using contemporary examples. Dividing the class into teams of five members, explain that each team member will be responsible for researching a president who was involved in forming Vietnam policy using the attached research prompt. Use a standard jigsaw puzzle to demonstrate how pieces interlock to create a whole picture. Using this example, each president will be a piece of the jigsaw puzzle that the student teams will create. Each "presidential piece" will comprise pictures, graphs, and keywords that reflect that president's policy.

Day 2

Using the attached research probe, students will begin research in the library. The librarian will revisit the INFOhio databases, emphasizing the difference between a database and a website. Students will remember to cite their sources using APA style. For homework, students begin designing jigsaw pieces using any construction material available.

Day 3

To finish research, students begin assembling a set of images, graphs, and keywords that reflect their president's contribution to Vietnam policy.

FIGURE 5.2 **Lesson Plan for Vietnam and the Presidential Jigsaw *(continued)***

Day 4

Students may mount their information on their puzzle pieces and begin to prepare their presentation.

Day 5

Students present their work to the class.

Resources and Technology

INFOhio:

- EBSCO*host*—High School
- American National Biography
- Britannica Online
- FirstGov
  The White House
  American Memory Project

The Vietnam Veterans Memorial Fund: www.teachvietnam.org

Assessment: Jigsaw projects will be evaluated with the following rubric:

Project Grading Rubric—200 Points Total

	Criteria	A Distinguished	B Proficient	C Average	D Attempted	Your score
Use of research time (30 points)	On task, used databases	30 Excellent	20 Satisfactory	10 Adequate	5 Unsuitable	
Facts/content (80 points)	Accurate, in-depth	80–72 More than required	71–68 Meets requirements	67–56 Finished, some errors	55–48 Mistakes, lacks depth	
Mechanics (40 points)	Spelling, grammar, references	40–38 Perfect	37–34 Few errors	33–28 Some errors	27–24 Many critical errors	
Presentation (50 points)	Neat, attention to detail, informative	50–45 Visually striking, good oral presentation	44–39 Appealing, oral presentation good	38–29 Legible, some oral flaws	28–22 Messy, oral presentation inadequate	
Comments (200 total points possible)						

Truman **Eisenhower** **Kennedy** **Johnson** **Nixon**

Research Probe

Consider the following questions when researching your president's involvement and creating your piece of the jigsaw. Remember to cite your source of information.

1. Name of president:

2. Dates in office:

(continued)

FIGURE 5.2 **Lesson Plan for Vietnam and the Presidential Jigsaw *(continued)***

3. Political party:

4. Political party in control of Congress:

5. Short summary of the president's policy on Vietnam:

6. What steps did this president take toward the conflict in Vietnam?

7. Did this president's decisions show a change in policy over time? Give examples.

8. Did this president increase or decrease the role of the United States in Vietnam when compared with the previous president?

9. How did this president keep the public informed of his decisions regarding Vietnam and the rest of Southeast Asia?

10. What is your evaluation of this president's policy on Vietnam?

A tip from your librarian: Save pictures, maps, graphs, and charts that are useful as you go along.

Source: INFOhio. (2003, November 2). *Lesson Plan: Vietnam and the Presidential Jigsaw.* Retrieved March 8, 2004, from www.infohio.org/Documents/ID/RomanPresidentialJigsaw200311.pdf. Reprinted by permission of INFOhio.

Before-Reading Activities

A B–D–A–centered lesson that includes activity and discussion before reading reduces the uncertainty that students bring to an assignment. Before-reading activities get students ready to read, to approach text material critically, and to seek answers to questions they have generated about the material. The before-reading dimension of a lesson, which is explained in Chapter 6, has also been called the *prereading* phase of instruction. During this instructional phase, a teacher often emphasizes one or more of the following: (1) motivating readers, (2) building and activating prior knowl-

FIGURE 5.3 **B–D–A Instructional Framework**

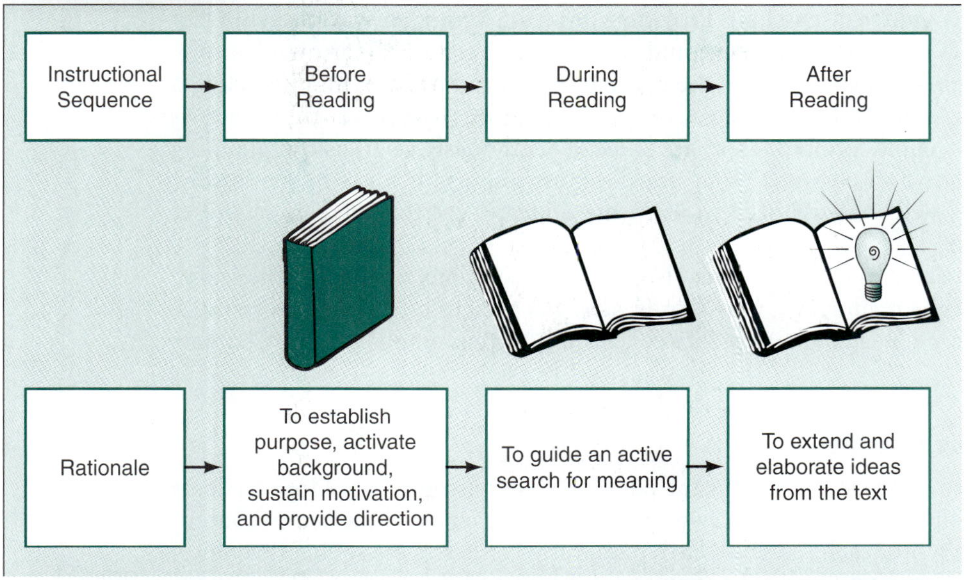

edge, (3) introducing key vocabulary and concepts, and (4) developing metacognitive awareness of the task demands of the assignment and the strategies necessary for effective learning.

A key factor related to motivation is activating students' interest in the text reading. However, concerning how to motivate students, we must first raise a fundamental question: Why should students be interested in this lesson? A teacher may even wish to consider whether he or she is interested in the material! If teachers are going to be models of enthusiasm for students, then the first step is to find something in the material about which to get really excited. Enthusiasm—it is almost too obvious to suggest—is contagious.

RESPONSE JOURNAL

Reflecting on your school experience, how did some of your teachers create interest in text readings in the before-reading phase of a text lesson?

Building and activating prior knowledge for a lesson and presenting key vocabulary and concepts are also essential to preparation before reading. In making decisions related to prior knowledge, it's important to review previous lessons in light of present material. What does yesterday's lesson have to do with today's? Will students make the connection to prevously studied material? Sometimes several minutes of review before forging on into uncharted realms of learning can make all the difference in linking new information to old. Furthermore, when deciding which vocabulary terms to single out for instruction, we emphasize three questions that should be considered: What keywords will students need to understand? Are all the terms equally important? Which new words carry heavy concept loads?

Before-reading activities may also include discussions that develop an awareness of the reading task at hand and of the strategies needed to handle the task effectively. These are metacognitive discussions. Providing direction is another way of saying that students will develop task knowledge and self-knowledge about their own learning strategies. Helping students analyze the reading task ahead of them and modeling a learning strategy that students will need during reading are two metacognitive activities that quickly come to mind. Here are some general questions to ask in planning for a metacognitive discussion: What are the most important ideas in the lesson? What strategies will students need to learn these ideas? Are the students *aware* of these strategies?

A B–D–A instructional framework also includes provisions for guiding the search for meaning during reading. In other words, students need to be shown how to think with texts as they engage in literacy-related learning, a topic emphasized in Chapters 6 through 10.

During-Reading Activities

Teachers easily recognize the important parts of a text assignment. Most students don't. Instead, they tend to read every passage in every chapter in the same monotonous way. Each word, each sentence, each paragraph is treated with equal reverence. No wonder a disconnect often exists between the text and the reader.

The disconnect between text and reader is especially noticeable in content areas where readers must interact with highly specialized and technical language. Nowhere, for example, is content literacy more challenging for students than in the reading of mathematics texts. Math texts are tersely written in highly condensed language. Students must perceive and decode mathematical symbols, construct meanings for specialized and technical vocabulary and concepts, analyze and interpret relationships, and apply interpretations to the solution of problems.

Study how two mathematics teachers adapt the B–D–A instructional framework to scaffold reader–text interactions during reading. The first teaches prealgebra classes in a middle school. The students are studying probability, and the objective of the teacher's lesson is to ensure that the class will be able to determine the probability of a simple event. During the before-reading phase of the lesson, the students explore the questions: Why do some sporting events, such as football, use the flipping of a coin to begin a game? Is the coin flip a fair way to decide which team will kick off? The questions tap into the students' prior knowledge and their conceptions (some naive, some sophisticated) of probability.

As part of the lesson, the teacher asks the students to use their math journals to write definitions of several terms associated with probability: *odds, chances, outcomes, events,* and *sample space.* The students' definitions are discussed as the teacher builds on what they know to arrive at a set of class definitions of the terms. He then pairs the students in "study buddy" teams and asks them to use what they already know about probability to read the assigned section from the textbook. The "study buddies" read the text section and complete the selective reading guide illustrated in Figure 5.4.

FIGURE 5.4 **Using a Selective Reading Guide in Math**

Page 236. Before reading, think about the ways in which we have defined *probability* in class discussion. Now compare our definitions with the one in the book. Develop in your own words a definition of *probability* based on what you know and what you have read.

Probability: ______________________

Page 236. Now read and define other key terms in this section.

Outcomes: ______________________

Events: ______________________

Sample space: ______________________

Page 236, Example 1. Read the example and answer the following:

What is the probability of rolling a 5? ______________________

How do you know? ______________________

Page 237, Example 2. Read this example slowly, and when you finish:

Define odds in favor: ______________________

Page 238, Example 3. Put on your thinking caps to answer the following:

What are the odds? ______________________

What is the difference between finding the probability and finding the odds? ______________________

____

Pages 238–240. You're on your own!

Complete problems 1–31 with your study buddy.

Together, the study buddies discuss the assigned material as they work through the guide. Selective reading guides, as we suggest in Chapter 10, are one way of engaging students in reading by providing a "road map" to the important concepts in the material.

The second teacher, a high school mathematics teacher, also adapts the B–D–A framework to guide students' engagement with the text and to help them make important connections between reading and mathematics. When she first started teaching, she noticed with some dismay that students almost never read the text. Nor did they talk about mathematics with one another. Therefore, she makes a conscious effort to incorporate literacy and cooperative learning principles whenever instructional situations warrant them.

One such situation occurred when her students were studying the concepts of ratio, proportion, and percentage. The focus of the lesson was a section that dealt with the development of scale drawings as an application of proportion. She initiated the lesson by having students take five minutes to write admit slips, a writing-to-learn strategy we introduce in Chapter 9. Admit slips are students' "tickets of admission" to the lesson. The teacher can use them in a variety of ways to find out what students are feeling and thinking as they begin the class period.

The teacher triggered admit slip writing with the prompt: "If you had a younger brother or sister in the sixth grade, how would you describe a scale drawing in words that he or she would understand?" Using half-sheets of paper distributed by the teacher, the students wrote freely for several minutes until instructed to "wind down" and complete the thoughts on which they were working. The teacher collected the admit slips and shared a few of the students' descriptions with the class. The discussion that followed revolved around the students' conceptions of scale drawings and what it means to be "in proportion."

The teacher then formed four-member cooperative groups to guide students' interactions with the text section on scale drawings. Each team was assigned to draw a scale model of the recreation room in its "dream house." First, the teams had to decide what facilities would be included in the recreation room. Once they developed the list of facilities, the team members read the text section and discussed how to develop a scale that would fit all of the facilities into the space provided for each team at the chalkboard. The lesson concluded with the teams describing their scale drawings. The teacher then asked the students to regroup and develop a list of the important ideas related to scale models.

After-Reading Activities

Guidance during reading bridges the gap between students and text so that students learn how to distinguish important from less important ideas, to perceive relationships, and to respond actively to meaning.

Ideas encountered before and during reading may need clarification and elaboration after reading. Postreading activities create a structure that refines emerging concepts. For example, a social studies teacher who was nearing completion of a unit on Southeast Asia asked her students to reflect on their reading by using the activity in Figure 5.5. The writing prompt in part II of the after-reading activity is based on an instructional practice called RAFT, which we describe in Chapter 9. The writing and follow-up discussion refined and extended the students' thinking about the ideas under study. The questions "Who is really best qualified?" and "Who is the specialist in each field?" prompted students to sort out what they had learned. The teacher provided just enough structure by listing topics from various facets of Southeast Asian culture to focus students' thinking and help them make distinctions.

Activities such as the one in Figure 5.5 extend thinking about ideas encountered during reading. Writing activities, study guides, and other after-reading practices are springboards to thinking and form the basis for discussing and articulating ideas developed through reading.

Some More Examples of B–D–A-Centered Lessons

How teachers adapt the B–D–A instructional framework depends on the students in the class, the text that they are studying, and the kinds of activities that will be

FIGURE 5.5 **Postreading Activity for a Southeast Asia Lesson**

I. *Directions:* A rice farmer, a Buddhist monk, a government official, and a geographer all feel competent to speak on any of the following topics. Who is really best qualified? Who is the specialist in each field? On the blank line preceding each topic, place the letter of the correct specialist.

A. Rice farmer
B. Buddhist monk
C. Government official
D. Geographer

_________ 1. The forested regions of Thailand
_________ 2. The life of Siddhārtha Gautama
_________ 3. The amount of rice exported each year
_________ 4. The monsoon rains in Southeast Asia
_________ 5. Harvesting rice
_________ 6. The causes of suffering
_________ 7. The art of meditation
_________ 8. The Me Nam River Basin
_________ 9. The amount of rice produced per acre
_________ 10. The pagodas in Thailand
_________ 11. The number of Buddhists living in Bangkok
_________ 12. The virtues of a simple life
_________ 13. The rice festival in Bangkok
_________ 14. The Temple of the Emerald Buddha
_________ 15. The attainment of Nirvana (perfect peace)

II. *Directions:* Pretend you are the rice farmer, the Buddhist monk, the government official, or the geographer. Write a "guest editorial" for the local newspaper revealing your professional attitude toward and opinion about the approaching monsoon season.

reflected in the lesson. Following are some examples of text-centered lessons in different content areas at different grade levels. As you study these lessons, notice how the teachers adapt the B–D–A framework in their lessons.

Middle School Science Class

Middle-level students were assigned a text selection on how bees communicate. The text told the story of Karl von Frisch, an entomologist who had studied bees for years, and focused on his experimental observations leading to the discovery of bees' communication behaviors. The teacher's objectives were to (1) involve students in an active reading and discussion of the text assignment and (2) have them experience some of the steps scientists go through when performing laboratory or field experiments. Study how she planned her instructional activities in Figure 5.6.

FIGURE 5.6 **B–D–A Activities in a Middle School Science Class**

I. Before Reading

A. Before introducing the text, determine what students now know about bees.

1. Who has observed bees close up?
2. What do you notice about bees that seems unique to them?
3. When you see a bee, is it usually by itself or in a group?
4. Why do you think bees swarm?

B. Connect students' responses to these questions to the text assignment. Introduce the story and its premise.

C. Form small groups of four students each, and direct each group to participate in the following situation:

Karl von Frisch worked with bees for many years. He was puzzled by something he had observed again and again. When he set up a table on which he placed little dishes of scented honey, he attracted bees. Usually, he had to wait hours or days for a bee to discover the feeding place. But as soon as one bee discovered it, many more came to it in a short time. Evidently, the first bee was able to communicate the news of food to the other bees in its hive.

Pretend that you are a scientist helping von Frisch discover how bees communicate. How do they tell each other where food is located? List ten things you could do to find out the answers to this question.

D. Have the students share their group's top five ideas with the class, and write them on the chalkboard.

II. During Reading

A. Assign the selection to be read in class.

B. During reading, direct students to note the similarities and differences between their ideas on the board and von Frisch's experimental procedures.

III. After Reading (Day 2)

A. Discuss the previous day's reading activity. How many of the students' ideas were similar to von Frisch's procedures? How many were different?

B. Extend students' understanding of the inquiry process that scientists such as von Frisch follow. Divide the class into groups of four students to work on the following exercise:

All scientists follow a pattern of research to find answers to the questions they have about different subjects. For example, von Frisch wanted to know about how bees communicated. He (1) formed a question, (2) formulated an experiment to answer the question, (3) observed his subjects in the experiment, and (4) answered the question based on his observations.

Now it's your turn! Tomorrow we are going on a field trip to the park to experiment with ants and food. Your first job as a scientist is to devise a question and an experiment to fit your question. After we return, you will write your observations and the answer to your question. You will be keeping notes on your experiment while we are in the park.

Question: ______________________________

Experiment: ______________________________

Observations: ______________________________

Answer: ______________________________

C. Conduct the experiment the next day at the park. Each group will be given a small amount of food to place near an existing anthill. The students will make notes and take them back to the classroom. Each group's discoveries will be discussed in class.

High School French Class

By way of contrast, study how a high school French teacher taught Guy de Maupassant's short story "L'Infirme" to an advanced class of language students. The story is about two men riding in a train. Henri Bonclair is sitting alone in a train car when another passenger, Revalière, enters the car. This fellow traveler is disabled, having lost his leg during the war. Bonclair wonders about the type of life he must lead. As he looks at the disabled man, Bonclair senses that he met him a few years earlier. He asks the man if he is not the person he met. Revalière is that man. Now Bonclair remembers that Revalière was to be married. He wonders if he got married before or after losing the leg or at all. Bonclair inquires. No, Revalière has not married, refusing to ask the girl to put up with a "deformed" man. However, he is on his way to see her, her husband, and her children. They are all very good friends. The French teacher formulated five objectives for the lesson:

1. To teach vocabulary dealing with the concept of "infirmity";
2. To foster students' ability to make inferences about the reading material from their own knowledge;
3. To foster students' ability to predict what will happen in the story in light of the background they bring to the story;
4. To foster students' ability to evaluate their predictions once they have read the story; and
5. To use the story as a basis for writing a dialogue in French.

Two of the activities used in the French teacher's plan, the *graphic organizer* and the *inferential strategy,* are explained in depth in later chapters. The steps in the activities section of the lesson plan are outlined in Figure 5.7 (pp. 142–143).

Middle School Music Class

A middle school music teacher combines literacy-related practices within the context of studying the components of an opera and engaging students in the understanding and appreciation of Richard Wagner's opera *The Flying Dutchman.* As part of the before-reading component of the lesson, students worked in teams to complete a *cloze activity sheet* (see Figure 5.8) in the form of a playbill. Cloze as an instructional activity is described in Chapter 8.

The playbill serves to activate students' prior knowledge about opera. Students fill in the playbill with the words and names provided at the bottom of the playbill activity sheet in Figure 5.8 (p. 144). When the student teams complete the activity, they share their answers with the class. The teacher then reads to the class a brief biographical sketch of Richard Wagner. She directs the student teams to check their playbills after listening to some of the events and highlights in Wagner's life to determine if the biographical sketch cleared up any of the teams' questions related to the cloze activity. Students then brainstorm what the opera *The Flying Dutchman* is about.

FIGURE 5.7 A B–D–A Lesson in a High School French Class

I. Before Reading

A. Begin the lesson by placing the title of the story on the board: "L'Infirme." Ask students to look at the title and compare it to a similar English word (or words). Determine very generally what the story is probably about (a handicapped person).

B. On the overhead, introduce keywords used in the story by displaying a *graphic organizer:*

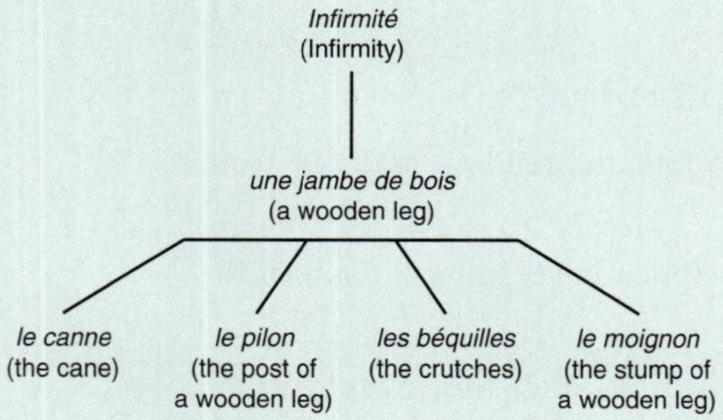

C. Use the *inferential strategy.* Ask and discuss with the class the following three sets of questions. Have the students write down their responses.

1. *Vous avez peut-être vu quelqu'un qui est très estropié à cause de la perte d'une jambe ou d'un bras. Qu'est-ce qui traverse votre esprit? De quoi est-ce que vous vous demandez?*
(You may have seen someone who is very crippled because of the loss of a leg or an arm. When you see such a person, what crosses your mind? What do you wonder about?)

2. *Dans l'histoire, Bonclair voit ce jeune infirme qui a perdu la jambe. Qu'est-ce que vous pensez traverse son esprit?*
(In the story, Bonclair sees this crippled young man who has lost his leg. What do you think crosses his mind?)

3. *Quand vous voyez quelqu'un qui a l'air vaguement familier, qu'est-ce que vous voulez faire? Qu'est-ce que vous faites? Quels sont souvent les résultats?*
(When you see someone who looks vaguely familiar, what do you want to do? What do you do? What are often the results?)

4. *Dans cette histoire, Bonclair se souvient vaguement qu'il a fait la connaissance de cet infirme. Prédites ce qu'il fera et prédites les résultats.*
(In this story, Bonclair remembers vaguely having met this cripple. Predict what he does and the results.)

5. *Imaginez que vous êtes fiancé(e) à un jeune homme ou à une jeune femme. Puis vous avez un accident qui vous rend estropié(e). Qu'est-ce que vous feriez? Voudriez-vous se marier? Pourriez-vous compter sur l'autre de vous aimer encore?*
(Imagine that you are engaged to a young man or woman. Then you have an accident that leaves you crippled. What would you do? Would you still want to marry? Could you still expect the other to love you?)

6. *Dans notre histoire, Revalière a eu un accident juste avant son marriage. Prédites ce qu'il fera et ce qu'il comptera de la jeune fille. Prédites les résultats.*
(In our story, Revalière has had an accident just before his marriage. Predict what he did and what he expected of the young woman. Predict the results.)

II. During Reading

A. Assign the reading, instructing the students to keep in mind their prior knowledge and predictions.

B. Ask them to note possible changes in their predictions.

III. After Reading

A. After the reading, conduct a follow-up discussion with the class. Relate their predictions to what actually happened, noting how our background

FIGURE 5.7 **A B–D–A Lesson in a High School French Class *(continued)***

knowledge and experience of the world lead us to think along certain lines.

B. Have the class form groups of four with at least one male and one female in each group. Establish the following situation:

Une jeune fille vient d'être estropiée dans un accident de natation. Son fiancé lui a téléphoné. Il veut lui parler. Qu'est-ce qu'il veut lui dire? On frappe à la porte. C'est lui.

(A young lady was recently crippled in a swimming accident. Her fiancé has called her. He wants to talk to her. What does he want to talk about? There is a knock at the door. It is he.)

1. Think together, drawing on your past knowledge or experience of situations like this. Write a fifteen- to twenty-line group dialogue in French between the girl and her fiancé. What might he have to tell her? How might she react?
2. Select a male and female student to present the group's dialogue to the class.

As part of the during-reading phase of the lesson, the teacher dims the lights in the classroom and invites students to close their eyes as they listen to the overture to *The Flying Dutchman*. In this context, the term *overture* is redefined by the class. After establishing the mood of the opera, students rethink their ideas about the story. During the next several class sessions, the teacher reads the story, stopping each day at a turning point of the story to pique students' curiosity. She ends each read-aloud with an enthusiastic "To be continued!" and then engages students in a discussion of the story that has occurred thus far. Toward the end of each discussion, she elicits predictions about what the students think will happen next. Throughout this process excerpts of the music are played at appropriate places in the lessons.

At the conclusion of the story, students enter the after-reading phase of the lesson. The teacher follows procedures associated with the discussion web strategy (see Chapter 7). The discussion web is a collaborative strategy that requires students to explore multiple perspectives around a key question. First, the students work in "think–pair–share" dyads to respond to the question, "Did Senta need to throw herself off the cliff into the sea?" from yes–no perspectives. They then form groups of four to share their perspectives in a larger forum and to reach a conclusion, which the groups share with the class.

These lesson activities all have the same underlying purpose. Each provides a set of experiences designed to move readers from preparation to engagement with the text to extension and elaboration of the concepts in the material under study.

How teachers plan instructional activities for content literacy lessons varies by grade level and the sophistication of the students. The same is true of developing plans for a unit of study. In the next section, we go beyond designing and planning lessons to decisions related to thematic learning involving multiple literacy experiences.

FIGURE 5.8 **Cloze Playbill for the Opera *The Flying Dutchman***

The Flying Dutchman

An ____________ by ____________

____________ in ____________ with ____________

subtitles on overhead screen

____________—Taken from a Norwegian legend

____________—The shores of Norway

____________—Maestro George Szell

Chorus—____________

____________—Constructed and designed by Marc Chagall

____________—Designed by Mademoiselle Choé

____________—The Cleveland Orchestra

____________—Aboard the ship

Dutchman—Sung by ____________

Daland—Sung by ____________

____________—On Shore

Senta—Sung by ____________

German	Act II	Setting	Spoken	Sung
Costumes	Choreographer	Conductor	Libretto	Scenery
Opera	Richard Wagner	Overture	Tenor	Baritone
English	Townspeople	Soprano	Sailors	Act I

Source: Reprinted by permission of Donna Kowallek Mitchell. Copyright © 2000.

Planning Units of Study

Units of study organize instruction around objectives, activities, print and nonprint resources, and inquiry experiences. A unit may be designed for a single discipline or may be interdisciplinary, integrating two or more content areas. In middle schools, where content area teachers are teamed in learning "communities" or "families," opportunities abound to develop interdisciplinary units. Interdisciplinary units require coordination and cooperation by all of the content area teachers teamed within a learning community. Team planning helps students make connections not otherwise possible among many knowledge domains. For example, a middle school teaching team organized an interdisciplinary unit around the theme of "Native Americans." They developed a four-week unit in which 130 seventh graders were "born" into one of sixteen Native American tribes. The students inquired into tribal lifestyles from many disciplinary perspectives and participated in a variety of activities to understand life as Native Americans both emotionally and intellectually.

myeducationlab

Go to the Assignments and Activities section of Topic 5: "Comprehension Strategies" in the MyEducationLab for your course and complete the activity "Using Text Features to Aid Comprehension" to consider how students can learn to use content area textbook features.

Components of a Well-Designed Unit

The unit of study is a planning tool that includes (1) a title reflecting the theme or topic of the unit, (2) the major concepts to be learned, (3) the texts and information sources to be studied by students, (4) the unit's instructional activities, and (5) provisions for assessing what students have learned from the unit.

Content Objectives

Content analysis is a major part of teacher preparation in the development of a unit of study. Content analysis results in the *what* of learning—the major concepts and understandings that students should learn from reading the unit materials. Through content analysis, the major concepts become the objectives for the unit. It doesn't matter whether these content objectives are stated in behavioral terms. What really matters is that you know which concepts students will interact with and develop. Therefore, it's important to decide on a manageable number of the most important understandings to be gained from the unit. This means setting priorities; it's impossible to cover every aspect of the material that students will read or to which they will be exposed.

A unit on spatial relationships for a high school art class provides an example of how a teacher planned content objectives, activities, and materials. First, she listed the major concepts to be taught in the unit:

1. Humans are aware of the space about them as functional, decorative, and communicative.
2. Space organized intuitively produces an aesthetic result, but a reasoned organization of space also leads to a pleasing outcome if design is considered.
3. Occupied and unoccupied space have positive and negative effects on mood and depth perception.
4. The illusion of depth can be created on a two-dimensional surface.

5. The direction and balance of lines or forms create feelings of tension, force, and equilibrium in the space that contains them.
6. Seldom in nature is the order of objects so perfect as to involve no focal point or force or tension.

Instructional Activities and Text Resources

The high school art teacher then developed the activities and identified the texts to be used in the unit (see Figure 5.9). As you study the figure, keep in mind that some of the text-related activities suggested are explored later in this book.

The actual framework of units will vary. For example, you might organize a unit entirely on a sequence of lessons from assignments in a single textbook. This type of organization is highly structured and is even restrictive in the sense that it often precludes the use of various kinds of other literature rich in content and substance. However, a unit of study can be planned so that the teacher will (1) use a single textbook to begin the unit and then branch out into multiple-text study and differentiated activities, (2) organize the unit entirely on individual or group inquiry and research, or (3) combine single-text instruction with multiple-text activities and inquiry.

Branching out provides the latitude to move from a single-text lesson to independent learning activities. The move from single- to multiple-information sources exposes students to a wide range of texts that may be better suited to their needs and interests. (See Figure 5.10 on page 148.)

Unit planning simply provides more options to coordinate a variety of information sources. In single-discipline units, B–D–A activities become an integral part of unit teaching.

Listing texts and resources is an important part of the planning process for a single-discipline unit. One reason a unit is so attractive as a means of organization is that the teacher can go beyond the textbook—or, for that matter, bypass it. A wide array of literature, both narrative and informational, gives students opportunities for an intense involvement in the theme or topic under study. Trade books, digital texts, pamphlets, periodicals, reference books, newspapers, and magazines are all potential alternative routes to acquiring information.

Moreover, the Internet has become a valuable planning resource for teachers in the development of units. You can access many useful ideas for integrating digital texts into units of study.

An Inquiry/Research Emphasis in Units of Study

Gathering, organizing, and sharing information are crucial to both academic success and success in our information-rich society. Inquiry should, therefore, play a major role in learning important content, and the process of inquiry should be woven into thematic units of study. *Standards for the English Language Arts* (1997), developed by IRA and NCTE, describes the fundamental characteristics of inquiry reading as follows: "Students conduct research on issues and interests by generating ideas and questions and by posing problems. They gather, evaluate, and synthesize data from

FIGURE 5.9 **Activities and Texts**

Text-Related Activities	*Texts*
1. Graphic organizer	Graham Collier, *Form, Space, and Vision*
2. Vocabulary and concept bulletin board	
3. Prereading	Chapter 3, Collier
4. Prereading	Chapters 6 and 7
5. Art journal	Chapters 6 and 7
6. K-W-L	Chapter 11
7. Vocabulary exercise	Chapter 3
8. Vocabulary exercise	Chapters 6 and 7
9. Vocabulary exercise	Chapter 11
10. Student's choice (list of projects for research study)	H. Botten, *Do You See What I See?* H. Helfman, *Creating Things That Move* D. McAgy, *Going for a Walk with a Line* L. Kaumpmann, *Creating with Space and Construction*
11. Hands-On	G. LeFrevre, *Junk Sculpture*
Ink dabs	J. Lynch, *Mobile Design*
Straw painting	
Dry seed arrangement	
Cardboard sculpture	
Positive—negative cutouts	
Perspective drawing	*Calder's Universe*
Large-scale class sculpture	
Mobiles	
Space frames	Displays of artist's works with questionnaires to be filled out about them
12. Filmstrip	
13. Field trip to studio of a sculptor	
14. Field trip to museum	
15. Learning corner	

a variety of sources (e.g., print and non-print texts, artifacts, and people) to communicate their discoveries in ways that suit their purpose and audience" (p. 7).

Steps and Stages Involved in Inquiry Projects

How teachers guide inquiry/research projects is the key to a successful unit. The process of inquiry, like the process of writing that we describe in Chapter 9, works best when it occurs in steps and stages. Each stage of an inquiry/research project requires

FIGURE 5.10 **"Branching Out" in a Thematic Unit: Using a Wide Range of Texts**

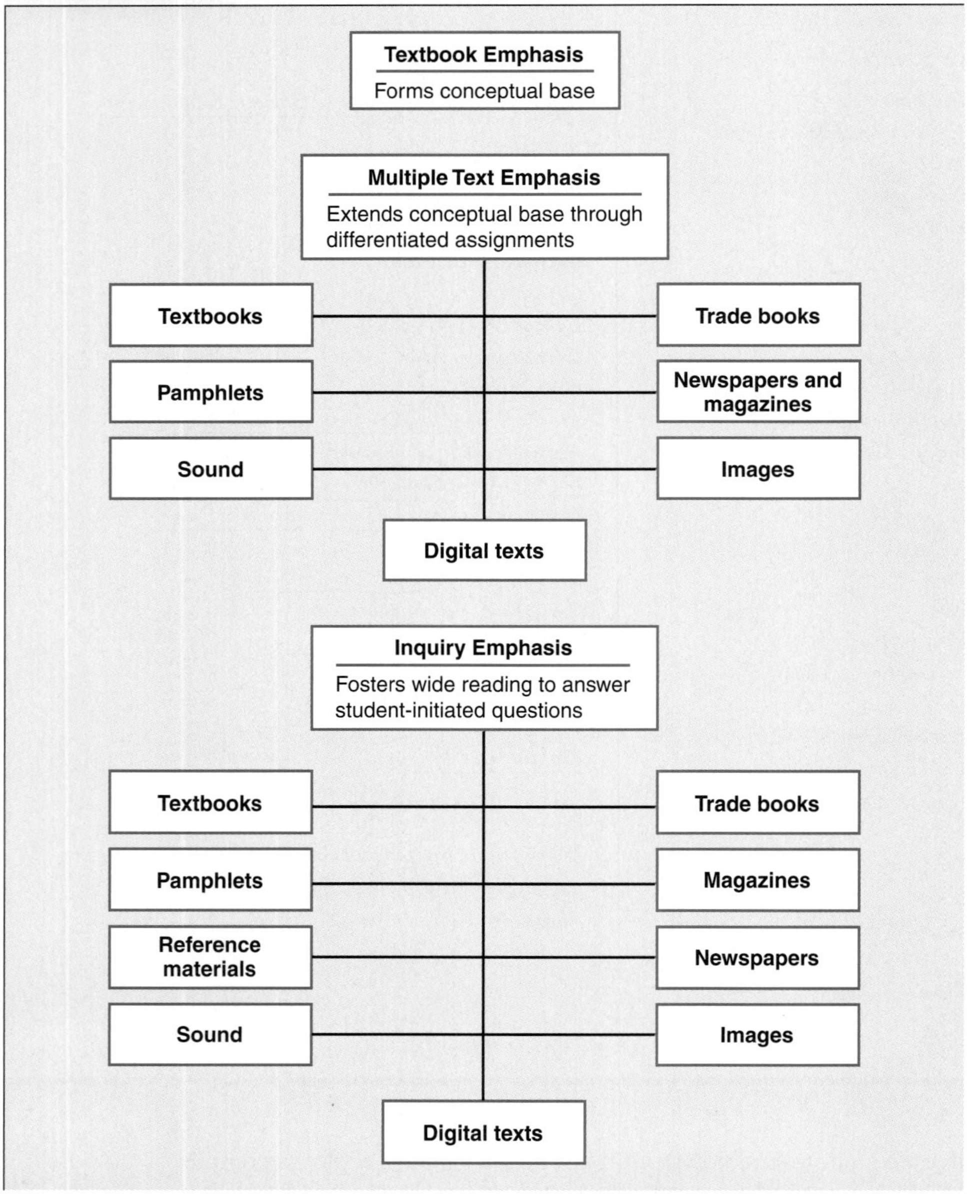

careful support by a teacher. In Box 5.1, we outline the stages and procedures for guiding inquiry/research.

When teachers simply assign and evaluate research reports, students often paraphrase whatever sources come to hand rather than actively pursuing information that

Evidence-Based Best Practices BOX 5.1

Procedures for Guiding Inquiry/Research Projects

I. Raise questions, identify interests, organize information.
   - A. Discuss interest areas related to the unit of study.
   - B. Engage in goal setting.
     1. Arouse curiosities.
     2. Create awareness of present levels of knowledge.
   - C. Pose questions relating to each area and/or subarea.
     1. "What do you want to find out?"
     2. "What do you want to know about _______?"
     3. Record the questions or topics.
     4. "What do you already know about _______?"
   - D. Organize information; have students make predictions about likely answers to gaps in knowledge.
     1. Accept all predictions as possible answers.
     2. Encourage thoughtful speculations in a non-threatening way.

II. Select materials.
   - A. Use visual materials.
     1. Trade books and encyclopedias
     2. Magazines, catalogs, directories
     3. Newspapers and comics
     4. Indexes, atlases, almanacs, dictionaries, readers' guides, computer catalogs
     5. Films, filmstrips, slides
     6. Videotapes, television programs
     7. Digital texts: CD-ROMs, website documents, videodisks
   - B. Use nonvisual materials.
     1. Audiotapes
     2. Records
     3. Radio programs
     4. Field trips
   - C. Use human resources.
     1. Interviews
     2. Letters
     3. On-site visits
     4. Discussion groups
     5. E-mail
     6. Listservs
   - D. Encourage self-selection of materials.
     1. "What can I understand?"
     2. "What gives me the best answers?"

III. Guide the information search.
   - A. Encourage active research.
     1. Reading
     2. Listening
     3. Observing
     4. Talking
     5. Writing
   - B. Facilitate with questions.
     1. "How are you doing?"
     2. "Can I help you?"
     3. "Do you have all the materials you need?"
     4. "Can I help you with ideas you don't understand?"
   - C. Have students keep records.
     1. Learning log that includes plans, procedures, notes, and rough drafts
     2. Book record cards
     3. Record of conferences with the teacher

IV. Consider different forms of writing.
   - A. Initiate a discussion of sharing techniques.
   - B. Encourage a variety of writing forms.
     1. Essay or paper
     2. Lecture to a specific audience
     3. Case study
     4. Story: adventure, science fiction, other genre
     5. Dialogue, conversation, interview
     6. Dramatization through scripts
     7. Commentary or editorial
     8. Thumbnail sketch

V. Guide the writing process.
   - A. Help students organize information.
   - B. Guide first-draft writing.
   - C. Encourage responding, revising, and rewriting.
   - D. "Publish" finished products.
     1. Individual presentations
     2. Classroom arrangement
     3. Class interaction

they are eager to share with others. Genuine inquiry is always a messy endeavor characterized by false starts, unexpected discoveries, changes in direction, and continual decision making. Too much guidance can be as dangerous as too little.

In an in-depth study of two middle school research projects, Rycik (1994) found that teachers may lose their focus on genuine inquiry as they establish procedures for guiding all students to complete a project successfully. The teachers in the study were very concerned with providing sufficient guidance, so they broke down their projects into a series of discrete steps (such as making note cards) that could be taught, completed, and evaluated separately. As the projects moved forward, the teachers gradually came to believe that mastering the procedure for each step was the primary outcome of the project, even more important than learning content information.

Rycik (1994) concluded that inquiry should not be confined to one big research paper because teachers cannot introduce and monitor the wide range of searching, reading, thinking, and writing skills that students need to complete such projects. Good researchers, like good writers, must learn their craft through frequent practice in a variety of contexts. This means that students should research from a variety of sources and express their findings for a variety of audiences in a variety of forms. Some recommendations for integrating research into the classroom routine include the following:

- *Make identifying questions and problems as important in your classroom as finding answers.*
- *Provide frequent opportunities to compare, contrast, and synthesize information from multiple sources.*
- *Present findings of research in a variety of products and formats,* including charts, graphs, and visual or performing arts.
- *Discuss possible sources for information* presented in the class or for answering questions posed by the teacher or students (e.g., personal interviews, diaries, experiments).

The teacher must carefully plan inquiry-centered projects, giving just the right amount of direction to allow students to explore and discover ideas on their own. The research process isn't a do-your-own-thing proposition; budding researchers need structure. Many a project has been wrecked on the shoals of nondirection. The trick is to strike a balance between teacher guidance and student self-reliance. A research project must have just enough structure to give students (1) a problem focus, (2) physical and intellectual freedom, (3) an environment in which they can obtain data, and (4) feedback situations in which to report the results of their research.

A Multiple-Text Emphasis in Units of Study

The literature-based movement in elementary schools serves as a prototype for the use of trade books in middle and high school classrooms. In addition, technology makes it possible to access and explore information sources through digital programs, electronic books, and the Internet. Internet inquiries and WebQuests provide excellent instructional frameworks for inquiry-centered learning. Although textbooks may be used to provide an information base, the foundation for individual and group inquiry into a theme or topic is built on students' use of multiple-information resources, both print and nonprint. Trade books (see Chapter 11) and digital texts, as we explained in Chapter 2, are geared to students' interests and inquiry needs.

myeducationlab

Go to the Assignments and Activities section of Topic 7: "Planning for Instruction" in the MyEducationLab for your course and complete the activity "Sharing Plans and Assignments with Students" and explore a sample lesson plan.

Say that in a middle grade classroom, students are engaged in a thematic unit on the environment. What might you observe over several weeks? For starters, the teacher may conduct several whole-class lessons at the beginning of the unit using the textbook to develop a conceptual framework for individual and group investigation. As the weeks progress, however, whole-class activity is less prevalent. Instead, small groups work on research projects or in discussion teams using Gary Paulsen's *Woodsong* (1990) and *Hatchet* (1987) and Roy Gallant's *Earth's Vanishing Forests* (1991). Individual students are also working on inquiries with books such as Paul Goble's *I Sing for the Animals* (1991) and Peter Parnall's *Marsh Cat* (1991) and *The Daywatchers* (1984).

In addition, the students are conducting research online, tapping into the rich information resources on the Internet. Several students investigate the websites of Environmental Science, the Rainforest Action Network, and the Global Recycling Network. Others explore software programs: Ozzie's World (Digital Impact), Zug's Adventures on Eco-Island (Zugware), Zurk's Rainforest (Soliel), and Imagination Express: Rainforest (Edmark). One or two students navigate the pages of electronic reference books, such as Grolier's Multimedia Encyclopedia (Grolier).

Toward the end of the unit, the class completes culminating activities, which may involve panel discussions, report writing, and oral presentations in which individuals or groups share knowledge gleaned from the various activities and texts. In this class, what you would observe is that everyone has something to contribute.

Active learning environments within units of study integrate whole-class, small-group, and individual learning activities. Whole-class presentation is an economical means of giving information to students when the classroom context lends itself to information sharing. A whole-class activity, for example, may be used to set the stage for a new thematic unit. The unit introduction, discussion of objectives, and background building can all take place within whole-class structure. However, the chief drawback of whole-class presentation is that it limits active participation among students. Although whole-class interaction provokes discussion to an extent, it cannot produce the volume of participation necessary to engage students in active learning situations. A viable alternative supported by a substantial body of research lies in the use of collaborative interactions between teacher and students and among students. These collaborative interactions are grounded in the principles underlying cooperative learning and small-group processes.

Planning Collaborative Interactions

Cooperative learning allows groups of students to pursue academic goals through collaboration in classroom instructional activities. The goals of cooperative learning, therefore, are to foster collaboration in a classroom context, to develop students' self-esteem in the process of learning, to encourage the development of positive group relationships, and to enhance academic achievement (Johnson, Johnson, & Holubec 1990). Cooperative groups facilitate active participation and should be a primary form of classroom organization when teachers bring students together to comprehend texts. The National Reading Panel's (NRP) review of research on text comprehension identifies cooperative learning as a scientifically supported comprehension strategy (NRP 2000). We agree with Duke and Pearson (2002), however, who view cooperative learning as an "instructional medium" that facilitates reading comprehension rather than an individual instructional strategy. Within the learning environment created by cooperative groups, students produce more ideas, participate more, and take greater intellectual risks. A cooperative group, with its limited audience, provides more opportunity for students to contribute ideas to a discussion and take chances in the process. The students can try out ideas without worrying about being wrong or sounding dumb—a fear that often accompanies risk taking in a whole-class situation.

Cooperative Learning

Engaged learners are socially interactive. Bringing learners and texts together in social collaboration to engage in discussions may be achieved through the use of cooperative learning groups. Many variations on cooperative group learning are possible. Several cooperative grouping patterns, in particular, work well within the context of content literacy practices and text-related discussions. The cooperative groups described in the following sections give you a feel for how students might collaborate in their interactions with texts and with one another as they extract and construct meaning to make sense out of what they are reading.

Jigsaw Groups

Interdependent team learning with texts may be achieved through *jigsaw groups* (Aronson 1978). Jigsaw teaching requires students to specialize in a content literacy task that contributes to an overall group objective. Jigsaw groups are composed of students divided heterogeneously into three- to six-member teams. Each student on a team becomes an expert on a subtopic of a theme or topic about which the class is reading. Not only is the student accountable for teaching the other members of the group about his or her subtopic but he or she is

RESPONSE JOURNAL

Describe how you would use the jigsaw strategy in your content area.

also responsible for learning the information other group members provide during the jigsaw discussions.

For example, a life science teacher in a middle school engages students in a thematic unit on the topic "birds." As part of the unit of study, he divides the class into five six-member jigsaw groups. Each member of a group is expected to become an expert on one of the following concepts in the unit: the relationship between birds and reptiles, the adaptation of various species of birds to their environment, the migration patterns of birds, the adaptation of birds for flight, the economic importance of birds, and the identification of various families and species.

As part of the jigsaw strategy, members of the different teams who share the same subtopic meet in temporary "expert groups" to discuss what they are reading and learning. Each of the expert groups has a variety of resource materials and texts made available by the teacher to help them explore and clarify their subtopics. When the members in each of the expert groups complete their tasks, they return to their jigsaw teams to teach and share what they have learned. As a jigsaw member presents his or her findings, the other members listen and take notes in preparation for a unit exam the teacher will give on the overall topic.

Student Teams Achievement Divisions (STAD)

Student teams lend themselves well to content area learning situations that combine whole-class discussion with follow-up small-group activity. The originator of STAD groups, Robert Slavin (1988), emphasizes the importance of achieving team learning goals but also recognizes that individual performance is important in cooperative groups.

STAD groups work this way: The teacher introduces a topic of study to the whole class, presents new information, and then divides the class into heterogeneous four-member groups of high-, average-, and low-achieving students to engage in follow-up team study. The goal of team study is to master the content presented in the whole-class discussion. The team members help each other by discussing the material, problem solving, comparing answers to guide material, and quizzing one another to ensure that each member knows the material. The students take periodic quizzes, prepared by the teacher, following team study. A team score is determined by the extent to which each member of the team improves over past performance. A system of team awards based on how well students perform individually ensures that team members will be interdependent for learning.

Learning Circles

Johnson and colleagues (1990) underscore the importance of positive interdependence through a cooperative learning model. Similar to STAD, learning circles mesh whole-group study with small-group interactions and discussion. Learning circles may comprise two to six members of varying abilities who come together to share text resources and help each other learn. All of the content literacy activities that we present in this book can be adapted to the type of interdependent learning teams that are suggested by Johnson and colleagues. However, cooperative groups don't run by themselves. You have to plan for the success of positive interdependence by teaching students how to use collaboration skills to work interdependently in teams and then facilitating the group process as students engage in discussion and interaction.

Johnson and colleagues (1990) suggest eighteen steps for structuring learning circles, some of which include specifying content objectives, deciding on the size of the group, assigning students to groups, arranging the room, planning instructional activities and guide material to promote interdependent learning, explaining the academic task, explaining the criteria for success, structuring the division of labor within the groups, structuring individual accountability and intergroup cooperation, monitoring students' behaviors, teaching the skills of collaboration, providing task assistance as needed, evaluating student learning, and assessing how well the teams functioned.

Group brainstorming, prediction, problem solving, mapping, and study strategies, all of which are discussed in Part Two, are easily woven into the fabric of cooperative learning circles. Coming to a group consensus on a variety of discussion tasks is an important outcome in cooperative learning groups. Students need to be shown how to engage cooperatively in consensus building as they decide what conclusions they can or cannot support as a result of their interactions with texts and one another.

Group Investigation

As we explained earlier in this chapter, students can be combined in teams of two to six to collaborate on inquiry topics that interest them within the context of a thematic unit and the major concepts of study. Each group selects a topic and cooperatively plans the inquiry in consultation with the teacher. Each research team, for example, decides how to investigate the topic, which tasks each member will be responsible for, and how the topic will be reported. The groups then conduct the investigation, synthesize their findings into a group presentation, and make their presentation to the entire class. The teacher's evaluation includes individual performance and the overall quality of the group presentation. In Figure 5.11, study how an American history teacher in high school sets up a group investigation project on the Revolutionary War.

Group Retellings

Group retellings underscore the importance of *conceptually related reading* in which each member of a cooperative group reads a different text on the same topic. For example, Wood (1987) illustrates the use of group retellings in a health class. Students of different abilities work in groups of three or more, reading timely articles or brochures on the topic of safety in the home. A magazine article might describe an eyewitness account of a home fire resulting from an electrical overload. A brochure from the local fire department might outline the precautions to take to avoid such a mishap, perhaps emphasizing the hazards associated with an overloaded circuit. A newspaper editorial might warn parents against leaving their children unattended and unfamiliar with safety hazards in the home.

RESPONSE JOURNAL

Describe how you would use the group retellings strategy in your content area.

FIGURE 5.11 **A Group Investigation Project for a Unit on the Revolutionary War**

Directions: Congratulations! You have been chosen to anchor the new series *TimeLine.* This show features the same type of in-depth interview as *NightLine,* except you have a time machine. You can go back in time and interview someone from the Revolution. To prevent changing the future, here are the rules:

1. Work in pairs. Both of you will do research and write the interview. Decide who will be the interviewer and who the interviewee. Decide on a historical interview date.
2. Your interviewee may be an actual historical figure (e.g., Paul Revere), or you may create a fictional eyewitness to a historical event (e.g., the Boston Tea Party).
3. Your research must be based on at least two sources, only one of which may be an encyclopedia. A bibliography must be included in the written interview turned in after the presentation.
4. Presentation
   a. Introduce the interviewee and briefly tell why this person is important or interesting.
   b. Your questions must stay within your time frame. You can't ask George Washington if he wants to be president; the office doesn't exist yet. You may ask him if he would like a political office in the future.
   c. The interviewee's answers must be reasonable and based on historical facts from your research.
   d. You are encouraged to include visual aids: pictures, cartoons, maps, props, and costumes.
   e. The interview should last no less than four minutes and no more than ten minutes.

Here is a list of possible subjects, or you may choose your own.

George Washington
Samuel Adams
Crispus Attucks
Thomas Jefferson
John Adams
Benjamin Franklin
Benedict Arnold
Francis Marion, the "Swamp Fox"
Marquis de Lafayette
Charles Cornwallis (British general)
Frederick North (British prime minister)
King George III
Haym Solomon (financier)
George Rogers Clark
John Dickinson
Thomas Paine
John Locke
Jean-Jacques Rousseau
Abigail Adams
James Arnistead (spy)
Deborah Sampson Gannett (soldier)
Patrick Henry
John Hancock
Ethan Allen
Peter Zenger
David Bushnell (submarine inventor)
Boston Massacre
Boston Tea Party
Reading and responding to the Declaration of Independence as a wealthy merchant or planter, a poor artisan or farmer, or a slave
Revolutionary battle or campaign of your choice
Treaty of Paris

After reading, each member of the group shares what he or she has read while the other members of the team listen and, at any point, share additional information and insights into the topic based on their reading. Group retellings capitalize on the pleasure derived from sharing newly learned information with a friend.

Small-Group Processes

Small-group learning is complex, and cooperative teams don't run by themselves. Students must know how to work together and how to use techniques they have been taught. The teacher, in turn, must know about small-group processes. The practical question is, How will individual students turn into cooperative groups? Anyone who has ever attempted small-group instruction in the classroom knows the dilemma associated with the question. Many conditions can confound team learning if plans are not made in advance; in particular, teachers must scaffold instruction around such matters as the size, composition, goals, and performance criteria of small groups and the division of labor within a group.

Group Size

The principle of "least group size" operates whenever you form learning teams. A group should be just large enough to include all the skills necessary to solve a problem or complete a task. A group that's larger than necessary provides less chance for individual participation and greater opportunity for conflict. If too many students are grouped together, there's bound to be a point of diminishing returns. The group size for content area reading should range from two to six members (depending, of course, on the type of reading task). Because most small-group activities involve discussion, three- or four-member groups are probably best.

Group Composition

Homogeneous grouping is often not necessary for discussion tasks. Both intellectual and nonintellectual factors influence a small group's performance, and the relationship between intelligence and small-group performance is often surprisingly low. Experiential and social background, interests, attitudes, and personality contribute greatly to the success of a cooperative group. Grouping solely by reading or intellectual ability shortchanges all students and robs discussion of diversity.

Students who struggle with reading shouldn't be relegated to tasks that require minimal thinking or low-level responses to content material. There is no quicker way to initiate misbehavior than to put students who find reading difficult together in a group. People learn from one another. A student whose background is less extensive than other students' can learn from them. The student who has reading difficulties needs good readers as models. Furthermore, the student who has trouble reading may in fact be a good listener and thinker who will contribute significantly to small-group discussion.

Group Goals and Tasks

Group learning is goal oriented. How the goals and the paths to task completion are perceived affects the amount and quality of involvement of the team members. If group goals are unclear, members' interest quickly wanes. Goals must also be directly related to the task. The conditions of the task must be clearly defined and must be understood by the individual members of the group.

Therefore, you should explain the criteria for task performance. For example, when students work with reading guides, such as those that are suggested in this book, they should attempt to adhere to such criteria as the following:

- *Each student should read the selection silently and complete each item of the guide individually or with others in the group,* depending on the teacher's specific directions.
- *Each item should be discussed by the group.*
- *If there is disagreement on any item, a group member must defend his or her position and show why there is disagreement.* This means going back into the selection to support one's position.
- *No one student should dominate a discussion or boss other members around.*
- *Each member should contribute something to each group discussion.*

As students work on literacy activities in their groups, the teacher can facilitate performance by reinforcing the criteria that have been established.

Positive Interdependence

Groups lack cohesiveness when learning is not cooperative but competitive and when students aren't interdependent in learning but work independently. However, since the 1970s, social scientists and instructional researchers have made great strides in understanding the problems of the competitive classroom. Researchers (Johnson & Johnson 1987; Slavin 1988) have studied the practical classroom applications of cooperative principles of learning. The bulk of their research suggests that cooperative small-group learning has positive effects on academic achievement and social relationships. Positive interdependence can be achieved through a variety of schemes in which students are rewarded for collaborative effort (Johnson & Johnson 1990). For example, a social studies teacher attempted to have students adhere to discussion behaviors during their interactions in small groups (these discussion behaviors were basically the same as those we discussed under performance criteria). Each small group earned a performance grade for discussing text assignments in a six-week thematic unit. Here's how the group members earned their grades:

RESPONSE JOURNAL

What is your reaction to the point system that the social studies teacher used to create positive interdependence among the small groups in his class?

1. The teacher observed each member in the group to monitor the use of the desired discussion behaviors.
2. On Fridays, each group earned a color reward worth a given number of points: green = 1 point, blue = 2 points, black = 3 points, and red = 4 points. The color that a group earned was based on how well it had performed according to the criteria for discussion.
3. Each member of the group received the color (and the points that went with it) that the whole group earned. Therefore, if one or two members of the group did not use the appropriate discussion behaviors, the entire group got a lower point award.

4. The color for each student in the class was noted on a learning incentive chart.
5. Each week, the small groups changed composition by random assignment.
6. The points attached to each color added up over the weeks. When the unit was completed, so many points resulted in a performance grade of A, B, C, or D.

What happened as a result of the reward system? On the Monday of each week that students were randomly assigned to new groups, they immediately went to the learning incentive chart to check the color received the previous week by each of the other members in their new group. Motivation was high. Group pressure caused individual students who had not received high points the previous week to concentrate on improving their performance in the new group.

Group Roles and Division of Labor

If cooperative groups are to be successful, members must divide the work of the group and understand their different roles within the group. Therefore, consider specifying complementary and interconnected responsibilities that the group must undertake to accomplish a joint task. Johnson and Johnson (1990) define several roles, which may vary by the nature of the task, for example:

Leader. The group leader facilitates the work of the group. Leadership skills include *giving directions* (reviewing instructions, restating the goals of the group, calling attention to time limits, offering procedures on how to complete the task most effectively), *summarizing* aloud what has been read or discussed, and *generating responses* by going beyond the first answer or conclusion and producing a number of plausible answers from which to choose.

Reader. The reader in the group is responsible for reading the group's material aloud so that the group members can understand and remember it.

Writer-recorder. The writer-recorder records the responses of the group on paper, edits what the group has written, and makes sure the group members check this work for content accuracy and completeness.

Checker. The checker makes sure the group is on target by checking on what is being learned by the members. The checker, therefore, may ask individuals within the group to explain or summarize the material being discussed.

Encourager. The encourager watches to make sure that all the members in the group are participating and invites reluctant or silent members to contribute.

If students are to understand the roles and the responsibilities of each role, you will need to develop in them a knowledge and an awareness of each. Discuss each role, demonstrate appropriate behavior and responses, role-play with students, coach, and provide feedback during actual group discussions.

Planning Discussions

Many of the instructional strategies and alternatives in this book are necessarily tied to discussion of one kind or another. Discussion allows students to respond to text, build concepts, clarify meaning, explore issues, share perspectives, and refine thinking. But effective discussions don't run by themselves. For a discussion to be successful, a teacher has to be willing to take a risk or two.

Whenever you initiate a discussion, its outcome is bound to be uncertain, especially if its purpose is to help students think critically and creatively about what they have read. Often a teacher abandons discussion for the safety of recitation, in which the outcome is far more predictable. A text discussion, however, should be neither a quiz show nor, at the opposite end of the continuum, a bull session. Yet, when discussions aren't carefully planned, students often feel an aimlessness or become easily threatened by the teacher's questions. Both being quizzed about text material and simply shooting the bull are apt to close doors on active text learning.

Different purposes for text discussion lead to the use of different types of discussions by content area teachers. *Guided discussions* and *reflective discussions* provide varying degrees of structure for students to talk about text as they interact with one another (Wilen, Ishler, Hutchison, & Kindsvatter 2004).

Guided Discussion

If your aim is to develop concepts, clarify meaning, and promote understanding, the most appropriate discussion may be *informational*. The main objective of an informational discussion is to help students grapple with issues and understand important concepts. When the discussion task is information centered, teachers use a *guided discussion*.

In a guided discussion, a teacher provides a moderate amount of scaffolding as he or she directs students to think about what they have read through the use of questions and/or teacher-developed guide material. Because the emphasis is on content understanding and clarification, it is important to recognize the central role of the teacher in a guided discussion. Your responsibilities lie in asking questions, in probing student responses when clarifications are needed to extend thinking, in encouraging student questions, and in providing information to keep the discussion on course. The potential problem, however, is domination of the discussion. Alvermann, Dillon, and O'Brien (1988) caution that, when overused, this role "can result in a discussion that more nearly resembles a lecture and frequently may confuse students, especially if they have been encouraged to assume more active roles in discussion" (p. 31).

> **myeducationlab**
> Go to the Assignments and Activities section of Topic 7: "Planning for Instruction" in the MyEducationLab for your course and view the clip "Selecting Reading Materials" to see how one teacher guides student understanding.

A guided discussion can easily take a *reflective turn*. When teachers consciously shift gears from guided discussion to reflective discussion, their roles in the discussion shift.

For example, Creech and Hale (2006) explain that discussion can be an important component of an inquiry approach in science classrooms, as teachers model their own problem-solving processes for students: "I model talking aloud about my own thinking processes and encourage students to 'think aloud' about how they make sense of what they are doing. Through this instructional conversation, students learn the *text* includes labs, data, and their own work, and that *reading* is an active problem-solving process" (p. 23).

Reflective Discussion

A reflective discussion is different from a guided discussion in several respects. The purpose of a reflective discussion is to require students to engage in critical and creative thinking as they solve problems, clarify values, explore controversial issues, and form and defend positions. A reflective discussion, then, presumes that students have a solid understanding of the important concepts they are studying. Without a basic knowledge and understanding of the ideas or issues under discussion, students cannot support opinions, make judgments, or justify and defend positions.

The teacher's role during a reflective discussion is that of participant. As a participant, you become a group member, so that you can contribute to the discussion by sharing ideas and expressing your own opinions: "Teachers can guide students to greater independence in learning by modeling different ways of responding and reacting to issues, commenting on others' points of view, and applying critical reading strategies to difficult concepts in the textbooks" (Alvermann et al. 1988, p. 31).

Creating an Environment for Discussion

Discussion is one of the major process strategies in the content area classroom. Because many of the strategies in this text revolve around discussion of some sort, we offer several suggestions for creating an environment in which discussion takes place, whether in small groups or in the whole class.

Arrange the Classroom to Facilitate Discussion

Arrange the room so that students can see each other and huddle in conversational groupings when they need to share ideas. A good way to determine how functional a classroom is for discussion is to select a discussion strategy that does not require continuous question asking. For example, brainstorming involves a good mixture of whole-class and small-group discussion. Students need to alternate their attention between the chalkboard (where the teacher or another student is writing down all the ideas offered within a specified time) and their small groups (where they might categorize the ideas) and back to the front of the room (for comparison of group categories and summarization). If students are able to participate in the various stages of brainstorming with a minimum of chair moving or other time-consuming movements, to see the board, and to converse with other students without undue disruption, the room arrangements are adequate or conducive to discussion.

Encourage Listening

Encourage a climate in which everyone is expected to be a good listener, including the teacher. Let each student speaker know that you are listening. As the teacher begins to talk less, students will talk more. Intervene to determine why some students are not listening to each other or to praise those who are unusually good role models for others. Accept all responses of students positively.

Try starting out with very small groups of no more than two or three students. Again, rather than use questions, have students react to a teacher-read statement (e.g., "Political primaries are a waste of time and money"). In the beginning, students may feel constrained to produce answers to questions to satisfy the teacher. A statement, however, serves as a possible answer and invites reaction and justification. Once a statement is given, set a timer or call time by your watch at two-minute intervals. During each interval, one student in the group may agree or disagree *without interruption*. After each group member has an opportunity to respond, the group summarizes all dialogue, and one person presents this summary to the class (Gold & Yellin 1982, pp. 550–552).

Establish a Goal for Discussion

Establish the meaning of the topic and the goal of the discussion: "Why are we talking about railroad routes and how do they relate to our unit on the Civil War?" Also, explain directions explicitly, and don't assume that students will know what to do. Many of the content area reading strategies in this book involve some group discussion. Frequently, strategies progress from independent, written responses to sharing, to comparing those responses in small groups, and then to pooling small-group reactions in a whole-class discussion. Without the guidance of a teacher who is aware of this process, group discussion tends to disintegrate.

Focus the Discussion

Keep the focus of the discussion on the central topic or core question or problem to be solved. Teachers may begin discussions by asking a question about a perplexing situation or by establishing a problem to be solved. From time to time, it may be necessary to refocus attention on the topic by piggybacking on comments made by particular students: "Terry brought out an excellent point about the Underground Railroad in northern Ohio. Does anyone else want to talk about this?" During small-group discussions, one tactic that keeps groups on task is reminding them of the amount of time remaining in the discussion.

Keeping the focus is one purpose for which teachers may legitimately question to clarify the topic. They may also want to make sure that they understood a particular student's comment: "Excuse me, would you repeat that?" Often, keeping the discussion focused will prevent the class from straying away from the task.

Avoid Squelching Discussion

Give students enough think time to reflect on possible answers before calling on someone or rephrasing your question. Moreover, try to avoid answering your own question. (One way to prevent yourself from doing this is to resist having a preset or "correct" answer in your own mind when you ask a question beyond a literal level of comprehension.) Do not interrupt students' responses or permit others to interrupt students' responses. Do, however, take a minute or two for you or a student to summarize and bring closure to a group discussion just as you would in any instructional strategy.

Both guided and reflective discussions may be conducted with the whole class or in small groups. A small-group discussion, whether guided or reflective, places the responsibility for learning squarely on students' shoulders. Because of the potential value of collaborative student interactions, we underscore the invaluable contribution of small-group discussions. Small-group learning opportunities help learners contribute ideas to a discussion and take chances in the process. The students can try out ideas without worrying about being wrong or sounding dumb—a fear that often accompanies risk taking in a whole-class situation.

LOOKING BACK LOOKING FORWARD

Planning is essential for content literacy and learning. It helps teachers to think through the goals, activities, texts, and strategies necessary to support students' learning with text. For example, the planning that goes into explicit strategy instruction helps teachers model and show students how to use literacy strategies to learn. Components of an explicit strategy instructional framework include awareness and explanation, modeling and demonstration, guided practice, and application.

In addition, B–D–A instructional frameworks help teachers to plan instructional activities at critical periods within the reading and discussion of a text that has been assigned to the whole class. This particular lesson structure focuses on what students do *b*efore, *d*uring, and *a*fter reading to facilitate text comprehension. A unit of study, however, helps teachers to organize instructional activities around inquiry projects and multiple texts. Unit planning gives the teacher much more latitude to coordinate resource materials and activities. Unit activities can be organized around the whole class, small groups, or individuals. An effective content classroom, organized around text lessons and units of study, thrives on collaborative interactions between teacher and students and among students and other students. These interactions are grounded in the principles of small-group processes, cooperative learning, and discussion.

In the next chapter, our emphasis turns to kindling student interest in text assignments and preparing them to think positively about what they will read. The importance of the role of prereading preparation in learning from text has often been neglected or underestimated in the content area classroom. Yet prereading activity is in many ways as important to the text learner as warm-up preparation is to the athlete. Let's find out why.

Minds On

1. You have probably seen some variation of the bumper sticker, "If you can read this, thank a teacher." In a small group, sitting in a circle, discuss how you feel about seeing this sticker and what you think it means. Select one member of your group to act as an observer, and use the questions that follow to record group interactions. Allow ten to fifteen minutes for discussion, and then ask the observer to share her or his list of questions and answers with the group.

   Observer's questions:

   a. Who raised questions during group discussion?
   b. Could most of the questions be answered yes or no, true or false?
   c. Who answered the questions?
   d. Who decided who would answer and when they would answer?
   e. Who kept the group on task?
   f. Did your seating arrangement change before or after the discussion?

   As a group, discuss the following:

   a. Did the discussion process described by the observer involve the sharing of ideas by group members with no one person asking or answering all the questions?
   b. What were the advantages and disadvantages of having the discussion progress without the rigid protocol of one person deciding who would answer and when?
   c. How would you contrast the effect of the seating in rows used in lecture question-and-answer sessions with the effect of the circle seating used in this discussion?

2. Join together with four or five other individuals who either teach or are planning to teach at approximately the same grade level. Imagine that you have just attended a cooperative learning workshop and you plan to incorporate what you learned into your teaching. What do you consider the single best cooperative activity for your grade level and why? Discuss how you would implement this approach with a selected topic. List any problems you expect might arise, and explain how you would solve them.

3. Recognizing that students with different abilities and interests learn differently, to what extent should a teacher attempt to organize a class so that all the students in the class will learn the same concepts and information? Would your answer be the same for a third-grade science class and a high school advanced physics class? What general guidelines can you develop as a group to help a new teacher organize learning to balance course content with individual differences? Also, what type of physical classroom design do you think would best facilitate your philosophy?

Hands On

1. Try the following experiment. Roll a standard 8½-by-11-inch sheet of paper into a tube 11 inches long and approximately 1 inch in diameter. Then hold the tube in your left hand and, keeping both eyes open, look through the tube with your left eye. Next, place your right hand, palm toward your face, against the side of the tube approximately half the distance

from your eye to the end of the tube. Angle the tube slightly so that the far end of the tube is behind your palm, and a hole should appear in your hand.

With a small group or individually, brainstorm how you might use this experiment as a prereading activity for a science lesson on the eye.

2. Team up with two other individuals. Designate one member of your group "observer," one "reader," and one "artist." The observer's task will be to make a written record of the actions of the reader and the artist. The artist will draw a triangle described by the reader in the following instructions:

    Draw a triangle so that one side is twice as long as one of the other two. Use one of the small sides as the base, and construct the triangle so that the longest side faces the left side of the paper. Design your triangle so that the longest side is three inches long. Make it exactly three inches if you have a ruler available, or estimate the length if you do not. Finally, assign the letters *a*, *b*, and *c* to each side of the triangle, designating the longest side as *c*.

    After the reader and the artist have completed the drawing, review the notes by the observer, and develop a written record of the intentions or reasons for each action previously recorded. For example, if the observer recorded that the reader turned back to reread the instructions, you might explain that the artist had forgotten a fact that he or she needed to understand.

    Finally, compare observations, make a class list of the learning strategies used by each group, and discuss which are successful approaches for a number of people. From this activity, what conclusions can you draw about the role of metacognition in reading to learn?

3. Bring your favorite book, magazine, poem, or drama to class. Develop a prereading activity that would provide the rationale for using this material, and introduce this piece. (This activity can be done in small groups of five or six or with the entire class.)

    Before your presentation, plan a series of entry questions and comments to match what you think others will say in response. Also, because you are introducing this material with a purpose in mind, the discussion should lead your small group to a particular point from which the next activity might begin.

    Be prepared to reach that departure point by a number of alternate routes. Prereading activities and discussions often remain detached from the reading/content activity, so that a novice is tempted to say, "That's enough talking. Let's get to the real lesson." The discussion or activity must be integral to the "real" lesson.

Here is the complete passage from the exercise at the conclusion of Chapter 1:

> Besides, Sir, we shall not fight our battles alone. There is a just God, who presides over the destinies of nations, who will raise up friends to fight our battles for us. The battle, Sir, is not to the strong alone: it is to the vigilant, the active, the brave. Besides, Sir, we have no election. If we were base enough to desire it, it is now too late to retire from the contest.
>
> There is no retreat, but in submission or slavery. Our chains are forged. Their clanking may be heard on the plains of Boston! The war is inevitable—and let it come—I repeat, Sir, let it come! It is in vain, Sir, to extenuate the matter. Gentlemen may cry, "Peace! Peace!" But there is no peace. The war has actually begun!
>
> The next gale that sweeps from the North will bring to our ears the clash of resounding arms! Our brethren are already in the field! Why stand we here idle? What is it that the Gentlemen wish? What would they have? Is life so dear, or peace too sweet, as to be purchased at the price of chains and slavery? Forbid it, Almighty God! I know not what course others may take, but as for me, give me liberty or give me death!

*e*RESOURCES

- Access useful ideas for content literacy lesson plans in your subject area by visiting the following sites: the Educator's Reference Desk **(www.eduref.org)**, the Ohio Resource Center **(www.ohiorc.org)**, and the Content Literacy Information Consortium (CLIC) **(http://curry.edschool.virginia.edu/go/clic)**.
- Access useful plans for inquiry projects and cooperative learning in your subject area by exploring Lesson Planet **(www.lessonplanet.com/directory/Education/Teacher_Resources/Lesson_Plans)** and Education World **(www.education-world.com)**.
- Explore ready-made plans for integrating electronic texts into units by visiting the Web Toolboxes **(www.ed.sc.edu/caw/toolbox.html)**.

CHAPTER 6

*That is what learning is.
You suddenly understand
something you've understood
all your life, but in a new way.*

—Doris Lessing

Activating Prior Knowledge and Interest

ORGANIZING PRINCIPLE

Activating prior knowledge and generating interest create an instructional context in which students will read with purpose and anticipation.

Learning happens. Most people outside the fields of cognitive psychology and education probably give little thought to how it happens or why it happens. In the quote that opens this chapter, Doris Lessing, recipient of the 2007 Nobel Prize for literature, provides one of the best commonsense definitions of learning that we have run across. As she suggests, learning is rooted in what we already know. Cognition—the process of knowing—is an active process that takes place in the brain. From a content literacy perspective, the essence of cognitive readiness is to prepare students to make connections between what they know and what they will learn. It is impossible to learn without prior knowledge.

Getting students cognitively ready to learn with text is no easy task. Teachers occasionally are perplexed by the behaviors of students who are capable of acquiring content through lecture and discussion but appear neither *ready* nor *willing* to read to learn. Readiness is a state of mind, a mental preparation for learning, a psychological predisposition. But readiness also entails an emotional stake in the

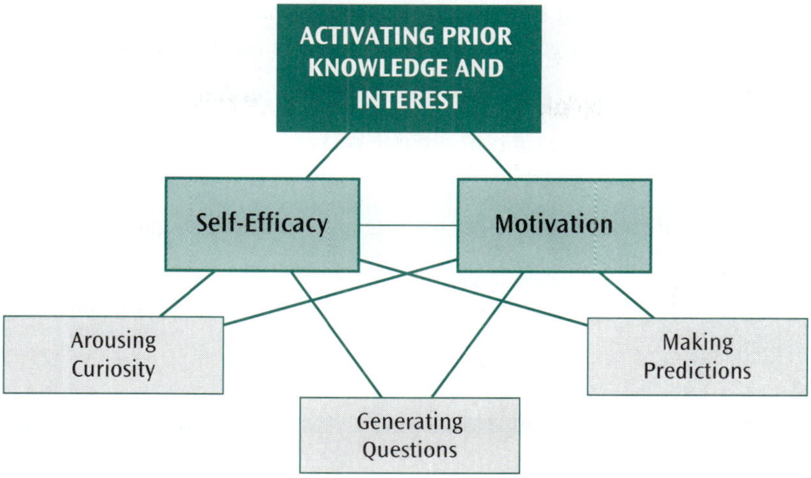

ideas and concepts under scrutiny and a willingness on the part of the students to *want* to engage in learning. Most students, we believe, would like to use reading to learn but don't believe that they have much chance of success.

Students *will* want to read when they have developed a sense of confidence in their ability to use reading to learn. Confident readers connect what they already know to what they are learning. They generate interest in the reading task at hand, even when the text is inherently dry or difficult. Preparing students to think purposefully about what they will read is implicit in the organizing principle for this chapter: **Activating prior knowledge and generating interest create an instructional context in which students will read with purpose and anticipation.**

FRAME OF MIND

1. Why do prereading strategies that activate prior knowledge and raise interest in the subject prepare students to approach text reading in a critical frame of mind?
2. How can meaningful learning be achieved with content area reading?
3. What are the relationships among curiosity arousal, conceptual conflict, and motivation?
4. How and why does a prediction strategy such as use of an anticipation guide facilitate reading comprehension?
5. What is the value of student-generated questions, and how might teachers help students ask questions as they read?

"Why can't we just read like in other classes? Why do we always have to think about what we read?" complained an irate high school junior in his history class. The teacher, who uses and adapts many of the instructional strategies suggested in this book, was momentarily caught off guard by the student's questions. But rather than dismiss them as the rantings of a malcontent, he turned the student's questions into a positive event by initiating a brief discussion about what it means and what it takes "to read like an historian."

The discussion was aimed at building and reinforcing students' concepts of reading as an active search for meaning—a process which, from a historian's perspective, involves detecting bias, analyzing and verifying information, inferring cause and effect, and thinking critically about ideas presented in text. Much of what transpired during the discussion boiled down to this: Active readers think *about* text, think *with* text, and think *through* text. "Historians," the teacher explained with more than a little enthusiasm, "actively search for meaning in everything they read. And that's what I expect from each of you."

Although the classroom incident just described is one of countless little dramas that occur daily in the context of teaching, for us it typifies two of the most powerful realities of content literacy: first, that many students are passive participants when it comes to reading to learn; and second, that caring and knowledgeable teachers can make a difference in the way students approach reading and learn with texts.

For many passive readers, learning with text remains a mysterious process. For most teachers, reading just happens, particularly when there is a strong purpose or a need to read in the first place. However, a great deal of uncertainty pervades reading for many students. The reading process remains a mystery to students who believe they have limited control over their chances of success with a reading assignment.

You can do a great deal to reduce the lack of control and the uncertainty that students bring to text learning situations. You can take the mystery out of learning with texts by generating students' interest in what they are reading, convincing them that they know more about the subject under study than they think they do, helping them actively connect what they do know to the content of the text, and making them aware of the strategies they need in order to construct meaning.

The challenge content area teachers face with reading to learn is not necessarily related to students' inability to handle the conceptual demands of academic texts. What students can do and what they choose to do are related but different instructional matters. Therefore, you need to create conditions that not only allow students to read effectively but also motivate them to want to read purposefully and meaningfully. ■

Self-Efficacy and Motivation

When students engage in content literacy activities, some feel confident in their ability to achieve success with reading and writing tasks. Others feel unsure and uncertain. Confident learners exhibit a high level of *self-efficacy* in content literacy situations; unsure learners, a low level. Self-efficacy refers to an "I can" belief in self that leads to a sense of competence. Bandura (1986) explains that self-efficacy refers to "people's judgment of their abilities to organize and execute courses of action required to attain designated types of performance" (p. 391). Self-efficacy is not concerned with the skills and strategies students bring to content literacy situations, but rather it focuses on students' estimations of their ability to apply whatever skills and strategies they bring to literacy learning. As Alvermann (2001) explains, self-efficacy contributes to the development of students' literacy identities. Before they can become lifelong readers, students must first view themselves as competent and capable readers.

RESPONSE JOURNAL

Think about your own self-efficacy as a learner. In which subject, if any, in your academic background have you judged yourself unable to succeed? How has low self-efficacy in the subject affected academic performance?

Recently, one of this textbook's authors published an article in *Educational Leadership* describing a crisis in self-confidence that nearly sabotaged his doctoral studies:

> Soon into the doctoral program, however, I found myself struggling with learning—and doubting myself—in ways that my students did. Although I could read a best-selling novel with ease . . . , I found myself taking similar amounts of time to read chapter assignments from my statistics and research methods textbooks—only to come up short in understanding what I had read. I soon eschewed reading these "incomprehensible" texts altogether in favor of taking copious notes and participating in study groups. During my first year of doctoral study, I often wondered why I had ever left the classroom. Was I out of my league? Not as smart or as wise as my fellow doctoral students. . . . On more than one occasion I thought about quitting and returning to classroom teaching where I had been successful. To encourage me to "stay with it," my wife, Jo Anne, purchased an "inspirational" poster and hung it prominently in my study area. The poster depicted several seagulls flying effortlessly across the sea with a caption from the ancient Roman poet Virgil, "They can because they think they can." Whenever I felt like caving into the pressures of doctoral study, I looked to the poster for confidence and, yes, a little bit of inspiration. (Vacca 2006, p. 56)

RTI *for Struggling Adolescent Learners* BOX 6.1

Strategy Interventions for Active Engagement and Comprehension

As we strongly suggest in all chapters related to reading comprehension, adolescents who struggle with learning must engage with texts that are appealing and appropriate. If students are not interacting with texts they find relevant, it can be difficult for teachers to determine whether low comprehension is related to a reading disability or to a simple lack of engagement with the text. RTI directs teachers and support staff to use appropriate assessments and strategy interventions that will more accurately reflect students' abilities. Middle and high school students, for example, need access to a variety of texts that range in both difficulty and content, including materials that they can and want to read. By providing this access, each student will have the opportunity to engage effectively with text and progress toward his or her learning goals.

Including an element of choice in content area reading practices is one way of ensuring that struggling readers have opportunities to comprehend texts suitable to their academic and intervention goals (NCTE 2006). If students can choose from a range of age- and ability-appropriate materials, including informational texts, teachers can capitalize on students' interests and strengths. When comprehension-related strategy interventions offer students a choice of materials that are appealing and pertinent to inquiry across the curriculum, struggling readers are more engaged. Allowing a reasonable level of autonomy can give struggling adolescent readers a sense of control over their own education, leading to higher motivation to continue reading.

The cognitive demands placed on a reader to comprehend text vary from subject matter to subject matter. Although Rich Vacca lacked the confidence to read statistical text at the beginning of his doctoral program, over time he developed comprehension strategies for reading these types of texts—and also confidence in his ability to do so. Several years after publishing the article, he received an e-mail from a cyber stranger with the subject line: "Thank you Professor Vacca." The letter, written by Jacquinne Reynolds, an eighth-grade teacher, remains one of the most rewarding surprises of Rich's career as an educator (see Box 6.2).

Self-efficacy and motivation are interrelated concepts. If students believe, for example, that they have a good chance to succeed at a reading task, they are likely to exhibit a willingness to engage in reading and to complete the task. Guthrie and Wigfield's (2000) model of reading engagement calls for instruction that underscores the importance of students' motivation in addition to their growth in conceptual knowledge, their use of comprehension strategies, and their social interaction in the classroom. The National Institute for Literacy (2007) explains that students who are motivated readers share several characteristics: They perceive that they have some level of control over their reading; they apply appropriate strategies in order to make complex reading tasks more manageable; and they display a high level of engagement in their reading experiences.

> **myeducationlab**
> Go to the Assignments and Activities section of Topic 3: "Motivation" in the MyEducationLab for your course and complete the activity "Engagement" and see educators demonstrate steps that create motivation.

By the time they enter middle school, students' motivation to read—particularly motivation that comes from their own authentic interests

BOX 6.2

E-mail from Jacquinne Reynolds

Dear Professor Vacca,

I just finished reading your article published in *Education Leadership,* Vol. 63, No. 5, 2006. You have no idea how much this article has inspired me. I am four months into a doctoral program and just this week I had thoughts of quitting. The reason is because I am having difficulty reading and understanding technical articles and finishing an assignment required next week. I have been doubting myself and questioning whether or not I should be in this program.

After reading your article I began to understand, as you put it, how self-efficacy and text comprehension go together. I have never had to read such in-depth literature before. Like you I love to read fiction. I can knock-out a novel or two in a few days, reading non-stop. However, reading the articles assigned each week for this class has been so difficult. It has been a real struggle to keep up with the reading assignments. I agree with your statement: "Whether or not a reader feels confident that he or she has the skills to handle a given reading situation makes a difference in that reader's approach." I have been doubting my ability to read and understand the articles I had to find to write a paper, and I have been deliberately stalling rather than writing my paper.

Reading your article has restored my confidence. If someone of your stature had these feelings and completed his course of study, what I am feeling is only human and I can succeed, too. I just wanted to write to you and say "thank you." Incidentally, my area of study is dealing with Literacy and African American Males in Urban School Districts. I teach eighth grade social studies in a small urban school district outside Flint, MI. I have young male students in all of my classes that are reading at third or fourth grade level. I will definitely consider using some of the strategies you suggested in this article.

Sincerely,

Jacquinne Reynolds

and desires to explore topics through reading—often declines. For struggling readers in particular, this decline in motivation is often compounded by the assessment and grouping practices common in middle and secondary schools. Some researchers such as Oldfather and Dahl (1994) suggest that part of this decline in students' motivation may be attributed to the limited emphasis middle and secondary teachers typically place on self-expression and personal response to reading. By fostering a learning environment that is response-centered, teachers can provide students with critical opportunities to explore texts, construct meaning, and make personal connections to content area topics.

Students' motivation for reading and learning with texts increases when they perceive that text is relevant to their own lives and when they believe that they are capable of generating credible responses to their reading of the text (Knickerbocker & Rycik 2002).

Bruner (1970, 1990), a pioneer in the field of cognitive psychology, suggested that the mind doesn't work apart from feeling and commitment. Learners make meaning when they exhibit an "inherent passion" for what is to be learned. How people construct meaning depends on their beliefs, mental states, intentions, desires, and commitments. Likewise, Eisner (1991) calls on us to celebrate thinking in schools by reminding us that brains may be born, but minds are made. Schools do not pay enough attention to students' curiosity and imagination. As a result, students disengage from active participation in the academic life of the classroom because there is little satisfaction to be gained from it. Unless students receive satisfaction from schoolwork, Eisner argues, there is little reason or motive to continue to pursue learning: "Thinking . . . should be prized not only because it leads to attractive destinations but because the journey itself is satisfying" (p. 40).

Given the current policy emphasis on accountability and adequate yearly progress as measured by high-stakes assessments (discussed in Chapter 4), teachers often find themselves torn between seeking to increase students' interest in content area subjects by supporting their motivation to learn and simply trying to fulfill externally imposed and, even arbitrary, achievement targets.

Nevertheless, effective teachers understand the importance of taking the time to make their subject areas relevant to students. In exploring matters of the mind, cognitive activity cannot be divorced from emotional involvement. Meaningful learning with texts occurs when students reap satisfaction from texts and a sense of accomplishment from reading. As Ivey and Fisher (2005) explain, "Teachers who understand their students' backgrounds, prior knowledge, interests, and motivations are much more likely to make the connections that adolescents crave" (p. 8).

Teachers can support students' motivation for reading by setting clear goals and expectations for reading, providing students with access to a variety of reading materials, and, when possible, allowing students a level of choice in selecting the texts they read (Brozo & Flyny 2007; Guthrie & Davis 2003). Teachers can also give students opportunities to interact with one another through shared reading experiences, and they can guide students in learning how to evaluating their own understanding of a text (Wigfield 2004; Reed, Schallert, Beth, & Woodruff 2004).

Two of the most appropriate questions that students can ask about a text are "What do I need to know?" and "How well do I already know it?" "What do I need to know?" prompts readers to activate their prior knowledge to make predictions and set purposes. It gets them thinking positively about what they are going to read. "How well do I already know it?" helps readers search their experience and knowledge to give support to tentative predictions and to help make plans for reading.

As simple as these two questions may seem on the surface, maturing readers rarely *know enough* about the reading process to ask them. "What do I need to know?" and "How well do I already know it?" require *metacognitive awareness* on the part of the learners. However, these two questions, when consciously raised and reflected on, put students on the road to regulating and monitoring their own reading behavior. It is never too early (or too late) to begin showing students how to set purposes by raising questions about the text.

In Chapter 1, we underscored the important role that prior knowledge plays in meaningful learning, so we won't belabor the point here, other than to reaffirm that prior knowledge activation is inescapably bound to one's purpose for reading and learning. As students ready themselves to learn with texts, they need to approach upcoming material in a critical frame of mind. Instructional scaffolding should make readers receptive to meaningful learning by creating a reference point for connecting the given (what one knows) with the new (the material to be learned). A frame of reference signals the connections students must make between the given and the new. They need to recognize how new material fits into the conceptual frameworks they already have. In Box 6.3, Aaron, an eighth-grade history teacher, uses an "ice cream sundae" strategy to activate his students' knowledge for and interest in the concept *assembly line*.

Conceptual conflicts are the key to creating motivational conditions in the classroom (Berlyne 1965). Should students be presented with situations that take the form of puzzlement, doubt, surprise, perplexity, contradiction, or ambiguity, they will be motivated to seek resolution. Why? The need within the learner is to resolve the conflict. As a result, the search for knowledge becomes a driving motivational force. When a question begins to gnaw at a learner, searching behavior is stimulated; learning occurs as the conceptual conflict resolves itself.

Arousing Curiosity

Arousing curiosity and activating prior knowledge are closely related instructional activities. Curiosity arousal gives students the chance to consider what they know already about the material to be read. Through your guidance, they are encouraged to make connections and to relate their knowledge to the text assignment. And further, they will recognize that there are problems—conceptual conflicts—to be resolved through reading. Arousing curiosity helps students raise questions that they can answer only by giving thought to what they read.

> **myeducationlab**
>
> Go to the Building Teaching Skills and Dispositions section of Topic 3: "Motivation" in the MyEducationLab for your course. As you complete the activity, note the strategies suggested for motivating students in all content areas.

Creating Story Impressions

Using story impressions is an instructional strategy that arouses curiosity and allows students to anticipate story content. Although teachers use story impressions with narrative text, it may also be used to create "text impressions" in content areas other than English language arts.

> **RESPONSE JOURNAL**
>
> How might you adapt story impressions to a content area other than English or history?

The story impressions strategy uses clue words associated with the setting, characters, and events in the story to help readers write their own versions of the story prior to reading. McGinley and Denner (1987), originators of the strategy, describe it this way: "Story impressions get readers to predict the events of the story that will be read, by providing them with fragments of the actual content. After reading the set of clues, the students are

Voices from the Classroom

BOX 6.3

Aaron

Eighth-Grade U.S. History Teacher

CHALLENGE

One of the great advancements during the Industrial Revolution was the assembly line. The concept of the assembly line is very abstract for most eighth-grade students to grasp. Many of these students have never been inside a factory and have no idea about how products are mass produced. I believe in actively building background knowledge and engaging students in the learning process. Doing so enables students to draw upon their own experiences to grasp a deeper understanding of the concepts being presented. Hands-on strategies are an excellent method for building and activating background knowledge that can help to make an abstract concept more concrete, and therefore, more understandable.

STRATEGY

To make the concept of assembly line production engaging and concrete, we assemble hot fudge sundaes together in class. Almost all of my students have had experience making and, of course, eating hot fudge sundaes. I try to connect these experiences to an in-class activity that will help them to understand how an assembly line works. As the students make the hot fudge sundaes, I interweave the concepts of the assembly line by making connections with the construction of their sundaes. First, I have each student write down the steps required to make a hot fudge sundae. Afterward, those steps are synthesized and the students discover that it takes about twenty to thirty steps to make a sundae, depending on the ingredients used. At this point, we discuss the importance of each identified step on an assembly line and how each step is dependent on the previous step.

In order to understand the concept of mass production, I choose one student to make an ice cream sundae following the specific steps the class identified. It usually takes the student between three to five minutes to make the sundae. Realizing it takes too long for one person to make the entire sundae, if each student in the class would like a sundae, we need to speed up the process. Each student in the class is assigned a specific step in the process of producing an ice cream sundae. Using this assembly line procedure, the students are able to produce an ice cream sundae in about eleven seconds. This illustrates to the students the efficiency of the assembly line in producing products quickly. However, sometimes too many goods are produced and that can lead to a glut of goods on the market, causing the price to fall because of too much supply.

Other unit concepts that I tie in with the assembly line includes the concept that this method of production provided jobs for many immigrants in the early 1900s who could not speak or read English. Reading and writing the language was not typically a necessary skill for assembly line workers of that era. Each worker was responsible for one specific step in the assembly process. Also, as worker safety became an increasing concern, legislation was passed to protect the workers and the government agency OSHA was formed. I illustrate the issue of worker safety by highlighting the messes students made as they assembled their sundaes. What if the fudge or whipped cream that had spilled all over the tables or on the students' hands had been battery acid or some other harmful chemical?

REFLECTION

Connecting students' knowledge of a familiar concept—the hot fudge sundae—to the new concept of an assembly line gives them a tangible representation of the new concept being presented. This engages students in making connections that they would not be able to make through just reading the textbook or listening to class lectures. Plus the students (and, of course, their teacher) get the added benefit of eating an ice cream sundae as part of the demonstration.

asked to render them comprehensible by using them to compose a story of their own in advance of reading the actual tale" (p. 249).

Fragments from the story, in the form of clue words and phrases, enable readers to form an overall impression of how the characters and events interact in the story. The clue words are selected directly from the story and are sequenced with arrows or lines to form a descriptive chain. The chain of clue words triggers impressions about the story. Students then write a "story prediction" that anticipates the events in the story.

The story impression example in Figure 6.1 was developed in preparation for students' reading of Jonathan Swift's classic, *Gulliver's Travels*. Based on the terms listed in the story chain, the students generated their prediction.

As McGinley and Denner (1987) explain, "The object, of course, is not for the student to guess the details or the exact relations among the events and characters of the story, but to simply compare his or her own story guess to the author's actual account" (p. 250). Box 6.4 (p. 176) outlines the steps to follow in the story impression strategy.

Notice in Figure 6.2 (p. 177) how a U.S. history teacher adapted story impressions to have students predict events leading up to the Boston Tea Party. In the space provided for a "text prediction," try writing what you think the text will be about. Compare your prediction with the one appearing on page 193.

CLASSROOM ARTIFACT **FIGURE 6.1** **Story Impression for *Gulliver's Travels***

Story Chain	Story Prediction
shipwrecked little people politics corruption giant science useless immortal talking horses insane morals	After being shipwrecked with a bunch of little people, a traveler, whose interest in politics was obvious but whose past was filled with corruption, decided to live off his giant bank account. He believed that science was useless and had failed him. Knowing he wasn't immortal, he decided to survive his ordeal by talking to sea horses, making people believe that he was insane. That way, he thought, they might not pay attention to his questionable morals.

Evidence-Based Best Practices **BOX 6.4**

Story Impressions

McGinley and Denner (1987) suggest the following steps to introduce story impressions to the class for the first time:

1. *Introduce the strategy.* Say to the students, "Today we're going to make up what we think this story *could* be about."
2. *Use large newsprint, a transparency, or interactive whiteboard to show students the story chain.* (See the left side of Figure 6.1 for an example.) Say, "Here are some clues about the story we're going to read." Explain that the students will use the clues to write their own version of the story and that after reading, they will compare what they wrote with the actual story.
3. *Read the clues together, and explain how the arrows link one clue to another in a logical order.* Then brainstorm story ideas that connect all of the clues in the order that they are presented, saying, "What do we think this story could be about?"
4. *Demonstrate how to write a story guess.* Use the ideas generated to write a class-composed story that links all of the clues. Use newsprint, the whiteboard, or a transparency for this purpose. Read the story prediction aloud with the students.
5. *Invite the students to read the actual story silently, or initiate a shared reading experience.* Afterward, discuss how the class-composed version is similar to and different from the author's story.
6. *For subsequent stories, use story impressions to have students write individual story predictions.* Or have them work in cooperative teams to write a group-composed story guess.

Establishing Problematic Perspectives

Creating problems to be solved or perspectives from which readers approach text material provides an imaginative entry into a text selection. For example, the teacher's role in creating problematic perspectives is (1) providing the time to discuss the problem, raising questions, and seeking possible solutions before reading and then (2) assigning the reading material that will help lead to resolution and conceptual development.

A social studies teacher and her students were exploring the development of early American settlements in a unit on colonial life. She presented the problem situation to her students as shown in Figure 6.3. The series of questions promoted an interest-filled discussion, putting students in a situation in which they had to rely on prior knowledge for responses.

Asking the students in the social studies class to approach reading by imagining that they were early European settlers placed them in a particular role. With the role came a perspective. Creating such a perspective has its underpinnings in a schema-theoretical view of the reading process.

RESPONSE JOURNAL
Create a problematic perspective on some topic of study in your content area.

One of the early studies of the Center for the Study of Reading at the University of Illinois pointed to the powerful role of perspective in comprehending text (Pichert & Anderson 1977). The researchers

FIGURE 6.2 Chain of Events Leading to the Boston Tea Party

Story Chain	Text Prediction
French and Indian War ↓ Stamp Act ↓ rights ↓ took away ↓ Parliament ↓ petitions ↓ repeal ↓ Sons of Liberty ↓ Townshend Acts ↓ boycott ↓ repeal ↓ tea tax ↓ Mohawk Indians ↓ Boston Tea Party	

FIGURE 6.3 A Problem Situation in a U.S. History Class

The time is 1680 and the place is Massachusetts. Imagine that you are early European settlers. You will want to try to think as you believe they may have thought and act as they might have acted. You and your group have petitioned the Great and General Court to be allowed to form a new town. After checking to make sure you are of good character and the land is fertile and can be defended, the court says yes. It grants you a five-mile-square plot of land. As proprietors of this land, you must plan a town. What buildings would you put in first? Second? Third? Later? Why? How would you divide the land among the many people who want to live there? Why? As proprietors, would you treat yourselves differently from the others? Why? How would you run the government?

showed just how important the reader's perspective can be. Two groups of readers were asked to read a passage about a house from one of two perspectives: a burglar or a house buyer. When readers who held the perspective of a house burglar read the story about going through the house, they recalled different information from those readers who approached the story from the perspective of a house buyer.

Creating a perspective (a role) for the student is one way to get into reading. Students in these roles find themselves solving problems that force them to use their knowledge and experience. In Figure 6.4, a high school teacher created a perspective for students before assigning a reading selection from an auto mechanics manual.

In preparation for reading the short story "Alas Babylon," an English teacher set up a perspective in which students' curiosity was aroused and their expectations of the story raised:

> The year is 2015. We are on the verge of a nuclear disaster. Through inside sources, you hear that the attack will occur within five days. What preparations will you consider making before the nuclear attack occurs?

The class considered the orienting question. After some discussion, the teacher initiated the activity in Figure 6.5. The students formed small groups, and each group was directed to come to a consensus on the twelve activities they would choose. Those items were chosen from the list in Figure 6.5.

From the small-group discussions came the recognition that the values, beliefs, and attitudes readers bring to a text shape their perspective as much as their background knowledge of a topic. For this reason, we suggest that when building the motivation for a text to be read, take into account, where appropriate, an examination of values, attitudes, and controversial issues related to the subject matter.

FIGURE 6.4 **Creating a Perspective in an Auto Mechanics Class**

You are the only mechanic on duty when a four-wheel-drive truck with a V-8 engine pulls in for repair. The truck has high mileage, and it appears that the problem may be a worn clutch disk. What tools do you think you will need? What procedures would you follow? Put your answers to these questions under the two following headings.

Tools Needed	Procedures
______________	______________________________
______________	______________________________
______________	______________________________
______________	______________________________
______________	______________________________

FIGURE 6.5 **Creating a Perspective in an English Class**

Assuming that your town and house will not be destroyed by the bomb and that you have enough time to prepare for the attack, which twelve activities from the following list will you choose?

________ 1. Buy a gun and ammunition to protect against looters.

________ 2. Cash in all CDs and take all the money out of your checking and savings accounts.

________ 3. Build a fireplace in your house.

________ 4. Buy firewood and charcoal.

________ 5. Buy extra tanks of gasoline and fill up your car.

________ 6. Purchase antibiotics and other medicines.

________ 7. Dig a latrine.

________ 8. Buy lumber, nails, and various other supplies.

________ 9. Plant fruit trees.

________ 10. Notify all your friends and relatives of the coming nuclear attack.

________ 11. Invest in books on canning and making candles and soap.

________ 12. Buy a few head of livestock from a farmer.

________ 13. Buy fishing equipment and a boat.

________ 14. Buy seeds of several different kinds of vegetables for a garden.

________ 15. Make friends with a farmer who has a horse and wagon.

________ 16. Shop at antique stores for kerosene lamps and large cooking pots.

________ 17. Buy a safe in which to hide your money.

________ 18. Buy foodstuffs.

Guided Imagery

Students' ability to visualize what they are reading is an important component for developing comprehension. Guided imagery allows students to explore concepts visually. Samples (1977) recommends guided imagery, among other things, as a means of

- Building an experience base for inquiry, discussion, and group work;
- Exploring and stretching concepts;
- Solving and clarifying problems;
- Exploring history and the future; and
- Exploring other lands and worlds.

Read the example in Figure 6.6; then close your eyes and do what it says.

FIGURE 6.6 A Guided Imagery Illustration

Close your eyes . . . tell all your muscles to relax. You are entering the space shuttle ten minutes before takeoff. Soon you feel it lift off . . . you look over at your companions and check their reactions. Now you are ready to take a reading of the instrument panel. As you relay the information to ground control, it is eleven minutes into the flight . . . you settle back into your chair and tell your fellow astronauts about your thoughts . . . about what you hope to see when the vehicle lands . . . about what you might touch and hear as you explore your destination. Finally, you drift off to sleep . . . picturing yourself returning to earth . . . seeing once again your friends and relations. You are back where you started . . . tell your muscles to move . . . open your eyes.

You may wish to have students discuss their "trips," which, of course, should parallel in some way the content of the reading selection to be assigned. In the classroom where this example was devised, students in a literature class participated in the imagery discussion before reading a short story on space travel. Discussion questions included, "How did you feel just before entering the space capsule? What were the reactions of your companions? Where did your exploration take you? Were there things that surprised you on the trip? Colors? Sounds?"

RESPONSE JOURNAL

Create a guided imagery scenario on a topic of study in your content area.

Some teachers will find themselves uncomfortable using guided imagery as an instructional strategy; others will not. However, it gives you an additional instructional option that will help students connect, in this case, what they "see" in their mind's eye to what they will read.

Content area teachers assess students' prior knowledge of and interest in a topic to be studied through authentic instructional practices. Box 6.5 describes an instructional strategy, PreP, designed by Langer (1981) to assess students' prior knowledge within an instructional context.

Making Predictions

Prediction strategies activate thought about the content before reading. Students must rely on what they know through previous study and experience to make educated guesses about the material to be read.

Why an educated guess? Smith (1988) defines predicting as the prior elimination of unlikely alternatives. He suggests:

> Readers do not normally attend to print with their minds blank, with no prior purpose and with no expectation of what they might find in the text. . . . The way readers look for meaning is not to consider all possibilities, nor to make reckless guesses about just one, but rather to predict within the most likely range of alternatives. . . . Readers can derive meaning from text because they bring expectations about meaning to text. (p. 163)

Evidence-Based Best Practices

BOX 6.5

PreP Procedure

Brainstorming is a key feature of the prereading plan (PreP), which may be used to estimate the levels of background knowledge that students bring to the text assignments.

Before beginning the PreP activity, the teacher should examine the text material for keywords (which represent major concepts to be developed), phrases, or pictures and then introduce the topic that is to be read, following the three-phase plan outlined by Langer (1981, p. 154):

1. *Initial associations with the concept.* In this first phase the teacher says, "Tell anything that comes to mind when . . ." (e.g., ". . . you hear the word *Congress*"). As each student tells what ideas initially came to mind, the teacher jots each response on the board. During this phase, the students have their first opportunity to find associations between the key concept and their prior knowledge. When this activity was carried out in a middle school class, one student, Bill, said, "Important people." Another student, Danette, said, "Washington, D.C."
2. *Reflections on initial associations.* During the second phase of PreP, the students are asked, "What made you think of . . . [the response given by a student]?" This phase helps the students develop awareness of their network of associations. They also have an opportunity to listen to each other's explanations, to interact, and to become aware of their changing ideas. Through this procedure, they may weigh, reject, accept, revise, and integrate some of the ideas that came to mind. When Bill was asked what made him think of important people, he said, "I saw them in the newspaper." When Danette was asked what made her think of Washington, D.C., she said, "Congress takes place there."
3. *Reformulation of knowledge.* In this phase, the teacher says, "Based on our discussion and before we read the text, have you any new ideas about . . . [e.g., Congress]?" This phase allows students to verbalize associations that have been elaborated or changed through the discussion. Because they have had a chance to probe their memories to elaborate on their prior knowledge, the responses elicited during the third phase are often more refined than those from the first. This time, Bill said, "Lawmakers of America," and Danette said, "U.S. government part that makes the laws."

Through observation and listening during PreP, content area teachers will find their students' knowledge can be divided into three broad levels. On one level are students who have *much* prior knowledge about the concept. These students are often able to define and draw analogies, make conceptual links, and think categorically. On the second level are students who may have *some* prior knowledge. These students can give examples and cite characteristics of the content but may be unable to see relationships or make connections between what they know and the new material. On the third level are students who have *little* background knowledge. They often respond to the PreP activity by making simple associations, often misassociating with the topic.

You can facilitate student-centered purposes by creating anticipation about the meaning of what will be read.

Anticipation Guides

An anticipation guide is a series of statements to which students must respond individually before reading the text. Their value lies in the discussion that takes place after the exercise. The teacher's role during discussion is to activate and agitate thought. As students connect their knowledge of the world to the prediction task, you must remain open to a wide range of responses. Draw on what students bring to the task, but remain nondirective in order to keep the discussion moving.

Anticipation guides may vary in format but not in purpose. In each case, the readers' expectations about meaning are raised before they read the text. Keep these six guidelines in mind in constructing and using an anticipation guide:

1. *Analyze the material to be read.* Determine the major ideas—implicit and explicit—with which students will interact.
2. *Write those ideas in short, clear declarative statements.* These statements should in some way reflect the world in which the students live or about which they know. Therefore, avoid abstractions whenever possible.
3. *Put these statements in a format that will elicit anticipation and prediction.*
4. *Discuss the students' predictions and anticipations before they read the text selection.*
5. *Assign the text selection.* Have the students evaluate the statements in light of the author's intent and purpose.
6. *Contrast the readers' predictions with the author's intended meaning.*

Adapting Anticipation Guides in Content Areas

A middle school social studies teacher prepared students for a reading assignment that contrasted the characteristics of the Northern and Southern soldiers in the Civil War. She began by writing "Johnny Reb" and "Billy Yank" in separate columns on the chalkboard. She asked students to think about what they already knew about the two soldiers: "How do you think they were alike? How were they different?" After some discussion, the teacher invited the students to participate in the anticipation activity in Figure 6.7.

Of course, each of the points highlighted in the statements was developed in the text selection. Not only did the students get a sense of the major ideas they would encounter in the text selection but they also read to see how well they had predicted which statements more accurately represented soldiers from the South and the North during the Civil War.

A science teacher began a weather unit by introducing a series of popular clichés about the weather. He asked his students to anticipate whether the clichés had a scientific basis (see Figure 6.8).

The before-reading discussion led the students to review and expand their concepts of scientific truth. Throughout different parts of the unit, the teacher returned to one or two of the clichés in the anticipation guide and suggested to the class that the textbook assignment would explain whether there was a scientific basis for each saying. Students were then directed to read to find out what the explanations were.

FIGURE 6.7 Anticipation Guide for a Civil War Lesson

Johnny Reb and Billy Yank were common soldiers of the Civil War. You will be reading about some of their basic differences in your textbook. What do you think those differences will be? Before reading your assignment, place the initials JR in front of the phrases that you think best describe Johnny Reb. Place the initials BY in front of the statements that best describe Billy Yank. Do not mark statements common to both.

_______ 1. More likely to be able to read and write
_______ 2. Best able to adjust to living in open areas
_______ 3. More likely to be from a rural setting
_______ 4. More interested in politics
_______ 5. More deeply religious
_______ 6. Often not able to sign his name
_______ 7. More apt to dislike regimentation of army life
_______ 8. More likely to speak slowly
_______ 9. More probably a Native American
_______ 10. More likely to be a common man in the social order

FIGURE 6.8 Anticipation Guide for Clichés About Weather

Directions: Put a check under "Likely" if you believe that the weather saying has any scientific basis; put a check under "Unlikely" if you believe that it has no scientific basis. Be ready to explain your choice.

Likely	**Unlikely**	
_______	_______	1. Red sky at night, sailors delight; red sky at morning, sailors take warning.
_______	_______	2. If you see a sunspot, there is going to be bad weather.
_______	_______	3. When the leaves turn under, it is going to storm.
_______	_______	4. If you see a hornet's nest high in a tree, a harsh winter is coming.
_______	_______	5. Aching bones mean a cold and rainy forecast.
_______	_______	6. If a groundhog sees his shadow, six more weeks of winter.
_______	_______	7. Rain before seven, sun by eleven.
_______	_______	8. If a cow lies down in a pasture, it is going to rain soon.
_______	_______	9. Sea gull, sea gull, sitting on the sand; it's never good weather while you're on land.

A health education teacher raised expectations and created anticipation for a chapter on the human immunodeficiency virus (HIV) and AIDS. Rather than prepare written statements, she conducted the anticipatory lesson as part of an introductory class discussion. She raised curiosity about the topic by asking students to participate in a strategy known as the "every-pupil response." She told the students that she would ask several questions about becoming infected with HIV. Every student was to respond to each question by giving a "thumbs up" if they agreed or a "thumbs down" if they disagreed. The class had to participate in unison and keep their thumbs up or down. After each question, the students shared their reasons for responding thumbs up or thumbs down. The questions were framed as follows: "Is it true that you can contract HIV by

- Having unprotected sex with an infected partner?"
- Kissing someone with HIV?"
- Sharing needles with an HIV-infected drug user?"
- Sharing a locker with an infected person?"
- Using a telephone after someone with HIV has used it?"
- Being bitten by a mosquito?"

The "oral anticipation guide" created lively discussion as students discussed some of their preconceived notions and misconceptions about HIV and AIDS.

Mathematics teachers also have been successful in their use of anticipation guides. In a precalculus class, the teacher introduced the activity in Figure 6.9 to begin the trigonometry section of the textbook. She created the anticipation guide to help students address their own knowledge about trigonometry and to create conceptual conflict for some of the more difficult sections of the chapter they would be studying.

Finally, a tenth-grade English teacher developed an anticipation guide for Elie Wiesel's book *Night*. The teacher had been relying mainly on the KWL strategy (see Chapter 7) for before-reading and after-reading discussions. She decided, as a change of pace, to use the anticipation guide in Figure 6.10 as an alternative to KWL. She adapted the anticipation guide format by asking students, before reading, to discuss their responses to a series of statements about the Holocaust. After reading *Night*, the students were then asked to revisit their original responses to the statements on the guide and to consider whether their reading confirmed or refuted their prereading responses. For the postreading discussion, the teacher placed a blank version of the anticipation guide on an overhead projector so that the students, as a class, could discuss how their knowledge and beliefs had changed as a result of the their reading of *Night*.

Imagine, Elaborate, Predict, and Confirm (IEPC)

Many students, particularly those who struggle with reading, have difficulty creating mental images as they read (Lenihan 2003). The imagine, elaborate, predict, and confirm (IEPC) strategy encourages students to use visual imagery to enhance their

FIGURE 6.9 Anticipation Guide for Preconceived Notions About Trigonometry

Directions: Put a check under "Likely" if you believe that the statement has any mathematical truth. Put a check under "Unlikely" if you believe that it has no mathematical truth. Be ready to explain your choices.

Likely	Unlikely	
________	________	Trigonometry deals with circles.
________	________	Angles have little importance in trigonometry.
________	________	Sailors use trigonometry in navigation.
________	________	Angles can be measured only in degrees.
________	________	Calculators are useless in trigonometry.
________	________	Trigonometry deals with triangles.
________	________	Trigonometry has no application in the real world.
________	________	Radians are used in measuring central angles.
________	________	Trigonometry has scientific uses.
________	________	Radians can be converted to degrees.

FIGURE 6.10 Anticipation Guide for *Night*

Directions: Read each of the following statements and, in the Before Reading column, place a plus (+) if you agree with the statement and a minus (–) if you disagree. Be prepared to support your responses during our class discussion. Later, after learning about the Holocaust, you will complete the After Reading column to see if any of your initial responses have changed. You'll be asked to discuss why you confirmed or changed your ideas from your before-reading responses.

Before Reading	Statement	After Reading
	The Holocaust took place only in Germany.	
	The Jews had plenty of time to escape so they could have avoided being sent to a concentration camp.	
	Jews were targeted because of their religion.	
	Other countries did not know what was happening to the Jews.	
	People in concentration camps were only killed if they broke a law.	
	Life in the concentration camps wasn't so bad for those who were too old or too young to work.	
	Survivors of the Holocaust just want to forget about what happened.	
	Jews were the only target of Hitler and the Nazis.	
	The Holocaust took place between WWI and WWII.	
	The term *Holocaust* was developed by the Jewish prisoners while they were at the camps.	

comprehension of a text selection. Figure 6.11 shows how a social studies teacher used the IEPC strategy to help her students to understand Theodore Taylor's book *The Cay.* Wood and Taylor (2005) explain the steps in implementing the IEPC strategy:

1. *Select a text passage or introduction to the text that contains content appropriate for developing imagery.* In the IEPC example illustrated in Figure 6.11, the teacher read a brief synopsis of the text to the students, which introduced them to the basic setting of the story and to the conflict that would develop in its plot.

2. *Imagine.* Have students close their eyes to imagine a scene from the book or text they are going to read. Encourage them to use experiences by thinking about the feelings, sights, smells, and tastes that they associate with the topic. Their images may emanate from the title of the text, a picture from the passage, or a passage read by the teachers. Ask students to share their images with a partner or with the group and to record their images in the I column of the IEPC chart. Students who were preparing to read *The Cay* imagined what it might be like to be stranded on a desert island with only one other person, whom they disliked or distrusted. They imagined the frustration that might result from being blind.

3. *Elaborate.* Once the students have heard initial responses from their classmates, ask them to think of additional details associated with the scene they have visualized. Ask questions that will prompt them to elaborate on the original images they described. Record their responses in the E column of the IEPC chart. The students preparing to read *The Cay* elaborated on their initial images by talking about what might have led to the dislike and distrust between the boys who were stranded on the island. They also elaborated on what it might feel like to experience a hurricane on the island, as the characters did in the story.

4. *Predict.* Have the students use their initial images and elaboration of those images to make predictions about the text they are going to read. Record those predictions in the P column of the IEPC. As Figure 6.11 shows, students offered a range of predictions about what might happen as *The Cay* unfolded and about how the characters might respond to their difficult predicament.

5. *Confirm.* During and after reading, encourage students to recall their predictions. Were they able to confirm their predictions or have they modified their predictions based on what they have learned from reading the text? Record their confirmations and modifications, using a different color marker for each, in the C column of the IEPC chart. As they read *The Cay,* the students looked carefully for passages and clues that would help them to identify which of their predictions were accurate and which needed to be modified. After reading the story, the students confirmed that their prediction that Phillip would learn not to judge people by the color of their skin proved to be accurate. In contrast, they recognized that their prediction that the characters would survive the storm together did not match what actually happened in the story.

FIGURE 6.11 IEPC Chart for *The Cay*

I	E	P	C
Being stranded on a desert island; feeling afraid Feeling suspicious of the person with whom you are stranded; wondering if they are going to harm you Being frustrated at not being able to see and not being able to do anything about it Seeing the dark rain clouds gather; wondering how long the storm will last and how strong it will be How will Phillip and Timothy survive?	Phillip and Timothy must have been terrified, especially after their boat was torpedoed. They must have been lonely, starving, exhausted. Phillip was white. Timothy was black. Phillip had been taught that black people were inferior. Will he overcome his prejudice? Phillip has lost his sight. He must feel helpless and angry because he is now dependent on Timothy. The wind is blowing furiously; waves are crashing on the shore; everything is soaked and flooded; it's hard to see or to walk.	Phillip and Timothy will learn to live together on the island. Timothy will help Phillip. Phillip will learn not to judge people by the color of their skin. Timothy and Phillip will survive the hurricane and they will be rescued and returned to civilization. Phillip will learn how to adjust to his blindness and Timothy and Phillip will remain friends.	Phillip disliked Timothy, but had to rely on him. Timothy took care of Phillip; Phillip learned to respect and care about Timothy. Phillip learns through Timothy's actions toward him that racism is wrong; he regains his sight, both physically and emotionally. Timothy dies in the hurricane protecting Phillip. Phillip holds Timothy's hand until he dies. Phillip is able to live because of what Timothy taught him.

Question Generation

Teaching students to generate their own questions about material to be read is an important prereading instructional goal. Teachers need to intentionally select strategies that will engage students in expressing their perceptions and developing understanding of text topics (Cook-Sather 2002). Neufeld (2005) suggests that, before reading a text, students ask and answer questions that will help them to read with a purpose, to recognize major characteristics of the texts, to activate their prior knowledge, and to make predictions about what they are about to read. By providing opportunities for students to generate questions and seek answers to those questions, teachers can support students in becoming strategic readers.

myeducationlab
Go to the Assignments and Activities section of Topic 3: "Motivation" in the MyEducationLab for your course and complete the activity "Using Questions to Motivate."

Active Comprehension

Teachers can use an active comprehension strategy when they *ask questions that beget questions in return*. You might, for example, focus attention on a picture or an illustration from a story or book and ask a question that induces student questions in response: "What would you like to know about the picture?" In return, invite the students to generate questions that focus on the details in the picture or its overarching message.

Or you might decide to read to students an opening paragraph or two from a text selection, enough to whet their appetites for the selection. Then ask, "What else would you like to know about _______?" Complete the question by focusing attention on some aspect of the selection that is pivotal to students' comprehension. It may be the main character of a story or the main topic of an expository text.

Active comprehension questions not only arouse interest and curiosity but also draw learners into the material. As a result, students will read to satisfy purposes and resolve conceptual conflicts that they have identified through their own questions. Let us examine several additional instructional strategies for engaging students in asking questions for reading.

ReQuest

ReQuest was originally devised as a one-on-one procedure for a remedial instructional context. Yet this strategy can easily be adapted to content area classrooms to help struggling readers think as they read. ReQuest encourages students to ask their own questions about the content material under study. Self-declared questions are forceful. They help students establish reasonable purposes for their reading. Manzo (1969) suggests the following steps for implementing the ReQuest strategy:

1. *Both the students and the teacher silently read the same segment of the text.* For students who have difficulty comprehending, Manzo recommends reading one sentence at a time. It can also be helpful to divide a longer, more complex text into smaller, more manageable sections. Then students and teacher can pause at the end of each small section and implement the ReQuest procedure. It is also helpful to inform the students before they begin reading that they will be asking the teacher questions about the text after they have read it.

2. *The teacher closes the book and is questioned about the passage by the students.*

3. *Next there is an exchange of roles.* The teacher queries the students about the text.

4. *On completion of the student–teacher exchange, the students and the teacher read the next segment of the text, pausing at the predetermined stopping point.* Steps 2 and 3 are then repeated.

5. *Students stop questioning and begin predicting.* At a suitable point in the text, when the students have processed enough information to make predictions about the remainder of the assignment, the exchange of questions stops. The teacher then asks prediction questions, "What do you think might happen in the remainder of the text? What has the author said or implied that makes you think so?" Divergent thinking is encouraged.

6. *Students are then assigned the remaining portion of the text to read independently.*
7. *The teacher facilitates a follow-up discussion of the material.*

Although the steps for ReQuest were devised for one-on-one instruction, they can be adapted for the content area classroom where students struggle with texts.

You can modify the ReQuest procedure to good advantage. For example, consider alternating the role of questioner after each question. By doing so, you will probably involve more students in the activity. Once students sense the types of questions that can be asked about a text passage, you might also try forming ReQuest teams. A ReQuest team composed of three or four students can be pitted against another ReQuest team. Your role is to facilitate the multiple actions resulting from the small-group formations.

Our own experiences with ReQuest suggest that students may consistently ask factual questions to stump the teacher or other students. Such questions succeed brilliantly because you are subject to the same restrictions imposed by short-term memory as the students. That you miss an answer or two is actually healthy—after all, to err is human.

However, when students ask only verbatim questions because they don't know how to ask any others, the situation is unhealthy. The sad fact is that some students don't know how to ask questions that will stimulate interpretive or applied levels of thinking. Therefore, your role as a good questioner during ReQuest is to provide a model from which students will learn. Over time, you will notice the difference in the quality of the student questions formulated. Box 6.6 shows how a civics and economics teacher used ReQuest with her class of predominantly English learners.

Expectation Outlines

Spiegel (1981) suggests the use of an expectation outline to help students ask questions about text. She recommends the expectation outline for factual material, but the strategy can be adapted to narrative studies as well. The expectation outline is developed on the chalkboard or an overhead projector transparency as students simply tell what they expect to learn from a reading selection.

If students are reading a factual selection, you may have them first take several minutes to preview the material. Then ask, "What do you think your assignment is going to be about?" Ask students to state their expectations in the form of questions. As they suggest questions, group related questions on the chalkboard or transparency. You also have the opportunity to ask students what prompted them to ask these questions in the first place. At this point, students may be encouraged to refer to the text to support their questions.

Once questions have been asked and grouped, the class labels each set of questions. Through discussion, students begin to see the major topics that will emerge from the reading. Help them to recognize that gaps may exist in the expectation outline of the assignment. For example, you may add a topic or two to the outline about which no questions were raised. On completion of the expectation outline, students read to answer the questions generated.

Evidence-Based Best Practices BOX 6.6

ReQuest Procedure

In a civics and economics class, a teacher applied the ReQuest strategy to help English learners understand the different branches of government in the United States. She related their understanding of the United States government to that of their native countries.

1. *Both the students and the teacher silently read the same segment of the text.* The teacher and the English learners read a section of the text about the structure of the United States government that outlined the three branches of government—legislative, judicial, and executive.

2. *The teacher closed the book and was questioned about the passage by the students.* The teacher encouraged students to make connections between the information in the text and their experiences with the governments of their native countries. She was prepared to answer questions about the information presented in the reading as well as to assimilate this information with students' existing knowledge of alternative government structures. For example, one student from Mexico noted that, although Mexico has a president, presidential elections in that country are held every six years, rather than every four years as they are in the United States. He went on to point out that there are no opportunities for reelection of a president in Mexico as there are in the United States.

3. *Next there was an exchange of roles.* The teacher then asked students questions about the text and encouraged them to make comparisons between the U.S. government and those of the countries with which they were familiar. For example, the teacher asked students to compare the civil liberties protected by the U.S. Constitution with those that are protected by the governments of their native counties. A student from Mexico referenced the individual and social rights established in the Constitution of Mexico and made comparisons to amendments in the U.S. Constitution.

4. *On completion of the student–teacher exchange, the class and the teacher read the next segment of the text.* Steps 2 and 3 were repeated.

5. *The teacher invited students to make predictions.* At this point in the lesson, the civics and economics teacher asked questions such as, "Now that we know how laws are created, what changes in legislation do you think might lie in the future?"

6. *Students were assigned a subsequent portion of the text to read silently.*

7. *The teacher facilitated a follow-up discussion of the material.*

For narrative materials, students may formulate their questions from the title of the selection or pictures or keywords and phrases in the selection. For example, direct students to preview a story by skimming through it quickly, studying the pictures and illustrations (if any), and jotting down five to ten keywords or phrases that appear to indicate the main direction of the story. As students suggest keywords and phrases, write them on the board and categorize them. Then ask students to state what they expect to find out from the story. Have them raise questions about its title, setting, characters, plot, and theme. As an alternative to questions, students may summarize their expectations by writing a paragraph about the story using the keywords and phrases that were jotted down and categorized.

Your Own Questions

A variation on the expectation outline is a strategy called *your own questions*. Here's how it works:

1. *Have students listen to or read a portion of the text from the beginning of a selection.*
2. *Ask students to write five to ten questions that they think will be answered by the remainder of the selection.*
3. *Discuss some of the questions asked by the students before reading.* Write the questions on the board.
4. *Have students read to determine whether the questions are answered.*
5. *After reading, ask the students to explain which questions were answered, which weren't, and why not.*

Strategies such as an expectation outline or your own questions teach students how to approach reading material with an inquisitive mind. These instructional strategies and the others presented in this chapter form a bridge between teacher-initiated guidance and independent learning behavior by students.

LOOKING BACK LOOKING FORWARD

Meaningful learning with texts occurs when students experience a sense of satisfaction with text and a feeling of accomplishment. In this chapter, the roles that self-efficacy and motivation play in purposeful learning was emphasized. Although some students may be skilled in reading and knowledgeable about the subject, they may not bring that skill and knowledge to bear in learning situations. It takes motivation, a sense of direction and purpose, and a teacher who knows how to create conditions in the classroom that allow students to establish their own motives for reading. One way to arouse curiosity about reading material is to encourage students to make connections among the key concepts to be studied. Another is to create conceptual conflict. Students will read to resolve conflicts arising from problem situations and perspectives and will use guided imagery to explore the ideas to be encountered during reading.

To reduce any uncertainty that students bring to reading material, you can help them raise questions and anticipate meaning by showing them how to connect what they already know to the new ideas presented in the text. The questions students raise as a result of predicting will guide them into the reading material and keep them on course. Anticipation guides, ReQuest, expectation outlines, and self-questioning are strategies for stimulating predictions and anticipation about the content.

In the next chapter, we explore ways to guide reading comprehension in the curriculum. A classroom teacher who encourages student engagement in reading brings learners and texts together to explore and construct meaning.

Minds On

1. Suppose you go to the library looking for a good book to read. You see a cart with a sign: "Current Best-Sellers." Because you have little familiarity with any of the books, how will you make a selection? How will you anticipate which book is for you? Because students rarely have the opportunity to select their course textbook, what can teachers do to help students make the book "fit"?

2. Divide your discussion group into two subgroups: individuals who are willing to take the position that all of the following statements are correct and those willing to argue that all of the statements are inaccurate. Discuss the pros and cons of each topic for five minutes. After you have finished, bring any items to the class as a whole that you believe could truly have been defended from either view, and be prepared to explain why or under what circumstances.

   a. Students are not qualified to ask their own questions about difficult content material.
   b. The old but still common practice of assigning reading in preparation for a discussion is, unfortunately, backward.
   c. Just as athletes need to warm up before a contest, readers need to warm up to get ready for text.
   d. Analyzing content vocabulary before reading is a sound instructional practice.
   e. Having students read a variety of materials on the subject matter will only confuse them.
   f. It is pointless to discuss most subjects with students before they read the text, because the varied social and economic backgrounds of the students make it possible for only a few to connect any relevant personal experience to the text subject.

3. Eliot Eisner believed that brains are born but minds are made. What do you believe is the teacher's role in a classroom filled with twenty-five brains waiting to be made into minds? Is the teacher the molder, shaper, and maker—that is, the only active partner? Is the teacher to serve as a model learner, a guide through knowledge, or a facilitator—that is, an equal or superior partner? Or do you see some happy medium? In your group, attempt to reach a consensus on what you consider to be the best role for a teacher in relation to these prompts.

Hands On

1. Try the following science experiment to activate prior knowledge and to stimulate interest in reading an explanation of the formula, *force equals pressure times area*. Bring the following materials to class: one 30-gallon garbage bag, duct tape, and a dozen straws. Flatten the trash bag on a table large enough for a volunteer to lie on with his or her upper body resting on the bag. Cut four small holes about nine inches apart along each of the edges of the two sides of the flattened bag that are perpendicular to the open end. Insert one straw in each opening. Next, tape each hole airtight. Tape the open end of the bag airtight as well. Ask a volunteer to lie on his or her back on top of the garbage bag on the table.

   Next, have eight individuals each select one straw, and explain that they will be attempting to lift the volunteer by blowing through the straws into the sealed bag. Before proceeding, however, invite the group to pose questions, draw on their prior knowledge, and anticipate why this experiment may succeed or fail. After the group has theorized about and discussed the problem, mention that the bag will break at a pressure of one pound per square inch, and ask if that fact changes their predictions. Finally, have the eight individuals attempt to inflate the bag by blowing into the straws simultaneously. As they do, be sure that someone stabilizes the volunteer so that he or she does not roll off the bag.

If the experiment works, the volunteer should rise several inches from the table. Break into small groups of five or six, and imagine that a science instructor has just used this experiment as an introduction to a chapter on the relationship between air pressure, force, and surface area. How motivated are the group members to read this chapter? As a group, discuss how science experiments may be used with anticipation guides, ReQuest, expectation outlines, and graphic organizers.

2. Team with a group of four or five other students. Before the next class, each member should collect three political cartoons, each using a different newspaper, magazine, or book. These cartoons may represent current or historical political issues.

   When you return to class, share the cartoons you found and discuss the knowledge the reader must already have in order to understand the humor. Select the one cartoon you found most enjoyable and list the background knowledge needed to understand it. When all groups have finished discussing and selecting, have each group read and explain its favorite cartoon to the whole class. As a large group, discuss how this activity illustrates the concept of prior knowledge when reading text. If there are art majors in the class, ask them to share the role of prior knowledge in viewing works of art.

3. Bring to class a nonfiction book or magazine article on a subject you enjoy. With a partner, practice the ReQuest strategy. On completion of the activity, join with two other pairs, and as a small group, discuss the effectiveness of the questioning, the successfulness of the learning that occurred, and your perceptions of the usefulness of this activity in a content area classroom.

TEXT PREDICTION (BY A STUDENT) FOR STORY IMPRESSIONS ACTIVITY IN FIGURE 6.2

Following the French and Indian War, England passed the Stamp Act to recover some of its war debts. Colonists complained that their right to vote on their own taxes had been taken away by Parliament. The Americans wrote petitions asking for the Stamp Act to be repealed. It was. Groups of colonists called the Sons of Liberty formed and carried on some rather rowdy activities. The Stamp Act was replaced by the Townshend Acts. Angry Americans boycotted all taxed products until England once again repealed the taxes—all except the tax on tea. One night a group of colonists, led by the Sons of Liberty, dressed as Mohawk Indians and threw tea overboard into the Boston harbor. This event was known as the Boston Tea Party.

*e*RESOURCES

- Find out more about self-efficacy and motivation by going to a special site created by Emory University (**www.des.emory.edu/mfp/self-efficacy.html**) to broaden the understanding of self-efficacy.
- Learn about question generation as a research-based comprehension strategy by going to Intervention Central (**www.interventioncentral.org/htmdocs/interventions/rdngcompr/qgen.php#topAnchor**). Identify some hints for using question generation as an instructional strategy in class. Explore Intervention Central more thoroughly for other intervention strategies (**www.interventioncentral.org**).

CHAPTER 7

I took a speed-reading course and read War and Peace in twenty minutes. It involves Russia.

—Woody Allen

Guiding Reading Comprehension

ORGANIZING PRINCIPLE

Teachers guide students' reading by (1) modeling how to read, think, and learn with texts; and (2) scaffolding instruction in the use of comprehension strategies that allow students to learn with text in meaningful ways.

Woody Allen's wry observation reminds us of how some students approach the reading of academic text: They read as fast as they can—eyes skimming over words, fingers flipping through the pages—to glean bits of information here and there in a mad dash to finish the reading assignment! How many times have teachers received one- or two-word answers (reminiscent of "It involves Russia") in response to thoughtful questions about assigned text? Superficial reading of academic text, more often than not, is devoid of thinking and learning.

Effective teachers, of course, always hope for more from their students. They set the bar high by challenging learners to develop ways of thinking that are essential for comprehending text and developing core concepts in a discipline. Through the instructional support they provide, teachers can build students' confidence and competence as readers by showing them how to use comprehension strategies to think deeply about text. A starting point for showing students how to read, think, and learn begins with the understanding that behind a text—whether print-based or nonprint in nature—is a real person doing real work. Writers, for example, believe that they have something worthwhile to say and reasons for saying it. Some write to entertain, others to inform. Authors like us do the

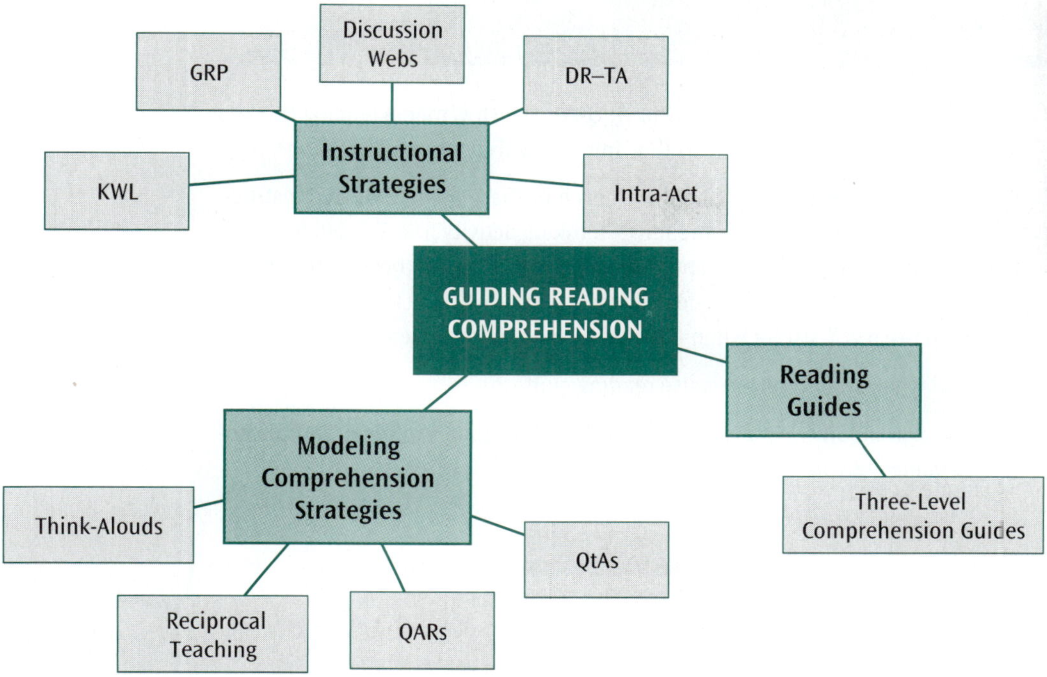

latter. When writers of informational texts talk directly to readers as we're doing now, linguists label the process *metadiscourse,* a mouthful of a word that describes what a writer does to engage the reader in thinking about the text.

Most readers don't consciously think about what a writer does to draw them into thoughtful interactions with the text. But an effective writer of academic text knows that when readers engage in the process, they think about what they are reading. Active, engaged reading always involves a dialogue between the reader and the text. As we learned in the previous chapter, engaged readers are motivated, knowledgeable, strategic, and socially interactive. They have much to contribute to the dialogue that takes place in the mind as they interact with texts to construct meaning. Yet in today's diverse classrooms, students may have trouble handling the conceptual demands of difficult text. How does a content area teacher guide comprehension in ways that model thinking strategies and engage and sustain students in discipline-specific learning, especially if the ideas encountered during reading are complex?

Earlier, we studied how activating prior knowledge before, during, and after reading is a critical instructional component of content literacy lessons. In this chapter, we extend the dialogue on reading comprehension as we explore strategies to think and learn with text. As the organizing principle for this chapter highlights: **Teachers guide students' reading by (1) modeling how to read, think, and learn with texts; and (2) scaffolding instruction in the use of comprehension strategies that allow students to learn with text in meaningful ways.**

FRAME OF MIND

1. How do think-alouds, reciprocal teaching, QARs, and QtAs model reading/thinking/learning strategies for students as they interact with texts in a discipline?
2. Describe the procedures associated with each of these literacy-related instructional strategies: KWL, directed reading–thinking activity (DR–TA), guided reading procedure (GRP), intra-act, and discussion web. How do these instructional strategies support thinking and learning with text? Which of these strategies may be particularly useful when adapted to your content area?
3. Why and when should teachers use reading guides?
4. How can you modify and adapt three-level reading guides to meet the conceptual demands of your discipline?

RESPONSE JOURNAL

What is your reaction to Socrates' explanation of what it means to think?

Although metaphors come and go, one that has been around since the ancient Greeks is as powerful today as it was centuries ago. In Plato's *Theaetetus,* written more than 2,000 years ago, Socrates is asked to explain what it means to think. He responds to his questioner by explaining that when the mind is thinking it is merely talking to itself, asking questions and answering them. Thinking is a conversation. It is a dialogue that you have with yourself in your mind. When a reader engages in a dialogue with text, the conversation metaphor puts an incredibly complex process—reading—into the context of what happens inside the minds of readers.

The conversations that take place between readers and texts transcend time and space. Texts make it possible to bring readers and authors together in content area classrooms. There is a catch, however. Thinking with texts requires students to participate actively in the conversation. A conversation works only when participants are involved and interacting with one another. Everyday conversations, for example, involve an exchange of ideas between two or more parties—a give-and-take dialogue—around topics of mutual interest and relevance.

Learning conversations in content area classrooms have similar characteristics, unless they break down or never get started. Dialogues easily turn into monologues when the transmission of information becomes more important than the sharing of ideas among students, teachers, and texts. Guiding the learning conversations that occur between the reader and the text is the subject of this chapter. ■

Modeling Comprehension Strategies

Students who struggle with text are usually unaware of strategies that will help them more effectively comprehend and make meaning. In this section, we explain several research-based practices that provide explicit instruction in the use of comprehension strategies (National Reading Panel 2000). Teachers from various disciplines can, with some modification, incorporate *think-alouds, reciprocal teaching, question–answer relationships (QARs),* and *questioning the author (QtA)* into their instructional routines to show students how to read, think, and learn with discipline-specific texts.

RESPONSE JOURNAL

Think-alouds, QARs, and reciprocal teaching are research-based instructional practices. Educators often describe a research-based instructional practice as a "best practice." What does the term *best practice* mean to you?

Using Think-Alouds to Model Comprehension Strategies

In think-alouds, teachers make their thinking explicit by verbalizing their thoughts while reading orally. The think-aloud strategy helps readers clarify their understanding of reading and their understanding of how to use strategies. Students will more clearly understand the strategies after a teacher uses think-alouds, because they can see how a mind actively responds to thinking through trouble spots and constructing meaning from the text (Davey 1983).

myeducationlab

Go to the Assignments and Activities section of Topic 5: "Comprehension Strategies" in the MyEducationLab for your course and complete the activity "Think-Alouds to Model Comprehension" to consider how think-alouds can be used.

There are five basic steps to follow when using think-alouds. First, select passages to read aloud that contain points of difficulty, ambiguities, contradictions, or unknown words. Second, while orally reading and modeling thinking aloud, have students follow silently and listen to how trouble spots are thought through. Third, have students work with partners to practice think-alouds by taking turns reading short, carefully prepared passages and sharing thoughts. Fourth, have students practice independently. Use a checklist similar to the one shown in Figure 7.1 to involve all students while verifying use of the procedures. Finally, to encourage transfer, integrate practice with other lessons and provide occasional demonstrations of how, why, and when to use think-alouds. Five points can be made during think-alouds:

1. Students should develop hypotheses by making predictions.
2. Students should develop images by describing pictures forming in their heads from the information being read.
3. Students should link new information with prior knowledge by sharing analogies.
4. Students should monitor comprehension by verbalizing a confusing point.
5. Students should regulate comprehension by demonstrating strategies.

FIGURE 7.1 Checklist for Self-Evaluation of Think-Alouds

While I was reading, how did I do? (Put an X in the appropriate column.)

	Not very much	A little bit	Much of the time	All of the time
Made predictions	______	______	______	______
Formed pictures	______	______	______	______
Used "like-a"	______	______	______	______
Found problems	______	______	______	______
Used fix-ups	______	______	______	______

Source: "Think Aloud—Modeling the Cognitive Processes of Reading Comprehension" by B. Davey, *Journal of Reading, 27*(1), 44–47. Copyright © 1983 by the International Reading Association. Reproduced with permission of International Reading Association via Copyright Clearance Center.

Let's look at how each of these points can be modeled in a middle school earth science class.

Develop Hypotheses by Making Predictions

Teachers might model how to develop hypotheses by making predictions from the title of a chapter or from subheadings within the chapter. Suppose you were teaching with an earth science text. You might say, "From the heading 'How Minerals Are Used,' I predict that this section will tell about things that are made out of different minerals." The text continues:

> Some of the most valuable minerals are found in ores. An **ore** is a mineral resource mined for profit. For example, bauxite (BAWK-sight) is an ore from which aluminum is taken. Iron is obtained from the ore called hematite (HEE-muh-tight). Bauxite and hematite are metallic minerals.
>
> Metallic minerals are metals or ores of metals. Gold, iron, and aluminum are examples of metals. Metals are important because of their many useful properties.
>
> One useful property of many metals is malleability (mal-ee-uh-BIL-uh-tee). **Malleability** is the ability to be hammered without breaking. Malleability allows a metal to be hammered into thin sheets.

Develop Images

To model how to develop imaging, at this point you might stop and say, "I have a picture in my head from a scene I saw in a movie about the Old West. I see a blacksmith pumping bellows in a forge to heat up an iron horseshoe. When the iron turns a reddish orange, he picks it up with his tongs, and he hammers. The sparks fly, but slowly the horseshoe changes shape to fit the horse's hoof." The text continues:

> Another property of many metals is ductility (duk-TIL-uh-tee). **Ductility** is the ability to be pulled and stretched without breaking. This property allows a metal to be pulled into thin wires.

Share Analogies

To model how to link new information with prior knowledge, you might share the following analogies. "This is like a time when I tried to eat a piece of pizza with extra cheese. Every time I took a bite, the cheese kept stretching and stretching into these long strings. It is also like a time when I went to the county fair and watched people make taffy. They got this glob of candy and put it on a machine that just kept pulling and stretching the taffy, but it never broke." The text continues:

> Metals share other properties as well. All metals conduct heat and electricity. Electrical appliances and machines need metals to conduct electricity. In addition, all metals have a shiny, metallic luster.

Monitor Comprehension

To model how to monitor comprehension, you can verbalize a confusing point: "This is telling me that metals have a metallic luster. I don't know what that is. I'm also confused because I thought this section was going to be about things that are made out of different minerals. This is different from what I expected."

Regulate Comprehension

To model how to correct lagging comprehension, you can demonstrate a strategy: "I'm confused about what *metallic luster* means, and I don't know why the authors are talking about this when I expected them to talk about stuff made out of minerals. Maybe if I ignore the term *metallic luster* and keep on reading, I'll be able to make some connections to what I expected and figure it all out." The text continues:

> Very shiny metals, like chromium, are often used for decorative purposes. Many metals are also strong. Titanium (tigh-TAY-nee-um), magnesium (mag-NEE-zee-um), and aluminum are metals that are both strong and lightweight. These properties make them ideal building materials for jet planes and spacecraft.

"Oh, they're talking about properties of metals that make them especially good for making certain things, like aluminum for jets because it is strong and lightweight. Now I understand why they're talking about properties. I'll bet chrome and chromium are just about the same, because I know chrome is the shiny stuff on cars. I think *metallic luster* must mean something like shiny because chromium reminds me of chrome."

Think-alouds are best used at the beginnings of lessons to help students learn the whats and hows of constructing meaning with text. The next teaching strategy, *reciprocal teaching,* is an excellent follow-up to think-alouds. Reciprocal teaching helps students learn how to apply the strategy learned during a think-aloud so that they can understand the author's message.

Using Reciprocal Teaching to Model Comprehension Strategies

When using reciprocal teaching, you model how to use four comprehension activities (generating questions, summarizing, predicting, and clarifying) while leading a dialogue (Brown & Palincsar 1984). Then students take turns assuming the teacher's role. A key to the effectiveness of this strategy is adjusting the task demand to support the students when difficulty occurs. That is, when students experience difficulty, you provide assistance by lowering the demands of the task. As the process goes on, you slowly withdraw support so that students continue learning. When planning a reciprocal teaching lesson, there are two phases. The first phase has five steps:

1. Find text selections that demonstrate the four comprehension activities.
2. Generate appropriate questions.
3. Generate predictions about each selection.
4. Locate summarizing sentences and develop summaries for each selection.
5. Note difficult vocabulary and concepts.

In the second phase, decisions are made about which comprehension activities to teach, based on the students' needs. It also helps determine students' present facility with the activities so that you are prepared to give needed support during the process. Once students are familiar with more than one strategy, reciprocal teaching can be used to model the decision-making process about which strategy to use.

Using Question–Answer Relationships (QARs) to Model Comprehension Strategies

Question–answer relationships (QARs) make explicit to students the relationships that exist among the type of question asked, the text, and the reader's prior knowledge. In the process of teaching QARs, you help students become aware of and skilled in using learning strategies to find the information they need to comprehend at different levels of response to the text (Raphael 1982, 1984, 1986).

The procedures for learning QARs can be taught directly to students by literacy specialists and can be reinforced by content area specialists. Keep in mind, however, that students may come to your class totally unaware of what information sources are available for seeking an answer, or they may not know when to use different sources. In this case, it is worth several days' effort to teach students the relationship between questions and answers. It may take up to three days to show students how to identify the information sources necessary to answer questions. The following steps, which we have adapted for content area situations, are suggested for teaching QARs:

1. *Introduce the concept of QARs.* Show students a chart or an overhead transparency containing a description of the four basic question–answer relationships. (We

recommend a chart that can be positioned in a prominent place in the classroom. Students may then refer to it throughout the content area lessons.) Point out the two broad categories of information sources: "In the text" and "In your head" (see Figure 7.2).

2. *Begin by assigning students several short passages from the textbook.* (These should be no more than two to five sentences in length.) Follow each reading with one question from each of the QAR categories on the chart. Then discuss the differences between a "right there" question and answer, a "think and search" question and answer, an "on your own" question and answer, and an "author and you" question and answer. Your explanations should be clear and complete. Reinforce the discussion by assigning several more short text passages and asking a question for each. Students will soon begin to catch on to the differences among the four QAR categories.

3. *Continue the second day by practicing with short passages.* Use one question for each QAR category per passage. First, give students a passage to read along with questions *and* answers *and* identified QARs. Why do the questions and answers represent one QAR and not another? Second, give students a passage along with questions and answers; this time they have to identify the QAR for each. Finally, give students passages, decide together which strategy to use, and have them write their responses.

4. *Review briefly on the third day.* Then assign a longer passage (75 to 200 words) with up to six questions (at least one each from the four QAR categories). First, have students work in groups to decide the QAR category for each question and the answers for each. Next, assign a second passage, comparable in length, with five questions for students to work on individually. Discuss their responses either in small groups or with the whole class. You may wish to work with several class members or colleagues to complete the QAR activity in Box 7.1. It was developed by a high school English teacher as part of a short story unit.

5. *Apply the QAR strategy to actual content area assignments.* For each question asked, students decide on the appropriate QAR strategy and write out their answers.

Once students are sensitive to the different information sources for different types of questions and know how to use these sources to respond to questions, variations can be made in the QAR strategy. For example, you might have students generate their own questions to text assignments—perhaps two for each QAR strategy. They then write down the answers to the questions as they understand them, except that they leave one question unanswered from the "think and search" category and one from the "on your own" or "author and you" category. These are questions about which the student would like to hear the views of others. During the discussion, students volunteer to ask their unanswered questions. The class is invited first to identify the

FIGURE 7.2 **Introducing QARs**

Where Are Answers to Questions Found?

In the Text:

Right There

The answer is in the text. The words used in the question and the words used for the answer can usually be found in the same sentences.

Think and Search

The answer is in the text, but the words used in the question and those used for the answer are not in the same sentence. You need to think about different parts of the text and how ideas can be put together before you can answer the question.

In Your Head:

Author and You

The answer is not in the text. You need to think about what you know, what the author says, and how they fit together.

On Your Own

The text got you thinking, but the answer is inside your head. The author can't help you much. So think about it, and use what you know already about the question.

Source: Adapted from "Teaching Question–Answer Relationships" by T. E. Raphael, *Reading Teacher, 39,* 516–520. Copyright © 1986 by the International Reading Association. Reproduced with permission of International Reading Association via Copyright Clearance Center.

Evidence-Based Best Practices **BOX 7.1**

QAR Awareness in a High School English Class

A high school English teacher develops students' awareness of QARs with the following guided practice activity. The teacher selects an excerpt from Richard Wilbur's *A Game of Catch* and asks students to answer a set of questions about the excerpt. The students are also asked to identify the QAR associated with each question.

> "Got your glove?" asked Glennie after a time. Scho obviously hadn't.
>
> "You could give me some easy grounders," said Scho. "But don't burn 'em."
>
> "All right," Glennie said. He moved off a little, so the three of them formed a triangle, and they passed the ball around for about five minutes, Monk tossing easy grounders to Scho, Scho throwing to Glennie, and Glennie burning them into Monk. After a while, Monk began to throw them back to Glennie once or twice before he let Scho have his grounder, and finally Monk gave Scho a fast, bumpy grounder that hopped over his shoulder and went into the brake on the other side of the street.
>
> "Not so hard," called Scho as he ran across to get it.
>
> "You should've had it," Monk shouted.
>
> It took Scho a little while to find the ball among the ferns and dead leaves, and when he saw it, he grabbed it up and threw it toward Glennie. It struck the trunk of the apple tree, bounced back at an angle, and rolled steadily and stupidly onto the cement apron in front of the firehouse, where one of the trucks was parked. Scho ran hard and stopped it just before it rolled under the truck, and this time he carried it back to his former position on the lawn and threw it carefully to Glennie. (*From "A Game of Catch," copyright 1953 by Richard Wilbur. Reprinted by permission of Harcourt, Inc. Originally appeared in* The New Yorker, *1953.*)

1. Question: What are the three boys doing?

   Answer: ______________________

   QAR: ______________________

2. Question: Why did Monk throw the ball so hard to Scho?

   Answer: ______________________

   QAR: ______________________

3. Question: Who was throwing the ball to Monk?

   Answer: ______________________

   QAR: ______________________

4. Question: How would you describe Scho's throwing ability?

   Answer: ______________________

   QAR: ______________________

5. Question: How would you characterize Monk?

   Answer: ______________________

   QAR: ______________________

6. Question: Why do friends sometimes get frustrated with one another?

   Answer: ______________________

   QAR: ______________________

question by QAR category and then to contribute answers, comments, or related questions about the material.

A second variation involves discussions of text. During question-and-answer exchanges, preface a question by saying, "This question is *right there* in the text," or "You'll have to *think and search* the text to answer," or "You're *on your own* with this one," or "The answer is a combination of the *author and you*. Think about what the author tells us and what we already know to try and come up with a reasonable response." Make sure that you pause several seconds or more for "think time." Think time, or "wait time," is critical to responding to textually implicit and schema-based questions.

Once students are familiar with QARs, they can be used in combination with a variety of interactive strategies that encourage readers to explore ideas through text discussions.

Questioning the Author (QtA)

Questioning the author (QtA) is a comprehension strategy that models for students the importance of asking questions while reading. Beck, McKeown, Hamilton, and Kucan (1997) devised the QtA strategy to demonstrate the kinds of questions students need to ask in order to think more deeply and construct meaning about segments of text as they read. Good readers act on the author's message. If what they are reading doesn't make sense to them, they generate questions about what the author says and means. When students struggle with text, however, they often do not have a clue about generating questions, let alone interacting with the author of text. Enter QtA instruction.

myeducationlab

Go to the Building Teaching Skills and Dispositions section of Topic 5: "Comprehension Strategies" in the MyEducationLab for your course. Use this activity to develop your skills in helping students gain the most from their texts.

The QtA strategy shows students how to read text closely as if the author were there to be challenged and questioned. QtA places value on the quality and depth of students' responses to the author's intent. It is important that students keep their minds active while reading as they engage in a dialogue with an author. Good readers monitor whether the author is making sense by asking questions such as, "What is the author trying to say here?" "What does the author mean?" "So what? What is the significance of the author's message?" "Does this make sense with what the author told us before?" "Does the author explain this clearly?" These questions are posed by the teacher to help students "take on" the author and understand that text material needs to be challenged.

Through QtA, students learn that authors are fallible and may not always express ideas in the easiest way for readers to understand. QtA builds metacognitive knowledge by making students aware of an important principle related to reading comprehension: *Not comprehending what the author is trying to say is not always the fault of the reader.* As a result, students come to view their roles as readers as "grappling with text" as they seek to make sense of the author's intent.

Planning a QtA Lesson

Planning QtA lessons for narrative or informational texts involves a three-stage process that requires the teacher to (1) identify major understandings and potential problems with a text prior to its use in class, (2) segment the text into logical stopping points for discussion, and (3) develop questions, or *queries,* that model and demonstrate how to "question the author." Box 7.2 examines the planning process.

When using QtA to comprehend stories, pose *narrative queries.* Through the use of narrative queries, students become familiar with an author's writing style as they strive to understand character, plot, and underlying story meaning. The following queries help students think about story characters: "How do things look for this character now?" "Given what the author has already told us about this character, what do you think the author is up to?" Understanding the story plot can be accomplished

Evidence-Based Best Practices BOX 7.2

Steps in a QtA Lesson

1. Analyze the text

- *Identify major understandings and potential problems that students may encounter during reading.*
- *Read the text closely and note the author's intent, the major ideas and themes, and any areas or potential obstacles in the material that could affect comprehension.*
- *Reflect on your own comprehension as you read the text.* Note any passages that you reread or pause to think about, knowing that these sections will most likely be problematic for students.

2. Segment the text

- *Determine where to stop the reading to initiate and develop discussion.* The text segments may not always fall at a page or paragraph break. You may want to stop reading after one sentence to ask a question.

3. Develop questions

- *Plan questions that will help students respond to what the author says and means.* These generic questions prompt students' responses to the text and encourage them to dig deeper and make sense of what they are reading. The following question guide will help you frame initiating and follow-up questions at different points in the lesson. Initiating questions at the beginning of the reading draw students' attention to the author's intent, whereas follow-up queries focus the direction of the discussion and assist students as they integrate and connect ideas. Follow-up questions help students determine why the author included certain ideas.

QTA QUESTION GUIDE

Initial questions at the beginning of the lesson:

- What is the author trying to say?
- What is the author's message?
- What is the author talking about?

Follow-up questions during reading help students make connections and inferences about the text:

- This is what the author says, but what does it mean?
- How does this text segment connect with what the author has already said?

Follow-up questions during reading help students with difficulties and confusions with the way the author presents information:

- Does the author make sense here?
- Did the author explain this clearly?
- What's missing? What do we need to find out?

Follow-up questions during reading clarify misinterpretations or make students aware that they made an inference (reinforce QARs):

- Did the author tell us that?
- Did the author say that or did you "think and search" to get the answer?

with queries such as these: "How has the author let you know that something has changed?" "How has the author settled this for us?"

Guiding the QtA Discussion

Beck and colleagues (1997) recommend the use of a variety of "discussion moves" to guide students:

Marking: Draw attention to certain ideas by either paraphrasing what a student said or by acknowledging its importance with statements such as "Good idea" or "That's an important observation."

Turning back: Make students responsible for figuring out ideas and turning back to the text for clarification.

Revoicing: Assist students as they express their ideas; filter the most important information and help students who are struggling to express their ideas by rephrasing their statements.

Modeling: Think aloud about an issue that is particularly difficult to understand, one that students are unable to reach without assistance.

Annotating: Provide information that is not in the text so that students can understand the concepts fully.

Recapping: Summarize the main ideas as a signal to move on in the lesson. Recapping can be done by either the teacher or the students.

The thoughtful use of questions is vital for classroom discussion. As learners actively explore and clarify meaning, guide the discussion as you progress from one text segment to the next.

Instructional Strategies

In this section, we describe several instructional strategies that engage students in reading, guide their interactions with texts, and help them to clarify and extend meaning. The instructional strategies that follow include (1) *KWL,* which stands for What do you *K*now? What do you *W*ant to know? What did you *L*earn? (2) *discussion webs,* (3) *guided reading procedure (GRP),* (4) *intra-act,* and (5) *directed reading–thinking activity* (DR–TA). Note the differences as well as the similarities of various instructional strategies emphasized in this section. Each can be adapted to serve any subject matter material. Think about the kinds of adaptations you will have to make with each instructional strategy to meet the particular needs of your content area.

The KWL Strategy

KWL is an instructional strategy that engages students in active text learning. The strategy begins with what students *know* about the topic to be studied, moves to what the students *want to know* as they generate questions about the topic, and leads to a record of what students *learn* as a result of their engagement in the strategy. Follow-up activities to KWL include discussion, the construction of graphic organizers, and summary writing to clarify and internalize what has been read.

KWL may be initiated with small groups of students or the whole class. When they develop confidence and competence with the KWL strategy, students may begin to use it for independent learning. KWL uses a strategy sheet, such as the one in Figure

FIGURE 7.3 A KWL Strategy Sheet

K—What I Know	W—What I Want to Know	L—What I Learned and Still Need to Learn

Categories of Information I Expect to Use

A.
B.
C.
D.
E.
F.
G.

Source: "K-W-L: A Teaching Model That Develops Active Reading in Expository Text" by D. M. Ogle, *The Reading Teacher, 39*(6), 564–570.

7.3. The procedures to follow in KWL revolve around the completion of the strategy sheet as part of the dynamics of student response and discussion.

Procedures for KWL

Here's how the KWL strategy works.

1. *Introduce the KWL strategy in conjunction with a new topic or text selection.* Before assigning a text, explain the strategy. Donna Ogle (1992), the originator of KWL, suggests that dialogue begin with the teacher saying

> It is important to first find out what we think we know about this topic. Then we want to anticipate how an author is likely to present and organize the information. From this assignment we can generate good questions to focus on reading and study. Our level of knowledge will determine to some extent how we will study. Then as we read we will make notes of questions that get answered and other new and important information we learn. During this process some new questions will probably occur to us; these we should also note so we can get clarification later. (p. 271)

In the process of explaining KWL, be sure that students understand *what* their role involves and *why* it is important for learners to examine what they know and to ask questions about topics that they will be reading and studying.

The next several steps allow you to model the KWL strategy with a group of learners or the entire class. Some students will find it difficult to complete the KWL strategy sheet on their own. Others will avoid taking risks or revealing what they know or don't know about a topic. Others simply won't be positively motivated. Modeling the KWL strategy reduces the initial risk and creates a willingness to engage in the process. Students who experience the modeling of the strategy quickly recognize its value as a learning tool.

2. *Identify what students think they know about the topic.* Engage the class in brainstorming, writing their ideas on the board or on an overhead transparency. Use the format of the KWL strategy sheet as you record students' ideas on the chalkboard or transparency. It's important to record everything that the students *think* they know about the topic, including their misconceptions. The key in this step is to get the class actively involved in making associations with the topic, not to evaluate the rightness or wrongness of the associations. Students will sometimes challenge one another's knowledge base. The teacher's role is to help learners recognize that differences exist in what they think they know. These differences can be used to help students frame questions.

3. *Generate a list of student questions.* Ask, "What do you want to know more about? What are you most interested in learning about?" As you write their questions on the chalkboard or transparency, recognize that you are again modeling for students what their role as learners should be: to ask questions about material to be studied.

When you have completed modeling the brainstorming and question-generation phases of KWL, have the students use their own strategy sheets to make decisions about what they personally think they know and about what they want to know more. Students, especially those who may be at risk in academic situations, may refer to the chalkboard or the overhead transparency to decide what to record in the first two columns.

4. *Anticipate the organization and structure of ideas that the author is likely to use in the text selection.* As part of preparation for reading, have students next use their knowledge and their questions to make predictions about the organization of the text. What major categories of information is the author likely to use to organize his or her ideas?

The teacher might ask, "How do you think the author of a text or article on _______ is likely to organize the information?" Have students focus on the ideas they have brainstormed and the questions they have raised to predict possible categories of information. As students make their predictions, record these on the board or transparency in the area suggested by the KWL strategy sheet. Then have students make individual choices on their own strategy sheets.

5. *Read the text selection to answer the questions.* As they engage in interactions with the text, the students write answers to their questions and make notes for new ideas and information in the L column of their strategy sheets. Again, the teacher's modeling is crucial to the success of this phase of KWL. Students may need a demonstration or two to understand how to record information in the L column.

Debrief students after they have read the text and have completed writing responses in the L column. First, invite them to share answers, recording these on the chalkboard or transparency. Then ask, "What new ideas did you come across that you didn't think you would find in the text?" Record and discuss the responses.

6. *Engage students in follow-up activities to clarify and extend learning.* Use KWL as a springboard into postreading activities to internalize student learning. Activities may include the construction of graphic organizers to clarify and retain ideas encountered during reading or the development of written summaries.

KWL Examples

In Christa Chaney's U.S. history class, students were beginning a study of the Vietnam War. Christa realized that her students would have little, if any, prior knowledge of and attitudes toward the Vietnam War, even though it's still part of our national consciousness. The students, in fact, were acutely aware of the war from recent popular movies and also from relatives who had participated in it.

However, Christa realized that although students might know something about the Vietnam War, they had probably had little opportunity to study it from the perspective of historians. This, then, was Christa's objective as a teacher of history: to help students approach the study of the Vietnam War—and understand the social, economic, and political forces surrounding it—from a historian's perspective.

Therefore, Christa believed that the KWL strategy would be an appropriate way to begin the unit. She believed that it would help students get in touch with what they knew (and didn't know) about the Vietnam War and raise questions that would guide their interactions with the materials that they would be studying.

Christa began KWL knowing that her students were familiar with its procedures, having participated in the strategy on several previous occasions in the class. Following the six steps, the class as a whole participated in brainstorming what they knew about the war and what they wanted to know. Christa recorded their ideas and questions on an overhead transparency and encouraged students' participation by asking such questions as, "What else do you know? Who knows someone who was in the war? What did he or she say about it? Who has read about the Vietnam War or seen a movie about it? What did you learn?"

As ideas and questions were recorded on the transparency, Christa asked the students to study the K column to anticipate categories of information that they might study in their textbook and other information sources that they would be using: "Do some of these ideas fit together to form major categories we might be studying?" She also asked the students to think about other wars they had studied—World Wars I and II, the U.S. Civil War, and the American Revolution: "When we study wars, are there underlying categories of information on which historians tend to focus?"

On completion of the whole-class activity, Christa invited her students to complete their strategy sheets, recording what they knew, what they wanted to find out more about, and what categories of information they expected to use.

Then, for homework, she assigned several sections from a textbook covering the Vietnam War and asked students to work on the L column on their own. Figure 7.4 shows how one student, Clayton, completed his strategy sheet.

FIGURE 7.4 **Clayton's KWL Strategy Sheet on the Vietnam War**

K—What I Know	W—What I Want to Know	L—What I Learned and Still Need to Learn
U.S. lost war	Why did we go to war?	Gulf of Tonkin Resolution made it legal for war but was not legally declared
protest marches and riots	Why did we lose?	French helped U.S.
movies made in 1960s	How many soldiers died?	Nixon withdrew troops because of fighting at home
jungle fighting	Who helped us?	Lottery used to draft soldiers
POWs	Who was president during war?	Antiwar movement at home
guerrilla fighting	On whose side were we?	55,000 Americans died plus thousands of innocent people
North and South fighting each other		Kennedy, Johnson, and Nixon were the presidents
U.S. soldiers suffered		Fought war to stop communism
the wall in Washington		

Categories of Information I Expect to Use

A. cause
B. results
C. U.S. involvement
D. type of fighting
E.
F.
G.

FIGURE 7.5 **Clayton's Summary in His Learning Log**

We fought the Vietnam War to stop communism. The U.S. Congress passed the Gulf of Tonkin Resolution, which said it was OK to go to war there, but the war was never declared a war—it was only called a conflict. The French and South Vietnamese people helped us, but it didn't matter. 55,000 Americans died fighting. People protested in the United States. Nixon withdrew the troops because of pressure to end the war at home.

As part of the next day's class, Christa asked the students to work in groups of four to share what they had found out about the war. They focused on the questions they had raised, as well as on new ideas they had not anticipated. When the groups completed their work, Christa brought the class together. She directed them to open their learning logs and write a summary of what they had learned from participating in KWL. Students used the L column on their strategy sheets to compose the summary. Clayton's summary is shown in Figure 7.5.

In Christa's class, the learning logs serve as history notebooks, in which students can record what they are learning, using a variety of writing-to-learn activities. (We explain learning logs and their uses more fully in Chapter 9.)

A high school math teacher adapted the KWL strategy to support his students' study of the Fibonacci numbers. Fibonacci numbers (a famous sequence of numbers that have been shown to occur in nature) are the direct result of a problem posed by a thirteenth-century mathematician, Leonardo of Pisa, on the regeneration of rabbits. The teacher used a math text from an enrichment unit to clarify and extend students' understanding of the Fibonacci numbers. The text selection, "Mathematics in Nature," illustrates the properties of the Fibonacci numbers and requires students to determine the relationships between these numbers and various phenomena in nature—for example, the leaves on a plant, the bracts on a pinecone, the curves on a seashell, or the spirals on a pineapple.

Before initiating the KWL strategy, the teacher used three props (a toy rabbit, a plant, and a pineapple) to arouse students' curiosity and to trigger their responses to the question, "What do these items have to do with mathematics?" After some exploratory talk, he then asked students, "What do you know about mathematics and nature?" The strategy sheet in Figure 7.6 illustrates the reader–text interactions that occurred as the teacher guided students through the steps in KWL.

Discussion Webs

Discussion webs encourage students to engage the text and each other in thoughtful discussion by creating a framework for students to explore texts and consider different sides of an issue in discussion before drawing conclusions. Donna Alvermann (1991) recommends discussion webs as an alternative to teacher-dominated discussions.

FIGURE 7.6 **A KWL Strategy Sheet in a Math Class**

K—What I Know	W—What I Want to Know	L—What I Learned and Still Need to Learn
planetary motion *spirals* *4 seasons* *landscaping* *geometric designs* *multiplying populations* *phases of the moon*	*What does a pineapple have to do with math?* *How are growth patterns in plants related to math?* *How is mathematics specifically related to nature?* *Where do bees fit?*	*Pineapples have hexagons on the surface that are arranged in sets of spirals.* *These spirals are related to Fibonacci numbers.* *Fibonacci numbers are found in leaf arrangements on plants.* *The rate that bees regenerate males is related to Fibonacci numbers.* *Who is this Fibonacci guy?* *What's the big deal about the "golden ratio"?*
Categories of Information I Expect to Use A. *Animals* B. *Plants* C. *Solar System* D. *Laws of Nature*		

The strategy uses cooperative learning principles that follow a think–pair–share discussion cycle (McTighe & Lyman 1988). The discussion cycle begins with students first thinking about the ideas they want to contribute to the discussion based on their interactions with the text. Then they meet in pairs to discuss their ideas with a partner. Partners then team with a different set of partners to resolve differences in perspective and to work toward a consensus about the issue under discussion. In the final phase of the discussion cycle, the two sets of partners, working as a foursome, select a spokesperson to share their ideas with the entire class.

The discussion web strategy uses a graphic display to scaffold students' thinking about the ideas they want to contribute to the discussion based on what they have read. The graphic display takes the shape of a web. In the center of the web is a question that is central to the reading. The question is posed in such a way that it reflects

FIGURE 7.7 **Discussion Web for *The Skin I'm In***

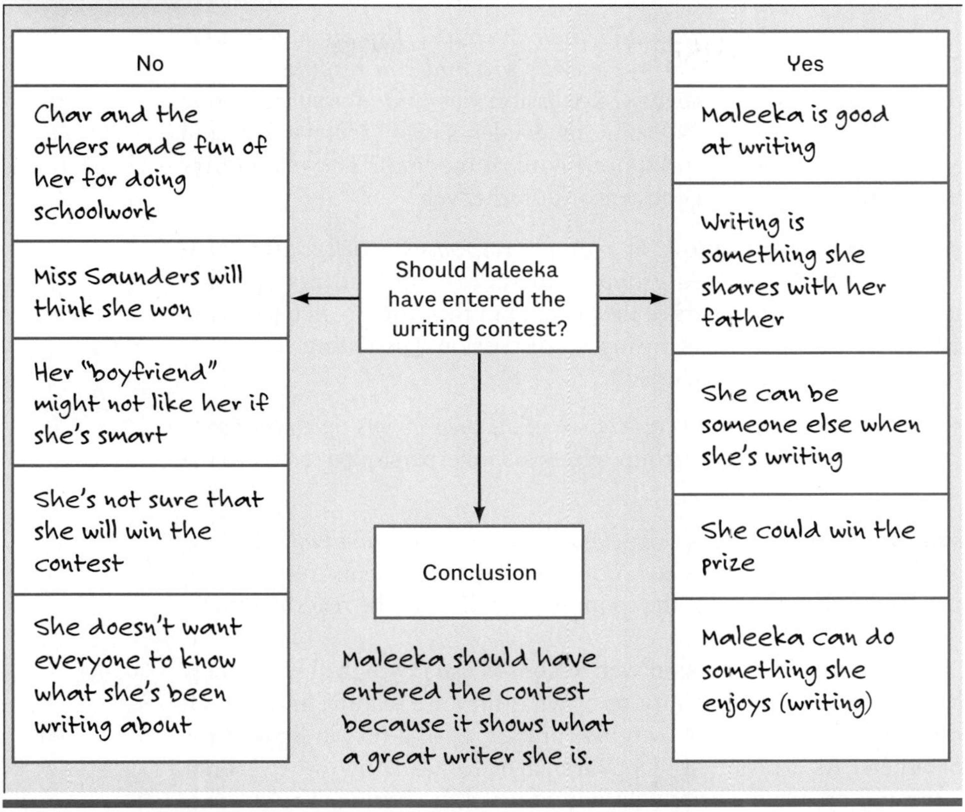

more than one point of view. Students explore the pros and cons of the question in the No and Yes columns of the web—first in pairs, and then in groups of four. The main goal of the four-member teams is to draw a conclusion based on their discussion of the web. Figure 7.7 illustrates a discussion web used after students had read Sharon Flake's book *The Skin I'm In,* winner of the 1999 Coretta Scott King Award. The book tells the story of Maleeka, a seventh grader in an inner-city school, who is torn between winning the approval of street-smart peers and pursuing her own academic capabilities. The question posed in the discussion web, "Should Maleeka have entered the writing contest?", invites students to consider one dilemma Maleeka faces as she works to resolve these conflicts.

RESPONSE JOURNAL
Why do you think discussion webs would help students read critically in your content area?

Procedures for the Discussion Web

Alvermann (1991) suggests an integrated lesson structure for the discussion web strategy that includes the following steps:

1. *Prepare your students for reading by activating prior knowledge, raising questions, and making predictions about the text.*
2. *Assign students to read the selection and then introduce the discussion web by having the students work in pairs to generate pro and con responses to the question.* The partners work on the same discussion web and take turns jotting down their reasons in the Yes and No columns. Students may use keywords and phrases to express their ideas and need not fill all of the lines. They should try to list an equal number of pro and con reasons on the web.
3. *Combine partners into groups of four to compare responses, work toward consensus, and reach a conclusion as a group.* Explain to your students that it is okay to disagree with other members of the group, but they should all try to keep an open mind as they listen to others during the discussion. Dissenting views may be aired during the whole-class discussion.
4. *Give each group three minutes to decide which of all the reasons given best supports the group's conclusion.* Each group selects a spokesperson to report to the whole class.
5. *Have your students follow up the whole-class discussion by individually writing their responses to the discussion web question.* Display the students' responses to the question in a prominent place in the room so that they can be read by others.

The level of participation in discussion web lessons is usually high. The strategy encourages students' individual interpretations of what they are reading and also allows them to formulate and refine their own interpretations of a text in light of the points of view of others. As a result, students are eager to hear how other groups reached a consensus and drew conclusions during whole-class sharing. The strategy works well with informational or narrative texts and can be adapted to the goals and purposes of most content area subjects.

Discussion Web Examples

Donna Mitchell, a music teacher, introduced her middle grade students to components of an opera by having them listen to Wagner's *The Flying Dutchman*. In Chapter 5, we discuss Mrs. Mitchell's lesson in detail. In the discussion, she activated students' prior knowledge of opera using a playbill that she constructed in the form of a modified cloze activity. As part of the lesson, Mrs. Mitchell also had students listen to the overture of the opera to set a mood and read to them portions of the story over several days. At the conclusion of the read-alouds, students entered the postreading stage of the lesson as they engaged in a discussion web activity. Study the discussion web in Figure 7.8 completed by one group of students in her class as they grappled with the question, "Did Senta need to throw herself off the cliff into the sea?"

Math teachers might also use the discussion web to help students consider relevant and irrelevant information in story problems. Study the discussion web in Figure 7.9, noting the adaptations the teacher made. In this illustration, the students worked

FIGURE 7.8 **Discussion Web for *The Flying Dutchman***

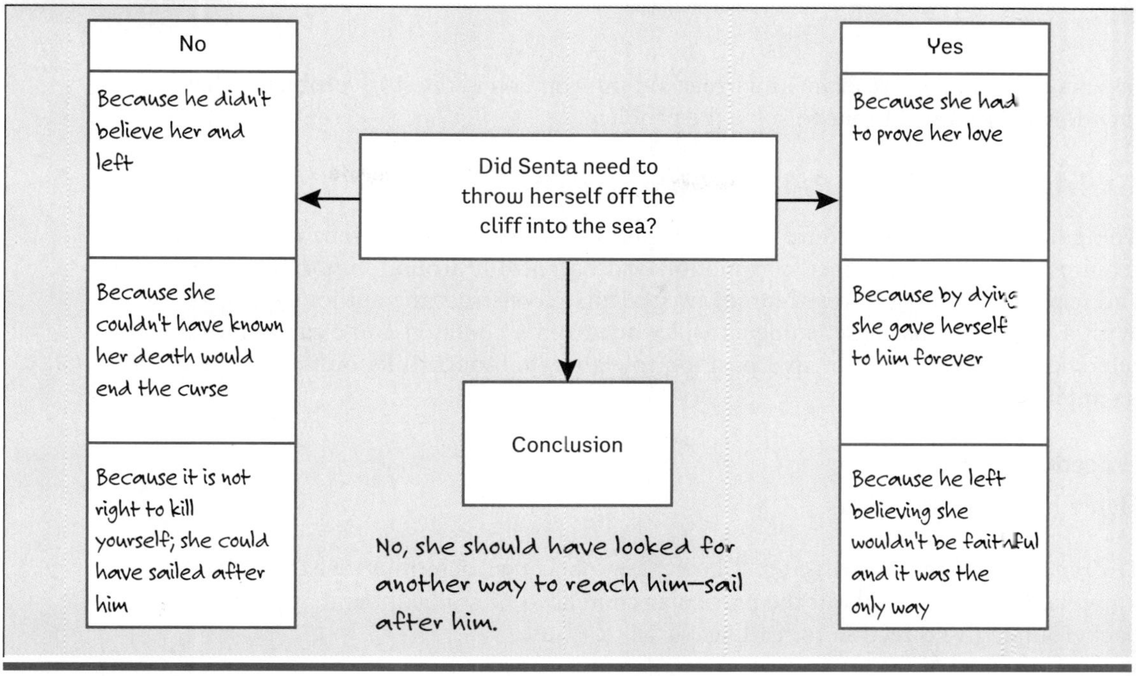

FIGURE 7.9 **Discussion Web for a Story Problem**

A U-Haul truck is driving through West Virginia. It is approaching a one-lane semicircular tunnel at a rate of fifty miles per hour. The truck is ten feet high, five feet wide, and twenty-five feet long. The tunnel has a radius of twelve feet and is 100 feet long. Will the truck fit through the tunnel?

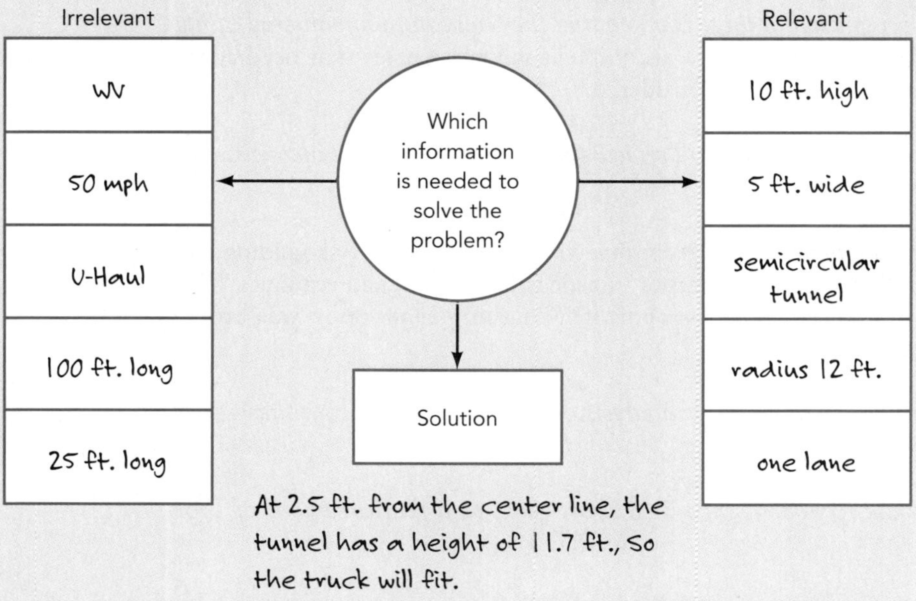

in pairs to distinguish relevant and irrelevant information in the story problem. They then formed groups of four to solve the problem.

Guided Reading Procedure (GRP)

The guided reading procedure (GRP) emphasizes close reading (Manzo 1975). It requires that students gather information and organize it around important ideas, and it places a premium on accuracy as students reconstruct the author's message. With a strong factual base, students will work from a common and clear frame of reference. They will then be in a position to elaborate thoughtfully on the text and its implications.

Procedures for GRP

Here's how the GRP works.

1. *Prepare students for reading.* Clarify key concepts; determine what students know and don't know about the particular content to be studied; build appropriate background; give direction to reading.

2. *Assign a reading selection.* Assign 500 to 900 words in the middle grades (approximately five to seven minutes of silent reading); 1,000 to 2,000 words for high school (approximately ten minutes). Provide general purpose to direct reading behavior. For example, "Read to remember all you can."

3. *As students finish reading, have them turn books face down.* Ask them to tell what they remember. Record it on the chalkboard in the fashion in which it is remembered.

4. *Help students recognize that there is much that they have not remembered or have represented incorrectly.* Simply, there are implicit inconsistencies that need correction and further information to be considered.

5. *Redirect students to their books and review the selection to correct inconsistencies and add further information.*

6. *Organize recorded remembrances into some kind of an outline.* Ask guiding, nonspecific questions: "What were the important ideas in the assigned reading? Which came first? What facts on the board support it? What important point was brought up next? What details followed?"

7. *Extend questioning to stimulate an analysis of the material and a synthesis of the ideas with previous learnings.*

8. *Provide immediate feedback, such as a short quiz, as a reinforcement of short-term memory.*

A GRP Example

Eighth graders were assigned a reading selection from the music education magazine *Pipeline*. The selection, "Percussion—Solid as Rock," concerns the development and uses of percussion instruments from ancient to modern times.

The teacher introduced the selection by giving some background. She then began a guided discussion by asking students to remember as much as they could as they read the assignment silently. The teacher recorded the collective memories of her students on a transparency, projecting responses onto an overhead screen. Then she asked, "Did you leave out any information that might be important?" Students were directed to review the selection to determine whether essential information was missing from the list on the screen. The teacher also asked, "Did you mix up some of the facts on the list? Did you misrepresent any of the information in the author's message?"

These questions are extremely important to the overall GRP procedure. The first question—"Did you leave out any information that might be important?"—encourages a review of the material. Students sense that some facts are more important than others. Further questioning at this point will help them distinguish essential from nonessential information. The second question—"Did you mix up some of the facts on the list?"—reinforces the importance of selective rereading and rehearsal because of the limitations imposed by short-term memory.

Next, the teacher asked the class to study the information recorded on the screen. The teacher directed the students to form pairs and then assigned the following task: "Which facts on the overhead can be grouped together? Organize the information around the important ideas in the selection. You have five minutes to complete the task."

On completion of the task the teacher encouraged students to share their work in whole-group discussion. Their groupings of facts were compared, refined, and extended. The teacher served as a facilitator, keeping the discussion moving, asking clarifying questions, and provoking thought. She then initiated the next task: "Let's organize the important ideas and related information. Let's make a map." Figure 7.10 shows what the students produced.

Outlining the mass of information will make students aware of the text relationships developed by the author. In Chapter 10 we explore several outlining procedures, such as semantic mapping, which help students produce the author's main ideas in relation to one another. Producing the author's organizational structure leads to more efficient recall at a later time and lays the groundwork for interpreting and applying the author's message. Once this common framework is developed, your questioning should lead to more divergent and abstract responding by the students.

The discussion "took off" after the outline was completed. The teacher asked several reflective questions that helped students associate their previous experiences and beliefs about drumming to the content under discussion. Cognitive performance centered on evaluation and application as students linked what they knew to what they were studying.

RESPONSE JOURNAL

How is the GRP similar to KWL? How is it different?

The final suggested step in the GRP is a short quiz, mainly to demonstrate in a dramatic way how successful the students can be with

FIGURE 7.10 Semantic Map of "Percussion—Solid as Rock"

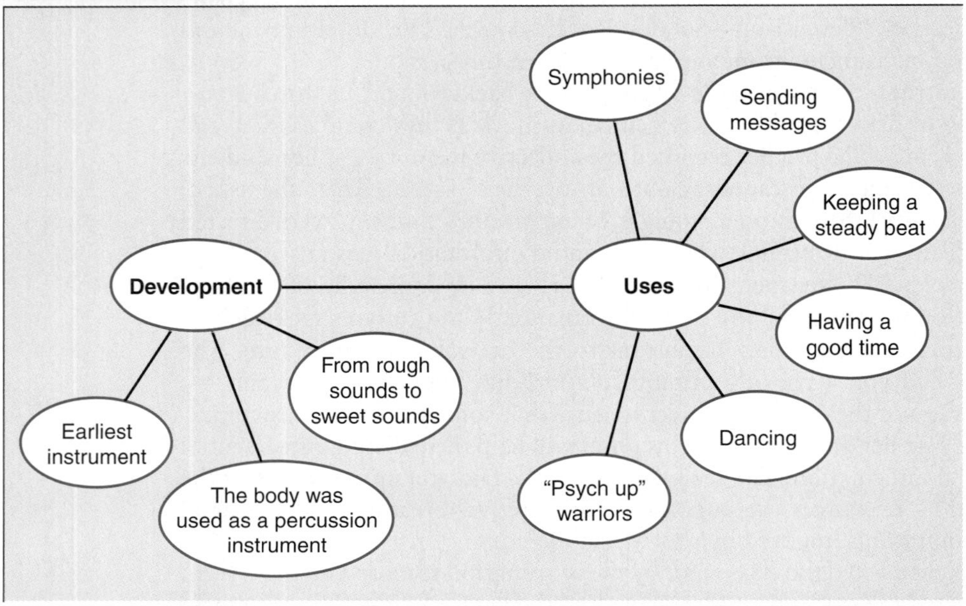

the reading material. The quiz should be viewed as positive reinforcement, not an interrogation check. Most of the students in this class earned perfect or near-perfect scores on the quiz—and this is as it should be.

Intra-Act

Intra-act lays the groundwork for reflective discussion. Pivotal to the intra-act strategy is the notion that students engage in a process of valuing as they reflect on what they have read. Hoffman (1979) suggests intra-act to provide readers with "the opportunity to experience rather than just talk about critical reading" (p. 608). According to Hoffman, students are more likely to read critically when they engage in a process of valuing. The valuing process allows students to respond actively to a text selection with thought and feeling.

The intra-act procedure can be used with a variety of reading materials—content area text assignments, historical documents, newspaper and magazine articles, narratives, and poetic material. The procedure requires the use of small groups whose members are asked to react to value statements based on the content of the text selection.

Procedures for Intra-Act

There are four phases in the intra-act procedure.

1. *Comprehension.* The comprehension phase promotes an understanding of the reading material to be learned. To begin this phase, the teacher follows effective prereading procedures by introducing the text reading, activating and building prior knowledge for the ideas to be encountered during reading, and inviting students to make predictions and speculate on the nature of the content to be learned. Building a frame of reference for upcoming text information is crucial to the overall success of the intra-act procedure.

Before inviting students to read the selection individually, the teacher forms small groups—intra-act teams—of four to six members. Assign a student from each group to serve as the team leader. The comprehension phase depends on the team leader's ability to initiate and sustain a discussion of the text. The team leader's responsibility is to lead a discussion by first summarizing what was read. The group members may contribute additional information about the selection or ask questions that seek clarification of the main ideas of the selection. The comprehension phase of the group discussion should be limited to seven to ten minutes.

2. *Relating.* The team leader is next responsible for shifting the discussion from the important ideas in the selection to the group's personal reactions and values related to the topic. Many times, this shift occurs naturally. However, if this is not the case, members should be encouraged by the team leader to contribute their own impressions and opinions. Discussion should again be limited to seven to ten minutes.

3. *Valuation.* Once group members have shared their personal reactions to the material, they are ready to participate in the valuation phase of the discussion. The teacher or team leader for each group distributes a game sheet. This game sheet contains a valuing exercise—a set of four declarative statements based on the selection's content. These value statements reflect opinions about the text selection and draw insights and fresh ideas from it. The purpose of the valuing exercise is to have students come to grips with what the material means to them by either agreeing (A) or disagreeing (D) with each statement. Figure 7.11 shows such a game sheet.

Study the game sheet in Figure 7.11. Note that students must first indicate on the game sheet their own reactions to the four value statements. Then, based on the previous discussion, they must predict how each of the other members of their group would respond. In the example of Figure 7.11, Joe disagreed with three of the statements. His predictions as to how other team members would respond are indicated by the circled letters underneath the individual names. Once the responding is complete, the students are ready for the reflective phase of the intra-act procedure.

4. *Reflection.* Begin the reflection phase of intra-act by scoring the game sheet. Group members take turns revealing how each responded to the four statements. As each member tells how he or she responded, the other members check whether their predictions agreed with that member's actual responses. During this phase, the teacher acts as a facilitator, noting how students responded but refraining from

FIGURE 7.11 **Joe's Game Sheet**

Name ____________________
Date ____________________
Total Score ____________________
Percentage
of Correct Predictions ____________

Names	Joe	Sharon	Paul	Colleen
1. Tobacco companies should be held responsible for the deaths of smokers from heart attacks and lung cancer.	A (D)	A + D	A + D	A – D
2. Smokers should be able to quit. They just need to really want to.	(A) D	A + D	A + D	A + D
3. The sale of cigarettes should be illegal just like the sale of cocaine or heroin.	A (D)	A + D	A + D	A + D
4. The government should spend money on programs to help people stop smoking.	A (D)	A – D	A + D	A – D

+: Joe's predictions were correct.
–: Joe's predictions were incorrect.

imposing a particular point of view on students. Instead, encourage students to reflect on what they have learned. According to Hoffman (1979), "It is very important that during this period students be allowed ample time to discuss, challenge, support and question one another's response. This interaction serves to separate opinions quickly arrived at from sound evaluative thinking" (p. 607).

Intra-act will require several classroom applications before students become accustomed to their roles during discussion. Repeated and extensive participation in intra-act will help students become fully aware of the task demands of the procedure. In the beginning, we recommend that on completion of an intra-act discussion, students engage in a whole-class discussion of the process in which they participated. Help students debrief: "What did we learn from our participation in intra-act? Why must all members of a group participate? How might discussion improve the next time we use intra-act?" Questions such as these make students sensitive to the purpose of the intra-act procedure (problem solving) and the role of each reader (critical analysis).

An Intra-Act Example

After students in a health education class read the article "Getting Hooked on Tobacco," four students, Joe, Sharon, Paul, and Colleen, met as a group to discuss their impressions. Joe, who was the group's team leader, began with a summary of the article and then gave his own reactions. Here's how Joe summarized the article's main ideas: "Well, basically the article says that the government says that tobacco makes you, you know, a drug addict, or something like that. It's like using cocaine or heroin. They say that people can't quit and they need more and more, so cigarettes should be like liquor and you have to get a license to sell them. The cigarette companies don't agree. Me too. I don't think a guy is going to go out and rob people just to get cigarettes. I mean, if he is that hard up, he would just quit."

After some clarifying discussion of what the article was about, the discussion shifted gears into the relating phase. Sharon reacted to the article this way: "Well, I don't think that a company should be allowed to sell stuff that kills people. And if all the people quit, the company would go out of business anyway, so it should just go out of business now because of a law."

Paul entered the conversation: "I think the guy was right who said if cigarettes were illegal the gangs would have gang wars to see who would get to sell them—just like they do with crack and cocaine right now. Besides, if people really want to kill themselves with smoking, they should be allowed. And if they don't, they should just quit. Right on the pack it says *quit.*"

Colleen replied, "It ain't so easy to quit. My dad tried, like, five times, and he finally had to get hypnotized to quit. And he wouldn't have started if he had to buy them from some gang or something. You get them from a store, and nobody ever asks you how old you are. Besides, who reads the warnings?"

When time for discussion was over, the valuation phase was initiated. Students were given a game sheet with these four value statements:

1. Tobacco companies should be held responsible for the deaths of smokers from heart attacks and lung cancer.
2. Smokers should be able to quit. They just need to really want to.
3. The sale of cigarettes should be illegal just like the sale of cocaine or heroin.
4. The government should spend money on programs to help people stop smoking.

Each student was asked to respond individually to the statements and then predict whether the other members of the group would agree or disagree with each statement. Joe's sheet is reproduced in Figure 7.11. From the discussion, he was pretty sure that Sharon would agree with the first statement because she had said that they "shouldn't be allowed to kill people." Similarly, he thought Paul would disagree because he thought people should "just quit." He was also pretty sure that Colleen would agree because she seemed to think it was bad that

RESPONSE JOURNAL

How is the intra-act strategy similar to discussion webs? How is it different?

you could just go into a store and buy cigarettes. He used similar reasons to predict the group members' reactions to the other statements.

As part of the reflection phase of intra-act, the group members shared what they had learned. Joe found that most of his predictions were correct. He was surprised to find out that Colleen did not agree with statement 1, but she explained that, "It's not the companies' fault that they sold something that's not illegal. First, they should make it illegal; then it's the companies' fault." Other members argued that her reasoning "didn't make sense" because the tobacco companies know that cigarettes are harmful. That debate was typical of the discussion that went on in all the groups as students worked out the ways in which the ideas presented in the text fit in with their own attitudes and beliefs.

Directed Reading–Thinking Activity (DR–TA)

The DR–TA fosters critical awareness and thinking by engaging learners in a process that involves prediction, verification, interpretation, and judgment. Much like the QtA, the teacher guides the reading and stimulates thinking through the frequent use of open-ended questions such as "What do you think?" "Why do you think so?" "Can you prove it?" The learning environment for a DR–TA lesson is critical to its success as an instructional practice. The teacher must be supportive and encouraging so as not to inhibit students' participation in the activity. As a rule, avoid inhibiting participation by refuting students' predictions. Wait time is also important. When posing an open-ended question, it is not unusual to pause for two, three, five, or even ten seconds for students to respond. Too often, the tendency is to slice the original question into smaller parts. Sometimes a teacher starts slicing too quickly out of a sense of frustration or anxiety rather than because of students' inability to respond. Silence may very well be an indication that hypothesis formation or other cognitive activities are taking place in the students' heads. So wait—and see what happens.

To prepare for a DR–TA with an informational text, analyze the material for its superordinate and subordinate concepts. What are the relevant concepts, ideas, relationships, and information in the material? The content analysis will help you decide on logical stopping points as you direct students through the reading.

For short stories and other narrative material, determine the key elements of the story: the *setting* (time and place, major characters) and the *events in the plot* (the initiating events or problem-generating situation, the protagonist's reaction to the event and his or her goal to resolve the problem, the set of attempts to achieve the goal, outcomes related to the protagonist's attempts to achieve the goal and resolve the problem, the character's reaction).

Once these elements have been identified, the teacher has a framework for deciding on logical stopping points within the story. In Figure 7.12, we indicate a general plan that may be followed or adapted for specific story lines. Notice that the suggested stopping points come at key junctures in a causal chain of events in the story line. Each juncture suggests a logical stopping point in that it assumes that the reader has

FIGURE 7.12 **Potential Stopping Points in a DR–TA for a Story Line with One Episode**

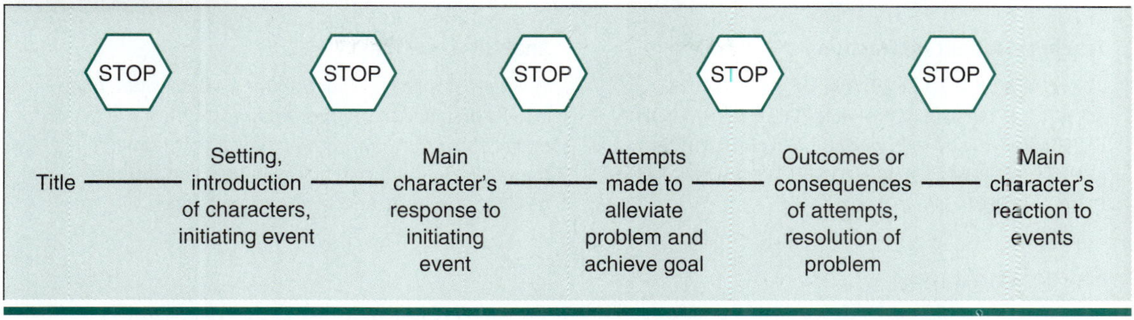

enough information from at least one preceding event to predict a future happening or event.

A DR–TA Example

In an eighth-grade science class, students were engaged in a study of a textbook chapter about the light spectrum (Davidson & Wilkerson 1988). Using a DR–TA framework, the teacher guided the students' interactions with the text material. Study an excerpt of the transcript from the beginning cycle of the DR–TA in Figure 7.13.

As you examine the transcript, note that teacher–student interactions are recorded in the left column of the box. The teacher's questions and comments are printed in capital letters, followed by the students' responses in lowercase letters. An analysis of the DR–TA lesson as it evolved is printed in the right column.

The transcript shows how the students used prior knowledge to anticipate the information that the text would reveal. As they shared what they expected to find, the students engaged in analyzing their pooled ideas. Their interactions with the teacher illustrate how a DR–TA instructional framework creates a need to know and helps readers declare purposes through anticipation and prediction making.

Once the purposes were established, the teacher assigned a section of the text chapter to be read. According to Davidson and Wilkerson (1988), two observers of the lesson:

> When students read the portion of the text they were directed to read, they read that infrared waves are invisible and that they are heat waves. Discussion, involving text ideas, students' previous ideas, and their reasoning abilities, showed that they discovered that infrared light is *not* one of the hottest colors because it is not a color. They also discovered that infrared waves are hot, since they are heat waves. The text supplied literal information. The discussion facilitated concept development and critical thinking. (p. 37)

Although the students' predictions were amiss in the initial cycle of questioning, the teacher chose not to evaluate or judge the predictions. She recognized that

FIGURE 7.13 Excerpt of a DR–TA Transcript from a Science Lesson on the Light Spectrum

Teacher–Student Interactions	Analysis of Lesson
I'D LIKE FOR YOU TO BEGIN BY JUST READING THIS ACTIVITY IN THIS SECTION. THEN TELL ME WHAT YOU EXPECT TO FIND IN THIS PASSAGE. YOU KNOW IT'S ABOUT LIGHT AND COLOR AND SPECTRUMS. WHAT ELSE DO YOU EXPECT THAT YOU WILL FIND?	The teacher directs students to read a description of an activity designed to produce a sun's spectrum with a prism. The activity includes holding a thermometer in the spectrum produced, placing a fluorite substance near the spectrum, and anticipating changes.
s: Heat	
WHY DO YOU SAY HEAT?	
s: Well, some of the colors are cooler.	The student's response is based on prior knowledge which she judges will be relevant.
DO YOU KNOW WHICH ONES WILL BE COOLER?	The teacher encourages the student to extend the response.
s: I think the darker ones.	
WHY DO YOU SAY THAT?	Teacher asks for justification.
s: They look cooler.	
THEY LOOK COOLER? OKAY.	Teacher accepts response, recognizing that the student has, in fact, generated a question to be answered in reading the text.
WHAT ELSE? DO YOU AGREE OR DISAGREE?	The teacher encourages other students to analyze this hypothesis or generate a different one.
s: Well, I agree with her on infrared and ultraviolet. They are probably the hottest colors you can get of the spectrum.	The student's response shows that he is evaluating the other student's response. Also, he uses specific vocabulary from his prior knowledge to extend the prediction.
ALL RIGHT. ANYBODY ELSE?	The teacher does not make a judgment about the validity of the predictions since that is the responsibility of the students as they read and discuss.
s: I think he is wrong.	A student disagrees.
WHY?	Teacher asks for justification.
s: Because whenever you melt steel, steel always turns red before it turns white. When it turns white, it melts completely.	The student analyzes the prior student's prediction and explains in terms of his own experience.
OKAY.	
s: You can't see infrared.	As stated, the student's response is a literal statement.
AND HOW WOULD THAT MAKE A DIFFERENCE IN WHAT HE JUST SAID?	The teacher assumes that there is a connection with the discussion and asks for explanation.
s: Well, he just said that it turned red before it turned white. And you can't see white, it's just a shade. Infrared you can't see—which would be just like sunlight. You can't see sunlight. So, I think it would be hotter.	In his extended response the student disagrees with the prior student's conclusion and explanation and uses an illustration from his prior knowledge which he feels is relevant to "prove" his point.

FIGURE 7.13 **Excerpt of a DR–TA Transcript *(continued)***

Teacher–Student Interactions	Analysis of Lesson
YOU THINK IT WOULD BE HOTTER?	The teacher does not point out the validity or lack of validity of either student's logic. She recognizes that both students are thinking critically and that they and others in the group will read to find clues to justify the concepts they are hypothesizing. She is consistent in her role as a facilitator of student discussion.
OKAY.	
ANYBODY ELSE?	
WELL, LET ME GIVE YOU THIS WHOLE FIRST PARAGRAPH. I WANT YOU TO READ TO THE BOTTOM OF THE PAGE AND THEN I WANT YOU TO GO TO THE TOP OF THE NEXT PAGE. IT WILL BE THE VERY TOP PARAGRAPH. COVER UP WHAT'S BELOW IT WITH YOUR PAPER. READ THAT FAR AND THEN STOP.	
(Students read silently.)	

Source: Reprinted with permission of Jane L. Davidson and Bonnie C. Wilkerson.

as readers interact with the text, more often than not they are able to clarify their misconceptions for themselves.

Reading Guides

RESPONSE JOURNAL

When you were a student, how helpful were worksheets in comprehending a text assignment?

What exactly is a reading guide? It has sometimes been compared to a "worksheet"—something students complete after reading, usually as homework. But reading guides do more than give students work to do. Guides, like worksheets, may consist of questions and activities related to the instructional material under study. One of the differences, however, between a reading guide and a worksheet is that students respond to the questions and activities in the guide *as* they read the text, not after. A reading guide provides instructional support as students need it. Moreover, a well-developed guide not only influences content acquisition but also prompts higher-order thinking.

Guides help students comprehend texts better than they would if left to their own resources. Over time, however, text learners should be weaned from this type of scaffolding as they develop the maturity and the learning strategies to interact with difficult texts without guide material. With this caveat in mind, let's explore the use of one type of reading guide that scaffolds learning at different levels of understanding: three-level comprehension guides.

Comprehension Levels

Because reading is a thoughtful process, it embraces the idea of levels of comprehension. Readers construct meaning at various levels of thinking and conceptual difficulty (Herber 1978). Figure 7.14 shows the different levels of comprehension.

At the *literal level,* students *read the lines* of the content material. They stay with print sufficiently to get the gist of the author's message. In simple terms, a literal recognition of that message determines what the author says. Searching for important literal information isn't an easy chore, particularly if readers haven't matured enough to know how to make the search or, even worse, haven't determined why they are searching in the first place. Most students can and will profit greatly from being shown how to recognize the essential information in the text.

Knowing what the author says is necessary but not sufficient in constructing meaning with text. Good readers search for conceptual complexity in material. They read at the *interpretive level—between the lines.* They focus not only on what authors say but also on what authors mean by what they say. The interpretive level delves into the author's intended meaning. How readers conceptualize implied ideas by integrating information into what they already know is part of the interpretive process. Recognizing the thought relationships that the author weaves together helps readers make inferences that are implicit in the material.

From time to time throughout this chapter, you have probably been trying to read us—not our words but us. And in the process of responding to our messages, you probably raised questions similar to these: "So what? What does this information mean to me? Does it make sense? Can I use these ideas for content instruction?"

FIGURE 7.14 **Levels of Comprehension**

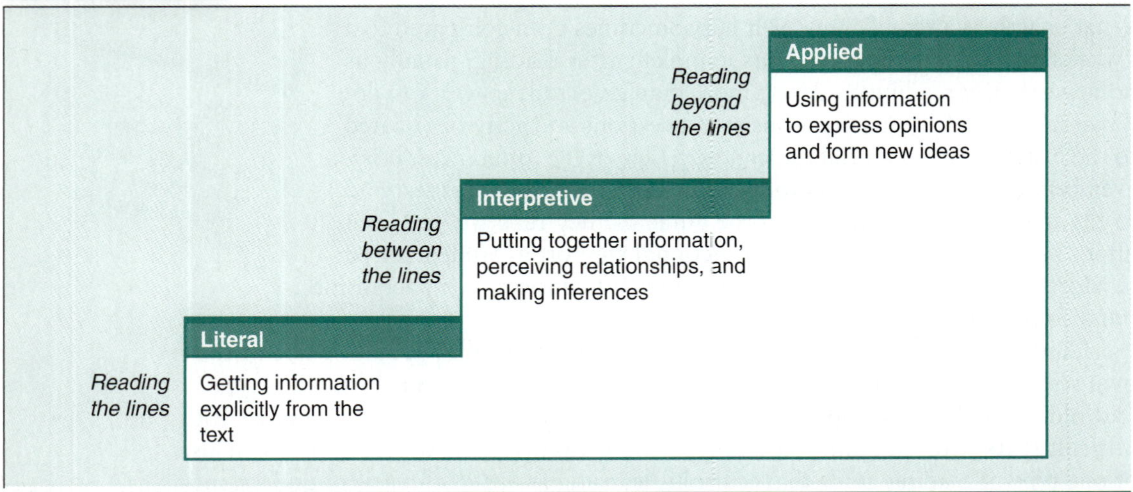

Your attempt to seek significance or relevance in what we say and mean is one signal that you are reading at the *applied level*. You are reading *beyond the lines*. Reading at the applied level is undoubtedly akin to critical reflection and discovery. When students construct meaning from text at the applied level, they know how to synthesize information—and to lay that synthesis alongside what they know already—to evaluate, question the author, think critically, and draw additional insights and fresh ideas from content material.

Three-Level Comprehension Guides

The levels-of-comprehension model that we have just introduced lends itself well to the development of guide material to engage students in reading. A three-level guide provides the framework in which students can interact with difficult texts at different levels of comprehension. One of the best ways to become familiar with the three-level guide is to experience one. Therefore, we invite you to participate in the following demonstration.

> **myeducationlab**
> Go to the Assignments and Activities section of Topic 5: "Comprehension Strategies" in the MyEducationLab for your course and complete the activity "Dimensions of Comprehension."

Preview the three-level guide in Figure 7.15; next, read "The Case of the Missing Ancestor." Then complete the three-level guide as you read the text or after reading.

THE CASE OF THE MISSING ANCESTOR

From the mid-1800s to the early 1900s, Europeans were actively searching for early ancestors. The Germans dug up the fossilized remnants of Neanderthal man and Heidelberg man. The French discovered not only ancient bones but also cave paintings done by early humans.

England, Charles Darwin's home, had no evidence of ancient ancestors. English scientists—both professionals and amateurs—began searching for fossils. Scarcely a cave was left unexplored, scarcely a stone was left unturned. Many scientists asked workers in gravel pits to watch for fossils.

In 1912, Charles Dawson, a part-time collector of fossils for the British Museum, wrote to Dr. Arthur Smith Woodward, keeper of the Natural History Department at the British Museum. Dawson claimed that a human skull he had found in a gravel pit in Piltdown Common, Sussex, "would rival Heidelberg man." Soon Woodward was digging in the gravel pit with Dawson and other eager volunteers. They found a separate jaw that, though apelike, included a canine tooth and two molars, worn down as if by human-type chewing. Flints and nonhuman fossils found at the same dig indicated that the finds were very old.

Despite arguments by some scientists that the jaw came from a chimpanzee or an orangutan, the discoverers reconstructed the skull and connected the jaw to it. They named the fossil *Eoanthropus dawsoni,* Dawson's "Dawn man," and said that it was much older than Neanderthal man. The find came to be known as Piltdown man.

The finds were X-rayed. One dental authority was suspicious of the canine; he said it was too young a tooth to show such wear. However, such contrary evidence was ignored in the general surge of enthusiasm. So the Piltdown man was acclaimed as an important find, a human in which the brain had evolved more quickly than the jaw.

FIGURE 7.15 **Three-Level Guide for "The Case of the Missing Ancestor"**

I. *Directions:* Check the statements that you believe say what the author says. Sometimes, the exact words are used; at other times, other words may be used.

_____ 1. The Germans discovered the fossilized remnants of the Neanderthal man and the Heidelberg man.

_____ 2. Charles Dawson found a human skull in a gravel pit in Piltdown Common, Sussex.

_____ 3. Charles Dawson was a professional archaeologist.

_____ 4. The fossil, labeled *Eoanthropus dawsoni,* became known as the Piltdown man.

_____ 5. The discovery of the Piltdown man was acclaimed as an important archaeological find.

_____ 6. Dental evidence regarding the Piltdown man was ignored.

II. *Directions:* Check the statements that you believe represent the author's *intended* meaning.

_____ 1. The English scientific community felt left out because important fossils had been found in other countries.

_____ 2. Good scientific practices were ignored by the people working with the Piltdown fossils.

_____ 3. Many scientists said that Piltdown was important because they wanted England to be important.

_____ 4. Dawson wanted to make himself famous, so he constructed a hoax.

III. *Directions:* Check the statements you agree with, and be ready to support your choices with ideas from the text and your own knowledge and beliefs.

_____ 1. Competition in scientific research may be dangerous.

_____ 2. Scientists, even good ones, can be fooled by poorly constructed hoaxes.

_____ 3. People often see only what they want to see.

_____ 4. A scientific "fact" is not always correct simply because many scientists believe strongly in it; theories are always open to question.

Beginning in the 1940s, the bones were subjected to modern tests. It is now believed that the skull was from a modern human and the jaw was from a modern ape, probably an orangutan. The animal fossils and flints were found to be very old, but not the types that have been found in England. Apparently, they had been placed in the gravel pit to make the finds more convincing. Why were the scientists and others fooled so easily? Perhaps the desire to find an "ancestor" may have interfered with careful scientific observation. (Alexander 1986)

Several comments are in order on your participation in the three-level guide demonstration. First of all, note that the three-level format gave you a "conscious experience" with comprehension levels as a process. Note also that as you proceeded through the process, you responded to and manipulated the important explicit and implicit ideas in the material. You may have sensed the relatedness of ideas as you moved within and among the levels.

Why did we direct you first to preview the guide and then to read the material? Because surveying helps create a predisposition to read the material. Previewing helps reduce the reader's uncertainty about the material to be read. You know what is coming. When we asked you to read the guide first, we hoped to raise your expectations about the author's message. By encountering some of the ideas before reading, you are in a better position to direct your search for information in the reading material that may be relevant.

You probably noted also that the declarative statements did not require you to produce answers to questions. Rather, you had to make decisions among likely alternatives; it's easier to recognize possible answers than to produce them.

Notice, too, that in a very positive way, the statements can serve as springboards for discussion and conversation about the content. Were students to react to guides *without* the opportunity to discuss and debate responses, the instructional material would soon deteriorate into busywork and paper shuffling.

RESPONSE JOURNAL

What do you think is the difference between responding to statements at different levels of comprehension versus responding to questions?

A final comment: Your maturity as a reader is probably such that you didn't need structured guidance for this selection, particularly at levels I and II. If you make the decision that certain segments of your text can be handled without reading guidance, don't construct guide material. A three-level guide is a means to growth in reading and growth through reading. It is not an end in itself.

Constructing Three-Level Comprehension Guides

Don't be misled by the apparent discreteness of comprehension levels. Don't, as Dale (1969) pronounced, suffer from "hardening of the categories." The term *levels* implies a cognitive hierarchy that may be more apocryphal than real. A reader doesn't necessarily read first for literal recognition, then interpretation, and finally application—although that may appear to be a logical sequence. Many readers, for instance, read text for overarching concepts and generalizations first and then search for evidence to support their inferences.

It is important to recognize that in reading, levels are probably interactive and inseparable. Nevertheless, the classroom teacher attempts to have students experience each aspect of the comprehension process as they read content material. In doing so, students adapt strategies as they interact with the material. They get a feel for the component processes within reading comprehension. They come to sense in an instructional setting what it means to make inferences, to use information as the basis for those inferences, and to rearrange or transform acquired understandings into what they know already in order to construct knowledge.

If guides were to be used with every text assignment every day, it would become counterproductive. One math teacher's evaluation of a three-level guide crystallizes this point: "The students said the guide actually helped them organize the author's ideas in their minds and helped them understand the material. I think the guide was successful, but I would not use it all the time because many of the assignments don't lend themselves to this type of activity." The three-level guide is only one instructional aid that helps students grow toward mature reading and independent learning.

Finally, we urge you also to consider guides as tools, not tests. Think of each statement in a three-level guide as a prompt that will initiate student discussion and reinforce the quality of the reader's interaction with text.

Before constructing a guide, the teacher has to decide the following: What important ideas should be emphasized? What are the students' competencies? What depth of understanding are the students expected to achieve? What is the difficulty of the material? Having made these decisions, consider these five guidelines:

1. *Begin construction of the guide at level II, the interpretive level.* Analyze the text selection, asking yourself, "What does the author mean?" Write down in your own words all inferences that make sense to you and that fit your content objectives. Make sure your statements are written simply and clearly (after all, you don't want to construct a guide to read the guide).

2. *Next, search the text for the propositions and explicit pieces of information needed to support the inferences you have chosen for level II.* Put these into statement form. You now have level I, the literal level.

3. *Decide whether you want to add a distractor or two to levels I and II.* We have found that a distractor maintains an active response to the information search, mainly because students sense that they cannot indiscriminately check every item and, therefore, must focus their information search more carefully.

4. *Develop statements for level III, the applied level.* Such statements represent additional insights or principles that can be drawn when relationships established by the author are combined with other ideas outside the text selection itself but inside the heads of your students. In other words, help students connect what they know already to what they read.

5. *Be flexible and adaptive.* Develop a format that will appeal to you and your students. Try to avoid crowding too much print on the reading guide.

A Three-Level Comprehension Guide Example

The format of a three-level guide will vary from one content area to another. The classroom example that follows serves only as a model. As you study it, think of ways that you will be able to adapt and apply the three-level construct to your discipline-specific materials. A middle grade teacher constructed the three-level guide in Figure 7.16 as part of a health unit. Notice how she uses question–answer relationships (QARs) as cues to direct students' responses. Students completed the guide individually and then discussed their responses in small groups.

FIGURE 7.16 **Three-Level Guide for a Health Lesson**

I. Right There! What did the author say?

Directions: Place a check on the line in front of the number if you think a statement can be found in the pages you read.

_____ 1. Every human being has feelings or emotions.

_____ 2. Research workers are studying the effects on the body of repeated use of marijuana.

_____ 3. You should try hard to hide your strong emotions, such as fear or anger.

_____ 4. Your feelings affect the way the body works.

_____ 5. You are likely to get angry at your parents or brothers or sisters more often than at other people.

II. Think and Search! What did the author mean?

Directions: Check the following statements that state what the author was trying to say in the pages you read.

_____ 1. Sometimes you act in a different way because of your mood.

_____ 2. Your emotional growth has been a continuing process since the day you were born.

_____ 3. The fact that marijuana hasn't been proved to be harmful means that it is safe to use.

_____ 4. Each time you successfully control angry or upset feelings, you grow a little.

III. On Your Own! Do you agree with these statements?

Directions: Check each statement that you can defend.

_____ 1. Escaping from problems does not solve them.

_____ 2. Decisions should be made on facts, not fantasies.

_____ 3. Getting drunk is a good way to have fun.

LOOKING BACK LOOKING FORWARD

Strategy-centered classrooms are places where students learn how to learn. Teachers support students' efforts to make meaning by guiding reading comprehension and modeling how to think and learn with texts. To this end, we explored several research-based comprehension strategies that show students how to be active, thoughtful readers: think-alouds, question–answer relationships (QARs), reciprocal teaching, and questioning the author (QtA). When these strategies are adapted to meet the textual and conceptual demands of a discipline, they not only model comprehension strategies but also engage learners in meaningful talk and discussion about the content under study.

Several comprehension-centered instructional strategies were also suggested to guide students' interactions with texts. These strategies are designed to help students clarify and extend meaning as they engage in reading. For example, KWL is a meaning-making strategy that engages students in active text learning and may be used with small groups of students or with an entire class. KWL comprises several steps that help learners examine what they know, what they want to know more about, and what they have learned from reading. The directed reading–thinking activity (DR–TA) was also described. DR–TA revolves around three guiding questions: (1) What do you think? (2) Why do you think so? (3) Can you prove it? The guided reading procedure (GRP) encourages close reading of difficult text, whereas the discussion web and intra-act strategies lay the groundwork for reflective discussion following the reading of text material.

In addition to comprehension strategies, teacher-prepared reading guides may also be used to guide reading. Three-level comprehension guides allow learners to interact with text, constructing meaning at different levels of thinking: literal, interpretive, and applied. In the next chapter, we focus on the building blocks of comprehension in a discipline: developing technical vocabulary and concepts. In particular, we examine the relationship between the vocabulary of a content area—its special and technical terms—and its concepts. How can a teacher help students to interact with the language of a discipline and, in the process, show them how to define, clarify, and extend their understanding of the concepts under study?

Minds On

1. Why and how will the instructional strategies that you have studied help you guide students in reading?
2. With a small group, create an intra-act guide sheet for this chapter. After you have finished, discuss any insights into reading gained from this activity.
3. Picture a content area class of twenty-five to thirty students (your choice of grade level and subject) from diverse backgrounds. Describe how you would use discussion webs and KWL strategies while maintaining high standards of content literacy and learning.
4. Select a popular book, film, or song that most members of your small group know. Discuss each of the following levels of comprehension communicated in that work: (a) literal (in the lines), (b) interpretive (between the lines), (c) applied (beyond the lines).

Hands On

1. Without sharing perceptions, each member of your group should read this short paragraph and follow the directions.

   An artist was talking enthusiastically about one of her favorite paintings to several people visiting the gallery when a woman approached her and offered to purchase the work. The owner of the gallery removed the painting from the wall. The painting was snatched from her hands, and the woman bolted through the front door into a waiting van, which sped down the street through a nearby red light and vanished into the night.

   Using the paragraph as a reference, respond to each of the following statements, in the order presented, by circling T (for true), F (for false), or ? (for unable to determine from the paragraph). Once you have characterized a statement as true, false, or questionable, you cannot change your answer.

a. The artist talked about one of her paintings.
T F ?

b. The thief was a woman.
T F ?

c. The crime appeared to be premeditated.
T F ?

d. This type of theft seems unlikely.
T F ?

e. The owner removed the painting from the wall.
T F ?

f. The owner was the artist.
T F ?

g. The woman who bolted through the door stole the painting.
T F ?

h. The person who snatched the painting from the owner's hands was the artist.
T F ?

i. A robbery didn't occur.
T F ?

Discuss the variety of possible answers based on your responses. What does this activity tell you about reader–text interactions?

2. Select a short informational article in a magazine or book, and make copies for each member of your group. Have each member of the group choose one of the following instructional strategies: (1) KWL (What do you *know?* About what do you *want to know* more? What did you *learn?*); (2) GRP (guided reading procedure); (3) intra-act; (4) DR–TA (directed reading–thinking activity); and (5) a discussion web. If there are more than five members in your group, duplicate strategies as needed.

   Using the same article, design a lesson around the strategy you have chosen and make copies to share with the members of the group. As you review the four different lessons prepared by your colleagues, what comparisons and contrasts can you make between these instructional strategies?

3. Select a short informational article in a magazine or book, and bring copies for each member of your group. Have each member of the group discuss the merits of one of the following instructional strategies: (1) guided discussion, (2) discussion web, (3) KWL, and (4) a three-level reading guide. If there are more than four members in your group, duplicate strategies as needed.

   Using the same article, design a lesson around the strategy you have discussed and make copies to share with the members of the group. As you review the four different lessons prepared by your colleagues, what comparisons and contrasts can you make between these instructional strategies?

eRESOURCES

- The following site is filled with ideas for engaging students in reading: **www.readingrockets.org.** Explore the site for ideas and research on how to support students' motivation to read. Discuss your findings in small groups.
- The National Reading Panel's focus on research-based strategies serves as a landmark in reading education. Review the Panel's findings on text comprehension (**www.nichd.nih.gov/publications/nrp/findings.cfm**).
- Use the keywords "QtA" or "Questioning the Author" and "KWL" or "KWL Strategies" to search for these two powerful comprehension strategies. Consider how you might use these strategies in your content area. Reading Quest provides examples for KWL (**www.readingquest.org/strat/kwl.html**) and QtA (**www.readingquest.org/strat/qta.html**).

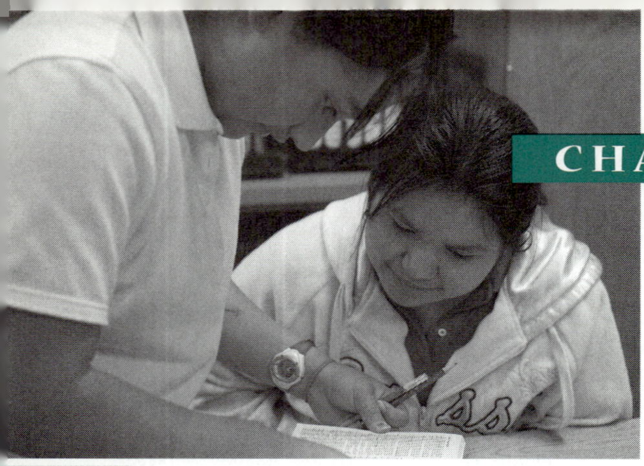

CHAPTER 8

Words are the model,
words are the tools,
words are the boards,
words are the nails.

—Richard Rhodes

Developing Vocabulary and Concepts

ORGANIZING PRINCIPLE

Teaching words well means giving students multiple opportunities to develop word meanings and learn how words are conceptually related to one another in the texts they are studying.

There is a strong connection between vocabulary knowledge and reading comprehension. If students are not familiar with most words they meet in print, they will undoubtedly have trouble understanding what they read. No wonder Richard Rhodes, an American journalist, historian, and author of fiction and nonfiction, suggests that words are the building materials students need to construct meaning as they read and learn with text. Technical vocabulary—words unique to a content area—are often unfamiliar to students, but are particularly important for disciplinary thinking and learning. The more experience students have with unfamiliar words and the more exposure they have to them, the more meaningful the words will become.

Vocabulary is as unique to a content area as fingerprints are to a human being. A content area is distinguishable by its language, particularly the technical terms that label the

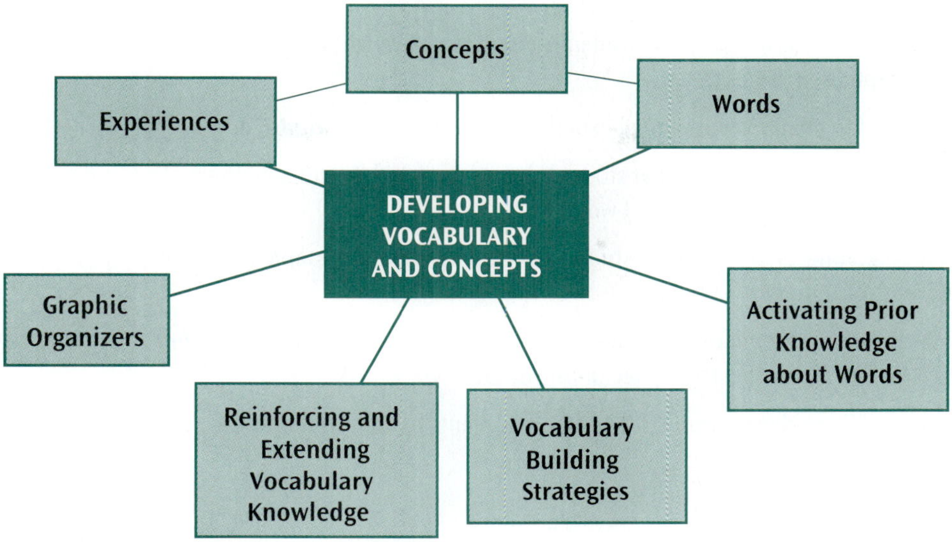

concepts undergirding the subject matter. Teachers know they must do something with the language of their content areas, but they often reduce instruction to routines that direct students to look up, define, memorize, and use content-specific words in sentences. Such practices divorce the study of vocabulary from an exploration of the subject matter. Learning vocabulary becomes an activity in itself—a separate one—rather than an integral part of learning academic content. Content area vocabulary must be taught *well enough* to remove potential barriers to students' understanding of texts in content areas. The organizing principle underscores the main premise of the chapter: **Teaching words well means giving students multiple opportunities to develop word meanings and learn how words are conceptually related to one another in the texts they are studying.**

FRAME OF MIND

1. Why should the language of an academic discipline be taught within the context of concept development?
2. What are the relationships among experiences, concepts, and words?
3. How can a teacher activate what students know about words and help them make connections among related words?
4. How do graphic organizers help students anticipate and understand important concepts in content area texts?
5. How do activities for vocabulary and concept development help students refine their knowledge of special and technical vocabulary?
6. How can knowledge of word structure help students to understand word meanings?

RESPONSE JOURNAL
What were some of your experiences with vocabulary instruction in content areas?

Fridays always seemed to be set aside for quizzes when we were students. And one of the quizzes most frequently given was the vocabulary test: "Look up these words for the week. Write out their definitions and memorize them. Then use each word in a complete sentence. You'll be tested on these terms on Friday."

Our vocabulary study seemed consistently to revolve around the dull routines of looking up, defining, and memorizing words and using them in sentences.

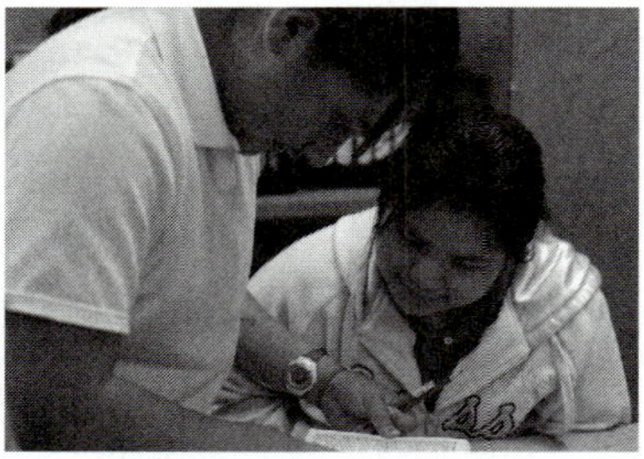

Such an instructional pattern resulted in meaningless, purposeless activity—an end in itself, rather than a means to an end. Although there was nothing inherently wrong with looking up, defining, and memorizing words and using them in sentences, the approach itself was too narrow for us to learn words in depth. Instead, we memorized definitions to pass the Friday quiz—and forgot them on Saturday.

Having students learn lists of words is based on the ill-founded notion that the acquisition of vocabulary is separate from the development of ideas and concepts in a content area. Teaching vocabulary often means assigning a list of words rather than exploring word meanings and relationships that contribute to students' conceptual awareness and understanding of a subject. Once teachers clarify the relationship between words and concepts, they are receptive to instructional alternatives. ■

One clarification that's quickly made involves the types of reading vocabulary found in textbooks. Three types of vocabulary are evident. The first type, *general vocabulary,* consists of everyday words with widely acknowledged meanings in common usage. The second, *special vocabulary,* is made up of words from everyday life, general vocabulary that take on specialized meanings when adapted to a particular content area. The third type, *technical vocabulary,* consists of words that have usage and application only in a particular subject matter field.

Special and technical terms are particularly bothersome when they're encountered in content material. Your participation in the demonstration in Figure 8.1 will illustrate why special and technical terms are likely candidates for vocabulary instruction in content areas. If your responses are similar to those of classroom teachers who have participated in this activity, several predictable outcomes are likely.

First of all, it is relatively easy for you to identify the content areas for several of the lists. Your knowledge and experience probably trigger instant recognition. You have a good working concept of many of the terms on these easy lists. You can put them to use in everyday situations that require listening, reading, writing, or speaking. They are your words. You own them.

Second, you probably recognize words in a few of the lists even though you may not be sure about the meanings of individual words. In lists 4 and 9, for example, you may be familiar with only one or two terms. Yet you are fairly sure that the terms in lists 4 and 9 exist as words despite the fact that you may not know what they mean. Your attitude toward these kinds of words is analogous to your saying to a stranger, "I think I've met you before but I'm not sure." Several of the words from the lists may be in your "twilight zone"; you have some knowledge about them, but their meanings are a "bit foggy, not sharply focused." *Trans fat* in list 7 is a case in point for some of us who have heard the term used in television commercials and may even have purchased foods with trans fat at the supermarket. Nevertheless, our guess is that we would be hard pressed to define or explain the meaning of *trans fat* with any precision.

Finally, in one or two cases a list may have completely stymied your efforts at identification. There simply is no connection between your prior knowledge and any of the terms. You probably are not even sure whether the terms in one list really exist as words.

Which content area did you identify for list 6? In truth, the terms in this list represent nonsense. They are bogus words that were invented to illustrate the point that many of the content terms in textbooks look the same way to students that the nonsense words in list 6 look to you. You're able to pronounce most of them with little trouble but are stymied when you try to connect them to your knowledge and experience. Students are stymied this way every day by real words that represent the key concepts of a content area.

The words in these lists are actually taken from middle and high school textbooks. Just think for a moment about the staggering conceptual demands we place on learners daily as they go from class to class. Terminology that they encounter in content material is often outside the scope of their normal speaking, writing, listening, and reading vocabularies. Special and technical terms often do not have concrete

FIGURE 8.1 **Vocabulary Demonstration Words in Content Areas**

Directions: In each of the nine blanks, fill in the name of the content area that includes all the terms in the list below:

1. ____________________

nationalism
imperialism
naturalism
instrumentalism
isolationist
radicalism
fundamentalist
anarchy

2. ____________________

forestry
ornithology
zoology
biology
entomology
botany
bacteriology
protista

3. ____________________

metaphor
allusion
irony
paradox
symbolism
imagery
simile

4. ____________________

prestissimo
adagio
larghetto
presto
allegro
largo
andante
tempo

5. ____________________

centimeter
milligram
deciliter
millisecond
kilometer
decimeter
kilogram
millimeter

6. ____________________

graffles
folutes
lesnics
raptiforms
cresnites
hygrolated
loors
chamlets

7. ____________________

trans fat
glycogen
monosaccharide
hydrogenation
enzymes
lyzine
cellulose

8. ____________________

octagon
hemisphere
decagon
hexagon
bisect
equilateral
quadrilateral
pentagon

9. ____________________

auricle
ventricle
tricuspid
semilunar
apex
mitral
aorta
myocardium

referents; they are abstract and must be learned through definition, application, and repeated exposure.

Your participation in this activity leads to several points about word knowledge and concepts in content areas. The activity is a good reminder that every academic discipline creates a unique language to represent its important concepts. This is why teaching vocabulary in content areas is too important to be incidental or accidental. Key concept words need to be taught directly and taught well.

Informational texts used in content area classes typically bring with them more challenging vocabulary demands than narrative or literary texts (Pearson, Hiebert, & Kamil 2007). Providing students with direct instruction in vocabulary has been found to influence comprehension of text more than any other factor (Bromley 2007). Students shouldn't be left to their own devices or subjected to the vagaries of a look up-and-define strategy as their only access to understanding the language of an academic discipline. Verbalizing a dictionary definition of a word and learning it by rote are quite different from encountering that word in a reading situation and constructing meaning for it based on conceptual knowledge and prior experiences.

> **myeducationlab**
> Go to the Assignments and Activities section of Topic 6: "Vocabulary and Fluency" in the MyEducationLab for your course and complete the activity "Intentional Vocabulary Instruction" to see how one teacher introduces new words.

Selecting specific vocabulary words for meaningful, direct instruction from the plethora of potential words that might be studied in a subject area can be a challenge for teachers. To provide guidance in doing so, Beck, McKeown, and Kucan (2002) categorize vocabulary words according to three tiers or levels:

Tier 1: Tier 1 words are basic high-frequency and high-utility words that are commonly used in everyday language. Tier I might include words such as *friend, move, eat,* and *home.* Native language speakers typically don't require direct instruction to understand Tier 1 words.

Tier 2: Tier 2 words are also high-frequency and high-utility words; however, words in this category are more commonly used by advanced or mature language users. Words such as *scalding, reprimand, clarify,* and *escapade* are examples of Tier 2 words. Vocabulary instruction is often needed in order for students to understand the meanings of these words.

Tier 3: Tier 3 words are low-frequency words, but words that are needed to understand a content area material. Tier 3 words are part of the language of a subject area and, as the vocabulary demonstration in Figure 8.1 illustrated, unique and integral to each subject area. Examples of Tier 3 words include words such as *Declaration of Independence, nucleus, quadratic equation,* and *palette.* Tier 3 words are those for which direct instruction is often required in content area classes.

Flanigan and Greenword (2007) extend Beck, McKeown, and Kucan's tier system for categorizing words for content area vocabulary instruction. Their model describes four levels specific to content area vocabulary words:

Level 1—Critical "Before" Words: Words that students must understand before they can begin to read a text and construct meaning from a text or passage.

Level 2—"Foot-in-the Door" Words: Words that students must understand at a basic level in order to gain a general understanding of a text.

Level 3—Critical "After" Words: Words that can be clarified after students have read a text; they tend to be words that students have seen or used in other contexts.

Level 4—Words Not to Teach: Words that students already understand, or words that appear in the text but do not pertain to the teacher's instructional objectives and are not critical to understanding the text.

In this chapter, we will show how to teach words well within the framework of subject matter learning. Teaching words well removes potential barriers to reading comprehension. It is no wonder that research has documented a strong link between vocabulary development and reading comprehension (National Reading Panel 2000; Pressley 2002a). Knowledge of word meanings, and the ability to use that knowledge effectively, contributes significantly to a student's reading and listening comprehension (Curtis & Longo 2001). When teachers understand *how* students acquire knowledge of vocabulary concepts, vocabulary instruction can be effectively integrated within the context of subject area learning (Blachowicz, Fisher, Ogle, & Watts-Taffe 2006).

Teaching words well involves helping students make connections between their prior knowledge and the vocabulary to be encountered in text and providing them with multiple opportunities to define, clarify, and extend their knowledge of words and concepts during the course of study. To begin, let's explore the connection that links direct experience to concepts and words. Understanding these connections lays the groundwork for teaching words, with the emphasis on learning.

RTI *for Struggling Adolescent Learners* — BOX 8.1

Responsiveness to Vocabulary and Concept Development

As the vocabulary strategy interventions in this chapter suggest, using a single approach to vocabulary and concept development, such as a traditional dictionary definition approach, will not adequately meet the learning needs of all students or the standards of individualized and intensive instruction as outlined by RTI directives. Struggling readers need both *direct* and *indirect* instruction to learn new vocabulary and concepts that can lead to improved comprehension (Bromley 2007). The National Reading Panel (2000) determined that direct instruction in vocabulary included preteaching words relevant to the unit or task and building students' knowledge of word morphology. Front-loading instruction by introducing new words or concepts allows students a greater chance at reading success through increased word knowledge and knowledge of skills and strategies that support independent reading comprehension. For Tier 1 accommodations, direct instruction may include whole-class or small-group instruction. For more intensive interventions, instruction would more likely be tailored to individual students' learning needs.

Struggling readers also need vocabulary instruction that is embedded in wide reading and strategy use that engages students in learning. After third grade, wide reading accounts for the largest source of vocabulary growth by far (Nagy 1988).

Experiences, Concepts, and Words

Words are labels for concepts. A single concept, however, represents much more than the meaning of a single word. It may take thousands of words to explain a concept. However, answers to the question, "What does it mean to know a word?" depend on how well we understand the relationships among direct experiences, concepts, and words.

RESPONSE JOURNAL

What are some words related to your content area that didn't exist ten years ago? One year ago? Why do you think these words are now in use?

Learning the meaning of new terms by reading definitions is only minimally effective. Concepts are learned by acting on and interacting with the environment. Students learn concepts best through direct, concrete, purposeful experiences (Nagy 1988). Learning is much more intense and meaningful when it develops through firsthand experience. However, in place of using direct experience, which is not always possible, students can develop and learn concepts through various levels of improvised or vicarious experience, which is often feasible in a classroom setting.

What Are Concepts?

Concepts create mental images, which may represent anything that can be grouped together by common features or similar criteria: objects, symbols, ideas, processes, or events. In this respect, concepts are similar to schemata. A concept hardly ever stands alone; instead, it is bound by a hierarchy of relationships. As a result, "most concepts do not represent a unique object or event but rather a general class linked by a common element or relationship" (Johnson & Pearson 1984, p. 33).

Bruner, Goodnow, and Austin (1977) suggest that we would be overwhelmed by the complexity of our environment if we were to respond to each object or event that we encountered as unique. Therefore, we invent categories (or form concepts) to reduce the complexity of our environment and the necessity for constant learning. For example, every feline need not have a different name; each is known as a *cat*. Although cats vary greatly, their common characteristics cause them to be referred to by the same general term. Thus, to facilitate communication, we invent words to name concepts.

Concept Relationships: An Example

Consider your concept for the word *ostrich*. What picture comes to mind? Your image of an ostrich might differ from ours, depending on your prior knowledge of the ostrich or the larger class to which it belongs, generally referred to as *land birds*. Moreover, your direct or vicarious experiences with birds may differ significantly from someone else's. Nevertheless, for any concept, we organize all our experiences and knowledge into conceptual hierarchies according to *class, example,* and *attribute* relations.

FIGURE 8.2 **A Concept Hierarchy Based on Class Relations**

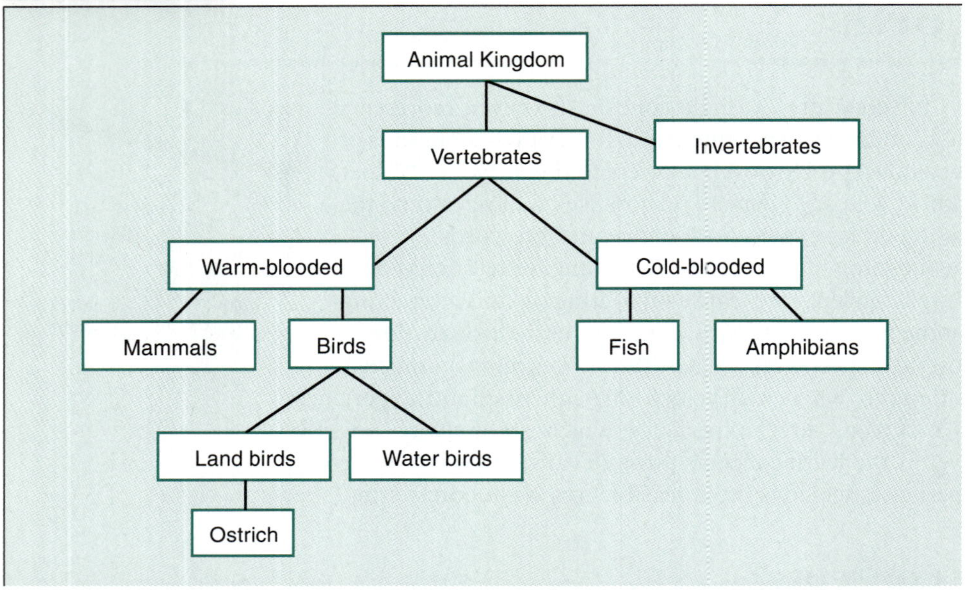

The concept *ostrich* is part of a more inclusive class or category called *land birds,* which is in turn subsumed under an even larger class of animals known as *warm-blooded vertebrates.* These class relations are depicted in Figure 8.2.

In any conceptual network, class relationships are organized in a *hierarchy* consisting of superordinate and subordinate concepts. In Figure 8.2, the superordinate concept is *animal kingdom. Vertebrates* and *invertebrates* are two classes within the animal kingdom; they are in a subordinate position in this hierarchy. *Vertebrates,* however—divided into two classes, *warm-blooded* and *cold-blooded*—are superordinate to *mammals, birds, fish,* and *amphibians,* which are types or subclasses of vertebrates. The concept *land birds,* subordinate to *birds* but superordinate to *ostrich,* completes the hierarchy.

For every concept, there are examples. An *example* is a member of any concept being considered. Class–example relations are complementary: Vertebrates and invertebrates are examples within the *animal kingdom;* mammals, birds, fish, and amphibians are examples of *vertebrates;* land birds are one example of *birds;* and so on.

Let's make *land birds* our target concept. What are some other examples of land birds in addition to the ostrich? *Penguin, emu,* and *rhea* are a few, as shown in Figure 8.3. We could have listed more examples of land birds. Instead, we now ask, "What do the ostrich, penguin, emu, and rhea have in common?" This question allows us to focus on their *relevant attributes,* the features, traits, properties, or characteristics common to every example of a particular group. In this case, the relevant attributes of land birds are the characteristics that determine whether the ostrich, penguin, emu, and rhea belong to the class of birds called *land birds.* An attribute is said to be *criti-*

FIGURE 8.3 Class–Example Relations for the Target Concept *Land Birds*

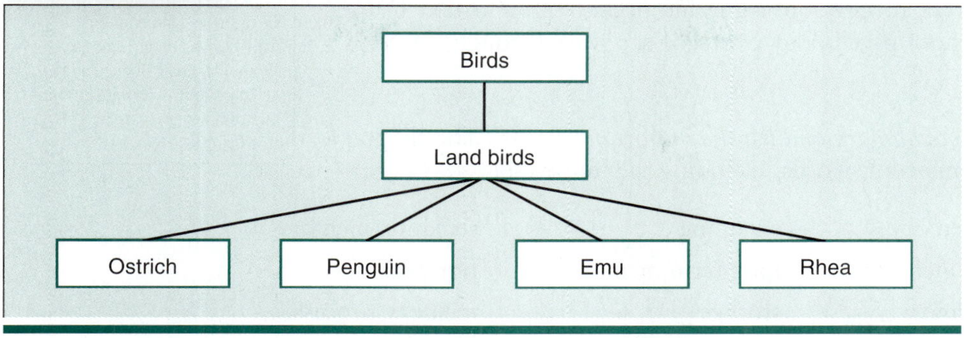

cal if it is a characteristic that is necessary to class membership. An attribute is said to be *variable* if it is shared by some but not all examples of the class.

Thus, we recognize that certain physical and social characteristics are shared by all land birds but that not every land bird has each feature. Virtually all land birds have feathers, wings, and beaks. They hatch from eggs and have two legs. They differ in color, size, habitat, and size of feet. Some land birds fly, and others, with small wings that cannot support their bodies in the air, do not. In what ways is the ostrich similar to other land birds? How is the ostrich different?

This brief discussion illustrates an important principle: *Teachers can help students build conceptual knowledge of content area terms by teaching and reinforcing the concept words in relation to other concept words.* This key instructional principle plays itself out in content area classrooms whenever students are actively making connections among the keywords in a lesson or unit of study.

Using Graphic Organizers to Make Connections Among Key Concepts

At the start of each chapter, we have asked you to use a "chapter overview" to organize your thoughts about the main ideas in the text. These ideas are presented within the framework of a *graphic organizer,* a diagram that uses content vocabulary to help students anticipate concepts and their relationships to one another in the reading material. These concepts are displayed in an arrangement of key technical terms relevant to the important concepts to be learned.

RESPONSE JOURNAL

Do you find the chapter overviews at the beginning of each chapter useful in preparing to study a chapter? Why? Why not?

Graphic organizers vary in format. One commonly used format to depict the hierarchical relationships among concept words is a "network tree" diagram. Keep in mind, network tree graphic organizers always show concepts in relation to other concepts. Let's take a closer look at how to construct and apply graphic organizers in the classroom.

A Graphic Organizer Walk-Through

myeducationlab
Go to the Assignments and Activities section of Topic 6: "Vocabulary and Fluency" in the MyEducationLab for your course and complete the activity "Clarifying Key Terms."

Suppose you were to develop a graphic organizer for a text chapter in a high school psychology course. Let's walk through the steps involved.

1. *Analyze the vocabulary and list the important words.* The chapter yields several important words, including the following:

episodic memory	encoding	semantic memory
short-term memory	long-term memory	retrieval
sensory memory	storage	memory processes

2. *Arrange the list of words.* Choose the word that represents the most inclusive concept, the one superordinate to all of the others. Next, choose the words classified immediately under the superordinate concepts and coordinate them with one another. Then choose the terms subordinate to the coordinate concepts. Your diagram may look like Figure 8.4.

3. *Add to the scheme vocabulary terms that you believe the students understand.* You add the following terms:

flashbulb memories	explicit memory	organizational systems
echoic	riding a bicycle	tip-of-the tongue phenomenon
iconic	visual codes	schema
working memory	acoustic codes	

4. *Evaluate the organizer.* The interrelationships among the key terms may look like Figure 8.5 once you evaluate the vocabulary arrangement.

FIGURE 8.4 Arrangement of Words on Memory in a Psychology Test

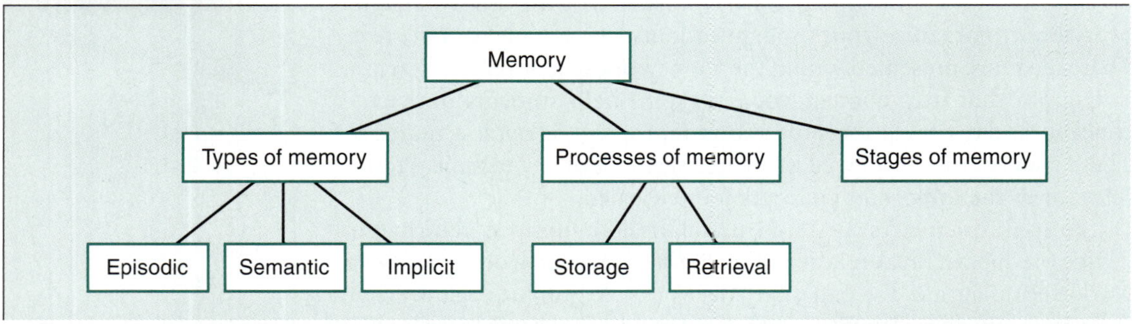

FIGURE 8.5 **Arrangement of Words on Memory After Evaluation of Organizer**

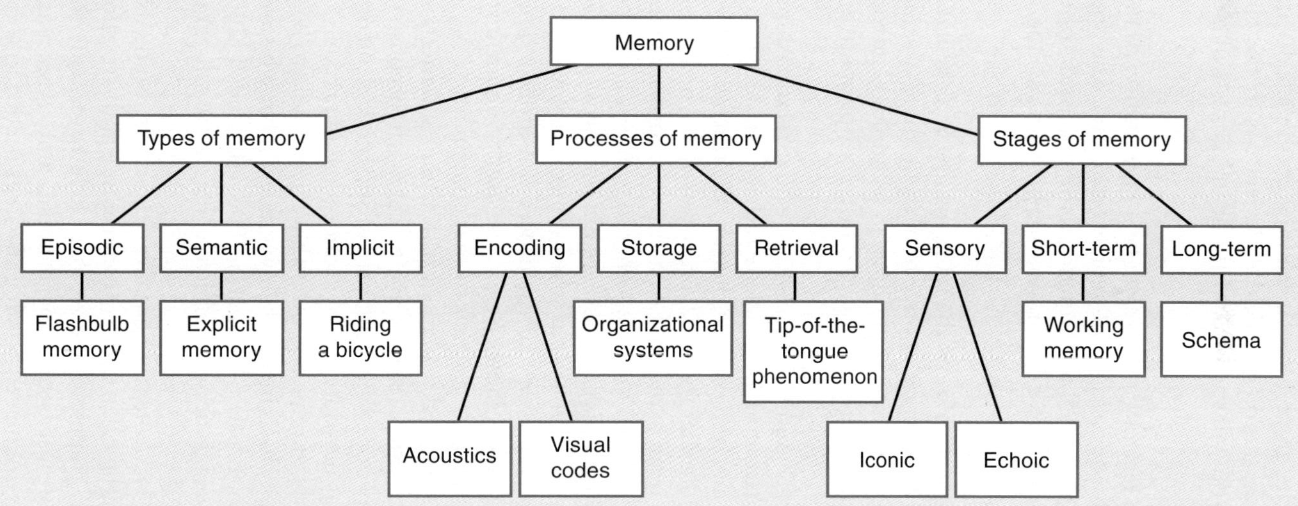

5. *Introduce the students to the learning task.* As you present the vocabulary relationships shown on the graphic organizer, create as much discussion as possible. Draw on students' understanding of and experience with the concepts the terms label. The discussions you will stimulate with the organizer will be worth the time it takes to construct it.

6. *As you complete the learning task, relate new information to the organizer.* This step is particularly useful as a study and review technique. The organizer becomes a study guide that can be referred to throughout the discussion of the material. Students should be encouraged to add information to flesh out the organizer as they develop concepts more fully.

Use a graphic organizer to show the relationships in a thematic unit, in a chapter, or in a subsection of a chapter. Notice how the graphic organizer in Figure 8.6, developed for a high school class in multimedia technology, introduced students to the different elements of PowerPoint and the different options available within each of those elements.

An art teacher used Figure 8.7 (p. 248) to show relationships among types of media used in art. She used an artist's palette rather than a tree diagram. After completing the entries for paint and ceramics herself, the teacher challenged her students to brainstorm other media that they had already used or knew about and to provide examples; she used the open areas on the palette to record students' associations.

When concepts are related to one another in terms of a chronological or linear order, the graphic organizer may be presented in the form of a time line (Parker & Jarolimek 1997). Time lines can be used when subject area material requires students to understand a sequence of events or the procedural order required to complete a given task. Figure 8.8 (p. 248) shows a time line used in an art history class to illustrate some of the major periods relevant to that content area.

Graphic organizers are easily adapted to learning situations in the elementary grades. For class presentation, elementary teachers often construct organizers on large sheets of chart paper or on bulletin boards. Still other elementary teachers draw pictures with words that illustrate the key concepts under study.

When used efficiently, graphic organizers have been found to be powerful learning tools for students whose achievement is below grade level or who are exhibiting learning difficulty (Guastello, Beasley, & Sinatra 2000). Baxendell (2003) offers the following research-based suggestions for effectively implementing graphic organizers:

1. *Be consistent when implementing graphic organizers.* Students who struggle to learn content area material often benefit from routine and structure. Using standard and familiar models of graphic organizers can help to provide that structure. For example, when reviewing a science or social studies unit, a tree diagram may be used to organize key concepts. When explaining the steps needed to solve a mathematical equation, a flowchart may best outline the necessary procedures.

2. *Use graphic organizers to coherently depict relationships between concepts.* For graphic organizers to be understandable, connections between concepts need to be

FIGURE 8.6 **A Graphic Organizer for Creating a PowerPoint Presentation**

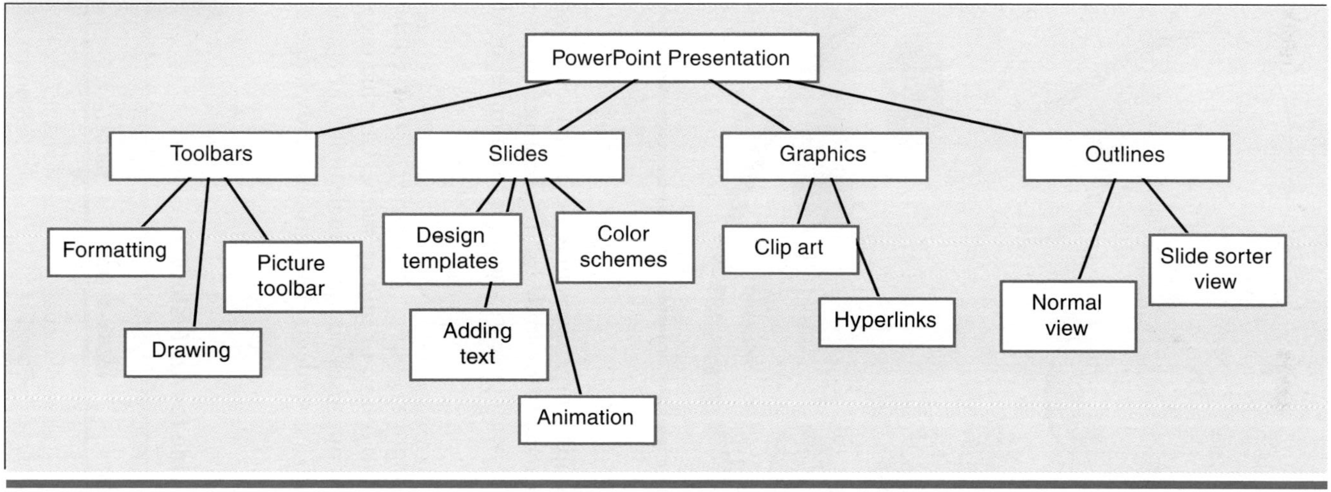

FIGURE 8.7 **A Graphic Organizer for Types of Media in Art**

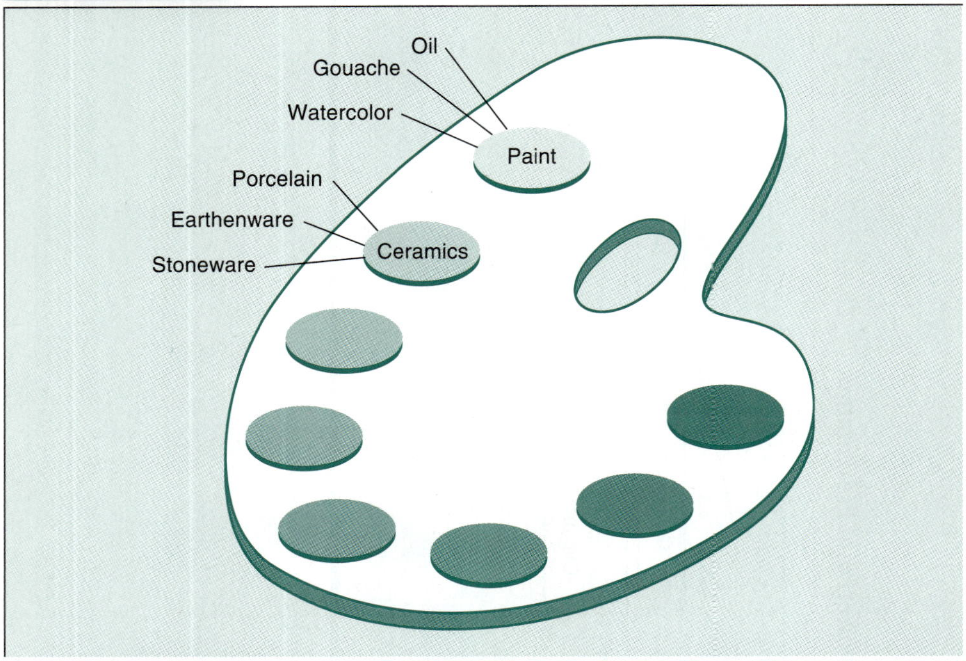

clear and straightforward. Graphic organizers that are cluttered or disorganized can confuse, rather than clarify, concepts for students. To construct coherent graphic organizers, use clear labels to connect concepts and limit the number of ideas presented in any single graphic organizer.

3. *Seek creative ways to integrate graphic organizers across content areas and throughout different stages of a lesson or unit of study.* Graphic organizers can be used and adapted for different purposes within a single unit. They can, for example, be used before reading to activate students' background knowledge and illuminate

FIGURE 8.8 **A Time Line for Art History**

1200s–1300s	1400s–1500s	1600s–1700s	1800s	1900s
Individualism in Italian Art	Italian Renaissance	Baroque Period of Europe	Romanticism, Impressionism, Abstract Art	Modernism

misconceptions students may have about the topic to be studied. Graphic organizers can also be used during reading to clarify and synthesize concepts and after reading as a form of review. Encouraging students to incorporate illustrations into their graphic organizers can enhance their understanding of the content.

Showing Students How to Make Their Own Connections

Graphic organizers may be used by teachers to build a frame of reference for students as they approach new material. However, in a more student-centered adaptation of the graphic organizer, the students work in cooperative groups and organize important concepts into their own graphic representations.

To make connections effectively, students must have some familiarity with the concepts in advance of their study of the material. In addition, student-constructed graphic organizers presume that the students are aware of the idea behind a graphic organizer. If they are not, you will need to give them a rationale and then model the construction of an organizer. Exposure to teacher-constructed graphic organizers from past lessons also creates awareness and provides models for the instructional strategy.

To introduce students to the process of making their own graphic organizers, follow these steps:

1. *Type the keywords and make copies for students.*
2. *Have them form small groups of two or three students each.*
3. *Distribute the list of terms and a packet of 3-by-5-inch index cards to each group.*
4. *Have the students write each word from the list on a separate card.* Then have them work together to decide on a spatial arrangement of the cards that depicts the major relationships among the words.
5. *As students work, provide assistance as needed.*
6. *Initiate a discussion of the constructed organizer.*

Before actually assigning a graphic organizer to students, you should prepare for the activity by carefully analyzing the vocabulary of the material to be learned. List all the terms that are essential for students to understand. Then add relevant terms that you believe the students already understand and will help them relate what they know to the new material. Finally, construct your own organizer.

The form of the student-constructed graphic organizer will undoubtedly differ from the teacher's arrangement. However, this difference in and of itself should not be a major source of concern. What is important is that the graphic organizer support students' abilities to anticipate connections through the key vocabulary terms in content materials.

Activating What Students Know About Words

Graphic organizers may be used to (1) activate students' prior knowledge of the vocabulary words in a text assignment or unit of study and (2) clarify their understanding of concepts as they study text. From a strategy perspective, students need to learn how to ask the question, "What do I know about these words?" When you use graphic organizers before reading or talking about key concepts, help the students build strategy awareness by exploring key terms before assigning text to read. In addition, consider the use of a quasi-instructional/informal assessment strategy known as Knowledge Rating (Blachowicz & Fisher 1996), illustrated on page 254.

Word Exploration

Word exploration is a *writing-to-learn* strategy that works well as a vocabulary activity. Before asking students to make connections between the words and their prior knowledge, a biology teacher asked them to explore what they knew about the concept of *natural selection* by writing in their learning logs.

A word exploration activity invites students to write quickly and spontaneously, a technique called *freewriting,* for no more than five minutes, without undue concern about spelling, neatness, grammar, or punctuation. The purpose of freewriting is to get down on paper everything that students know about the topic or target concept. Students write freely for themselves, not for an audience, so the mechanical, surface features of language, such as spelling, are not important.

Word explorations activate schemata and jog long-term memory, allowing students to dig deep into the recesses of their minds to gather thoughts about a topic. Examine one of the word explorations for the target concept *natural selection:*

> Natural selection means that nature selects—kills off—does away with the weak so only the strong make it. Like we were studying in class last time things get so competitive even among us for grades and jobs etc. The homeless are having trouble living with no place to call home except the street and nothing to eat. That's as good an example of natural selection as I can think of for now.

The teacher has several of the students share their word explorations with the class, either reading them verbatim or talking through what they have written, and notes similarities and differences in the students' concepts. The teacher then relates their initial associations to the concept and asks the students to make further connections: "How does your personal understanding of the idea *natural selection* fit in with some of the relationships that you see?"

Brainstorming

An alternative to word exploration, brainstorming is a procedure that quickly allows students to generate what they know about a key concept. In brainstorming, the students can access their prior knowledge in relation to the target concept. Brainstorming involves two basic steps that can be adapted easily to content objectives: (1) The teacher identifies a key concept that reflects one of the main topics to be studied in the text, and (2) students work in small groups to generate a list of words related to the concept in a given number of seconds.

List–Group–Label

Hilda Taba (1967) suggests an extension of brainstorming that she calls "list–group–label." When the brainstorming activity is over and *lists* of words have been generated by the students, have the class form learning teams to *group* the words into logical arrangements. Then invite the teams to *label* each arrangement. Once the list–group–label activity is completed, ask the students to make predictions about the content to be studied. For example, you might ask, "How does the title of the text (or thematic unit) relate to your groups of words?" or "Describe why you decided to group certain words together on one list rather than place them on a different list."

Wood (2001) suggests list–group–label–write as a variation of the original list–group–label strategy. Once they have completed the *list, group,* and *label* steps in the strategy, ask students, working individually or in pairs, to *write* a sentence or paragraph using the words from one of the lists. This writing task provides students with an opportunity to synthesize their understanding of how the words are related. It also illuminates important background knowledge that students bring to the text or unit, as well as any misconceptions that will need to be addressed as their study of the topic proceeds.

A teacher initiated a brainstorming activity in her high school geometry class. The students, working in small groups, were asked to list in four minutes as many words as possible that were related to geometry. Then the groups shared their lists of geometry words as the teacher created a master list on the board from the individual entries of the groups. She also wrote three categories on the board—Angles, Shapes, and Measures—and asked the groups to classify each word from the master list under one of the categories. Here's how one group organized some of the words from the master list:

ANGLES	SHAPES	MEASURES
acute	polygon	circumference
right	trapezoid	protractor
obtuse	triangle	radius
	circle	area
	square	perimeter

Note that in this example, the teacher provided the categories. She recognized that students needed the additional structure to be successful with this particular task. As a result of the activity, students were able to share what they knew with other members of the class and the teacher was able to identify gaps in students' understanding of concepts that could be addressed through subsequent readings and class discussions.

Word Sorts

Like brainstorming, word sorts require students to classify words into categories based on their prior knowledge. However, unlike brainstorming, students do not generate a list of words for a target concept. Instead, the teacher identifies the keywords from the unit of study and invites the students to sort them into logical arrangements of two or more.

A word sort is a simple yet valuable activity. Individually or in small groups, students literally sort out technical terms that are written on cards or listed on an exercise sheet. The object of word sorting is to group words into different categories by looking for shared features among their meanings. According to Gillet and Kita (1979), a word sort gives students the opportunity "to teach and learn from each other while discussing and examining words together" (pp. 541–542).

Gillet and Kita (1979) also explain that there are two types of word sorts: the *open sort* and the *closed sort*. Both are easily adapted to any content area. In the closed sort, students know in advance of sorting what the main categories are. In other words, the criterion that the words in a group must share is stated. In a middle grade music class, students were studying the qualities of various "instrument families" of the orchestra. The music teacher assigned the class to work in pairs to sort musical instruments into four categories representing the major orchestral families: strings, woodwinds, brass, and percussion. Figure 8.9 represents the closed sort developed by one collaborative "think–pair–share" group.

FIGURE 8.9 **Closed Sort for Musical Instruments**

Strings (bow or plucked)	**Woodwinds (single or double reed)**	**Brass (lips vibrate in mouthpiece)**	**Percussion (sounds of striking)**
Violin	Flute	Trumpet	Timpani
Viola	Piccolo	Trombone	Bass drum
Cello	Oboe	French horn	Chimes
Harp	Clarinet		Xylophone
	Saxophone		Bells
	Bassoon		Triangle
			Snare drum

Open sorts prompt divergent and inductive reasoning. No category or criterion for grouping is known in advance of sorting. Students must search for meanings and discover relationships among technical terms without the benefit of any structure.

Study how an art teacher activated what students knew about words associated with pottery making by using the open word sort strategy. She asked the high school students to work in collaborative pairs to arrange the following words into possible groups and to predict the concept categories in which the words would be classified:

jordan	lead	Cornwall stone	sgraffito
ball	chrome	cone	roka
antimony	slip	wheel	leather
cobalt	scale	bisque	hard
mortar	kaolin	stoneware	oxidation

Three categories that students formed were *types of clay, pottery tools,* and *coloring agents.*

Open word sorts can be used before or after reading. Before reading, a word sort serves as an activation strategy to help learners make predictive connections among the words. After reading, word sorts enable students to clarify and extend their understanding of the conceptual relationships.

Knowledge Ratings

As the procedure implies, knowledge ratings get readers to analyze what they know about a topic. Blachowicz (1986) recommends that teachers present students with a list of vocabulary in a survey-like format in which students must analyze each word individually, as in the two examples in Box 8.2.

A follow-up discussion might revolve around questions such as these: Which are the hardest words? Which do you think most of the class doesn't know? Which are the easiest ones? Which will most of us know? Students should be encouraged within the context of the discussion to share what they know about the words. In this way the teacher can assess and get some idea of the state of knowledge the class brings to the text reading or a larger unit of study.

myeducationlab

Go to the Assignments and Activities section of Topic 6: "Vocabulary and Fluency" in the MyEducationLab for your course and complete the activity "Assessing Content Vocabulary Knowledge" and consider how new vocabulary can be applied.

These procedures are all a part of prereading preparation. Naturally it would be foolhardy to use all of these procedures at one time, but one or two in combination set the stage for students to read with some confidence in and competence with the language of the text.

Before considering a variety of extension activities that put students in the position of clarifying and refining their knowledge of words and concepts, consider two strategies that permit text learners to define words in relation to the contexts in which they are used: the vocabulary self-collection strategy (VSS) and concept of definition (CD) procedure.

Evidence-Based Best Practices

BOX 8.2

Two Examples of Knowledge Ratings

Knowledge Rating*

How much do you know about these words?

	Can Define	Have Seen/Heard	?
exponent	X		
intersection	X		
domain			X
intercept		X	
slope		X	
parabola			X
origin		X	
vertex		X	
irrationals	X		
union		X	
coefficient		X	

*From a unit on quadratic functions and systems of equations in a high school math class.

Knowledge Rating*

How much do you know about these words?

	A Lot!	Have Seen/Heard	Not Much
publication design			
color schemes			
font schemes			
layout			
page content			
background fill			
website options			
design gallery			

*From a newspaper unit using Microsoft Publisher in a middle school language arts class.

Defining Words in the Context of Their Use

The vocabulary self-collection strategy (VSS) and concept of definition word maps (CD word maps) are two instructional strategies that make students aware of and build learning strategies for defining words. Both activities invite students to use their texts to determine how words are defined in their natural context.

Vocabulary Self-Collection Strategy

Vocabulary self-collection strategy (VSS) promotes the long-term acquisition of language in an academic discipline (Haggard 1986). As a result of the repeated use of the strategy, students learn how to make decisions related to the importance of concepts and how to use context to determine what words mean. The VSS strategy has been found to be effective for teaching word meaning in context to students across ability levels (Harmon, Hedrick, Wood, & Gress 2005) and for helping students to build independence as word learners (Ruddell & Shearer 2002). VSS begins once students read and discuss a text assignment. The teacher asks students, who are divided into teams, to nominate one word that they would like to learn more about. The word must be important enough for the team to share it with the class. The teacher also nominates a word. Here are several suggested steps in VSS:

1. *Divide the class into nominating teams of two to five students.* Together the students on a nominating team decide which word to select for emphasis in the text selection.
2. *Present the word that each team has selected to the entire class.* A spokesperson for each team identifies the nominated word and responds to the following questions:
   a. *Where is the word found in the text?* The spokesperson reads the passage in which the word is located or describes the context in which the word is used.
   b. *What do the team members think the word means?* The team decides on what the word means in the context in which it is used. They must use information from the surrounding context and may also consult reference resources.
   c. *Why did the team think the class should learn the word?* The team must tell the class why the word is important enough to single out for emphasis.

To introduce VSS to the students, the teacher first presents his or her nominated word to the class, modeling how to respond to the three questions. During the team presentations, the teacher facilitates the discussion, writes the nominated words on the board with their meanings, and invites class members to contribute additional clarifications of the words.

To conclude the class session, students record all the nominated words and their meanings in a section of their learning logs or in a separate vocabulary notebook. These lists may be used for review and study. As a consequence of VSS, the teacher has a set of student-generated words that can be incorporated into a variety of follow-up vocabulary activities, as suggested in the next section.

Concept of Definition Word Maps

Although VSS provides opportunities to define and explore the meanings of words used in text readings, many students are not aware of the types of information that contribute to the meaning of a concept. Nor have they internalized a strategy for defining a concept based on the information available to them. In addition, words in a text passage often provide only partial contextual information for defining the meaning of a concept.

Concept of definition (CD) word maps provide a framework for organizing conceptual information in the process of defining a word (Schwartz 1988; Schwartz & Raphael 1985). Conceptual information can be organized in terms of three types of relationships: the general class or category in which the concept belongs, the attributes or properties of the concept and those that distinguish it from other members of the category, and examples or illustrations of the concept. Students from elementary school through high school can use CD word maps to learn how to construct meaning for unknown words encountered in texts.

CD word map instruction supports vocabulary and concept learning by helping students internalize a strategy for defining and clarifying the meaning of unknown words. The hierarchical structure of a concept has an organizational pattern that is reflected by the general structure of a CD word map (see Figure 8.10).

In the center of the CD word map, students write the concept being studied. Working outward, they then write the word that best describes the general class or superordinate concept that includes the target concept. The answer to "What is it?" is the general class or category. Students then provide at least three examples of the concept as well as three properties by responding, respectively, to the questions, "What are some examples?" and "What is it like?" Comparison of the target concept is also possible when students think of an additional concept that belongs to the general class but is different from the concept being studied. Figure 8.11 provides an example of a CD word map for the word *tiger.*

RESPONSE JOURNAL

Select a concept from your content area and develop a CD word map for it.

Schwartz (1988) recommends a detailed plan for modeling CD word maps with students. The plan includes demonstrating the value of CD word mapping by connecting its purpose to how people use organizational patterns to aid memory and interpretation; introducing the general structure of a CD word map, explaining how the three probes define a concept, and walking students through the completion of a word map; and applying CD word mapping to an actual text selection.

Two caveats are relevant to CD word map instruction: CD word maps work best with concept words that function as nouns, but the procedure may be used, with some adaptation, with action words as well. Also, a potential misuse of CD word mapping

FIGURE 8.10 General Structure for a CD Word Map

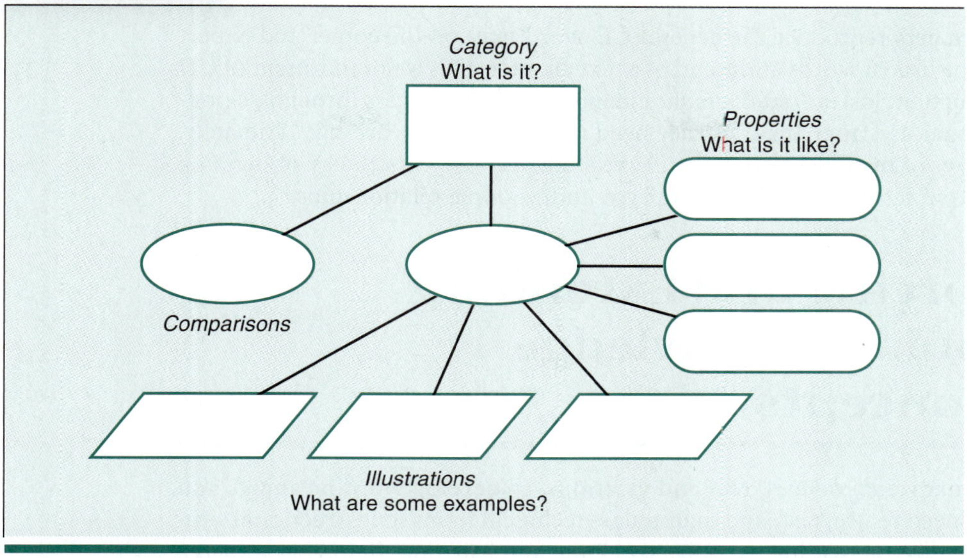

Source: "Learning to Learn: Vocabulary in Content Area Textbooks" by R. Schwartz, *Journal of Reading, 32*(2), 108–118. Copyright © 1988 by the International Reading Association. Reproduced with permission of International Reading Association via Copyright Clearance Center.

FIGURE 8.11 CD Word Map for the Word *Tiger*

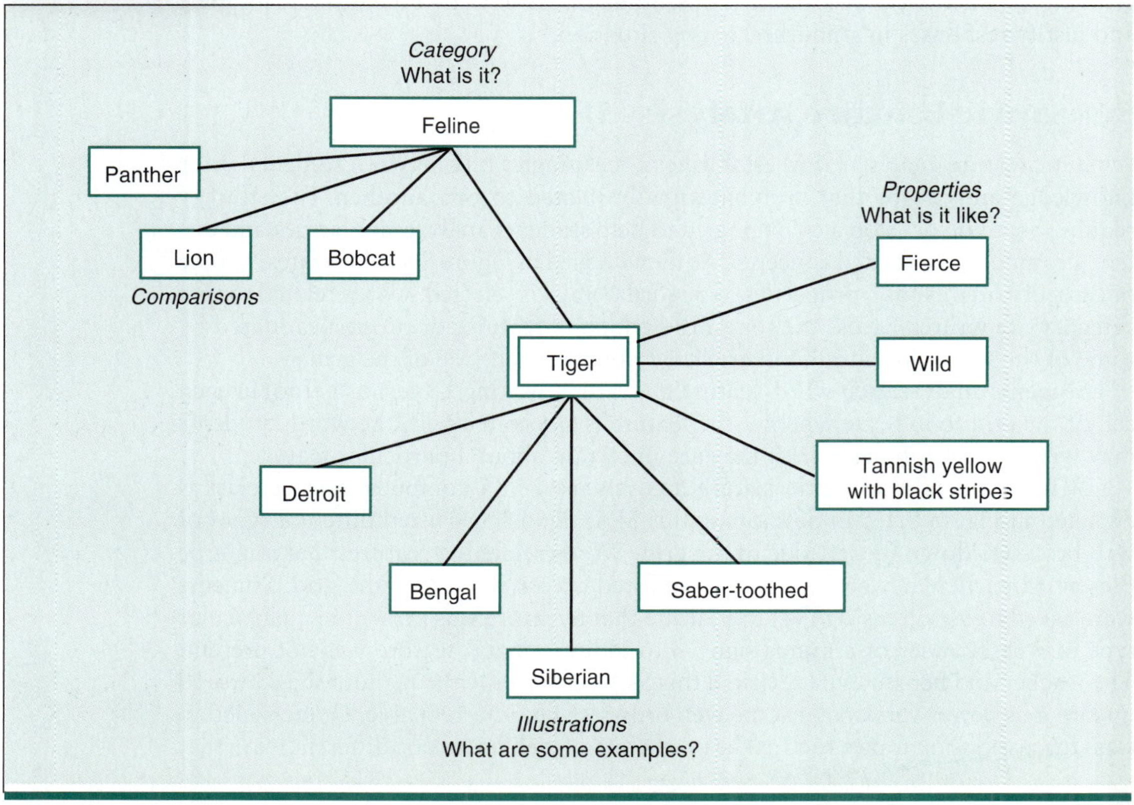

occurs when teachers reproduce the general CD word map on the copier and expect students to define lists of words at the end of a text chapter. This is not the intent of CD word map instruction. Instead, students should internalize the process through demonstration and actual use, applying it as they need it in actual text learning. Ultimately, the goal of CD word map instruction is to have students own the strategy of defining unknown words in terms of category, property, and example relationships.

Reinforcing and Extending Vocabulary Knowledge and Concepts

Students need many experiences, real and vicarious, to develop word meanings and concepts. They need to use, test, and manipulate technical terms in instructional situations that capitalize on reading, writing, speaking, and listening. In having students do these things, you create the kind of natural language environment that is needed to extend vocabulary and concept development. Various vocabulary extension activities can be useful in this respect.

These activities should be completed individually by students and then discussed either in small groups or in the class as a whole. The oral interaction in team learning gives more students a chance to use terms. Students can exchange ideas, share insights, and justify responses in a nonthreatening situation.

Semantic Feature Analysis (SFA)

Semantic feature analysis (SFA) establishes a meaningful link between students' prior knowledge and words that are conceptually related to one another. The strategy requires that you develop a chart or grid to help students analyze similarities and differences among the related concepts. As the SFA grid in Figure 8.12 illustrates, a topic or category (in this case, properties of quadrilaterals) is selected, words related to that category are written across the top of the grid, and features or properties shared by some of the words in the column are listed down the left side of the grid.

Students analyze each word, feature by feature, writing Y (yes) or N (no) in each cell of the grid to indicate whether the feature is associated with the word. Students may write a question mark (?) if they are uncertain about a particular feature.

A variation of a semantic feature analysis used in a computer science class is depicted in Figure 8.13. In developing this SFA, the teacher listed different types of web browsers down the left side of the grid. Words related to features that might be present in particular web browsers were listed across the top of the grid. Students were asked to use a plus sign (+) to indicate that a feature was present in a particular type of web browser or a minus sign (–) to indicate that a feature was not present. The teacher and her students revisited this SFA periodically throughout the course to update it as newer versions of some web browsers became available. Doing so led to class discussions on topics such as the marketing of web browsers, different ways that

FIGURE 8.12 **A Semantic Feature Analysis for Geometry**

Directions: Determine which of these properties is found in the four quadrilaterals listed. Mark "Y" or "N" in each box.

	Parallelogram	Rectangle	Rhombus	Square
Diagonals bisect each other.				
Diagonals are congruent.				
Each diagonal bisects a pair of opposite angles.				
Diagonals form two pairs of congruent triangles.				
Diagonals form four congruent triangles.				
Diagonals are perpendicular to each other.				

web servers ensure the security of customers who communicate and shop online, and technology's influence on the way people conduct everyday tasks such as information gathering, shopping, and bill paying.

As a teaching activity, SFA is easily suited to before- or after-reading instructional routines. If you used it before reading to activate what students know about words,

FIGURE 8.13 **A Semantic Feature Analysis for Computer Applications**

Directions: Determine which of these properties is found in the web browsers listed.

	RSS Support	Support for Active X	Google Search from Toolbar	Tabbed Browsing	Pop-Up Blocking	Themes/ Skins
Firefox						
Internet Explorer						
Opera						
Safari						

Voices from the Classroom

BOX 8.3

Tracy

Tenth-Grade Biology Teacher

CHALLENGE

I noticed that students in my biology class seemed to have difficulty retaining information about specific concepts and vocabulary. Therefore, I wanted to incorporate strategies that would engage students more actively in learning important biology terms. In the past, I've had my students create vocabulary posters as part of their homework assignments. When studying the human body systems, students illustrated a given concept or term with a drawing, clip art, or a photo to help them remember the information. For example, when learning about the functions of the heart, some students represented this concept with an illustration of a pump, including gasoline pump, bike pump, or even someone pumping iron. Students spent a lot of time on the assignment and enjoyed the activity but they didn't seem to remember the concepts and the vocabulary.

STRATEGY

In order to help students process the connections between a given concept and its meaning, I continued to incorporate the homework assignment of illustrating the vocabulary word. However, this time, I asked students to add some written explanation of why they made their decision to illustrate the concept the way they did. For example, if a student used a balloon to illustrate the bladder, I would expect them to write something about how the bladder is like a balloon (i.e., because it can stretch and hold things). By writing-to-learn, I hoped that students would be able to add the information to their long-term memory. More recently, I used the Semantic Feature Analysis as an informal assessment to see what students had learned so far about our topic of the excretory system. I began by creating a chart, shown below, with specific vocabulary, facts, and concepts chosen to summarize the topic we had been studying. I modeled the activity first by doing an example with my students. Then, they continued independently by analyzing each concept and marking the column with a + or – to indicate if the words were conceptually related to one another. They did well on those.

Excretory System	Lungs	Skin	Kidneys	Liver
Excretes waters				
Excretes urea				
Excretes carbon dioxide				
Excretes urine				

REFLECTION

After enhancing the vocabulary illustration activity with a written component and by incorporating the Semantic Feature Analysis, students in my biology class were better able to create a meaningful link between concepts, their meanings, and their relationships to various body systems. Their performance on a quiz showed that students consistently had a better recall and a better understanding of the terms and concepts. When we reviewed for the quiz, the students seemed more confident in their answers where previously they tended to fish for the information and responses. Scores on the quiz itself improved compared to scores on previous quizzes. Even the typically struggling students scored 90 percent or above. Prior to using the Semantic Feature Analysis as a learning tool, these students performed inconsistently on assessments with scores ranging from 70 percent to 100 percent. Now the majority were at a mastery level.

Students were engaged during the Semantic Feature Analysis activity. They viewed it as a puzzle or game, and it was easy and fun for them to complete it. The novelty of the activity helped too. There was not a lot of writing, but they had to know the information in order to complete the activity successfully. Perhaps in the future, I will have students write a statement after completing the Semantic Feature Analysis to explain their thinking and to tie all of the information together. I have also created a Semantic Feature Analysis to review for the midterm exam. I hope that organizing and categorizing information will help students to spark their memory and to summarize the information learned in class.

Review for Midterm	**Nervous System**	**Endocrine System**
Carries electrical messages		
Carries chemical messages		
Carries messages on neurons		
Carries messages in blood stream		
Controls reactions to stimulus		
Involves brain and spinal cord		
Involves glands		
Message must jump over gap known as synapse		
Neurotransmitter must fit receptors on dendrite		
Involves hormones		
Involves receptors		
Involves target cells		
Hormones must fit receptor on target cell		
Involves neurotransmitters		
Involves dendrites		
Involves axons		
Message travels slower (minutes, hours, days)		
Message travels very fast (less than one second)		

recognize that they can return to the SFA after reading to clarify and reformulate some of their initial responses on the SFA grid. In Box 8.3, Voices from the Classroom, read how Tracy devised an effective SFA strategy for her biology class.

Categorization Activities

Vocabulary extension exercises involving categorization require students to determine relationships among technical terms much as word sorts do. Students are usually given four to six words per grouping and asked to do something with them. That something depends on the format used in the exercise. For example, you can give students sets of words and ask them to circle in each set the word that includes the others. This exercise demands that students perceive common attributes or examples in relation to a more inclusive concept and to distinguish superordinate from subordinate terms. Following is an example from an eighth-grade social studies class.

Directions: Circle the word in each group that includes the others.

1. government	2. throne
council	coronation
judges	crown
governor	church

A variation on this format directs students to cross out the word that does not belong and then to explain in a word or phrase the relationship that exists among the common items, as illustrated in the following example.

Directions: Cross out the word in each set that does not belong. On the line above the set, write the word or phrase that explains the relationship among the remaining three words.

1. _______	2. _______
drama	time
comedy	character
epic	place
tragedy	action

Concept Circles

One of the most versatile activities we have observed at a wide range of grade levels is the concept circle. Concept circles provide still another format and opportunity for studying words critically—for students to relate words conceptually to one another. A concept circle may simply involve putting words or phrases in the sections of a circle and directing students to describe or name the concept relationship among the sections. The example in Figure 8.14 is from a middle grade science lesson.

In addition, you might direct students to shade in the section of a concept circle containing a word or phrase that *does not relate* to the words or phrases in the other sections of the circle and then identify the concept relationships that exist among the remaining sections (see Figure 8.15).

Finally, you can modify a concept circle by leaving one or two sections of the circle empty, as in Figure 8.16. Direct students to fill in the empty section with a word or two that relates in some way to the terms in the other sections of the concept circles. Students must then justify their word choice by identifying the overarching concept depicted by the circle.

As you can see, concept circles serve the same function as categorization activities. However, students respond positively to the visual aspect of manipulating the sections in a circle. Whereas categorization exercises sometimes seem like tests to students, concept circles are fun to do.

FIGURE 8.14 The Concept Circle

Directions:
Name the planet represented by all of the sections in the circle.

1. ______________________

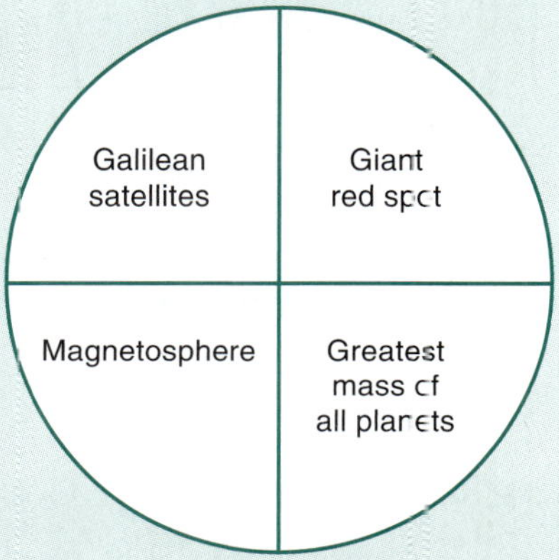

FIGURE 8.15 A Variation on the Concept Circle

Directions:
Shade in the section that does not relate to the words in the other sections. Then name the concept.

1. ______________________

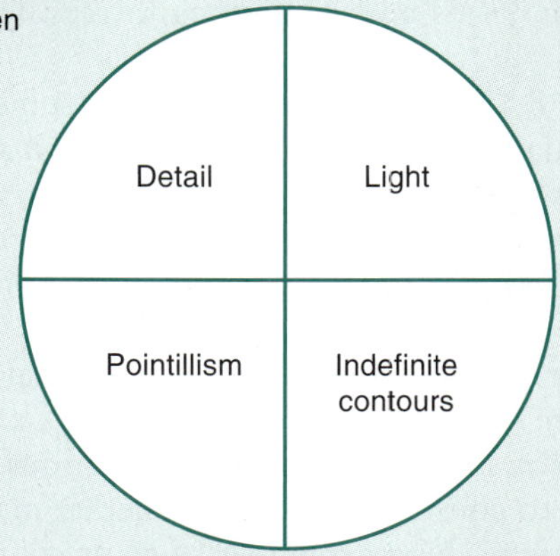

FIGURE 8.16 **Another Variation on the Concept Circle**

Directions:
Add an additional example to the circle, and then name the concept depicted by the circle.

Name ____________________

Magic Squares

The magic square activity is by no means new or novel, yet it has a way of reviving even the most mundane matching exercise. We have seen the magic square used successfully in elementary and secondary grades as well as in graduate courses. Here's how a magic square works. An activity sheet has two columns, one for content area terms and one for definitions or other distinguishing statements such as characteristics or examples (see Figure 8.17). Direct students to match terms with definitions. In doing so, they must take into account the letters signaling the terms and the numbers signaling the definitions. The students then put the number of a definition in the proper space (denoted by the letter of the term) in the "magic square answer box." If their matchups are correct, they will form a magic square. That is, the numerical total will be the same for each row across and each column down the answer box. This total forms the puzzle's "magic number." Students need to add up the rows and columns to check if they're coming up with the same number each time. If not, they should go back to the terms and definitions to reevaluate their answers.

The magic square exercise in Figure 8.17 is from a family and consumer studies class. Try it. Its magic number is 15. Analyze the mental maneuvers that you went through to determine the correct number combinations. In some cases, you undoubtedly knew the answers outright. You may have made several educated guesses on others. Did you try to beat the number system? Imagine the possibilities for small-group interaction.

Many teachers are intrigued by the possibilities offered by the magic square, but they remain wary of its construction: "I can't spend hours figuring out number combinations." This is a legitimate concern. Luckily, the eight combinations in Figure 8.18 make magic square activities easy to construct. You can generate many more combinations from the eight patterns simply by rearranging rows or columns (see Figure 8.19 on page 266).

FIGURE 8.17 Magic Squares: Analyzing Food Labels

Directions: Select the best answer for each of the terms from the numbered definitions. Put the number in the proper space in the magic square box. If the totals of the numbers are the same both across and down, you have found the magic number!

A. Serving size
B. Servings per container
C. Calories
D. Fat, cholesterol, sodium
E. Fiber, vitamins
F. Trans fats, protein, and sugars
G. Percent daily value
H. 2,000
I. Footnote

1. Provides recommended dietary information for important nutrients, including fats, sodium, and fiber
2. The nutrients listed first should be limited
3. How many portions are in a package
4. Eating enough of these nutrients can improve your health and help reduce the risk of some diseases and conditions
5. Provides a measure of how much energy you get from a serving of this food
6. Recommendations for key nutrients but only for a 2,000 calorie daily diet
7. Influences the number of calories and all the nutrient amounts listed on the top part of the label
8. Recommended daily caloric intake
9. Nutrients without a percent daily value

A	B	C
D	E	F
G	H	I

Source: Information taken from the FDA website: www.cfsan.fda.gov/~dms/foodlab.html.

FIGURE 8.18 A Model of Magic Square Combinations

7	3	5
2	4	9
6	8	1

0* 15**

10	8	6
2	9	13
12	7	5

4* 24**

7	11	8
10	12	4
9	3	14

5* 26**

9	2	7
4	6	8
5	10	3

1* 18**

9	7	5
1	8	12
11	6	4

3* 21**

16	2	3	13
5	11	10	8
9	7	6	12
4	14	15	1

0* 34**

19	2	15	23	6
25	8	16	4	12
1	14	22	10	18
7	20	3	11	24
13	21	9	17	5

0* 65**

2	7	18	12
8	5	11	15
13	17	6	3
16	10	4	9

0* 39**

* Foils needed in answer column
** Magic number

Notice that the single asterisk in Figure 8.18 denotes the number of foils needed so that several of the combinations can be completed. For example, the magic number combination of 18 requires one foil in the number 1 slot that will not match with any of the corresponding items in the matching exercise. To complete the combination, the number 10 is added. Therefore, when you develop a matching activity for combination 18, there will be ten items in one column and nine in the other, with item 1 being the foil.

FIGURE 8.19 **Variations on Magic Square Combinations**

7	3	5
2	4	9
6	8	1

→

8	1	6
3	5	7
4	9	2

or

6	1	8
7	5	3
2	9	4

Vocabulary-Building Strategies

myeducationlab

Go to the Assignments and Activities section of Topic 6: "Vocabulary and Fluency" in the MyEducationLab for your course and complete the activity "Content Vocabulary and English Learners."

Showing learners how to construct meaning for unfamiliar words encountered during reading helps them develop strategies needed to monitor comprehension and increase their own vocabularies. Demonstrating how to use *context, word structure,* and the *dictionary* provides students with several basic strategies for vocabulary learning that will last a lifetime. With these strategies, students can search for information clues while reading so that they can approximate the meanings of unknown words. These clues often reveal enough meaning to allow readers who struggle with text to continue reading without "short-circuiting" the process and giving up because the text does not make sense.

You can scaffold the use of vocabulary-building strategies before assigning material to be read. If one or more words represent key concepts—and the words lend themselves to demonstration—you can model the inquiry process necessary to construct meaning. The demonstration is brief, often lasting no more than five minutes. There are three types of demonstrations that will make students aware of vocabulary-building strategies. The first is to model how to make sense of a word in the context of its use, the second involves an analysis of a word's structure, and the third combines context and word structure. Usually these demonstrations require the use of visuals, such as an overhead transparency or a whiteboard. After the brief demonstration, guide students to practice and apply the strategy that you just modeled so that they can become proficient in its use.

Using Context to Approximate Meaning

Constructing meaning from context is one of the most useful strategies at the command of proficient readers. Showing readers who struggle how to make use of context builds confidence and competence and teaches the inquiry process necessary to unlock the meaning of troublesome technical and general vocabulary encountered during reading. Using context involves using information surrounding a difficult word to help reveal its meaning. Every reader makes some use of context automatically. Strategy instruction, however, is needed when the text provides a *deliberate context* to help the reader with concept terms that are especially difficult. Often the text author will anticipate that certain words will be troublesome and will provide information clues and contextual aids to help readers with meaning. In these instances, students will benefit from a strategy that allows them to use the deliberate context to construct meaning.

The use of context is mostly a matter of inference. Inference requires readers to see an explicit or implicit relationship between an unfamiliar word and its context or to connect what they know already with the unknown term. It can't be assumed that students will perceive these relationships or make the connections on their own. Most students who struggle with text simply don't know how to use a deliberate context provided by an author. Three kinds of information in particular are useful to struggling readers: *typographic, syntactic,* and *semantic* clues.

Typographic Clues

Typographic or format clues make use of footnotes, italics, boldface print, parenthetical definitions, pictures, graphs, charts, and the like. A typographic clue provides a clear-cut connection and a direct reference to an unknown word. Many students tend to gloss over a typographic aid instead of using it to spotlight the meaning of a difficult term. The teacher can rivet attention to these aids with minimal expenditure of class time.

For example, consider the way a science teacher modeled a strategy for revealing the meaning of the word *enzymes,* which was presented in boldface type in the text. Before assigning a text section titled "Osmosis in Living Cells," the teacher asked students to turn to page 241. Then he asked, "Which word in the section on osmosis stands out among the others?" The students quickly spotted the word *enzymes.* "Why do you think this word is highlighted in boldface type?" he asked. A student replied, "I guess it must be important." Another student said, "Maybe because it has something to do with osmosis—whatever that is." The teacher nodded approvingly and then asked the class to see if they could figure out what *enzymes* meant by reading this sentence: "Chemical substances called **enzymes** are produced by cells to break down large starch molecules into small sugar molecules."

The science teacher continued the demonstration by asking two questions: "What are enzymes?" and "What do they do?" The students responded easily. The teacher concluded the walk-through with these words: "Words that are put in large letters or boldfaced print are important. If you pay attention to them as we just did, you will have little trouble figuring out what they mean. There are four other words in boldfaced type in your reading assignment. Look for them as you read and try to figure out what they mean."

Syntactic and Semantic Clues

Syntactic and semantic clues in content materials should not be treated separately. The grammatical relationships among words in a sentence or the structural arrangement among sentences in a passage often helps clarify the meaning of a particular word.

Syntactic and semantic clues are much more subtle than typographic clues. Table 8.1 presents a summary of the most frequently encountered syntactic and semantic clues.

Help students visualize the inquiry process necessary to reveal meaning. For example, if a *definition clue* is used, as in this example from Table 8.1: "Entomology is the study of insects, and biologists who specialize in this field are called entomologists," it may be appropriate first to display the term. During the modeling discussion, you can then show how *is* and *are called* provide information clues that reveal meaning for *entomology* and *entomologists.* A simple strategy would be to cross out *is* and *are called* in the sentence and replace them with equal signs (=):

> Entomology ~~is~~ = the study of insects, and biologists who specialize in this field ~~are called~~ = entomologists.

A brief discussion will reinforce the function of the verb forms *is* and *are called* in the sentence.

The definition clue is the least subtle of the syntactic and semantic clues. However, all the clues in Table 8.1 require students to make inferential leaps. Consider one of the examples from the mood and tone clue: "The tormented animal screeched with horror and writhed in pain as it tried desperately to escape from the hunter's trap." Suppose this sentence came from a short story about to be assigned in an English class. Assume also that many of the students would have trouble with the word *tormented* as it is used in the sentence. If students are to make the connection between *tormented* and the mood created by the information clues, the teacher will have to ask several effective clarifying questions.

The demonstration begins with the teacher writing the word *tormented* on the board. She asks, "You may have heard or read this word before, but how many of you think that you know what it means?" Student definitions are put on the board. The teacher then writes the sentence on the board. "Which of the definitions on the board do you think best fits the word *tormented* when it's used in this sentence?" She encourages students to support their choices. If none fits, she will ask for more definitions now that students have seen the sentence. She continues questioning, "Are there any other words or phrases in the sentence that help us get a feel for the meaning of *tormented?* Which ones?"

The inquiry into the meaning of *tormented* continues in this fashion. The information clues *(screeched with horror, writhed in pain, desperately)* that establish the mood are underlined and discussed. The teacher concludes the modeling activity by writing five new words on the board and explaining, "These words are also in the story that you are about to read. As you come across them, stop and think. How do the words or phrases or sentences surrounding each word create a certain feeling or mood that will allow you to understand what each one means?"

When modeling the use of context in Table 8.1, it's important for students to discover the information clues. It's also important for the teacher to relate the demonstration to several additional words to be encountered in the assignment. Instruction of this type will have a significant cumulative effect. If students are shown how to use contextual clues for two or three words each week, over the course of an academic year they will have 80 to 120 applications in the process.

TABLE 8.1

Synctactic and Semantic Contextual Clues

Type of Clue	Explanation	Examples
1. Definition	The author equates the unknown word to the known or more familiar, usually using a form of the verb *be*.	*Entomology* **is** the study of insects, and biologists who specialize in this field **are called** *entomologists.* A *critical review* **is** an attempt to evaluate the worth of a piece of writing.
2. Linked synonyms	The author pairs the unknown word with familiar synonyms or closely related words in a series.	Kunte Kinte was the victim of **cruel, evil,** *malevolent,* and **brutal** slave traders. The senator from Connecticut possessed the traits of an honest and just leader: **wisdom, judgment,** *sagacity.*
3. Direct description: examples, modifiers, restatements	The author reveals the meaning of an unknown word by providing additional information in the form of appositives, phrases, clauses, or sentences.	*Example clue:* Undigested material **such as fruit skins, outer parts of grain, and the stringlike parts of some vegetables** forms *roughage.* *Modifier clues: Pictographic writing,* **which was the actual drawing of animals, people, and events,** is the forerunner of written language. *Algae,* **nonvascular plants that are as abundant in water as grasses are on land,** have often been called "grasses of many waters." *Restatement clue:* A billion dollars a year is spent on *health quackery.* **In other words, each year in the United States, millions of dollars are spent on worthless treatments and useless gadgets to "cure" various illnesses.**
4. Contrast	The author reveals the meaning of an unknown word by contrasting it with an antonym or a phrase that is opposite in meaning.	You have probably seen animals perform tricks at the zoo, on television, or in a circus. Maybe you taught a dog to fetch a newspaper. **But learning tricks—usually for a reward—is very different from** *cognitive problem solving.* It wasn't a *Conestoga* like Pa's folks came in. **Instead, it was just an old farm wagon drawn by one tired horse.**
5. Cause and effect	The author establishes a cause-and-effect relationship in which the meaning of an unknown word can be hypothesized.	The *domestication* of animals probably began when young animals were caught or strayed into camps. **As a result, people enjoyed staying with them and made pets of them.** A family is *egalitarian* **when both husband and wife make decisions together and share responsibilities equally.**
6. Mood and tone	The author sets a mood (ironic, satirical, serious, funny, etc.) in which the meaning of an unknown word can be hypothesized.	A sense of *resignation* engulfed my thoughts as **the feeling of cold grayness was everywhere around me.** The *tormented* animal **screeched with horror and writhed in pain as it tried desperately to escape** from the hunter's trap.

*Italics denote the unknown words. Boldface type represents information clues that trigger context revelation.

Context-Related Activities

Readers who build and use contextual knowledge are able to recognize fine shades of meaning in the way words are used. They know the concept behind the word well enough to use that concept in different contexts. In the following sections, we suggest two ways to extend a student's contextual knowledge of content area terms.

Modified Cloze Passages

Cloze passages (discussed in Chapter 4) can be created to reinforce technical vocabulary. However, the teacher usually modifies the procedure for teaching purposes. Every *n*th word, for example, needn't be deleted. The modified cloze passage will vary in length. Typically, a 200- to 500-word text segment yields sufficient technical vocabulary to make the activity worthwhile.

Should you consider developing a modified cloze passage on a segment of text from a reading assignment, make sure that the text passage is one of the most important parts of the assignment. Depending on your objectives, students can supply the missing words either before or after reading the entire assignment. If they work on the cloze activity before reading, use the subsequent discussion to build meaning for key terms and to raise expectations for the assignment as a whole. If you assign the cloze passage after reading, it will reinforce concepts attained through reading.

On completing a brief prereading discussion on the causes of the Civil War, an American history teacher assigned a cloze passage before students read the entire introduction for homework. See how well you fare on the first part of the exercise.

> What caused the Civil War? Was it inevitable? To what extent and in what ways was slavery to blame? To what extent was each region of the nation at fault? Which were more decisive—the intellectual or the emotional issues?
>
> > Any consideration of the (1) of the war must include the problem of (2). In his second inaugural address, Abraham Lincoln said that slavery was "somehow the cause of the war." The critical word is "(3)." Some (4) maintain that the moral issue had to be solved, the nation had to face the (5), and the slaves had to be (6). Another group of historians asserts that the war was not fought over (7). In their view, slavery served as an (8) focal point for more fundamental (9) involving two different (10) of the Constitution. All of these views have merit, but no single view has won unanimous support.
> >
> > *(Answers can be found on page 276.)*

OPIN

OPIN is a meaning-extending vocabulary strategy developed by Frank Greene of McGill University. OPIN provides another example of context-based reinforcement and extension. OPIN stands for *opinion* and also plays on the term *cloze*.

Here's how OPIN works. Divide the class into groups of three. Distribute exercise sentences, one to each student. Each student must complete each exercise sentence individually. Then each group member must convince the other two members that his or her word choice is the best. If no agreement is reached on the best word for each sentence, each member of the group can speak to the class for his or her individual choice. When all groups have finished, have the class discuss each group's choices. The only rule of discussion is that each choice must be accompanied by a reasonable defense or justification. Answers such as "Because ours is best" are not acceptable.

OPIN exercise sentences can be constructed for any content area. Here are sample sentences from science, social studies, and family and consumer studies:

SCIENCE

1. A plant's ________ go into the soil.
2. The earth gets heat and ________ from the sun.
3. Some animals, such as birds and ________, are nibblers.

SOCIAL STUDIES

1. We cannot talk about ________ in America without discussing the homeless.
2. The thought of ________ or revolution would be necessary because property owners would fight to hold on to their land.
3. Charts and graphs are used to ________ information.

FAMILY AND CONSUMER STUDIES

1. Vitamin C is ________ from the small intestine and circulates to every tissue.
2. Washing time for cottons and linens is eight to ten minutes unless the clothes are badly ________.

(Answers can be found on page 276.)

OPIN encourages differing opinions about which word should be inserted in a blank space. In one sense, the exercise is open to discussion, and as a result, it reinforces the role of prior knowledge and experiences in the decisions that each group makes. The opportunity to "argue" one's responses in the group leads not only to continued motivation but also to a discussion of word meanings and variations.

In addition to emphasizing context as a vocabulary-building strategy, showing learners how to approximate word meaning through *word structure* is another important aspect of vocabulary building.

Word Structure

A word itself provides information clues about its meaning. The smallest unit of meaning in a word is called a *morpheme*. Analyzing a word's structure, *morphemic analysis*, is a second vocabulary-building strategy that students can use to predict meaning.

When readers encounter an unknown word, they can reduce the number of feasible guesses about its meaning considerably by approaching the whole word and identifying its parts. When students use morphemic analysis in combination with context, they have a powerful strategy at their command. The relationship between morphology knowledge and vocabulary development appears to be reciprocal: Students who have acquired larger vocabularies tend to have a greater understanding of morphology, and building an understanding of morphology helps students to expand their vocabularies (Kieffer & Lesaux 2007).

myeducationlab

Go to the Building Teaching Skills and Dispositions section of Topic 6: "Vocabulary and Fluency" in the MyEducationLab for your course. Use this activity to develop your skills in helping students broaden their vocabulary.

Student readers often find long words daunting. A long or polysyllabic word falls within one of four categories:

1. *Compound words made up of two known words joined together.* Examples: *commonwealth, matchmaker.*
2. *Words containing a recognizable stem to which an affix (a prefix, combining form, or suffix) has been added.* Examples: *surmountable, deoxygenize, unsystematic, microscope.*
3. *Words that can be analyzed into familiar and regular pronounceable units.* Examples: *undulate, calcify, subterfuge, strangulate.*
4. *Words that contain irregular pronounceable units so that there is no sure pronunciation unless one consults a dictionary.* Examples: *louver, indictment.*

Content vocabulary terms from categories 1 and 2 (compound words and recognizable stems and affixes) are the best candidates for instruction. You can readily demonstrate techniques for predicting the meanings of these words because each of their isolated parts will always represent a meaning unit.

In some instances, a word from category 3 may also be selected for emphasis. However, there is no guarantee that students will bring prior knowledge and experience to words that comprise the third category. Long phonemically regular words lend themselves to syllabication. Syllabication involves breaking words into pronounceable sound units or syllables. The word *undulate,* for example, can be syllabicated (un-du-late). However, the syllable *un* is not a meaning-bearing prefix.

Many words from category 3 are derived from Latin or Greek. Students who struggle with texts will find these words especially difficult to analyze for meaning because of their lack of familiarity with Latin or Greek roots. Occasionally, a word such as *strangulate* (derived from the Latin *strangulatus*) can be taught because students may recognize the familiar word *strangle.* They might then be shown how to link *strangle* to the verb suffix *-ate* (which means "to cause to become") to hypothesize a meaning for *strangulate.* Unfortunately, the verb suffix *-ate* has multiple meanings, and the teacher should be quick to point this out to students. This procedure is shaky, but it has some payoff.

Words from category 2 warrant instruction, because English root words are more recognizable, obviously, than Latin or Greek ones. Whenever feasible, teach the principles of structural word analysis using terms that have English roots. Certain affixes are more helpful than others, and knowing which affixes to emphasize during instruction will minimize students' confusion.

The most helpful affixes are the combining forms, prefixes, or suffixes that have single, invariant meanings. (See Appendix B.)

Many other commonly used prefixes have more than one meaning or have several shades of meaning. Because of their widespread use in content terminology, you should also consider these variant-meaning prefixes for functional teaching. (See Appendix C for a list of prefixes with varying meanings.)

The tables of affixes are resources for you. Don't be misled into thinking that students should learn long lists of affixes in isolation to help in analyzing word structure. This approach is neither practical nor functional. We recommend instead that students be taught affixes as they are needed to analyze the structure of terms that will appear in a reading assignment.

For example, an English teacher modeled how to analyze the meaning of *pandemonium* before students were to encounter the term in an assignment from *One Flew over the Cuckoo's Nest.* She wrote the word on the board—pan*demon*ium—underlining the English base word *demon,* and asked students for several synonyms for the word. Student responses included *witch, devil, monster,* and *wicked people.*

Then she explained that *-ium* was a noun suffix meaning "a place of." "Now let's take a look at *pan.* Sheila, have you ever heard of the Pan American Games? They are similar to the Olympics, but what do you think is a major difference between the Olympics and the Pan American Games?" Sheila and several students responded to the question. A brief discussion led the students to conclude the Pan American Games, like the Olympics, are a series of athletic contests; however, unlike the Olympics, only countries in North, Central, and South America and the Caribbean participate in the Pan American Games. The teacher affirmed the students' conclusions and noted that Pan American means quite literally, "all the Americas." Further discussion centered around the word *panoramic.* Through this process, relating the known to the unknown, students decided that *pan* meant "all."

"Now, back to *pandemonium.* 'A place of all the demons.' What would this place be like?" Students were quick to respond. The demonstration was completed with two additional points. The teacher asked the class to find the place in *One Flew over the Cuckoo's Nest* where *pandemonium* was used and read the paragraph. Then she asked them to refine their predictions of the meaning of *pandemonium.* Next the teacher discussed the origin of the word—which the English poet John Milton coined in his epic poem *Paradise Lost.* Pandemonium was the capital of hell, the place where all the demons and devils congregated—figuratively speaking, where "all hell broke loose."

Using the Dictionary as a Strategic Resource

The use of context and word structure are strategies that give struggling readers insight into the meanings of unknown words. Rarely does context or word structure help learners derive precise definitions for keywords. Instead, these vocabulary-building strategies keep readers on the right track so that they are able to follow a text without getting bogged down or giving up.

There are times, however, when context and word structure reveal little about a word's meaning. In these instances, or when a precise definition is needed, a dictionary is a logical alternative and a valuable resource for students.

Knowing when to use a dictionary is as important as knowing how to use it. A content teacher should incorporate dictionary usage into ongoing plans but should avoid a very common pitfall in the process of doing so. When asked, "What does this word mean?" the teacher shouldn't automatically reply, "Look it up in the dictionary."

To some students, "Look it up in the dictionary" is another way of saying "Don't bug me" or "I really don't have the time or the inclination to help you." From an instructional perspective, that hard-to-come-by teachable moment is lost whenever we routinely suggest to students to look up a word in a conventional or electronic dictionary.

One way to make the dictionary a functional resource is to use it to verify educated guesses about word meaning revealed through context or word structure. For example, if a student asks you for the meaning of a vocabulary term, an effective tactic is to bounce the question right back: "What do you think it means? Let's look at the way it's used. Are there any clues to its meaning?" If students are satisfied with an educated guess because it makes sense, the word need not be looked up. But if students are still unsure of the word's meaning, the dictionary is there.

When students go into a dictionary or an online vocabulary site to verify or to determine a precise definition, more often than not they need supervision to make good decisions. Keep these tips in mind as you work on dictionary usage.

1. *Help students determine the "best fit" between a word and its definition.* Students must often choose the most appropriate definition from several. This poses a real dilemma for young learners. Your interactions will help them make the best choice of a definition and will provide a behavior model for making such a choice.

2. *If you do assign a list of words to look up in a dictionary, choose them selectively.* A few words are better than many. The chances are greater that students will learn several key terms thoroughly than that they will develop vague notions about many.

3. *Help students with the pronunciation key in a glossary or dictionary as the need arises.* This does not mean, however, that you will teach skills associated with the use of a pronunciation key in isolated lessons. Instead, it means guiding and reinforcing students' abilities to use a pronunciation key as they study the content of your course.

Vocabulary development is a gradual process, "the result of many encounters with a word towards a more precise grasp of the concept the word represents" (Parry 1993, p. 127). If this is the case, students who struggle with demanding text material will benefit from vocabulary-building strategies that make use of context clues, word structure, and appropriate uses of reference tools such as the dictionary.

LOOKING BACK LOOKING FORWARD

A strong relationship exists between vocabulary knowledge and reading comprehension. In this chapter, we shared numerous examples of what it means to teach words well: giving students multiple opportunities to build vocabulary knowledge, to learn how words are conceptually related to one another, and to learn how they are defined contextually in the material that students are studying. Vocabulary activities provide students the multiple experiences they need to use and manipulate words in different situations. Conceptual and definitional activities provide the framework needed to study words critically. Various types of concept activities—such as semantic feature analysis, concept of definition word maps, word sorts, categories, concept circles, and magic squares—reinforce and extend students' abilities to perceive relationships among the words they are studying.

In the next chapter we underscore the interrelationships between reading, thinking, and writing processes as we explore the role of writing in content area learning. The ideas presented in the chapter are intended to show how writing activity can and must go beyond "mechanical uses" in the content classroom.

Minds On

1. A few of your students come to you and ask why they aren't using dictionaries to help them learn vocabulary words as they did last year. What is your response? Justify your response.
2. Each of the following statements should be randomly assigned to members of your group. Your task with your drawn statement is to play the devil's advocate. Imagine that you are in a conference with other teachers, all of whom have the same child in their classes. One member of the teaching team, represented by the other members of your discussion group, makes the statement you've selected, and you totally disagree. Argue to these teachers why you believe this statement is false. Members of the teaching team must respond with counterarguments, using classroom examples for support whenever possible.
   a. Students who are interested and enthusiastic are more likely to learn the vocabulary of a content area subject.
   b. Students need to know how to inquire into the meanings of unknown words by using context analysis and dictionary skills.
   c. An atmosphere for vocabulary reinforcement is created by activities involving speaking, listening, writing, and reading.
   d. Vocabulary reinforcement provides opportunities for students to increase their knowledge of the technical vocabulary of a subject.
   e. Vocabulary taught and reinforced within the framework of concept development enhances reading comprehension.
   f. Vocabulary knowledge and reading comprehension have a strong relationship.

   Were there any statements that you had difficulty contradicting? If so, pose these to the class as a whole, and solicit perspectives from other groups.
3. Your principal notices that your history class spends a lot of time working in pairs and groups on vocabulary, and she doesn't understand why this is necessary "just to learn words." As a group, compose a letter to her explaining the importance of student interaction in learning the vocabulary of any content area.

Hands On

1. The class should be organized into four groups. Two groups will represent alien life forms and two will represent human beings. Each group meets for fifteen to twenty minutes. Working separately, each alien group will create five or six statements in their own "alien" language. The humans will organize strategies for decoding the messages they will receive.

   After the time has elapsed, each alien group meets with a human group and the aliens make their statements. If possible, the aliens will attempt to respond to the humans' questions with keywords or phrases. Next, with the alien and human groups switched, the process is repeated. Finally, as a whole class, discuss your success or lack of success in translating in relation to what you have learned about vocabulary and concepts.

2. Examine the following list of vocabulary words taken from this chapter:

general vocabulary	comprehension
technical vocabulary	conceptual level
special vocabulary	concept circles
concept	OPIN
word sorts (open, closed)	word puzzles
brainstorming	magic squares
semantic word maps	prior knowledge
knowledge ratings	target concept
syntactic and semantic contextual aids	cognitive operations
semantic feature analysis	joining
freewriting	excluding
modified cloze passages	selecting
context	implying

Team with three other members of the class, and with this list of words, each create one of the following:

a. Two conceptually related activities, such as a set of concept circles and a closed word sort
b. A context activity that presents the key concept words in meaningful sentence contexts
c. A semantic word map or a semantic feature analysis

Follow this activity with a discussion of the advantages and disadvantages of each approach and of the appropriate time during a unit to use each.

ANSWERS TO CLOZE PASSAGE

1. causes 2. slavery 3. somehow 4. historians 5. crisis 6. freed 7. slavery 8. emotional 9. issues 10. interpretations

POSSIBLE ANSWERS TO OPIN EXERCISES

Science: 1. roots 2. radiation 3. rodents

Social Studies: 1. poverty 2. violence 3. organize

Family and Consumer Studies: 1. absorbed 2. soiled

*e*RESOURCES

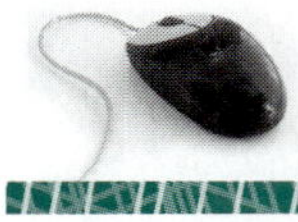

- Discovery Education offers a site that allows users to create word puzzles (**http://puzzlemaker.discoveryeducation.com**). Design a puzzle based on vocabulary words from a chapter of a content area text. Seek out vocabulary-building strategies in your content area by using the keywords "vocabulary + lessons + (content area)" to conduct an Internet search. Many links will come up. Consider the value of each site and identify the best sites.
- TeacherVision offers downloadable graphic organizers for immediate use (**www.teachervision.fen.com/graphic-organizers/printable/6293.html**). Explore the Internet further for content-specific graphic organizers by using the keywords "graphic organizers + (content area)."

CHAPTER 9

I write entirely to find out what I'm thinking . . . and what it means.

—Joan Didion

Writing Across the Curriculum

ORGANIZING PRINCIPLE

Writing facilitates learning by helping students to explore, clarify, and think deeply about the ideas and concepts they encounter in reading.

Writing mirrors thinking. Although award-winning novelist Joan Didion writes to tell a good story, she also writes for insight—for an understanding of the inner meaning of her thoughts. Writing, thinking, and meaning-making are tied together in ways that cannot be disentangled. In content area classrooms, teachers use a variety of instructional activities and strategies to put into play the power of writing to facilitate thinking and learning in their disciplines.

In other chapters, we have recommended instructional strategies involving writing to support students' comprehension of texts. In this chapter, however, our intent is to highlight and reaffirm the powerful learning opportunities that arise whenever teachers link reading to writing in the lessons that they plan. A classroom environment that supports reading and writing invites students to explore ideas, clarify meaning, and construct knowledge. When reading and writing are taught in tandem, the union influences

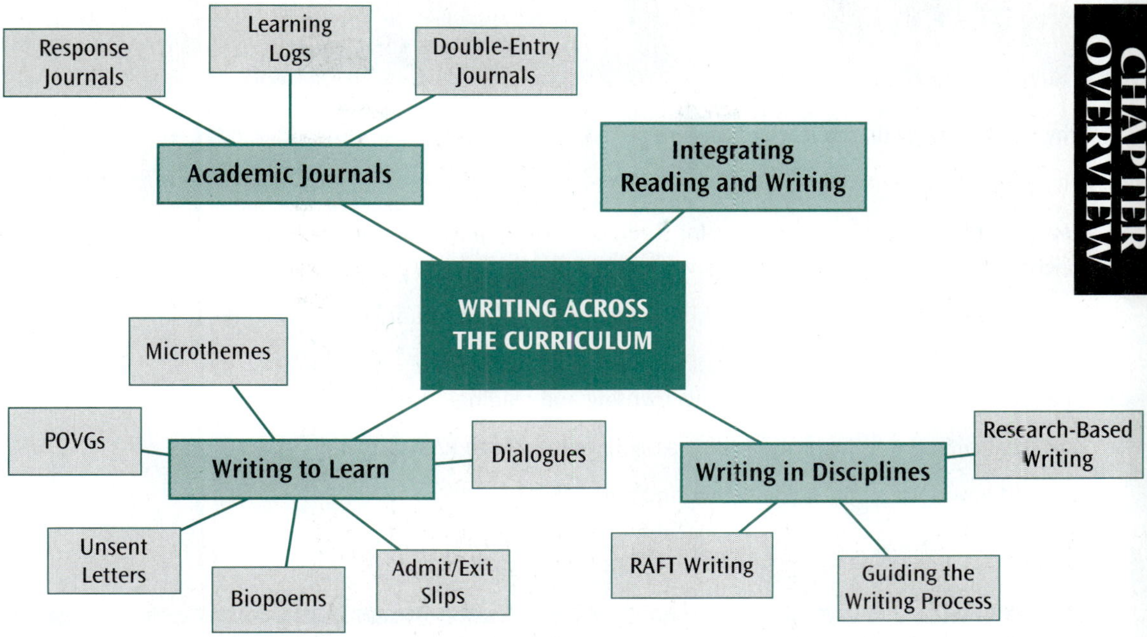

content learning in ways not possible when students read without writing or write without reading. When teachers invite a class to write before or after reading, they motivate students to use writing to think about what they will read and to explore and think more deeply about the ideas they have read.

Reading and writing are taught in some classrooms as if they bear little relationship to each other. The result has often been to sever the powerful bonds for meaning-making that exist between reading and writing. There's little to be gained from teaching reading apart from writing. The organizing principle reflects this notion: **Writing facilitates learning by helping students to explore, clarify, and think deeply about the ideas and concepts they encounter in reading.**

FRAME OF MIND

1. Why emphasize writing to learn in content areas?
2. Why integrate writing and reading?
3. How might teachers create occasions for students to write to read and to read to write?
4. How can teachers use exploratory writing activities to motivate students to read and write?
5. How can teachers use journals to connect writing and reading?
6. How can teachers develop essay writing assignments through RAFT activities?
7. Why and how do teachers guide the writing process?

Simon, born in 1994, is a digital native. For millions of adolescents born in the 1990s, digital technologies were a reality and already a significant part of the cultural landscape. From the time he received his first handheld Nintendo Game Boy as a preschooler, Simon has grown up with video games, computers, the Internet, mobile phones, Facebook, and his beloved MP3 player. Like most teenagers immersed in new literacies, Simon probably doesn't think of himself as a writer, but writing is a significant part of his young life. Why the paradox?

As researchers at the Pew Internet and American Life Project report in their groundbreaking study, *Writing, Technology and Teens:*

> Most teenagers spend a considerable amount of their life composing text, but they do not think that a lot of the material they create electronically is *real* writing. The act of exchanging e-mails, instant messages, texts, and social network posts is communication that carries the same weight to teens as phone calls and between-class hallway greetings. (Lenhart, Arafeh, Smith, & Macgill 2008, p. i)

Using a combination of focus groups from various regions of the United States and telephone surveys, the Pew research team documented many interesting phenomena about adolescents' personal identities in relation to technology and writing. The role of digital technologies in the lives of adolescents is quite evident in these findings: 75 percent of teens have a cell phone, 93 percent use the Internet, 68 percent of online teens use instant messaging, and nearly 75 percent have created content for the Internet. Figure 9.1 summarizes the Pew findings.

Writing in a digital medium, however, has not been without its controversies. There is a prevailing notion, for example, that texting and instant messaging are harming adolescents' ability to use language effectively in their writing. In his book *Txting: The Gr8 Db8*, David Crystal (2008a) dispels the texting controversy as myth. According to Crystal, a British linguist, there is little empirical evidence that texting adversely affects writing. In an online article for *The Guardian,* Crystal (2008b) examines the recent phenomenon of "txt poetry" to illustrate his point. In the article, he discusses the linguistic skill involved in crafting a txt poem like "txt commndmnts," written by children's author and poet Norman Silver:

TXT COMMNDMNTS

1. u shall luv ur mobil fone with all ur hart
2. u & ur fone shall neva b apart
3. u shall nt lust aftr ur neibrs fone nor thiev
4. u shall b prepard @ all times 2 tXt & 2 recv
5. u shall use LOL & othr acronyms in conversatns
6. u shall b zappy with ur ast*r*sks & exc!matns!!
7. u shall abbrevi8 & rite words like theyr sed
8. u shall nt speak 2 sum1 face2face if u cn msg em insted
9. u shall nt shout with capitls XEPT IN DIRE EMERGNCY+
10. u shall nt consult a ninglish dictnry (Published by txtcafe.com 2006)

Silver's poem, a playful parody on the ten commandments, is inventive and humorous in its construction. Yet it says much about literacy and the conventions of texting as e-communication in a twenty-first-century society. Crystal is quick to suggest that children and teenagers would not be good at texting if they had not already developed extensive written language skill and sensitivity:

> Before you can write and play with abbreviated forms, you need to have a sense of how the sounds of your language relate to the letters. You need to know that there are such things as alternative spellings. If you are aware that your texting behaviour is different, you must have already intuited that there is such a thing as a standard. If you are using such abbreviations as lol and brb ("be right back"), you must have developed a sensitivity to the communicative needs of your textees. (Crystal 2008b)

Texting, instant messaging, or posts on Facebook represent different types of *social writing*. The majority of today's adolescents, as the Pew study discovered, do not identify social writing as "real writing," but do recognize the importance of *academic writing* in their school lives. Interestingly, teenagers perceive academic writing tasks to be limited in scope, that is, short

FIGURE 9.1 **Writing, Technology, and Teens: Summary of Findings**

- Even though teens are heavily embedded in a tech-rich world, they do not believe that communication over the Internet or text messaging is writing.
- The impact of technology on writing is hardly a frivolous issue because most believe that good writing is important to teens' future success.
- Teens are motivated to write by relevant topics, high expectations, an interested audience, and opportunities to write creatively.
- Writing for school is a nearly everyday activity for teens, but most assignments are short.
- Teens believe that the writing instruction they receive in school could be improved.
- Nonschool writing, while less common than school writing, is still widespread among teens.
- Multichannel teens and gadget owners do not write any more—or less—than their counterparts, but bloggers are more prolific.
- Teens more often write by hand for both out-of-school writing and school work.
- As tech-savvy as they are, teens do not believe that writing with computers makes a big difference in the quality of their writing.
- Parents are generally more positive than their teen children about the effect of computers and text-based communication tools on their child's writing.
- Teens enjoy nonschool writing and, to a lesser extent, the writing they do for school.

Source: Lenhart, A., Arafeh, S., Smith, A., & Rankin Macgill, A. (April 24, 2008). *Writing, Technology and Teens.* Washington, DC: Pew Internet & American Life Project. Retrieved May 2009, from www.pewinternet.org/~media/Files/Reports/2008/PIP_Writing_Report_FINAL3.pdf. Reprinted by permission.

responses to homework questions—a conclusion that many writing researchers have formed since the 1980s (Langer & Applebee 1987; National Commission on Writing 2003)

Students in content literacy situations need varied and frequent experiences with writing and reading as tools for learning. There are at least three good reasons for teachers to take a second look at the role of writing in their classrooms. First, writing improves thinking. Second, it facilitates learning. Third, writing is closely connected to reading.

Content area teachers usually have second thoughts about assigning writing in their classrooms because of preconceived notions of what the teaching of writing may entail. Writing isn't generally thought of as basic to thinking and learning in a discipline. Teachers of every discipline share in the responsibility of showing students how to think and write as scientists, historians, mathematicians, and literary critics do. When students engage in writing as a way of knowing, they are thinking on paper (Moore, Moore, Cunningham, & Cunningham 2006). ■

Integrating Reading and Writing

There is no better way to think about a subject than to have the occasion to read and write about it. However, reading and writing don't necessarily guarantee improved thinking or learning. Students can go through the motions of reading and writing, lacking purpose and commitment, or they can work thoughtfully to construct meaning, make discoveries, and think deeply about a subject. Classrooms that integrate reading and writing lend encouragement to students who are maturing as readers and writers and provide instructional support so that readers and writers can play with ideas, explore concepts, clarify meaning, and elaborate on what they are learning.

Reading and Writing as Composing Processes

Reading and writing are acts of composing because readers and writers are involved in an ongoing, dynamic process of constructing meaning (Tierney & Pearson 1983). Composing processes are more obvious in writing than in reading: The writer, initially facing a blank page or screen, constructs a text. The text is a visible entity and reflects the writer's thinking on paper. Less obvious is the "text"—the configuration of meanings—that students compose or construct in their own minds as they read.

Think of reading and writing as two sides of the same coin. Whereas the writer works to make a text sensible, the reader works to make sense from a text. As a result, the two processes, rooted in language, are intertwined and share common cognitive and sociocultural characteristics. Both reading and writing, for example, involve purpose, commitment, schema activation, planning, working with ideas, revision and rethinking, and monitoring. Both processes occur within a social, communicative context. Skilled writers are mindful of their content (the subject about

RTI for Struggling Adolescent Learners

BOX 9.1

Responsive Teaching for At-Risk Writers

Students who struggle with academic learning tasks typically find writing activities difficult to accomplish. Increasingly intensive instruction linked to specific skills and strategies is often needed before struggling learners are able to successfully complete independent writing activities. RTI models encourage schools to support at-risk writers by incorporating strategy instruction across the curriculum. In this chapter, we will provide many Tier 1 strategy interventions to help content area teachers in disciplinary learning situations.

If students continue to struggle with writing after Tier 1 instruction, typical Tier 2 accommodations might include explicit small-group or individualized strategy instruction to produce abbreviated writing assignments. This is especially useful for students with specific writing disabilities. When students have difficulty writing, it is helpful to break down assignments into smaller, more manageable tasks. Teachers can modify the requirements of a particular writing assignment or divide writing prompts into a series of adapted steps, allowing struggling writers to focus on a single idea or concept. Struggling writers also benefit from the use of computers to explore ideas as well as to check documents for spelling and grammar, allowing them to focus on content rather than proofreading. Voice recognition software supports students who face physical and cognitive challenges that impede their ability to write.

As we demonstrate in this chapter, writing to learn activities can also be used to support other types of literacy interventions. *Learning logs* can help students monitor their own comprehension and implement fix-up strategies when they encounter reading difficulties. *Exploratory writing* allows students to identify gaps between their prior knowledge and text content. Structured assignments such as *double-entry journals* allow students to process content from multiple perspectives, or at multiple times, to aid in comprehension.

which they are writing) and also of their audiences (the readers for whom they write). Skilled readers are mindful of a text's content and are also aware that they engage in transactions with its author.

The relationships between reading and writing have been a source of inquiry by language researchers since the mid-1970s (Close, Hull, & Langer 2005). Several broad conclusions about the links between reading and writing can be drawn: Good readers are often good writers, and vice versa; students who write well tend to read more than those who do not write well; wide reading improves writing; and students who are good readers and writers perceive themselves as such and are more likely to engage in reading and writing on their own.

Why connect reading and writing in instructional contexts? From a content literacy perspective, writing about ideas and concepts encountered in texts will improve students' acquisition of content more than simply reading without writing. When reading and writing are taught in concert, the union fosters problem solving and makes thinking and learning more powerful than if reading or writing is engaged in separately.

Reading and Writing as Exploration, Motivation, and Clarification

RESPONSE JOURNAL

Why should exploratory writing be encouraged in content area classrooms?

When teachers integrate writing and reading, they help students use writing to *think about what they will read* and to *understand what they have read.* Writing may be used as a motivational tool to catapult students into reading. It is also one of the most effective ways for students to understand something they have read. Teachers can put students into writing-to-read or reading-to-write situations because the writing process is a powerful tool for exploring and clarifying meaning.

Writers engage in a process of exploration and clarification as they go about the task of making meaning. They progress from exploring meaning to clarifying it as they continue to work with a piece of writing. A writer's first efforts are an initial attempt to think on paper or screen. The more writers work with ideas put on paper or screen, the more they are able to revise, rethink, and clarify what they have to say about a subject.

Occasions to write on content subjects before reading and after reading create opportunities to learn content in concert with reading. Students who experience the integration of writing and reading are likely to learn more content, to understand it better, and to remember it longer. This is the case because writing, whether before or after reading, promotes thinking, but in different ways. Writing a summary after reading (see Chapter 10), for example, is likely to result in greater understanding and retention of important information. However, another type of writing—let's say an essay—may trigger the analysis, synthesis, and elaboration of ideas encountered in reading and class discussion.

The International Network of Writing Across the Curriculum (INWAC), an informal community of teachers, researchers, and institutions who champion the development and use of writing strategies in content areas, identifies two major instructional components for disciplinary writing: writing to learn (WTL) and writing in disciplines (WID). Let's take a closer look at each component. How are they alike? How are they different?

Writing to Learn (WTL)

Instructional activities that support WTL are by their very nature short and informal writing tasks. The writing that these activities produce is often tentative and unfinished. When students engage in WTL, they explore ideas and clarify what they are thinking about in relation to a subject under study. Before reading, WTL activities help students tap into prior knowledge and make connections between the "old" (what they already know) and the "new" (what they will be learning about). For example, many content area teachers combine a prereading activity such as brainstorming with five or so minutes of "quick-writing," in which students write freely and spontaneously on what they know and on what they hope to learn from more in-depth reading and study. After reading, quick-writing activities such as *microthemes* are useful in helping students to summarize and extend their thoughts about a subject.

WTL should not be confused with *learning to write*. Students learn to write formally from the time they enter school and continue learning to write throughout their lives. Language arts and English teachers, entrusted with the primary responsibility for students' writing development, teach learners how to engage in the process of writing as a central component of learning to write. In this chapter, we discuss the content area teacher's role in guiding the writing process when students are engaged in more elaborate writing assignments such as essays and research papers.

A variety of instructional activities may be used for WTL, including microthemes, POVGs, unsent letters, biopoems, dialogues, and admit/exit slips. Having students write regularly in various kinds of journals is also an important component of writing to learn in content area classrooms.

Microthemes

More isn't necessarily better when getting students to think and learn by writing. In fact, brevity is the key to writing an effective microtheme. A microtheme is a brief piece of writing that results in a great deal of thinking (Bean, Drenk, & Lee 1982). Think of microthemes as miniessays. Teachers often require students to write a microtheme on one side of an index card or half-sheet of paper. A 5-by-8 inch index card is a lot less threatening for students than the prospect of writing a full-blown essay.

Microthemes can be assigned for a variety of purposes, including analyzing and synthesizing information and ideas encountered in reading, writing summaries, or taking a stand on an important issue. In a biology class, for example, students were involved in an ecological study of organisms in short river communities along the western coast of Florida. One of the readings dealt with community relationships in the life of river turtles. As part of the unit, the teacher assigned a variety of WTL activities, including microthemes. One of the microthemes helped students to reflect on and synthesize information related to river turtle life. After much discussion of the topic, the teacher distributed index cards and assigned the following microtheme in the form of two questions: What relationships to other organisms does an adult river turtle have in this river community? How do these relationships differ from those of a young river turtle?

Before writing, students were asked to jot down notes and key points from the text and class discussions that they might use in the microtheme. Since words were at a premium, students had to be concise, yet complete. Here's what Jaycee wrote on her index card:

> Adult river turtles have got both direct and indirect relationships with other organisms in this river community. Direct relationships include eating many of the plants that grow in the river. Other organisms eat and live off of the river turtle. Leeches suck on

their blood like vampires while other animals eat the turtles eggs. When there in the water river turtles can be food for certain fish, herons, and even a kind of snapping turtle. Indirect relationships are when turtles compete for a food source like tape grass with another organism. Young river turtles differ from adult river turtles. Young turtles can be carnivorous as well as herbivorous. They are also more likely to be eaten by preteters than adult turtles. When both young and adult turtles die they become food for decomposers that return all the substances in the turtles body to the nonliving world.

Jaycee's microtheme is fairly fact-laden and accurate in its description of direct and indirect relationships. Although she has some spelling errors (i.e., *preteters*) and grammatical miscues, these are to be expected in quick-writing activities. Jaycee and her classmates shared their microthemes in "study buddy" groups and also had an opportunity to raise questions in a whole-class follow-up discussion. The teacher then gave students an opportunity to make content changes or add information to their index cards. Although a grade is not assigned to individual microthemes, the teacher has students save their themes to use as "study cards" for unit tests. Other teachers may choose to grade microthemes by assigning points based on a scale of 1 to 5, with 5 being rated as excellent.

POVGs

A POVG (point of view guide) connects writing to reading in a creative, nonthreatening manner (Wood 1988; Wood, Lapp, Flood, & Taylor 2008). POVGs are designed to trigger thoughtful reading and writing by having students "get inside the skin" of a character or a subject under study. Several key characteristics of POVGs include the following:

- POVGs are questions presented in an *interview* format that allow students to think about text from different points of view and perspectives.
- POVGs encourage *speculation, inferential thinking,* and *elaboration* by placing students in *role-play* situations.
- POVGs engage students in writing to learn by having them *actively contribute their own experiences* to the role.
- POVGs require *first-person* writing on the part of students as they respond to a situation.

POVGs can fit into a microtheme format or stand alone as a reading-writing-to-learn activity. In the sample microtheme above, Jaycee's language is formal, textbook-like, and somewhat stilted. However, POVG writing usually results in more informal, playful language as students assume a role and write in the first person. Jaycee's biology teacher also adapts a microtheme format to include POVG-type responses. In the unit on turtle life in a river community, notice how the teacher switched from very academic questions in the microtheme example to a role-play situation:

> Situation: You are about to be interviewed as if you are a young river turtle living in a river community along the west coast of Florida.
>
> Question: As a young river turtle, what is your typical day like?

Before writing their responses on index cards, students are assigned to read the text and take notes. Notice how Jaycee's language changes as she assumes the role of a young river turtle:

> I get up in the morning thinking about the long day ahead of me. When I leave my veggie pad, the first thing I do is pick up the newspaper and check out the obitcheries to see how the musk turtles are doing. They been having it rough lately. Then I go to the local resterant where I feed on snails, worms and water insects. As I make my way back to my floating mat of vegetation I don't got any fears until I see my mom and dad chomping away at the only thing that will protect me later in life. Tape grass. At this point, I'm thinking, Is this good parental behavior? After a hard days work, I go back to my veggie pad and dream of the day I become an adult. Will I do the same thing to my kids?

The structure of a POVG is easily adapted to learning situations in science, social studies, history, or English language arts. In a high school American history class studying the Great Depression, students are assigned to go online to the PBS website, American Experience, to read how farmers from the Great Plains fled to California during the Dust Bowl of the 1930s (www.pbs.org/wgbh/amex/dustbowl/peopleevents). The teacher's POVG establishes a situation for writing based on three questions:

> It's 1936. You were a farmer in Oklahoma during the Dust Bowl in which "the land just blew away." The bank foreclosed on your farm and you and your family were forced to move west to California in search of work and a new life. You have been living in California for two years. You are about to be interviewed by a writer from *Collier's Magazine*. First

read the text and then write your responses fully for each of the questions in the first person.

1. What was it like when you reached California? Describe how you were treated.
2. What kind of farmwork did you find in California? Was it different from what you expected in your former life as a farmer in Oklahoma?
3. Why did you give up migrant farming to move to a "shacktown" called "Okieville"? Describe what life was like for you and your family in Okieville.

POVGs may be devised for a single lesson or a unit of study. Figure 9.2 provides an example of a POVG from a middle school team unit on slavery in the United States.

FIGURE 9.2 **Point of View Guide for *From Slave Ship to Freedom Road***

On the Ship

You have recently been abducted from your home. You find yourself on a ship sailing to an unknown destination. There is much suffering aboard ship. You hear bodies being thrown overboard on a regular basis. What thoughts and feelings are going through your head?

The Auction Block

You are a plantation owner at a slave auction. You have $900.00 to spend. You must decide between purchasing an adolescent female or a thirty-year-old male. Which one do you choose and why?

Running Away

You are a slave working in the fields. You witness the "patterollers" dragging back Samuel, a runaway slave, for the second time. What are your thoughts? What do you think will happen to Samuel? Will this incident change your behavior in any way?

Business

You own a large plantation. Economic times are hard. Your business might fail. What do you need to do to keep your business going? What part, if any, does slavery play in your plans?

Underground Railroad

You are a white Christian who has been helping slaves escape through the Underground Railroad. Does the recently passed Fugitive Slave Act of 1850 change your behavior or attitudes? Are you willing to risk going to jail for someone you don't know? Why?

Civil War

You are a black slave living in an area where battles of the Civil War are being fought. You are planning to escape to join up with Union soldiers and fight in the war. Why is it so important to you to fight in this war?

Freedom and Change

The Union soldiers have come to the plantation. They said you are free. What does "freedom" mean to you? What problems do you have now that you didn't have before? How would you describe the emotions that you are feeling?

The POVG is designed to have students write to learn throughout the unit from a slave's perspective at different historical points. *From Slave Ship to Freedom Road,* a trade book by Julius Lester, became the basis for daily read-alouds by the teacher, followed by POVG writing in student response journals. Later in the chapter we will explain more fully the use of a response journal for WTL experiences. Also, Chapter 11 includes a discussion of read-alouds and the use of trade books for disciplinary learning.

Unsent Letters

Like POVGs, the WTL activity known as *unsent letters* establishes a role-play situation in which students are asked to write letters in response to the material they are studying. The activity requires the use of imagination and often demands that writers engage in interpretive and evaluative thinking (Smith 2002). In an inner-city middle school in Cleveland, Ohio, a social studies teacher asked students to write an unsent letter to Barack Obama, written shortly after his election as the forty-fourth president of the United States. Since this was a letter to the president, the teacher's only proviso to the students was not to use slang in their writing. Shelby's letter reflects both personal and informative writing:

Dear President Obama,

I can't begin to tell you how amazing it is you got elected president of the United States. It's just too sweet to put in words. My gramma says its never going to happen in her life time. Everybody in my family thought so too. They never were going to see the day a black man gets elected president. But you proved everybody wrong. America was ready for you. You sure did it and we're all so proud to be living in this country today. I really liked seeing you on TV dancing with your beautiful wife when Beyoncé was singing. I know being president isn't going to be easy. There's lots of problems that need fixing. The economy isn't good. There's a war. But you got elected because Americans believe in you. Your a natural born leader, your smart too. I'm a couple years older than Malia. The look in her eyes when you were sworn in is the same one I had. I know you will make all Americans proud.

Sincerely,

Shelby

A high school English teacher uses unsent letters to help students think more deeply about short stories. One of the stories, "Thank You, M'am" by Langston Hughes, is about Roger, a fourteen-year-old African American youth who makes the mistake of trying to steal the purse of Mrs. Luella Bates Washington Jones. He wants money to buy a pair of blue suede shoes. However, since Luella Jones is a very large woman, Roger fails to overpower her. Instead of having him arrested, she takes Roger home and feeds him supper. Before Roger leaves, Mrs. Jones gives him money to buy his shoes, tells him never to mug anyone again, and says that she wishes that he would behave himself. Roger barely says, "Thank you," as Mrs. Jones closes the door and he never sees her again.

When the class finished discussing the story, students were asked to write an unsent letter to Mrs. Jones from Roger fifteen years after the incident occurred. Here's Scott's letter:

Dear Mrs. Luella Bates Washington Jones,

I'm Roger. Remember me? You probably don't, but 15 years ago I came up behind you and tried to steal your purse. Instead of turning me in you gave me a warm meal and 10 dollars to buy a pair of shoes. After I left your house, I never tried to steal again. I am now married and we have a little girl name Luella after you. We were driving through the neighborhood and passed your house. I wanted to stop, but decided not to. So I'm writing this letter to say thank you, m'am and return the 10 dollars you gave me. I now counsel street kids about breaking the law and doing the right thing. I hope you remember me and that this letter let's you know how your act of kindness turned my life around.

Sincerely,

Roger

Unsent letters direct students' thinking with particular audiences in mind. Biopoems, by contrast, require students to play with ideas using precise language in a poetic framework.

Biopoems

A *biopoem* allows students to reflect on large amounts of material within a poetic form. The biopoem follows a pattern that enables writers to synthesize what they have learned about a person, place, thing, concept, or event under study. For example, study the following pattern for a person or character:

RESPONSE JOURNAL

What is your reaction to the use of a biopoem as a writing-to-learn activity?

Line 1. First name

Line 2. Four traits that describe character

Line 3. Relative ("brother," "sister," "daughter," etc.) of ________________

Line 4. Lover of ________________ (list three things or people)

Line 5. Who feels ________________ (three items)

Line 6. Who needs ________________ (three items)

Line 7. Who fears ________________ (three items)

Line 8. Who gives ________________ (three items)

Line 9. Who would like to see ________________ (three items)

Line 10. Resident of ________________

Line 11. Last name

Study how a health education teacher adapted the preceding pattern as part of a unit on HIV and AIDS awareness. After several days of studying the topic, the teacher introduced the biopoem strategy and explained how it could be useful in learning. She shared several biopoems from previous years that students had written on various topics and then discussed the biopoem format and clarified any questions that students might have about the writing task. She invited students to write a biopoem about AIDS by applying what they learned to an imaginary person. One of the students in the health class "invented" Valerie and then wrote the biopoem that follows:

Valerie,
Thin, tired, sad, confused.
She asks: "Why me?"
  "How will I deal with this?"
  "Will I be alone?"

Valerie,
She needs love,
  support,
  care,
  and advice.

Valerie,
She fears dying,
  being alone,
  feeling rejected.

Valerie,
She would like to see a cure,
Her family's approval,
Friends who care.

Valerie,
Your neighbor next door
A resident of Anywhere, U.S.A.
Valerie

A geometry teacher adapted the biopoem format for use in her class. Rather than write about a person, students were assigned a biopoem to describe the characteristics of a concept they were studying. Here's how one student described a trapezoid:

Trape
I've got two legs, two bases, and four angles,
My family includes sister Square and brothers Rhombus and Rectangle.
I need one pair of parallel sides
and each pair of base angles to be congruent.
I fear two pairs of parallel sides and also fear only three sides to it.
I would like to see the pyramids in Egypt some day.
Resident of Polygon
Zoid

Biopoems, as you can see, help students to synthesize their learning as they play with ideas in a format that provides an alternative to prose writing.

Admit Slips and Exit Slips

Admit slips are brief comments written by students on index cards or half-sheets of paper at the very beginning of class. The purpose of the admit slip is to have students react to what they are studying or to what's happening in class. Students are asked to respond to questions such as

What's confusing you about _________?

What problems did you have with your text assignment?

What would you like to get off your chest?

What do you like (dislike) about _________?

The admit slips are collected by the teacher and read aloud (with no indication of the authorship of individual comments) as a way of beginning class discussion. Admit slips build a trusting relationship between teacher and students and contribute to a sense of community in the classroom.

In an algebra class, where students had been studying complex numbers, the teacher asked the class to use admit slips to explain difficulties students had with one of their homework assignments. One student wrote, "I didn't know where to start." Several other students made similar comments. The teacher was able to use the written feedback to address some of the problems that students had with the assignment.

An *exit slip,* as you might anticipate, is a variation on the admit slip. Toward the end of class, the teacher asks students for exit slips as a way of bringing closure to what was learned. An exit slip question might require students to summarize, synthesize, evaluate, or project.

In the algebra class, exit slips were used toward the end of the class to introduce a new unit on imaginary numbers. The teacher asked students to write for several minutes as they reflected on the question "Why do you think we are studying about imaginary numbers after we studied the discriminant?" One student wrote, "Because the discriminant can be negative and I didn't know what kind of a number $\sqrt{-1}$ was. I guessing [*sic*] it must be imaginary. Right?" The teacher was able to sort through the exit slip responses and use them to introduce the new unit.

The several minutes devoted to exit slip writing are often quite revealing of the day's lesson and establish a direction for the next class.

Academic Journals

Because journals serve a variety of real-life purposes, not the least of which is to write about things that are important to us, they have withstood the test of time. Artists, scientists, novelists, historical figures, mathematicians, dancers, politicians, teachers, children, athletes—all kinds of people—have kept journals. Some journals—diaries, for example—are meant to be private and are not intended to be read by anyone but the writer. Sometimes, however, a diary makes its way into the public domain and affects readers in powerful ways. Anne Frank, probably the world's most famous child diarist, kept a personal journal of her innermost thoughts, fears, hopes, and experiences while hiding from the Nazis during World War II. Having read her diary, who hasn't been moved to think and feel more deeply about the tragic consequences of the Holocaust?

Other journals are more work related than personal in that writers record observations and experiences that will be useful, insightful, or instructive. In more than forty notebooks, Leonardo da Vinci recorded artistic ideas, detailed sketches of the human anatomy, elaborate plans for flying machines, and even his dreams. Novelists throughout literary history have used journals to record ideas, happenings, and conversations that have served to stimulate their imaginations and provide material for their writing. Even in a professional sport such as baseball, it is not unusual for hitters to keep a log of their at-bats: who the pitcher was, what the situation was (e.g., runner on base or bases empty), what types of pitches were thrown, and what the outcome of each at-bat was.

Academic journals also serve a variety of purposes. They help students generate ideas, create a record of thoughts and feelings in response to what they are reading, and explore their own lives and concerns in relation to what they are reading and learning. Academic journals create a context for learning in which students interact with information personally as they explore and clarify ideas, issues, and concepts under study. These journals may be used as springboards for class discussion or as mind stretchers that extend thinking, solve problems, or stimulate imagination. All forms of writing and written expression can be incorporated into academic journal writing, from doodles and sketches to poems and letters to comments, explanations, and reactions.

Three types of journals in particular have made a difference in content literacy situations: *response journals, double-entry journals,* and *learning logs*. Each of these can be used in an instructional context to help students explore literary and informational texts. Teachers who use academic journals in their classes encourage students to use everyday, expressive language to write about what they are studying, in the same way that they encourage students to use talk to explore ideas during discussion. When expressive language is missing from students' journal writing, the students do not experience the kind of internal talk that allows them to explore and clarify meaning in ways that are personal and crucial to thinking on paper or on screen.

When writing in academic journals, students need not attempt to sound "academic," even though they are writing about ideas and information of importance in various disciplines. Like the writing activities previously discussed in this chapter, journal entries need to be judged on the writer's ability to communicate and explore ideas, not on the quality of handwriting or the number of spelling and grammatical errors in the writing. Journal writing underscores informal learning. It relieves teachers of the burden of correction so that they can focus on students' thinking, and it creates a nonthreatening situation for students who may be hesitant to take risks because they are overly concerned about the mechanics of writing (e.g., handwriting, neatness, spelling, and punctuation).

Response Journals

Response journals create permanent records of what readers are feeling and thinking as they interact with texts. A response journal allows students to record their thoughts about texts and emotional reactions to them. Teachers may use prompts to trigger students' feelings and thoughts about a subject or may invite students to respond freely to what they are reading and doing in class. Prompts include questions, visual stimuli, read-alouds, or situations created to stimulate thinking. An earth science teacher, for example, might ask students to place themselves in the role of a water molecule as they describe what it's like to travel through the water cycle. Examine how Mike, a low-achieving ninth grader who didn't like to write, responded in his journal entry:

> **myeducationlab**
> Go to the Assignments and Activities section of Topic 4: "Writing" in the MyEducationLab for your course and complete the activity "Written Response" to see how one student used facts to support her opinions.

> My name is Moe, its short for Molecule. I was born in a cloud when I was condensed on a dust particle. My neverending life story goes like this.

> During Moes life he had a great time boncing into his friends. He grew up in the cloud and became bigger and heavier. Moe became so heavy that one night lightning struck and he fell out of his cloud as a raindrop. He landed in a farmers field where this leavy plant sucked him up. Moe became a small section of a leave on the plant and their he absorbed sunlight and other things. One day a cow came by and ate Moes leave. He was now part of the cow.
>
> Well you can guess the rest. The farmer ate the cow and Moe became part of the farmer. One day the farmer was working in the field, he started sweating and thats when Moe escaped. He transpirated into the air as a molecule again. Free at last he rejoined a group of new friends in a cloud and the cycle went on.

Mike's teacher was pleased by his journal entry, mechanical errors and all. On homework questions, he usually wrote short, incoherent answers. In this entry, however, he interacted playfully with the information in the text and demonstrated his understanding of the water cycle.

Historical Character Journals

Role-playing is an excellent prompt for response journal writing. A history teacher may invite students to assume the role of a historical character and to view events and happenings from the character's perspective. In Claudia Finley's U.S. history class, students keep journals of events that took place in American history from the perspective of a fictitious historical family that each student created. The families witness all of the events that take place in American history and write their reactions to these events. Finley scaffolds the journal writing assignment with the guidesheet in Figure 9.3. Study the guidesheet, and then read several entries from one student's journal in Figure 9.4 (pages 297–298).

Sketchbooks in Art

A high school art teacher incorporates a sketchbook into his courses to guide students' thinking and responses to what they are learning and studying in class. As an introduction to the sketchbook, the class discusses reasons for keeping a sketchbook, which the teacher adapted from a model used by McIntosh (1991):

- *What should you include in your sketchbook?* New ideas, sketches, concepts, designs, redesigns, words, notes from class, drawings to show understanding, reflections on the class, questions that you have, and new things you've learned.
- *When should you include entries in your sketchbook?* (1) After each class; (2) anytime an insight or a design idea or question hits you; (3) anytime, so keep the sketchbook handy and visible in your work area.
- *Why should you draw and write in your sketchbook?* (1) It will record your ideas and ideas you might otherwise forget; (2) it will record and note your growth; (3) it will facilitate your learning, problem solving, idea forming, research, reading, and discussion in class.

FIGURE 9.3 A Guidesheet for Historical Character Journals

To help you develop your historical character, use the information that you have gained about the American colonies and your own background knowledge.

Who is your character?

1. What is your character's name? How old is your character? Is he or she married? (*Note:* How old were people when they married during his or her time?)

   ____

   ____

2. Who else is in your character's family? How old is each of these people? (*Note:* What happened to a lot of children during this time?)

   ____

   ____

3. Where does your character live?

   ____

   ____

4. What does your character do for a living? Is he or she rich or poor?

   ____

   ____

5. What religion is your character? What attitude does he or she have toward religion?

   ____

   ____

6. How much education does your character have?

   ____

   ____

7. Was your character born in the United States, Europe, or Africa? If he or she was born in Europe, in what country?

   ____

   ____

8. How does your character feel about people who are "different" in skin color, religion, social or economic class, or nationality?

   ____

   ____

   a. Skin color? (*Note:* This may depend on where he or she lives.)

      ____

   b. Religion?

      ____

   c. Social or economic class?

      ____

   d. Nationality?

      ____

9. How does your character feel about being part of a colony instead of living in an independent country?

   ____

   ____

   ____

CLASSROOM ARTIFACT **FIGURE 9.4** **Historical Character Journal Entries**

1770

My name is Victoria Black and I'm thirteen years old. We are a Protestant family and we attend church regularly. It's a social as well as religious occasion for us. We stay all day and my mother gossips with all of the neighbors. I've made a few friends there but usually I stay with my sister. I have long blond hair and sparkling blue eyes in my mother's words. I'm learning how to take care of the home and cook lately. My mother says it's important because soon enough I'll be married. I think she wants me to marry one of the boys from town whose father is a popular lawyer. I have an older sister Sarah who is fifteen and has just gotten married. My parents are Mathew and Elizabeth Black, they are becoming older and mother has been sick lately. We worry very much for them and say prayers daily. We live on Mander Plantation in Trenton, Pennsylvania, where my father grows cotton and some tobacco. We have many indentured servants which we treat very nicely. I've become close with a couple of them. Usually when servants' time has expired my father will give them some land to start up their lives. Because we are more north we haven't any African slaves yet. My father is planning a trip out east to buy some slaves later this month. I'm still not sure if buying people is the right thing to do but my brother told me he doesn't think they're real people. I don't know how my father feels on this, he must think it's alright. My father is very confused about what's going on with the British. He doesn't understand why the colonists think they even have a chance at fighting and winning with the British. He thinks the war will be over in no time.

1778

I'm married now to William Brown, a new lawyer for Pennsylvania. We have two children, Mary and Richard Brown. They are still both very young, Mary is six and Richard is four and I'm expecting another soon! William is for the Revolutionary War. He feels the Brits are not being sensible with their laws for us. The taxation has bothered us greatly. Each week we scramble for money. Even though William is a lawyer, it's still hard to get started and receive reasonable wages. The British have also gone too far with the quartering act. We had British soldiers knock on our door last week asking for food. William was outraged. He says we have to have a revolution and win, if we want to survive and live happily. William said things are just going to get worse and worse. I don't think things could get any worse. I do

(continued)

CLASSROOM ARTIFACT **FIGURE 9.4** **Historical Character Journal Entries *(continued)***

worry about this war, for my brothers and William. Hopefully neither of them will be in the militia. We are already hearing of some battles, which sound awful. We are starting to go to church and pray every day now for our family and country.

1779-1781

William and my brothers are going to be in the militia. I'm very worried for them. William feels what he's doing is right for the country. We seem to be winning some of the battles, which is surprising. The women and children from our church gather every day and pray for our brothers and husbands. We all try our hardest to stay on our feet and have enough food for everyone. Some weeks it's difficult. We feel that all of our money is going to taxes. We pray that the end will be here soon. I had a baby boy which we named Daniel Brown. It will be hard to raise these children alone. Before William goes to the militia I'm going to visit my mother, she's dying and I'd like to say goodbye to her.

- *How should you write and draw entries in your sketchbook?* You can express yourself in sketches and drawings; in single words, questions, or short phrases; in long, flowing sentences; in designs and redesigns; in diagrams, graphs, and overlays; or in colors.
- *Remember, the sketchbook is yours, and it reflects how perceptive you are with your ideas and how creative you are in your thought processes!*

Examine several of the students' sketchbook entries in Figure 9.5.

Math Journals

Math teachers use response journals in a variety of ways. They may invite students to write a "math autobiography" in which they describe their feelings and prior experiences as math learners. Rose (1989) suggests the following prompt for a biographical narrative in math:

> Write about any mathematical experiences you have had. The narratives should be told as stories, with as much detail and description as possible. Include your thoughts, reactions, and feelings about the entire experience. (p. 24)

CLASSROOM ARTIFACT **FIGURE 9.5** **Entries from a Sketchbook**

Van Gogh vs. Gauguin

—I like Van Gogh much better
—Gauguin is nice but too showy
—I like elegance of Van Gogh
—Self-portraits are really challenging
—Van Gogh—master directionalist
—Unbelievable that he (Van Gogh) had no training!

—I like looking at different artists. Even though I know these people are masters, I love their work.
—I could never do that without lots of training!!

Impressionists

—Pretty
—Watercolory
—Really masterful handling of paint (watercolor)
—Saw them at Smithsonian

Question
When am I going to work larger?
I liked what we did on the computer—hope I get a chance to work with it again.

Questions
Why is it that I always draw late at night or early in the morning?
Shouldn't I start thinking about painting?
Will I ever understand color mixing?
Will I ever understand doing pencil directions?
Will I learn to stretch a canvas?

Looking to the future
—I don't use this sketchbook to do sketches—I like it more as a log
—Paint!! (probably a final problem)

If students need more scaffolding than the prompt, Rose recommends having them complete and write elaborations on sentences, such as

My most positive experience with math was ______________________
My background in math is ______________________
I liked math until ______________________
Math makes me feel ______________________
If I were a math teacher, I'd ______________________

The content of math journals may also include exploratory writing activities, summaries, letters, student-constructed word problems and theorem definitions, descriptions of mathematical processes, calculations and solutions to problems, and feelings about the course. Examine, for example, the journal entries in Figures 9.6 and 9.7.

Double-Entry Journals (DEJs)

A double-entry journal (DEJ) is a versatile adaptation of the response journal. As the name implies, DEJs allow students to record dual entries that are conceptually related. In doing so, students juxtapose their thoughts and feelings according to the prompts they are given for making the entries. To create a two-column format for a DEJ, have students divide sheets of notebook paper in half lengthwise. As an alternative, younger writers may need more room to write their entries than a divided page allows. They find that it is easier to use the entire left page of a notebook as one column and the right page as the other column.

CLASSROOM ARTIFACT **FIGURE 9.6** **Journal Entry in Response to the Prompt, "What Goes Through Your Mind When You Do a Proof?"**

October 7

When I look at something I have to prove, the answer is always so obvious to me, I don't know what to write. This confuses me more because then I just write down one thing. Even though I understand it, no one else could. I don't use postulates & theorems because I have no idea which is which. So if you gave me a proof, I could probably prove it, but just not mathematically using big words.

CLASSROOM ARTIFACT **FIGURE 9.7** **Journal Entry in Response to the Prompt, "Explain to Someone How to Bisect an Angle"**

9/4

How to Draw a Bisected Angle

Make an acute angle. Label it $\angle ABC$ — making Point A on one ray, B at the vertex, or point where rays meet, and C on the other ray. Now, with a compass, draw an arc of any measurement which will cross both rays. Next, use your compass to measure the distance between the two points you made by making the arc and keep the measurement locked on your protractor. Now, put the point of your compass on one of the arc points and make a slash in the middle of the angle. Do the same from the other dot on the other ray. The slash marks should cross in the center. Make a point where the slashes cross. Label it Point D. Draw a ray starting at Point B going through Point D. $\overrightarrow{BD}$ now bisects $\angle ABC$.

Purposes for Using DEJs

DEJs serve a variety of functions. In the left column of the journal, students may be prompted to select words, short quotes, or passages from the text that interest them or evoke strong responses. In this column, they write the word, quote, or passage verbatim or use their own words to describe what is said in the text. In the right column, the students record their reactions, interpretations, and responses to the text segments they have selected. As part of a science unit on the solar system, for example, middle level students used double-entry journals as an occasion to explore their own personal meanings for the concept of the solar system. In the left column, they responded to the question, "What is it?" In the right column, the students reflected on the question, "What does it mean to you?" Study the entries that three of the students wrote in the "What is it?" column. Then compare the three corresponding entries from the right column, "What does it mean to you?"

WHAT IS THE SOLAR SYSTEM?	WHAT DOES IT MEAN TO YOU?
It is nine planets, along with asteroid belts, stars, black holes, and so on.	The solar system is a mystery to me. I know the planets and stuff, but how did it come into being? Galileo had something to do with the solar system, but I'm not sure exactly what. I would like to find out more about it.

(continued)

WHAT IS THE SOLAR SYSTEM?	WHAT DOES IT MEAN TO YOU?
It is planets and stars. Earth is the third planet from the sun. It is the only planet with water. Stars are huge many much greater than the sun in size.	The solar system reminds me of a white haired scientist who is always studying the big vast opening in the sky. When I look at the sky at night I see tiny twinkling lights. People tell me that they're planets but I think they're stars. I see constellations but I don't recognize them. I am not a white haired scientist yet.
The nine planets are not very interesting to me and I won't bother to go through them. But I did memorize the order of the planets by this sentance. *M*y *v*ery *e*ager *m*other *j*ust *s*erved *u*s *n*ine *p*izzas. Take the beginning letters to remind you of each planet.	When I think about what the solar system means to me, I think about an unknown universe, which could be much larger than we think it is. I start to think about science fiction stories that I have read, alien beings and creatures that are in the universe some place.

Examples of DEJs in English and Math Classrooms

In an eighth-grade language arts class, Harry Noden and his students were engaged in a unit on the Yukon and Jack London's *Call of the Wild*. As part of the core book study of London's classic novel about the adventures of a sled dog named Buck, Noden arranged for a sled dog team demonstration by a group of local residents who participate in dog sledding as a hobby. His class was excited by the demonstration, which took place on the school's grounds. The next day, the class used double-entry journals to reflect on the experience. In the left column, they responded to the question, "What did you learn from the demonstration?" In the right column, they reflected on the question, "How did the demonstration help you better understand the novel?" Examine some of the students' entries in Figure 9.8.

Mathematics teachers have also been encouraged to use double-entry journals to help students solve word problems (Tobias 1989). In the left column, a teacher might direct students to engage in "thinking out loud" as they work on a word problem. In the right column, the students go about solving the problem, providing a layout of their sketches and calculations. Tobias noticed that as students began to use the two-column format to think about their problem-solving processes, they focused on posing two kinds of questions: "What is making the problem difficult for me? What could I do to make it easier for myself?" Here is one student's "thinking out loud" entry in response to this problem: *A car goes 20,000 miles on a long trip, rotating its five tires (including the spare) regularly and frequently. How many miles will any one tire have driven on the road?*

> I assume there is a formula for solving this problem, but I have forgotten (if I ever knew) what it is.
>
> I am being confused by the word "rotate." Simply by driving, we cause our tires to turn or "rotate" on the road. But "rotate" means something else in this problem. I had better concentrate on that.
>
> I wonder how many miles each tire will have gone while in the trunk? Is this a useful approach? Let me try. (p. 52)

CLASSROOM ARTIFACT **FIGURE 9.8** **Entries from a Double-Entry Journal Assignment for *The Call of the Wild***

What did you learn from the demonstration?	How did the demonstration help you better understand the novel?
I learned that although dogs just look big and cuddly they really can work. When people take the time they can teach their dog anything. Yet that saying also applies to life. **[Alex]**	I never realized how hard it was for Buck to pull the sled. It takes a lot of work.
It was excellent. I learned that the owners and the dogs were a family and extremely hard workers. I learned how hard a race could be and the risk involved. I'm glad I got to see the dogs and their personalities. **[Marcus]**	It proved to me how Buck needed to be treated with praise and discipline and equality. That way you get a wonderful dog and a companion for life.
I learned about how they trained their dogs and that they need as much or more love and attention as they do discipline. **[Jennifer]**	It helped me understand the book better because it showed how unique Buck is compared to the other dogs. Also what a dog sled looks like and what Buck might have looked like. It made the story come alive more.

Tobias explains that using this unorthodox approach, trying to find the number of miles that any one tire will have traveled in the trunk of the car, is a productive way to solve the problem. In the right column, the student calculated the correct answer by dividing 5 tires into 20,000 miles to get 4,000 miles per tire in the trunk. He then subtracted 4,000 miles from the total 20,000 miles driven, yielding the correct answer: Each tire, rotated onto the four on-road positions, traveled a total of 16,000 miles.

Learning Logs

Learning logs add still another dimension to personal learning in content area classrooms (Bangert-Drowns, Hurley, & Wilkinson 2004). The strategy is simple to implement but must be used regularly to be effective. As is the case with response and double-entry journals, students keep an ongoing record of learning *as it happens* in a notebook or loose-leaf binder. They write in their own language, not necessarily for others to read but to themselves, about what they are learning. Entries in logs influence learning by revealing problems and concerns.

There is no one way to use learning logs, although teachers often prefer allowing five or ten minutes at the end of a period for students to respond to process questions such as, What did I understand about the work we did in class today? What didn't I understand? At what point in the lesson did I get confused? What did I like or dislike about class today? The logs can be kept in a box and stored in the classroom. The teacher then reviews them during or after school to see what the students are learning and to recognize their concerns and problems. Let's take a look at how several teachers integrate logs into their instructional contexts.

Learning Logs in Math Classrooms

Two math teachers report using learning logs with much success in their classrooms. Kennedy (1985), a middle school teacher, has designed what he calls a "writing in math" program in which learning logs are a key feature. In addition to the preceding process questions, he likes to ask students about what they're wondering. What specific questions do they have about the material being studied? He also finds that logs are effective for "making notes." According to Kennedy, the distinction between *taking* and *making* notes is central to the use of learning logs: "Taking notes is copying someone else's information; *making notes* is writing interpretive comments and personal reminders such as 'Ask about this' or just 'Why?' " (p. 61).

A high school algebra teacher introduces learning logs to her class this way:

> From time to time, I'll be asking you to write down in your logs how you went about learning a particular topic in this class. In other words, can you capture that moment when things finally made sense to you and how you felt? And can you express the frustration that might have preceded this moment? (Pradl & Mayher 1985, p. 5)

Students may at first be tentative about writing and unsure of what to say or reveal—after all, journal writing is reflective and personal. It takes a trusting atmosphere to open up to the teacher. However, to win the trust of students, teachers, such as the algebra teacher, refrain from making judgmental or evaluative comments when students admit a lack of understanding of what's happening in class. If a trusting relationship exists, students will soon recognize the value of logs, although perhaps not as enthusiastically as one high school student:

> This journal has got to be the best thing that's hit this chemistry class. For once the teacher has direct communication with every member of the class. No matter how shy the student is they can get their lack of understanding across to the teacher. . . . These journals act as a "hot line" to and from the teacher. I feel this journal has helped me and everyone that I know in class. The only thing wrong is we should have started these on the first day of school!! In every class! (Pradl & Mayher 1985, p. 6)

The algebra teacher's students probably feel the same way about their algebra class. Here are some of the things that they do in their logs. For starters, the teacher likes to introduce a new topic by asking students to jot down their predictions and expectations of what the topic may involve. She also has her students write down their understanding of any new theorem that is introduced. After students believe that they have learned a theorem well, they use their logs to imagine how they might explain the theorem to another, less well-informed person, such as a younger sister or brother.

Both Kennedy and the algebra teacher use logs to have students create word problems that are then used to challenge other members of the class. Kennedy (1985) likes to have students write different kinds of word problems in their learning logs: "Sometimes I have them supply the data (for example, 'Write a problem involving the use of percent'); other times I supply the data (for example, 'Write a problem using the numbers 200, 400, and 600')" (p. 61).

Most journal activities require thinking but do not demand a finished product. Students soon learn to write without the fear of making errors. However, there are times when students should know in advance that their journal entries will be read aloud in class. According to Levine (1985), this is when students often produce their best writing because they are composing for an audience of peers. Josh, for example, an eighth grader, wrote about a lab experiment this way:

> Today in class we did a demo to try and find effective ways of recovering the solute from a solution.
>
> Several people came up with ideas as to how we could do this. A few people suggested filtering the solution, and others thought heating the solution so it evaporated would bring the solute back.
>
> First we tried filtering a copper sulfate solution but found that process didn't work. Evidently the crystals had dissolved to such an extent, that they were too small to be gathered by the filter paper.
>
> We then heated the solution and found we were far more successful than in our first try. Approximately thirteen minutes after we began heating the solution, a ring of copper sulfate crystals appeared in the bowl where the solution was. Eventually all the liquid evaporated leaving only the crystals. Quite obviously I learned that to recover the solute

from a solution you can heat the solution. I also learned not to bother trying to filter the solution. (p. 45)

Journal writing allows students such as Josh to express what's on their minds honestly and without pretense. In Box 9.2, Voices from the Classroom, follow the introduction of collaborative math journaling in a middle school unit on fractions.

Writing in Disciplines

WTL activities, as we have shown, provide students with numerous informal opportunities to explore and clarify ideas and concepts. A second instructional component of academic writing—known as writing in disciplines (WID)—involves more formal, elaborate, and well-thought-out writing on the part of students. Although there are aspects of academic writing that cut across all disciplines, each discipline has its specific *writing forms, styles,* and *conventions* that students must consider and follow as they engage in WID assignments. As the Writing in the Disciplines website put it, "The demands of writing a history paper or a sociology paper are, as most students quickly discover, very different from those of writing an English essay or business report" (Writing in the Disciplines 2001).

myeducationlab

Go to the Building Teaching Skills and Dispositions section of Topic 4: "Writing" in the MyEducationLab for your course. Completing the activity will help you work with students to develop their writing skills.

As important as a research paper is to learning in most, if not all, disciplines, other forms of writing are also essential: position papers, progress reports, lab and field reports, interpretive essays, reviews, project proposals, and journal or newspaper articles. Figure 9.9 (p. 308) provides an extensive listing of writing forms that are an integral part of WID writing assignments.

RAFT Writing

The key to thoughtful writing begins with the design of the assignment itself. The teacher's primary concern should be how to make an assignment *explicit* without stifling interest or the spirit of inquiry. An assignment should provide more than a subject to write on. This is where RAFT can make a difference in students' approach to writing.

RAFT is an acronym that stands for *r*ole, *a*udience, *f*orm, and *t*opic. RAFT allows teachers to create *prompts* for many types of discipline-specific writing assignments (Holston & Santa 1985). What constitutes an effective writing prompt for academic assignments? Suppose you were assigned one of the following topics to write on, based on text readings and class discussion:

- Batiking
- The role of the laser beam in the future
- Nuclear disarmament

Voices from the Classroom

BOX 9.2

Wendy

Middle School Teacher and Literacy Coach

CHALLENGE

Math teachers in my school often struggle to find the time to blend high-level thinking skills with writing. In my own classroom, I found the use of collaborative math journals to be particularly effective for addressing this challenge. When I introduced the strategy to my colleagues, many were familiar with math journals, but for most of them, the concept of using it as a tool for collaborative learning was new. By pairing students in teams to write and respond to each other's math journal entries, students engage in discussing not just the "what" but also the "why and "how" of their problem-solving processes. The collaborative effort also allows students to draw upon one another's strengths.

STRATEGY

When I first presented the idea of using collaborative math journals, some teachers were skeptical. They were concerned that journaling time would take up too much class time or that it would encourage idle chit-chat among the students. Mrs. Thomas, however, agreed to give it a try when teaching a unit on fractions. When she initially presented this to her students, students were put off by the idea of writing in math class. "I was just in language arts class writing," one student said, "why do I have to write in here too?" For most students though, the idea of a math journal grew on them the more they used it. Mrs. Thomas had her students use the journal for their daily warm-up, in which they reviewed the previous day's material. At the end of each class, she asked them to write to their partner about the topic covered in that day's class, and she offered a writing prompt to those who weren't sure where to begin. She also used the collaborative math journal as an organizational tool in conjunction with another strategy, the KWL chart. She said that, as their journal use became more routine, students became more comfortable with journaling and began to make it "more of their own" by abbreviating and using symbols that were meaningful to them.

Students' test scores consistently showed their increasing understanding of the mathematics content covered in class. Mrs. Thomas believed that, for many students, journaling contributed to this understanding. When asked about their reflections of collaborative math journaling, twelve students out of twenty reported positive reactions to their journal use. "It was like writing in a diary," one student commented. "I liked getting a note from someone, but not getting in trouble for passing a note at school," said another.

REFLECTION

As with just about any strategy, not every student responded favorably. Five students, two of whom struggled with writing, did not like using the journal at all. "It was just too hard," one explained. "Too much work for math," said another. So, while not every student loved it, many found collaborative math journaling useful and enjoyable for communicating the problem-solving processes involved in their mathematics learning. As a literacy coach, I learned a great deal by working together with Mrs. Thomas to develop innovative ways to adapt collaborative math journaling to specific topics and student needs.

FIGURE 9.9 Some Discourse Forms for Content Area Writing

- Journals and diaries (real or imaginary)
- Biographical sketches
- Anecdotes and stories:
  - From experience
  - As told by others
- Thumbnail sketches:
  - Of famous people
  - Of places
  - Of content ideas
  - Of historical events
- Guess who/what descriptions
- Letters:
  - Personal reactions
  - Observations
  - Public/informational
  - Persuasive:
    - To the editor
    - To public officials
  - To imaginary people
  - From imaginary places
- Requests
- Case studies:
  - School problems
  - Local issues
  - National concerns
  - Historical problems
  - Scientific issues
- Songs and ballads
- Demonstrations
- Poster displays
- Reviews:
  - Books (including textbooks)
  - Films
  - Outside reading
  - Television programs
  - Documentaries
- Historical "you are there" scenes
- Science notes:
  - Observations
  - Science notebook
  - Reading reports
  - Lab reports
- Written debates
- Taking a stand:
  - School issues
  - Family problems
  - State or national issues
  - Moral questions
- Books and booklets
- Informational monographs
- Radio scripts
- TV scenarios and scripts
- Dramatic scripts
- Notes for improvised drama
- Cartoons and cartoon strips
- Slide show scripts
- Puzzles and word searches
- Prophecy and predictions
- Photos and captions
- Collage, montage, mobile, sculpture
- Applications
- Memos
- Résumés and summaries
- Poems
- Plays
- Stories
- Fantasy
- Adventure
- Science fiction
- Historical stories
- Dialogues and conversations
- Children's books
- Telegrams
- Editorials
- Commentaries
- Responses and rebuttals
- Newspaper "fillers"
- Fact books or fact sheets
- School newspaper stories
- Stories or essays for local papers
- Proposals
- Math:
  - Story problems
  - Solutions to problems
  - Record books
  - Notes and observations
- Responses to literature
- Utopian proposals
- Practical proposals
- Interviews:
  - Actual
  - Imaginary
- Directions:
  - How-to
  - School or neighborhood guide
  - Survival manual
- Dictionaries and lexicons
- Technical reports
- Future options, notes on:
  - Careers, employment
  - School and training
  - Military/public service

Source: Teaching Writing in the Content Areas: Senior High School by Stephen Tchudi and JoAnne Yates. Copyright © 1983, National Education Association. Reprinted with permission.

No doubt, some of you would probably begin writing on one of the topics without hesitation. Perhaps you already know a great deal about the subject, have strong feelings about it, and can change the direction of the discourse without much difficulty. Others, however, may resist or even resent the activity. Your questions might echo the following concerns: Why do I want to write about any of these topics in the first place? For whom am I writing? Will I write a paragraph? A book? The most experienced writer must come to grips with questions such as these, and with even more complicated ones: How will I treat my subject? What role will I take? If anything, the questions raise to awareness the *rhetorical context*—the writer's *role*, the *audience*, the *form* of the writing, and the writer's *topic*—that most writing assignments should provide. A context for writing allows students to assess the writer's relationship to the subject of the writing (the topic) and to the reader (the audience for whom the writing is intended).

RESPONSE JOURNAL

Develop a RAFT writing activity for a topic in your content area.

A good writing activity, then, *situates* students in the writing task. Instead of asking students to write about how to batik, give students a RAFT.

> To show that you understand how batiking works, imagine that you are giving a demonstration at an arts-and-crafts show. Describe the steps and procedures involved in the process of batiking to a group of onlookers, recognizing that they know little about the process but are curious enough to find out more.

This example creates a context for writing. It suggests the writer's role (the student providing a batiking demonstration), the writer's audience (observers of the demonstration), the form of the writing (a how-to demonstration), and the topic (the process of batiking). RAFT writing prompts contrived situations and audiences in the context of what is being read or studied. However, they are far from trivial, nonacademic, or inconsequential. Instead, when students "become" someone else, they must look at situations in a nontraditional way. After writing, they can compare different perspectives on the same issue and examine the validity of the viewpoints that were taken.

Or take, as another example, the nuclear disarmament topic:

> The debate over nuclear disarmament has countries and people taking different sides of the argument. There are some who argue that nuclear proliferation will lead to nuclear war or nuclear terrorism. There are others who contend that the nuclear arms race is the only way to maintain peace in the world.
>
> You have been selected to write a position paper for the class in which you debate your side of the argument. Another student has been selected to defend an opposing position. The class will then vote on the most persuasive of the two positions. Once you have investigated the issue thoroughly, write a paper to convince as many classmates as possible that your position is the best one.

As you can see from the two examples, each creates a lifelike context, each identifies a purpose and an audience, and each suggests the writer's stance and a format—that is, a demonstration or a position paper. In each case, students will not necessarily make the assumption that the teacher is the audience, even though ultimately the teacher will evaluate the written product.

Research-Based Writing

Research projects pave the way for writing at every stage of the process, whether writing involves drawing up a project schedule, choosing a topic, formulating research questions, making an outline, taking notes, preparing a first draft, revising and editing, or completing the paper. Teachers who carefully plan research projects give just the right amount of direction to allow students to explore and discover ideas on their own. Research isn't a do-your-own-thing proposition. Novice researchers need structure. A research project must have just enough structure to give students (1) a problem focus, (2) physical and intellectual freedom, (3) an environment in which they can obtain data, and (4) guidance in writing and reporting the results of their research. See Box 5.1 on page 149 to review an outline of various aspects of the procedures for guiding research projects.

Ideally, research arises out of students' questions about the topic under study. A puzzling situation may arouse curiosity and interest. We recommend using questions such as the following to initiate research:

How is _____ different from _____? How are they alike?

What has changed from the way it used to be?

What can we learn from the past?

What caused ______ to happen? Why did it turn out that way?

What will happen next? How will it end?

How can we find out?

Which way is best?

What does this mean to you? How does this idea apply to other situations?

As a result of questioning, students should become aware of their present level of knowledge and the gaps that exist in what they know. They can use the questioning session to identify a problem. You might ask, "What do you want to find out?" During the planning stage of a research project, the emphasis should be on further analysis of each individual or group problem, breaking it down into a sequence of manageable parts and activities. The teacher facilitates by helping students to clarify problems. As students progress in their research, data collection and interpretation become integral stages of the inquiry. Students will need the physical and intellectual freedom to investigate their problems. They will also need an environment—a library or media center—where they will have access to a variety of informational materials, including print and electronic sources.

The teacher's role during data collection and interpretation is that of a resource. Your questions will help the students interpret data or perhaps raise new questions, reorganize ideas, or modify plans: "How are you doing? How can I help? Are you finding it difficult to obtain materials? Which ideas are giving you trouble?" This role is very similar to that of guiding the actual writing of the research project.

Guiding the Writing Process

Getting started with the actual writing of a paper or research report can be difficult, even terrifying. In the *Zits* cartoon, Jeremy delays writing until the night before his paper is due as he struggles with the all-too-familiar writer's block that all writers experience at one time or another. Waiting until the night before to write a paper is not good strategy!

One of the teacher's first instructional tasks is to make students aware that the writing process occurs in stages. It's the rare writer who leaps in a single bound from an idea-in-head to a finished product on paper. The stages of the writing process may be defined broadly as *discovery, drafting,* and *revising*. Table 9.1 presents an overview of these stages.

These stages are by no means neat and orderly. Few writers proceed from stage to stage in a linear sequence. Instead, writing is a *recursive* process; that is to say, writing is a back-and-forth activity. As teachers we want to engage students in the use of discovery strategies to explore and generate ideas and make plans before writing a draft, but once they are engaged in the physical act of composing a draft, writers often discover new ideas, reformulate plans, rewrite, and revise.

The Discovery Stage

What students do before writing is as important as what they do before reading. Discovery strategies involve planning, building and activating prior knowledge, setting goals, and getting ready for the task at hand. In other words, discovery refers to everything that students do before putting words on paper for a first draft. The term *prewriting* is often used interchangeably with *discovery,* but it

RESPONSE JOURNAL

What kinds of discovery strategies do you use to get started with an important writing assignment?

Source: Zits © Zits Partnership, King Features Syndicate.

TABLE 9.1

Stages in the Writing Process
Discovery
■ Exploring and generating ideas ■ Finding a topic ■ Making plans (Audience? Form? Voice?) ■ Getting started
Drafting
■ Getting ideas down on paper ■ Sticking to the task ■ Developing fluency and coherence
Revising
■ Revising for meaning ■ Responding to the writing ■ Organizing for clarity ■ Editing and proofreading for the conventions of writing, word choice, syntax ■ Polishing

is somewhat misleading because students often engage in some form of writing before working on a draft.

Discovery is what the writer consciously or unconsciously does to get energized and motivated—to get ideas out in the open, to explore what to say and how to say it: What will I include? What's a good way to start? Who is my audience? What form should my writing take? Scaffolding the use of discovery strategies in a classroom involves any support activity or experience that motivates a student to write, generates ideas for writing, or focuses attention on a particular subject. Students can be guided to think about a topic in relation to a perceived audience and the form that a piece of writing will take. A teacher who recognizes that the writing process must slow down at the beginning will help students discover that they have something to say and that they want to say it.

Getting started on the right foot is what the discovery stage is all about. Generating talk about an assignment or research project before writing buys time for students to gather ideas and organize them for writing. Discussion before writing is as crucial to success as discussion before reading.

Drafting

The drafting stage involves getting ideas down on paper in a fluent and coherent fashion. The writer drafts a text with an audience (readers) in mind.

If students are primed for writing through discovery strategies, first drafts should develop without undue struggle. The use of in-class time for drafting is as important as allotting in-class time for reading. In both cases, teachers can regulate and monitor the process much more effectively. For example, while students are writing, a teacher's time shouldn't be occupied grading papers or attending to other unrelated tasks.

The drafting stage should be a time to confer individually with students who are having trouble using what they know to tackle the writing task. Serve as a sounding board or play devil's advocate: "How does what we studied in class for the past few days relate to your topic?" or "I don't quite understand what you're getting at. Let's talk about what you're trying to say."

Revising

Revising a text is hard work. Student writers often think that *rewriting* is a dirty word. They mistake it for recopying—emphasizing neatness rather than an opportunity to rethink a paper. This is why good writing often reflects good rewriting. From a content area learning perspective, rewriting is the catalyst for clarifying and extending concepts under study. Revising text hinges on the feedback students receive between first and second drafts.

RESPONSE JOURNAL

When you write a draft of an academic writing assignment, do you seek feedback before revising it? If not, why not? As a skilled writer, do you need feedback from a peer or an instructor?

Teacher feedback is always important, but it's often too demanding and time consuming to be the sole vehicle for response. It may also lack the *immediacy* that student writers need to "try out" their ideas on an audience—especially if teachers are accustomed to taking home a stack of papers and writing comments on each one. The "paper load" soon becomes unmanageable and self-defeating. An alternative is to have students respond to the writing of other students. By working together in "response groups," students can give reactions, ask questions, and make suggestions to their peers. These responses to writing-in-progress lead to revision and refinement during rewriting.

myeducationlab

Go to the Assignments and Activities section of Topic 4: "Writing" in the MyEducationLab for your course and complete the activity "Peer Editing" to see how one teacher has students help each other develop their writing skills.

Once feedback is given on the content and organization of a draft, students can begin to edit and proofread their texts for spelling, punctuation, capitalization, word choice, and syntax. Accuracy counts. Cleaning up a text shouldn't be neglected, but student writers in particular must recognize that concern about proofreading and editing comes toward the end of the process.

LOOKING BACK LOOKING FORWARD

In this chapter, we focused on writing to emphasize the powerful bonds between reading and writing. Content area learning, in fact, is more within the reach of students when writing and reading are integrated throughout the curriculum. The combination of reading and writing in a classroom improves achievement and instructional efficiency. When students write in content area classrooms, they are involved in a process of manipulating, clarifying, discovering, and synthesizing ideas. The writing process is a powerful strategy for helping students gain insight into course objectives.

The uses of writing have been noticeably limited in content area classrooms. Writing has often been restricted to noncomposing activities such as filling in the blanks on worksheets and practice exercises, writing one-paragraph-or-less responses to study questions, or taking notes. The role of writing in content areas should be broadened because of its potentially powerful and motivating effect on thinking and learning.

Because writing promotes different types of learning, students should have many different occasions to write. Students should participate in exploratory writing activities, journal-keeping, and discipline-specific forms of writing. Informal writing activities, such as the unsent letter, place students in a role-playing situation in which they are asked to write letters about the material being studied. Additional activities include biopoems, microthemes, POVGS, dialogues, and admit/exit slips. Journals, one of the most versatile writing-to-learn strategies, entail students' responding to text as they keep ongoing records of learning while it happens, in a notebook or loose-leaf binder. When students use response journals, double-entry journals, or learning logs, they soon learn to write without the fear of making mechanical errors. Students should also engage in RAFT writing assignments that are task explicit. An explicit RAFT assignment helps students determine the role, the audience, the form of the writing, as well as the topic.

Moreover, writing should be thought of and taught as a process. When students develop process-related writing strategies, they will be in a better position to generate ideas, set goals, organize, draft, and revise. The writing process occurs in stages; it is not necessarily a linear sequence of events but more of a recursive, back-and-forth activity. The stages of writing explored in this chapter were defined broadly as discovery, drafting, and revising. Discovery-related writing strategies motivate students to explore and generate ideas for the writing, set purposes, and do some preliminary organizing for writing. As students discover what to write about, they draft ideas into words on paper or on the computer screen. Drafting itself is a form of discovery and may lead to new ideas and plans for the writer. Revising strategies help students to rethink what they have drafted, making changes that improve both the content and organization of the writing.

The next chapter examines what it means to study. Studying texts requires students to engage in purposeful independent learning activities. Organizing information, summarizing chunks of information, taking notes, and conducting and reporting inquiry-centered research are examples of learner-directed strategies.

Minds On

1. Each member of your group should select one of the following roles to play: (a) a language arts teacher who believes that correct mechanics are the heart of good writing, (b) a science teacher who assigns students a variety of writing-to-learn projects, (c) a history teacher who believes that writing is the job of the language arts department, (d) a math teacher who uses math journals to aid in students' comprehension, and (e) an administrator who lacks a philosophical view and is listening to form an opinion.

   Imagine that this group is eating lunch in the faculty lounge at a middle school where you teach. The language arts teacher turns to the science teacher and says, "My students were telling me that in the writing assignment you gave, you told them not to worry about mechanics, that you were interested mainly in their content and form. I wish you wouldn't make statements like that. After all, I'm trying to teach these kids to write correctly." Continue the discussion in each of your roles.

2. What strategies do you believe would be most useful in making writing assignments meaningful for learning?

3. Your group should divide into two teams, one pro and one con. Review each of the following four statements, and discuss from your assigned view the pros and cons of each issue. After you have discussed all four statements, take an "agree" or "disagree" vote on each statement, and discuss what you really believe about the issue.

   a. We write to discover meaning (to understand) and to communicate meaning to others (to be understood).

b. Writing is an incidental tool in learning and relatively unconnected to reading.

c. Writing to learn is a catalyst for reading and studying course material.

d. Students need to know the writer's role, audience, and form, and topic for a writing assignment.

4. At the start of the chapter, we wrote, "When reading and writing are taught in tandem, the union influences content learning in ways not possible when students read without writing or write without reading." Drawing on your experience and the text, discuss some specific examples that support this thesis.

Hands On

1. In the center of a blank sheet of paper, write the name of the first color that comes to your mind. Circle that color. Let your mind wander, and quickly write down all descriptive words or phrases that come to your mind that are related to that color word. Connect the words logically, creating clusters. Next, see what images these relationships suggest to you. Write a piece (a poem, a story, or an essay) based on your clusters. Exchange papers, and in pairs, comment on

   a. The best phrase in your partner's piece

   b. What needs explanation or clarification

   c. The central idea of the piece

   With your partner, discuss how this exercise illustrates the characteristics of writing to learn.

2. Work with a partner. Your task is to observe the other during the following activity and to record the characteristics of the other's approach to writing. For example, you might describe the writer pausing, sighing, gazing off, writing hurriedly, scratching out, and erasing. At the end of the activity, share your written description with the partner you observed to see if your observations match the writer's own perceptions.

   For this activity, write down seven pairs of rhyming words, and then recopy the pairs, alternating words (e.g., *hot, see, not, me*). Next, give your list of rhymes to your partner and have him or her write lines of poetry, using each word on the list as the final word in a line of the poem.

   What did you learn from both observing and being observed as a writer?

3. Take part in the following activities:

   a. Brainstorm by clustering associations with the topic "writing in school."

   b. Use this cluster to write a first draft of your experiences with writing in school.

   c. Meet with a small group. Share your draft by reading it aloud to your group. Receive formative evaluation on your piece, and respond to the writing presented by others in your group. Make notes about possible changes that might be made in a second draft of your piece.

   d. Revise your draft.

   e. Describe for the class your experiences during this activity. Was this a helpful process? Discuss implications for your own teaching.

e RESOURCES

- The following site contains thousands of story problems for enhancing critical thinking and problem-solving skills: **www.mathstories.com.** Many of the problems are based on children's literature. Browse the site and, working in small groups, write your own story problems based on content area topics of interest.

- Use the keywords "double-entry journal," "double-entry journal + classroom lessons," and "RAFT writing strategies" to complete a search of these powerful writing strategies. Consider how you might use these strategies in your content area. Of all the sites that come up in your searches, identify the sites with the most complete information and lessons.

CHAPTER 10

Study without reflection is a waste of time.

—Confucius

Studying Text

ORGANIZING PRINCIPLE

Studying text helps students make connections and think more deeply about ideas encountered during reading.

Studying text is an active, persistent, demanding process that takes place inside the head. It requires not only concentrated effort but also reflective thinking. Confucius got it right. Studying is a waste of time *if* students go through the motions of studying without thinking deeply about what they have read.

Students who study texts are self-directed, deliberate in their plans and actions, and conscious of their goals. They have reasons for studying, whether their purposes involve acquiring, organizing, summarizing, or using information and ideas. Studying text is hard work. It requires readers to be disciplined and patient with print. But because they are deliberate in their plans and actions and conscious of their goals, students who study text not only know how to work hard but also know how to work smart.

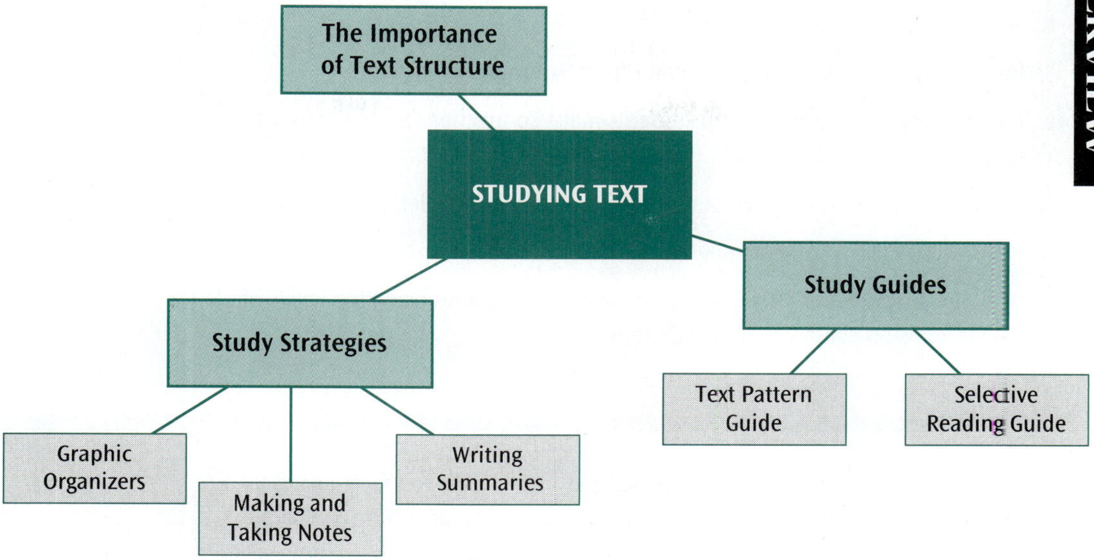

To work smart, students need to develop strategies for studying. Putting study strategies to good use is directly related to students' knowledge and awareness of what it means to study. As they become more aware of studying text, students look for *structure*—how the important information and ideas are organized in text—in everything they read. The organizing principle suggests that one important aspect of studying is to show students how to use the structure of ideas in text to their advantage: **Studying text helps students make connections and think more deeply about ideas encountered during reading.**

FRAME OF MIND

1. What does it mean to work smart?
2. How is internal text structure different from external text structure?
3. How do graphic organizers help students make connections among important ideas?
4. What note-taking frameworks and procedures can you model for your students?
5. How can you show students how to summarize information?
6. What are study guides? How can you develop study guides using the levels-of-comprehension construct and text patterns?

The poster caught our attention immediately. It had just gone up on the bulletin board in Julie Meyer's classroom. "School Daze: From A to Z" defined significant school activities in the lives of students, each beginning with a letter of the alphabet. The entry for the letter *S* just happened to be the subject of this chapter. It read, "STUDY: *Those precious moments between texting, video games, movies, sports, food, personal grooming, and general lollygagging when one opens one's school books—and falls asleep.*"

Though some students might agree that study is a quick cure for insomnia, few of us would deny that studying texts is one of the most frequent and predominant activities in schools today. The older students become, the more they are expected to learn with texts.

It's not uncommon to find a teacher prefacing text assignments by urging students to "study the material." And some students do. They are able to study effectively because they know what it means to *approach* a text assignment: to *analyze* the reading task at hand, to *make plans* for reading, and then to *use strategies* to suit their purposes for studying. Students who approach texts in this way achieve a level of independence because they are in charge of their own learning.

RESPONSE JOURNAL
How is studying a text different from reading it?

Other students, less skilled in reading and studying, wage a continual battle with texts. Some probably wonder why teachers make a big deal out of studying in the first place. For them, the exhortation to "study the material" goes in one ear and out the other. Others try to cope with the demands of study. Yet they are apt to equate studying texts with rote memorization, cramming "meaningless" material into short-term memory.

Whenever teachers urge students to study, they probably have something definite in mind. Whatever that something is, it shouldn't remain an ambiguous or unattainable classroom goal. All too often, the problem for students is that they aren't aware of what it means to study, let alone to use study strategies.

Today's students need to learn how to work smart. Working smart involves knowing when and when not to take shortcuts; it's knowing how to triumph over the everyday cognitive demands that are a natural part of classroom life.

Knowing how to work smart requires time and patience. Studying is a process that is learned inductively through trial and error and the repeated use of different strategies in different learning situations. And this is where teachers have a role to play. Through the instructional support you provide, students discover that some strategies work better for them than others in different learning situations.

More often than not, however, students will tell you that they study to pass tests. Fair enough. They are quick to associate studying with memorizing information. A concept of study that includes retention has merit. But too many students spend too much time using up too much energy on what often becomes their only strategy: rote memorization. Rote memorizing leads to short-lived recall of unrelated bits and pieces of information. Alternatives to rote memorization should be taught and reinforced when and where they count the most: in a content area classroom.

Studying text *is* hard work. Cultivating a repertoire of study strategies to "get the important ideas straight in your head" is essential. Showing students how to distinguish important from less important ideas is one of the key aspects of studying texts effectively. ■

The Importance of Text Structure

Authors impose structure—an organization among ideas—on their writing. Perceiving structure in text material improves learning and retention. When students are shown how to see relationships among concepts and bits of essential information, they are in a better position to respond to meaning and to distinguish important from less important ideas.

Educational psychologists from Thorndike (1917) to Kintsch (1977) and Meyer and Rice (1984) have shown that text structure is a crucial variable in learning and memory. Likewise, for more than fifty years, reading educators have underscored the recognition and use of organization as essential processes underlying comprehension and retention (Herber 1978; Niles 1965; Salisbury 1934; Smith 1964).

The primary purpose of many content area texts is to provide users with information. To make information readily accessible, authors use external and internal structural features. *External text structure* is characterized by a text's overall instructional design—its format features. Its *internal text structure* is reflected by the interrelationships among ideas in the text as well as by the subordination of some ideas to others.

External Text Structure

Printed and electronic texts contain certain format features—organizational aids—that are built into the text to facilitate reading. This book, for example, contains a *preface*, a *table of contents*, *appendixes*, a *bibliography*, and *indexes*. These aids, along with the *title page* and *dedication,* are called the *front matter* and *end matter* of a book. Of course, textbooks vary in the amount of front and end matter they contain. These aids can be valuable tools for prospective users of a textbook. Yet the novice reader hardly acknowledges their presence in texts, let alone uses them to advantage.

In addition, each chapter of a textbook usually has *introductory* or *summary statements, headings, graphs, charts, illustrations,* and *guide questions.*

Organizational aids, whether in electronic or printed texts, are potentially valuable—if they are not skipped or glossed over by readers. Headings, for example, are inserted in the text to divide it into logical units. Headings strategically placed in a text should guide the reader by highlighting major ideas.

Within a text, authors use an internal structure to connect ideas logically in a coherent whole. Internal text structure might vary from passage to passage, depending on the author's purpose. These structures, or patterns of organization, within a text are closely associated with informational writing. Read Box 10.1 to learn how a high school civics and economics teacher works with his students on these structures.

RESPONSE JOURNAL

Why do some students ignore external orgainzational aids as tools for studying?

Internal Text Structure

Content area texts are written to inform. This is why exposition is the primary mode of discourse found in informational texts. This is not to say that some authors don't, at times, attempt to persuade or entertain their readers. They may. However, their primary business is to *tell, show, describe,* or *explain.* It stands to reason that the more logically connected one idea is to another, depending on the author's informative purpose, the more coherent the description or explanation is.

myeducationlab

Go to the Assignments and Activities section of Topic 5: "Comprehension Strategies" in the MyEducationLab for your course and complete the activity "Using Text Features to Aid Comprehension" to see how one teacher familiarizes her students with expository text features.

Skilled readers search for structure in a text and can readily differentiate the important ideas from less important ideas in the material. Research has shown that good readers know how to look for major thought relationships (Meyer, Brandt, & Bluth 1980; Taylor 1980). They approach a reading assignment looking for a predominant *text pattern* or organization that will tie together the ideas contained throughout the text passage.

Text patterns represent the different types of logical connections among the important and less important ideas in informational material. A case can be made for five text patterns that seem to predominate in informational writing: *description, sequence, comparison and contrast, cause and effect,* and *problem and solution.* Here are descriptions and examples of these text structures.

Description

The description text pattern involves providing information about a topic, concept, event, object, person, idea, and so on (facts, characteristics, traits, features), usually

Voices from the Classroom

BOX 10.1

David
High School Civics and Economics Teacher

CHALLENGE

Civics and economics are integral components of my students' personal and academic success. While the curriculum supports their understanding of citizenship and government, students must also pass an end of course exam that is part of their graduation requirement. One of the biggest challenges they face is trying to read and understand their textbooks.

STRATEGY

I teach them how to evaluate the external text structure of chapters and use this framework to support their understanding before, during, and after reading. Our textbook is organized by topical units, such as citizenship, government, and economic systems. Chapters within each unit are structured differently to accommodate the different types of information they present. Before starting each chapter, I ask students to scan the chapter to determine the format of the text and record any headings. This will become an outline for their notes. Students also look for boldfaced or italicized words to determine if there are any unfamiliar terms. When they find unfamiliar words, they are taught to reference the text glossary or definitions provided within the chapter so they will understand the word when they encounter it during reading. Through this preview, students can begin to frame their perception of the material.

During reading, students use visual clues to check their comprehension of material. In our books, figures, photos, maps, and graphs serve to support understanding of subject matter. If they don't see the connection between the visual clues and the text, I tell students to reread the selection. If they still struggle with the material, they are directed to use any of the other fix-up strategies we have learned, such as referring back to previous passages or looking ahead to see if the main idea provides a meaningful context for the information in the chapter.

After reading, I ask students to review their notes and discuss their insights and questions with a classmate. This allows students to check their own understanding while considering another student's perspective on the material. This discussion serves to clear up misunderstandings and leads to a deeper comprehension of the content, while allowing students to work collaboratively towards a curricular goal.

REFLECTION

Using an evaluation of text structure to guide reading and note taking gives students concrete guidelines for processes that are often overwhelming to adolescent readers. Instead of using an arbitrary organizer, students learn to frame their processing of a text on the structure of the material itself. Students then build on their knowledge to comprehend concepts throughout the academic year as well as in subsequent social studies classes. They are better prepared to successfully complete their standardized exam in fulfillment of part of their graduation requirements, and, more importantly, students begin to see the relevance of our curriculum for understanding broader world events.

qualifying the listing by criteria such as size or importance. This pattern connects ideas through description by listing the important characteristics or attributes of the topic under consideration. The description pattern is one of the most common ways of organizing texts. Here is an example:

> There were several points in the fight for freedom of religion. One point was that religion and government should be kept apart. Americans did not want any form of a national church as was the case in England. Americans made sure that no person would be denied his or her religious beliefs.

Sequence

The sequence text pattern involves putting facts, events, or concepts into a sequence. The author traces the development of the topic or gives the steps in the process. Time reference may be explicit or implicit, but a sequence is evident in the pattern. The following paragraph illustrates the pattern:

> John F. Kennedy was the Democratic candidate for president when in October 1960 he first suggested there should be a Peace Corps. After he was elected, Kennedy asked his brother-in-law, Sargent Shriver, to help set up a Peace Corps. In March 1961, Kennedy gave an order to create the organization. It wasn't until September that Congress approved the Peace Corps and appropriated the money to run it for one year.

Comparison and Contrast

The comparison-and-contrast text pattern involves pointing out likenesses (comparison) and/or differences (contrast) among facts, people, events, concepts, and so on. Study this example:

> Castles were built for defense, not comfort. In spite of some books and movies that have made them attractive, castles were cold, dark, gloomy places to live. Rooms were small and not the least bit charming. Except for the great central hall or the kitchen, there were no fires to keep the rooms heated. Not only was there a lack of furniture, but what was there was uncomfortable.

Cause and Effect

The cause-and-effect text pattern involves showing how facts, events, or concepts (effects) happen or come into being because of other facts, events, or concepts (causes). Examine this paragraph for causes and effects:

> The fire was started by sparks from a campfire left by a careless camper. Thousands of acres of important watershed burned before the fire was brought under control. As a result of the fire, trees and the grasslands on the slopes of the valley were gone. Smoking black stumps were all that remained of tall pine trees.

Problem and Solution

The problem-and-solution text pattern involves showing the development of a problem and one or more solutions to the problem. Consider the following example:

> The skyrocketing price of oil in the 1970s created a serious problem for many Americans. The oil companies responded to the high cost of purchasing oil by searching for new oil supplies. This resulted in new deposits being found in some Third World nations, such as Nigeria. Oil companies also began drilling for oil on the ocean floor, and scientists discovered ways to extract oil from a rock known as *oil shale*.

Signal Words in Text Structure

Authors often showcase text patterns by giving readers clues or signals to help them figure out the structure being used. Readers usually become aware of the pattern if they are looking for the signals. A signal may be a word or a phrase that helps the reader follow the writer's thoughts.

Figure 10.1 shows signal words that authors often use to call attention to the organizational patterns just defined.

FIGURE 10.1 **Signal Words and Phrases Used in Various Text Structures**

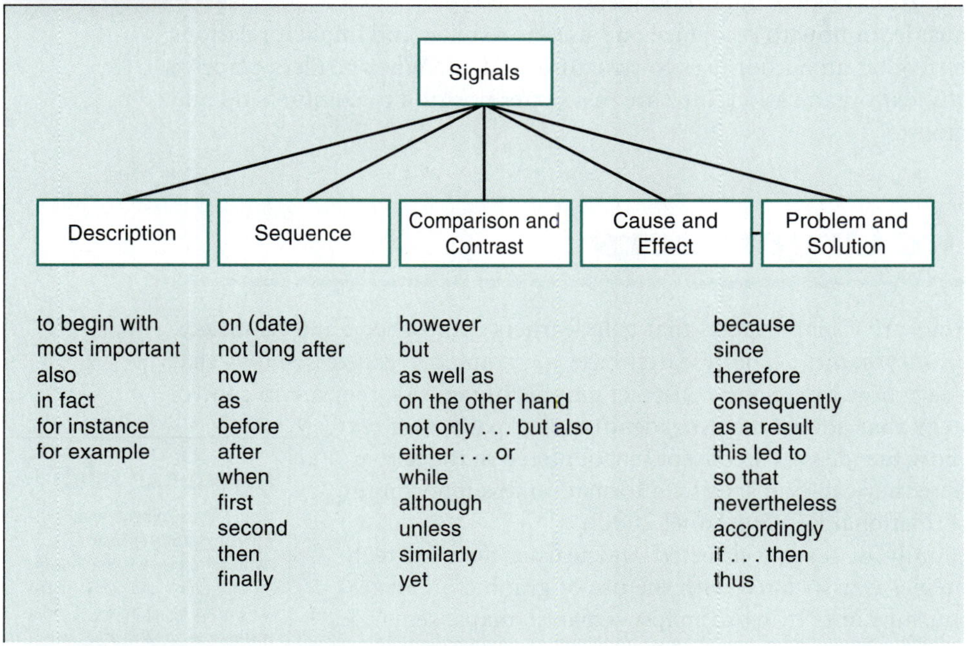

Awareness of the pattern of *long stretches* of text is especially helpful in planning reading assignments. In selecting from a passage of several paragraphs or several pages, teachers first need to determine whether a predominant text pattern is contained in the material. This is no easy task.

Informational writing is complex. Authors do not write in neat, perfectly identifiable patterns. Within the individual paragraphs of a text assignment, several kinds of thought relationships often exist. Suppose an author begins a passage by stating a problem. In telling about the development of the problem, the author *describes* a set of events that contributed to the problem. Or perhaps the author *compares* or *contrasts* the problem under consideration with another problem. In subsequent paragraphs, the *solutions* or attempts at solutions to the problem are stated. In presenting the solutions, the author uses heavy description and explanation. These descriptions and explanations are logically organized in a *sequence*.

The difficulty that teachers face is analyzing the overall text pattern, even though several types of thought relationships are probably embedded in the material. Analyzing a text for a predominant pattern depends in part on how clearly an author represents the relationships in the text.

Several guidelines follow for analyzing text patterns. First, survey the text for the most important idea in the selection. Are there any explicit signal words that indicate a pattern that will tie together the ideas throughout the passage? Second, study the content of the text for additional important ideas. Are these ideas logically connected to the most important idea? Is a pattern evident? Third, outline or diagram the relationships among the superordinate and subordinate ideas in the selection. Use the diagram to specify the major relationships contained in the text structure and to sort out the important from the less important ideas.

Students must learn how to recognize and use the explicit and implicit relations in the text patterns that an author uses to structure content. When readers perceive and interact with text organization, they are in a better position to comprehend and retain information.

Graphic Organizers

Graphic organizers are visual displays that help learners comprehend and retain *textually important information.* The research base for graphic organizers shows that when students learn how to use and construct graphic organizers, they are in control of a study strategy that allows them to identify what parts of a text are important, how the ideas and concepts encountered in the text are related, and where they can find specific information to support more important ideas (National Reading Panel 2000).

> **myeducationlab**
> Go to the Assignments and Activities section of Topic 4: "Writing" in the MyEducationLab for your course and complete the activity "Mapping" to see how one teacher uses graphic organizers.

An entire family of teacher-directed and learner-directed techniques and strategies is associated with the use of graphic organizers to depict relationships in text: word maps, semantic maps, semantic webs, flowcharts, concept matrices, and tree diagrams, to name a few. Although it is easy to get confused by the plethora of labels, a rose by any other name is still a rose.

What these techniques and strategies have in common is that they help students interact with and outline textually important information. For example, when students read a text with an appropriate graphic organizer in mind, they focus on important ideas and relationships. And when they construct their own graphic organizers, as we discussed in Chapter 8, they become actively involved in outlining those ideas and relationships.

Outlining helps students clarify relationships. Developing an outline is analogous to fitting together the pieces in a puzzle. Think of a puzzle piece as a separate idea and a text as the whole. Outlining strategies can be used effectively to facilitate a careful analysis and synthesis of the relationships in a text. They can form the basis for critical discussion and evaluation of the author's main points.

Problems arise when students are restricted in the way they must depict relationships spatially on paper or on a screen. The word *outlining* for most of us immediately conjures up an image of the "correct" or "classic" format that we have all learned at one time or another but have probably failed to use regularly in real-life study situations. The classic form of outlining has the student represent the relatedness of information in linear form:

I. Main Idea
  A. Idea supporting I
    1. Detail supporting A
    2. Detail supporting A
      a. Detail supporting 2
      b. Detail supporting 2
  B. Idea supporting I
    1. Detail supporting B
    2. Detail supporting B
II. Main Idea

This conventional format represents a hierarchical ordering of ideas at different levels of subordination. Roman numerals signal the major or superordinate concepts in a text section; capital letters, the supporting or coordinate concepts; Arabic numbers, the supporting or subordinate details; and lowercase letters, the subsubordinate details.

Some readers have trouble using a restricted form of outlining. Initially, at least, they need a more visual display than the one offered by the conventional format. And this is where graphic organizers can play a critical role in the development of independent learners.

To show students how to use and construct graphic organizers, begin by assessing how students usually outline text material. Do they have a sense of subordination among ideas? Do they have strategies for connecting major and minor concepts? Do they use alternatives to the conventional format? Make them aware of the rationale for organizing information through outlining. The jigsaw puzzle analogy—fitting pieces of information together into a coherent whole—works well for this purpose. Assessment and building awareness set the stage for illustrating, modeling, and applying the strategies. Box 10.2 outlines the steps used to build strategic knowledge and skills related to students' use of graphic organizers.

Evidence-Based Best Practices

BOX 10.2

GRAPHIC ORGANIZERS

To introduce students to various kinds of graphic organizers that may be applicable to texts in your content area, Jones, Pierce, and Hunter (1988–1989) suggest some of the following steps:

1. *Present an example of a graphic organizer that corresponds to the type of outline you plan to teach.* For example, suppose that a text that students will read is organized around a cause-and-effect text pattern. First, preview the text with the students. Help them discover features of the text that may signal the pattern. Make students aware that the title, subheads, and signal words provide them with clues to the structure of the text. Then ask questions that are pertinent to the pattern—for example, What happens in this reading? What causes it to happen? What are the important factors that cause these effects?

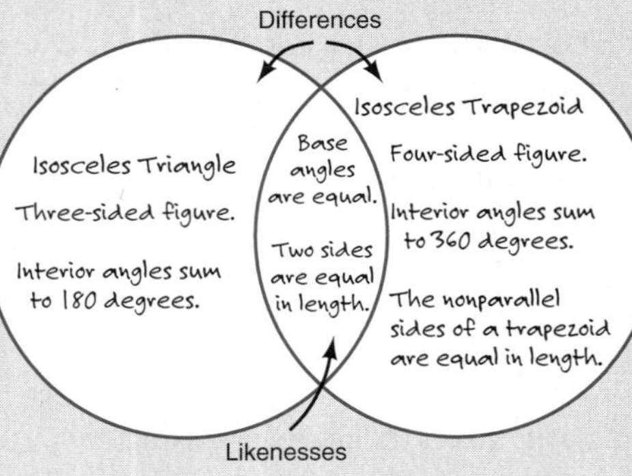

2. *Demonstrate how to construct a graphic outline.* Suppose that math students have completed a reading about the differences between isosceles triangles and isosceles trapezoids. Show them how to construct a *Venn diagram* to map how they are alike and different. Next, refer to the comparison and contrast questions you raised in the preview. Guide students through the procedures that lead to the development of the Venn diagram: First, on an overhead transparency, present an example of a partially completed Venn graphic. Second, have students review the text and offer suggestions to help complete the graphic. The accompanying graphic display shows a class-constructed rendering of the Venn diagram. Third, develop procedural knowledge by discussing when to use the Venn graphic and why.
3. *Coach students in the use of the graphic outline and give them opportunities to practice.* If other texts represent a particular text pattern that you have already demonstrated with the class, encourage students individually or in teams to construct their own graphic outlines and to use their constructions as the basis for class discussion.

Using Graphic Organizers to Reflect Text Patterns

Students can be shown how to construct maps and other types of visual displays to reflect the text patterns authors use to organize ideas. According to Jones, Pierce, and Hunter (1988–1989), "A fundamental rule in constructing graphic organizers is that the structure of the graphic should reflect the structure of the text it represents" (p. 21).

Jones and her colleagues recommend a variety of possible graphic organizer representations that reflect different text patterns. These "generic" outlines are illustrated in Appendix D. What follows are classroom examples of how some of these outlines might be developed in content area classrooms.

Comparison-and-Contrast Matrix

In addition to the Venn diagram and graphic organizers, a teacher can show students how a comparison and contrast pattern serves to organize ideas in a text through the use of a matrix outline. A comparison and contrast matrix shows similarities and differences between two or more things (people, places, events, concepts, processes, etc.). Readers compare and contrast the target concepts listed across the top of the matrix according to attributes, properties, or characteristics listed along the left side. Study the two examples of a comparison and contrast matrix in Figure 10.2 (p. 328). High school students used the biology example to outline the likenesses and differences of fungi and algae. Precalculus students used the matrix outline to compare and contrast conic sections (parabola, ellipse, and hyperbola).

Problem-and-Solution Outline

This graphic representation depicts a problem, attempted solutions, the result or outcomes associated with the attempted solutions, and the end result. It works equally well with narrative or informational texts to display the central problem in a story or the problem and solution text pattern. Figure 10.3 (p. 329) illustrates a problem and solution outline developed by students as part of a class reading of *Monster* by Walter Dean Myers. In studying characterization and plot, students were asked to evaluate the choices made by the main character in the story, Steve. The book is written as a screenplay created by Steve to explain his experience awaiting trial for the murder of a store owner during a robbery, for which Steve may or may not have been serving as a lookout. Throughout the book, Steve reevaluates his decision to be at the store in the first place, and struggles with the perception many have of him as a consequence of his possible participation in the robbery. The students completed a problem and solution outline to analyze the impact that Steve's choices may have had on his life. The teacher introduced the outline. Students worked in pairs to complete the outline and then shared their responses with the whole class.

FIGURE 10.2 **Comparison-and-Contrast Matrices for Biology (a) and Precalculus (b)**

(a)	Fungi	Algae
Body Structure		
Food Source		
Method or reproduction		
Living environment		

(b)	Parabola	Ellipse	Hyperbola
Sketch two examples			
Equation in standard form			
Special characteristics			
Foci (focal points)			
Line(s) of symmetry			

FIGURE 10.3 **Problem-and-Solution Outline for Walter Dean Myers's *Monster***

Problem

Who has the problem?

Steve Harmon

What was the problem?

Should he be a lookout during the robbery or should he stand up to his friends?

Why was it a problem?

If he stands up to his friends he could get beaten up; if he serves as the lookout soemone else could get hurt and he could go to jail.

Solutions

Attempted Solutions	Outcomes
Steve goes to the store but doesn't commit to being the lookout	Steve endes up getting caught and going on trial
Steve claims he is not guilty during the trial	Everyone wonders if he is innocent or just trying to get out of trouble

End Result

Steve finds himself on trial for murder and is upset that everyone thinks he is a "monster" for getting involved in a robbery that results in murder. Even though he ends up being found not guilty, Steve knows some people will always believe he was guilty and that he made bad decisions.

Network Tree

The network tree is based on the same principle as the graphic organizers introduced in Chapter 8 and used in the chapter organizers in this book. That is to say, it represents the network of relationships that exists between superordinate concepts and subordinate concepts. It can be used to show causal information or to describe a central idea in relation to its attributes and examples. Notice how math students explored relationships in the quadratic formula by using the network tree illustrated in Figure 10.4.

Series-of-Events Chain

The series-of-events chain may be used with narrative material to show the chain of events that lead to the resolution of conflict in a story. It may also be used with informational text to reflect the sequence pattern in a text. It may include any sequence of events, including the steps in a linear procedure, the chain of events (effects) caused by some event, or the stages of something. Scientific and historical texts are often organized in a sequence pattern and lend themselves well to this type of graphic display. A science class, for example, might be asked to map the sequence of steps in the scientific method by using a series-of-events chain. After reading about the scientific method, students might make an outline similar to the one in Figure 10.5.

FIGURE 10.4 **Network Tree for the Quadratic Formula**

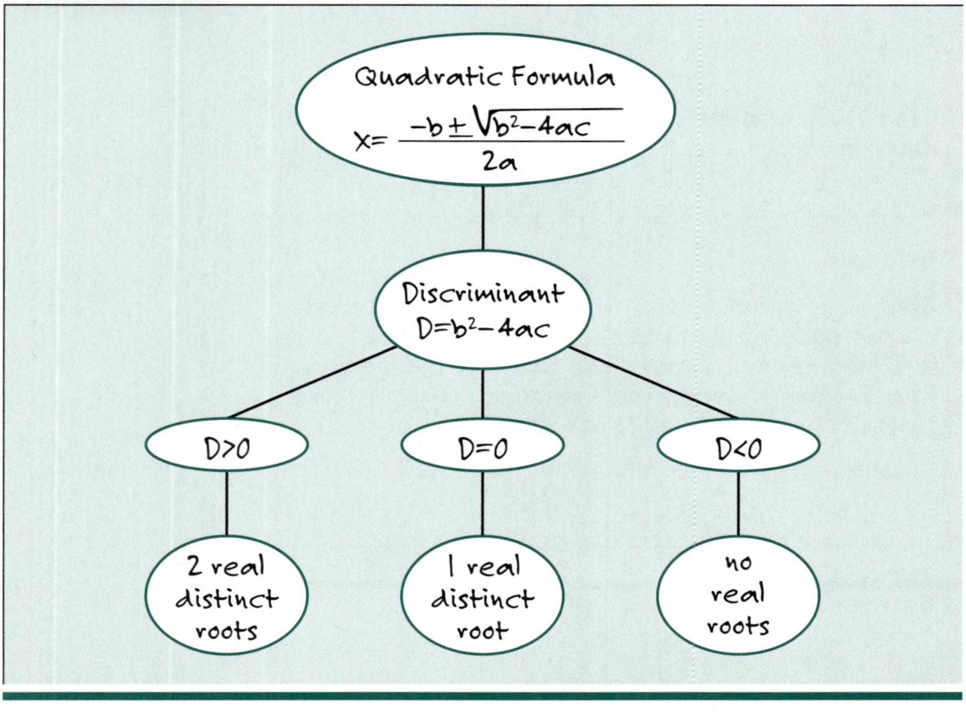

FIGURE 10.5 **Series-of-Events Chain for the Scientific Method**

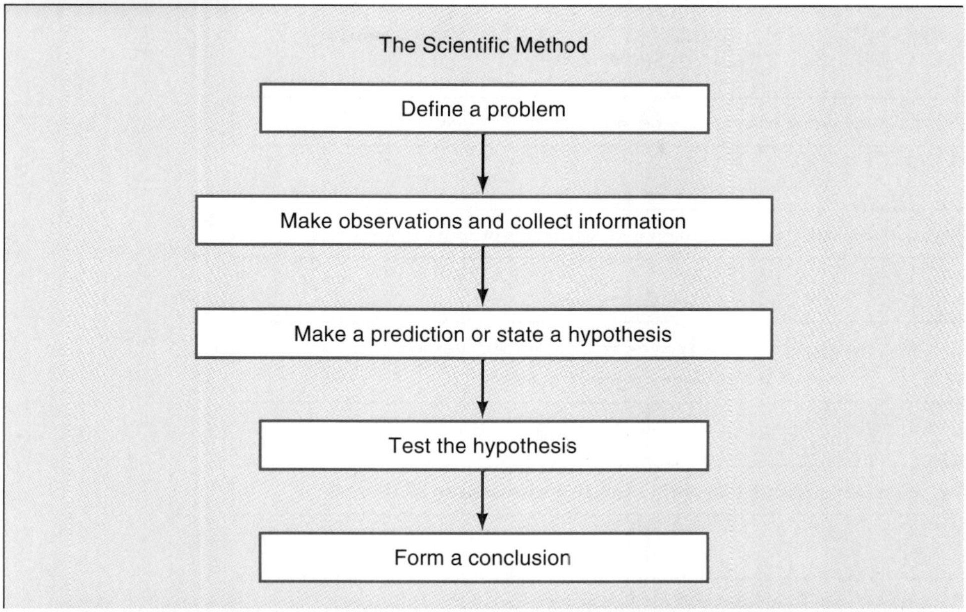

In an English class, students read an excerpt from *My Bondage and My Freedom,* by Frederick Douglass, the famous American slave, abolitionist, and journalist. Douglass writes about the reasons for and purposes of the Negro spirituals that slaves sang and the effects that these songs had on his life. The teacher assigned the text selection to be read in class and then divided the students into learning circles (four-member teams) to work through the sequence of events that had led to Douglass's hatred of slavery. The series-of-events chain in Figure 10.6 illustrates the work of one of the learning circles.

Appendix D illustrates additional types of graphic organizers that may be adapted to different content areas. Closely associated with the use of graphic organizers is an instructional scaffold that involves questioning.

Using Questions with Graphic Organizers

Graphic organizers and questions related to them go hand in hand. Buehl (1991), for example, lists the types of questions associated with the problem-and-solution, cause-and-effect, and comparison-and-contrast patterns.

PROBLEM AND SOLUTION

1. What is the problem?
2. Who has the problem?

CLASSROOM ARTIFACT **FIGURE 10.6** **Series-of-Events Chain for an Excerpt from *My Bondage and My Freedom***

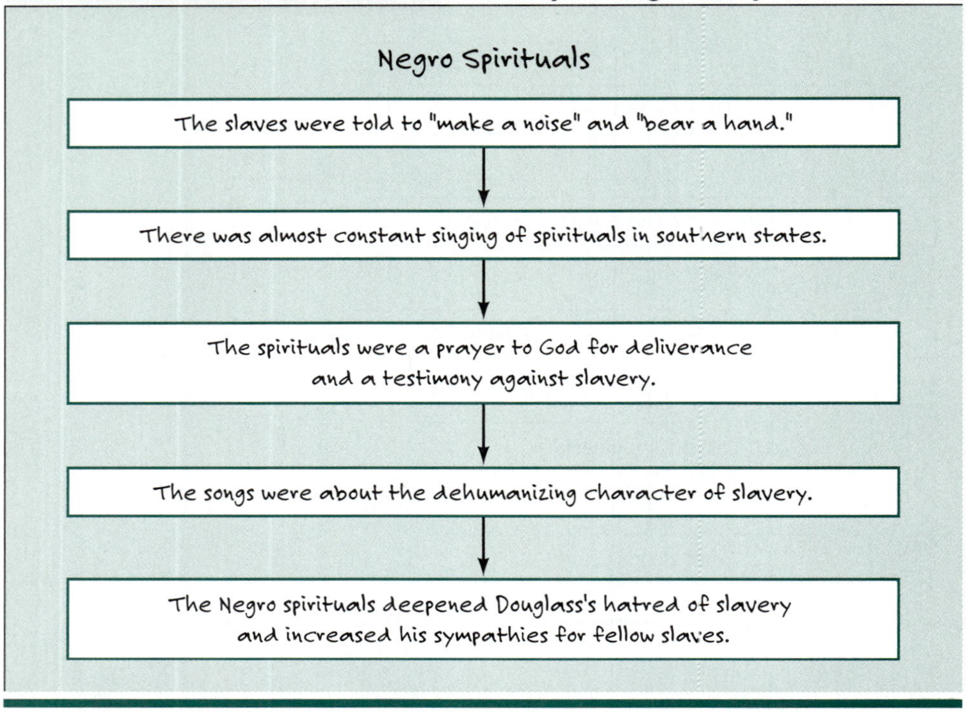

3. What is causing the problem?
4. What are the effects of the problem?
5. Who is trying to solve the problem?
6. What solutions are attempted?
7. What are the results of these solutions?
8. Is the problem solved? Do any new problems develop because of the solutions?

CAUSE AND EFFECT

1. What happens?
2. What causes it to happen?
3. What are the important elements or factors that cause this effect?
4. How are these factors or elements interrelated?
5. Will this result always happen from these causes? Why or why not?
6. How would the result change if the elements or factors were different?

COMPARISON AND CONTRAST

1. What items are being compared and contrasted?
2. What categories of attributes can be used to compare and contrast the items?
3. How are the items alike or similar?
4. How are the items not alike or different?
5. What are the most important qualities or attributes that make the items similar?
6. What are the most important qualities or attributes that make the items different?
7. In terms of the qualities that are most important, are the items more alike or more different?

Additional questions associated with graphic organizers are provided in Appendix D. There are many benefits to learning how to use and construct graphic organizers, not the least of which is that they make it easier for students to find and reorganize important ideas and information in the text.

Another type of graphic display is the semantic, or cognitive, map. Maps are based on the same principles as graphic organizers.

Semantic (Cognitive) Mapping

A popular graphic representation, often called a *semantic map* or a *cognitive map*, helps students identify important ideas and shows how these ideas fit together. Teachers avoid the problem of teaching a restricted, conventional outline format. Instead, the students are responsible for creating a logical arrangement among keywords or phrases that connect main ideas to subordinate information. When maps are used, instruction should proceed from teacher-guided modeling and illustration to student-generated productions. A semantic map has three basic components:

1. *Core question or concept.* The question or concept (stated as a keyword or phrase) that establishes the main focus of the map. All the ideas generated for the map by the students are related in some way to the core question or concept.
2. *Strands.* The subordinate ideas generated by the students that help clarify the question or explain the concept.
3. *Supports.* The details, inferences, and generalizations that are related to each strand. These supports clarify the strands and distinguish one strand from another.

Students use the semantic map as an organization tool that visually illustrates the categories and relationships associated with the core question or concept under study. To model and illustrate the use of a semantic map, a middle school social studies teacher guided students through the process. The class began a unit on Ohio's early settlements. As part of the prereading discussion, four questions were raised for the class to ponder: What do you think were the three most important early settlements in Ohio? What do you think these settlements had in common? How were they different?

In what ways might the location of a settlement be important to the survival of the settlers? Predictions were made and discussed and led naturally to the text assignment.

The teacher assigned the material, directing the students to read with the purpose of confirming or modifying their predictions about the early settlements. After reading, the students formed small groups. Each group listed everything its members could remember about the settlements on index cards, with one piece of information per card.

In the center of the whiteboard, the teacher wrote "The First Ohio Settlements" and circled the phrase. She then asked students to provide the main strands that helped answer the question and clarify the concept "What were Ohio's most important early settlements?" The students responded by contrasting their predictions to the explanations in the text assignment. The teacher began to build the semantic map on the board by explaining how strands help students answer the questions and understand the main concept.

Next, she asked the students to work in their groups to sort the cards that had been compiled according to each of the settlements depicted on the semantic map. Through discussion, questioning, and think-aloud probes, the class completed the semantic map depicted in Figure 10.7.

FIGURE 10.7 Semantic Map: The First Ohio Settlements

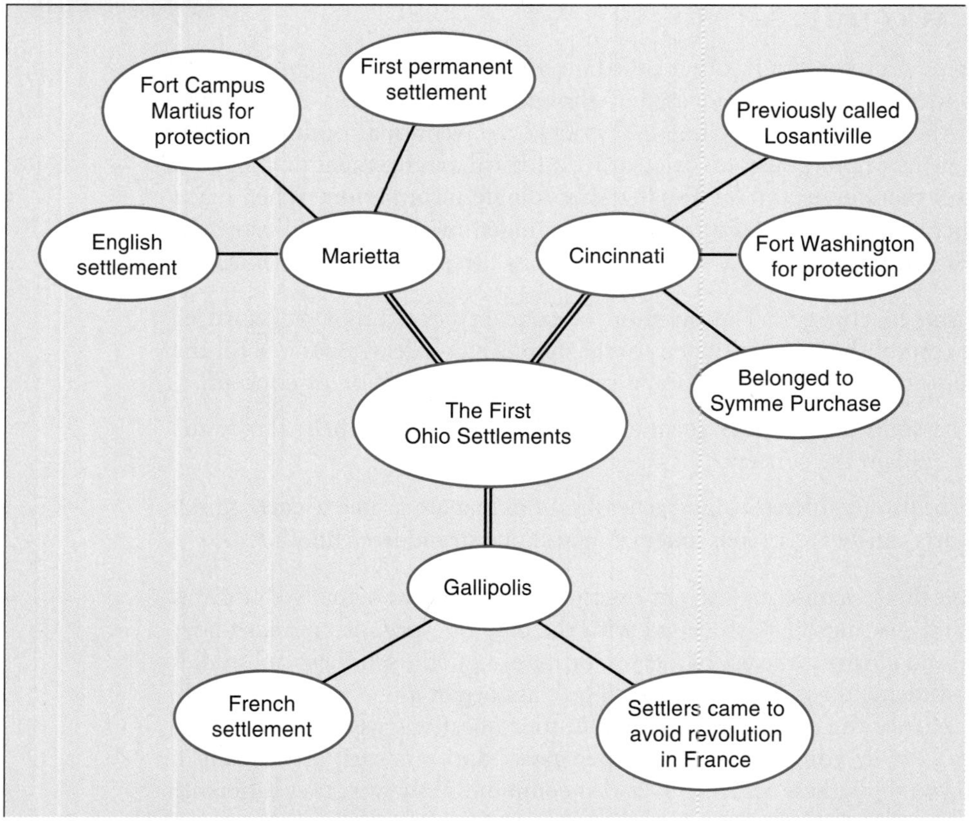

Some teachers prefer to distinguish strands from supports through the use of lines. Notice that in Figure 10.7, a double line connects the strands to the core concept. Supports are linked to each web strand by single lines. With younger students, some teachers also recommend using different-colored chalk to distinguish one strand from another.

With appropriate modeling, explanation, and experience, students soon understand the why, what, and how of semantic maps and can begin to develop maps by themselves. We suggest that the teacher begin by providing the core question or concept. Students can then compare and contrast their individual productions in a follow-up discussion. Of course, text assignments should also be given in which students identify the core concept on their own and then generate the structures that support and explain it. In addition to using graphic outlines, teachers can develop study guides (discussed later in this chapter) to help students discern text patterns.

Writing Summaries

Summarizing involves reducing a text to its main points. To become adept at summary writing, students must be able to discern and analyze text structure. If they are insensitive to the organization of ideas and events in expository or narrative writing, students will find it difficult to distinguish important from less important information. Good summarizers, therefore, guard against including information that is not important in the text passage being condensed. Immature text learners, by contrast, tend to *retell* rather than condense information, often including in their summaries interesting but nonessential tidbits from the passage. Good summarizers write in their own words but are careful to maintain the author's point of view and to stick closely to the sequence of ideas or events as presented in the reading selection (Friend 2000–2001). When important ideas are not explicitly stated in the material, good summary writers create their own topic sentences to reflect textually implicit main ideas.

> **myeducationlab**
> Go to the Assignments and Activities section of Topic 4: "Writing" in the MyEducationLab for your course and complete the activity "Summarizing/Writing in Science." Consider how students write summaries in the various content areas.

Box 10.3 outlines the "rules" to follow in developing a well-written summary.

Using GRASP to Write a Summary

Teachers can show students how to summarize information through the guided reading procedure (GRP) as explained in Chapter 7. After students have read a text passage, they turn the books face down and try to remember everything that was important in the passage. What they recall is recorded by the teacher on the whiteboard. Seize this opportune moment to show students how to delete trivial and repetitious information from the list of ideas on the board. As part of the procedure, the students are given a chance to return to the passage, review it, and make sure that the list contains all of the information germane to the text.

When this step is completed, the teacher then guides the students to organize the information using a graphic outline format. Here is where students can be shown

Evidence-Based Best Practices

BOX 10.3

Writing a Summary

Kintsch and van Dijk (1978) were among the first to formulate a set of basic rules for summarization based on analyses of how people summarize effectively. Others have modified and adapted these rules, but generally, students must follow these procedures:

1. *Include no unnecessary detail.* In preparing a summary, students must learn not to include trivial and repetitious information from a text passage.
2. *Collapse lists.* When a text passage includes examples, details, actions, or traits, students must learn how to condense these into broader categories of information. With frequent exposure to instructional activities, such as graphic organizers, vocabulary categorization exercises, and outlining strategies, students soon become aware that similar items of information can be encompassed by more inclusive concepts. They must learn to summarize information by collapsing a list of details and thinking of a keyword or phrase that names its concept. Study the examples that Hare and Borchardt (1984) give: "If you saw a list like eyes, ears, neck, arms, and legs, you could say 'body parts.' Or, if you saw a list like ice skating, skiing, or sledding, you could say 'winter sports'" (p. 66).
3. *Use topic sentences.* Expository text sometimes contains explicit topic sentences that preview a paragraph. However, if a paragraph doesn't have a topic sentence, students must learn to create their own for a summary. This is probably the most difficult demand placed on maturing learners.
4. *Integrate information.* Summarizers must learn how to use keywords, phrases, and explicit and invented topic sentences to compose a summary. The first three rules help students do the basic work of summarizing. In other words, the rules *prepare* students for writing the summary. Yet when they actually put ideas into words, they must integrate the information into a coherent piece of writing.
5. *Polish the summary.* Because writing often follows a composing process, students must learn to revise a *draft* of a summary into a more organized, natural-sounding piece of writing. While rethinking a summary, students will get a firmer grasp on the main points of the material and will state them clearly.

how to collapse individual pieces of information from a list into conceptual categories. These categories can be the bases for identifying or creating topic sentences. The students can then integrate the main points into a summary.

Figure 10.8 shows how students in one science class adapted the GRP to summarize information they recalled from an article they read about planets. Following a model developed by Hayes (1989), the teacher modeled the development and writing of an effective summary by guiding students through a procedure called GRASP (guided reading and summarizing procedure). After following the initial steps of the GRP, the teacher recorded students' initial recollections of what they had read in the article on planets. Then, after rereading, students' additions and corrections to their first recollections were recorded.

The students then organized the information from these notes into the following categories: the planets, the movement of the planets, and changes in beliefs about

FIGURE 10.8 **Details Remembered from an Article on the Planets**

Students' First Recollections	Additions or Corrections
Ptolemy thought the planets orbited the Earth	Orbited the Sun
Kepler found that the planets orbited in a specific pattern	Pattern is elliptical
Nine planets in our solar system	Currently, there are eight planets (Pluto was downgraded)
Planets consistently orbit the sun from a certain distance	Order: Mercury, Venus, Earth, Mars, Jupiter, Saturn, Uranus, Neptune
Mathematicians can calculate the movements of the planets	Movement was previously thought to be controlled by gods. Movements based on geometry and based on pull of gravity
Many planets have smaller bodies (moons) that orbit around them	Moons orbit Mars, Jupiter, Saturn, Earth, Uranus, Neptune, and Pluto

the planets. These categories, along with the subordinate information associated with each, became the basis for writing the summary. The teacher walked the students through the summary-writing process as a whole class. First, the students were asked to contribute sentences to the summary based on the outline information that they had organized together. Then the teacher invited their suggestions for revising the summary into a coherent message. Figure 10.9 displays part of the completed summary, as revised by the class.

FIGURE 10.9 The Planet Summary, as Revised by the Students

While once Ptolemy thought that we had nine planets and they ~~circled~~ *orbited* around the Earth, we now know our solar system is a group of eight planets that ~~circle~~ *orbit* the sun in ~~a circle.~~ *an ellipse* Some planets also have ~~things~~ smaller bodies^ *, called moons,* moving around them.

Polishing a Summary

As you can see from the revised summary in Figure 10.9, a good summary often reflects a process of writing *and* rewriting. Teaching students how to write a polished summary is often a neglected aspect of instruction. When students reduce large segments of text, the condensation is often stilted. It sounds unnatural. We are convinced that students will learn and understand the main points better and retain them longer when they attempt to create a more natural-sounding summary that communicates the selection's main ideas to an audience—for example, the teacher or other students. Rewriting in a classroom is often preceded by *response* to a draft by peers and teacher. We dealt in much more detail with responding and revising in Chapter 9. Here, however, let us suggest the following:

- *Compare a well-developed summary that the teacher has written with the summaries written by the students.* Contrasting the teacher's version with the student productions leads to valuable process discussions on such subjects as the use of introductory and concluding statements; the value of connectives, such as *and* and *because,* to show how ideas can be linked; and the need to paraphrase—that is, to put ideas into one's own words to convey the author's main points.
- *Present the class with three summaries.* One is good in that it contains all the main points and flows smoothly. The second is OK; it contains most of the main points but is somewhat stilted in its writing. The third is poor in content and form. Let the class rate and discuss the three summaries.
- *Team students in pairs or triads, and let them read their summaries to one another.* Student response groups are one of the most effective means of obtaining feedback on writing in progress.
- *In lieu of response groups, ask the whole class to respond.* With prior permission from several students, discuss their summaries. What are the merits of each one, and how could they be improved in content and form?

The real learning potential of summary writing lies in students' using their own language to convey the author's main ideas.

Making Notes, Taking Notes

Effective study activities for acting on and remembering material involve making notes as well as taking notes. Notes can be written on study cards (index cards) or in a learning log that is kept expressly for the purpose of compiling written reactions to and reflections on text readings.

Note making should avoid verbatim text reproductions. Instead, notes can be used to paraphrase, summarize, react critically, question, or respond personally to what is read. Whatever form the notes take, students need to become aware of the different types of notes that can be written and should then be shown how to write them.

> **myeducationlab**
> Go to the Assignments and Activities section of Topic 3: "Study Skills and Strategies" in the MyEducationLab for your course and complete the activity "Note-Taking Hints" to review a document designed to help students take notes.

Text Annotations

Text annotations describe the different kinds of notes students can write. Several are particularly appropriate for middle grade and secondary school students. For example, read the following passage. Then study each of the notes made by a high school student, shown in Figures 10.10 through 10.13.

> Unpleasantness for those trading illegally in wild animals and their products is escalating around the world. Within the past decade government after government has passed laws to restrict or prohibit the sale of wildlife seriously depleted by hunting and habitat destruction. With legal channels pinched, animal dealers have resorted to nefarious schemes to continue the flow.
>
> Wildlife is big business. Exotic-bird collectors will pay $10,000 for a hyacinth macaw. . . . In New York I tried on a pair of trendy western boots trimmed in lizard skin. The price? "Two hundred thirty five," the clerk said, with an archness suggesting that most of his customers didn't bother to ask. . . .
>
> These items are being sold legally. But somewhere in the dim beginnings of their trail through commerce, they may have been acquired illegally. . . .
>
> This fascination with wildlife within the affluent nations of the world adds to the disappearance of animals in the less developed countries. In between stand the illegal traders willing to circumvent the wildlife-protection laws to satisfy the demand and their own pocketbooks. . . .
>
> Wildlife smuggling is costing the U.S. millions of dollars to control and is denying income to the treasury of any nation that would otherwise receive duty from legal imports. It has spread diseases that would have been detected in legal quarantine periods. . . . An irreversible effect of illegal trade could be the extinction of animal species that are finding fewer and fewer places to hide. (Grove 1981)

FIGURE 10.10 A Summary Note

The illegal trading of wildlife and their products is a profitable business in affluent countries around the world. The continuation of such trade threatens both developed and underdeveloped nations economically and ecologically. More recent laws are making this illegal trade much more difficult to carry out.

The *summary note,* as you might surmise, condenses the main ideas of a text selection into a concise statement. Summary notes are characterized by their brevity, clarity, and conciseness. When a note summarizes expository material, it should clearly distinguish the important ideas in the author's presentation from supporting information and detail. When the summary note involves narrative material, such as a story, it should include a synopsis containing the major story elements. Examine the example of a summary note from a student's note card in Figure 10.10.

FIGURE 10.11 A Thesis Note

Illegal wild animal trade is a very profitable business. Illegal wildlife trade is a threat to humans and their environment. More laws throughout the world can restrict this activity.

The *thesis note* answers the question "What is the main point the author has tried to get across to the reader?" The thesis note has a telegram-like character. It is incisively stated yet unambiguous in its identification of the author's main proposition. The thesis note for a story identifies its theme. Study the example in Figure 10.11.

The *critical note* captures the reader's reaction or response to the author's thesis. It answers the question "So what?" In writing critical notes, the reader should first state the author's thesis, then state the reader's position in relation to the thesis, and finally, defend or expand on the position taken. See Figure 10.12.

The *question note* raises a significant issue in the form of a question. The question is the result of what the reader thinks is the most germane or significant aspect of what he or she has read. See Figure 10.13.

FIGURE 10.12 A Critical Note

The trading of wildlife for high profits is something all of us will pay for ultimately. Countries are being cheated out of needed revenues. Even more important, the future of species of animals is being threatened. The money-minded traders also give little thought to the spread of disease that could be avoided by legal quarantines. All nations need to cooperate to pass stricter laws to control or prohibit the trade of wildlife for temporary luxury.

FIGURE 10.13 A Question Note

(Should illegal wildlife trade be allowed to continue or, at least, be ignored, after unsuccessful attempts to stop it?) The author says that it is becoming more unpleasant for illegal traders of wildlife and their products because of more laws instituted by governments around the world. He also cites serious economic and ecological reasons not to give up the fight.

Showing students how to write different types of notes begins with assessment; leads to awareness and knowledge building, modeling, and practice; and culminates in application. First, assign a text selection and ask students to make whatever notes they wish. Second, have the class analyze the assessment, share student notes, and discuss difficulties in making notes. Use the assessment discussion to make students aware of the importance of making notes as a strategy for learning and retention.

Third, build students' knowledge for note making by helping them recognize and define the various kinds of text notes that can be written.

As part of a growing understanding of the different types of notes, students should be able to tell a well-written note from a poorly written one. Have the class read a short passage, followed by several examples of a certain type of note, one well written and the others flawed in some way. For example, a discussion of critical notes may include one illustration of a good critical note, one that lacks the note maker's position, and another that fails to defend or develop the position taken.

Note-Taking Procedures

Walter Pauk's (1978) response to the question, "Why take notes?" is profound in its simplicity: "Because we forget." More than 50 percent of the material read or heard in class is forgotten in a matter of minutes. A system of taking and making notes triggers recall and supports retention. When teaching students how to take notes, modeling and practice should follow naturally from awareness and knowledge building. Teachers can guide students through the process of making and taking different types of notes by sharing their thought processes. For example, a teacher might show how a note is written and revised using a think-aloud procedure. Students can then practice note making individually and in peer groups of two or three. Peer-group interaction is typically nonthreatening and can lead to notes that can be duplicated, compared, and evaluated by the class with teacher direction.

To facilitate the application of note-taking procedures to reading tasks across content areas, we suggest that students write notes regularly and in a variety of forms, such as learning logs, study cards, or on their computers. Note-taking procedures can take many forms. In this section, we highlight a few of those forms: reading logs, annotations, T-notes, and Cornell notes.

Reading Logs

Notes written in reading logs serve two purposes: They can aid students in organizing and synthesizing important information as they read a text and they can serve as a tool for clarifying and reviewing text material. Gomez and Gomez (2007) suggest double-entry reading logs as note-making tools that can help students organize key details about complex topics and teachers to gain information about student learning that can aid them in planning subsequent instruction. Students can, for example, use an argument/evidence double-entry reading log, shown in Figure 10.14, to distinguish main ideas or arguments found in a text from the evidence presented to support each main idea or argument. Similarly, a vocabulary or concept double-entry reading log, shown in Figure 10.15, can be used to help students identify those vocabulary

FIGURE 10.14 **Argument Evidence Double-Entry Reading Log**

Main ideas or arguments from a text:	Evidence to support each main idea or argument:

FIGURE 10.15 **Vocabulary/Concept Double-Entry Reading Log**

Challenging terms from the text:	My interpretation of each term:

concepts that they find difficult to understand. They can use the left-hand column of the double-entry log to list challenging terms and the right-hand column to write their interpretations of those terms. Later, following class discussions or additional readings that clarify these terms, students can revisit their double-entry logs by adding or revising the information they contain.

Annotations

Annotations can be used as a cognitive literacy strategy across content areas to help students to understand text structure, identify and analyze important concepts, and communicate their understanding of those concepts (Pressley 2006). Zywica and Gomez (2008) applied text annotation as part of their multiyear Adolescent Literacy Support Project. They found the strategy to be particularly useful when charts, graphs, and illustrations are frequently embedded in the text. The text annotation system they described was designed to help students to identify different components within a single text. As they read, students mark the text with annotation symbols that represent key concepts, questions, or transition points. Some of the text annotation symbols that students used as they read an article for a science class included the following:

- A rectangle around key content vocabulary
- A triangle around difficult or confusing words
- A double underline for main ideas or important points
- A single underline for supporting evidence
- An arrow for procedural words
- An asterisk for transition words
- A question mark for confusing information

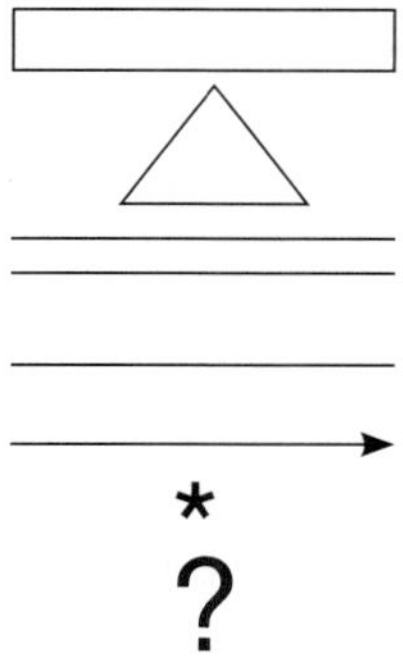

We recommend that teachers model the use of annotations and gradually introduce annotation symbols to students by selecting symbols that are most appropriate for organizing and understanding a particular text. Students should not be expected to use all of the annotation symbols at their disposal when reading a single text. As Zywica and Gomez remind us, the purpose of annotating text is to provide a framework to support students' understanding of concepts presented in a text, not to create busywork in addition to the reading. The text annotation procedure can be conducted as a whole-class activity, in which students take turns identifying various components of a text that is visible to the group through an overhead projector or whiteboard. Students can also work in pairs or in small groups to annotate a text, and in doing so can deliberate about correctly identifying elements such as the main ideas and supporting evidence.

T-Notes

T-notes provide a simple but effective framework for organizing information presented in texts. As Burke (2002) explains, teachers can adapt T-notes to help students compare and contrast concepts or to identify patterns across texts. The T-note example pictured in Figure 10.16 was used as a note-taking device for a text selection about different systems of government in a high school civics and economic class. Students used the left-hand side of the T-note to record information from the text that pertained to important points about capitalism; they used the right-hand side to record information in the text that pertained to communism. At the bottom of the T-note, they wrote a statement in which they summarized their understanding of the main idea presented in their reading.

myeducationlab

Go to the Assignments and Activities section of Topic 8: "Study Skills and Strategies" in the MyEducationLab for your course and complete the activity "Cornell Notes" to see one teacher demonstrate this key study strategy.

Cornell Notes

A tried and true note-taking procedure common in many schools is the Cornell system developed by Walter Pauk in 1966. Cornell notes, as they are commonly called, can be used both as a note-taking procedure

FIGURE 10.16 T-Note for Systems of Government

Name ______________________ Date ______________

Subject ______________________ Period ______________

Systems of Government

Capitalism	Communism
■ Wealth is privately owned ■ Market economy; laissez-faire ■ Free trade; consumers have choice ■ Means for industrialization of many countries in 19th and 20th centuries ■ Adam Smith is the "father" of capitalist ideals ■ Can lead to monopolies ■ People work for personal advancement ■ Allows people to change their social station by working hard	■ Wealth is commonly owned ■ Society regulates production to ensure everyone is equal ■ Communist state controls production and eliminates choice ■ Communists believed industrialization and capitalism caused poor conditions of working class ■ Karl Marx is the "father" of communism ■ People work for common good ■ Eliminates economic and social classes

In this box, write a summary statement that shows your interpretation of what you have read.

While communism allows everyone to work together toward an equitable society, capitalism allows everyone an opportunity to make a better life through hard work and perseverance.

for recording important information during class lectures and as a study tool to review and extend concepts covered in class. Figure 10.17 shows the basic framework of Cornell notes. Students write details from a class lecture in the right-hand column. Soon after the lecture, student use the left-hand column to record questions or list key concepts that are based on the detailed notes they wrote during the lecture. Once students have had time to respond to those questions and to reflect on the material, they can use the space at the bottom of the page to write a summary statement, a synthesis of key points covered, or additional questions they need to address. Pauk and Ross (2007) recommend that students follow the sequence below when using Cornell notes:

1. *Record.* During a class lecture, record the important points addressed in the lecture in the right-hand column.

FIGURE 10.17 **Cornell Notes**

Name ______________________ Date ______________________

Topic ______________________ Subject ______________________

Questions or key concepts based on lecture notes or reading:	Important details from class lecture or reading:

A summary statement, list of key points learned from the lecture or reading, or questions from your reflection that you still need to address:

2. *Question.* As soon after the class as possible, use the left-hand column to develop questions about the material based on the notes you have written in the right-hand column.
3. *Recite.* Cover the notes you have taken during class and try to answer the questions you have written.
4. *Reflect.* Reflect on the material by asking and answering questions such as: How does this new information fit with what I already know? What new information have I acquired? Why is this information important?
5. *Review.* Spend time every week reviewing your notes. This consistent and sequential review of the material can help you to form connections and to analyze thoroughly the concepts presented. Consistent review can also aid in preparing for a unit assessment.

Note-taking procedures such as T-notes and Cornell notes can provide a study guide framework that helps students better comprehend texts. Over time, as students develop the maturity and the learning strategies to interact with difficult texts, the need for study guides is typically reduced. Until that time, however, study guides can provide students with support for navigating complex content area texts. In Chapter 7, we suggested the use of three-level comprehension guides for scaffolding learning at different levels of understanding. Text pattern guides and selective reading guides are also useful for helping students study difficult text.

Study Guides

Text patterns are difficult for some readers to discern, but once students become aware of the importance of organization and learn how to search for relationships in text, they are in a better position to use information more effectively and to comprehend material more thoroughly.

> **myeducationlab**
> Go to the Building Teaching Skills and Dispositions section of Topic 8: "Study Skills and Strategies" in the MyEducationLab for your course. Complete the activity to learn to use active teaching techniques to help students develop autonomy over learning.

Text Pattern Guides

A study guide based on text patterns helps students perceive and use the major text relationships that predominate in the reading material. As you consider developing a study guide for text patterns, you may find it useful first to read through the text selection and identify a predominant pattern; and second, to develop an exercise in which students can react to the structure of the relationships represented by the pattern.

A middle school teacher prepared a matching activity to illustrate the cause-and-effect pattern for students who were studying a unit titled "The Native American: A Search for Identity." One reading selection from the unit material dealt with Jenny, an adolescent member of the Blackfoot tribe, who commits suicide.

The teacher asked, "Why did Jenny take her life?" The question led to a before-reading discussion. The students offered several predictions. The teacher then suggested that the reading assignment was written in a predominantly cause-and-effect pattern. He discussed this type of pattern, and the students contributed several examples. Then he gave them the study guide in Figure 10.18 to complete as they read the selection.

The class read for two purposes: to see whether their predictions were accurate and to follow the cause-and-effect relationships in the material. Notice that the social studies teacher included page numbers after the causes listed on the guide. These helped students focus their attention on the relevant portions of the text. First, the students read the selection silently; then they worked in groups of four to complete the study guide.

A second example, the comparison-and-contrast study guide in Figure 10.19, shows how the format of a guide will differ with the nature of the material (in this case, narrative) and the teacher's objectives. Juniors in an English class used the study guide to discuss changes in character in the story "A Split Cherry Tree."

FIGURE 10.18 Cause–Effect Study Guide for "The Native American: A Search for Identity"

Directions: Select from the Causes column at the left the cause that led to each effect in the Effects column at the right. Put the letter of each effect next to its cause in the space provided.

Causes

_______ 1. Jenny takes an overdose of pills (p. 9).

_______ 2. The buffalo herds have been destroyed, and hunger threatens (p. 10).

_______ 3. Native Americans remain untrained for skilled jobs (p. 10).

_______ 4. The temperature reaches 50 degrees below zero (p. 10).

_______ 5. There are terrible living conditions (no jobs, poor homes, and so on) (p. 10).

_______ 6. Pride and hope have vanished from the Blackfeet (p. 11).

_______ 7. Because we're Native Americans (p. 12).

_______ 8. The old world of the Native Americans is crumbling and the new world of the whites rejects them (p. 13).

_______ 9. The attitude of the Bureau of Indian Affairs (p. 13).

Effects

a. Unemployment rate for the Blackfeet is about 50 percent.
b. The first victim of this life is pride.
c. Blackfeet have become dependent on whites' help for survival.
d. Blackfeet turn to liquor.
e. Native Americans are robbed of their self-confidence.
f. They are always downgraded.
g. Eighty percent of the Blackfeet must have governmental help.
h. *Hope* is a word that has little meaning.
i. She kills herself.

FIGURE 10.19 Comparison–Contrast Study Guide for "A Split Cherry Tree"

Directions: Consider Pa's attitude (how he feels) toward the following characters and concepts. Note that the columns ask you to consider his attitudes toward these things twice—the way he is at the beginning of the story (pp. 147–152) and the way you think he is at the end of the story. Whenever possible, note the page numbers on which this attitude is described or hinted.

Characters and Concepts	Pa's Attitude at the Beginning of the Story	Pa's Attitude at the End of the Story
Punishment		
Dave		
Professor Herbert		
School		
His own work		
His son's future		
Himself		

Selective Reading Guides

Selective reading guides show students how to think with print. The effective use of questions combined with signaling techniques helps model how readers interact with text when reading and studying.

Cunningham and Shablak (1975) indicate that content area teachers can impart tremendous insight into *how* to acquire text information through a selective reading guide:

RESPONSE JOURNAL

Which study guide—text pattern or selective—is more appropriate for your content area? Why?

> The teacher begins . . . by determining the overall purpose for a particular reading assignment. Second, he selects those sections of the reading which are necessary to achieve this purpose.
>
> Most important . . . he eliminates from the assignment any and all sections that are irrelevant to the purpose. Third, for those relevant sections that remain, the teacher determines, *based on his own model reading behaviors,* what a student must operationally do to achieve the purpose—step by step, section by section. (p. 381; emphasis added)

The premise behind the selective reading guide is that, though teachers understand how to process information from their own content area, students do not yet possess the necessary processing skills. A selective reading guide can help to guide students' reading of content area texts. Figure 10.20 illustrates how a selective reading guide was used by a marketing teacher in one Career and Technical Education (CTE) department as he guided his students toward developing consumer awareness and an

FIGURE 10.20 Selective Reading Guide for a Marketing Class

Chapter 20: Internet as Place

Page 365: Read the introduction. List the ways in which students can use the Internet to support their school work.

Page 366: What is e-commerce? List several examples of businesses that rely on e-commerce.

Page 368: Use a Venn diagram to compare and contrast a dot-com business with a traditional business.

Pages 370–376: Skim the section on "The Internet as Retail Place." List both the positive and negative attributes of online shopping.

Page 376, Figure 29.9: The Better Business Bureau website illustrated in the text gives guidelines for responsible practices for online businesses. Based on your experiences with online shopping, what additional guidelines would you add to this list?

Page 376: The author states that many customers prefer to shop in traditional stores. Do you agree? Do you prefer to shop online or in traditional stores? Why?

Pages 379–381: Skim the section "Future of e-tailing." List the advantages and disadvantages of online shopping. Which do you think will have a more powerful impact on customers in the future?

FIGURE 10.21 A Reading Road Map

Life Functions of Bacteria

Location	Speed	Mission
Start		Before reading: Write down what comes to mind about the following: Living things —— Bacteria —— Plants and food Bacteria: Asexual reproduction; Animals and food
Life functions of bacteria pp. 111–112	Read quickly	1. Where are bacteria found?
Heterotrophs and autotrophs p. 112	Slow down, write	2. Fill in the chart below with some information given about each: Heterotroph | Autotroph Parasites | Saprophytes
Endospores pp. 112–113	Slow, think, write	3. Tell why the formation of endospores is important to a bacterium's survival.
Binary fission p. 113	Stop, think, write	4. How does what you do when the weather becomes too cold compare to what a bacterial cell does if its environment becomes too cold?
	Read quickly	5. Briefly describe binary fission.
	Stop, think, write	6. Bacteria don't cover everything on earth because they die almost as quickly as they reproduce. What do you think causes bacteria to die?
Stop		Think about what you've just learned. Without looking back in your book, jot down what you remember about each of the following: Autotrophs Heterotrophs Endospores Reproduction of bacteria

understanding of a market economy. His selective reading guide for a chapter from Clark, Sobel, and Basteri's text *Marketing Dynamics* uses both written questions and signals to help students in processing material from their text.

For struggling readers, teachers add a visual dimension to the guide. Study the guide in Figure 10.21 (p. 349), developed by a middle school science teacher. Notice how he guides students through the life functions of bacteria by using various kinds of cues, signals, and statements. The guide provides location cues to focus students' attention on relevant segments of text, speed signals to model flexibility in reading, and mission statements that initiate tasks that help students think and learn with texts.

LOOKING BACK LOOKING FORWARD

Teaching students how to study texts involves showing them how to become independent learners. In this chapter, we used the role that text structure plays to illustrate how you can teach students to use learner-directed strategies that involve constructing graphic organizers, writing summaries, and making and taking notes.

Understanding how authors organize their ideas is a powerful factor in learning with texts. Because authors write to communicate, they organize ideas to make them accessible to readers. A well-organized text is a considerate one. The text patterns that authors use to organize their ideas revolve around description, sequence, comparison and contrast, cause and effect, and problem and solution. The more students perceive text patterns, the more likely they are to remember and interpret the ideas they encounter in reading.

Graphic organizers help students outline important information that is reflected in the text patterns that authors use to organize ideas. The construction of graphic organizers allows students to map the relationships that exist among the ideas presented in text. This strategy is a valuable tool for comprehending and retaining information.

Students who engage in summarizing what they have read often gain greater understanding and retention of the main ideas in text. Students need to become aware of summarization rules and to receive instruction in how to use these rules to write and polish a summary.

Notes are part of another useful strategy for studying text. Making notes allows students to reflect on and react to important ideas in text.

In addition to the development of study strategies, teachers develop study guides to engage students in text comprehension and learning. With the use of guides, teachers provide instructional support to allow students to interact with and respond to difficult texts in meaningful ways. We explored and illustrated two types of guides: text pattern guides and selective reading guides. Text pattern guides help students to follow the predominant text structures in reading assignments. Selective reading guides show students how to think with text by modeling reading behaviors necessary to read effectively.

How do teachers incorporate instructional practices and strategies into lessons *before, during,* and *after* assigning texts to read? In the next chapter, we explore the use of trade books in content literacy lessons and units of study. Trade books, like digital texts, are an alternative to textbooks.

Minds On

1. A member of the board of education has been quoted as saying that she is opposed to "spoon-feeding" high school students. After a board meeting one evening, you have an opportunity to talk with her. You explain that there is a difference between "spoon-feeding" students and helping them to "work smart." As a group, discuss how you might justify supporting students' studying through the use of techniques such as graphic organizers, summaries, and note taking.

2. Following an in-service program on using graphic organizers, you notice that some teachers in your building are preparing a semantic map for every assignment, whereas others, who say they don't have time, never use them. Your principal asks you, as a member of a team, to prepare a one-page sheet of guidelines for the use of graphic organizers in which you suggest when, why, and how various graphic displays should be used. What would you include in this guide?

3. Imagine that your group is team-teaching an interdisciplinary unit on the Civil War. Each member of your group should select (a) a content area and (b) one of the text patterns described in this chapter (sequence, comparison and contrast, problem and solution, cause and effect, or description). After reviewing some materials on the art, history, music, politics, science, mathematics, and literature of the Civil War, discuss how you might make use of a selected text pattern to teach a concept.

4. As part of an effort to improve school achievement in content area subjects, the curriculum director of your school system has suggested implementing a mandatory study skills course for all high school first-year students. As a team, compose a memo explaining why and how studying can be effectively taught when content area teachers are also involved in the delivery of instruction.

5. The basic premise of a study guide is to provide instructional support for students for whom the text is too difficult to handle independently. How might guides be especially well suited to below-level students who have low self-esteem and little confidence in their ability to meet success with content material? In what ways will the purpose of meeting the individual needs of academically at-risk students be better served through their use? Provide specific examples when possible.

6. Reflect on the use of study guides in each of the content areas. Do you agree or disagree with the following statements:

   a. Study guides provide students with direction and organization for their reading.
   b. Study guides give students the chance to respond to texts in meaningful ways.
   c. Study guides are not meant to be used every day or with every reading assignment; that would reduce their effectiveness.
   d. Levels of comprehension are not as discrete as they may seem, but their division and treatment as separate entities are necessary to address various aspects of comprehension.
   e. If students become used to the support study guides offer, they will always be teacher dependent.

7. If a study guide is offered as an independent activity, students will get little out of it; failure will be just as frequent as with the traditional question-laden worksheet. Students need to be led through the use of study guides, sometimes working independently, sometimes working together. Reflect on the role of the content teacher in designing and using guides for learning.

Hands On

1. Design a semantic map for a science lesson on the characteristics of the planets. Create what you consider the most effective design for that specific content.

2. Using either problem and solution, cause and effect, or comparison and contrast, construct a graphic organizer for a passage from an informational text. Share your representation with members of your group, and discuss how some topics seem appropriate for one specific organizational pattern, whereas others might be organized in a variety of ways.

3. Distribute one card to each member of the class. Ask the students to write down the name of an individual they believe has made a significant contribution to society. Emphasize that the contribution may be in either a specific area of knowledge (art, music, science, literature, politics) or a nonspecific area such as acts of humanitarianism or environmental activism.

   Next, announce that the task of the class will be to create clusters of cards with names that have a common focus. Give each student in the class three minutes to find one partner whose card name relates to his or her own. Then have each team of partners locate another team whose names can be classified together. Explain that, if necessary, groups may redefine their common focus to create clusters. As a whole class, share the focus categories developed by each group.

   Finally, repeat the process, but do not allow any group to use the same common focus. Discuss how this activity relates to the process of outlining.

4. Imagine that one of your colleagues asks students to write summaries of what they are reading in class but does not provide explicit instruction on how to summarize a text effectively. You have observed that many of your colleague's students are frustrated by the task or are simply copying summaries written by other students. With a member of your group, create a dialogue in which you discuss some instructional alternatives that will lead students to writing summaries effectively. As a group, discuss the suggestions you found effective and recommend some others that might help students work smart.

5. In a small group, read a short selection from a current news story, magazine article, textbook selection, or electronic media source. Write examples of the different kinds of notes that can be made from the text. Compare your group's notes with those of other groups, and discuss the different thinking tasks each type of note required, as well as the further use of each note in a classroom teaching situation.

6. In a small group, compile a list of study strategies that the group members use as well as the purposes for which they are used. Categorize the strategies into different groupings according to their perceived purposes. Display the strategies on an overhead or a whiteboard for a discussion of commonalities and suggestions for studying texts.

*e*RESOURCES

- Find more examples of graphic organizers by going to the Graphic Organizer Index at **www.graphic.org/goindex.html.** Conduct your own Internet search using the keywords "semantic maps + lesson plans." Go to Lesson Planet (**www.lessonplanet.com**) to see what comes up when you search for semantic mapping on this site.

CHAPTER 11

I don't believe in the kind of magic in my books. But, I do believe something very magical can happen when you read a good book.

—J. K. Rowling

Learning with Trade Books

ORGANIZING PRINCIPLE

Instructional practices involving the use of trade books in content areas help to extend and enrich the curriculum.

Books are assuming a more dynamic role in the lives of adolescents. With the help of movies and other media, we have seen an explosion in adolescents' reading for pleasure, especially in terms of graphic novels and fantasy. People of all ages have succumbed to the magic of J. K. Rowling's fantastical *Harry Potter* novels; they have continued to voraciously consume her books, even after watching the blockbuster movies. Stephenie Meyer's *Twilight* series has sparked the same phenomenal response. These books fly off the shelves in major bookstores. Today's adolescents are spending hours engaged in an array of literacy pursuits—reading and writing fan fiction, blogging, text messaging, and so on. Literacy clearly plays an important role in their lives. So, why aren't these same students clamoring for books in the classroom?

Today's classrooms must align books with the contemporary needs and interests of diverse student populations. By becoming more knowledgeable about trade books, teachers can better equip themselves to meet the academic, linguistic, social, and emotional needs of today's students. Books are made to be read for a variety of purposes, not the least of which is to learn. Books also serve as vehicles for change, social justice, and agency. Trade books, the subject of this chapter, should not be confused with textbooks. Trade books are

Written in collaboration with Barbara Moss and Virginia Loh, San Diego State University.

CHAPTER OVERVIEW

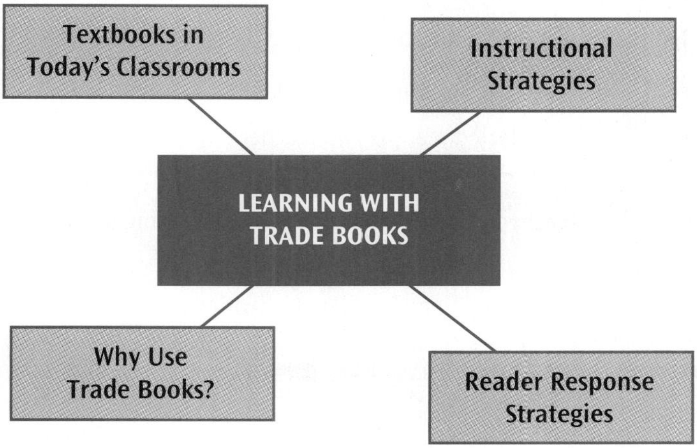

published for distribution to the general public through booksellers. On the other hand, textbooks are distributed directly to school districts and selected by school boards and other policy makers. It's important to acknowledge that textbooks do play an important role in content area learning; however, they also have their limitations.

We make the case, as we did in Chapter 2, that in today's rapidly changing classrooms, textbooks by themselves are not enough. Students need access to a range of reading materials, and trade books are a veritable mother lode of fiction and nonfiction texts that connect to curricular areas and state standards. Trade books—whether picture books, fiction, nonfiction, or poetry—have the potential to motivate students with intense involvement in a subject and the power to develop in-depth understanding in ways not imagined a few years ago. Furthermore, by engaging students in active response to trade books, we heighten their interest and understanding of text content. By introducing students to trade books that reflect the contemporary realities of diverse cultures and classes, we increase their self-awareness and cultural understanding. We also engage students whose cultures and realities may not be represented in the canon or in textbooks.

Should textbooks be abandoned? Certainly not. Our point in this chapter is to underscore the value of integrating a variety of print and multimedia environments into the curriculum. The organizing principle for this chapter looks beyond the often limiting role of textbooks in content areas: **Instructional practices involving the use of trade books in content areas help to extend and enrich the curriculum.**

FRAME OF MIND

1. What are some problems associated with textbook use?
2. Why use trade books to learn subject matter?
3. How can teachers create classroom libraries in content area classrooms?
4. What should the roles of self-selected reading and teacher read-alouds be in the content area classroom?
5. What are some ways that teachers can engage students in responding to the trade books they read?
6. How can teachers involve students in inquiry-related activities?

In describing his 2007 Caldecott Award–winning book *The Invention of Hugo Cabret,* Brian Selznick states, "I think of my book as kind of like a cousin to graphic novels and a cousin to picture books, and a cousin to the cinema. . . . It's definitely related to the cinema and the way cinema tells its story, but it's not quite any of these things" (Adlit.org 2008). In their creative uses of form, themes, and genre, today's authors are changing the definition of children's and young adult literature.

Many contemporary books are no longer literature solely for children or young adults; these books are read by people of all ages. As noted earlier, crossover novels such as J. K. Rowling's *Harry Potter* series, Stephenie Meyer's *Twilight* saga, and many other books are seen in the hands of the young and old alike.

New formats such as the *graphic novel* (the comic book version of a novel), new forms such as *narrative verse* (a novel written in poetic form), and the increased blurring of genre are making books more appealing to wider audiences. Given the changing demographics of our student populations, it is reassuring that there is such variety in children's and young adult literature. To entice and encourage a new generation of readers, trade books must reflect their diverse needs and interests.

In order to nurture a culture of reading, students need trade books in their content area classrooms—books that take them to different places, let them live different lives, and be different people. Students need books that captivate them, nurture their souls, and capitalize on their interests. Readers need books that let them see themselves and satisfy their need to know about the world around them.

In many ways, the content area classroom is the perfect place for students to connect with books because it affords students opportunities to build webs of meaning about a topic through a variety of sources. Through such experiences, students engage in meaning-making by evaluating information, connecting ideas across sources, comparing and contrasting information, and reflecting on meaning. In this chapter, we explore the complementary roles of textbooks and trade books in the classroom as well as the unique ways in which responses to trade books can enhance and extend content learning experiences. In general, we also make a strong case for using trade books—trade books that reflect the contemporary realities of our students, that present multiple perspectives, and that advocate for agency and change. ■

Textbooks in Today's Classrooms

A familiar ritual occurs in classrooms practically everywhere at the beginning of each school year. The ritual, of course, is the "distribution of textbooks" captured brilliantly in the accompanying *Funky Winkerbean* cartoon.

Textbooks are more the rule than the exception in most classrooms. Estimates suggest that 75 to 90 percent of classrooms in the United States use textbooks almost exclusively (Palmer & Stewart 1997). Les Moore, the teacher in the cartoon, mouths the words that many teachers have either spoken aloud or thought about as part of the "distribution of textbooks" ritual. Textbooks, after all, are expensive. School districts, depending on their size, invest hundreds of thousands of dollars on a textbook adoption. Textbooks are purchased to last several years or more before the next adoption period. Mr. Moore expects his course textbooks to be returned at the end of the year in the same condition as the beginning of the year: "Although," he says somewhat wryly, "some signs of use would be nice!"

The cartoon hits home. Textbooks remain unread by too many students, even though teachers attempt to use textbooks with the best of intentions. Often we have heard teachers note with regret that students "simply don't read assigned textbook material anymore." Yet, it's not that the majority of students can't read. Most choose not to, primarily because they have never been shown how to think and learn with textbooks.

Reasons Teachers Use Textbooks

Textbooks are, for most teachers, essential classroom tools. They act as blueprints for learning in particular content areas. And in today's standards-driven environment, they provide coverage of content in particular disciplines that may well appear on high-stakes tests of some kind. Time constraints in a standards-driven curriculum are real. Teachers feel enormous pressure to cover a certain amount of content in a specified amount of time before students move on to the next chapter or unit of study. Teachers who operate under time constraints often view textbooks as efficient informational resources that support what students are studying in a particular subject at

Source: Funky Winkerbean © Batom, Inc. North American Syndicate.

a particular time. Textbook-driven instruction relies on lecturing and other means of information giving when content coverage is the primary purpose. For these reasons and others, content area teaching often involves the use of one type of text—the textbook—often to the exclusion of other types of texts.

Problems with Using Textbooks

Textbooks are not without problems, though. Because of their encyclopedic nature, most textbooks do not treat subject matter with the breadth and depth necessary to fully develop ideas and concepts.

RESPONSE JOURNAL

Based on your own school experiences, what do you believe are some of the problems associated with textbook-only instruction?

A case in point is the 2007 edition of *The Americans* published by McDougal-Littell. The textbook, more than 1,000 pages in length, is written for a comprehensive high school U.S. history curriculum. Its design is attractive and inviting: full of eye-catching and instructionally helpful features, including black-and-white and color photos, maps, tables, graphs, cartoons, and a wide variety of instructional features (key vocabulary, questions, graphic organizers, and capsule main idea statements) for each chapter. All of these design features serve several purposes: to support students' reading, to make learning more visual and appealing, and to break up written text into manageable chunks of writing that won't overwhelm students, despite the overall 1,000-plus pages of the textbook.

Moreover, *The Americans* is written in an appealing, descriptive manner to capture students' interest and hold their attention. Take, for example, a sample passage from a section of the textbook describing the United States' decision to enter World War I:

> A light drizzle fell on Washington on April 2, 1917, as senators, representatives, and members of the Supreme Court, and other guests crowded into the Capitol building to hear President Wilson deliver his war resolution.
>
> Congress passed the resolution a few days later. With the hope of neutrality finally shattered, U.S. troops would follow the stream of American money and munitions that had been heading to the Allies throughout the war. But Wilson's plea to make the world "safe for democracy" wasn't just political posturing.
>
> Indeed, Wilson and many Americans truly believed that the United States had to join the war to pave the way for a future order of peace and freedom and a resolved but anxious nation held its breath as the United States prepared for war. (Danzer 2007, p. 586)

The passage cleverly uses words and phrases such as "light drizzle," "the hope of neutrality shattered," and "anxious nation held its breath" to re-create the atmosphere and tension surrounding the U.S. decision to enter World War I. However, the coverage of Wilson's war resolution and the events surrounding the decision to go to war is limited to several short paragraphs. Even though coverage is cursory at best, the text description accomplishes its purpose: to chronicle events and people and to give readers the "flavor" of the political, economic, and social forces underlying the United States' entry into World War I.

This example illustrates a problem with textbooks in general. They aren't designed to provide in-depth coverage. A textbook conveys a body of knowledge and casts a wide net in an effort to cover as much information as possible. No wonder textbooks are often described as being "a mile wide and an inch deep."

As state standards require even more content coverage, textbooks must include an ever greater number of topics. Space limitations require that textbooks merely mention people or topics, often omitting important background information on particular topics. This can result in students having superficial knowledge of many topics, but little in-depth knowledge of any.

Experts have identified at least four other concerns with textbooks: (1) They are often "inconsiderate" of their readers, (2) they may contain inaccuracies, (3) they are often written at high levels of difficulty, and (4) they lack appeal for students.

Inconsiderate Texts

"Inconsiderate texts" contain writing that may be confusing and lack clear organization. Textbooks tend to jump from topic to topic, rather than using generally accepted patterns of exposition, such as cause–effect, sequence, or comparison and contrast. Many of these texts are often written in a descriptive mode, which makes retention of material more difficult.

Inaccuracy

A second concern about textbooks is that of accuracy. Television news shows have focused on this issue. For example, *20/20* reported several years ago that textbooks are rife with errors. In fact, it featured a concerned parent who found 113 errors in a current edition of a best-selling science textbook! Further concerns about accuracy relate to the fact that students in many schools are using outdated textbooks because of budget constraints.

Inappropriate Reading Level

Another critical concern is that textbooks are often written well above the reading level of their intended audiences. Of today's students, 25 to 40 percent are reading, or attempting to read, textbooks that are well beyond their reading levels (Schoenbach, Greenleaf, Cziko, & Hurwitz 1999). For struggling readers or English learners, the gap between reader and textbook can be as great as three to five years. This coupled with students' lack of prior knowledge for text content can create a situation in which the textbook becomes little more than furniture.

Negative Student Reactions

Finally, students themselves express reservations about their textbooks. When eleventh- and twelfth-grade students in physics classes were queried about the use of their textbooks, one student stated flatly, "I don't mess with the textbook. It's confusing." Another responded, "I should be telling you that the text is the best way to learn information. I would tell you that for all my other classes. I learn by reading, and I read a lot. But I just can't understand this textbook. It's way above my head." These revealing comments came from interviews that were part of a study on the use of texts in science classes (Hynd, McNish, Guzzetti, Lay, & Fowler 1994). The researchers, who interviewed a mix of students in general and college-prep science classes, were struck by the similarities in the students' comments, despite assumed differences in ability, motivation, and background. Various student comments revealed insightful perspectives, including the beliefs that textbooks assume too much student knowledge, that textbooks need fuller explanations and more relevant examples, and that textbooks should be better organized.

As these examples illustrate, when reading merely chronicles of events, students dismiss (and miss) the power of text to inform and transform their lives. When a textbook is the only source of information in a particular content area class, students come to connect the content of a particular subject with what are sometimes dull, lifeless textbooks. When the textbook becomes the curriculum, students are denied the range of perspectives and opportunities for critical thinking.

Why Use Trade Books?

Trade books, rich in narrative and informational content, can provide a valuable complement to most textbooks. Trade books can transport students to different places and times in ways that textbooks can't. Trade books can also relate experiences and perspectives that may have been excluded in textbooks. Learning with trade books involves exposure to many different genres and forms, all of which are potential sources of information for the active learner. Teaching trade books using a critical literacy framework allows teachers to push students to read the world (Freire 1970/2000), and ultimately learn about their place in this world. For example, a nonfiction or fiction trade book has the potential to be a magnifying glass that enlarges and enhances the reader's personal interactions with a subject. When teachers use textbooks and trade books in tandem, they help learners think critically about content and, perhaps more importantly, they also help them think about the larger questions of the world.

> **myeducationlab**
> Go to the Assignments and Activities section of Topic 8: "Study Skills and Strategies" in the MyEducationLab for your course and complete the activity "Organization of Nonfiction" to see how one teacher explains expository text structures.

The use of literature in the classroom can challenge and stimulate student thinking on a range of important issues with particular relevance to the world today, including immigration, globalization, and much more. It is imperative that teachers place thought-provoking books in the hands and minds of students. As Aidan Chambers (1973) notes, good literature both comforts and subverts. As teenagers seek to construct and establish their identities, trade books with social justice themes may help give them a sense of agency and also help them empathize, which is a motivating factor needed for social change (Goodman 2002). Furthermore, teachers need to acknowledge the power of trade books and guide students toward a more critical lens. According to critical literacy theorists (Bean & Moni 2003; Foss 2002; Morgan

1997), texts position the readers to assume a stance; in order to develop citizens and future leaders, teachers need to teach students how to think critically.

Today's trade books can provide an effective complement to textbooks in virtually any subject. The best trade books overcome many of the limitations of content area texts discussed in the previous section. They provide depth, considerate and accurate information, material at a variety of reading levels, and motivation for learning. For example, high-quality trade books can supply the depth of information that space limitations prevent textbooks from providing. Consider the brief textbook treatment of World War I you might find in a history text. Many outstanding trade books provide in-depth accounts of that event in history, such as *The First World War* (Keegan 2003). Making a case for using picture books in secondary classrooms, *Faithful Elephants* (Tsuchiya 1988) offers a different perspective on World War II, encouraging empathy and cross-cultural understanding. Trade books can fulfill the need for story and provide the emotional dimension so lacking in textbooks. Unlike textbooks, they move students' minds and their hearts.

In addition, trade books, nonfiction titles in particular, often contain information that is written and organized in ways that make information more interesting and accessible. The best nonfiction books are more than "baskets of facts"; they speak to young readers personally through informal, engaging writing styles. Their clear, reader-friendly explanations of scientific principles or processes can be extremely helpful to students. In addition, authors of trade books take enormous pains to ensure accuracy. In a speech in Columbus, Ohio, Jim Murphy explained that *each fact* in his award-winning nonfiction title *The Great Fire* (Murphy 1998) was checked for accuracy at least three times. Similarly, authors of multicultural trade books cite deliberate and diligent research of a variety of sources in order to produce culturally authentic works (Loh 2006).

Trade books can help teachers differentiate instruction by meeting the range of reading levels in their classrooms. By using a variety of trade books at different levels, teachers can match students with books they can read. Instead of having all students read the same textbooks, students can read a variety of different trade books about a particular topic. This allows teachers to give students books at their independent reading levels, a practice that has been associated with gains in achievement.

Furthermore, exposure to nonfiction literature gives students much needed practice reading expository text, which unlike narrative, does not typically involve characters, plots, or settings. This type of text is typically less familiar to students than narrative and more difficult for them to read. The reality is that many students do not know how to read to learn with informational texts because their school experiences have been limited to textbook-only reading. For some students the only historical, mathematics, or science materials they will ever read in a lifetime are in textbooks.

Trade books help readers at all levels develop greater understanding of content-related concepts. Historical fiction titles, for example, provide a framework for remembering, understanding, and evaluating historical content. The same holds for content in science and other subject areas. Popular science books, both fact and fiction, provide background knowledge for science concepts covered in class and help students relate these concepts to their everyday lives.

Finally, trade books have the power to motivate students to read more. The compelling visual qualities of today's nonfiction books make them many students' favorite out-of-school reading. Authors of nonfiction not only inform but also entertain. Consider, for example, *Phineas Gage: A Gruesome but True Story About Brain Science* (Fleischman 2002). In 1848, Phineas Gage had a three-and-a-half-foot iron rod blasted through his head and survived. Despite his recovery, Gage's personality underwent a drastic transformation. He changed from a reliable, respected foreman to an unpredictable and temperamental man who eventually lost his job. The focus of the book is not simply on what happened to Gage, but on what neurologists have learned and continue to learn today about the workings of the human brain. Because of its lively writing and extraordinary visuals, this amazing book provides background information about the human brain in a format sure to motivate even those students who have little initial interest in the topic.

Authors of fiction engage students through characters that remind readers of themselves and their peers. Many titles address students' emotional needs because they are written from the viewpoint of students. People of all ages and backgrounds are attracted to books that speak to them in some personal way. For many female students, for example, Ann Brashares's (2001) best-selling *Sisterhood of the Traveling Pants* collection speaks of the powerful bonds of friendship and its potential to transform lives. For males of any ethnicity, but especially Native Americans, Sherman Alexie's (2007) *The Absolutely True Diary of a Part-Time Indian* speaks of the trials and tribulations of forging multiple cultural identities. Today's young adult literature is more edgy than in the past, and one could argue, more representative of today's teens. Because of this, today's young adult books are likely to appeal to a wider audience than ever before, and as a result teens will be more likely to read such books.

Capturing students' attention and promoting the habit of lifelong reading provide a major rationale for using trade books. Of all the goals for literacy instruction, there is none more critical than creating students who read independently. Independent reading provides practice and pleasure, and develops passion for books. It affords students an opportunity to "get lost in a book"—to be so engaged in reading that one loses track of time, of place, of everything but the power of a text to transport and transform us. Repeated experiences that involve true engagement with books help students develop a love of reading that may last a lifetime. When students are given opportunities to interact with quality trade books, they have a better chance of becoming lifelong readers. Textbooks alone cannot motivate students to continue their learning, particularly in the case of reluctant or academically diverse readers, who are often frustrated and defeated by textbooks in the first place. There is no substitute for a good book.

Learning with Trade Books

When students have opportunities to learn with trade books, they are in a position to explore and interact with many kinds of texts, both fiction and nonfiction. Today's trade books are better than ever. They are written by authors in touch with the emotions and experiences of today's young people and address an enormous range of themes and genre. They present characters and events from virtually every ethnic and cultural group in accurate and meaningful circumstances and settings.

Today's trade books offer teachers a variety of genres, ranging from easy-to-read titles using engaging formats to extremely sophisticated explorations of complex topics. Trade books can serve the needs of every student in every academic area. The greatest challenge for teachers is deciding which books to choose from the enormous selection available. Figure 11.1 (p. 364) provides a list of references to help teachers select good books for their classrooms.

Nonfiction Books

Nonfiction trade books have, in recent years, moved from the shadows into the spotlight of literary excellence. Nonfiction books, which include informational books and biographies, are not glorified textbooks. They connect with readers through writing that is not strictly objective in tone and literal in content, but that engages contemporary readers. These books contain elements of fiction that flesh out historical details and provide an element of entertainment. This "new journalism" (Donelson & Nilsen 1997) represents the kind of meaty material that entertains students at the same time it informs.

For many students, nonfiction is the literature of choice for out-of-school reading. Many students report a fascination with facts and a "need to know" that drives their reading choices. Despite its popularity, nonfiction seldom makes its way into content area classrooms. Because of this, nonfiction trade books are a largely untapped resource with great potential for motivating readers. By using nonfiction trade books in the classroom, teachers can bridge the gap between students' in- and out-of-school reading, and capitalize on their interest in this genre.

The wide array of nonfiction books available for the classroom can help teachers enliven classroom instruction in every content area. No single book will satisfy all readers, but teachers will find many titles that can spark student learning. Using nonfiction in the classroom can:

- Deepen student knowledge of real people, places, and phenomena of the present and the past;
- Provide in-depth, up-to-date information;
- Help students see how knowledge in different domains is organized, used, and related;
- Develop student familiarity with the language and vocabulary of a discipline;
- Improve student comprehension of expository text, a skill required for survival in the Information Age; and
- Provide insights into contemporary issues of interest to teens that get little attention in textbooks.

The range of topics available, the variety of formats, and the varying levels of difficulty make these books an indispensable resource for content area classrooms.

FIGURE 11.1 Trade Book Selection Guide for Children and Adolescents

The ALAN Review (Assembly on Literature for Adolescents, National Council of Teachers of English). Published three times a year; articles and "Clip and File" reviews. Urbana, IL: National Council of Teachers of English. http://scholar.lib.vt.edu/ejournals/ALAN

Appraisal: Children's Science Books for Young People. Published quarterly by Children's Science Book Review Committee. Reviews written by children's librarians and subject specialists.

Association for Library Service to Children. (1995). *The Newbery & Caldecott Awards: A guide to the medal and honor books.* Chicago: American Library Association. Provides short annotations for the winners and runners-up of ALA-sponsored awards. www.ala.org/ala/alsc/awardsscholarships/literaryawds/literary related.htm

Book Links: Connecting Books, Libraries, and Classrooms. Published six times a year by the American Library Association to help teachers integrate literature into the curriculum; bibliographies in different genres and subjects; suggestions for innovative use in the classroom. www.ala.org/ala/productsandpublications/periodicals/booklinks/booklinks.htm

Booklist. Published twice monthly by the American Library Association. Reviews of children's trade books and nonprint materials (video, audio, and computer software). Approximate grade levels are given; separate listing for nonfiction books. www.ala.org/ala/booklist/booklist.htm

Books for the Teenage Reader. Published annually by the Office of Young Adult Services, New York Public Library. Recommendations from young adult librarians in the various branches of the New York Public Library. http://teenlink.nypl.org/bta1.cfm

Bulletin of the Center for Children's Books. Published monthly by the University of Chicago Press; detailed reviews and possible curriculum uses are noted. http://bccb.lis.uiuc.edu

Carter, B. (2000). *Best books for young adults* (2nd ed). Chicago: American Library Association. This classic book contains lists of 1,800 books arranged by topics including animals, romance, and survival.

Children's Books: Awards and Prizes. New York: Children's Book Council. Award-winning titles as well as state "Children's Choice" awards for exemplary trade books. www.cbcbooks.org

Christenbury, L. (Ed.). (1995). *Books for you: A booklist for senior high students* (11th ed.). Urbana, IL: National Council of Teachers of English. Provides annotations for both fiction and nonfiction written for students, organized into fifty categories.

Friedberg, J. B. (1992). *Portraying persons with disabilities: An annotated bibliography of non-fiction for children and teenagers* (2nd ed.). New Providence, NJ: Bowker. Provides comprehensive listings of nonfiction dealing with physical, mental, and emotional disabilities.

Gillespie, J. T., & Barr, C. (2004). *Best books for high school readers: Grades 9–12.* Englewood, CO: Libraries Unlimited. Lists 12,000 fiction and nonfiction titles published between 2001 and 2003, recommended in at least two sources and organized thematically.

Gorman, M. (2003). *Getting graphic: Using graphic novels to promote literacy with preteens and teens.* New York: Linworth Publishing. Provides an introduction to teaching with graphic novels and includes a bibliography of fifty graphic novels suitable for sixth grade, as well as suggestions for using these books in the classroom.

Helbig, A., & Perkins, A. R. (2000). *Many peoples, one land: A guide to new multicultural literature for children and young adults.* Westport, CT: Greenwood Press. Provides an extensive listing of titles featuring African Americans, Asian Americans, Hispanic Americans, and Native Americans.

The Horn Book Magazine. Published six times a year by Horn Book, Inc.; articles by noted children's authors, illustrators, and critics on aspects of children's literature, including its use in the classroom. Nonfiction books are reviewed in a separate section. www.hbook.com/publications/magazine/default.asp

International Reading Association. "Children's Choices," a list of exemplary, "reader-friendly" children's literature, is published every October in *The Reading Teacher.* www.reading.org/resources/tools/choices_childrens.html

McClure, A. A., & Kristo, J. (Ed.). (2002). *Adventuring with books: A booklist for pre-K–grade 6* (13th ed.). Urbana, IL: National Council of Teachers of English.

FIGURE 11.1 Trade Book Selection Guide for Children and Adolescents *(continued)*

Summaries of hundreds of books arranged by genre and topic within content areas.

Miller-Lachman, L. (1992). *Our family, our friends, our world: An annotated guide to significant multicultural books for children and teenagers.* New Providence, NJ: Reed Publishing. Comprehensive reference work includes 1,000 of the best English-language fiction and nonfiction multicultural books published since 1970. Each chapter introduces a culture, a map of the region, and an annotated list of books for preschool through grade twelve.

Notable Children's Trade Books in the Field of Social Studies. National Council for the Social Studies. Published yearly in the spring issue of *Social Education;* annotates notable fiction and nonfiction books, primarily for children in grades K–8. www.socialstudies.org/resources/notable

Outstanding Science Trade Books for Students K–12. National Science Teachers Association. Published each year in the spring issue of *Science and Children;* contains information consistent with current scientific knowledge; is pleasing in format; illustrated; and is nonsexist, nonracist, and nonviolent.

Rand, D., & Parker, T. T. (2000). *Black books galore! Guide to great African American children's books about girls.* New York: Jossey-Bass. Featuring 360 books arranged alphabetically by title, this book provides descriptions, notes awards, and spotlights well-known authors and illustrators.

Rosow, L. V. (1996). *Light 'n lively reads for ESL, adult and teen readers.* Englewood, CO: Libraries Unlimited. Books are arranged in seventeen different thematic units. Each unit lists picture books, thin books, challenging books, book chapters and "strong passages," newspaper and magazine articles, and suggested activities related to each theme.

School Library Journal. Published by R. R. Bowker; articles on all aspects of children's literature, including its use in content areas; reviews by school and public librarians. www.schoollibraryjournal.com

Totten, H. L., & Brown, R. W. (1995). *Culturally diverse library collections for children.* New York: Neal-Schuman. Includes annotations on Native Americans, Asian Americans, Hispanic Americans, and African Americans.

Topics addressed in nonfiction trade books range from art to zoology. Formats range from encyclopedic treatments of topics like David Macaulay's (2008) *The Way We Work,* which describes the design and functions of the human body, to tightly focused, narrowly defined topics such as Karen Beil's (1999) *Fire in Their Eyes: Wildfires and the People Who Fight Them.*

There are outstanding biographies and autobiographies of all sorts of people, including rock stars (*John Lennon: All I Want Is the Truth* [Partridge 2005]), writers (*e.e. cummings: A Poet's Life* [Reef 2006]), athletes (Lance Armstrong and Sally Jenkins's [2001] *It's Not About the Bike: My Journey Back to Life*), composers (*This Land Was Made for You and Me: The Life and Songs of Woody Guthrie* [Partridge 2002]), scientists (*Genius: A Photobiography of Albert Einstein* [Delano 2005]), artists (*Chuck Close, Up Close* [Greenberg & Jordan 1998]), and ordinary teens who find themselves in extraordinary situations (*A Long Way Gone: Memoirs of a Boy Soldier* [Beah 2007], the tragic account of a former child soldier in Sierra Leone). There are books that recount real-life adventures such as *Shipwreck at the Bottom of the World: The Extraordinary True Story of Shackleton and the* Endurance (Armstrong 1998)

Evidence-Based Best Practices BOX 11.1

Appreciating Art and Artists Through the Use of Trade Books

Today's nonfiction trade books offer teachers rich opportunities to involve students in learning about artists and analyzing their works. Art teacher Carole Newman has found many ways to create literacy activities that serve to extend student learning in her middle school art classes. One project that she typically involves her students in is the study of the lives and work of famous artists. This project combines reading, writing, and artistic expression. She begins this project by providing her students with a wide array of artists' biographies. These include books from the *Lives of the Artists* series, artists' biographies by Jan Greenberg and Diane Stanley, and many others. Some of the artists students study include Diego Rivera, Frida Kahlo, Marc Chagall, Pablo Picasso, Jackson Pollack, Edgar Degas, Claude Monet, Georgia O'Keefe, and so on.

Students identify an artist they wish to learn about, and select and read a book about the artist's life. Students are required to identify five important facts about the artist's life and prepare an in-depth analysis of two of the artist's works. As part of this analysis, students record their observations about the works in a learning log. Finally, students create their own artwork, employing the style and media used by the artist under study. They share their findings through group presentations where they present information about the artists and their works as well as their original artistic creations.

and *Team Moon: How 400,000 People Landed Apollo 11 on the Moon* (Thimmesh 2006). Other titles address contemporary issues of concern to people the world over, including AIDS, climate change, and homelessness. There are collections of interviews written with young readers in mind such as *Colors of Freedom: Immigrant Stories* (Bode 2000), which presents the voices of teen immigrants from such places as Afghanistan, El Salvador, India, Cuba, and China. In addition, there are first-person accounts of teens who make disastrous mistakes, such as *Hole in My Life* (Gantos 2002), about a teenager who discovered his passion for writing in prison and went on to become a beloved children's author. Figure 11.2 lists additional nonfiction titles useful for various content areas.

Perhaps the greatest difficulty teachers face when selecting nonfiction for the classroom is deciding which books to choose from the large number available. An important point to keep in mind is that variety truly is the spice of life where reading and learning are concerned. No one book will satisfy all readers. The point of using nonfiction trade books in the classroom is to expose students to more than one point of view in a way that is both informational and readable. Although many nonfiction books sound like textbooks packaged in pretty covers, teachers can select quality books by considering the five A's:

1. The authority of the author
2. The accuracy of text content
3. The appropriateness of the book for its audience

RESPONSE JOURNAL

Select several nonfiction trade books related to your discipline. Use the five As to evaluate the books, and identify one title that you think represents a quality book. Explain why you made the choice you did, what content-related objectives the book could help you meet, and how you might use the book in your classroom.

FIGURE 11.2 **Nonfiction Trade Books for Content Area Classrooms**

Science

Burns, L. G. (2007). *Tracking trash: Flotsam, jetsam, and the science of ocean motion.* Boston: Houghton Mifflin.

Dash, J. (2000). *The longitude prize.* New York: Farrar, Straus & Giroux.

Delano, M. F. (2005). *Genius: A photobiography of Albert Einstein.* Washington, DC: National Geographic.

Dendy, L. (2005). *Guinea pig scientists: Bold self-experimenters in science and medicine.* New York: Henry Holt.

Dingle, A. (2007). *The periodic table: Elements with style.* Boston: Houghton Mifflin/Kingfishers.

Farrell, J. (2005). *Invisible allies: Microbes that shape our lives.* New York: Farrar, Straus & Giroux.

Fleischman, J. (2002). *Phineas Gage: A gruesome but true story about brain science.* Boston: Houghton Mifflin.

Giblin, J. (1995). *When plague strikes: The black death, smallpox, AIDS.* New York: HarperCollins.

Jenkins, S. (2002). *Life on earth: The story of evolution.* Boston: Houghton Mifflin.

Pearce, F. (2007). *Earth then and now.* New York: Firefly.

Thimmesh, C. (2000). *Girls think of everything: Stories of ingenious inventions by women.* New York: Houghton Mifflin.

Thimmesh, C. (2006). *Team moon: How 400,000 people landed Apollo 11 on the moon.* New York: Houghton Mifflin.

Social Studies

Armstrong, J. (2002). *Shattered: Stories of children and war.* New York: Knopf.

Bartoletti, S. C. (2001). *Black potatoes: The story of the great Irish famine, 1845–1850.* Boston: Houghton Mifflin.

Bitton-Jackson, L. (1997). *I have lived a thousand years: Growing up in the Holocaust.* New York: Simon & Schuster.

Bode, J. (2000). *The colors of freedom: Immigrant stories.* New York: Franklin Watts.

Calabro, M. (1999). *The perilous journey of the Donner party.* New York: Clarion Books.

Cooper, M. (2002). *Remembering Manzanar: Life in a Japanese relocation camp.* New York: Clarion Books.

Deem, J. M. (2005). *Bodies from the ash: Life and death in ancient Pompeii.* Boston: Houghton Mifflin.

Fleming, C. (2008). *The Lincolns: A scrapbook look at Abraham and Mary.* New York: Schwartz & Wade Books.

Hoose, P. M. (2001). *We Were There, Too! Young People in U.S. History.* New York: Farrar, Straus & Giroux.

Oppenheim, J. (2006). *Dear Miss Breed: True stories of the Japanese American incarceration during World War II and a librarian who made a difference.* New York: Scholastic.

Raddatz, M. (2007). *The long road home: A story of war and family.* New York: Penguin.

Schanzer, R. (2004). *George vs. George: The American Revolution as seen from both sides.* Washington, DC: National Geographic.

Art and Music

Beckett, W. (1999). *My favorite things: 75 works of art from around the world.* New York: Abrams.

Byrd, R. (2003). *Leonardo, beautiful dreamer.* New York: Dutton.

Greenberg, J., & Jordan, S. (2004). *Andy Warhol: Prince of pop.* New York: Delacorte.

Greenberg, J., & Jordan, S. (1998). *Chuck Close: Up close.* New York: DK.

Grody, S., & Prigoff, J. (2007). *Graffiti LA: Street styles and art.* New York: Harry N. Abrams.

Marsalis, W. (1995). *Marsalis on music.* New York: Norton.

Mühlberger, R. (1993). *What makes a Monet a Monet?* New York: New York Metropolitan Museum of Art/Viking.

Myers, W. D. (2006). *Jazz.* New York: Holiday House.

Health and Physical Education

Armstrong, L., & Jenkins, S. (2001). *It's not about the bike: My journey back to life.* New York: Berkley Books.

Blumenthal, K. (2005). *Let me play! The story of Title IX: The law that changed the future of girls in America.* New York: Atheneum.

Canfield, J. (2000). *Chicken soup for the sports fan's soul: 101 stories of insight, inspiration and laughter in the world.* Deerfield, FL: HCI.

Chryssicas, M. K. (2007). *Breathe: Yoga for teens.* DK.

Shivack, N. (2007). *Inside out: Portrait of an eating disorder.* New York: Simon & Schuster.

4. The literary artistry
5. The appearance of the book (Moss 2003, pp. 123–124)

Table 11.1 suggests questions teachers can consider in relationship to each of the five A's as they select nonfiction books.

Classroom uses for nonfiction are limitless but are most often thought of in reference to student report writing or inquiry projects. Nonfiction trade books have many other excellent uses as well. For example, they can help students consider multiple perspectives related to a particular issue.

One interesting way to use nonfiction involves pairing fiction with nonfiction. Judy Hendershot involved her middle graders in reading the historical novel *Out of the Dust* (Hesse 1997) as part of a social studies unit on the Depression. During this time she read aloud the nonfiction title *Children of the Great Depression* (Freedman 2005). Through this pairing of fiction with nonfiction, students developed deeper understanding of the experiences of the children who suffered through the greatest economic downturn in American history. The first title exposes students to the harsh experiences of the female narrator during this time. The second provides a somewhat wider view, helping students understand the causes of the Depression as well as its impact on children across the country.

TABLE 11.1

The Five A's for Evaluating Nonfiction Trade Books

Criteria	Questions to Ask
Authority	Does the author identify and credit experts consulted during the research process?
Accuracy	Is text content accurate? Are maps, graphs, charts, and other visual aids presented clearly? Does the author distinguish between facts and theories?
Appropriateness	Is information presented in ways appropriate to the intended audience? Does the author show respect for the reader? Is information effectively organized?
Literary artistry	Does the book have literary artistry? Does the author use literary devices to make information come alive? Is the author's style engaging?
Attractiveness	Is the appearance and layout of the book likely to entice readers?

Source: B. Moss. (2003). *Exploring the Literature of Fact: Children's Nonfiction Trade Books in the Elementary Classroom.* New York: Guilford Press. Reprinted by permission of Guilford Press.

Evidence-Based Best Practices **BOX 11.2**

Linking Physical Education with Literacy Learning

Teacher Tona Wilson at Monroe Clark Middle School in San Diego makes literacy learning an integral part of her physical education classes. She uses read-alouds on a regular basis, for example, to teach students concepts related to health and physical education. She often reads aloud from books such as *Wilma Unlimited* (Krull 2000) or *Chicken Soup for the Sports Fan's Soul* (Canfield 2000). She regularly reads short newspaper and magazine articles about current events related to sports. These read-alouds provide a rich source for discussion and help students recognize the importance of health and physical education in their everyday lives.

Tona uses her strong knowledge of trade books related to sports to encourage her students to read in school and out of school. In order to become better acquainted with her students' sports-related interests, Tona has each student complete a survey about their sports-related preferences and extracurricular activities. This provides her with information that enables her to recommend particular titles to her students that relate to their interests in soccer, baseball, dance, or field hockey. She regularly consults with reading teachers at the school who provide assistance in locating books for students with particular interests.

Another literacy-related activity Tona involves her students in is a research project she calls "bioboards." Bioboards involve her students in using trade books to research sports figures from the past or present. Students are required to locate information related to the person's life and (1) create a time line of the sport figure's life, (2) identify great sports moments in his or her life, (3) research the schools the person attended and sports participation in school, and (4) create color pictures depicting selected events and write captions explaining each picture. Each student displays his or her information on an 11-by-17-inch board and presents it to the other members of the class.

As they learn about different types of games, students regularly engage in shared and guided reading activities that teach them about the history, rules, and methods of scoring. They then work with partners incorporating what they have learned about these games to create their own new games, such as racquetball soccer. In these and many other ways, Tona Wilson helps her students see the many values of literacy as they learn about health and physical education.

Picture Books

All too often, middle and high school teachers think of picture books as suitable only for the primary grades. However, the picture book format is broad and has, particularly recently, been adapted for students of all ages. Picture books encompass every genre and cover a wide range of subjects. They can be used to enhance instruction in every content area.

In picture books art and text work together to tell a story. Picture books typically average around thirty-two pages in length, and their illustrations represent a wide range of media from collage to cut paper. These books are works of art that can represent an area of study in and of themselves. Picture books are more than visual feasts though; they contain the rich vocabulary and lyrical language characteristic of the finest literature. Picture books fall into four general categories: wordless books, picture books with minimal text, picture storybooks, and illustrated books.

myeducationlab

Go to the Assignments and Activities section of Topic 3: "Motivation" in the MyEducationLab for your course and complete the activity "Using Picture Books to Motivate Adolescents" to see how one teacher uses a picture book as a model for writing.

1. *Wordless books.* Illustrations tell the story completely; no text is involved. Tom Feelings's (1995) *The Middle Passage: White Ships/Black Cargo* portrays the cruel experience of slavery through powerful illustrations that transcend the need for words.

2. *Picture books with minimal text.* The illustrations in these books continue to tell the story, but words are used to enhance the pictures. *Mysteries of Harris Burdick* (Van Allsburg 1984) is an example of a book with minimal text.

3. *Picture storybooks.* Interdependent story and illustrations are central to the telling of the tale. *Show Way* (Woodson 2005), which describes an African American family's tradition of making quilts originally designed as secret maps for runaway slaves, is an excellent example of a picture storybook in which illustration and text work together to create a seamless whole.

4. *Illustrated books.* These have more words than pictures, but the illustrations illuminate the text in important ways. A stunning example is Kadir Nelson's (2008) *We Are the Ship.* This amazing book was the 2008 winner of the Coretta Scott King Award, which recognizes an African American author and illustrator of outstanding books for children and young adults. Nelson, an extraordinary artist and storyteller, tells the story of the Negro Baseball Leagues from the 1920s to the 1940s. His breathtaking illustrations portray the forgotten players of that time with grace and strength.

Many picture books suitable for middle and high school students are written to appeal to all age groups. Increasingly, however, picture books are written specifically with older readers in mind. Walter Dean Myers's (2002) *Patrol: An American Soldier in Vietnam* provides a vivid example of this trend. This unusual and gripping book combines mixed-media collages with a riveting poem about a young soldier's fear, confusion, and fatigue. Its in-depth focus and emotional content help readers connect with the realities of war for the typical foot soldier.

Picture books can scaffold student understanding of a range of topics through formats that intrigue rather than intimidate. Picture books provide students with background knowledge about people, places, events, and experiences. They can ground students in cognitive concepts critical for understanding a variety of content area subjects. Because picture books with a multicultural focus are increasing in availability, they can also provide rich opportunities for promoting cultural diversity.

Picture books are a particularly rich resource for struggling readers and English language learners. Illustrations aid comprehension, and the manageable length and limited amount of print in picture books enhance their appeal to students for whom reading is a challenge. Because of their accessible format, picture books can motivate these students to read, and independent, enjoyable reading experiences can lead to reading that continues after the bell has rung, an important correlate to increased reading achievement.

Picture books lend themselves to use in virtually every content area. Math and science concepts can come alive though illustrated nonfiction picture books. *Go Figure!*

A Totally Cool Book About Numbers (Ball 2005) takes a lively look at the history of mathematics, number theory, logic, and more through puzzles and problems to solve. *Anno's Math Games II* (Anno 1989) inspires critical analysis of the notion of sets and logical possibilities presented in the detailed illustrations. The science-related biography *The Man Who Made Time Travel* (Lasky 2003) relates the story of John Harrison, who devoted thirty-five years of his life to solving the problem of tracking longitude in shipboard navigation. *Gregor Mendel, the Friar Who Grew Peas* (Bardoe 2006) gives glimpses of the life and work of a man whose name is known to every biology student.

Picture books can also build bridges between the past and present. Many excellent titles focus on events surrounding World War II. In *Hidden Child* (2005), Isaac Millman describes his childhood in France as a Jewish boy hiding from the Nazis. *Home of the Brave* (Say 2002) presents an enigmatic, haunting view of the internment of the Japanese during World War II. In *The Butter Battle Book* (1984), Dr. Seuss explores the illogical nature of war and poses the question, Which country will "push the button" first?

When author and illustrator Peter Sís's (2007) teenaged children asked him to describe his own youth, Sís responded with an extraordinary combination of graphic novel and picture book, *The Wall: Growing Up Behind the Iron Curtain.* Because words alone could not tell the story, he used period photographs, crosshatch drawings, and journal entries to describe the conflict between his need to pursue his creative instincts and the oppressive communist government in Czechoslovakia. The book provides a vivid portrayal of a world of darkness unimaginable to most of today's students, and could give world history classes a personal glimpse of life under a totalitarian regime.

Illustrated picture books are useful in the English classroom as well. Bruce Coville's (1997) *William Shakespeare's Macbeth* provides an easy-to-read complement to Shakespeare's original work. A similar picture book adaptation of *The Necklace* is also available. Picture book versions of poems are increasingly popular, and combine traditional texts with dramatic illustrations. The vivid illustrations in *Cremation of Sam McGee* (Service 1986), for example, provide an interesting visual counterpart to this tale of the Yukon during the Gold Rush.

Illustrated books also deal with individuals who have made significant contributions to the arts. Kathleen Krull's *Lives of the Musicians: Good Times, Bad Times (and What the Neighbors Thought)* (1993) and *Lives of the Artists: Masterpieces, Messes (and What the Neighbors Thought)* (1995) give lighthearted, amusing glimpses of well-known musicians and artists. Each thumbnail sketch is only a few pages long, making them ideal for short read-alouds in music and art classes.

These picture books and countless others can be integrated into your content area. They can be used with older students as interesting schema builders, anticipatory sets to begin lessons, models for quality writing, motivators for learning, read-alouds, and springboards into discussion and writing. Figure 11.3 (p. 372) provides examples of picture books useful for content area classrooms at all grade levels.

FIGURE 11.3 **Picture Books for Middle and High School Classrooms**

Aliki. (1999). *William Shakespeare and the Globe.* New York: HarperCollins.

Bunting, E. (1984). *Smoky night.* Ill. D. Diaz. Orlando, FL: Harcourt Brace.

Burleigh, R. (1997). *Hoops.* Ill. S. T. Johnson. San Diego, CA: Silver Whistle.

Chekhov, A. (1991). *Kashtonka.* Trans. R. Povear. Ill. B. Moser. New York: Putnam.

Coville, B. (1997). *William Shakespeare's Macbeth.* Ill. G. Kelly. New York: Dial.

deMaupassant, G. (1993). *The necklace.* Ill. G. Kelly. New York: Creative Editions.

Feelings, T. (1995). *The middle passage: White ships/black cargo.* New York: Dial.

Fox, M. (2000). *Feathers and fools.* Ill. N. Wilton. San Diego, CA: Voyager.

Garland, S. (1993). *The lotus seed.* Ill. T. Kiuchi. San Diego, CA: Harcourt.

Giblin, J. (1994). *Thomas Jefferson: A picture book biography.* Ill. M. Dooling. New York: Scholastic.

Golenbock, P. (1990). *Teammates.* Ill. P. Bacon. San Diego: Harcourt Brace Jovanovich.

Goodall, J. (1979). *The story of an English village.* New York: Atheneum.

Hoyt-Goldsmith, D. (1994). *Day of the dead: A Mexican-American celebration.* Ill. L. Migdale. New York: Holiday House.

Igus, T. (1998). *I see the rhythm.* San Francisco: Children's Book Press.

Innocenti, R. (1985). *Rose Blanche.* San Diego, CA: Creative Editions.

Krull, K. (1993). *Lives of the musicians: Good times, bad times (and what the neighbors thought).* Ill. K. Hewitt. San Diego, CA: Harcourt Brace.

Krull, K. (1995). *Lives of the artists: Masterpieces, messes (and what the neighbors thought).* Ill. K. Hewitt. San Diego, CA: Harcourt Brace.

Krull, K. (1997). *Lives of the athletes: Thrills, spills (and what the neighbors thought).* Ill. K. Hewitt. San Diego, CA: Harcourt Brace.

Krull, K. (2000). *Wilma unlimited: How Wilma Rudolph became the world's fastest woman.* Ill. D. Diaz. San Diego, CA: Harcourt Brace.

Krull, K. (2003). *Harvesting hope: The story of Cesar Chavez.* San Diego, CA: Harcourt.

Lasky, K. (1994). *The librarian who measured the earth.* Ill. K. Hawkes. Boston: Little, Brown.

Lasky, K. (2003). *The man who made time travel.* Ill. K. Hawkes. New York: Farrar, Straus & Giroux.

Lauber, P. (1996). *Hurricanes: Earth's mightiest storms.* New York: Scholastic Press.

Lindbergh, R., & Brown, R. (1992). *A view from the air: Charles Lindbergh's earth and sky.* New York: Viking.

Lowe, S. (1990). *Walden.* Ill. R. Sabuda. New York: Philomel.

Macauley, D. (1973). *Cathedral: The story of its construction.* Boston: Houghton Mifflin.

Macauley, D. (1998). *The new way things work.* Boston: Houghton Mifflin.

Maruki, T. (1980). *Hiroshima no pika.* New York: Lothrop, Lee & Shepard.

Myers, W. D. (2002). *Patrol: An American soldier in Vietnam.* New York: HarperCollins.

Noyes, A. (1983). *The highwayman.* Ill. C. Mikolaychak. New York: Lothrop, Lee & Shepard.

Peacock, L. (1998). *Crossing the Delaware: A history in many voices.* Ill. W. L. Krudop. New York: Atheneum.

Polacco, P. (1994). *Pink and say.* New York: Scholastic.

Price, L. (1990). *Aida.* Ill. L. & D. Dillon. San Diego, CA: Harcourt Brace.

Rappaport, D. (2001). *Martin's big words: The life of Dr. Martin Luther King, Jr.* Ill. B. Collier. New York: Hyperion.

Raschka, C. (1997). *Mysterious Thelonious.* New York: Orchard.

Ryan, P. M. *When Marian sang: The true recital of Marian Anderson.* Ill. B. Selznick. New York: Scholastic.

Rylant, C. (1984). *Waiting to waltz: A childhood.* Ill. S. Gammell. New York: Bradbury.

Say, A. (2002). *Home of the brave.* Boston: Houghton Mifflin.

Service, R. (1986). *The cremation of Sam McGee.* Ill. T. Harrison. New York: Greenwillow.

Seuss, Dr. (1984). *The butter battle book.* New York: Random House.

Simon, S. (1990). *Oceans.* New York: Morrow Junior Books.

Stanley, D. (1996). *Leonardo da Vinci.* New York: Morrow.

Stanley, D. (2000). *Michelangelo.* New York: HarperCollins.

Tsuchiya, Y. (1988). *Faithful elephants: A true story of people, animals and war.* Trans. T. Kykes. Ill. Ted Lewin. Boston: Houghton Mifflin.

Van Allsburg, C. (1984). *Mysteries of Harris Burdick.* Boston: Houghton Mifflin.

Wisniewski, D. (1996). *Golem.* New York: Clarion Books.

Yolen, J. (1992). *Encounter.* Ill. D. Shannon. San Diego, CA: Harcourt Brace Jovanovich.

Fiction Books

Fiction entices readers to interact with texts from a number of different perspectives that are impossible to achieve in nonfiction alone. Genres such as fantasy, traditional works (e.g., folktales and myths), historical fiction, and realistic fiction help readers step outside their everyday world for a while to consider a different subject or perspective. In doing so, readers learn to see the world through a different lens, a skill that is necessary for personal and societal change and development.

For some students, fiction books are better bait than nonfiction books, which some students perceive as too similar to textbooks. Students tend to read books about protagonists who are the same age or older; rarely do they read books in which the protagonist is younger. Crossover novels, books that appeal to both teenagers and adults and that are marketed to both audiences (Hunt 2007), have blurred the lines between young adult and adult literature. Crossover novels break from the tradition of young adult fiction through their (1) extended length, (2) sophisticated language, (3) unique narrative formats, (4) challenging vocabulary, (5) inclusion of adult characters, and (6) mature themes and topics. According to Hunt (2007), "The crossover novel requires more serious concentration from young readers and helps move them from the pleasures of light reading to the pleasures of literary reading."

Books such as Khaled Hosseini's (2007) *A Thousand Splendid Suns* and Jeanette Walls's (2006) *The Glass Castle: A Memoir* are good examples of this trend. They demonstrate high standards of literary quality yet appeal to a young adult audience. In recognition of the appeal of the crossover phenomenon, the American Library Association now recognizes ten adult books annually that have special appeal to teenage readers through its Alex Awards.

One contributing factor to the increase in fiction reading could be the popularity of movie adaptations. Students tend to read books that have been made into movies. This is easily corroborated in major bookstores; following the release of the movies, bookshelves are stocked with copies of the original texts. Popular young adult books such as *Coraline* (Gaiman 2006), *Holes* (Sachar 1998), *Speak* (Anderson 1999), *The Sisterhood of the Traveling Pants* (Brashares 2001), and many more have been made into successful motion pictures. It is relevant to note that there have also been several occasions in which movies have been adapted into books. In the classroom, teachers can encourage critical discussions of the similarities and differences in plot and character development by studying the author's and the film director's decisions.

Currently, fantasy is a hot genre for teens. Stories about vampires, dragons, and superheroes never cease to engage and amaze young adult readers. Although fantasy seems an unlikely addition to the required reading list in a content area classroom, consider the possibilities for a moment. Jane Yolen's series *The Pit Dragon Trilogy* (1996), which takes place on a planet called Austar IV, provides young readers with much to consider about the need to improve and change modern social conditions. Nancy Farmer's (2002) *The House of the Scorpion,* set in a futuristic society, offers a profound perspective on cloning and immigration. We can see ourselves more objectively when we consider our lives from the distance of these stories. In this way, fantasy and science fiction books can serve as a springboard for deeper discussions about big ideas.

Poetry and drama provide fascinating insights into a myriad of topics. From Nikki Grimes's (2002) *Bronx Masquerade,* about urban high school students who share their writing in a poetry slam, to Naomi Shihab Nye's (2002) *19 Varieties of Gazelle: Poems of the Middle East,* these genres provide personal glimpses into the human experience. *A Wreath for Emmett Till,* Marilyn Nelson's (2005) moving tribute to the life of the African American boy who was the victim of a racially motivated murder in 1955, is an extraordinary work. This series of fifteen sonnets is multilayered and unsparing in its honesty.

Poetry titles like *Big Talk: Poems for Four Voices* (Fleischman 2000), *Joyful Noise: Poems for Two Voices* (Fleischman 1988), and *Math Talk: Mathematical Ideas in Poems for Two Voices* (Pappas 1993) have real performance potential in the secondary classroom. The poems in each of these titles were designed to be read aloud. English teachers might use these books as models for students to create their own poems in multiple voices. Poetry slams, too, can provide a motivating and engaging way to engage teens in writing and reading their own poetry.

Other texts provide classroom performance opportunities as well. Gary Soto's (1997) *Novio Boy: A Play* is a lighthearted story about young love in a Mexican American community, with realistic characters and familiar situations that students will identify with. For teachers who don't want to tackle group plays, Chamber Stephens's (2002) *Magnificent Monologues for Teens* provides single-character sketches covering a range of topics of interest to teens. Also, the 2007 Newbery winner, *Good Masters! Sweet Ladies!: Voices from a Medieval Village* (Schlitz 2007) offers a wide range of monologues from the perspectives of medieval youth.

Realistic fiction books run the gamut from problem realism, to sports stories, to mysteries, to adventure, to romance. Young adults have long gravitated toward titles about young people engaged in personal struggles; they like to read stories that reflect their trials and tribulations, real and perceived. *The First Part Last* (Johnson 2003), for example, is a powerful novel that describes a teenaged father struggling to raise an infant on his own. *When Zachary Beaver Came to Town* (Holt 1999) is the poignant story of Toby, a boy in a small Texas town, who befriends Zachary, "the world's fattest boy," and discovers that his own problems aren't as bad as they seem. *Jerk, California* (Friesen 2008) describes a teenage boy who survives the torment of living with Tourette's syndrome and discovers the truth about his real father and a family he has never known.

The popularity and demand for "edgy" books, ones that address serious subjects such as sex, drugs, abuse, and so on, suggests that today's young people crave books that speak to them and not about them or for them. Teens want to read authentic stories about real dramas and traumas. *Go Ask Alice* (Anonymous 1971) has compelled young readers for more than three decades with its story of a teen addict whose life is spiraling out of control. *Impulse* by Ellen Hopkins (2008) reveals the inner turmoils of three teens placed in a psychiatric hospital after failed suicide attempts. *Speak* by Laurie Halse Anderson (1999) is about a girl dealing with date rape. *Skud* (2004) by

Dennis Foon addresses male violence and *Paranoid Park* (2008) by Blake Nelson is about an accidental homicide.

Realistic fiction is a perennial teen favorite; historical fiction, while less popular, has the potential to give the past a pulse. Historical fiction can put a human face on history in ways that textbooks can't. Through vicarious involvement in the lives of characters who never actually existed, but who are placed in times and places that actually did, teens can participate in the most triumphant or the most terrible moments in history. Laurie Halse Anderson's (2000) *Fever 1793* is a dramatic account of a little-known historical event, the yellow fever epidemic in Philadelphia, and demonstrates how a young woman's strength of character helped her survive events that turn her world upside down. Markus Zusak's (2007) *The Book Thief* reveals a compelling story of Nazi Germany during World War II, as narrated by Death. Another extraordinary book set during the time of the Holocaust is *The Boy in the Striped Pajamas* (Boyne 2006), the unlikely story of a friendship between two children in a concentration camp, one an inmate and one the child of the commandant. This is historical fiction at its best—a moving story of the power of friendship in a world gone mad.

Many worthy works of fiction are found on the annual *Young Adults' Choices List,* sponsored by the International Reading Association. This list reflects the book choices of teens themselves, including titles dealing with social and political issues, such as drunk driving, women's rights, death, and war. The host of fiction books available can do much to enhance and clarify the content curriculum. An author's ability to bring lifelike characters into sharp focus against a real-world setting results in compelling reading. Showing students how authors use different points of view toward history is explored in Box 11.3.

Books for Unmotivated Readers

Meeting the needs of reluctant readers is a perennial challenge for all teachers. Now more than ever before, however, there are easy-to-read titles on a range of topics relevant to today's content area classroom. In addition to picture books, reluctant readers often respond positively to short books (those with fewer than 100 pages), series books, and graphic novels.

RESPONSE JOURNAL

How can trade books help you address the needs of reluctant readers in the classroom? What advantages might they have over textbooks?

Short but intriguing fiction titles such as *Stuck in Neutral* (Trueman 2001) are sure to captivate those readers who do not readily connect with books. Shawn McDaniel, the main character and narrator of the story, has cerebral palsy and cannot walk, talk, or focus his eyes. As the story progresses, the reader comes to understand the strange world that Shawn inhabits, a world rich with experiences that he is unable to communicate to others. As the story progresses, Shawn becomes increasingly concerned about his father's attitude toward him, and he panics when he begins to think that his father is considering killing him to stop his suffering. This moving book raises a number of issues related to euthanasia and is sure to provoke interesting discussions.

Evidence-Based Best Practices

BOX 11.3

Exploring Different Points of View Toward Historical Events

The use of trade books can help expose students to a variety of perspectives in relationship to particular historical events. Students typically study world explorers as part of social studies at both the middle and high school levels. The use of trade books can offer perspectives about historical events beyond those provided in the textbook. By providing students with a wide variety of texts, they can reflect on the ways in which history is not only reported but also interpreted by writers. Consider, for example, the events surrounding Christopher Columbus's discovery of the New World. Trade books from the historical fiction, nonfiction, and picture book genres provide dramatically different portrayals of that event.

Social studies teacher Robert Wells involves his students in examining these different points of view. He uses six different biographies and historical fiction titles for this lesson. Two of these are *Pedro's Journal* (Conrad 1991), a fictionalized account of Columbus's voyage, narrated by Pedro, a ship's boy who accompanied Columbus on his journey, and Jane Yolen's *Encounter* (1992), an account of Columbus's arrival told from the point of view of a Taino Indian boy.

Robert divides students into groups based on the books they are reading and directs students to look at each book's account of the events of October 12, 1492. He focuses groups' reading, asking them to think about the following questions as they read: What are the events that take place as Columbus lands? What is the author's point of view toward Columbus? How does the author describe the native people Columbus meets? What is Columbus's attitude toward the natives?

After students have read their books, Robert leads the whole class in completing a data chart that compares the answers to the questions found in each of the books. The students then engage in a discussion about why the accounts of the same events are different. They reflect on the sources each author used to create the account, as well as the reasons authors who consulted the same sources might provide different accounts. Through this discussion, students gain understanding of the idea of history as interpretation, rather than fact.

Dozens of other fiction and nonfiction titles can captivate reluctant readers. In *Thirteen Reasons Why* (Asher 2007), a teenage girl sends her classmate a package of cassette tapes that explain her recent suicide. Clay and other teens within her circle of friends are forced to consider how their actions may have contributed to her death. Series books continue to have great appeal for reluctant readers; fantasy and romance titles are particularly popular with teens who may not love to read. The *Star Wars, Cirque du Freak, Circle of Magic,* and *Young Wizards* series help satisfy teen interests in fantasy. The *Luxe* series, teen romance books set at the turn of the century, is popular with female teen readers. Informational series such as Dorling Kindersley's *Eyewitness Books* are extremely appealing to students who enjoy reading about the real world.

Graphic novels are an incredibly rich resource for reluctant readers. Graphic novels employ sophisticated relationships among words and images that can promote critical thinking in ways that words alone cannot. They can be particularly useful for students who find it difficult to visualize what is happening in a text; the graphics support the text and help students get at the meaning of the text. They can also be useful for those students who reject the texts typically found in classrooms. The unique combination of the visual and verbal may be the catalyst that turns a reluctant reader into a ravenous one. Finally, for students who are "Generation Visual" (Lyga 2004)—that is, they spend most of their time "wired" in some way, whether playing video games or exploring MySpace—these books can provide a familiar visual format.

Graphic novels can engage students in both fictional and factual topics, particularly when they are as well written as Art Spiegelman's (1986) *Maus: A Survivor's Tale*. In this book, the story of the Holocaust is vividly told with the Nazis depicted as cats and the Jewish people as mice. Rather than detracting from the seriousness of the subject, the cartoon format lends force to the plight of the Nazis' victims. More recent graphic novels that are popular with students include *American Born Chinese* (Yang 2008), which won the highly coveted Michael L. Printz award for young adult literature. This sophisticated text is made up of three individual plotlines: one focused on Chinese folk hero Monkey King; one focused on Jin Wang, an Asian American middle school student who doesn't fit in at school; and one focused on the plight of Danny, a teenager shamed by his Chinese cousin. Gareth Hinds's (2007) *Beowulf* uses full-color illustrations and mixed media to relate this legendary story to a modern audience. *Malcolm X: A Graphic Biography* (Helfer 2006) describes the events of its subject's life with drama and conflict.

Instructional Strategies for Using Trade Books

A recent study of exemplary content area instruction found a key commonality among effective teachers: All of them used multiple texts with a range of formats and difficulty levels (Allington & Johnston 2002). These teachers capitalized on the myriad uses for trade books in the content area classroom and used them to enhance and extend students' content area literacy learning. This section will identify ways that teachers can organize students for literature study. Virtually all of these ways of using literature can enhance objectives for student learning in every content area.

> **myeducationlab**
> Go to the Building Teaching Skills and Dispositions section of Topic 10: "Struggling Readers" in the MyEducationLab for your course. Complete the activity to learn to use active teaching techniques to meet the needs of struggling readers.

In Box 11.4, we learn how an American history teacher taught eighth graders with immigrant parents by reading about their historical roots in trade books.

Creating Classroom Libraries and Text Sets

Several key components are necessary to create a multitext content area classroom. First and foremost, content area teachers need to acquire books related to their content area. These books can be used to stock classroom libraries, both for large- and small-group reading and for individual inquiry. Locating books for these purposes

Voices from the Classroom

BOX 11.4

Garrett

Eighth-Grade American History Teacher

CHALLENGE

Trade books provide an effective complement to textbook content for disengaged, unmotivated readers who have difficulty completing textbook assignments. Garrett Sampson's eighth-grade American history class in an urban middle school in San Diego was involved in a unit of study entitled Immigration: Past and Present. Student interest in the topic was high because of the recent demonstrations against proposed legislation that would penalize undocumented workers. Many students in the class had parents who had come to this country from Mexico, and almost all of them knew someone who had entered the United States illegally. "My students knew something about the reasons for the demonstrations, but knew little about the history of immigration in this country or the specifics of the proposed legislation," said Garrett.

STRATEGY

Garrett began the unit by reading aloud, which is an easy way to build student background knowledge about new topics of study. He read Katherine Krull's (2003) picture book biography *Harvesting Hope: The Story of Cesar Chavez,* stopping periodically to engage students in a discussion of the events of Chavez's life. When he finished reading, he asked students to reflect on Chavez's philosophy of resistance, which involved nonviolent protest. He asked students to think about the similarities and differences between Chavez's protests on behalf of California's migrant workers and the recent protests related to immigration. Students engaged in a lively discussion of these issues and Garrett recorded these on a chart that students could refer to in the future.

Following the read-aloud, Garrett introduced students to the book *Voices from the Fields,* which contains interviews with the children of migrant workers. Garrett asked the students to read the interviews to discover the issues that migrant workers still encounter today. He paired up students and gave each pair one interview to read silently. After they read, he combined three pairs of students. Each of the three pairs met and shared their interview with the group. Following this, each group identified three issues that migrant workers still face. The groups reported out and the entire class discussed the challenges faced by migrant workers of the past and present. Garrett asked students to respond to the following question: How was the cause of migrant workers in Cesar Chavez's day similar to the cause of immigrants today? Students drew many parallels between the situations of the two groups.

The next day, Garrett showed students primary source photographs from Russell Freedman's (1995) *Immigrant Kids,* which portrays immigrant children in New York at the turn of the century. He read brief excerpts from this book, providing students with rich examples of the daily life of these immigrant children. At this point, he had students pair up again to read brief profiles from Bode's (2000) *The Colors of Freedom: Immigrant Stories,* which describes the lives of modern-day immigrant teens. This reading experience helped students learn about the American immigrant experience from the perspective of teens from all over the world. Students then completed a Venn diagram comparing the experiences of immigrants at the turn of the century with those today.

Finally, Garrett had students read two brief point–counterpoint articles from the Internet about what should be done about undocumented workers. One article supported deportation, while the other recommended amnesty. Students worked in groups to complete a discussion web that examined the question, Should undocumented workers be allowed to stay in this country? Students discussed their views and tried to come to consensus about what the best solution to the immigration problem might be.

REFLECTION

Through the use of literature and multiple text types, Garrett engaged his typically unmotivated textbook learners in reading, writing, and thinking about a variety of texts that explore different issues related to immigration. He provided them with short, engaging texts that built their background knowledge, stimulated discussion, and were relevant to student's own lives.

is always a challenge, but resourceful teachers have found that library book sales, garage sales, and book clubs such as Scholastic and Trumpet are good resources for obtaining inexpensive books.

A classroom library is a critical component of a multitext classroom. By creating a classroom library of books at a range of reading levels and in a variety of genres including picture books, poetry, historical fiction, biography, and informational books, teachers increase students' access to books and help motive them to learn. Other resources such as magazines and newspapers are equally appropriate for inclusion in a content area classroom library. To meet the diverse reading needs and interests of today's students, as well as the variety of ways that trade books can be used in the content area classrooms, classroom libraries should include a wide range of titles, addressing a variety of topics and reading levels.

What kinds of books might be found in a classroom library in an American history class? Good choices include survey books about history such as *A History of Us* (Hakim 1999), the highly acclaimed series by Joy Hakim that speaks directly to students about historical events using a conversational style. Historical fiction, for example Avi's (2008) *The Seer of Shadows,* combines history with a thrilling story, in this case, the Victorian obsession with the spirit world and a photographer who hatches a scheme to get rich quick by exploiting that obsession. Titles by authors such as Ann Rinaldi and Russell Freedman could add to this collection. The nonfiction *5,000 Miles to Freedom: Ellen and William Craft's Flight from Slavery* (Fradin & Fradin 2006) uses photographs, letters, and newspaper accounts to document the true adventure of the Crafts as they escaped from slavery to freedom in the North. Easy-to-read picture book biographies, such as *The Amazing Life of Benjamin Franklin* (Giblin 2000), also have a place in the classroom library. Hundreds of informational titles could round out such a collection, including books by renowned young adult authors like Jim Murphy and many others.

However these titles, excellent as they are, might not appeal to less motivated students. Middle and high school students enjoy books with humor and comic books.

For that reason, the teacher might consider *Cartoon History of the United States* (Gonick 1991), a satirical vision of American history. Other amusing titles, including *So You Want to Be President?* (St. George 2000) and *Explorers Who Got Lost* (Sansevere-Dreher, Dreher, & Renfro 1994), debunk some of the myths about our presidents and famous explorers of the past. Magazines like *National Geographic World, Cobblestone,* or *Time for Kids* could round out such a collection.

In addition to a range of titles broadly related to a content area discipline, teachers will want to create text sets related more specifically to particular units of study within a content area. Text sets involve assembling a variety of titles that span a range of difficulty levels and include a range of resources, including books as well as other sources such as magazines, websites, newspaper articles, and so on. A sample text set related to the Civil War appears in Figure 11.4. These text sets can be used in myriad ways: for independent, self-selected reading, individual inquiry, or idea circles.

RESPONSE JOURNAL

Create a text set of six books related to your discipline. Be sure to select books from a variety of genres and difficulty levels. Describe the books you selected and why you chose those particular books. What kinds of connections exist across the texts? How might you use the books to capitalize on those connections?

Self-Selected Reading

Organized, systematic efforts to make independent reading central in the lives of students are essential. Such experiences can create adolescents who want to continue reading after the bell has rung and "read like a wolf eats," as author Gary Paulsen describes the ravenous hunger for books that consumes book lovers. All too often, in today's standardized test–driven culture, we forget the importance of independent reading. Hundreds of studies document the fact that the more time students spend reading, the higher their reading achievement. To encourage reading and demonstrate its importance, many secondary schools provide uninterrupted sustained silent reading time, sometimes referred to as SSR time or DEAR (Drop Everything and Read). At one San Diego high school, a separate twenty-five minute period is allocated each day for sustained silent reading time. During this time, everyone—teachers, students, and even construction workers at the school site—reads. Uninterrupted sustained silent reading time lets students practice reading and read for their own purposes and pleasure. Students self-select materials other than their textbooks. They can read books, magazines, or newspapers from home or obtain texts from the school or classroom library that relate to personal interests.

Providing access to a range of text types during sustained silent reading time can increase student motivation for reading, because it involves letting students read about topics of interest to them. Silent reading of self-selected books is an effective way to promote the type of engaged reading that has been shown to increase achievement (Guthrie, Schafer, & Huang 2001).

Simply providing time for SSR, however, may not be sufficient to ensure that students benefit from this time. Pilgreen (2000) identifies eight factors of SSR success: (1) access to books, (2) appealing books that address student interests, (3) classroom environments that encourage reading as a social activity, (4) encouragement from

FIGURE 11.4 **Text Set on the Civil War**

Picture Books

Ackerman, N. (1990). *The tin heart.* Ill. Michael Hays. New York: Atheneum. This picture book describes the effect of the Civil War on the friendship of two young girls who live on opposite sides of the Mason-Dixon line.

Lyon, G. E. (1991). *Cecil's story.* Ill. P. Catalanotto. New York: Orchard. A picture book title that describes the apprehensions of a young boy whose father may need to leave home to serve in the Civil War.

Turner, A. (1987). *Nettie's trip south.* Ill. Ron Himler. New York: Macmillan. A young girl travels south during the 1850s and discovers firsthand the horrors of slavery.

Winter, J. (1992). *Follow the drinking gourd.* New York: Dragonfly. Slaves escape to freedom through the lyrics of a folk song that provide directions for following the Underground Railroad.

Plays

Davis, O. (1978). *Escape to freedom: A play about Frederick Douglass.* New York: Viking Penguin. This compelling play exposes young readers to the incredible life of Frederick Douglass.

Folktales

Hamilton, V. (1985). *The people could fly.* Ill. L. & D. Dillon. New York: Knopf. A collection of American Black folktales narrated in authentic dialect.

Nolen, J. (2005). *Big Jabe.* Ill. Kadir Nelson. New York: Amistad. A tall tale about an African American baby who improves life for the slaves on a plantation.

Historical Fiction

Hahn, M. D. (2005). *Hear the wind blow.* New York: Clarion Books. The story of a thirteen-year-old Virginia boy whose life is changed forever when a Confederate soldier he hides in his home is discovered by the Yankees.

Hansen, J. (1986). *Which way freedom?* New York: Walker. Describes the life of an escaped slave who serves in the Civil War.

Hunt, I. (1964) *Across five Aprils.* New York: Follett. Describes how the Creighton family of southern Illinois struggled with the impact of the Civil War.

Reeder, C. (1989). *Shades of gray.* New York: Macmillan. Twelve-year-old Will Page, the orphaned son of a Confederate soldier, must live with his Uncle Jed, who refused to fight for the Confederacy.

Nonfiction

Armstrong, J. (2005). *Photo by Brady: A picture of the Civil War.* New York: Atheneum. Armstrong tells the fascinating story of the life of Brady and his indelible mark on history.

Fleming, T. (1988). *Band of brothers: West Point in the Civil War.* New York: Walker. Describes men who were friends and classmates at West Point and later served in the Civil War, often fighting against one another.

Lester, J. (1968). *To be a slave.* Ill. T. Feelings. New York: Dutton. Using the actual words of his subjects, Lester portrays life as it existed for slaves in this country.

Murphy, J. (1990). *The boys' war.* New York: Clarion Books. Diaries, letters and original photographs tells the story of young boys who participated in the Civil War.

Silvey, A. (2008). *I'll pass for your comrade: Women soldiers in the Civil War.* New York: Atheneum. Describes the women who posed as men to fight in the Civil War and how they coped with daily life as soldiers in a world dominated by men.

Warren, A. (2009). *Under siege: Three children at the Civil War battle for Vicksburg.* New York: Farrar, Straus & Giroux. Uses primary sources to tell the story of children who survived this battle by living in a cave.

Websites

American Memory—Primary Source Photographs of the Civil War
http://memory.loc.gov

The Civil War Home Page—Comprehensive Website Related to the Civil War
www.civilwar.com

teachers and parents, (5) staff training in SSR, (6) nonaccountability in terms of tests of knowledge or book reports, (7) follow-up activities that can encourage further reading, and (8) distributed time to read that includes short periods of fifteen to twenty minutes at least twice a week. Fisher (2004) argues that SSR programs should not consist of isolated instances in which certain teachers engage students in reading, but rather need to be schoolwide initiatives that represent a larger emphasis on staff development, collaboration between teachers and students, and effective administrative leadership.

Effective sustained silent reading programs have a number of benefits:

- They increase the amount of time students spend reading during the school day.
- They help students develop interest in a subject.
- They build knowledge that helps students read and learn more about a topic.
- They provide a basis for researching a particular topic.
- They familiarize students with different formats and genres used to report information that can be models for their own research and writing. (Worthy, Broaddus, & Ivey 2001)

Teacher Read-Alouds

Students in Maria Prieto's ninth-grade English class read excerpts from *The Diary of Anne Frank* (Frank 1967) in their literature anthology every year. This year she decided to enrich her students' study of the diary by reading aloud the informational book *Anne Frank: Beyond the Diary* (van der Rol & Verhoeven 1993). This visually appealing text contains background on the Frank family, including their move from Germany to Amsterdam, photographs of the diary itself, artifacts, maps of the "secret annex," and a heartbreaking primary source document—the Nazis' typewritten list of Frank family members targeted for arrest. Maria described her use of the book in the following way:

> Before my students start reading the diary, I read aloud Chapters 1 and 2. These chapters provide important background about Anne's life and information about Hitler's rise to power. I put the map of the "secret annex" that appears in the book on the document camera to give students a spatial understanding of the place where the Franks and the van Daans lived. Then my students read the diary. After they've completed their reading of the diary, I read chapters which describe how the Frank family was arrested and the later discovery of the diary. Finally, I read the section of the book that describes Anne's life after the arrest at the concentration camp at Bergen Belsen. After each reading, I passed the book around so that students could more closely examine the photographs. They were very interested in the book. I put several copies of the book in the classroom library and a number of students read it on their own after reading the diary.

This example demonstrates a number of purposes that content area read-alouds can accomplish. First, read-alouds can provide important background information that enhances student understanding of assigned readings. Maria's use of the map of the secret annex, for example, helped students visualize the setting for Anne Frank's experiences. Secondly, the read-aloud extended and enhanced the content in the diary itself by describing the rest of Anne Frank's tragic story. Third, reading aloud can spur student interest in a topic. After hearing a book read aloud, students are much more likely to pick up books this topic, and related ones, on their own.

Reading aloud is considered by many experts to be the single most important activity in developing student literacy ability, regardless of age. Reading aloud provides literary experiences in a supportive context and exposure to the various forms of written language, both narrative and expository. As students listen to literature, they unconsciously absorb its rhythms, structures, and cadences. Read-alouds give struggling readers access to information in the more difficult texts commonly used in content area classrooms.

In addition, read-alouds provide a way for teachers to demonstrate for students the mental processes used to make sense of what they are reading. These processes can become evident to students through many of the strategies described in this book, including think-alouds, directed reading–listening activities, and many others. Read-aloud experiences should go beyond brief isolated experiences during which the teacher reads and students listen. These "bigger" read-aloud experiences should be interactive, with students actively engaged in thinking, questioning, clarifying, and summarizing texts (Ivey 2002). Finally, read-alouds provide opportunities for response to literature that can lead to engagement and further understanding of content. These will be described in the following section.

Based on hundreds of read-aloud experiences, Barbara Erickson (1996) offers the following guidelines for middle and high school teachers who wish to incorporate reading aloud in their classes:

- Hold students' interest
- Stimulate discussion
- Reflect authors from many cultures
- Match the social and emotional levels of the listeners

Erickson also suggests that teachers prepare for read-alouds carefully by first practicing the work. She recommends that initial read-alouds last no longer than fifteen minutes. Furthermore, she advocates using pictures and props to heighten student interest and increase understanding of text content.

Read-alouds can include books from a variety of genres, including poetry, short stories, fiction, nonfiction, magazine articles, or even plays. Sharon Creech's (2001) *Love That Dog* is a perfect read-aloud for an English class; it uses free verse to explore the ways that poetry helps a young boy express his grief about losing his beloved dog. The poetic picture book *I See the Rhythm* (Igus 1998) is an ideal music class read-aloud. This stunning book traces the history of African American music through dramatic visuals and rhythmic poetry. An outstanding read-aloud for a world history class studying ancient civilizations is *Bodies from the Ash* (Deem 2005). This title provides fascinating glimpses of life in ancient Pompeii, based on the clues provided by the plaster cast remains of the unfortunate men, women, and children who died there.

At the beginning of a science lesson, an excerpt from a book read aloud to the class or a picture book can provide an enjoyable preview of the lesson's contents. In this way, trade books play a supporting role by introducing a part of or perspective on the lesson that entices students to want to learn more. The verbal imagery of the text or the visual stimuli of picture books appeal to all age groups and should help to activate schemata that are crucial to further learning. For example, an excellent introduction to a study of the planets is Elaine Scott's (2007) *When Is a Planet Not a Planet? The Story of Pluto*. In this clearly written text she outlines the history of the discovery of the planets and compares the work of scientists today with those of the past. Her explanation of modern-day scientists' skepticism surrounding Pluto's status as a planet and their development of new definitions for the term provide current information about what constitutes of a planet and the existence of dwarf planets.

RESPONSE JOURNAL

Identify a read-aloud book that you might use to introduce a unit or topic of study. Plan a lesson around the book, identifying follow-up discussion questions that you might use after you have read the book aloud.

Read-alouds need not be cover to cover. Reading excerpts from books, magazines, newspaper articles, or webpages can sometimes be more effective than longer read-alouds. "Bits and pieces" read-alouds include reading picture captions from nonfiction titles to provide "sneak previews" of books. Short read-alouds focusing on biographical profiles from any of the Kathleen Krull *Lives of* books can provide an engaging way to interest students in artists, musicians, presidents, and so on.

Group Models for Studying Trade Books

As teachers become increasingly convinced of the value of using literature in content area classrooms, they will want students to experience literature in increasingly varied ways. They may decide that students can benefit from "breaking out" of the textbook to engage in reading trade books, or they may use literature in connection with units of study. Many teachers use the additional time provided by block scheduling to engage students in reading and discussing trade books. One of the most challenging aspects of using literature in the classroom—whether fiction or nonfiction—is grouping students for instruction. The grouping pattern of choice depends on the teacher's and students' goals and purposes for using the literature. The following section will explain four different grouping models that teachers might wish to use as they involve students in studying content-related literature.

Whole-Group/Single-Book Model

Sometimes teachers want all students in a class to have a common reading experience centered on the same book. On these occasions they may use a whole-group model in which all students read the same book. Science teacher Ken Blake wanted to extend his textbook's treatment of outer space and space travel. He decided to involve his students in reading *Team Moon: How 400,000 People Landed Apollo 11 on the Moon* (Thimmesh 2006).

Because this was the first time he had used literature to supplement the textbook, he decided to use the whole-group/single-book model. He purchased twenty-five copies of the book, and each student read the book. Students then participated in large- and small-group discussions about a variety of topics, including the work of the astronauts during the flight and the discoveries they made as they explored the moon. Students also compared and contrasted information in their textbook to that found in this book. They considered the challenges posed by the expedition and debated the importance of sending astronauts for further explorations of the moon.

Small-Groups/Multiple-Books Model

A second model for using literature is the small-groups/multiple-books model. With this model, students work in small groups to read different books related to a common theme. Alan Trent used multiple copies of several fiction and nonfiction titles to supplement textbook content and enrich his students' study of the Civil War. Students formed groups based on their selection of one of four different books: *Hear the Wind Blow* (Hahn 2003), *The War Within: A Novel of the Civil War* (Matas 2001), *Fields of Fury: The American Civil War* (McPherson 2002), and *The Boys' War: Confederate and Union Soldiers Talk About the Civil War* (Murphy 1990). Students read and discussed each title in their small groups over a two-week period. Using the jigsaw strategy, students then formed new groups in which they shared their information. They then shared the information obtained from one another with the larger group through creative extensions, including projects, dramatic presentations, and debates.

RESPONSE JOURNAL

Identify three different trade books related to your discipline that students could read in small groups. Select titles that provide different points of view about a particular topic or issue related to your content area. Identify two ways that students in each group might share the perspective provided by the book they read with other members of the class.

Individual Inquiry Model

Individual inquiry is an increasingly popular method to involve students in research by letting them explore issues of personal interest. As part of inquiry experiences, students generate ideas and questions and pose problems. Through their research projects, students investigate topics and collect, analyze, and organize information. Students later present this information through a project or report. By using several sources about the same topic, students can examine multiple points of view and evaluate the accuracy of information.

Inquiry projects can combine fiction with nonfiction. In an inquiry project with high school students, English teacher Joan Kaywell (1994) linked fiction and nonfiction books. Her class first generated a list of problems affecting today's teens such as anorexia nervosa, stress, suicide, pregnancy, sexual abuse, and so on. The class narrowed the number of topics to five and formed inquiry groups based on each topic. At this point, each student in a group selected and read a different young adult novel related to the identified problem.

After reading their novels, students used nonfiction materials to conduct research about the problem posed in their novel. Each student found at least one nonfiction source and cited a minimum of ten facts related to the topic. Students then reconvened in small groups where they pooled these facts and selected twenty-five facts to be included in an information sheet about the problem. They discussed source credibility, recency, and relevancy of information as they narrowed down their lists. They then presented this information to the larger group.

Reader Response Strategies

Reader response refers to the way a person reacts to hearing or reading a piece of literature. It describes the unique interaction that occurs between a reader's mind and heart and a particular literary text (Hancock 2007). Reader responses are dynamic, fluid, and varied. Different readers construct different meanings from texts; no two readers interpret the same work in the same way.

Why should content area teachers be interested in responses to literature? Research suggests that students grow in several different areas when engaged in response-based activities:

- They develop ownership of their reading and their responses.
- They make personal connections with literature.
- They gain appreciation for multiple interpretations and tolerance for ambiguity.
- They become more critical readers and attain higher levels of thinking and richer understandings of literature.
- They increase their repertoire of responses to literature.
- They begin to view themselves as successful readers.
- They develop greater awareness of the literary quality of a work. (Spiegel 1998)

Involving students in response to literature can help content area teachers meet many important goals related to developing student thinking skills. Response activities can help to develop critical thinkers: Students who can examine different sides of an argument respond more thoughtfully to texts and more thoroughly understand the ways texts work.

Response-centered classrooms can help students grow in their understanding and appreciation of nonfiction just as surely as fiction. Teachers often assume that nonfiction literature will elicit only efferent responses, but studies have found that readers do respond aesthetically to nonfiction (Hancock 2007). Effective teachers guide students' responses to biographies and informational books in ways that encourage both efferent and aesthetic responses. By providing a supportive context and engaging activities that promote both oral and written responses, teachers can extend and deepen students' literary experiences with both nonfiction and fiction.

The rest of this chapter is devoted to examples of instructional strategies teachers can use to promote responses to literature. Strategies for promoting responses range from writing to drama to inquiry-driven idea circles. All of the strategies described are designed to help teachers encourage meaningful student responses, both aesthetic and efferent, to the excellent literature available today. Through reader response experiences, students can make personal connections between texts and their lives, reflect on what these books have to teach them, and deepen their involvement with literature.

Writing as a Reader Response

Writing in response to reading, whether fiction or nonfiction, allows learners to share their thoughts and feelings about a text. It can help students construct meanings of texts at the same time it improves writing fluency. Writing in response to nonfiction can evoke feelings and enhance learning of text content. As noted in Chapter 9, "writing to learn" can help students think about what they will be reading or reflect on what has been read. It can improve understanding of difficult concepts, increase retention of information, prompt learners to elaborate on and manipulate ideas, and help them gain insight into the author's craft. A variety of written response activities encourages students to think in different ways. Some response activities described in this section focus on helping students respond emotionally to texts, others on helping them process information or record what they have learned. Some of the activities are formal, while others are informal in nature.

Reflective Writing

One of the many excellent ideas presented in Stephanie Harvey and Anne Goudvis's (2007) *Strategies That Work* is the idea of asking students to use writing to reflect on the mental connections they make between the texts they are reading and their own lives. As students grow in sophistication, they develop the ability to recognize the mental connections they make between the texts they read and other texts, as well as between the texts they are reading and the wider world. Harvey and Goudis refer to these connections as *text-to-self, text-to-text,* and *text-to-world* connections, respectively. It is possible for students to make these connections with books from any genre.

Text-to-self connections arise when readers feel personal connections with text events or character's emotions. Harvey recommends using memoirs or realistic fiction to help students develop skills in making text-to-self connections, because reader identification with characters can be particularly strong in these types of texts. Saying "It reminds me of . . ." can prompt students to reflect on these types of connections.

Text-to-text connections involve connecting ideas across texts. The concept of *text* can be broadened here; students might connect text content to a movie or song, for example. These connections include comparing characters' personalities and actions, story events and plot lines, and lesson themes or messages in stories; finding common themes, writing styles, or perspectives in an author's work; and comparing the treatment of common themes by different authors.

Text-to-world connections are the most sophisticated connections students can make. With these types of connections, students reflect on the relationship between the content of the text and the wider world. This could include connections related to world events, issues, or concerns.

Post-It Notes

Harvey recommends that teachers use think-alouds and other text demonstrations to model for students how readers naturally create these connections. After this modeling occurs, students can begin to record the various kinds of connections on Post-it notes as they read, jotting down words or phrases that explain the thoughts or feelings that occur to them as they read. As they read and record these connections, students can code text-to-self connections (T-S), text-to-text connections (T-T), and text-to-world connections (T-W). Students should not focus solely on recording and categorizing their connections, but should reflect on how the connection has led them to greater understanding of the text. These notes can serve as the basis for rich postreading discussions about the kinds of thinking students have done as they read. In addition, these notes can often evolve into longer written pieces.

Expository Texts as Models for Writing

Students need a variety of writing experiences in the classroom, including experience in writing nonnarrative texts. One way to involve students in informational writing is by having them use information trade books as models for their own writing. These books can serve as models for brief, short-term writing experiences or extended, long-term experiences.

The Important Book (Brown 1949), though a picture book, can serve as a model for information writing in many content areas. Each paragraph of this book states an important characteristic, or main idea, about a common object. This trait is followed by supporting details that further enhance the description of the object and then a restatement of the main idea. Leslie Hughes, a middle school science teacher, used this text structure during a review of a unit on oceans. The teacher read the model to the class and provided students with the following text frame:

The important thing about _______ is ___________.

Students then formed writing groups and were assigned particular topics related to oceans. They identified the main ideas related to their topic and inserted it into the text frame. They provided supporting details and concluded the writing with a restatement of the main idea. An example of one student's effort follows:

> The important thing about a tide pool is that it contains a community of plants and animals. Tide pools are left in rocky basins and shallow hollows as low tide causes ocean water to go back out to sea. These basins of sea water contain plants, crabs, periwinkles, and other plant and animal life. But the important thing about tide pools is that they contain a community of plants and animals.

Dozens of nonfiction books can provide models for inquiry-related writing. *My Season with Penguins: An Antarctic Journal* (Webb 2000) is a field journal maintained by biologist Sophie Webb. This title could serve as a model for students' own field journals in a science class. Examples of books that model the use of interviews and oral history abound. One of the finest is *Oh Freedom! Kids Talk About the Civil Rights Movement* (King & Osborne 1997). This book was actually created by young people; the students interviewed friends, family members, and neighbors who told the story of the civil rights movement from their own perspectives. The result is an amazing oral history of that turbulent time. Teachers could involve students in conducting their own oral history interviews related to topics of study in a social studies class.

Process Drama as a Heuristic

Responding to literature through drama provides a wealth of opportunities for enhancing student engagement in learning. *Process drama* experiences allow students to establish an imaginary world in which they experience fictional roles and situations. Process drama differs from other forms of drama in that it does not involve the use of scripts; instead students themselves compose and rehearse episodes that continue over time, and audience is integral to the process (O'Neill 1995). Like reading, drama requires that students make meaning based on the reading that they have done. However, with drama, this meaning-making takes on a visual component. That is, students externalize the visual images they create from a text and incorporate thought, language, and movement to demonstrate their learning. Through drama, they enter the world of the text, whether fiction or nonfiction, which lets students observe and reflect on that world.

Students reshape learning obtained through print into a dramatic form. Dramatic activities encourage changes in student thinking and promote positive experiences with literature. Many struggling readers have difficulty creating mental images as they read. Dramatic activities scaffold this image making in a motivating and meaningful way.

These activities can generate interest and help students enter a text, seeing and feeling the emotions of the characters or experiencing the events described. By combining reading with dramatic experiences, teachers help students enhance their oral language skills through listening and speaking, thereby developing vocabulary and reading fluency. Dramatic activities encourage learners to listen for cues and learn to use their voices to convey emotion. In addition, they help students develop self-confidence and cooperative learning skills. These activities also offer a natural entry point into the world of writing; students can move from simply dramatizing the words of others to creating their own scripts that can be performed.

For many students, drama heightens understanding of the often dense and complex expository material found in today's nonfiction. It can enhance student understanding of both technical vocabulary and specific content-related concepts. It can motivate students to explore the content of these books more deeply. Most of all, it can bring abstract information to life, making it concrete and therefore comprehensible, which can be particularly helpful for struggling readers or English language learners.

Dramatic responses to literature have other benefits as well. Responses of this type require in-depth familiarity with the text to be dramatized. Generally learners need repeated exposure to a text before they can formulate a response to it. This repeated exposure could be particularly beneficial for struggling readers.

Improvisational Drama

Improvisational drama involves students in active response to literature and encourages them to use their imaginations. It is beneficial for students of all ages, many of whom find dramatic play extremely motivating. Improvisational responses to fiction and nonfiction help students mediate texts in ways that make them interesting, memorable, and comprehensible. When creating improvisational drama, teachers create structures that allow students to explore important themes found in the books they read. In one scene in *The Giver* (Lowry 1993), for example, Jonas and the Giver talk about the fact that Jonas could be lost and that all his received memories could be released on people who have never experienced painful memories. In an improvisation based on this book, students could assume roles as members of the society and receive memories for the first time. They could describe this event and the feelings they experience as a result of it (Temple, Martinez, Yokota, & Naylor 2005). Through this dramatic activity, students deepen their understanding of *The Giver* and the people whose lives it explores. Such experiences provide a nice change of pace in the classroom. Students not only enjoy these activities but also appear to retain much of the information presented as a result of the dramatizations.

Other more structured forms of dramatic response can sensitize students to expository text organization. For example, after reading *The Heart and Blood (How Our Bodies Work)* (Burgess 1988) a middle grade teacher involved her students in a dramatic activity designed to demonstrate the sequence by which blood flows through the heart. One half of the class carried red sheets of construction paper to represent oxygenated blood and the other carried blue to represent deoxygenated blood. Eight students then paired up to act as valve gatekeepers. Student desks were arranged in the shape of the heart, and stations represented the lungs and other body parts. Students moved around the room, simulating the flow of blood through the heart and other organs, then wrote about the activity in their learning logs (Moss 2003).

Pantomime

Pantomime is another form of response useful with content-related texts. It requires learners to communicate using their bodies, without relying on verbal communication. Students might enjoy creating pantomimes in response to Aliki's (1983) *A Medieval*

Feast. This particular book contains many scenes that students could pantomime, including depictions of turning boars on the spit, fencing fields, and sounding trumpets (Stewig & Buege 1994). Nicholas Reeves's (1992) *Into the Mummy's Tomb* could stimulate dramatizations of building of the pyramids, the burial of Tutankhamen, the process of mummification, or the purposes of the artifacts found in the tomb.

Tableau

Tableau or snapshot drama is another motivational dramatic response activity. Tableaus are silent performances that involve three-dimensional representations. A tableau typically involves no movement, talking, or props, only gestures. Students freeze moments in time and demonstrate the physical or emotional relationships and character gestures or activities. Typically, teachers give students time to plan their tableau in small groups. Each group comes to the front of the class and the teacher gives a "one, two, three, freeze" cue. The audience then discusses the tableau, offering their interpretations of what they see.

This activity works extremely well with all kinds of texts, including poetry, fantasies, realistic fiction, biographies, or information books. For example, small groups could create tableaus related to selected poems from Cynthia Rylant's (1984) *Waiting to Waltz*. Or, small groups of students could select and read different texts related to a common theme and select a scene to dramatize. Each person in the group would assume a role in the drama. After practicing, students could create their "frozen moments." The other students in the class could then attempt to identify the scene portrayed.

Readers Theatre

Readers theatre differs from process drama in that it involves oral presentation of a script by two or more readers. No props, costumes, or memorization of lines is required. Students must, however, read their parts fluently, with appropriate dramatic flair. Readers theatre is often used with folktales or narrative text, but can be used with nonfiction as well.

Information books and biographies with dialogue are easily adapted to this format, but picture books, short stories, or excerpts from longer books can also be quite effective. The following guidelines can help teachers adapt nonfiction texts to a readers theatre script:

1. Select an interesting section of text containing the desired content.
2. Reproduce the text.
3. Delete lines not critical to the content being emphasized, including those that indicate that a character is speaking.
4. Decide how to divide the parts for the readers. Assign dialogue to appropriate characters. With some texts, it will be necessary to rewrite text as dialogue or with multiple narrators. Changing third-person point of view to first-person (I or we) can create effective narration.

5. Add a prologue to introduce the script in storylike fashion. If needed, a postscript can be added to bring closure to the script.
6. Label the readers' parts by placing the speaker's name in the left-hand margin, followed by a colon.
7. After the script is finished, ask others to read it aloud. Students can then make revisions based on what they hear. Give students time to read and rehearse their parts (Young & Vardell 1993).

An obvious next step is to involve students in selecting books from which they can develop their own readers theatre scripts. Through this activity, learners develop critical thinking skills, make decisions, work cooperatively, and practice the process of revision.

Idea Circles

Another excellent way for students to respond to trade books is through the use of idea circles. Idea circles represent the small-group/multiple-text model of organizing the classroom for literature study. They involve students in small-group peer-led discussions of concepts fueled by reading experiences with multiple texts (Guthrie & McCann 1996). Idea circles are an ideal way to promote peer-directed conceptual understanding of virtually any aspect of content area learning. This conceptual learning involves three basic ingredients: facts, relationships between facts, and explanations.

Idea circles not only engage students in learning about science and social studies, but they also require engagement in a variety of literacy activities, including locating information, evaluating the quality and relevance of information, summarizing information for their peers, and determining relationships among information found in a variety of sources. They require that students learn to integrate information, ideas, and viewpoints. In addition, they involve students in a variety of important collaborative processes including turn taking, maintaining group member participation, and coaching one another in the use of literacy strategies (Guthrie & McCann 1996).

Idea circles share some things in common with literature circles. Like literature circles, they involve three to six students in directed small-group discussions. Like literature circles, idea circles are peer led and involve student-generated rules. However, idea circles involve students in discussion surrounding the learning of a particular concept, rather than a discussion centering on a single literary text. In literature circle discussions, students may have conflicting interpretations of a piece of literature. With idea circles, students work together to create a common understanding of a concept by constructing abstract understanding from facts and details. Another difference between literature circles and idea circles is in the use of texts. With literature circles, students all read and respond to a single text. With idea circles, each student may interact with a different text in preparation for the group discussion. Then during the discussion, students share the unique information that they have found. Furthermore, idea circle discussions require the use of informational rather than literary texts.

The teacher begins the idea circle experience by presenting students with a goal in the form of a topic or question. An example of a question might be, "What is a desert?" Before the idea circle meets, students can either read extensively from relevant informational trade books or read and discuss their findings concurrently. Information that students bring to the group comes from prior experiences and discussions with others, as well as from their readings. In their groups, students exchange facts, discuss relationships among ideas, and offer explanations. As this linking together of facts continues, students create a conceptual framework around a topic or question. Individuals offer information, check it against the information found by others, and discuss more deeply. Students continually challenge one another regarding the accuracy and relevance of their information. Through this checking, students are encouraged to search for information, comprehend the texts being used, and synthesize information from multiple sources. When conflicts arise, students search their sources to clarify conflicting information. Ultimately, the group must weave together the important details that all students contribute.

Getting Started with Idea Circles

Here's how to use idea circles in your classroom:

1. Decide whether to engage the entire class in idea circles simultaneously or start with a single team and gradually add more.
2. Identify appropriate topics of study. The topic should be interesting, explanatory, and expansive. In addition, the topic should contain natural categories or subtopics.
3. Set clear goals for what each group should accomplish during their discussions. Students may complete data charts, semantic maps, or other graphic organizers.
4. Provide students with a rich array of trade books and other resources at a variety of levels related to the topic under study.
5. Make sure students have read and learned about the topic before participating in the idea circle.
6. Post student-generated interaction rules so that students know how to function in their groups.

When used as part of a unit of study, idea circles are most effective when placed at the middle or end of a unit.

During a social studies exploration of the mound-building tribes in Ohio, teacher Ann Craig involved her students in an inquiry project using idea circles.

She divided students into three different groups, with each assigned to study a different mound-builder tribe—the Hopewells, the Adenas, and the Fort Ancient. Ms. Craig focused student inquiry through questions like these: What were some of the purposes of the mounds? Where did each tribe live in Ohio? Why are they no longer in existence? Students consulted a variety of different sources, including trade books, textbooks, websites, and so on, to locate answers to these questions. Finally, the groups were reconfigured so that each contained an Adena expert, a Hopewell expert, and a Fort Ancient expert. The final product for the idea circle was for each group to complete a data chart comparing and contrasting each of the three tribes.

As you can see, books have the power to expand our vision, link us with people from the past, present, and future, and widen our vision of the world. The dialogue that is created between a book and its reader can be a powerful one—it can confuse or perplex us, unnerve us, move us to laughter or tears, or urge us to social action. It can satisfy our curiosity or make us see old ideas in completely new ways. By complementing textbook content with trade books and involving students in opportunities to respond to those books, we can help to ensure that students view the work of the scientist, the historian, or the musician as more than just knowing the facts about a topic—recognizing that such work involves interpretation, reflection, and consideration of multiple points of view.

Using Technology to Respond to Literature

Today's students are technology savvy. They have grown up with cell phones, the Internet, and iPods. They memorized e-mail addresses before house addresses. Teenagers spend a great deal of time on the Internet, communicating, networking, and gaming. As we stated in Chapter 1, teachers need to understand that these activities are acts of literacy. Students are reading and writing and critically thinking, even as they "play." To maintain student interest and to use what they already know, teachers can capitalize on students' digital immersion to further their learning and comprehension of texts. Teachers may even be able to raise the status of reading in the personal lives of students.

Students are forming book clubs (among other clubs) on social networks such as MySpace and Facebook. Such venues enable students from a variety of places to participate in online discussions about anything. The efficacy of book clubs relies on the contributions of members; as people negotiate thoughts, opinions, and interpretations, greater understanding is achieved. Teachers can set up an Internet community of readers and facilitate reading discussions that go beyond the classroom. Per social networking norms, responses are brief and unedited, but the key here is quantity, not necessarily quality. Also, the comments are documented and can be saved for future analysis. In the classroom, teachers can ask students to elaborate and explicate.

Blogging

Blogging about books can also be effective. Two popular blogging sites for adolescents are LiveJournal (www.livejournal.com) and Blogger (www.blogger.com). As we saw in earlier chapters, many students write and read blogs on a daily basis. These blogs may not necessarily be about books, as people blog about anything and everything under the sun. However, teachers can encourage students to blog about books and also to read other people's blogs about books. All bloggers also have a space for comments and questions. Again, it is customary to write many short responses. The idea is to help students build momentum around reading and writing about reading. For this generation, it is probably easier to build a sense of community via the Internet.

The fan fiction sites are fascinating, especially www.fanfiction.net. Fan fiction is a phenomenon that was around long before the Internet; however, it is becoming a popular vehicle for young readers and writers. Essentially, fans write fictional pieces in the same vein as their idols and publish these pieces online. For example, *Harry Potter* fans have the opportunity to make up fiction about the famous magician; fans have written about Harry's married life with Ginny, his early years with the Dursleys, his inner monologues, and so on, in the manner of J. K. Rowling. In this manner, fans can fill in gaps, write from the perspective of secondary characters, and/or extend or elaborate on specific scenes. Fans can also write literary crossovers (e.g., Harry Potter in Dante's *Inferno*).

There are rules for fan fiction. Fans cannot contribute pieces "out of canon," meaning fans must be true to the author or genre. Pieces generally include the following components: disclaimer, peer-review process (space for comments), rating, short commentary about context, and a request for reviews. True to their stage of development, adolescent fan fiction writers want approval and feedback. These writers are doing everything that we want them to do in the classroom: They are negotiating and navigating texts and they are writing and revising based on critical feedback. Why not make this a classroom assignment?

Googledocs

Googledocs is another great tool for encouraging collaborative writing. The key to using these various Internet practices is to recognize that users, in this case our adolescent students, are seeking attention and collaboration by participating and contributing to a social and public network. That being said, Googledocs allows students to work on and to share a single doc. All one needs is a gmail.com address, which is free of charge. All the members of a Googlegroup have access to Googledocs and can actively view and make changes to a particular document in real time.

Technology allows us to extend learning beyond the four walls of the classroom; it also gives us an opportunity to connect with our students and to motivate them. It provides students with choices about when and where they log in. As active members of their respective Internet communities, students experience pride of ownership in their writing and thoughts. Teachers do need to explain the advantages and disadvantages of making personal lives and thoughts public, as teenagers tend to forget that their published words have permanence.

LOOKING BACK LOOKING FORWARD

Trade books in content area classrooms can extend and enrich information across the curriculum. Textbooks generally are unable to treat subject matter with the depth and breadth necessary to fully develop ideas and concepts and engage students in critical inquiry. Trade books have the potential to capture students' interests and imagination in people, places, events, and ideas.

Whereas textbooks compress information, trade books provide students with intensive and extensive involvement in a subject. Trade books offer students a variety of interesting, relevant, and comprehensible text experiences. With trade books, students are likely to develop an interest in and an emotional commitment to a subject. Trade books are schema builders. Reading books helps students generate background knowledge and provides them with vicarious experiences. Many kinds of trade books, both nonfiction and fiction, can be used in tandem with textbooks.

Access to books within the content area classroom helps ensure that students are exposed to content in a variety of formats. By creating classroom libraries, providing time for reading, and reading aloud to students, teachers increase the possibility that students will become lifelong readers.

By involving students in reading and responding to trade books through writing, drama, and inquiry activities such as idea circles, teachers move students from the solitary act of reading to building community around texts through peer interaction. In sharing their responses to literature, whether written or oral, students learn to reflect more deeply on the meanings of texts and connect more personally to the texts that they read. They begin to see that reactions to texts are as varied as the students in a particular classroom, and that by understanding each person's response to a text we come to understand our humanity and ourselves more fully.

In the concluding chapter of this book, we focus our attention on the role of the *literacy coach* as an instructional support for teachers. The literacy coach often collaborates with a schoolwide academic team to develop and implement a comprehensive plan to increase students' academic achievement. The work of literacy coaches varies from school to school. Often, however, it involves organizing professional development workshops for content area teachers, observing and providing feedback on classroom instruction, modeling effective literacy strategies, and leading all teachers in ongoing reflection and inquiry about their classroom practices.

Minds On

1. Read this statement: "One way of thinking about a textbook is that it takes a subject and distills it to its minimal essentials. In doing so, a textbook runs the risk of taking world-shaking events, monumental discoveries, profound insights, intriguing and faraway places, colorful and influential people, and life's mysteries and processes and compressing them into a series of matter-of-fact statements." Can you think of a book you have read that opened new or more perspectives on a topic of which you had previously had only textbook knowledge? What do you believe is the ideal balance between the use of textbooks and the use of fiction books, nonfiction books, and picture books in a content classroom?

2. To what extent do you believe students should participate in the selection of documents from websites for use in a content course? Would you answer this question differently for students of various ages?

3. You are one of only a few content area teachers in your school who regularly reads aloud to

their students. After observing you, your principal suggests that teacher read-alouds represent a waste of instructional time that might be used more profitably. Write a letter to the principal that provides a thoughtful response to this criticism.

4. Reflect on some of the reader response activities you have experienced as a student, either in middle school, high school, or college. These could include discussions, dramatic activities, writing, or other types of activities. How did participation in these kinds of activities influence your understanding of or reaction to the text you were studying?

Hands On

1. Select two nonfiction trade books that you are considering for use in the classroom. The two titles should relate to the same topic—preferably one your students are actually studying. Read the two books, and analyze them in terms of their quality, using the criteria identified in Table 11.1. Which book do you think is most appropriate for use in the classroom and why? Then compare the two titles in terms of their treatment of the topic. How are they alike? How are they different? In what ways do they support or extend information provided in the textbook? Come to class prepared to share your analysis.
2. Select two picture books that you might coordinate with a particular unit you now teach or with a unit you have planned or observed. Explain why you chose these particular books and how you will use them to motivate your students. Describe the activities that will follow the initial use or reading of the book.
3. Create a text set consisting of at least six titles related to a topic of study in your classroom. Select at least one of the books from the text set and plan a read-aloud lesson using the book. Then, decide how your students might respond to the book through discussion, writing, or drama. Come to class prepared to read the book and have your classmates participate in the response activity.

eRESOURCES

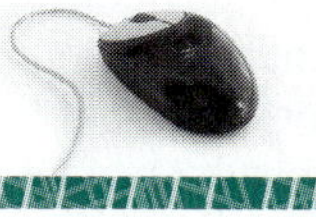

- There are many websites that will help you locate books of interest to your students. Visit one of the following sites that provide useful information on children's literature: the Children's Literature Web Guide (**www.ucalgary.ca/~dkbrown**) and the Assembly on Literature for Adolescents Review (ALAN Review) (**http://scholar.lib.vt.edu/ejournals/ALAN**). Browse these sites for information relevant to your content area. Share your findings in small groups and discuss the ways teachers might use these sites.
- To find lesson plans and resources for using literature, go to **www.cloudnet.com/~edrbsass/edadolescentlit.htm**. Explore the various lessons for your own content area.

CHAPTER 12

For every problem there is one solution which is simple, neat, and wrong.

—H. L. Mencken

Literacy Coaching

ORGANIZING PRINCIPLE

Literacy coaches contribute to the development and implementation of planned, reflective, and inquiry-based professional development leading to improved instruction.

Teachers are professionals. Their preparation does not end with their initial licensure but is an ongoing process, much like that of a developing reader and writer. To be sure, a certain amount of growth occurs naturally, as colleagues observe each other teach, share worthwhile innovations and strategies, and make decisions about instruction. Yet teachers also need purposeful, planned support similar to that given students who are developing core ideas and concepts in content areas.

Teachers are at different stages in their careers, as well as different levels of expertise in their craft. The National Council for Accreditation of Teacher Education (NCATE, 2009) describes the continuum of educator preparation and development. First, teachers acquire subject matter and general knowledge; next, they refine their content knowledge and build a foundation of pedagogical knowledge and skills; then, they work as a student teacher or intern, often receiving an initial or novice teaching license in the process. As they continue to build their experience and skills, teachers progress to securing a professional license, and can eventually achieve advanced license in an area of specialization. Ongoing professional development is essential for progressing through the more advanced levels of this continuum. Literacy coaches provide support by understanding that diversity exists

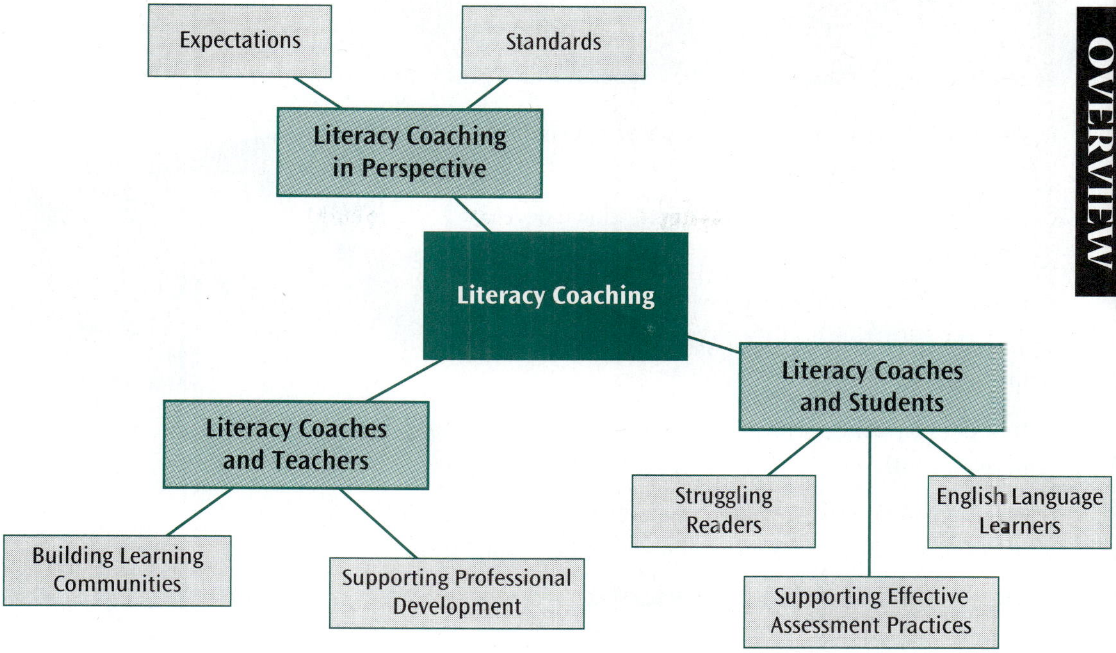

among teachers and by planning for active and meaningful adult learning in professional communities.

When coaches learn to reflect on what is happening in classrooms, and to tap into the immense body of practical knowledge acquired through teaching experience, they can help to facilitate more reflective teaching and effective professional growth. Engaging in collaboration with colleagues and participating in strategies such as writing, dialogue, problem solving, and technology use provide support for teachers who seek to improve their teaching. In doing so, teachers become both targets and agents of change (Bean 2004).

To avoid becoming a target, effective literacy coaches and teachers alike know there are few "right" or quick solutions. Working with teachers and students in content areas demands an authentic problem-solving process in order to promote growth and change. And that takes time.

In this chapter, we begin with an overview of how the role of the literacy coach has evolved through the years, explain the current expectations of that role, and summarize the recommended standards by professional organizations for middle and high school literacy coaching. We discuss how coaches can work effectively with teachers by building learning communities, conferring with teachers, and supporting professional development. Examples are provided of literacy coaches supporting teachers in their work with struggling readers, English language learners, and different assessment systems. The organizing principle of this chapter underscores the role of literacy coaching in creating powerful adult learning situations: **Literacy coaches contribute to the development and implementation of planned, reflective, and inquiry-based professional development leading to improved instruction.**

FRAME OF MIND

1. Why is it important for teachers to participate in ongoing professional development?
2. How can literacy coaches support professional development for teachers?
3. How has the role of the literacy coach changed over time?
4. What are the current expectations and standards for literacy coaches?
5. How does building a school learning community support professional development?
6. What can literacy coaches do to support struggling readers, English language learners, and effective assessment practices in schools?

Literacy Coaching in Perspective

Including specialists in schools as part of the literacy team to provide guidance for classroom teachers and address students' literacy issues is widely accepted. The roles these educators fulfill, however, have changed over the years (Mraz, Algozzine, & Watson 2008). During the 1960s the primary responsibility of the reading specialist was to work directly with struggling readers in small groups or in pull-out programs, where students received specialized instruction outside of their regular classrooms. Often, there was little collaboration between the classroom teacher and the specialist about the type of instruction a student received in the pull-out setting (Dole 2004). As concerns about the effectiveness of these programs led to a shift toward in-class collaborative instruction between reading specialists and classroom teachers, the specialist's role was expanded from working solely with students to shared leadership and coaching responsibilities to improve the quality of classroom instruction (Bean 2004; Bean, Cassidy, Grumet, Shelton, & Wallis 2002).

Recent policy initiatives, such as the No Child Left Behind Act (U.S. Department of Education 2001), and the development of standards and mandated assessments have prompted policy makers to examine both literacy practices and the preparation and continuing education of those responsible for implementing literacy programs (Bean 2004; Fulton & Porter 2000). Shifting the role of a reading specialist from teaching students to coaching teachers has been one initiative designed to improve reading instruction by providing ongoing, consistent, and relevant professional development to teachers.

How does a literacy coach differ from a traditional reading specialist? Some middle and high school literacy coaches continue to work with small groups of students on a limited basis (Guth & Pettengill 2005). Appropriate assistance for students with severe reading difficulties remains a priority, and schools often rely on literacy professionals to provide support for these students (IRA 2005). At long last, there is recognition that literacy coaches need to be familiar with the characteristics of adult learners so that they can more effectively offer guidance and support to teachers who want to refine their instructional practices.

Titles used to describe reading professionals vary greatly from region to region and often from school to school. In many states, "reading specialist" is a certification or licensure earned by teachers through advanced preparation (usually a master's degree) related to reading or literacy. Many reports advocate that coaches hold this certificate before coaching, if at all possible (e.g., Guth & Pettengill 2005; IRA 2005; Sturtevant 2003). Other common titles for individuals engaged in literacy coaching include academic facilitator, literacy facilitator, curriculum coach, and academic coach (IRA 2006).

Current Expectations for Literacy Coaches

To support teachers in meeting the needs of diverse adolescents, districts across North America are hiring literacy coaches whose primary role is to provide continuing professional development for teachers. Although the new role of the literacy coach is similar to the role that some reading professionals held in secondary schools as early as the 1960s and 1970s, when schools with federal grant funds hired reading specialists to provide "resource" assistance to other teachers (Anders 2002), today literacy coaches often have more multifaceted roles than their predecessors. As Sturtevant (2003) and Toll (2005) explain, literacy coaches in middle and high schools are seen as teacher leaders and may be expected to do the following:

- Mentor individual teachers
- Model and observe in classrooms
- Work with study groups and teacher teams
- Lead a schoolwide literacy council
- Advise administrators on the school literacy program
- Collaborate with literacy coaches in other schools
- Administer and monitor literacy assessments
- Work with parents and/or community groups

The list of potential responsibilities for literacy coaches can be overwhelming, especially when one considers that middle and high schools with hundreds or thousands of students often have only one literacy coach. In other schools, the position of literacy coach may be held by a professional who also has teaching responsibilities. The Alliance for Excellent Education, an education advocacy group in Washington, D.C., recommends that schools hire one coach for every twenty teachers, for maximum effectiveness (Hall 2004). It is also important for educators in local districts and schools to create school plans that clarify what is expected of literacy coaches (NASSP 2005). Coaches should participate in this process and the outcomes should be communicated to all constituency groups, including teachers and administrators.

RTI for Struggling Adolescent Learners

BOX 12.1

The Role of Literacy Coaches

As we emphasize throughout this chapter, literacy coaches provide essential leadership for schools to address the needs of all learners, including struggling readers and writers. RTI in practice increases the need for literacy coaches and specialists in schools (IRA 2008; Stecker, Fuchs, & Fuchs 2008). Because RTI requires schools to implement evidence-based practices and prepare effective teachers, literacy coaches serve a valuable role in offering professional development to faculty and staff. Literacy coaches, as we discuss in detail in this chapter, can organize workshops and study groups to help teachers understand the variety of reasons students may struggle with reading in content area classes.

Understanding the learner and the nature of the reading tasks required in content area curricula is the first step toward developing instruction that helps students become more successful in meeting the literacy demands of school. A next step would be to help teachers develop expertise in using appropriate literacy strategies in their teaching. For example, after learning the importance of activating and building background knowledge, study group members might explore different types of anticipatory activities to use with their classes. Literacy coaches could then model lessons for teachers in different grade levels or in different content areas and observe and conference with teachers as they try out new ideas. Literacy coaches could also work with small groups of teachers or individuals to look at student work samples and assess what types of difficulties students are having. Although instruction focused on literacy improvement in the content classroom would benefit all students, significantly struggling adolescent learners would arguably gain the most through new access to core curriculum texts that previously may have been beyond their grasp.

Moreover, we contend that literacy coaches can provide leadership in professional collaboration among specialists in the school. At many middle and high schools, individual and small-group instruction for struggling learners is provided by a mix of special education teachers, ESOL teachers, speech language pathologists, certified reading teachers, paraprofessionals, and volunteer tutors. Literacy coaches, as leaders of the school literacy program, can provide an invaluable service by encouraging communication among these groups and by helping them work together to provide effective services for students. Coaches can also work collaboratively with library and media specialists to develop a collection of print and technological resources to meet the needs of struggling readers, and they can help teachers review potential materials and programs designed for struggling readers before purchases are made.

At a whole-school level, literacy coaches often organize literacy leadership teams (NASSP 2005). Literacy teams conduct assessments about the overall literacy achievement and needs of different groups of learners and then systematically plan ways to support both student learning and the professional development of teachers. Although struggling readers are a diverse group and can be defined in a wide variety of ways, all students in middle or high school who struggle to meet course expectations due to difficulties in reading need specialized attention in the school literacy plan.

Mraz, Algozzine, and Kissel (2009) describe the roles of the literacy coach, as illustrated in Figure 12.1. Coaches help teachers *plan for instruction.* Effective instruction is not as simple as selecting a content area textbook and then assigning students to read and answer questions at the end of each chapter. Effective instruction requires teachers to be knowledgeable and reflective about their instructional practice and the research that informs it. Teachers must apply that knowledge to their instructional decision-making process in order to meet the diverse learning needs of students. Through ongoing collaboration and problem solving, literacy coaches can help teachers to plan reflective and effective instruction for their students.

Coaches support teachers in *developing manageable routines.* Managing includes organizing materials needed for instruction, scheduling time productively, and creating an engaging learning environment. Literacy coaches also help teachers prepare for instruction by offering support and advice on setting and communicating expectations and rules to students, communicating the consequences of desired and undesired behaviors, and handling disruptions effectively and efficiently.

Delivering instruction involves presenting content, monitoring student learning, and adjusting instruction. Each of these elements can be supported by effective

FIGURE 12.1 Roles of Literacy Coaches

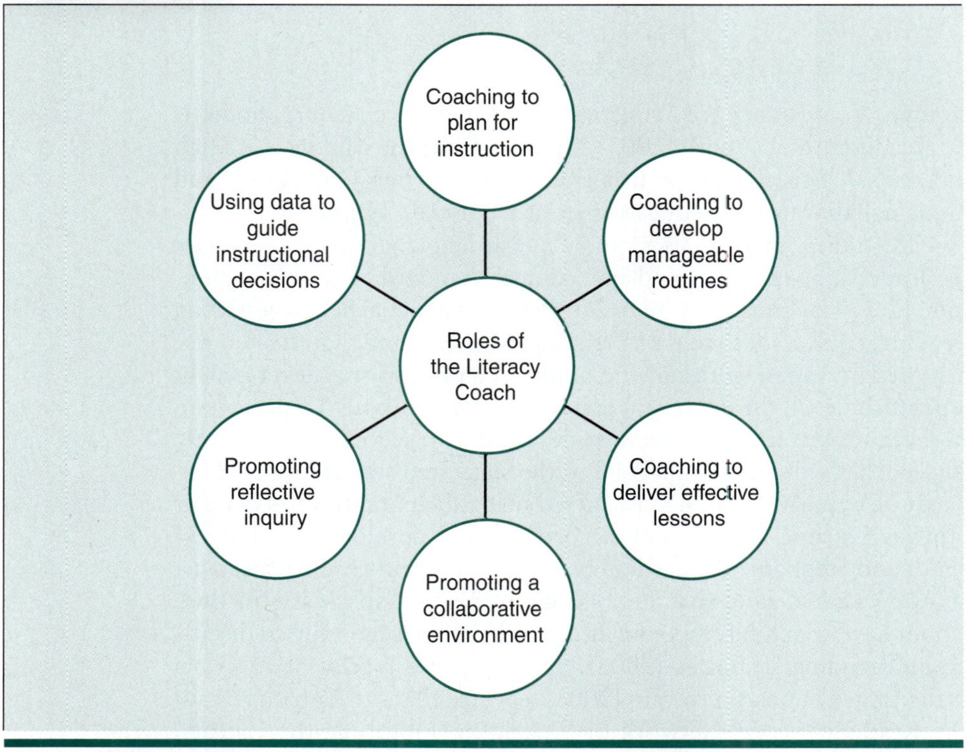

Source: Adapted from Mraz, M., Algozzine, R., & Kissel, B. (2009). *The Literacy Coach's Companion.* Thousand Oaks, CA, and Newark, DE: Corwin Press and the International Reading Association.

coaching. Once plans for content area instruction have been developed, literacy coaches work with teachers to implement those lessons.

In addition to working with individual teachers, literacy coaches work to create and *promote a collaborative environment*. As Mraz, Algozzine, and Kissel (2009) explain, "The teacher–coach relationship is reciprocal: Teachers learn from coaches, coaches learn from teachers and both learn from students" (p. 12). Effective literacy coaches foster collaborative environments by encouraging teachers to share their insights, knowledge, beliefs, and experiences during coaching conversations and professional development sessions.

Effective literacy coaches *promote reflective inquiry*. They encourage teachers to think reflectively about their teaching practice. That is, literacy coaches encourage teachers to review the instructional decisions they have made and to determine the extent to which those decisions were effective for their students.

Finally, coaches collaborate with teachers to *use data to guide instructional decisions*. Analysis of these data, which can include both formal and informal assessments such as those described in Chapter 4, helps assess the degree to which student learning outcomes have been achieved. Several factors contribute to effective assessment practices. These include monitoring student understanding and engaged time, maintaining records of students' progress, informing students about their progress, using data to make decisions, and making judgments about students' performance (Algozzine & Ysseldyke 2006).

Standards for Literacy Coaching

An important source of assistance for implementing a literacy coaching model is the International Reading Association's (2005) "Standards for the Middle and High School Literacy Coach." This document was created over a two-year period and represents a unique collaboration of educators in professional organizations in literacy, science, social studies, mathematics, and English language arts. It sets four standards—three leadership standards and one content standard—which are summarized in Figure 12.2. The standards advocate that literacy coaches have strong preparation in reading, equivalent to that of a reading specialist, and that their course work also include preparation in working with adults as a professional development specialist. On a practical level, the document states that the standards "represent an ideal" (p. 5), and because literacy coaching in middle and high schools is a relatively new concept, few coaches will initially meet all of the suggested standards.

As coaches acquire requisite skills, it's crucial to bolster their abilities and counter their isolation through strong and continuing professional development. For example, Nancy Guth and Stephanie Pettenfill, a reading supervisor–reading specialist team from Stafford, Virginia, note that middle school reading specialists in their district (all of whom have coaching responsibilities) meet at least monthly to discuss reading research and reading strategies (2005). Similarly, in a review of coaching programs across the United States, Sturtevant (2003) reported that the Alabama Reading Initiative, the Reading Success Network of WestEd in California, the Chicago Reading Initiative, and others all included strong professional development components for literacy coaches. Toll (2005) goes a step further, advising coaches to become

FIGURE 12.2 **Recommended Standards for Middle and High School Literacy Coaches**

Standard 1: Skillful Collaborators

Collaborate with School Literacy Team—collaborate with school level literacy team to determine schoolwide literacy strengths and needs and develop and implement a literacy program.

Promote Positive Relationships Among School Staff—establish and emphasize positive relationships related to the role of support versus evaluative.

Foundations of Literacy—share with teachers an integrated body of research about how students become successful readers, writers, and communicators.

Family Literacy—serve as a resource to families (e.g., provide information to parents about how they can support their child's reading development at home).

Standard 2: Skillful Job-Embedded Coaches

Provide Professional Development—related to literacy strategies in reading, writing, vocabulary, etc., and helping teachers to develop effective instruction.

Conduct Demo Lessons—demonstrate instructional strategies and provide ongoing support to teachers as they try the strategies themselves.

Engage in Classroom Coaching (One-on-One)—observe teachers in a nonthreatening manner in order to provide feedback through reflective dialogue.

Support Content Area Reading—discuss and share strategies and ideas to enhance content area reading and writing.

Differentiated Instruction—work with teachers to develop and implement differentiated instruction to meet the needs of individual learners.

Organize Materials—assist teachers in selection and analysis of content area text and instructional materials.

Standard 3: Skillful Evaluators of Literacy Needs

Support Effective Assessment Practices—lead faculty in understanding, selecting, and using multiple forms of assessments as diagnostic tools to guide instructional decision making and enhance both teacher and program effectiveness.

Analyze Data and Monitor Student Progress—meet with teachers to examine student work and evaluate their success while analyzing trends and results.

Conduct Assessment—conduct assessment for individuals or groups of students.

Standard 4: Skillful Instructional Strategists

Possess Content Area Knowledge—know how reading and writing processes relate with the various disciplines (i.e., English language arts, math, science, and social studies).

Provide Instruction—for individuals or small groups of students who are struggling readers (push-in, pull-out, or both settings).

Source: Adapted from International Reading Association (IRA). (2005). *Standards for Middle and High School Literacy Coaches.* Newark, DE: Author.

proactive in their own professional development by building a support system of other coaches outside of their own schools.

Overall, the role of the middle or high school literacy coach is important because coaches can have great impact on a school's literacy program, teacher professional development, and student learning. However, the potential roles for a coach are so numerous that coaches who are asked to do too much too quickly can easily feel overwhelmed and ineffective. School leaders, in consultation with literacy coaches, need to develop long-term plans that do not attempt to accomplish everything in the first year or two. In addition, districts need to provide continuing professional development and a sufficient cadre of coaches to really make a difference. With thoughtful planning and solid support, literacy coaches can help schools and teachers create learning environments that support, motivate, and guide adolescent literacy learners.

Literacy Coaches and Teachers

There are several ways in which literacy coaches work with teachers, administrators, and other school constituents to enhance literacy instruction. Building learning communities is an important component of effective professional development. School learning communities are teams of people who share knowledge, engage in periodic reviews of achievements or challenges, and work together to improve the overall learning of students (DuFour 2003). Together, team members reflect on teaching and learning and work toward developing a shared vision for the school (Marzano 2003).

Building Learning Communities: A Closer Look

The literacy coach facilitates a collaborative learning environment by working with various participants who contribute to the development of student learning. The community participants include administrative personnel such as principals, directors, and assistant principals; teachers, both veterans and newcomers; and parents and caregivers.

In addition to helping individual teachers within content area classrooms, the literacy coach is responsible for bringing groups of school members together in productive and meaningful ways. As Mraz, Algozzine, and Kissel (2009) explain, when teachers, parents, administrators, students, and coaches establish effective learning communities they work together to do the following:

- Strengthen their own professional knowledge
- Problem solve
- Celebrate successes and acknowledge challenges
- Build community
- Enhance instruction
- Discover ways to meet individual student needs

Though the school as a whole may strive to be a cohesive learning community, different constituencies within the school community may come together for different purposes at different times. For example, learning communities can encompass teacher–coach, teacher–teacher, and principal–coach interactions.

Here's how one middle school learning community worked: A group of six teachers met voluntarily each month throughout the school year to discuss the successes and challenges they experienced as they worked to develop integrated units among content area classes. As part of their conversation about how to effectively address the changes brought about by this integration initiative, the group members, led by the literacy coach, read Moore and Whitfield's (2008) article "Musing: A Way to Inform and Inspire Pedagogy Through Self-Reflection." After reading and discussing the article with colleagues, Jen Boysko, a fifth-grade teacher, wrote the following:

> I feel that I reflect on my lessons constantly. It seems as if I am always thinking about what I might say next, or how that lesson could have been different. I recognize that, as an educator, reflecting plays a crucial part in being successful. I did not realize, however, that there are levels of reflecting. When I *react,* I usually just discuss what happened in class that day with a coworker or peer. Unfortunately, I seem to react more to frustrating situations or when I know a lesson was not delivered well. I need to reflect more on things that did go well so that I can continue that behavior or habit, and even possibly improve on it. I *elaborate* those reflections at grade-level meetings when I compare strategies in the classroom with what other teachers are doing. It often takes me back to what I already did, and where I need to go. I *contemplate* insights and thoughts about a classroom situation, both academic and social, to seek out further assistance from my peers or school facilitators. Reflecting is not always an easy process. Realizing that change is needed and moving forward with an action plan is far more difficult than to just think about it.

At their next meeting together, Jen shared some of her insights about reflective teaching, and the group together talked about their own experiences with the change process and brainstormed advice for moving forward. "Continuing development is the mark of a true professional, an ongoing effort that is never complete. Educators committed to attaining and remaining at the top of their profession invest much energy in staying informed and increasing their skills. They are then in a position to exercise leadership among colleagues" (Danielson 1996, p. 115). Literacy coaches help to facilitate this process.

Conferring with Teachers

"The most beneficial learning activities are those that are embedded in the work that educators do" (Easton 2008, p. 748). Examples of enbedded learning activities include book studies, lesson analysis, study groups, data analysis, classroom visits, and teacher–coach conversations. Schools and districts undertaking major projects or changes increasingly include teachers and literacy coaches in designing, planning, and implementing these new ideas, which often require a considerable investment of time and mental energy. When viewed as authentic professional growth opportunities, however, professional educators find the time to become involved. In addition to the personal knowledge and experience gained through participation, teachers and literacy coaches are able to interact with one another on a level different from that of the classroom, thereby making an enhanced contribution to the education of students.

"Relationships with colleagues are an important element of teachers' contributions to the school and district. Professional educators are generous with their expertise and willingly share materials and insights, particularly with those less experienced than they" (Danielson 1996, p. 113). The essence of collaboration is conversation—colleagues sitting down together and engaging in serious dialogue about the nuts and bolts of teaching.

Whether the topic involves developing common curricular themes, integrating technology, reading an article from a professional publication, or writing about experiences, the activity of teachers and literacy coaches sharing ideas and insights with one another is a powerful one. The rapport and trust that grows between individuals break down the walls of isolation that can exist when teachers work alone in their classrooms. Teachers and literacy coaches exchange roles and become learners from each other, gaining from each other's perspectives and expertise. Just as teachers and coaches try to realize the potential of students by maximizing their strengths, so too can they grow as professionals by learning from one another. This can and should be an ongoing process—across experience levels and subjects taught.

Professional knowledge is enriched when teachers and coaches come together to discuss instructional practices. These conversations are at the heart of literacy coaching. Rapport and trust are created when literacy coaches and teachers engage in meaningful conversations (Blachowicz, Obrochta, & Fogelberg 2005). Teacher–coach conferences can serve several purposes. For example, teachers and coaches may work to connect a school- or districtwide literacy initiative to classroom instruction, or coaches and teachers may engage in genuine inquiry about strategies that could support student learning in content area classes. These conferences provide the literacy coach with an opportunity to establish a relationship of trust by listening carefully, maintaining confidentiality, and following through on coaching commitments (Bean & DeFord 2007). Through collaborative dialogue with teachers, coaches can promote a shared vision of the school's literacy goals, use student data to inform instructional decisions, and encourage instructional discussions to continue through ongoing professional development (Shankilin 2006).

Mraz, Algozzine, and Kissel (2009) suggest that coaches use five phases when conducting conferences with teachers, keeping in mind that a conference should be a dialogue between the teacher and the coach, not a lecture or evaluation on the part of the coach:

1. *Ask questions.* These initial questions can be related to the lesson, to student responses, or to connections between the lesson observed and the broader curriculum or unit of study.
2. *Explain what the coach notices.* State observations, objectively describing behaviors and events without imposing a judgment on what was observed.
3. *Offer a coaching point when it is appropriate to do so.* If there are several areas for which coaching points could be offered, select one as the main priority.

4. *Brainstorm next steps.* The coach and the teacher should determine together next steps for both the teacher and the coach. For example, the teacher and the coach may agree on a particular strategy that the teacher would like to try in his or her class; a time should be scheduled for a follow-up conference to discuss the successes and challenges of this strategy application.

5. *Link to literature.* Suggest and locate practitioner and research articles or books concerning an aspect of literacy learning that is relevant to the teacher; offer to read and discuss these with the teacher at a later time.

Creating partnerships is not simply a matter of goodwill. True collaboration creates a sense of connectedness that brings with it responsibility. When teachers make connections, they form a community, thereby counteracting the isolation that pervades the teaching profession. As Griffin put it, "when teachers are engaged together in thinking aloud about their work and its consequences, the results are a greater sense of professionalism and a stronger and more cohesive instructional program" (Griffin 1991, p. 250). In Box 12.2, Lynne, a middle school literacy coach, recounts her own efforts to confer with teachers to improve literacy learning for students across content areas.

Supporting Professional Development

What constitutes high-quality professional development? The findings of a two-year study by the National Foundation for the Improvement of Education (NFIE) indicate that gains in teacher learning are greatest when faculty schoolwide collaborate to examine student performance results and decide collectively what steps need to be taken to improve those results (Renyi 1998). Similarly, Richardson (2003) identified seven characteristics that were evident in successful professional development initiatives. Professional development was most successful when it

1. Was schoolwide;
2. Was long-term and included follow-up;
3. Encouraged collegiality;
4. Sought consensus among participants on goals;
5. Received support from administrators;
6. Received adequate funding for materials, consultants, and staffing; and
7. Acknowledged participants' existing beliefs and instructional practices.

High-quality professional development is not a one-stop workshop or isolated event. It is, as Renyi (1998) described, "an ethos—a way of being where learning is suffused throughout the teachers' working lives" (pp. 73–74). Box 12.3 (p. 412), Voices from the Classroom, describes one high school's effort to implement a high-quality professional development initiative in order to improve reading across content area classes.

Voices from the Classroom

BOX 12.2

Lynne

Middle School Literacy Coach

CHALLENGE

As a literacy coach, I collaborate with teachers on how to help students to read and understand expository texts. Together, we try to teach our students the skills they need to read critically and to make connections between texts in one subject area and broader circumstances beyond the classroom. However, with so much material to cover and so few hours in the school day, it is tempting for teachers to resort to traditional, and often ineffective, assign-and-tell routines: The teacher lectures during the class period, and then for homework, assigns a text selection for the students to read on their own. Students then answer a series of questions about their reading, and, when they return to class the next day, the teacher tells them about the text they have supposedly read. Even students with limited reading skills are able to answer these literal questions with a high degree of accuracy just by matching the words in the questions with similar words in the text. They simply copy the material from the text on to their paper and they have completed the assignment. Sound familiar? This instructional method creates a false illusion about reading proficiency. I have found that the ineffectiveness of this method is often revealed when students are tested on the material in a way that requires them to make connections or to apply their knowledge of the concepts presented in their reading.

STRATEGY

To help teachers move beyond assign-and-tell routines, I often work with them to plan and implement the application of the before-, during-, and after-reading (B–D–A) model to their lesson or unit of study [as described in Chapter 5]. The initial plan we develop together is not static. It is continuously modified as the material is taught and as learners need change.

Before reading the text, I talk with the teacher to select a before-reading strategy that will allow the teacher to introduce the topic and encourage the students to make connections between their prior knowledge and the new topic. There are many strategies available to teachers for activating students' prior knowledge. Sometimes, I need to point out that, far from being one more thing to add to a teacher's to-do list, using an appropriate before-reading strategy allows the teacher to assess the knowledge students bring, or do not bring, to the subject matter.

Next, we talk together about strategies that could be used for monitoring students' understanding of the topic during the reading process. I find this step to be especially important with content area material. Often, if students fail to understand an earlier section of the text, the text that follows will be incomprehensible to them as well. Key vocabulary needs to be identified; structures inherent in expository texts need to be emphasized; discussion and explanation of pertinent facts need to be highlighted as students read. We brainstorm, and often I model, strategies that can address these key steps in the learning process.

Finally, I conference with teachers to select instructional strategies to be used after the students have completed the reading. This step is crucial in developing higher-order thinking skills. It can also be an opportunity to guide students through the process of analyzing, synthesizing, comparing, contrasting, and making connections.

REFLECTION

When a teacher models and scaffolds the material throughout the reading process, students can develop critical literacy skills that are necessary for understanding content area texts. If these critical reading skills are not developed, the false illusion of reading proficiency through the use of the all too familiar assign-and-tell routines will continue to persist and students will continue to struggle with content area text in middle and high school classrooms. As a literacy coach, I can collaborate with teachers to develop systematic and well-planned alternatives that are likely to be more effective. It feels like a win–win situation to me and, I hope, for my colleagues as well.

Teachers who want a successful content area reading program in their school need more than knowledge and enthusiasm if this important aspect of instruction is to become a reality. Certain support strategies can be used to increase success as colleagues engage in what can best be described as a process of change. As teachers work together to grow professionally it is essential that change initiatives receive necessary support. One way to begin this process is to conduct a needs assessment, such as the one pictured in Figure 12.3, to determine the learning priorities that teachers have for their own

FIGURE 12.3 **Sample Needs Assessment Survey**

Welcome to the new semester. As we begin to make our professional development plans for the coming months, we would like to know what area or topics interest you the most. For each of the items listed below, please indicate your interest in including that topic in this semester's professional development plan using the following scale:

1 = I am comfortable with this topic and do not need a lot of help in this area.

2 = I would like to refresh or refine my knowledge of this topic.

3 = This is a priority for me and I would like to learn a lot more about it.

Topic	Interest Level		
Integrating new literacies into my teaching	1	2	3
Assessing student performance	1	2	3
Locating appropriate texts	1	2	3
Applying strategies for enhancing student engagement	1	2	3
Applying strategies for activating students' background knowledge	1	2	3
Applying strategies for vocabulary learning	1	2	3
Applying study strategies	1	2	3
Applying strategies for improving students' writing	1	2	3

Voices from the Classroom

BOX 12.3

Jean
High School Literacy Coach

CHALLENGE

In an era of high-stakes accountability, pressure falls on teachers to ensure that students understand subject area material and can demonstrate that knowledge effectively on mandated standardized tests. This can be a tall order for secondary students who struggle with basic reading, let alone with the highly specialized subject area texts and multiple transitions throughout the day, with each course and each teacher having different requirements and different instructional approaches. In our school, we have found that many students struggle to comprehend curriculum materials and to meet the wide ranging demands of high school courses.

STRATEGY

To support students as they strive to understand content and to streamline the transitions within the school day, our school created a schoolwide professional development initiative to support teachers in learning and applying effective strategies for content area reading. Because so few of our high school teachers had received substantive coursework on content area reading strategies in their preservice preparation programs, many were either unaware of what strategies were available to them, or unsure of how to incorporate them into courses that were already filled to the brim with required content.

To begin our initiative, teachers, literacy coaches, and school administrators worked together to form a schoolwide reading program that was integrated across content areas and engaged all members of the school community as both learners and teachers: English teachers showed other teachers how to administer and analyze an informal reading inventory; literacy coaches modeled how to assess students' reading ability and how to differentiate instruction so that content area texts would be accessible to students of varying reading levels; the school media specialist provided a workshop on how to locate supplemental curriculum materials to match students' reading levels; each content area team investigated and selected reading strategies that they believed would best support their specialized course content. Throughout the school year, teachers formed peer support teams to discuss their successes and challenges encountered when implementing new content area reading strategies. In addition to the informal conversations that occurred among teachers throughout the school year, literacy coaches provided formal content area reading workshops as part of ongoing professional development.

REFLECTION

Some teachers remained resistant to the additional responsibility of reading instruction in content area classrooms. However, most teachers were responsive to this professional development initiative, particularly when they observed growth in their students' understanding of subject area material. Their efforts were concentrated, consistent, and supported by peers and administrators. Having a degree of control over the strategies they selected and the manner in which they used them seemed to give teachers a voice throughout this initiative and a sense of autonomy over the application of strategies in their courses. In my book, that's as good as it gets!

FIGURE 12.4 **Strategies to Support Change**

- Peer collaboration to develop instructional strategies and assessments
- Observations in one another's classrooms in one's own or another building
- Mentoring programs for new teachers or experienced teachers who are new to a grade level
- Small-group seminars that include time for reflective dialogue
- Reading and discussion of professional literature with colleagues
- Peer support teams (peers share questions, concerns, and ideas for solutions as they seek to implement changes in their teaching and literacy programs)
- Peer coaching (feedback is given to teachers by teachers as strategies are applied with students)
- Lesson demonstrations
- Guided practice (a literacy coach leads participants in applying strategies)
- Opportunities to attend conferences or to hear speakers on topical issues
- Follow-up sessions related to conferences or workshops attended
- Threaded discussions via e-mail or Blackboard
- A professional development Website where teachers can share resources, ideas for lesson plans, and relevant data

Source: Reprinted by permission of the publisher. From Shelley B. Wepner and Dorothy S. Strickland, editors, *The Administration and Supervision of Reading Programs,* fourth edition. New York: Teachers College Press.

professional growth. Such an assessment can guide the work of the literacy coach as individual and schoolwide literacy goals are pursued. During professional development, relevant experiences, such as those listed in Figure 12.4, need to be provided by teachers and for teachers who want to grow in their ability to deliver content area reading strategies. The literacy coach can facilitate the application of these strategies.

Literacy Coaches and Students

In supporting the work of teachers, literacy coaches can play an important part in developing programs that directly affect students. The following examples describe how the work of a literacy coach can support struggling readers, English language learners, and effective overall assessment practices within a school.

Supporting Struggling Readers

Literacy coaches provide essential leadership for schools to address the needs of all learners, including their struggling readers. On a whole-school level, literacy coaches often organize literacy leadership teams (NASSP 2005). This team can conduct a needs assessment about the overall literacy achievement and needs of different groups of learners and then systematically plan ways to support both student and teacher learning. Although "struggling readers" are a diverse group and can be defined in a wide variety of ways, all students in middle and high school who struggle to meet course expectations due to difficulties in reading need special attention in the school literacy plan.

myeducationlab

Go to the Assignments and Activities section of Topic 8: "Study Skills and Strategies" in the MyEducationLab for your course. Complete the activity "Differentiating Study Strategies" and consider how teachers can help all students succeed.

Teachers' professional development should also be addressed, based on teachers' questions and concerns as well as the students' needs identified by the school needs assessment. Literacy coaches can organize workshops and study groups to help teachers understand the variety of reasons students may struggle with reading in content area classes. Understanding learners and the nature of the reading tasks required in content courses is a first step toward developing instruction that helps students become more successful in meeting literacy demands. A next step would be to help teachers develop expertise in using appropriate literacy strategies in their teaching. For example, after learning the importance of activating and building background knowledge, study group members might explore several types of anticipatory activities to use with their classes. Literacy coaches can then model lessons for teachers in different grade levels or in different content areas, and observe and conference with teachers as they try out new ideas.

Literacy coaches can also work with small groups of teachers or individuals to look at students' work samples and assess what types of difficulties students are having. Although instruction focused on literacy improvement in the content classroom would benefit all students, those who are struggling to comprehend content area texts will arguably gain the most through new access to a curriculum that previously may have been beyond their grasp.

Literacy coaches also can provide leadership in collaboration among specialists in the school. Learners who struggle in reading may have one or more classifications, such as "learning disabled." At many secondary schools, individual and small-group instruction for struggling readers is provided by a mix of special education teachers, ESOL teachers, speech-language pathologists, certified reading teachers and specialists, paraprofessionals, and volunteer tutors. Literacy coaches, as leaders of the school literacy program, can provide an invaluable service by encouraging communication among these groups and by helping them work together to provide effective services for students. Coaches can also work collaboratively with library and media specialists to develop a collection of print and technological resources to meet the needs of struggling readers, and they can help teachers review potential materials or programs designed for struggling readers before purchases are made.

Supporting English Language Learners

Literacy coaches can provide support for English learners in a variety of ways. First, they can ensure that their school's literacy plan considers the needs of these students. As García and Godina (2004) note, "few school districts have developed coherent programs of instruction at the middle and high school levels to address the various needs of English language learners" (p. 306). Students learning English at the secondary level are a widely varied group, and details related to cultural, educational, and language background are important to consider. For example, some students arrive in the United

States or Canada as teens with a history of limited formal schooling in their home countries; some of them have experienced great trauma in war-torn countries before their arrival. Others enter school with educational backgrounds similar to their North American counterparts. Some English learner students are not new immigrants, but have been in English language programs for a number of years.

> **myeducationlab**
> Go to the Assignments and Activities section of Topic 2: "Assessment" in the MyEducationLab for your course and complete the activity "Differentiated Assessment" and hear one teacher's thoughts on providing effective instruction for all of her students.

It is also important for coaches and literacy councils to understand features of their school's English language program and how it may affect student achievement. Information related to how students are assessed, assigned to ESL or bilingual education classes, and transitioned to general education classes is important to consider. Specialist teachers who work with English learners should, of course, participate on the school literacy council and can provide valuable information on both student needs as well as regulations that affect services for this population.

In addition, the literacy coach can collaborate with the ESL or bilingual education teachers to create a staff development program that helps all teachers in the school understand the needs of English learners. In many schools, content teachers are likely to have students with a range of levels of English proficiency in their classrooms. This may be a new circumstance for many content teachers, who can benefit from workshops and study groups that explore the best ways to merge content teaching with support for the English learner. Content teachers may need assistance from coaches, for example, in locating appropriate materials, understanding students' background knowledge, and learning appropriate strategies for teaching and assessment. ELL and bilingual education teachers may also benefit from the literacy coach's help in adding to their repertoire of strategies for improving the reading, writing, and communication of their students.

Literacy coaches also can assist their school in building communication with the families of their English learners and helping the school's program become more culturally responsive. For example, as coaches successfully advocate for the use of materials representing a wide variety of cultural groups, all students can expand their understanding of the world and see themselves in the curriculum. Many literacy coaches have been effective in supporting English learners and others by creating links that extend beyond the school. This might include developing internships that lead to jobs or college, or bringing business people, government employees, or college students to the school to serve as mentors or tutors.

Supporting Effective Assessment Practices

As part of providing literacy program leadership, a literacy coach can play an important role in a school's assessment program. First, it is important that the literacy coach work with the school's administrators and literacy council to conduct an assessment of the overall needs of their school. This assessment might include a survey of teachers related to their knowledge of teaching practices and views on school improvement; a review of standardized test scores for different grade levels and subpopulations; interviews with school leaders and representatives of different departments; and focus groups of students and parents that discuss students' literacy practices, goals, and needs. The literacy council can also evaluate the current assessment program, taking time to consider whether it provides information that truly informs teaching and learning. With these data, the literacy council can make recommendations about ways the school could better meet the needs of students in literacy and learning.

myeducationlab

To enhance your understanding of Response to Intervention, go to the IRIS Center Resource section of Topic 10: "Struggling Readers" in the MyEducationLab for your course and complete the module entitled "RTI (Part 3): Reading Instruction."

Moreover, literacy coaches working directly with teachers and teams of teachers can help them select, create, and use assessments to their best advantage. Teachers may need to update their knowledge on principles of assessment, including the purposes of different types of assessments and ways to interpret assessment information for parents and students. Although teachers in many secondary schools feel great pressure related to statewide high-stakes tests, as Afflerbach (2004) notes, most high-stakes tests receive money, media attention, and time "all out of proportion to the benefits they provide" (p. 386). Because of this, coaches need to encourage teachers to use a wide variety of assessments that give useful information to inform instruction. Departmental meetings, schoolwide workshops, or smaller study groups may be helpful in this regard. Teachers may also benefit from one-on-one work with literacy coaches to review students' work samples and discuss what they show about students' literacy skills and understanding of course concepts. This discussion, in turn, provides a catalyst for the coach and teacher to consider teaching strategies that might be beneficial. Adolescent students can also participate in self-reflection on their own progress, possibly using portfolios that include work from a term or a year.

Two common problems related to assessment plague many literacy coaches. The first is that coaches are sometimes put in charge of the schoolwide literacy assessment program, including state-mandated tests. Supervisors need to be aware that assigning this responsibility to a literacy coach means that he or she likely will have time for little else. As Guth and Pettengill (2005) note, an additional and related concern is that "one paradigm for assessment . . . is that of the reading specialist doing the reading assessments and the classroom teachers doing the teaching" (p. 60). Teachers must share in assessment responsibilities to gain a better understanding of their students' strengths and needs. Conversely, coaches mentor teachers by modeling lessons in their classrooms, thus gaining insight into dilemmas teachers face as well as curricular and student characteristics.

LOOKING BACK LOOKING FORWARD

The roles and titles of literacy coaches have changed over the years, and standards and expectations for literacy coaches have emerged that bring more consistency to the work of literacy coaches. Literacy coaches contribute to inquiry-based professional development in content area classrooms that leads to professional growth for teachers and improved instruction for students. Literacy coaches influence instructional practices designed to serve the diverse literacy needs of students, including struggling readers and English language learners, and they can guide the assessment practices used within the school. By building learning communities, conferring with teachers, and supporting ongoing professional development, literacy coaches create powerful learning environments for all members of the school community. Reflecting on her own professional journey, high school teacher Sarah Van Wyhe explained:

> The experiences I've had and the knowledge I've gained over the past year have made me think how the next thirty might be. Doors may open to

different job opportunities, and some I may try to walk through. Right now, I will stay in Mobile Unit #13 that welcomes around eighty teenagers Monday through Friday, one hundred eighty days a year. The difference will be that, when they walk through my door, I will be better able to prepare them for a bright future. I will be a more reflective practitioner who seeks research-based best practices to use in my classroom. I will be confident all my students can learn when taught effective strategies that go with them when they leave. I hope to apply what I have learned, and will continue to learn, in order to become a more effective teacher every day. I will share what I can with my coworkers, they will share ideas with me, and together we will help to shape the future.

Minds On

1. Reflect on a time when you teamed with a literacy coach or a teacher on a project. What were some of the benefits to students and teachers derived from the collaboration? What were some of the drawbacks?
2. Examine the following professional development needs: (a) to become familiar with research and to use it to inform instructional practices, (b) to reconsider one's own beliefs in order to come to a better understanding of one's own teaching practices, and (c) to explore alternative strategies for improving one's teaching and learning. Where would you place your own professional needs, and how do they compare with those of others in your group?
3. Imagine that you are part of a committee in charge of planning a professional development program for teachers in your school. How would you determine what that professional development program should encompass? What factors would you consider as you prepared to implement that program?

Hands On

1. Think of a content area class that you have recently observed. If you were a literacy coach preparing to conduct a conference with the teacher of that class, what questions and comments would you include in that conference? How would you structure the conference so that it was supportive and interactive?
2. Team with several people in the class to develop ideas that could be used by a literacy coach to support teachers in your school as they work to meet the needs of struggling readers and English language learners.
3. Review the summary of Recommended Standards for Middle and High School Literacy Coaches outlined in Figure 12.2. Discuss these standards with a literacy coach to determine how the coach attempts to address these standards and the challenges encountered when doing so.

*e*RESOURCES

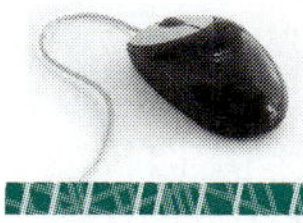

- Select an article from the Literacy Coaching Clearinghouse website (**www.literacycoachingonline.org**) and discuss with colleagues how the article connects to the work of literacy coaches in your school or district. What suggestions would you offer for enhancing the work of the coach based on the article you read?
- Explore the collection of NCTE's online resources for literacy coaches (**www1.ncte.org/store/books/language/118000.htm**) and select resources that are most relevant to your content area. Explain how you might incorporate the resources you selected into your content area instruction.

APPENDIX A

Ordeal by Cheque

Los Angeles, Calif. Aug. 30th 19 03 No. ____
HOLLYWOOD STATE BANK 90-984
6801 Santa Monica Boulevard
Pay to the order of Goosie Gander Baby Shoppe $48.50
One hundred & forty eight —— 50/ Dollars
Lawrence Exeter

Los Angeles, Calif. Sept 2nd 19 03 No. ____
HOLLYWOOD STATE BANK 90-984
6801 Santa Monica Boulevard
Pay to the order of Hollywood Hospital $100.00
One hundred —— xx Dollars
Lawrence Exeter

Los Angeles, Calif. Oct. 3rd 19 03 No. ____
HOLLYWOOD STATE BANK 90-984
6801 Santa Monica Boulevard
Pay to the order of Dr. David M. McCoy $476.00
Four hundred & seventy five —— xx Dollars
Lawrence Exeter Sr.

Los Angeles, Calif. Dec 19th 19 03 No. ____
HOLLYWOOD STATE BANK 90-984
6801 Santa Monica Boulevard
Pay to the order of California Toyland Co. $83.20
Eighty Three —— 20/ Dollars
Lawrence Exeter, Sr.

Los Angeles, Calif. Oct. 6th 19 09 No. ____
HOLLYWOOD STATE BANK 90-984
6801 Santa Monica Boulevard
Pay to the order of Palisades School for Boys $1,250.00
Twelve hundred & fifty —— xx Dollars
Lawrence Exeter Sr.

Los Angeles, Calif. Apr. 18th 19 10 No. ____
HOLLYWOOD STATE BANK 90-984
6801 Santa Monica Boulevard
Pay to the order of City Bicycle Co. $52.50
Fifty two —— 50/ Dollars
Lawrence Exeter Sr.

Los Angeles, Calif. Aug 26th 19 15 No. ____
HOLLYWOOD STATE BANK 90-984
6801 Santa Monica Boulevard
Pay to the order of Columbia Military Acad. $2,150.00
Twenty-one hundred & fifty —— xx Dollars
Lawrence Exeter Sr.

Los Angeles, Calif. Sept 3rd 19 21 No. ____
HOLLYWOOD STATE BANK 90-984
6801 Santa Monica Boulevard
Pay to the order of Hollywood Cadillac Co. $3,885.00
Thirty eight hundred & eighty five xx Dollars
Lawrence Exeter Sr.

Los Angeles, Calif. Sept. 7th 19 21 No. ____
HOLLYWOOD STATE BANK 90-984
6801 Santa Monica Boulevard
Pay to the order of Wilshire Auto Repair Service $288.76
Two hundred & eighty-eight —— 76/ Dollars
Lawrence Exeter Sr.

Los Angeles, Calif. Oct. 15th 19 21 No. ____
HOLLYWOOD STATE BANK 90-984
6801 Santa Monica Boulevard
Pay to the order of Stanford University $339.00
Three hundred & thirty-nine —— xx Dollars
Lawrence Exeter Sr.

Los Angeles, Calif. June 1st 19 23 No. ____
HOLLYWOOD STATE BANK 90-984
6801 Santa Monica Boulevard
Pay to the order of Miss Daisy Windsor $25,000.00
Twenty-five thousand —— xx Dollars
Lawrence Exeter Sr.

Los Angeles, Calif. June 9th 1923 No.____
HOLLYWOOD STATE BANK 90-984
6801 Santa Monica Boulevard
Pay to the order of French Line, Ile de France $585.00
Five hundred + eighty-five ——xx Dollars
Lawrence Exeter Sr.

Los Angeles, Calif. Aug. 23rd 1923 No.____
HOLLYWOOD STATE BANK 90-984
6801 Santa Monica Boulevard
Pay to the order of Banque de France $5,000.00
Five thousand ——xx Dollars
Lawrence Exeter Sr.

Los Angeles, Calif. Feb. 13th 1926 No.____
HOLLYWOOD STATE BANK 90-984
6801 Santa Monica Boulevard
Pay to the order of University Club Florists $76.50
Seventy-six ——50/ Dollars
Lawrence Exeter Sr.

Los Angeles, Calif. June 22nd 1926 No.____
HOLLYWOOD STATE BANK 90-984
6801 Santa Monica Boulevard
Pay to the order of University Club Florists $312.75
Three hundred & twelve ——75/ Dollars
Lawrence Exeter Sr.

Los Angeles, Calif. Aug 11th 1926 No.____
HOLLYWOOD STATE BANK 90-984
6801 Santa Monica Boulevard
Pay to the order of Riviera Heights Land Co. $56,000.00
Fifty-six Thousand ——xx Dollars
Lawrence Exeter Sr.

Los Angeles, Calif. Oct. 30th 1926 No.____
HOLLYWOOD STATE BANK 90-984
6801 Santa Monica Boulevard
Pay to the order of Renaissance Interior Decorators $22,000.00
Twenty-two thousand ——xx Dollars
Lawrence Exeter Sr.

Los Angeles, Calif. Nov. 18th 1926 No.____
HOLLYWOOD STATE BANK 90-984
6801 Santa Monica Boulevard
Pay to the order of Beverly Diamond + Gift Shoppe $678.45
Six hundred + seventy-eight ——45/ Dollars
Lawrence Epeter Sr.

Los Angeles, Calif. Nov. 16th 1926 No.____
HOLLYWOOD STATE BANK 90-984
6801 Santa Monica Boulevard
Pay to the order of Hawaii Steamship Co. $560.00
Five hundred + sixty ——xx Dollars
Lawrence Epeter Sr.

Los Angeles, Calif. Nov. 21st 1926 No.____
HOLLYWOOD STATE BANK 90-984
6801 Santa Monica Boulevard
Pay to the order of Lawrence Epeter, Junior $200,000.00
Two hundred thousand ——xx Dollars
Lawrence Epeter Sr.

Los Angeles, Calif. Nov. 22nd 1926 No.____
HOLLYWOOD STATE BANK 90-984
6801 Santa Monica Boulevard
Pay to the order of Ambassador Hotel $2,250.00
Twenty-two hundred + fifty ——xx Dollars
Lawrence Epeter Sr.

Los Angeles, Calif. Dec. 1st 1926 No.____
HOLLYWOOD STATE BANK 90-984
6801 Santa Monica Boulevard
Pay to the order of University Club Florists $183.50
One hundred + eighty-three ——50/ Dollars
Lawrence Exeter Sr.

Los Angeles, Calif. Feb. 18 1927 No.____
HOLLYWOOD STATE BANK 90-984
6801 Santa Monica Boulevard
Pay to the order of Cocoanut Grove Sweet Shoppe $27.00
Twenty seven ——— Dollars
Lawrence Epeter Jr.

LOS ANGELES, CALIF. July 16, 1927 No. ____
HOLLYWOOD STATE BANK 90-984
6801 SANTA MONICA BOULEVARD
PAY TO THE ORDER OF Parisian Gown Shoppe $925.00
Nine hundred, twenty five ~~ DOLLARS
Lawrence Expeter Jr.

LOS ANGELES, CALIF. Dec. 1, 1927 No. ____
HOLLYWOOD STATE BANK 90-984
6801 SANTA MONICA BOULEVARD
PAY TO THE ORDER OF Anita Lingerie Salon $750.00
Seven hundred, fifty ~~ DOLLARS
Lawrence Expeter Jr.

LOS ANGELES, CALIF. April 1, 1928 No. ____
HOLLYWOOD STATE BANK 90-984
6801 SANTA MONICA BOULEVARD
PAY TO THE ORDER OF Parisian Gown Shoppe $1,150.00
Eleven hundred, fifty ~~ DOLLARS
Lawrence Expeter, Jr.

LOS ANGELES, CALIF. Nov. 1, 1928 No. ____
HOLLYWOOD STATE BANK 90-984
6801 SANTA MONICA BOULEVARD
PAY TO THE ORDER OF Moderne Sportte Shoppe $562.00
Five hundred, sixty two ~~ DOLLARS
Lawrence Expeter, Jr.

LOS ANGELES, CALIF. July 1, 1929 No. ____
HOLLYWOOD STATE BANK 90-984
6801 SANTA MONICA BOULEVARD
PAY TO THE ORDER OF The Bootery $145.25
One hundred, forty-five ~ 25/100 DOLLARS
Lawrence Expeter, Jr.

LOS ANGELES, CALIF. Aug. 23, 1929 No. ____
HOLLYWOOD STATE BANK 90-984
6801 SANTA MONICA BOULEVARD
PAY TO THE ORDER OF Tony Spagoni $126.00
One hundred, twenty six ~ DOLLARS
Lawrence Expeter Jr.

LOS ANGELES, CALIF. Aug. 30, 1929 No. ____
HOLLYWOOD STATE BANK 90-984
6801 SANTA MONICA BOULEVARD
PAY TO THE ORDER OF Tony Spagoni $126.00
One hundred, twenty six ~~ DOLLARS
Lawrence Expeter, Jr.

LOS ANGELES, CALIF. May 25, 1930 No. ____
HOLLYWOOD STATE BANK 90-984
6801 SANTA MONICA BOULEVARD
PAY TO THE ORDER OF University Club Florists $87.00
Eighty seven ~~ DOLLARS
Lawrence Expeter Jr.

LOS ANGELES, CALIF. May 28, 1930 No. ____
HOLLYWOOD STATE BANK 90-984
6801 SANTA MONICA BOULEVARD
PAY TO THE ORDER OF Broadway Diamond Co. $575.00
Five hundred, seventy five ~ DOLLARS
Lawrence Expeter Jr.

LOS ANGELES, CALIF. Nov. 13, 1930 No. ____
HOLLYWOOD STATE BANK 90-984
6801 SANTA MONICA BOULEVARD
PAY TO THE ORDER OF Miss Flossie Wentworth $50,000.00
Fifty thousand ~~ DOLLARS
Lawrence Expeter, Jr.

LOS ANGELES, CALIF. Nov. 14, 1930 No. ____
HOLLYWOOD STATE BANK 90-984
6801 SANTA MONICA BOULEVARD
PAY TO THE ORDER OF Wall & Smith, attys. at Law $525.00
Five hundred, twenty five ~ DOLLARS
Lawrence Expeter, Jr.

LOS ANGELES, CALIF. Nov. 15, 1930 No. ____
HOLLYWOOD STATE BANK 90-984
6801 SANTA MONICA BOULEVARD
PAY TO THE ORDER OF Mrs. Lawrence Expeter, Jr. $5000.00
Five thousand ~~ DOLLARS
Lawrence Expeter, Jr.

Los Angeles, Calif. June 20 1931 No. ____
HOLLYWOOD STATE BANK 90-984
6801 Santa Monica Boulevard
Pay to the order of Clerk, Reno Municipal Court $52.00
Fifty-two ——— Dollars
Lawrence Exeter, Jr.

Los Angeles, Calif. June 20 1931 No. ____
HOLLYWOOD STATE BANK 90-984
6801 Santa Monica Boulevard
Pay to the order of Marie Wharton Exeter $175,000.00
One hundred seventy five thousand — Dollars
Lawrence Exeter, Jr.

Los Angeles, Calif. June 20 1931 No. ____
HOLLYWOOD STATE BANK 90-984
6801 Santa Monica Boulevard
Pay to the order of Walker & Walker $700.00
Seven hundred ——— Dollars
Lawrence Exeter, Jr.

Los Angeles, Calif. June 20 1931 No. ____
HOLLYWOOD STATE BANK 90-984
6801 Santa Monica Boulevard
Pay to the order of Wall & Smith $450.00
Four hundred fifty ——— Dollars
Lawrence Exeter, Jr.

Los Angeles, Calif. July 1 1931 No. ____
HOLLYWOOD STATE BANK 90-984
6801 Santa Monica Boulevard
Pay to the order of Tony Spagoni $100.00
One hundred ——— Dollars
Lawrence Exeter, Jr.

Los Angeles, Calif. July 2 1931 No. ____
HOLLYWOOD STATE BANK 90-984
6801 Santa Monica Boulevard
Pay to the order of Tony Spagoni $100.00
One hundred ——— Dollars
Lawrence Exeter, Jr.

Los Angeles, Calif. July 3 1931 No. ____
HOLLYWOOD STATE BANK 90-984
6801 Santa Monica Boulevard
Pay to the order of Peter Ventizzi $25.00
Twenty-five ——— Dollars
Lawrence Exeter

Los Angeles, Calif. July 5th 1931 No. ____
HOLLYWOOD STATE BANK 90-984
6801 Santa Monica Boulevard
Pay to the order of Hollywood Hospital $100.00
One hundred ——— xx Dollars
Lawrence Exeter, Sr.

Los Angeles, Calif. July 15th 1931 No. ____
HOLLYWOOD STATE BANK 90-984
6801 Santa Monica Boulevard
Pay to the order of Dr. David M. McCoy $175.00
One hundred + seventy-five — xx Dollars
Lawrence Exeter, ~~Sr.~~

Los Angeles, Calif. July 16th 1931 No. ____
HOLLYWOOD STATE BANK 90-984
6801 Santa Monica Boulevard
Pay to the order of Hollywood Mortuary $1,280.00
Twelve hundred + eighty — xx Dollars
Lawrence Exeter

APPENDIX B

Affixes with Invariant Meanings

AFFIX	MEANING	EXAMPLE
Combining Forms		
anthropo-	man	anthropoid
auto-	self	autonomous
biblio-	book	bibliography
bio-	life	biology
centro-, centri-	center	centrifugal
cosmo-	universe	cosmonaut
heter-, hetero-	different	heterogeneous
homo-	same	homogeneous
hydro-	water	hydroplane
iso-	equal	isometric
lith-, litho-	stone	lithography
micro-	small	microscope
mono-	one	monocyte
neuro-	nerve	neurologist
omni-	all	omnibus
pan-	all	panchromatic
penta-	five	pentamerous
phil-, philo-	love	philanthropist
phono-	sound	phonology
photo-	light	photosynthesis
pneumo-	air, respiration	pneumonia
poly-	many	polygon

AFFIX	MEANING	EXAMPLE
proto-	before, first in time	prototype
pseudo-	false	pseudonym
tele-	far	television
uni-	one	unicellular
Prefixes		
apo-	separate or detached from	apocarpous
circum-	around	circumvent
co-, col-, com-, con-, cor-	together or with	combine
equi-	equal	equivalent
extra-	in addition	extraordinary
intra-	within	intratext
mal-	bad	malpractice
mis-	wrong	mistreatment
non-	not	nonsense
syn-	together or with	synthesis
Noun Suffixes		
-ana	collection	Americana
-archy	rule or government	oligarchy
-ard, -art	person who does something to excess	drunkard, braggart
-aster	inferiority or fraudulence	poetaster
-bility	quality or state of being	capability
-chrome	pigment, color	autochrome
-cide	murder or killing of	insecticide
-fication, -ation	action or process of	classification, dramatization
-gram	something written or drawn	diagram
-graph	writing, recording, drawing	telegraph, lithograph
-graphy	descriptive science of a specific subject or field	planography, oceanography
-ics	science or art of	graphics, athletics
-itis	inflammation or inflammatory disease	bronchitis
-latry	worship of	bibliolatry

AFFIX	MEANING	EXAMPLE
-meter	measuring device	barometer
-metry	science or process of measuring	photometry
-ology, -logy	science, theory, or study of	phraseology, paleontology
-phobia	fear	hypnophobia
-phore	bearer or producer	semaphore
-scope	instrument for observing or detecting	telescope
-scopy	viewing, seeing, or observing	microscopy
-ance, -ation, -ion, -ism, -dom, -ery, -mony, -ment, -tion	quality, state, or condition; action or result of an action	tolerance, adoration, truism, matrimony, government, sanction
-er, -eer, -ess, -ier, -ster, -ist, -trix	agent, doer	helper, engineer, countess, youngster, shootist, executrix
Adjective Suffixes		
-able, -ible	worthy of or inclined to	debatable, knowledgeable
-aceous, -ative, -ish, -ive, -itious	pertaining to	impish, foolish, additive, fictitious
-acious	tendency toward or abundance of	fallacious
-est	most	greatest
-ferous	bearing, producing	crystalliferous
-fic	making, causing, or creating	horrific
-fold	multiplied by	fivefold
-form	having the form of	cuneiform
-ful	full of or having the quality of	masterful, useful, armful
-genous	generating or producing	androgenous, endogenous
-ic	characteristic of	seismic, microscopic
-less	lacking	toothless
-like	similar to	lifelike
-most	most	innermost
-ous, -ose	possessing, full of	joyous, grandiose
-wise	manner, direction, or positions	clockwise

APPENDIX C

Commonly Used Prefixes with Varying Meanings

PREFIX	MEANING	EXAMPLE
ab-	from, away, off	abhor, abnormal, abdicate
ad-	to, toward	adhere, adjoin
ante-	before, in front of, earlier than	antecedent, antediluvian
anti-	opposite of, hostile to	antitoxin, antisocial
be-	make, against, to a great degree	bemoan, belittle, befuddle
bi-	two, twice	biped, bivalve
de-	away, opposite of, reduce	deactivate, devalue, devitalize
dia-	through, across	diameter, diagonal
dis-	opposite of, apart, away	dissatisfy, disarm, disjointed
en-	cause to be, put in or on	enable, engulf
epi-	upon, after	epitaph, epilogue, epidermis
ex-	out of, former, apart, away	excrete, exposition
hyper-	above, beyond, excessive	hyperphysical, hypersensitive
hypo-	under, less than normal	hypodermic, hypotension
in-, il-, im-, ir-	not, in, into, within	inept, indoors
inter-	between, among	interscholastic, interstellar
neo-	new, young	neophyte, neo-Nazi
ortho-	straight, corrective	orthotropic, orthopedic
per-	through, very	permanent, perjury

PREFIX	MEANING	EXAMPLE
peri-	around, near, enclosing	perimeter, perihelion
post-	after, behind	postwar, postorbital
pre-	before, in place, time, rank, order	preview, prevail
pro-	before, forward, for, in favor of	production, prothorax, pro-American
re-	again, back	react, recoil
sub-, sur-, sug-, sup-	under, beneath	subordinate, subsoil, substation
super-	above, over, in addition	superhuman, superlative, superordinate
syn-	with, together	synthesis, synchronize
trans-	across, beyond, through	transatlantic, transconfiguration, transaction
ultra-	beyond in space, excessive	ultraviolet, ultramodern
un-	not, the opposite of	unable, unbind

APPENDIX D

Graphic Organizers with Text Frames

Graphic organizers are visual illustrations of verbal statements. Frames are sets of questions or categories that are fundamental to understanding a given topic. Here we show nine "generic" graphic forms with their corresponding frames. Examples of topics that could be represented by each graphic form are also given. These graphics show at a glance the key parts of the whole and their relations, helping the learner to comprehend text and solve problems.

Spider Map

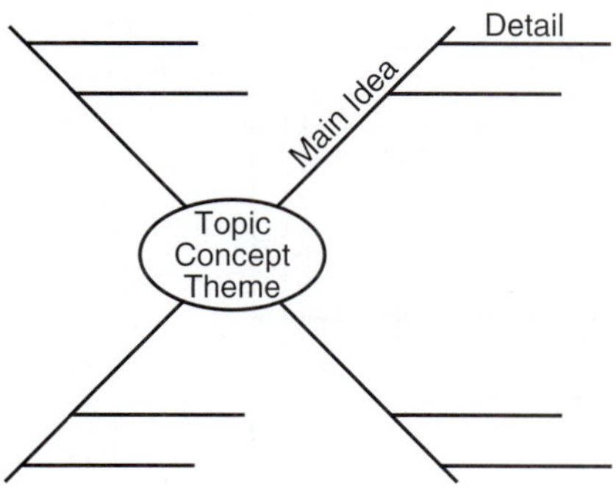

Used to describe a central idea: a thing (a geographic region), process (meiosis), concept (altruism), or proposition with support (experimental drugs should be available to AIDS victims). Key frame questions: What is the central idea? What are its attributes? What are its functions?

Series-of-Events Chain

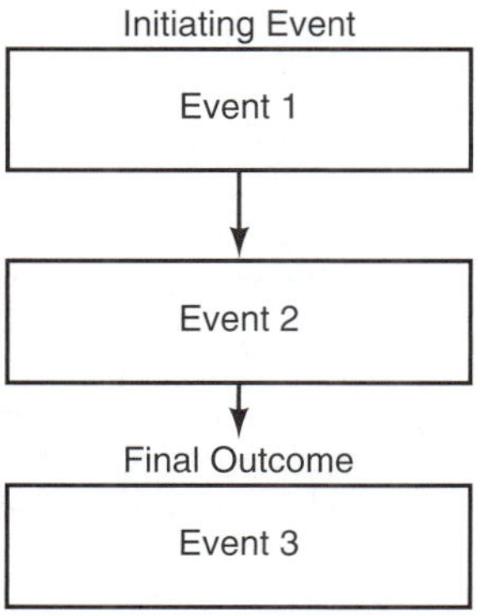

Used to describe the stages of something (the life cycle of a primate); the steps in a linear procedure (how to neutralize an acid); a sequence of events (how feudalism led to the formation of nation-states); or the goals, actions, and outcomes of a historical figure or character in a novel (the rise and fall of Napoléon). Key frame questions: What is the object, procedure, or initiating event? What are the stages or steps? How do they lead to one another? What is the final outcome?

Used for time lines showing historical events or ages (grade levels in school), degrees of something (weight), shades of meaning (Likert scales), or ratings scales (achievement in school). Key frame questions: What is being scaled? What are the end points?

Continuum/Scale

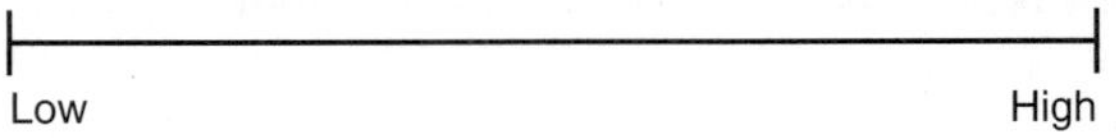

Compare/Contrast Matrix

	Name 1	Name 2
Attribute 1		
Attribute 2		
Attribute 3		

Used to show similarities and differences between two things (people, places, events, ideas, etc.). Key frame questions: What things are being compared? How are they similar? How are they different?

Used to represent a problem, attempted solutions, and results (the national debt). Key frame questions: What was the problem? Who had the problem? Why was it a problem? What attempts were made to solve the problem? Did those attempts succeed?

Problem/Solution Outline

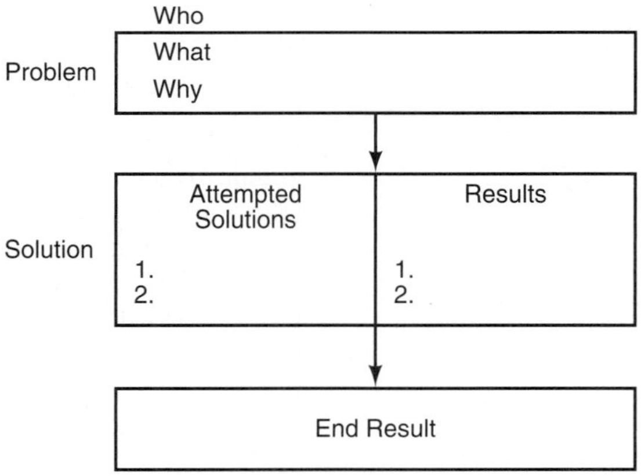

Network Tree

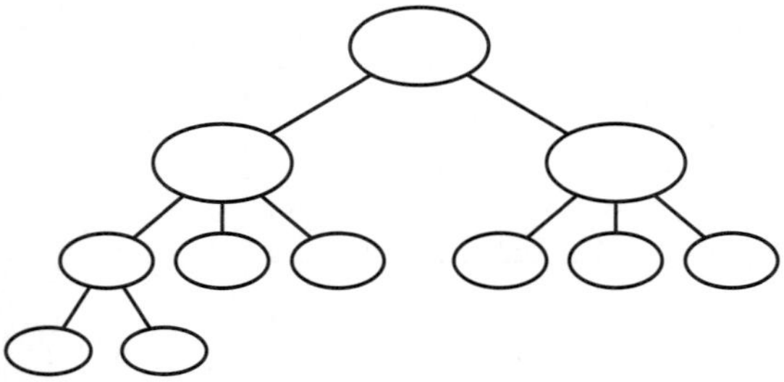

Used to show causal information (causes of poverty), a hierarchy (types of insects), or branching procedures (the circulatory system). Key frame questions: What is the superordinate category? What are the subordinate categories? How are they related? How many levels are there?

Human Interaction Outline

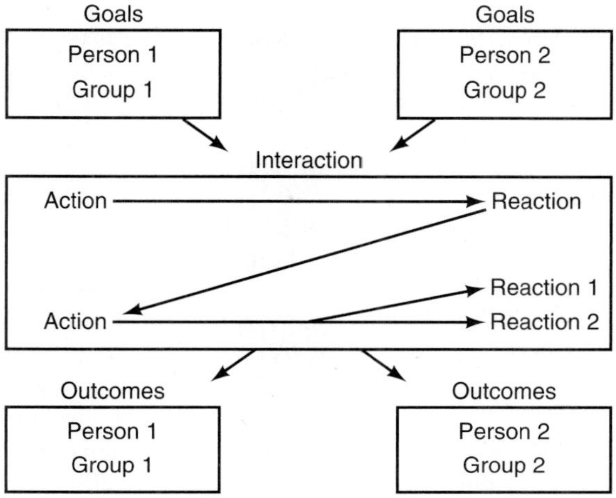

Used to show the nature of an interaction between persons or groups (European settlers and Native Americans). Key frame questions: Who are the persons or groups? Did they conflict or cooperate? What was the outcome for each person or group?

Fishbone Map

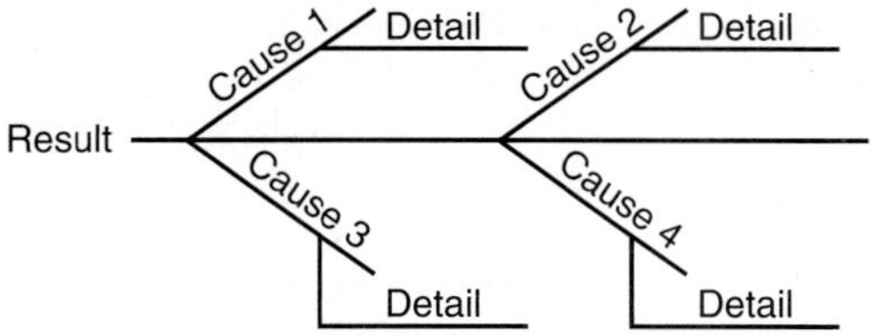

Used to show the causal interaction of a complex event (an election, a nuclear explosion) or complex phenomenon (juvenile deliquency, learning disabilities). Key frame questions: What are the factors that cause *X*? How do they relate? Are the factors that cause *X* the same as those that cause *X* to persist?

Cycle

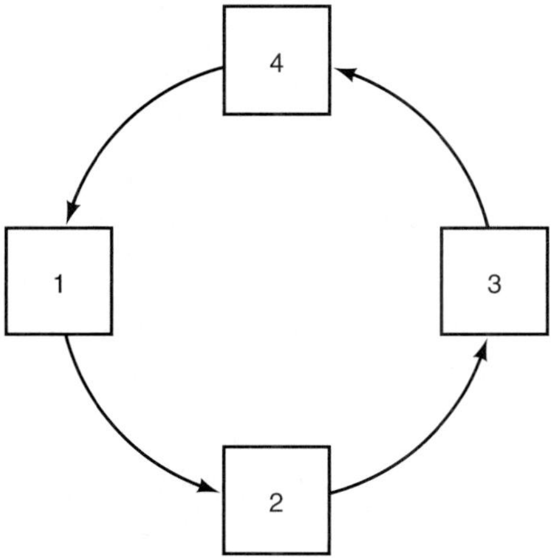

Used to show how a series of events interact to produce a set of results again and again (weather phenomena, cycles of achievement and failure, the life cycle). Key frame questions: What are the critical events in the cycle? How are they related? In what ways are they self-reinforcing?

References

Abrams, S. (2000). *Using journals with reluctant writers: Building portfolios for middle and high school students.* Thousand Oaks, CA: Corwin Press.

Ackerman, N. (1990). *The tin heart.* Ill. M. Hays. New York: Atheneum.

Adlit.org. (2008). Brian Selznick. Retrieved March 1, 2009, from www.adlit.org/transcript_display/19677

Afflerbach, P. (2004). *National Reading Conference policy brief: High-stakes testing and reading assessment.* Oak Creek, WI: National Reading Conference.

Alexander, P. (1986). *Silver Burdett biology.* Morristown, NJ: Silver Burdett.

Alexie, S. (2007). *The absolutely true diary of a part-time Indian.* New York: Little, Brown.

Algozzine, B., & Ysseldyke, J. E. (2006). *Effective instruction for students with special needs.* Thousand Oaks, CA: Corwin Press.

Aliki. (1983). *A medieval feast.* New York: Crowell.

Aliki. (1999). *William Shakespeare and the Globe.* New York: HarperCollins.

Allen, M. B. (2003). *Eight questions on teacher preparation: What does the research say?* Denver, CO: Education Commission of the States.

Alliance for Excellent Education. (2006). *Policy brief: Why the crisis in adolescent literacy demands a national response.* Washington, DC: Author.

Allington, R., & Johnston, P. H. (Eds.). (2002). *Reading to learn: Lessons from exemplary fourth-grade classrooms.* New York: Guilford Press.

Allington, R. L. (2001). *What really matters for struggling readers: Designing research-based programs.* New York: Longman.

Allington, R. L., & Strange, M. (1980). *Learning through reading in the content areas.* Lexington, MA: Heath.

Alvarez, M. C. (1996). Explorers of the universe: Students using the World Wide Web to improve their reading and writing. In B. Neate (Ed.), *Literacy saves lives* (pp. 140–145). Herts, UK: United Kingdom Reading Association.

Alvermann, D. E. (1991). The discussion web: A graphic aid for learning across the curriculum. *Reading Teacher, 45*(2), 92–99.

Alvermann, D. E. (2001). Reading adolescents' reading identities: Looking back to see ahead. *Journal of Adolescent & Adult Literacy, 44,* 676–690.

Alvermann, D. E., Dillon, D. R., & O'Brien, D. G. (1988). *Using discussion to promote reading comprehension.* Newark, DE: International Reading Association.

Alvermann, D. E., & Moore, D. W. (1991). Secondary school reading. In P. D. Pearson, R. Barr, M. L. Kamil, & P. Mosenthal (Eds.), *Handbook of reading research* (2nd ed., pp. 951–983). New York: Longman.

Alvermann, D. E., Swafford, J., & Montero, K. M. (2004). *Content area literacy instruction for the elementary grades.* Boston: Allyn & Bacon.

Ames, L. J. (1986). *Draw fifty cars, trucks, and motorcycles.* Garden City, NY: Doubleday.

Anders, P. L. (2002). Secondary reading programs: A story of what was. In D. L. Schallert, C. M. Fairbanks, J. Worthy, B. Maloch, & J. V. Hoffman (Eds.), *51st yearbook of the National Reading Conference* (pp. 82–93). Oak Creek, WI: National Reading Conference.

Anderson, D. L. (1999). *Using projects in the mathematics classroom to enhance instruction and incorporate history of mathematics.* Paper presented at the National Council of Teachers of Mathematics annual conference, San Francisco, CA.

Anderson, L. H. (1999). *Speak.* New York: Farrar, Strauss & Giroux.

Anderson, L. H. (2000). *Fever 1793.* New York: Simon & Schuster.

Anderson, R. C., & Freebody, P. (1981). Vocabulary knowledge. In J. T. Guthrie (Ed.), *Comprehension and teaching: Research perspectives* (pp. 77–117). Newark, DE: International Reading Association.

Anderson-Inman, L., & Horney, M. (1997). Electronic books for secondary students. *Journal of Adolescent & Adult Literacy, 40*(6), 486–491.

Anno, M. (1989). *Anno's math games II.* New York: Philomel.

Anonymous. (1971). *Go ask Alice.* New York: Simon Pulse.

Applebee, A. N. (1991). Environments for language teaching and learning: Contemporary issues and future directions. In J. Flood, J. M. Jensen, D. Lapp, & J. R. Squire (Eds.), *Handbook of research on teaching the English language arts* (pp. 549–558). New York: Macmillan.

Armbruster, B. B. (2000). Responding to informative prose. In R. Indrisano & J. R. Squire (Eds.), *Perspectives on writing: Research, theory, and practice.* Newark, DE: International Reading Association.

Armbruster, B. B., & Anderson, T. H. (1981). *Content area textbooks.* Reading Education Report No. 23. Urbana: University of Illinois Center for the Study of Reading.

Armbruster, B. B., & Anderson, T. H. (1985). Frames: Structure for informational texts. In D. H. Jonassen (Ed.), *Technology of text* (pp. 331–346). Englewood Cliffs, NJ: Education Technology Publications.

Armstrong, J. (1998). *Shipwreck at the bottom of the world: The extraordinary true story of Shackleton and the* Endurance. New York: Crown.

Armstrong, J. (2002). *Shattered: Stories of children and war.* New York: Knopf.

Armstrong, L., & Jenkins, S. (2001). *It's not about the bike: My journey back to life.* New York: Berkley Books.

Aronson, E. (1978). *The jigsaw classroom.* Beverly Hills, CA: Sage.

Aronson, M. (1998). *Art attack: A short cultural history of the avant-garde.* New York: Clarion Books.

Artley, A. S. (1975). Words, words, words. *Language Arts, 52,* 1067–1072.

Asher, J. (2007). *Thirteen reasons why.* New York: Penguin.

Atkin, S. B. (1993). *Voices from the fields: Children of migrant farmworkers tell their stories.* Boston: Little, Brown.

Atwell, N. (1990). Introduction. In N. Atwell (Ed.), *Coming to know: Writing to learn in intermediate grades* (pp. xi–xxiii). Portsmouth, NH: Heinemann.

Atwell, N. (1998). *In the middle: New understandings about writing, reading, and learning* (2nd ed.). Portsmouth, NH: Heinemann.

Au, K. H. (1993). *Literacy instruction in multicultural settings.* Orlando: Harcourt Brace.

Au, K. H., & Mason, J. M. (1981). Social organizational factors in learning to read: The balance of rights hypothesis. *Reading Research Quarterly, 17*(1), 115–152.

Avi. (2008). *The seer of shadows.* New York: HarperCollins.

Baker, F. W. (2009). *State standards which include elements of media literacy.* Retrieved February 5, 2009, from www.frankwbaker.com/state_lit.htm

Baker, J. (1991). *Window.* New York: Greenwillow.

Baker, L. (1991). Metacognition, reading, and science education. In C. M. Santa & D. E. Alvermann (Eds.), *Science learning: Processes and applications* (pp. 12–13). Newark, DE: International Reading Association.

Baker, L., & Brown, A. (1984). Cognitive monitoring in reading. In J. Flood (Ed.), *Understanding reading comprehension* (pp. 21–44). Newark, DE: International Reading Association.

Ball, J. (2005). *Go figure! A totally cool book about numbers.* New York: DK Children.

Ballard, R. D. (1988). *Exploring the Titanic.* New York: Scholastic.

Bamford, R. A., & Kristo, J. V. (Eds.). (1998). *Making facts come alive: Choosing quality nonfiction literature K–8.* Needham Heights, MA: Christopher Gordon.

Bandura, A. (1986). *Social foundations of thought and action: A social cognitive theory.* Englewood Cliffs, NJ: Prentice Hall.

Bangert-Drowns, R. L., Hurley, M. M., & Wilkinson, B. (2004). The effects of school-based writing-to-learn interventions on academic achievement: A meta-analysis. *Review of Educational Research, 74,* 29–58.

Banks, A. B. (2008). *An introduction to multicultural education* (4th ed.). Boston: Pearson.

Banks, J. A. (2001). *Cultural diversity and education: Foundations, curriculum, and teaching* (4th ed.). Boston: Allyn & Bacon.

Bardoe, C. (2006). *Gregor Mendel: The friar who grew peas.* New York: Abrams Books.

Barnes, D. (1995). Talking and learning in the classroom: An introduction. *Primary Voices K–6, 3*(1), 2–7.

Barnitz, J. G. (1994). Discourse diversity: Principles for authentic talk and literacy instruction. *Journal of Reading, 37*(7), 586–591.

Barrentine, S. J. (1999). *Reading assessment: Principles and practices for elementary teachers.* Newark, DE: International Reading Association.

Barron, R. F. (1969). The use of vocabulary as an advance organizer. In H. L. Herber & P. L. Sanders (Eds.), *Research in reading in the content areas: First report* (pp. 29–39). Syracuse, NY: Syracuse University Reading and Language Arts Center.

Barron, R. F., & Earle, R. (1973). An approach for vocabulary development. In H. L. Herber & R. F. Barron (Eds.), *Research in reading in the content areas: Second report* (pp. 51–63). Syracuse, NY: Syracuse University Reading and Language Arts Center.

Barron, R. F., & Stone, F. (1973, December). *The effect of student constructed graphic post organizers upon learning of vocabulary relationships from a passage of social studies content.* Paper presented at the meeting of the National Reading Conference, Houston, TX.

Bartoletti, S. C. (2001). *Black potatoes: The story of the great Irish famine, 1845–1850.* Boston: Houghton Mifflin.

Bartoletti, S. C. (2006). *Hitler youth: Growing up in Hitler's shadow.* New York: Scholastic.

Barton, D., & Hamilton, M. (1998). *Local literacies: Reading and writing in one community.* London: Routledge.

Barton, J. (1995). Conducting effective classroom discussions. *Journal of Reading, 38*(5), 346–350.

Baxendell, B. W. (2003). Consistent, coherent, creative: The 3 C's of graphic organizers. *Teaching Exceptional Children, 35,* 46–53.

Beah, I. (2007). *A long way gone: Memoirs of a boy soldier.* New York: Farrar, Straus & Giroux.

Beals, M. P. (1995). *Warriors don't cry: A searing memoir of the battle to integrate Little Rock.* New York: Washington Square Press.

Beaman, B. (1985). Writing to learn social studies. In A. R. Gere (Ed.), *Roots in sawdust: Writing to learn across the disciplines* (pp. 50–60). Urbana, IL: National Council of Teachers of English.

Bean, J. C., Drenk, D., & Lee, F. D. (1982). Microtheme strategies for developing cognitive skills. In C. W. Griffin (Ed.), *New directions for teaching and learning.* San Francisco: Jossey-Bass.

Bean, R. M. (2004). Promoting effective literacy instruction: The challenge for literacy coaches. *The California Reader, 37*(3), 58–63.

Bean, R. M., Cassidy, J., Grumet, J. E., Shelton, D. S., & Wallis, S. R. (2002). What do reading specialists do? Results from a national survey. *The Reading Teacher, 55*(8), 736–744.

Bean, R. M., & DeFord, D. (2007). *Do's and don'ts for literacy coaches: Advice from the field.* Retrieved November 1, 2007, from the Literacy Coaching Clearinghouse website, www.literacycoachingonline.org

Bean, T. W. (2001). An update on reading in the content areas: Social constructionist dimensions. *Reading Online, 5*(5). Retrieved October 5, 2005, from www.readingonline.org/articles/art_index.asp?HREF=handbook/bean/index.html

Bean, T. W., & Moni, K. (2003). Developing students' critical literacy: Exploring identity construction in young adult fiction. *Journal of Adolescent & Adult Literacy, 46*(8), 638–648.

Beatty, P. (1987). *Charley Skedaddle.* New York: Morrow.

Beck, I. L., McKeown, M. G., Hamilton, R. L., & Kucan, L. (1997). *Questioning the author: An approach for enhancing student engagement in text.* Newark, DE: International Reading Association.

Beck, I. L., McKeown, M. G., & Kucan, L. (2002). *Bringing words to life: Robust vocabulary instruction.* New York: Guilford Press.

Beebe, B. F. (1968). *African elephants.* New York: McKay.

Beil, K. M. (1999). *Fire in their eyes: Wildfires and the people who fight them.* San Diego: Harcourt Brace.

Berger, M. (1986). *Atoms, molecules, and quarks.* New York: Putnam.

Berlyne, D. E. (1965). *Structure and direction of thinking.* New York: Wiley.

Berman, I., & Biancarosa, G. (2005). *Reading to achieve: A governor's guide to adolescent literacy.* Washington, DC: National Governor's Association for Best Practices.

Bernhardt, E. B. (1998). Socio-historical perspectives on language teaching in modern America. In H. Byrnes (Ed.), *Perspectives in research and scholarship in second language learning* (pp. 39–57). New York: Modern Language Association.

Bernhardt, E. B., & Kamil, M. L. (1998). Literacy instruction for non-native speakers of English. In M. Graves, B. Graves, & C. Watts (Eds.), *Teaching reading in the 21st century* (pp. 432–475). Boston: Allyn & Bacon.

Betts, E. (1950). *Foundations of reading* (rev. ed.). New York: American Book Company.

Biancarosa, G., & Snow, C. (2004). *Reading next: A vision for action and research in middle and high school literacy.* Report to Carnegie Corporation of New York. Washington, DC: Alliance for Excellent Education. Retrieved June 25, 2007, from www.all4ed.org/publications/ReadingNext/ReadingNext.pdf

Bishop, R. S. (2003). Reframing the debate about cultural authenticity. In D. L. Fox & K. G. Short (Eds.), *Stories matter: The complexity of cultural authenticity in children's literature* (pp. 25–37). Urbana, IL: National Council of Teachers of English.

Bitton-Jackson, L. (1997). *I have lived a thousand years: Growing up in the Holocaust.* New York: Simon & Schuster.

Blachowicz, C. (1986). Making connections: Alternatives to the vocabulary notebook. *Journal of Reading, 29,* 643–649.

Blachowicz, C., & Fisher, P. (1996). *Teaching vocabulary in all classrooms.* Columbus, OH: Merrill.

Blachowicz, C., Obrochta, C., & Fogelberg, E. (2005). Literacy coaching for change. *Educational Leadership, 62*(6), 55–58.

Blachowicz, C. Z., Fisher, P. J. L., Ogle, D., & Watts-Taffe, S. (2006). Vocabulary: Questions from the classroom. *Reading Research Quarterly, 41*(4), 524–539.

Bleich, D. (1978). *Subjective criticism.* Baltimore: Johns Hopkins University Press.

Blohm, J. M., & Lapinsky, T. (2006). *Kids like me: Voices of the immigrant experience.* Boston: Intercultural Press.

Blumenthal, K. (2005). *Let me play: The story of Title IX: The law that changed the future of girls in America.* New York: Atheneum.

Bode, J. (1989). *New kids on the block: Oral histories of immigrant teens.* New York: Franklin Watts.

Bode, J. (2000). *Colors of freedom: Immigrant stories.* New York: Franklin Watts.

Boykin, A. W. (1978). Psychological/behavioral verve in academic/task performance: Pre-theoretical considerations. *Journal of Negro Education, 47*(4), 343–354.

Boykin, A. W. (1984). Reading achievement and the social-cultural frame of reference of Afro-American students. *Journal of Negro Education, 53*(4), 464–473.

Boyne, J. (2006). *The boy in the striped pajamas.* New York: Fickling.

Brashares, A. (2001). *Sisterhood of the traveling pants.* New York: Delacorte.

Britton, J. (1970). *Language and learning.* London: Allen Lane.

Bromley, K. (2007). Nine things every teacher should know about words and vocabulary instruction. *Journal of Adolescent and Adult Literacy, 50*(7), 528–537.

Brown, A. L. (1978). Knowing when, where, and how to remember: A problem of metacognition. In R. Glaser (Ed.), *Advances in instructional psychology* (pp. 117–175). Mahwah, NJ: Erlbaum.

Brown, A. L., Bransford, J. W., Ferrara, R. F., & Campione, J. (1983). Learning, remembering, and understanding. In J. Flavell & E. Markham (Eds.), *Handbook of child psychology* (pp. 393–451). New York: Wiley.

Brown, A. L., & Palincsar, A. S. (1982). Inducing strategic learning from texts by means of informed, self-control training. *Topics in Learning and Learning Disabilities, 2,* 1–17.

Brown, A. L., & Palincsar, A. S. (1984). Reciprocal teaching of comprehension-fostering and comprehension-monitoring activities. *Cognition and Instruction, 1,* 117–175.

Brown, D. (1987). *Principles of language learning and teaching.* Englewood Cliffs, NJ: Prentice Hall.

Brown, M. W. (1949). *The important book.* Ill. L. Weisgard. New York: Harper & Row.

Brozo, W. G. (1989). Applying a reader response heuristic to expository text. *Journal of Reading, 32,* 140–145.

Brozo, W. G. (1990). Learning how at-risk readers learn best: A case for interactive assessment. *Journal of Reading, 33,* 522–527.

Brozo, W. G., & Flyny, E. S. (2007). Content literacy: Fundamental toolkit elements. *Reading Teacher, 61*(2), 192–194.

Brozo, W. G., & Tomlinson, C. M. (1986). Literature: The key to lively content courses. *Reading Teacher, 40,* 288–293.

Bruce, B. C. (2002). Diversity and critical social engagement: How changing technologies enable new modes of literacy in changing circumstances.

In D. E. Alvermann (Ed.), *Adolescents and literacies in a digital world* (pp. 1–18). New York: Peter Lang.

Bruner, J. (1961). The act of discovery. *Harvard Educational Review, 31*, 21–32.

Bruner, J. (1970). The skill of relevance or the relevance of skills. *Saturday Review, 53*.

Bruner, J. (1986). *Actual minds, possible worlds.* Cambridge, MA: Harvard University Press.

Bruner, J. (1990). *Acts of meaning.* Cambridge, MA: Harvard University Press.

Bruner, J., Goodnow, J., & Austin, G. (1977). *A study of thinking.* New York: Science Editions.

Buckingham, D. (1993). *Reading audiences: Young people and the media.* Manchester, UK: Manchester University Press.

Buckingham, D. (2003). *Media education: Literacy, learning and contemporary culture.* Cambridge, UK: Polity.

Buehl, D. (1991, Spring). Frames of mind. *The Exchange: Newsletter of the IRA Secondary Reading Interest Group*, pp. 4–5.

Buehl, D. (2009). Linking research to practice in disciplinary instruction: An interview by David Moore. *Journal of Adolescent and Adult Literacy, 52*(6), 535–537.

Buehl, D., & Moore, D. (2009). Linking research to practice in disciplinary instruction. *Journal of Adolescent and Adult Literacy, 52*(6), 535–537.

Bunting, E. (1994). *Smoky night.* Ill. D. Diaz. Orlando, FL: Harcourt Brace.

Burgess, J. (1988). *The heart and blood (How our bodies work).* Englewood Cliffs, NJ: Silver Burdett.

Burke, J. (2002). *Tools for thought: Graphic organizers for your classroom.* Portsmouth, NH: Heinemann.

Burleigh, R. (1997). *Hoops.* Ill. S. T. Johnson. San Diego, CA: Silver Whistle.

Bustle, L. S. (2004). The role of visual representation in the assessment of learning. *Journal of Adolescent & Adult Literacy, 47*, 416–423.

Cai, M. (1994). Images of Chinese and Chinese Americans mirrored in picture books. *Children's Literature in Education, 25*, 169–191.

Calabro, M. (1999). *The perilous journey of the Donner Party.* New York: Clarion Books.

Camp, G. (1982). *A successful curriculum for remedial writers.* Berkeley: National Writing Project, University of California.

Campano, G. (2007). *Immigrant students and literacy: Reading, writing, and remembering.* New York: Teachers College Press.

Canfield, J. (2000). *Chicken soup for the sports fan's soul: 101 stories of insight, inspiration and laughter in the world.* Deerfield, FL: HCI.

Carlo, M. S., August, D., McLaughlin, B., Snow, C. E., Dressler, C., Lippman, D. N., Lively, T. J., & White, C. E. (2004). Closing the gap: Addressing the vocabulary needs of English-language learners in bilingual and mainstream classrooms. *Reading Research Quarterly, 39*(2), 188–215.

Carr, E., & Ogle, D. (1987). K-W-L Plus: A strategy for comprehension and summarization. *Journal of Reading, 30*, 626–631.

Carter, B. (2000). *Best books for young adults.* Chicago: American Library Association.

Carter, B., & Abrahamson, R. F. (1990). *Nonfiction for young adults: From delight to wisdom.* Phoenix, AZ: Oryx Press.

Cassidy, J., & Cassidy, D. (2009, February/March). What's hot in adolescent literacy. *Reading Today, 26*(4), 1, 8, 9.

Cazden, C. (2001). *Classroom discourse: The language of teaching and learning.* Portsmouth, NH: Heinemann.

Chambers, A. (1973). *Introducing books to children.* London: Heinemann.

Chang, I. (1991). *A separate battle: Women and the Civil War.* New York: Scholastic.

Chekhov, A. (1991). *Kashtanka.* Trans. R. Povear. Ill. B. Moser. New York: Putnam.

Clark, B., Sobel, J., & Basteri, C. G. (2006). *Marketing dynamics.* Tinley, IL: Goodheart-Wilcox.

Clark, R. P. (1987). *Free to write: A journalist teaches young writers.* Portsmouth, NH: Heinemann.

Clary, D., Oglan, V., & Styslinger, M. (2008). *It is not just about content: Preparing content area teachers to be literacy leaders.* Retrieved February 12, 2009, from the Literacy Coaching Clearinghouse website, www.literacycoachingonline.org

Close, E. A., Hull, M., & Langer, J. A. (2005). Writing and reading relationships in literacy learning. In

R. Indrisano & J. A. Paratore (Eds.), *Learning to write, writing to learn: Theory and research in practice* (pp. 67–79). Newark, DE: International Reading Association.

Coiro, J. (2003). Reading comprehension on the Internet: Expanding our understanding of reading comprehension to encompass new literacies. *Reading Teacher, 56,* 458–464.

Collins, J. L. (1997). *Strategies for struggling writers.* New York: Guilford Press.

Cone, M. (1992). *Come back, salmon: How a group of dedicated kids adopted Pigeon Creek and brought it back to life.* Photo. S. Wheelwright. San Francisco: Sierra Club Books for Children.

Congressional Digest. (1999, August–September). The federal role in education: 1999–2000 policy debate topic. *Congressional Digest,* 193.

Conley, M. (2008). Cognitive strategy instruction for adolescents: What we know about the promise, what we don't know about the potential. *Harvard Educational Review, 78*(1), 84–106.

Conrad, P. (1991). *Pedro's journal.* New York: Scholastic.

Considine, B., Horton, J., & Moorman, G. (2009). Teaching and reading the millennial generation through media literacy. *Journal of Adolescent and Adult Literacy, 52*(6), 471–481.

Cook-Sather, A. (2002). Authorizing students' perspectives: Toward trust, dialogue, and change in education. *Educational Researcher, 31*(4), 3–14.

Cooney, T., Bell, K., Fisher-Cauble, D., & Sanchez, W. (1996). The demands of alternative assessment: What teachers say. *Mathematics Teacher, 89,* 484–487.

Cooper, M. (2002). *Remembering Manzanar: Life in a Japanese relocation camp.* New York: Clarion Books.

Cope, B., & Kalantzis, M. (Eds.). (2000). *Multiliteracies: Literacy learning and the design of social futures.* London: Routledge.

Cover, R. (1989). *Cultural diversity training.* A paper presented at a conference on issues in multicultural education, Chapel Hill, NC.

Coville, B. (1997). *William Shakespeare's Macbeth.* Ill. G. Kelly. New York: Dial.

Creech, J., & Hale, G. (2006). Literacy in science: A natural fit, promoting student literacy through inquiry. *The Science Teacher, 73*(2), 22–27.

Creech, S. (1996). *Walk two moons.* New York: HarperCollins.

Creech, S. (2001). *Love that dog.* New York: HarperTrophy.

Crue, W. (1932, February). Ordeal by cheque. *Vanity Fair.*

Crutcher, C. (1989). *Athletic shorts.* New York: Greenwillow.

Crystal, D. (2008a). *Txting: The Gr8 Db8.* Oxford, England: Oxford University Press.

Crystal, D. (2008b). Texting. *English Language Teaching (ELT) Journal, 62*(1), 77–83.

Cummins, J. (1981). The role of primary language development in promoting educational success for language minority students. In J. Cummins (Ed.), *Schooling and language minority students: A theoretical framework* (pp. 3–49). Los Angeles: Evaluation, Dissemination, and Assessment Center, California State University at Los Angeles.

Cummins, J. (1986). Empowering minority students: A framework for intervention. *Harvard Educational Review, 56*(1), 18–36.

Cummins, J. (1994). The acquisition of English as a second language. In K. Spangenberg-Urbschat & R. Pritchard (Eds.), *Kids come in all languages: Reading instruction for ESL students* (pp. 36–62). Newark, DE: International Reading Association.

Cunningham, R., & Shablak, S. (1975). Selective reading guide-o-rama: The content teacher's best friend. *Journal of Reading, 18,* 380–382.

Curry, J. (1989). The role of reading instruction in mathematics. In D. Lapp, J. Flood, & N. Farnan (Eds.), *Content area reading and learning: Instructional strategies* (pp. 187–197). Upper Saddle River, NJ: Prentice Hall.

Curtis, M. E., & Longo, A. M. (2001). Teaching vocabulary to adolescents to improve comprehension. *Reading Online, 5*(4). Retrieved August 8, 2005, from www.readingonline.org/articles/art_index.asp?HREF=curtis/index.html

Dale, E. (1969). Things to come. *Newsletter, 34,* 1–8.

Daniels, H. (1994). *Literature circles: Voice and choice in book clubs and reading groups* (2nd ed.). York, ME: Stenhouse.

Danielson, C. (1996). *Enhancing professional practice: A framework for teaching.* Alexandria, VA: Association for Supervision and Curriculum Development.

Danzer, G. A. (2007). *The Americans: Reconstruction to the 21st century.* New York: McDougall Littell.

Darling-Hammond, L. (2003). Standards and assessments: Where we are and what we need. *Teachers College Record.* Retrieved April 10, 2008, from www.tcrecord.org/Content.asp?ContentID=11109

Darling-Hammond, L., & Baratz-Snowden, J. (2005). *A good teacher in every classroom: Preparing the highly qualified teachers our children deserve.* San Francisco: Jossey-Bass.

Dash, J. (2000). *The longitude prize.* New York: Farrar, Straus & Giroux.

Davey, B. (1983). Think aloud: Modeling the cognitive processes of reading comprehension. *Journal of Reading, 27,* 44–47.

Davidson, J. L., & Wilkerson, B. C. (1988). *Directed reading-thinking activities.* Monroe, NY: Trillium Press.

Davis, O. (1978). *Escape to freedom: A play about Frederick Douglass.* New York: Viking Penguin.

Dean, Z. (2007). *The A-List.* New York: Poppy.

Deem, J. M. (2005). *Bodies from the ash: Life and death in ancient Pompeii.* Boston: Houghton Mifflin.

Deighton, L. (1970). *Vocabulary development in the classroom.* New York: Teachers College Press.

Delano, M. F. (2005). *Genius: A photobiography of Albert Einstein.* Washington, DC: National Geographic.

Delpit, L. D. (1988). The silenced dialogue: Power and pedagogy in educating other people's children. *Harvard Educational Review, 58,* 280–298.

deMaupassant, G. (1993). *The necklace.* Ill. G. Kelly. New York: Creative Editions.

Dessen, S. (2006). *That summer.* New York: Viking.

Dessen, S. (2009). *Lock and key.* New York: Puffin.

Dewey, J. (1899/1980). *The school and society.* Carbondale: Southern Illinois University Press.

Diaz, C. F. (2001). *Multicultural education for the twenty-first century.* New York: Longman.

Díaz-Rico, L. T. (2008). *Strategies for teaching English learners* (2nd ed.). Boston: Pearson.

Díaz-Rico, L. T., & Weed, K. Z. (2002). *The cross-cultural, language, and academic development handbook: A complete K–12 reference guide.* Boston: Allyn & Bacon.

Dillon, D. R. (1989). Showing them that I want them to learn and that I care about who they are: A micro-ethnography on the social organization of a secondary low-track English-reading classroom. *American Educational Research Association Journal, 26,* 227–259.

Dillon, S. (2005, August 23). Connecticut sues the U.S. over school testing [Electronic version]. *The New York Times.*

Dillon, S. (2008, October 13). Under No Child Left Behind, even solid schools falter. [Electronic version]. *The New York Times.*

Dole, J. (2004). The changing role of the reading specialist in school reform. *The Reading Teacher, 57,* 462–471.

Donelson, K. L., & Nilsen, A. P. (1997). *Literature for today's young adults* (5th ed.). New York: Longman.

Draper, R. J. (2008). Redefining content area literacy teacher education: Finding my voice through collaboration. *Harvard Educational Review, 78*(1), 60–83.

Dreher, P. (2000). Electronic poetry: Student-constructed hypermedia. *English Journal, 90*(2), 68–73.

Duffelmeyer, F. A., & Baum, D. D. (1992). The extended anticipation guide revisited. *Journal of Reading, 35*(8), 654–656.

Duffy, G. G. (1983). From turn taking to sense making: Broadening the concept of reading teacher effectiveness. *Journal of Educational Research, 76,* 134–139.

DuFour, R. (2003). Building a professional learning community. *School Administrator, 60*(5), 13–18.

DuFour, R., & Eaker, R. (1998). *Professional learning communities at work: Best practices for enhancing student achievement.* Reston, VA: Association for Supervision and Curriculum Development.

Duke, N. K., & Pearson, P. D. (2002). Effective practices for developing reading comprehension. In A. E. Farstrup & S. J. Samuels (Eds.), *What research has to say about reading instruction* (3rd ed., pp. 205–242). Newark, DE: International Reading Association.

Dyer, D. (1997). *Jack London: A biography.* New York: Scholastic.

Eanet, M., & Manzo, A. V. (1976). REAP: A strategy for improving reading/writing/study skills. *Journal of Reading, 19,* 647–652.

Easton, L. B. (2008). From professional development to professional learning. *Phi Delta Kappan, 89*(10), 755–759, 761.

Echevarria, J., & Graves, A. (2003). *Sheltered content instruction: Teaching English-language learners with diverse abilities* (2nd ed.). Boston: Allyn & Bacon.

Echevarria, J., Vogt, M., & Short, D. J. (2008). *Making content comprehensible for English language learners: The SIOP model* (3rd ed.). Boston: Allyn & Bacon.

Echlin, H. (2007). *Digital discussion: Take your class to the Internet.* Retrieved September 8, 2008, from www.edutopia.org/whats-next-2007-Blog

Education Commission of the States (ECS). (2004). *ECS report to the nation: State implementation of the No Child Left Behind Act, executive summary.* Retrieved May 16, 2006, from www.esc.org

Education Commission of the States (ECS). (2006). *Recent state policies/activities.* Retrieved May 16, 2006, from www.ecs.org/ecs/ecsat.nsf

Education Commission of the States (ECS). (2008). Assessment: High-stakes/competency—pros & cons. Retrieved September 21, 2008, from www.ecs.org/html/issuesSection.asp?print=true&issueID=12

Edwards, P. (1967). *Equiano's travels: The interesting narrative of the life of Olaudah Equiano or Gustavus Vassa, the African.* New York: Praeger.

Eisner, E. (1997). Cognition and representation: A way to pursue the American dream? *Phi Delta Kappan, 78,* 349–353.

Eisner, E. W. (1985). *The educational imagination: On the design and evaluation of school programs* (2nd ed.). New York: Macmillan.

Eisner, E. W. (1991). The celebration of thinking. *Maine Scholar, 4,* 39–52.

Eisner, W. (2000). *New York: The big city.* New York: DC Comics.

Epstein, S., & Epstein, B. W. (1978). *Dr. Beaumont and the man with a hole in his stomach.* New York: Coward McCann & Geoghegan.

Erickson, B. (1996). Read-alouds reluctant readers relish. *Journal of Adolescent & Adult Literacy, 40*(3), 212–215.

Evans, C. W., Leija, A. J., & Falkner, T R. (2001). *Math links: Teaching the NCTM 2000 standards through children's literature.* Englewood, CO: Teacher Ideas Press.

Faltis, C. J., & Coulter, C. A. (2004). *Teaching English learners and immigrant students in secondary schools.* Upper Saddle River, NJ: Pearson.

Farmer, N. (2002). *The house of the scorpion.* New York: Atheneum/Richard Jackson.

Farr, R. (1992). Putting it all together: Solving the reading assessment puzzle. *Reading Teacher, 46,* 26–37.

Farr, R., & Tone, B. (1998). *Assessment portfolio and performance* (2nd ed.). Orlando, FL: Harcourt Brace.

Farrell, J. (2005). *Invisible allies: Microbes that shape our lives.* New York: Farrar, Straus & Giroux.

Feelings, T. (1995). *The middle passage: White ships, black cargo.* New York: Dial.

Fetterman, D. M. (1989). *Ethnography step by step.* Thousand Oaks, CA: Sage.

Fillmore, L. (1981). Cultural perspectives on second language learning. *TESL Reporter, 14,* 23–31.

Finn, P. (1999). *Literacy with an attitude: Educating working class students in their own self-interest.* Albany: SUNY Press.

Fisher, D. (2004). Setting the "opportunity to read" standards: Resuscitating the SSR program in an urban high school. *Journal of Adolescent & Adult Literacy, 48,* 138–149.

Fisher, D., & Frey, N. (2003). Writing instruction for struggling adolescent readers: A gradual release model. *Journal of Adolescent & Adult Literacy, 46,* 396–405.

Fisher, D., Frey, N., & ElWardi, R. (2005). Creating independent writers and thinkers in secondary schools. In R. Indrisano & J. A. Paratore (Eds.), *Learning to write, writing to learn: Theory and research in practice.* Newark, DE: International Reading Association.

Flanigan, K., & Greenwood, S. C. (2007). Effective content vocabulary instruction in the middle: Matching students, purposes, words, and strategies. *Journal of Adolescent & Adult Literacy, 51*(3), 226–238.

Flavell, J. H. (1976). Metacognitive aspects of problem solving. In L. B. Resnick (Ed.), *The nature of intelligence* (pp. 38–62). Mahwah, NJ: Erlbaum.

Flavell, J. H. (1981). Cognitive monitoring. In P. Dickson (Ed.), *Communication skills.* Orlando, FL: Academic Press.

Fleischman, J. (2002). *Phineas Gage: A gruesome but true story about brain science.* Boston: Houghton Mifflin.

Fleischman, P. (1988). *Joyful noise: Poems for two voices.* New York: HarperCollins.

Fleischman, P. (2000). *Big talk: Poems for four voices.* New York: Candlewick.

Fleming, T. (1988). *Band of brothers: West Point in the Civil War.* New York: Walker.

Foon, D. (2004). *Skud.* Canada: Groundwood Books.

Foss, A. (2002). Peeling the onion: Teaching critical literacy with students of privilege. *Language Arts, 79*(5), 393–403.

Fox, M. (2000). *Feathers and fools.* Ill. N. Wilton. San Diego, CA: Voyager.

Fradin, D., & Fradin, J. (2006). *5,000 miles to freedom: Ellen and William Craft's flight from slavery.* Washington, DC: National Geographic.

Frank, A. (1967). *Anne Frank: The diary of a young girl.* New York: Doubleday.

Freedman, R. (1995). *Immigrant kids.* New York: Puffin.

Freedman, R. (2000). *Give me liberty! The story of the Declaration of Independence.* New York: Holiday House.

Freedman, R. (2005). *Children of the Great Depression.* New York: Clarion Books.

Freeman, E. B., & Person, D. G. (1998). *Connecting informational children's books with content area learning.* Boston: Allyn & Bacon.

Freire, P. (1970/2000). *Pedagogy of the oppressed.* New York: Continuum.

Friend, R. (2000–2001). Teaching summarization as a content area strategy. *Journal of Adolescent & Adult Literacy, 44,* 320–329.

Friesen, J. (2008). *Jerk, California.* New York: Penguin.

Fry, E. (1977). Fry's readability graph: Clarifications, validity, and extension to level 17. *Journal of Reading, 21,* 242–252.

Fulton, M., & Porter, M. (2000). *Common state strategies to improve student reading.* Denver, CO: ECS.

Gagne, R. (1970). *The conditions of learning.* New York: Holt, Rinehart, and Winston.

Gaiman, N. (2006). *Coraline.* New York: HarperCollins.

Gallant, R. A. (1991). *Earth's vanishing forests.* New York: Macmillan.

Gallo, D. R. (2007). *First crossing: Stories about teen immigrants.* Cambridge, MA: Candlewick Press.

Gambrell, L. B. (1980). Think-time: Implications for reading instruction. *Reading Teacher, 33,* 143–146.

Gantos, J. (2002). *Hole in my life.* New York: Farrar, Straus & Giroux.

Garcia, E. (2002). *Student cultural diversity: Understanding and meeting the challenge* (3rd ed.). Boston: Houghton Mifflin.

García, G. E., & Godina, H. (2004). Addressing the literacy needs of adolescent English language learners. In T. Jetton & J. A. Dole (Eds.), *Adolescent literacy research and practice* (pp. 304–320). New York: Guilford Press.

Garland, S. (1993). *The lotus seed.* Ill. T. Kiuchi. San Diego, CA: Harcourt.

Gee, J. P. (1996). *Social linguistics and literacies: Ideology in discourses* (2nd ed.). London: Falmer Press.

Gere, A. R. (Ed.). (1985). *Roots in the sawdust: Writing to learn across the disciplines.* Urbana, IL: National Council of Teachers of English.

Gersten, R., & Jimenez, R. (1994). A delicate balance: Enhancing literature instruction for students of English as a second language. *Reading Teacher, 47,* 438–449.

Giblin, J. (1994). *Thomas Jefferson: A picture book biography.* Ill. M. Dooling. New York: Scholastic.

Giblin, J. C. (1995). *When plague strikes: The Black Death, smallpox, AIDS.* New York: HarperCollins.

Giblin, J. C. (2000). *The amazing life of Benjamin Franklin.* Ill. M. Dooling. New York: Scholastic.

Giblin, J. (2000). More than just the facts: A hundred years of children's nonfiction. *The Horn Book, 76,* 413–424.

Giblin, J. (2002). *The life and death of Adolf Hitler.* New York: Clarion Books.

Gillet, J., & Kita, M. J. (1979). Words, kids, and categories. *Reading Teacher, 32,* 538–542.

Goble, P. (1991). *I sing for the animals.* New York: Bradbury.

Gold, P., & Yellin, D. (1982). Be the focus: A psycho-educational technique for use with unmotivated learners. *Journal of Reading, 25*(5), 550–552.

Golenbock, P. (1990). *Teammates.* Ill. P. Bacon. San Diego, CA: Harcourt Brace Jovanovich.

Gomez, L. M., & Gomez, K. (2007). Reading for learning: Literacy supports for 21st century work. *Phi Delta Kappan, 89*(3), 224–228.

Gonick, L. (1991). *Cartoon history of the United States.* New York: HarperCollins.

Goodall, J. (1979). *The story of an English village.* New York: Atheneum.

Goodlad, J. (1984). *A place called school.* New York: McGraw-Hill.

Goodman, D. J. (2000). Motivating people from privileged groups to support social justice. *Teachers College Record, 102,* 1061–1086

Goodman, K., & Goodman, Y. (1978). *Reading of American children whose language is a stable rural dialect of English or a language other than English.* Washington, DC: National Institute of Education. (ERIC Document Reproduction Service No. ED173754)

Goodrich, F., & Hackett, A. (2000). *The diary of Anne Frank: Play and related readings.* New York: Dramatists Play Service.

Graham, S. (2005). Strategy instruction and the teaching of writing: A meta-analysis. In C. A. MacArthur, S. Graham, & J. Fitzgerald (Eds.), *Handbook of writing research.* New York: Guilford Press.

Gray, W. S. (1925). *Summary of investigations related to reading* (Supplementary Educational Monographs, No. 28). Chicago: University of Chicago Press.

Gredler, M. E., & Johnson, R. L. (2004). *Assessment in the literacy classroom.* Boston: Pearson.

Greenberg, J., & Jordan, S. (1998). *Chuck Close: Up close.* New York: DK.

Greene, B. (1999). *Summer of my German soldier.* New York: Puffin Books.

Greene, M. (1997). Metaphors and multiples: Representation, the arts, and history. *Phi Delta Kappan, 78,* 387–394.

Greenlee-Moore, M. E., & Smith, L. L. (1996). Interactive computer software: The effects on young children's reading achievement. *Reading Psychology, 17,* 43–64.

Griffin, G. A. (1991). Interactive staff development: Using what we know. In A. Lieberman & L. Miller (Eds.), *Staff development for education in the '90s* (pp. 243–258). New York: Teachers College Press.

Grimes, N. (2002). *Bronx masquerade.* New York: Speak.

Grove, N. (1981, March). Wild cargo: The business of smuggling animals. *National Geographic, 159,* 287–315.

Gruenewald, M. M. (2005). *Looking like the enemy: My story of imprisonment in Japanese American internment camps.* Troutdale, OR: New Sage Press.

Guastello, E. F., Beasley, T. M., & Sinatra, R. C. (2000). Concept mapping effects on science content comprehension of low-achieving inner-city seventh graders. *Remedial and Special Education, 21,* 356–365.

Guilfoyle, C. (2006). NCLB: Is there life beyond testing? *Educational Leadership, 64*(3), 8–13.

Gunderson, L. (2007). *English-only instruction and immigrant students in secondary schools: A critical examination.* Mahwah, NJ: Erlbaum.

Gunderson, L. (2009, February). *Where are the English Language Learners?* Paper presented at English Language Learner Institute at the Annual Convention of the International Reading Association, Phoenix, AZ.

Guth, N. D., & Pettengill, S. S. (2005). *Leading a successful reading program: Administrators and reading specialists working together to make it happen.* Newark, DE: International Reading Association.

Guthrie, J. T., & Davis, M. H. (2003). Motivating struggling readers in middle school through an engagement model of classroom practice. *Reading and Writing Quarterly, 19,* 59–85.

Guthrie, J. T., & Humenick, N. M. (2004). Motivating students to read: Evidence for classroom practices that increase reading motivation and achievement. In P. McCardle & V. Chhabra (Eds.), *The voice of evidence in reading research* (pp. 329–354). Baltimore: Brookes.

Guthrie, J. T., & McCann, A. D. (1996). Idea circles: Peer collaborations for conceptual learning. In L. B. Gambrell & J. F. Almasi (Eds.), *Lively discusssions! Fostering engaged reading* (pp. 87–105). Newark, DE: International Reading Association.

Guthrie, J. T., Schafer, W. D., & Huang, C. (2001). Benefits of opportunity to read and balanced instruction on the NAEP. *Journal of Educational Research, 94,* 145–162.

Guthrie, J. T., & Wigfield, A. (1997). Reading engagement: A rationale for theory and teaching. In J. T. Guthrie & A. Wigfield (Eds.), *Reading engagement: Motivating readers through integrated instruction* (pp. 1–12). Newark, DE: International Reading Association.

Guthrie, J. T., & Wigfield, A. (2000). Engagement and motivation in reading. In M. Kamil, P. Mosenthal, P. D. Pearson, & R. Barr (Eds.), *Handbook of reading research, Vol. III* (pp. 403–424). Mahwah, NJ: Erlbaum.

Hadaway, N. L., Vardell, S. M., & Young, T. A. (2002). *Literature-based instruction with English language learners*. Boston: Allyn & Bacon.

Haggard, M. R. (1986). The vocabulary self-collection strategy: Using student interest and world knowledge to enhance vocabulary growth. *Journal of Reading, 29*, 634–642.

Hahn, M. D. (2003). *Hear the wind blow.* New York: Clarion Books.

Hakim, J. (1999). *A history of US.* New York: Oxford University Press.

Hall, B. (2004). *Literacy coaches: An evolving role.* Retrieved October 21, 2006, from www.carnegie.org/reporter/09literacy/index.html

Halliday, M., & Hasan, R. (1976). *Cohesion in English*. London: Longman.

Hamilton, V. (1985). *The people could fly: American black folktales*. New York: Knopf.

Hamilton, V. (1988). *In the beginning: Creation stories from around the world*. Orlando, FL: Harcourt Brace.

Hancock, M. (2007). *A celebration of literature and response: Children, books, and teachers in K–8 classrooms* (3rd ed.). New York: Prentice Hall.

Hancock, M. R. (1993). Exploring and extending personal response through literature journals. *Reading Teacher, 46*, 466–474.

Hansen, J. (1986). *Which way freedom?* New York: Walker.

Hare, V. C., & Borchardt, K. M. (1984). Direct instruction of summarization skills. *Reading Research Quarterly, 20*, 62–78.

Harmon, J. M., Hedrick, W. B., Wood, K., & Gress, M. (2005). Vocabulary self-selection: A study of middle-school students' word selections from expository texts. *Reading Writing Quarterly, 26*, 313–333.

Hart, P. D., & Teeter, R. M. (2002). *A national priority: Americans speak on teacher quality.* Princeton, NJ: Educational Testing Service.

Harvey, S. (1998). *Nonfiction matters: Reading, writing, and research in grades 3–8*. Portland, ME: Stenhouse.

Harvey, S., & Goudvis, A. (2000). *Strategies that work: Teaching comprehension to enhance understanding*. York, ME: Stenhouse.

Harvey, S., & Goudvis, A. (2007). *Strategies that work: Teaching comprehension for understanding and engagement.* York, ME: Stenhouse.

Hayes, D. A. (1989). Helping students grasp the knack of writing summaries. *Journal of Reading, 33*, 96–101.

Haynes, J. (2007). *Getting started with English language learners: How educators can meet the challenge*. Alexandria, VA: Association for Supervision and Curriculum Development.

Healy, M. K. (1982). Using student response groups in the classroom. In G. Camp (Ed.), *Teaching writing: Essays from the Bay Area writing project* (pp. 266–290). Portsmouth, NH: Boyton-Cook.

Heath, S. (1983). *Ways with words: Language, life, and work in communities and classrooms*. Cambridge, MA: Harvard University Press.

Heath, S., & Mangiola, L. (1989). *Children of promise: Literate activity on linguistically and culturally diverse classrooms*. Washington, DC: National Education Association.

Helfer, A. (2006). *Malcolm X: A graphic biography.* New York: Farrar, Straus & Giroux.

Herber, H. L. (1964). Teaching reading and physics simultaneously. In J. A. Figurel (Ed.), *Improvement of reading through classroom practice. Proceedings of the 9th Annual Convention of the International Reading Association, 9*, 84–85.

Herber, H. L. (1970). *Teaching reading in content areas*. Englewood Cliffs, NJ: Prentice Hall.

Herber, H. L. (1978). *Teaching reading in content areas* (2nd ed.). Upper Saddle River, NJ: Prentice Hall.

Hesse, K. (1997). *Out of the dust*. New York: Scholastic.

Hibbing, A. N., & Rankin-Erickson, J. L. (2003). A picture is worth a thousand words: Using visual images to improve comprehension for middle school struggling readers. *Reading Teacher, 56,* 758–770.

Hickam, H. (1998). *Rocket boys.* New York: Delacorte.

Hinds, G. (2007). *Beowulf.* New York: Candlewick.

Hobbs, R., & Frost, R. (2003). Measuring the acquisition of media-literacy skills. *Reading Research Quarterly, 38,* 330–355.

Hobbs, W. (1989). *Bearstone.* New York: Atheneum.

Hoffman, J. V. (1979). The intra-act procedure for critical reading. *Journal of Reading, 22,* 605–608.

Hoffman, J. V. (1992). Critical reading/thinking across the curriculum: Using I-charts to support learning. *Language Arts, 69,* 121–127.

Hoffman, J. V., Au, K. H., Harrison, C., Paris, S. G., Pearson, P. D., Santa, C. M., Silver, S. H., & Valencia, S. W. (1999). High-stakes assessments in reading: Consequences, concerns, and common sense. In S. J. Barrentine (Ed.), *Reading assessment: Principles and practices for elementary teachers* (pp. 21–34). Newark, DE: International Reading Association.

Holston, V., & Santa, C. (1985). RAFT: A method of writing across the curriculum that works. *Journal of Reading, 28,* 456–457.

Holt, K. W. (1999). *When Zachary Beaver came to town.* New York: Holt.

Homer, C. (1979). A direct reading-thinking activity for content areas. In R. T. Vacca & J. A. Meagher (Eds.), *Reading through content* (pp. 41–48). Storrs: University Publications and the University of Connecticut Reading-Language Arts Center.

Honey, M. (1999). *Bitter fruit: African American women in World War II.* Columbia: University of Missouri Press.

Hoose, P. M. (2001). *We were there, too! Young people in U.S. history.* New York: Farrar, Straus & Giroux.

Hopkins, E. (2008). *Impulse.* New York: Margaret K. McElderry.

Hosseini, K. (2007). *A thousand splendid suns.* New York: Riverhead.

Hoyt-Goldsmith, D. (1994). *Day of the Dead: A Mexican-American celebration.* Photo. L. Migdale. New York: Holiday House.

Huey, E. (1908). *The psychology and pedagogy of reading.* New York: Macmillan.

Hunt, I. (1964). *Across five Aprils.* New York: Follett.

Hunt, J. (2007, March/April). Redefining the young adult novel. *Horn Book.* 2007. Retrieved February 14, 2009, from www.hbook.com/magazine/articles/2007/mar07_hunt.asp

Hymes, D. (1972). On communicative competence. In J. Pride & J. Holmes (Eds.), *Sociolinguistics.* Harmondsworth, UK: Penguin.

Hynd, C. R., McNish, M. E., Guzzetti, B., Lay, K., & Fowler, P. (1994). *What high school students say about their science texts.* Paper presented at the annual meeting of the College Reading Association, New Orleans.

Igoa, C. (1995). *The inner world of the immigrant student.* Mahwah, NJ: Lawrence Erlbaum.

Igus, T. (1998). *I see the rhythm.* San Francisco: Children's Book Press.

Innocenti, R. (1985). *Rose Blanche.* San Diego, CA: Creative Editions.

International Reading Association. (1999a). *Adolescent literacy position statement.* Newark, DE: Author.

International Reading Association. (1999b). *High-stakes assessments in reading: A position paper of the International Reading Association.* Newark, DE: Author.

International Reading Association. (2005). *Standards for middle and high school literacy coaches.* Newark, DE: Author. Retrieved March 1, 2006, from www.reading.org/downloads/resources/597coaching_standards.pdf

International Reading Association. (2006). *Standards for reading professionals.* Retrieved July 6, 2006, from www.reading.org/styleguide/standards_reading_profs.html

International Reading Association. (2006). *Standards for middle and high school literacy coaches.* Newark, DE: Author.

International Reading Association. (2008). *Implications for reading teachers in response to intervention (RTI).* Retrieved October 9, 2008, from www.reading.org/downloads/resources/rti0707_implications.pdf

International Reading Association and National Council of Teachers of English. (1997). *Standards for the English language arts.* Newark, DE: Author.

Irwin, J. W., & Davis, C. A. (1980). Assessing readability: The checklist approach. *Journal of Reading, 24,* 124–130.

Ivey, G. (2002). Getting started: Manageable literacy practices. *Educational Leadership, 60,* 20–23.

Ivey, G., & Broaddus, K. (2001). "Just plain reading": A survey of what makes students want to read in middle school classrooms. *Reading Research Quarterly, 36,* 350–377.

Ivey, G., & Fisher, D. (2005). Learning from what doesn't work. *Educational Leadership, 63*(2), 8–15.

Izzo, A., & Schmidt, P. R. (2006). A successful ABC's in-service project: Supporting culturally responsive teaching. In P. R. Schmidt & C. Finkbeiner (Eds.), *ABC's of cultural understanding and communication: National and international adaptations* (pp. 19–42). Greenwich, CT: Information Age Publishing.

Jackson, F. (1994). Seven strategies to support culturally responsive pedagogy. *Journal of Reading, 37,* 298–303.

Jackson, R. (1975). *Inside hitting with Reggie Jackson.* Chicago: Regnery.

James, F. (2004). *Response to intervention in the Individuals with Disabilities Education Act (IDEA) 2004.* Retrieved November 19, 2008, from www.reading.org/downloads/resources/IDEA_RTI /report.pdf

Jasper, K. C. (1995). The limits of technology. *English Journal, 84*(6), 16–17.

Jenkins, S. (2002). *Life on earth: The story of evolution.* Boston: Houghton Mifflin

Jimenez, R., & Gamez, A. (1996). Literature-based cognitive strategy instruction for middle school Latina/o students. *Journal of Adolescent & Adult Literacy, 40*(2), 84–91.

Jimenez, R., Garcia, G., & Pearson, P. D. (1995). Three children, two languages, and strategic reading: Case studies in bilingual/monolingual reading. *American Educational Research Journal, 32,* 67–97.

Jimenez, R., Garcia, G., & Pearson, P. D. (1996). The reading strategies of bilingual Latina/o students who are successful English readers: Opportunities and obstacles. *Reading Research Quarterly, 32*(1), 90–112.

Johnson, A. (2003). *The first part last.* New York: Simon Pulse.

Johnson, D. D., & Pearson, P. D. (1984). *Teaching reading vocabulary* (2nd ed.). Fort Worth, TX: Holt, Rinehart, and Winston.

Johnson, D. W., & Johnson, R. T. (1987). *Learning together and alone: Cooperative, conjunctive, and individualistic learning* (2nd ed.). Englewood Cliffs, NJ: Prentice Hall.

Johnson, D. W., & Johnson, R. T. (1990). *Learning together and alone: Cooperative, conjunctive, and individualistic learning* (3rd ed.). Upper Saddle River, NJ: Prentice Hall.

Johnson, D. W., Johnson, R. T., & Holubec, E. J. (1990). *Circles of learning: Cooperation in the classroom* (3rd ed.). Edina, MN: Interaction Book.

Johnson, D. W., & Steele, V. (1996). So many words, so little time: Helping college ESL learners acquire vocabulary-building strategies. *Journal of Adolescent & Adult Literacy, 39,* 348–357.

Johnson, E., Mellard, D. F., Fuchs, D., & McKnight, M. A. (2006). *Responsiveness to intervention: How to do it.* Lawrence, KS: National Research Center on Learning Disabilities.

Jones, B. F., Pierce, J., & Hunter, B. (1988–1989). Teaching students to construct graphic representations. *Educational Leadership, 46*(4), 20–25.

Kamil, M. (2003). *Adolescents and literacy: Reading for the 21st century.* Washington, DC: Alliance for Excellent Education.

Kang, H. (1994). Helping second language readers learn from content area text through collaboration and support. *Journal of Reading, 37,* 646–652.

Kaplan, L. S., & Owings, W. A. (2003). The politics of teacher quality. *Phi Delta Kappan, 84*(9), 687–692.

Karchmer, R. A., Mallette, M. H., Kara-Soteriou, J., & Leu, D. J. (2005). *Innovative approaches to literacy education: Using the Internet to support new literacies.* Newark, DE: International Reading Association.

Kaywell, J. (1994). Using young adult fiction and nonfiction to produce critical readers. *The ALAN Review, 21,* 1–6.

Keegan, J. (2003). *The first world war.* New York: Random House.

Kieffer, M. J., & Lesaux, N. K. (2007). Breaking down words to build meaning: Morphology, vocabulary, and reading, comprehension in the urban classroom. *The Reading Teacher, 61*(2), 134–144.

Kennedy, B. (1985). Writing letters to learn math. *Learning, 13,* 58–61.

King, C., & Osborne, L. B. (1997). *Oh freedom! Kids talk about the civil rights movement with the people who made it happen.* New York: Knopf.

Kinney, J. (2007). *The diary of a wimpy kid.* New York: Abrams Books.

Kintsch, W. (1977). On comprehending stories. In M. A. Just & P. A. Carpenter (Eds.), *Cognitive processes in comprehension* (pp. 360–401). Mahwah, NJ: Erlbaum.

Kintsch, W., & van Dijk, T. (1978). Toward a model of text comprehension and production. *Psychological Review, 85,* 363–394.

Kirby, D., Liner, T., & Vinz, M. (1988). *Inside out: Developmental strategies for teaching writing* (2nd ed.). Montclair, NJ: Boynton/Cook.

Kist, W. (2000). Beginning to create the new literacy classroom: What does the new literacy look like? *Journal of Adolescent & Adult Literacy, 43,* 710–718.

Kist, W. (2005). *New literacies in action: Teaching and learning in multiple media.* New York: Teachers College Press.

Kist, W. (2007a). Basement new literacies: Dialogue with a first-year teacher. *English Journal, 97*(1), 43–48.

Kist, W. (2007b). Vocabulary media journals: Finding multimedia to define words. In M. T. Christel & S. Sullivan (Eds.), *Lesson plans for creating media-rich classrooms* (pp. 23–29). Urbana, IL: National Council of Teachers of English.

Kist, W. (2010). *The socially networked classroom: Teaching in the new media age.* Thousand Oaks, CA: Corwin Press.

Kitchen, B. (1993). *And so they build.* New York: Dial.

Klein, N. (2000). *No logo: Taking aim at the brand bullies.* New York: Picador.

Klein, S. P., Hamilton, L. S., McCaffrey, D. F., & Stecher, B. M. (2000). *Issue paper: What do test scores in Texas tell us?* Santa Monica, CA: Rand.

Knickerbocker, J. L., & Rycik, J. (2002). Growing into literature: Adolescents' literary interpretation and appreciation. *Journal of Adolescent & Adult Literacy, 46*(3), 196–208.

Knoeller, C. P. (1994). Negotiating interpretations of text: The role of student-led discussions in understanding literature. *Journal of Reading, 37,* 572–580.

Koretz, D. M. (2008). *Measuring up: What educational testing really tells us.* Cambridge, MA: Harvard University Press.

Koretz, D., & Barron, S. T. (1998). *The validity of gains in scores on the Kentucky Instructional Results Information System.* Santa Monica, CA: Rand.

Kress, G. (2003). *Literacy in the new media age.* London: Routledge.

Krogness, M. (1995). *Just teach me, Mrs K: Talking, reading, and writing with resistant adolescent learners.* Portsmouth, NH: Heinemann.

Krull, K. (1993). *Lives of the musicians: Good times, bad times (and what the neighbors thought).* Ill. K. Hewitt. San Diego, CA: Harcourt Brace Jovanovich.

Krull, K. (1995). *Lives of the artists: Masterpieces, messes (and what the neighbors thought).* Ill. K. Hewitt. San Diego, CA: Harcourt Brace.

Krull, K. (1997). *Lives of the athletes: Thrills, spills (and what the neighbors thought).* Ill K. Hewitt. San Diego, CA: Harcourt Brace.

Krull, K. (2000). *Wilma unlimited: How Wilma Rudolph became the world's fastest woman.* Ill. D. Diaz. San Diego, CA: Harcourt Brace.

Krull, K. (2003). *Harvesting hope: The story of Cesar Chavez.* San Diego, CA: Harcourt.

Kubey, R., & Baker, F. (1999, October 27). Has media literacy found a curricular foothold? *Education Week.* Retrieved August 27, 2008, from www.frankwbaker.com/edweek.htm

Ladson-Billings, G. (1994). *The dreamkeepers: Successful teachers of African American students.* San Francisco: Jossey-Bass.

Ladson-Billings, G. (1995). Toward a theory of culturally relevant pedagogy. *American Educational Research Journal, 32,* 465–491.

Ladson-Billings, G. (1999). Preparing teachers for diverse student populations: A critical race theory perspective. In A. I. Nejad & P. D. Pearson (Eds.), *Review of research in education* (Vol. 24, pp. 211–247). Washington, DC: American Education Research Association.

Langer, J. A. (1981). From theory to practice: A prereading plan. *Journal of Reading, 25,* 152–156.

Langer, J. A., & Applebee, A. N. (1987). *How writing shapes thinking.* Urbana, IL: National Council of Teachers of English.

Langer, J. A., & Flihan, S. (2000). Writing and reading relationships: Constructive tasks. In R.

Indrisano & J. R. Squire (Eds.), *Perspectives on writing: Research, theory, and practice.* Newark, DE: International Reading Association.

Langstaff, J. (1991). *Climbing Jacob's ladder.* New York: Macmillan.

Lankshear, C., & Knobel, M. (2003). *New literacies: Changing knowledge and classroom learning.* Buckingham, UK: Open University Press.

Lapp, D., Fisher, D., Flood, J., & Cabello, A. (2001). An integrated approach to the teaching and assessment of language arts. In S. Hurley & J. V. Tinajero (Eds.), *Literacy assessment of second language learners* (pp. 11–26). Boston: Allyn & Bacon.

Lapp, D., & Flood, J. (1995). Strategies for gaining access to the information superhighway: Off the side street and on to the main road. *Reading Teacher, 48,* 432–436.

Lasky, K. (1994). *The librarian who measured the earth.* Ill. K. Hawkes. New York: Little, Brown.

Lasky, K. (2003). *The man who made time travel.* Ill. K. Hawkes. New York: Farrar, Straus & Giroux.

Lauber, P. (1986). *Volcano: The eruption and healing of Mount St. Helens.* New York: Bradbury Press.

Lauber, P. (1996). *Hurricanes: Earth's mightiest storms.* New York: Scholastic.

Lawrence, L. (1985). *Children of the dust.* New York: HarperCollins.

Lee, C. D. (2004, Winter/Spring). Literacy in the academic disciplines and the needs of adolescent struggling readers. *Voices in Urban Education (VUE),* 14–19.

Leffland, E. (1979). *Rumors of peace.* New York: Harper & Row.

Leland, C. H., & Harste, J. C. (1994). Multiple ways of knowing: Curriculum in a new key. *Language Arts, 71,* 337–345.

Lenhart, A., Arafeh, S., Smith, A., & Macgill, A. (2008). *Writing, technology, and teens.* Washington, DC: Pew Internet and American Life Project.

Lenihan, G. (2003). Reading with adolescents: Constructing meaning together. *Journal of Adolescent & Adult Literacy, 47*(1), 8–12.

Lenters, K. (2006). Resistance, struggle, and the adolescent reader. *Journal of Adolescent and Adult Literacy, 50*(2), 136–146.

Lester, J. (1968). *To be a slave.* New York: Dial Press.

Lester, J. D. (1984). *Writing research papers: A complete guide* (4th ed.). Glenview, IL: Scott Foresman.

Leu, D. J., Jr. (1996). Sarah's secret: Social aspects of literacy and learning in a digital information age. *Reading Teacher, 50,* 162–165.

Leu, D. J., Jr. (2000). Literacy and technology: Deictic consequences for literacy education in an information age. In M. L. Kamil, P. M. Mosenthal, P. D. Pearson, & R. Barr (Eds.), *Handbook of reading research* (Vol. 3, pp. 743–770). Mahwah, NJ: Erlbaum.

Leu, D. J., Jr. (2002). The new literacies: Research on reading instruction with the Internet. In A. E. Farstrup & S. J. Samuels (Eds.), *What research has to say about reading instruction* (pp. 310–336). Newark, DE: International Reading Association.

Leu, D. J., Coiro, J., Castek, J., Hartman, D. K., Henry, L. A., & Reinking, D. (2008). Research on instruction and assessment in the new literacies of online reading comprehension. In C. C. Block, S. Parris, & P. Afflerbach (Eds.), *Comprehension instruction: Research-based best practices.* New York: Guilford Press.

Leu, D. J., Jr., & Leu, D. D. (2000). *Teaching with the Internet: Lessons from the classroom* (3rd ed.). Norwood, MA: Christopher-Gordon.

Leu, D. J., Leu, D. D., & Coiro, J. (2006). *Teaching with the Internet K–12: New literacies for new times (*4th ed.). Norwood, MA: Christopher-Gordon.

Levin, E. (1992). *If you traveled west in a covered wagon.* New York: Scholastic.

Levin, E. (1996). *If your name was changed at Ellis Island.* New York: Scholastic.

Levine, D. S. (1985). The biggest thing I learned but it really doesn't have to do with science. . . . *Language Arts, 62,* 43–47.

Li, G. (2005). *Culturally contested pedagogy: Battles of literacy and schooling between mainstream teachers and Asian immigrant parents.* Albany: SUNY Press.

Li, G. (2009). *Multicultural families, home literacies, and mainstream schooling.* Charlotte, NC: Information Age Publishing.

Lin, G. (2007). *The year of the dog.* Boston: Little, Brown.

Lindbergh, R., & Brown, R. (1992). *A view from the air: Charles Lindbergh's earth and sky.* New York: Viking.

Linek, W. M. (1991). Grading and evaluation techniques for whole language teachers. *Language Arts, 68,* 125–132.

Lipsky, D. K., & Gartner, A. (1997). *Inclusion and school reform: Transforming America's classrooms.* Baltimore: Paul H. Brookes.

Little Soldier, L. (1989). Cooperative learning and the Native American student. *Phi Delta Kappan, 71,* 161–163.

Llewellyn, C. (1991). *Under the sea.* New York: Simon & Schuster.

Loh, V. (2006). Quantity and quality: The need for culturally authentic trade books in Asian American young adult literature. *The ALAN Review,* 34(1), 36–53.

Lowe, S. (1990). *Walden.* Ill. R. Sabuda. New York: Philomel.

Lowry, L. (1993). *The giver.* New York: Houghton Mifflin.

Lyga, A. W. (2004). *Graphic novels in your media center.* Colorado Springs, CO: Libraries Unlimited.

Lyon, G. E. (1991). *Cecil's story.* New York: Orchard.

Ma, W. (2004). *Intellectual gazing: Participatory learning in a graduate seminar.* Unpublished doctoral dissertation, University at Buffalo.

Ma, W. (2007). Dialoging internally: Participatory learning in a graduate seminar. In C. C. Park, R. Endo, S. J. Lee, & X. L. Rong (Eds.), *Asian American education: Acculturation, literacy development, and learning* (pp. 167–195). Charlotte, NC: Information Age Publishing.

Ma, W. (2008). Participatory dialogue and participatory learning in a discussion-based graduate seminar. *Journal of Literacy Research, 40*(2), 220–249.

Macaulay, D. (1973). *Cathedral: The story of its construction.* Boston: Houghton Mifflin.

Macaulay, D. (1978). *Castle.* Boston: Houghton Mifflin.

Macaulay, D. (1982). *Pyramid.* Boston: Houghton Mifflin.

Macaulay, D. (1998). *The new way things work.* Boston: Houghton Mifflin.

Macaulay, D. (2008). *The way we work.* Boston: Houghton Mifflin.

MacGinitie, W. H. (1993). Some limits of assessment. *Journal of Reading, 36,* 556–560.

Maguire, K. (2001). *Governors find education bill faults.* Retrieved October 2002 from www.speakout.com/cgi-bin/edt/im.display.printable?client.id=speakout&story.id=10037

Malinowski, B. (1954). *Magic, science and religion and other essays.* New York: Doubleday.

Manzo, A. V. (1969). The ReQuest procedure. *Journal of Reading, 11,* 123–126.

Manzo, A. V. (1975). Guided reading procedure. *Journal of Reading, 18,* 287–291.

Manzo, A., Manzo, U., & Estes, T. (2001). *Content area literacy: Interactive teaching for interactive learning.* New York: Wiley.

Marsalis, W. (1995). *Marsalis on music.* New York: Norton.

Maruki, T. (1980). *Hiroshima no pika.* New York: Lothrop, Lee & Shepard.

Marzano, R. J. (2003). *What works in schools: Translating research into action.* Alexandria, VA: Association for Supervision and Curriculum Development.

Massell, D., Kirst, M., & Hoppe, M. (1997). *Persistence and change: Standards-based reforms in nine states.* Consortium for Policy Research in Education, University of Pennsylvania, Graduate School of Education. Washington, DC: U.S. Department of Education.

Matas, C. (2001). *The war within: A novel of the Civil War.* New York: Simon & Schuster.

Matthew, K. (1996). What do children think of CD-ROM storybooks? *Texas Reading Report, 18,* 6.

McColl, A. (2005). Tough call: Is No Child Left Behind constitutional? [Electronic version]. *Phi Delta Kappan, 86*(6), 604–610.

McCullen, C. (1998). The electronic thread: Research and assessment on the Internet. *Middle Ground, 1*(3), 7–9.

McGinley, W. J., & Denner, P. R. (1987). Story impressions: A pre-reading/writing activity. *Journal of Reading, 31,* 248–253.

McIntosh, M. (1991, September). No time for writing in your class? *Mathematics Teacher,* pp. 423–433.

McKenna, M. C., & Robinson, R. D. (2006). *Teaching through text: Reading and writing in the content areas* (4th ed.). Boston: Pearson.

McKeon, C. (2001). E-mail as a motivating literacy event for one student: Donna's case. *Reading Research and Instruction, 40*(3), 185–202.

McKinley, R. (1978). *Beauty: A retelling of the story of* Beauty and the Beast. New York: HarperCollins.

McLaren, P. (1989). *Life in schools: An introduction to critical pedagogy in the foundations of education.* New York: Longman.

McPherson, J. (2002). *Fields of fury: The American Civil War.* New York: Atheneum.

McTighe, J., & Lyman, F. T. (1988). Cueing thinking in the classroom: The promise of theory-embedded tools. *Educational Leadership, 45*(7), 18–24.

Merkley, D. M., & Jefferies, D. (2001). Guidelines for implementing a graphic organizer. *Reading Teacher, 54,* 350–357.

MetaMetrics (2008). *The Lexile framework for reading: FAQ.* Retrieved September 19, 2008, from www.lexile.com/DesktopDefault.aspx?view=ed&tabindex=6&tabid=18

Meyer, B. J. F., Brandt, D., & Bluth, G. (1980). Use of top-level structure in text: Key for reading comprehension of ninth-grade students. *Reading Research Quarterly, 16,* 72–103.

Meyer, B. J. F., & Rice, E. (1984). The structure of text. In P. D. Pearson (Ed.), *Handbook of reading research* (pp. 319–352). New York: Longman.

Miholic, V. (1994). An inventory to pique students' metacognitive awareness. *Journal of Reading, 38*(2), 84–86.

Mike, D. G. (1996). Internet in the schools: A literacy perspective. *Journal of Adolescent and Adult Literacy, 40,* 4–13.

Miller, T. (1998). The place of picture books in middle-level classrooms. *Journal of Adolescent and Adult Literacy, 41*(5), 376–382.

Millman, I. (2005). *Hidden child.* New York: Farrar, Straus & Giroux.

Moje, E. B. (2007). Developing socially just subject-matter instruction: A review of the literature on disciplinary literacy. In N. L. Parker (Ed.), *Review of research in education* (pp. 1–44). Washington, DC: American Educational Research Association.

Moje, E. B. (2008). Responsive literacy teaching in secondary school content areas. In M. W. Conley, J. R. Freidhoff, M. B. Sherry, & S. F. Tuckey (Eds.), *Meeting the challenge of adolescent literacy* (pp. 58–87). New York: Guilford Press.

Moje, E. B., Ciechanowski, K. M., Kramer, K., Ellis, L., Carrillo, R., & Collazo, T. (2004). Working toward third space in content area literacy: An examination of everyday funds of knowledge and discourse. *Reading Research Quarterly, 39*(1), 38–70.

Moje, E., Overby, M., Tysvaer, N., & Morris, K. (2008). The complex world of adolescent literacy: Myths, motivations, and mysteries. *Harvard Educational Review, 78*(1), 107–154.

Moje, E. B., Young, J. P., Readence, J. E., & Moore, D. W. (2000). Reinventing adolescent literacy for new times: Perennial and millennial issues. *Journal of Adolescent & Adult Literacy 43,* 400–410.

Moll, L. (1994). Literacy research in community and classrooms: A sociocultural approach. In R. B. Ruddell & H. Singer (Eds.), *Theoretical models and processes in reading.* Newark, DE: International Reading Association.

Moll, L. C. (1992). Bilingual classroom studies and community analysis: Recent trends. *Educational Researcher, 21*(2), 20–24.

Moore, D. W., Bean, T. W., Birdyshaw, D., & Rycik, J. A. (1999). *Adolescent literacy: A position statement for the Commission on Adolescent Literacy of the International Reading Association.* Newark, DE: International Reading Association.

Moore, D., Moore, S., Cunningham, P., & Cunningham, J. (2006). *Developing readers and writers in the content areas K–12.* Boston: Allyn & Bacon.

Moore, J., & Whitfield, V. F. (2008). Musing: A way to inform and inspire pedagogy through self-reflection. *Reading Teacher, 6*(17), 586–588.

Moore, M. T. (2004). Issues and trends in writing instruction. In R. Robinson, M. McKenna, & J. Wedman (Eds.), *Issues and trends in literacy education* (3rd ed.). Boston: Allyn & Bacon.

Morgan, W. (1997). *Critical literacy in the classroom: The art of the possible.* New York: Routledge.

Moss, B. (1995). Using children's nonfiction tradebooks as read-alouds (Teacher's notebook). *Language Arts, 72,* 122–126.

Moss, B. (2003). *Exploring the literature of fact: Children's nonfiction trade books in the elementary classroom.* New York: Guilford Press.

Mraz, M. (2000). The literacy program selection process from the perspective of school district administrators. *Ohio Reading Teacher, 34*(2), 40–48.

Mraz, M. (2002). Factors that influence policy decisions in literacy: Perspectives of key policy informants. Ph.D. dissertation, Kent State University.

Mraz, M., Algozzine, B., & Kissel, B. (2009). *The literacy coach's companion.* Thousand Oaks, CA, and Newark, DE: Corwin Press and the International Reading Association.

Mraz, M., Algozzine, B., & Watson, P. (2008). Perceptions and expectations of roles and responsibilities of literacy coaching. *Literacy Research and Instruction, 47,* 141–157.

Mraz, M., Vacca, J. V., & Vintinner, J. P. (2008). Professional development. In S. Wepner & D. Strickland (Eds.), *The administration and supervision of reading programs* (4th ed., pp. 133–143). New York: Teachers College Press.

Mühlberger, R. (1993). *What makes a Monet a Monet?* New York: Metropolitan Museum of Art/Viking.

Murphy, J. (1990). *The boys' war: Confederate and Union soldiers talk about the Civil War.* New York: Clarion Books.

Murphy, J. (1992). *The long road to Gettysburg.* New York: Clarion Books.

Murphy, J. (1998). *The great fire.* New York: Clarion.

Murray, D. M. (1980). Writing as process: How writing finds its own meaning. In T. R. Donovan & B. W. McClelland (Eds.), *Eight approaches to teaching composition* (pp. 80–97). Urbana, IL: National Council of Teachers of English.

Myers, W. D. (1991). *Now is your time!: The African-American struggle for freedom.* New York: HarperCollins.

Myers, W. D. (2001). *Monster.* New York: Amistad.

Myers, W. D. (2002). *Patrol: An American soldier in Vietnam.* Ill. A. Grifalconi. New York: HarperCollins.

Nagy, W. E. (1988). *Teaching vocabulary to improve reading comprehension.* Newark, DE: International Reading Association.

National Association of Secondary School Principals (NASSP). (2005). Creating a culture of literacy: A guide for middle and high school principals. Retrieved March 30, 2006, from www.principals.org/s_nassp/sec.asp

National Center for Educational Statistics. (2007). *The nation's report card: Reading 2007.* Retrieved April 17, 2009, from www.nces.ed.gov/pubSearch/pubinfo.asp?pubid=2007496

National Commission on Writing. (2003). *The neglected R: The need for a writing revolution.* Retrieved from www.writingcommission.org

National Council for Accreditation of Teacher Education. (2009). *A continuum of educator preparation and development.* Washington DC: Author.

National Council of Teachers of English (NCTE). (2006). *NCTE principles of adolescent literacy reform: A policy research brief.* Retrieved July 7, 2007, from www.ncte.org/library/NCTEFiles/Resources/PolicyResearch/AdolLitResearchBrief.pdf

National Council of Teachers of Mathematics (NCTM). (2000). *Principles and standards for school mathematics.* Washington, DC: Author.

National Institute for Literacy (2007). *What content-area teachers should know about adolescent literacy.* Washington DC: National Institute of Child Health and Human Development (NICHD).

National Middle School Association (NMSA). (2005). *Highly qualified: A balanced approach.* Retrieved September 28, 2006, from www.nmsa.org

National Middle School Association (NMSA), National Association of Elementary School Principals (NAESP), and the National Association of Secondary School Principals (NASSP). (2004). *Highly qualified: A balanced approach.* Retrieved April 14, 2006, from www.nmsa.org/portals/o/pdf/about/position_statements/EdWeek.pdf

National Reading Panel. (2000). *Teaching children to read: An evidence-based assessment of the scientific research literature on reading and its implications for reading instruction* (National Institute of Health Pub. No. 00-4769). Washington, DC: National Institute of Child Health and Human Development.

National School Boards Association. (2006). *The next chapter: A school board guide to improving adolescent literacy.* Alexandria, VA: Author. Retrieved May 18, 2008, from www.nsba.org

Neal, J. C., & Moore, K. (1991). *The Very Hungry Caterpillar* meets *Beowulf* in secondary classrooms. *Journal of Reading, 35,* 290–296.

Neill, M. (2003). Leaving children behind: How No Child Left Behind will fail our children. *Phi Delta Kappan, 85*(3), 225–228.

Neilsen, L. (2006). Playing for real: Performative texts and adolescent identities. In D. Alvermann, K. Hinchman, S. Phelps, & S. Waff (Eds.), *Reconceptualizing the literacies in adolescents' lives* (pp. 5–28). Mahwah, NJ: Erlbaum.

Nelson, B. (2008). *Paranoid park.* New York: Puffin.

Nelson, J. (1978). Readability: Some cautions for the content area teacher. *Journal of Reading, 21,* 620–625.

Nelson, K. (2008). *We are the ship: The story of Negro league baseball.* New York: Hyperion.

Nelson, M. (2005). *A wreath for Emmitt Till.* New York: Houghton Mifflin Harcourt.

Neufeld, P. (2005). Comprehension instruction in content area classes. *Reading Teacher, 59*(4), 302–312.

Newcomb, N. (2007). Psychology's role in mathematics and science education. *Research Report.* Washington, DC: American Psychological Association:

Newell, G. (1984). Learning from writing in two content areas: A case study/protocol analysis. *Research in the Teaching of English, 18,* 205–287.

New London Group. (1996). A pedagogy of multiliteracies: Designing social futures. *Harvard Education Review* 66(1), 60–92.

Nichols, S. L., & Berliner, D. C. (2007). *Collateral damage: How high-stakes testing corrupts America's schools.* Cambridge, MA: Harvard Education Press.

Nichols, S. L., & Berliner, D. C. (2008). Testing the joy out of learning. *Educational Leadership, 65*(6), 14–18.

Nichols, W. D., Wood, K. D., & Rickelman, R. (2001). Using technology to engage students in reading and writing. *Middle School Journal, 32*(5), 45–50.

Nieto, S. (2002). *Language, culture, and teaching: Critical perspectives for a new century.* Mahwah, NJ: Erlbaum.

Niles, O. (1965). Organization perceived. In H. L. Herber (Ed.), *Developing study skills in secondary schools* (pp. 36–46). Newark, DE: International Reading Association.

Noden, H. R. (1995). A journey through cyberspace: Reading and writing in a virtual school. *English Journal 84*(6), 19–26.

Noden, H. R., & Vacca, R. T. (1994). *Whole language in middle and secondary classrooms.* New York: HarperCollins.

North Carolina Department of Public Instruction (NCDPI). (2008). *ABCs/AYP accountability report.* Retrieved October 2008 from www.ncpublicschools.org/abcs

North Carolina Public Schools. (2003). *The ABC's accountability model.* Retrieved October 2002 from www.ncpublicschools.org/abcs

Noyes, A. (1983). *The highwayman.* Ill. C. Mikolaychak. New York: Lothrop, Lee & Shepard.

Nye, N. S. (2002). *19 varieties of gazelle: Poems of the Middle East.* New York: HarperCollins.

Nye, R. (1968). *Beowulf: A new telling.* New York: Hill.

Oakes, J. (1985). *Keeping track: How schools structure inequality.* New Haven, CT: Yale University Press.

O'Brien, R. C. (1975). *Z for Zachariah.* New York: Atheneum.

Ogle, D. (1986). KWL: A teaching model that develops active reading of expository text. *Reading Teacher, 39,* 564–570.

Ogle, D. M. (1992). KWL in action: Secondary teachers find applications that work. In E. K. Dishner, T. W. Bean, J. E. Readence, & D. W. Moore (Eds.), *Reading in the content areas: Improving classroom instruction* (3rd ed., pp. 270–281). Dubuque, IA: Kendall-Hunt.

Ohio Department of Education. (2003). *Ohio administrative codes and rules links: Rule 3301-13-01.* Retrieved September 2003 from www.ode.state.oh.us/ proficiency/rules.asp?pfv=True

Oldfather, P., & Dahl, K. (1994). Toward a social constructivist reconceptualization of intrinsic motivation for literacy learning. *Journal of Reading Behavior, 26,* 139–158.

O'Neill, C. (1995). *Drama worlds: A framework for process drama.* Portsmouth, NH: Heinemann.

Osborne, A. B. (1996). Practice into theory into practice: Culturally relevant pedagogy for students we have marginalized and normalized. *Anthropology and Education Quarterly, 27*(3), 285–314.

Palmatier, R. (1973). A notetaking system for learning. *Journal of Reading, 17,* 36–39.

Palmer, R. G., & Stewart, R. A. (1997). Nonfiction trade books in content area instruction: Realities and potential. *Journal of Adolescent and Adult Literacy, 40,* 630–641.

Pang, V. O., & Cheng, L. L. (Eds.). (1998). *Struggling to be heard: The unmet needs of Asian Pacific American children.* Albany: SUNY Press.

Papert, S. (1980). *Mindstorms: Children, computers, and powerful ideas.* New York: Basic Books.

Pappas, T. (1993). *Math talk: Mathematical ideas in poems for two voices.* New York: Wide World.

Paris, S., & Meyers, M. (1981). Comprehension monitoring, memory, and study strategies of good and poor readers. *Journal of Reading Behavior, 13,* 5–22.

Parker, W. C., & Jarolimek, J. (1997). *Social studies in elementary education.* Upper Saddle River, NJ: Prentice Hall.

Parnall, P. (1984). *The daywatchers.* New York: Macmillan.

Parnall, P. (1991). *Marsh cat.* New York: Macmillan.

Parry, K. (1993). Too many words: Learning the vocabulary of an academic subject. In T. Huckin, M. Haynes, & J. Coady (Eds.), *Second language reading and vocabulary learning* (pp. 109–129). Norwood, NJ: Ablex.

Parsons, L. (2001). *Response journals revisted: Maximizing learning through reading, writing, viewing, discussing, and thinking.* Markham, ON: Pembroke.

Partridge, E. (2002). *This land was made for you and me: The life and songs of Woody Guthrie.* New York: Viking.

Partridge, E. (2005). *John Lennon: All I want is the truth.* New York: Viking.

Patterson, N. G. (2000). Hypertext and the changing roles of readers. *English Journal, 90*(2), 74–80.

Pauk, W. (1978). A notetaking format: Magical but not automatic. *Reading World, 16,* 96–97.

Pauk, W., & Ross, J. Q. O. (2007). *How to study in college.* Boston: Houghton Mifflin Harcourt.

Paulsen, G. (1987). *Hatchet.* New York: Viking Penguin.

Paulsen, G. (1989). *The winter room.* New York: Harcourt Brace.

Paulsen, G. (1990). *Woodsong.* New York: Macmillan.

Payne, R. (2003). *Framework for understanding poverty* (3rd ed.). Highlands, TX: Aha! Process.

Payne, R., DeVol, P., & Smith, T. (2005). *Bridges out of poverty: Strategies for professionals and communities.* Highlands, TX: Aha! Process.

Peacock, L. (1998). *Crossing the Delaware: A history in many voices.* Ill. W. L. Krudop. New York: Atheneum.

Pearce, D. L. (1983). Guidelines for the use and evaluation of writing in content classrooms. *Journal of Reading, 27,* 212–218.

Pearson, P. D. (1974–1975). The effects of grammatical complexity on children's comprehension, recall, and conception of certain semantic relations. *Reading Research Quarterly, 10,* 155–192.

Pearson, P. D. (1982). *A context for instructional research and reading comprehension* (Technical Report No. 230). Urbana: University of Illinois Center for the Study of Reading.

Pearson, P. D., & Johnson, D. (1978). *Teaching reading comprehension.* Fort Worth, TX: Holt, Rinehart and Winston.

Pearson. P. D., Hiebert, E. H., & Kamil, M. (2007). Vocabulary assessment: What we know and what we need to learn. *Reading Research Quarterly, 42*(2), 282–296.

Pearson, P. D., & Spiro, R. (1982). The new buzz word in reading as schema. *Instructor, 89,* 46–48.

Peregoy, S. F., & Boyle, O. F. (2001). *Reading, writing, and learning in ESL: A resource book for K–12 teachers* (3rd ed.). New York: Longman.

Peregoy, S. F., & Boyle, O. F. (2008). *Reading, writing, and learning in ESL: A resource book for teaching K–12 English learners* (5th ed.). Boston: Pearson.

Perie, M., Grigg, W., & Donahue, P. (2005). *The nation's report card: Reading 2005* (NCES 2006-451). Washington, DC: U.S. Department of Education.

Pew Internet and American Life Study (2006). *Internet penetration and access.* Retrieved August 28, 2008, from www.pewinternet.org/topics.asp?page=2&c=3

Pew Internet and American Life Study (2008). *Home broadband 2008.* Retrieved August 28, 2008, from www.pewinternet.org/topics.asp?page=1&c=3

Pichert, J. W., & Anderson, R. C. (1977). Taking different perspectives on a story. *Journal of Educational Psychology, 69,* 309–315.

Pilgreen, J. (2000). *How to organize and manage a sustained silent reading program.* Portsmouth, NH: Heinemann.

Plucker, J. A., Spradlin, T. E., Cline, K. P., & Wolf, K. M. (2005). *Education policy brief: No Child Left Behind, Spring 2005 implementation update* [Electronic version]. Bloomington, IN: Center for Evaluation & Education Policy.

Polacco, P. (1994). *Pink and say.* New York: Philomel.

Pradl, G. M., & Mayher, J. S. (1985). Reinvigorating learning through writing. *Educational Leadership, 42,* 4–8.

Preble, L. (2006). *Queen Geek series.* New York: Berkeley.

Pressley, M. (2000). What should comprehension instruction be the instruction of? In M. Kamil, P. Mosenthal, P. D. Pearson, & R. Barr (Eds.), *Handbook of reading research* (Vol. 3, pp. 545–562). Mahwah, NJ: Erlbaum.

Pressley, M. (2002a). Comprehension instruction: What makes sense now, what might make sense soon. *Reading Online, 5*(2). Retrieved October 3, 2005, from www.readingonline.org/articles/art_index.asp?HREF=/articles/handbook/pressley/index.htm

Pressley, M. (2002b). *Reading instruction that works: The case for balanced reading.* New York: Guilford Press.

Pressley, M. (2006). *Reading instruction that works: The case for balanced instruction.* New York: Guilford Press.

Price, L. (1990). *Aida.* Ill. L. Dillon & D. Dillon. San Diego: Harcourt Brace.

RAND Reading Study Group. (2002). *Reading for understanding: Toward an R&D program in reading comprehension.* Santa Monica, CA: Science and Technology Policy Institute, Rand Education.

Randall, S. N. (1996). Information charts: A strategy for organizing students' research. *Journal of Adolescent and Adult Literacy, 39,* 536–542.

Ransom, K. A., Santa, C. M., Williams, C. K., Farstrup, A. E., Au, K. H., Baker, B. M., et al. (1999). High-stakes assessments in reading: A position statement of the International Reading Association. *Journal of Adolescent and Adult Literacy, 43*(3), 305–312.

Raphael, T. E. (1982). Question-answering strategies for children. *Reading Teacher, 36,* 186–191.

Raphael, T. E. (1984). Teaching learners about sources of information for answering comprehension questions. *Journal of Reading, 27,* 303–311.

Raphael, T. E. (1986). Teaching question–answer relationships. *Reading Teacher, 39,* 516–520.

Rappaport, D. (2001). *Martin's big words: The life of Dr. Martin Luther King, Jr.* Ill. B. Collier. New York: Hyperion.

Raschka, C. (1997). *Mysterious Thelonious.* New York: Orchard.

Ray, D. (1990). *A nation torn: The story of how the Civil War began.* New York: Scholastic.

Readence, J. E. (2002). Adolescent literacy. In B. J. Guzzetti (Ed.), *Literacy in America: An encyclopedia of history, theory, and practice* (pp. 13–15). Santa Barbara, CA: ABC-CLIO.

Reed, J. H., Schallert, D. L., Beth, A. D., & Woodruff, A. L. (2004). Motivated reader, engaged writer: The role of motivation in the literate acts of adolescents. In T. L. Jetton & J. A. Dole (Eds.), *Adolescent literacy research and practice* (pp. 251–282). New York: Guilford Press.

Reeder, C. (1989). *Shades of gray.* New York: Macmillan.

Reef, C. (2006). *e.e. cummings: A poet's life.* New York: Clarion Books.

Reeves, N. (1992). *Into the mummy's tomb: The real-life discovery of Tutankhamun's treasures.* New York: Scholastic/Madison.

Reinking, D. (1995). Reading and writing with computers: Literacy research in a post-typographic world. In K. A. Hinchman, D. J. Leu, Jr., & C. K. Kinzer (Eds.), *Perspectives on literacy research and practice* (pp. 17–33). Chicago: National Reading Conference.

Reinking, D. (1997). Me and my hypertext: A multiple digression analysis of technology and literacy. *Reading Teacher, 50,* 626–643.

Reinking, D. (1998). Synthesizing technological transformations of literacy in a post-typographic world. In D. Reinking, M. McKenna, L. D. Labbo, & R. Kieffer (Eds.), *Handbook of literacy and technology: Transformations in a post-typographic world* (pp. xi–xxx). Mahwah, NJ: Erlbaum.

Reinking, D. (2003). Multimedia and engaged reading in a digital world. In L. Verhoeven & C. Snow (Eds.), *Creating a world of engaged readers.* Mahwah, NJ: Erlbaum.

Renyi, J. (1998). Building learning into the teaching job. *Educational Leadership, 55*(5), 70–74.

Reyes, M., & Molner, L. (1999). Instruction strategies for second-language learners in the content areas. *Journal of Reading, 35,* 96–103.

Reyhner, J., & Garcia, R. L. (1989). Helping minorities read better: Problems and promises. *Reading Research and Instruction, 28*(3), 84–91.

Richardson, V. (2003). The dilemmas of professional development. *Phi Delta Kappan, 84,* 401–406.

Rico, G. L. (1983). *Writing the natural way: Using right-brain techniques to release your expressive powers.* Los Angeles: Tarcher.

Ride, S., & Okie, S. (1986). *To space and back.* New York: Lothrop, Lee & Shepard.

Roberts, P. (1985). Speech communities. In V. Clark, P. Escholz, & A. Rosa (Eds.), *Language* (4th ed.). New York: St. Martin's Press.

Roby, T. (1987). Commonplaces, questions, and modes of discussion. In J. T. Dillon (Ed.), *Classroom questions and discussion* (pp. 134–169). Norwood, NJ: Ablex.

Rodrigues, R. J. (1983). Tools for developing prewriting skills. *English Journal, 72,* 58–60.

Rodriguez, L. J. (1993). *Always running: La vida loca: Gang days in L.A.* New York: Touchstone.

Rohmer, H. (Ed.). (1997). *Just like me: Stories and self-portraits by fourteen artists.* San Francisco: Children's Book Press.

Rohmer, H. (Ed.). (1999). *Honoring our ancestors: Stories and pictures by fourteen artists.* San Francisco: Children's Book Press.

Rose, B. (1989). Writing and mathematics: Theory and practice. In P. Connolly & T. Vilardi (Eds.), *Writing to learn mathematics and science* (pp. 19–30). New York: Teachers College Press.

Rose, S. A., & Fernlund, P. M. (1997). Using technology for powerful social studies learning. *Social Education, 13*(6), 160–166.

Rosenblatt, L. (1938/1995). *Literature as exploration.* (5th ed.). New York: Modern Language Association.

Rosenblatt, L. M. (1982). The literary transaction: Evocation and response. *Theory into Practice, 21,* 268–277.

Ruddell, M. R., & Shearer, B. A. (2002). "Extraordinary," "tremendous," "exhilarating," "magnificent": Middle school at-risk students become avid word learners with the Vocabulary Self-Collection Strategy (VSS). *Journal of Adolescent and Adult Literacy, 45,* 352–363.

Rumelhart, D. E. (1982). Schemata: The building blocks of cognition. In J. Guthrie (Ed.), *Comprehension and teaching: Research reviews* (pp. 3–26). Newark, DE: International Reading Association.

Ryan, P. M. (2000). *Esperanza rising.* New York: Scholastic.

Ryan, P. M. (2002). *When Marian sang: The true recital of Marian Anderson.* Ill. B. Selznick. New York: Scholastic.

Rycik, J. A. (1994). *An exploration of student library research projects in seventh grade English and social studies classes.* Unpublished doctoral dissertation, Kent State University.

Rylant, C. (1984). *Waiting to waltz: A childhood.* Ill. S. Gammell. New York: Bradbury.

Sachar, L. (1998). *Holes.* New York: Farrar, Strauss & Giroux

Salisbury, R. (1934). A study of the transfer effects of training in logical organization *Journal of Educational Research, 28,* 241–254.

Samples, R. (1977). *The whole school book: Teaching and learning late in the 20th century.* Reading, MA: Addison-Wesley.

Sanders, T. (2004). *No time to waste: The vital role of college and university leaders in improving science and mathematics education* Paper presented at the invitational conference of Teacher Preparation and Institutions of Higher Education: Mathematics and Science Content Knowledge, Washington, DC.

Sansevere-Dreher, D., Dreher, D., & Renfro, E. (1994). *Explorers who got lost.* New York: Tor Books.

Santa, C. M., & Havens, L. T. (1991). Learning through writing. In C. M. Santa & D. E. Alvermann (Eds.), *Science learning: Processes and applications* (pp. 122–133). Newark, DE: International Reading Association.

Say, A. (1990). *El Chino.* Boston: Houghton Mifflin.

Say, A. (2002). *Home of the brave.* Boston: Houghton Mifflin.

Schlitz, L. A. (2007). *Good masters! Sweet ladies!: Voices from a medieval village.* New York: Candlewick.

Schmar-Dobler, E. (2003). Reading on the Internet: The link between literacy and technology. *Journal of Adolescent & Adult Literacy, 47,* 30–85.

Schmidt, P. R. (1998). The ABC's of cultural understanding and communication. *Equity and Excellence in Education, 31*(2), 28–38.

Schmidt, P. R. (1999a). KWLQ: Inquiry and literacy learning in science. *Reading Teacher, 52*(6), 789–792.

Schmidt, P. R. (1999b). Know thyself and understand others. *Language Arts, 76*(4), 332–340.

Schmidt, P. R. (2000). Teachers connecting and communicating with families for literacy development. In T. Shanahan & F. Rodriguez-Brown (Eds.), *National reading conference yearbook* (49th ed., pp. 194–208). Chicago: National Reading Conference.

Schmidt, P. R. (2001). The power to empower. In P. R. Schmidt & P. B. Mosenthal (Eds.), *Reconceptualizing literacy in the new age of multiculturalism and pluralism* (pp. 389–433). Greenwich, CT: Information Age Publishing.

Schmidt, P. R. (2003). *Culturally relevant pedagogy: A study of successful in-service.* Paper presented at the annual meeting of the National Reading Conference, Scottsdale, AZ.

Schmidt, P. R. (2005a). Culturally responsive instruction: Promoting literacy in secondary content areas. *Adolescent Literacy.* Naperville, IL: Learning Point Associates. Retrieved from www.learningpt.org

Schmidt, P. R. (Ed.). (2005b). *Preparing educators to communicate and connect with families and communities.* Greenwich, CT: Information Age Publishing.

Schmidt, P. R. (2008, December). Secondary preservice teacher preparation for culturally responsive literacy teaching. Paper presented at the 58th Annual Meeting of the National Reading Conference, Orlando, FL.

Schmidt, P. R., & Finkbeiner, C. (2006). ABC's of cultural understanding and communication: National and international adaptations. Greenwich, CT: Information Age Publishing.

Schmidt, P. R., & Ma, W. (2006). *50 literacy strategies for culturally responsive teaching, K–8.* Chicago: Corwin Press.

Schoenbach, R., Greenleaf, C., Cziko, C., & Hurwitz, L. (1999). *Reading for understanding: A guide to improving reading in middle and high school classrooms.* San Francisco: Jossey-Bass.

Scholastic. (2006). *The kids and family reading report.* Retrieved August 30, 2008, from www.scholastic.com/aboutscholastic/news/readingreport.htm

Scholastic. (2008). *The 2008 kids and family reading report.* Retrieved August 30, 2008, from www.scholastic.com/aboutscholastic/news/readingreport.htm

Schumm, J. S., & Mangrum, C. T., II. (1991). FLIP: A framework for content area reading. *Journal of Reading, 35,* 120–124.

Schwartz, D. (1998). *G is for Googol.* New York: Tricycle Press.

Schwartz, R. M. (1988). Learning to learn: Vocabulary in content area textbooks. *Journal of Reading, 32,* 108–117.

Schwartz, R. M., & Raphael, T. E. (1985). Concept of definition: A key to improving students' vocabulary. *Reading Teacher, 39,* 198–204.

Sciezka, J. (2005). *Guys write for Guys Read.* New York: Viking.

Scott, E. (2007). *When is a planet not a planet? The story of Pluto.* New York: Clarion Books.

Selznick, B. (2007). *The Invention of Hugo Cabret.* New York: Scholastic Press.

Sender, R. M. (1986). *The cage.* New York: Macmillan.

Service, R. (1986). *The cremation of Sam McGee.* Ill. T. Harrison. New York: Greenwillow.

Seuss, Dr. (1984). *The butter battle book.* New York: Random House.

Shanahan, T. (Ed.). (1990). *Reading and writing together: New perspectives for the classroom.* Norwood, MA: Christopher-Gordon.

Shanahan, T., & Shanahan, C. (2008). Teaching disciplinary literacy to adolescents: Rethinking content-area literacy. *Harvard Educational Review, 78*(1), 40–59.

Shanklin, N. (2006). *What are the characteristics of effective literacy coaching?* Retrieved November 1, 2007, from www.literacycoachingonline.org

Shanks, A. Z. (1982). *Busted lives: Dialogues with kids in jail.* New York: Delacorte.

Short, K., Harste, J., & Burke, C. (1996). *Creating classrooms for authors and inquirers.* Portsmouth, NH: Heinemann.

Shulman, L. (1987). Learning to teach. *AAHE Bulletin,* 5–6.

Simon, S. (1990). *Oceans.* New York: Morrow.

Singer, H. (1978). Active comprehension: From answering to asking questions. *Reading Teacher, 31,* 901–908.

Sis, P. (2007). *The wall: Growing up behind the iron curtain.* New York: Farrar, Straus & Giroux.

Skinner, R. A., & Staresina, L. N. (2004). State of the states [Electronic version]. *Education Week, 23*(7), 97–99.

Slavin, R. E. (1987). Synthesis of research on cooperative learning. *Educational Leadership, 48*(5), 72–82.

Slavin, R. E. (1988). Cooperative learning and student achievement. In R. E. Slavin (Ed.), *School and classroom organization.* Hillsdale, NJ: Erlbaum.

Smith, D. B. (1973). *A taste of blackberries.* New York: HarperCollins.

Smith, F. (1988). *Understanding reading* (4th ed.). Hillsdale, NJ: Erlbaum.

Smith, L. (2002). *Unsent letters: Writing as a way to resolve and renew.* San Francisco: Walking Stick Press.

Smith, N. B. (1964). Patterns of writing in different subject areas. *Journal of Reading, 7,* 31–37.

Soto, G. (1997). *Novio boy: A play.* San Diego, CA: Harcourt Brace.

Spellings, M. (2005). *A highly qualified teacher in every classroom: The secretary's annual report on teacher quality, 2005.* Retrieved August 5, 2006, from www.title2.org/secReport05.htm

Spencer, S. L., & Vavra, S. A. (2009). *The perfect norm.* Charlotte, NC: Information Age Publishing.

Spiegel, D. L. (1981). Six alternatives to the directed reading activity. *Reading Teacher, 34,* 914–922.

Spiegel, D. L. (1998). Reader response approaches and the growth of readers. *Language Arts, 76,* 41–48.

Spiegelman, A. (1986). *Maus: A survivor's tale.* New York: Pantheon.

Spivey, N. M. (1984). *Discourse synthesis: Constructing texts in reading and writing.* Newark, DE: International Reading Association.

St. George, J. (2000). *So you want to be president?* New York: Philomel.

Stanley, D. (1996). *Leonardo da Vinci.* New York: Morrow.

Stanley, D. (2000). *Michelangelo.* New York: HarperCollins.

Stanley, J. (1992). *Children of the dust bowl: The true story of the school at Weedpatch Camp.* New York: Clarion Books.

Staples, S. F. (1991). *Shabanu: Daughter of the wind.* New York: Random House.

Stecker, P. M., Fuchs, D., & Fuchs, L. S. (2008). Progress monitoring as essential practice within Response to Intervention. *Rural Special Education Quarterly, 27,* 10–17.

Stephens, C. (2002). *Magnificent monologues for teens.* New York: Sandcastle.

Stewig, J. W., & Buege, C. (1994). *Dramatizing literature in whole language classrooms.* New York: Teachers College Press.

Street, B. (1995). *Social literacies: Critical approaches to literacy in development, ethnography and education.* New York: Longman.

Sturtevant, E. (1992). *Content literacy activities in high school social studies: Two case studies in a multicultural setting.* Unpublished doctoral dissertation, Kent State University.

Sturtevant, E. G. (2003). *The literacy coach: A key to improving teaching and learning in secondary schools.* Washington, DC: Alliance for Excellent Education. Retrieved July 6, 2006, from www.all4ed.org/publications/LiteracyCoach.pdf

Suid, M., & Lincoln, W. (1989). *Recipes for writing: Motivation, skills, and activities.* Menlo Park, CA: Addison-Wesley.

Sutherland, Z., & Arbuthnot, M. H. (1986). *Children and books* (7th ed.). Glenview, IL: Scott Foresman.

Taba, H. (1967). *Teacher's handbook for elementary social studies.* Reading, MA: Addison-Wesley.

Tan, S. (2007). *The arrival.* New York: Arthur A. Levine.

Tatum, A. (2000). Breaking down barriers that disenfranchise African American adolescent readers in low-level tracks. In P. Mason & J. S. Schumm (Eds.), *Promising practices for urban reading instruction* (pp. 98–118). Newark, DE: International Reading Association

Tatum, A. (2005). *Teaching reading to black adolescent males: Closing the achievement gap.* Portland, ME: Stenhouse.

Taylor, B. (1980). Children's memory of expository text after reading. *Reading Research Quarterly, 15,* 399–411.

Taylor, T. (1969). *The cay.* New York: Harcourt.

Tchudi, S., & Yates, J. (1983). *Teaching writing in the content areas: Senior high school.* Washington, DC: National Education Association.

Temple, C., Martinez, M., Yokota, J., & Naylor, A. (2005). *Children's books in children's hands: An introduction to their literature.* Boston: Allyn & Bacon.

Thimmesh, C. (2000). *Girls think of everything: Stories of ingenious inventions by women.* Boston: Houghton Mifflin.

Thimmesh, C. (2006). *Team moon: How 400,000 people landed Apollo 11 on the moon.* New York: Houghton Mifflin.

Thoman, E., & Jolls, T. (2008). *Literacy for the 21st century.* Retrieved January 4, 2009, from www.medlit.org

Thompson, W. I. (1981). *The time falling bodies take to light: Mythology, sexuality, and the origins of culture.* New York: St. Martin's Press.

Thorndike, E. (1917). Reading and reasoning: A study of mistakes in paragraph reading. *Journal of Educational Psychology, 8,* 323–332.

Tierney, R. J. (1998). Literacy assessment reform: Shifting beliefs, principled possibilities, and emerging practices. *Reading Teacher, 51,* 374–390.

Tierney, R. J. (2002). An ethical chasm: Jurisdiction, jurisprudence, and the literacy profession. *Journal of Adolescent and Adult Literacy, 45*(4), 260–276.

Tierney, R. J., Carter, M. A., & Desai, L. E. (1991). *Portfolio assessment in the reading-writing classroom.* Norwood, MA: Christopher-Gordon.

Tierney, R. J., & Pearson, P. D. (1983). Toward a composing model of reading. *Language Arts, 60,* 568–580.

Tierney, R. J., & Pearson, P. D. (1992). A revisionist perspective on "Learning to learn from texts: A framework for improving classroom practice." In E. K. Dishner, T. W. Bean, J. E. Readence, & D. W. Moore (Eds.), *Reading in the content areas: Improving classroom instruction* (3rd ed., pp. 82–86). Dubuque, IA: Kendall/Hunt.

Tierney, R. J., & Shanahan, T. (1991). Research on reading-writing relationships: Interactions, transactions, and outcomes. In P. D. Pearson, R. Barr, M. Kamil, & P. Mosenthal (Eds.), *Handbook of reading research* (2nd ed., pp. 246–280). New York: Longman.

Tobias, S. (1989). Writing to learn science and mathematics. In P. Connolly & T. Vilardi (Eds.), *Writing to learn mathematics and science* (pp. 47–61). New York: Teachers College Press.

Toll, C. A. (2005). *The literacy coach's survival guide: Essential questions and practical answers.* Newark, DE: International Reading Association.

Topping, D. H., & McManus, R. (2002). *Real reading, real writing: Content area strategies.* Portsmouth, NH: Heinemann.

Toppo, G. (2001). *Education bill could affect funding.* Retrieved from www.speakout.com/cgi-in/udt/im.display.printable?client.id=speakout&story.id=9967

Torgesen, J. K., Houston, D. D., Rissman, L. M., Decker, S. M., Roberts, G., Vaughn, S., Wexler, J., Francis, D. J., Rivera, M. O., & Lesaux, N. (2007). *Academic literacy instruction for adolescents: A guidance document from the Center on Instruction.* Portsmouth, NH: RMC Research Corporation, Center on Instruction. Retrieved May 19, 2008, from www.centeroninstruction.org

Trueman, T. (2001). *Stuck in neutral.* New York: HarperTempest.

Tse, L. (2001). *Why don't they learn English? Separating fact from fallacy in the U.S. language debate.* New York: Teachers College Press.

Tsuchiya, Y. (1988). *Faithful elephants: A true story of people, animals and war.* Trans. T. Kykes. Ill. T. Lewin. Boston: Houghton Mifflin.

Turner, A. (1987). *Nettie's trip south.* Ill. R. Himler. New York: Macmillan.

Ung, L. (2000). *First they killed my father: A daughter of Cambodia remembers.* New York: Perennial Press.

U.S. Census Bureau. (2000). *Population estimates.* Retrieved November 9, 2005, from www.census.gov/popest/estimates.php

U.S. Department of Education (2001). *The No Child Left Behind Act of 2001.* Retrieved on January 11, 2002, from www.ed.gov/offices/OESE/esea/NCLBexecumm.pdf

Vacca, J. L., Vacca, R. T., Gove, M. K., Burkey, L., Lenhart, L., & McKeon, C. (2002). *Reading and learning to read* (5th ed.). Boston: Allyn & Bacon.

Vacca, R. T. (1975). Development of a functional reading strategy: Implications for content area instruction. *Journal of Educational Research, 69,* 108–112.

Vacca, R. T. (1977). An investigation of a functional reading strategy in seventh-grade social studies. In H. L. Herber & R. T. Vacca (Eds.), *Research in reading in the content areas: Third report* (pp. 101–118). Syracuse, NY: Syracuse University Reading and Language Arts Center.

Vacca, R. T. (1998). Literacy issues in focus: Let's not marginalize adolescent literacy. *Journal of Adolescent and Adult Literacy, 41*(8), 604–610.

Vacca, R. T. (2002a). Content literacy. In B. J. Guzzetti (Ed.), *Literacy in America: An encyclopedia of history, theory, and practice* (pp. 101–104). Santa Barbara, CA: ABC-CLIO.

Vacca, R. T. (2002b). Making a difference in adolescents' school lives: Visible and invisible aspects of content area reading. In A. E. Farstrup & S. J. Samuels (Eds.), *What research has to say about reading instruction* (3rd ed., pp. 184–204). Newark, DE: International Reading Association.

Vacca, R. T. (2006). They can because they think they can. *Educational Leadership, 63*(5), 56–59.

Vacca, R. T., & Alvermann, D. E. (1998, October). The crisis in adolescent literacy: Is it real or imagined? *NASSP Bulletin, 82,* 4–9.

Vacca, R. T., & Padak, N. D. (1990). Who's at risk in reading? *Journal of Reading, 33,* 486–489.

Vacca, R. T., & Vacca, J. L. (2000). Writing across the curriculum. In R. Indrisano & J. R. Squire (Eds.), *Perspectives on writing: Research, theory, and practice* (pp. 214–232). Newark, DE: International Reading Association.

Valdes, G., & Figueroa, R. A. (1994). *Bilingualism and testing: A special case bias.* Norwood, NJ: Ablex.

Valencia, S. (1990). A portfolio approach to classroom reading assessment: The whys, whats, and hows. *Reading Teacher, 43,* 338–340.

Valencia, S., McGinley, W. J., & Pearson, P. D. (1990). *Assessing reading and writing: Building a more complete picture for middle school assessment.* Urbana: University of Illinois, Center for the Study of Reading.

Van Allsburg, C. (1984). *Mysteries of Harris Burdick.* Boston: Houghton Mifflin.

Van Allsburg, C. (1990). *Just a dream.* Boston: Houghton Mifflin.

van der Rol, R., & Verhoeven, R. (1993). *Anne Frank: Beyond the diary.* New York: Viking.

Vardell, S. M., & Copeland, K. A. (1992). Reading aloud and responding to nonfiction: Let's talk about it. In E. B. Freeman & D. G. Person (Eds.), *Using nonfiction trade books in the elementary classroom: From ants to zeppelins* (pp. 76–85). Urbana, IL: National Council of Teachers of English.

Vogt, M. E., & Echevarria, J. (2008). *99 ideas and activities for teaching English learners with the SIOP model.* Boston: Pearson.

Von Ziegesar, C. (2002). *Gossip girl.* New York: Poppy.

Vygotsky, L. S. (1934/1986). *Thought and language.* Cambridge, MA: MIT Press.

Walker, B. J. (1991, February-March). Convention highlights reading assessment changes. *Reading Today,* 20.

Walls, J. (2006). *The glass castle: A memoir.* New York: Scribner.

Walpole, S., & McKenna, M. (2004). Intervention programs. In *The literacy coach's handbook.* New York: Guilford Press.

Walsh, K., & Snyder, E. (2004). *NCTQ reports: Searching the attic for highly qualified teachers.* National Council on Teacher Quality. Retrieved February 2005, from www.ctredpol.org/pubs/Forum15November2004/WalshPaper.pdf

Wang, M. C., Reynolds, M. C., & Walberg, H. J. (1994–1995). Serving students at the margins. *Educational Leadership, 52*(4), 12–17.

Watkins, D. A., & Biggs, J. B. (Eds.). (1996). *The Chinese learner: Cultural, psychological, and contextual influences.* Hong Kong: University of Hong Kong Press.

Webb, S. (2000). *My season with penguins: An Antarctic journal.* Boston: Houghton Mifflin.

Weiss, M. J., & Weiss, H. S. (2002). *Big city cool: Short stories about urban youth.* New York: Persea Books.

Wenglinski, H. (2000). *How teaching matters: Bringing the classroom back into discussions of teacher quality.* Princeton, NJ: Educational Testing Service. Retrieved from www.ets.org/Media/Education_topics/pdf/teamat.pdf

Whitin, P. (2002). Leading into literature circles through the sketch-to-stretch strategy. *Reading Teacher, 55,* 444–450.

Wiesel, E. (2006). *Night.* New York: Hill and Wang.

Wigfield, A. (2004). Motivation for reading during the early adolescent and adolescent years. In D. S. Strickland & D. E. Alvermann (Eds.). *Bridging the literacy achievement gap, grades 4–12* (pp. 251–282). New York: Teachers College Press.

Wilcox, S. (1997). Using the assessment of students' learning to reshape thinking. *Mathematics Teacher, 90,* 223–229.

Wilen, W., Ishler, L., Hutchison, J., & Kindsvatter, R. (2004). *Dynamics of effective secondary teaching* (5th ed.). Boston: Allyn & Bacon.

Wilkinson, L. E., & Silliman, E. R. (2000). Classroom language and literacy learning. In M. Kamil, P. Mosenthal, P. D. Pearson, & R. Barr (Eds.), *Handbook of reading research* (Vol. 3, pp. 337–360). Mahwah, NJ: Erlbaum.

Williams, B. (1995). *The Internet for teachers.* Foster City, CA: IDG Books Worldwide.

Willinsky, J. (1990). *The new literacy: Redefining reading and writing in the schools.* New York: Routledge.

Wills, J., & Mehan, H. (1996). Recognizing diversity within a common historical narrative: The challenge to teaching history and social studies. *Multicultural Education, 4*(1), 4–11.

Wisconsin Historical Society. (2009). *Thinking like a historian.* Retrieved May 4, 2009, from www.wisconsinhistory.org/ThinkingLikeaHistorian

Wise, B. (2009, February). Adolescent literacy: The cornerstone of student success. *Journal of Adolescent & Adult Literacy, 52,* 369–375.

Wisniewski, D. (1996). *Golem.* New York: Clarion.

Wixson, K. K., Boskey, A. B., Yochum, M. M., & Alvermann, D. E. (1984). An interview for assessing students' perceptions of classroom reading tasks. *Reading Teacher, 37,* 346–353.

Wong, J. L. (2007). *Seeing Emily.* New York: Amulet Books.

Wood, K. D. (1987). Fostering cooperative learning in middle and secondary classrooms. *Journal of Reading, 31,* 10–18.

Wood, K. D. (1988). Changing perspective to improve comprehension. *Middle School Journal, 22*(3), 52–56.

Wood, K. D. (2001). *Literacy strategies across the subject areas: Process-oriented blackline masters for the K–12 classroom.* Boston: Allyn & Bacon.

Wood, K. D., Lapp, D., Flood, J., & Taylor, D. B. (2008). *Guiding readers through text: Study guides for new times* (2nd ed.). Newark, DE: International Reading Association.

Wood, K. D., & Taylor, D. B. (2005). *Literacy strategies across the subject areas: Process-oriented blackline masters for the K–12 classroom* (2nd ed.). Boston: Allyn & Bacon.

Woodson, J. (2005). *Show way.* New York: Putnam.

Worthy, J., Broaddus, K., & Ivey, G. (2001). *Pathways to independence: Reading, writing, and learning in grades 3–8.* New York: Guilford Press.

Writing in the Disciplines. (2001). *Writing in the disciplines.* Retrieved June 2009 from www.cariboo.bc.ca/disciplines

Yang, G. L. (2008). *American born Chinese.* New York: Square Fish Press.

Yokota, J. (1993). Issues in selecting multicultural literature for children and adolescents. *Language Arts, 20,* 156–167.

Yolen, J. (1992). *Encounter.* Ill. D. Shannon. San Diego, CA: Harcourt Brace Jovanovich.

Yolen, J. (1996). *The pit dragon trilogy.* San Diego, CA: Magic Carpet/Harcourt Brace.

Young, T. A., & Vardell, S. M. (1993). Weaving readers theatre and nonfiction into the curriculum. *Reading Teacher, 46,* 396–406.

Zastrow, C., & Janc, H. (2006). *The condition of liberal arts in America's public schools: A report to the Carnegie Corporation of New York.* Washington, DC: Council for Basic Education.

Zhensun, Z., & Low, A. (1991). *A young painter: The life and paintings of Wang Yani.* New York: Scholastic.

Zusack, M. (2007). *The book thief.* New York: Knopf.

Zywica, J., & Gomez, K. (2008). Annotating to support learning in the content areas: Teaching and learning science. *Journal of Adolescent and Adult Literacy, 52*(2), 155–165.

Name Index

Subject Index